Government in the
American Economy

GOVERNMENT in the AMERICAN ECONOMY
Conventional and Radical Studies on the Growth of State Economic Power

Robert B. Carson, Jerry Ingles, Douglas McLaud, Editors

State University College
Oneonta, New York

D. C. HEATH AND COMPANY
Lexington, Massachusetts   Toronto   London

Published simultaneously in Canada.

Printed in the United States of America.

International Standard Book Number: 0-669-83261-8

Library of Congress Catalog Card Number: 72-9009

*To our wives, Marjorie,
Estílita, and Pauline, and
the kids, James and Sarah,
Juan William and Rebecca,
Amy Susan and Lori Ann*

Preface

While discussing the general state and present tendencies of the social sciences in America, the eminent economic historian Thomas Cochran has observed:

> Writing that openly argues for a new ideology or shows a missionary bias in favor of radical change in major institutions is regarded as unscholarly and unreliable. This may explain why the battles in American scholarship are so often over methods.[1]

Although the following collection of readings is not specifically intended to lay out a "new ideology" or create a "missionary bias," it clearly attempts to present a new view of the American economic system in general and of the discipline of economics in particular. The proposed change of view is basically simple: namely, to examine in a systematic way the profound institutional and theoretical changes that have been wrought upon the American economic system by the enlargement of government power and influence in the economy and society over the past half century. If the editors consciously project any particular bias in the following selection of readings it is simply an attempt to get at the roots and the meaning of this growing governmental power by exploring a wide variety of readings and critiques on the issue.

The questions raised are of course more than mere "economic" questions. They go well beyond issues of production, consumption, and resource allocation. And, for anyone faintly familiar with the traditional jargon and practices of the economics profession, it will be obvious that this approach to the matter of "government in the economy" is quite different from that offered in the basic textbook or the usual set of elementary lectures. Although most economists are doubtless aware of the immediacy and complexity of this issue, traditional economics, at least in its elementary forms, consistently begs the question. Government is somehow just *there*. It is an independent variable or an exogenous factor. It is not integrated into a holistic view of the economic system. The student is introduced to the usual microeconomic models of supply and demand, competition, monopoly, factor allocation, and so forth, without the "government variable," and then, after demonstration of some mastery of these problems, the effects of taxes and transfers, antitrust regulation, and so on, are plugged into the general model. Similarly, the macroeconomic tools of monetary and fiscal policy are approached as if they were theoretically (and practically) detached from government's actual role

[1] Thomas Cochran, "Economic History, Old and New," *American Historical Review*, LXXIV, No. 5 (June, 1969), 1565.

in business cycle and growth conditions. To be sure, the economist is always admitting that government is there, and he spends much of his time explaining the special economic conditions and roles of government in the economy, but he almost always does this in a detached and unintegrated way.

John Galbraith once observed that, in economics, too much time was spent fighting skirmishes ". . . with blank cartridges for ground that has already been won in a war that is over."[2] To a very considerable extent this is the discipline's situation in the "government and the economy" question. That government does, and perhaps must, play a staggeringly important role in the economy and that economic theory and policy are useless without such a recognition is a war that was won a long time ago in American economics. The admission of this fact, however, has rarely led to a systematic and balanced critique of the problem. The real meaning in institutional and personal political-economic terms has been evaded while methodological skirmishes continually break out here and there. Most practicing economists, whether they are looking closely at their students' bored responses to the discipline's emphasis on often irrelevant problems of technique and method or the general public's growing concern about the growth of government, are surely aware that government's economic role in the society can no longer be treated as a mere variation of a theoretic model.

The growing popular recognition of the dimensions of government's role in the economy and the swelling reaction against it is a comparatively recent event. Certainly the sources of reaction are numerous and diverse, ranging from the alienated and disaffected young, the traditional conservative opponents of state power, the recently emerged and increasingly articulate New Left academics and radical political activists, down to the ordinary taxpayer, oppressed and confused by rising taxes and prices and dwindling job security. The crucible of Vietnam and the failure of the twin crusades against poverty and racism at home, of course, provided the backdrop to the recent growing antagonism and opposition to the enlargement of the state's power. To sort out causes and effects of these trends here is really not important; however, it is obvious that Americans of all political views have traveled a long way since President Johnson assured us, in 1965, that the expansion of federal economic and political power was producing a new American consensus, a Great Society. As his economic advisors put it:

> After years of ideological controversy, we have grown used to the new relationship among Government, households, business, labor and agriculture. The tired slogans that made constructive discourse difficult have lost their meaning for most Americans.
>
> It has become abundantly clear that our society wants neither to turn backward the clock of history nor to discuss our present problems in a doctrinaire or partisan spirit.[3]

[2] John K. Galbraith, *Economics and the Art of Controversy* (New York: Vintage Books, 1959), p. 105.
[3] *The Economic Report of the President, 1965*, p. 145.

Only a half dozen years later President Nixon found it possible to devote a State of the Union address to the problems of too much government, and, taking a popular slogan from the radical Left, could urge, at least rhetorically, that "power should be returned to the people."[4]

The point is that many Americans have become profoundly confused by the development and the direction of state power and are divided illogically and inconsistently on whether to support or oppose this or that expression of state authority. The following collection of readings, although scarcely hiding the various writer's biases, is not intended so much as a resolution of what should be the "proper" role for the state as simply a summary of the issues and the choices. The organizational technique of the book is to contrast the views of those who essentially are defenders of the economic and political extension of the state (the conventional wisdom) and those who hold to a radical (both left and right) opposition to such developments.

After the introductory essay summarizing trends and magnitudes of state economic growth, the readings introduce theoretical discussions of state economic power from both historical and more recent perspectives. Then they move to some critical studies of the historical development of state power in America. The final and longest section of the readings takes up, issue by issue, some of the leading problems involved in a present-day study of the state in the economy. The reader will find each section prefaced with the editors' introductory comments, and each section concludes with discussion questions. An annotated bibliography gives sources for further readings.

A concluding essay is offered by the editors in an attempt to pull together the diverse and conflicting arguments and analysis set out in the readings and to elaborate, in a critical way, on the above-cited need for a more integrated and analytic study of the growing problem of "government in the economy."

[4] This was the thrust of his *State of the Union* message of 1971.

Contents

Government in the American Economy

PART I

Dimensions and Trends in the Development of State Economic Power

Beginning in late 1969, increasing through 1970, and continuing into the first half of 1971, the American economy showed the unmistakable signs of running into serious difficulty. Although there was fairly wide disagreement among economists on the exact sequence or causal relations among the economic developments, a list of the more dangerous indicators could be practically unanimously agreed upon by mid-1971. Inflation, which had been building since 1967, continued to soar at an annual rate of more than 7 per cent. Unemployment stood at over 5 million or approximately 6 per cent of the work force. Manufacturing output indices continued to be sluggish and few businessmen or bankers offered much optimism about the output trends for the immediate future. The inflationary push was making American labor increasingly restive; indeed, more militant union talk was circulating publicly and privately than most Americans could recall since the end of World War II, and the prospect for extensive and protracted strikes was very great. Moreover, quietly and without much public notice by most Americans, the United States international trade situation was also steadily worsening, so that 1971 appeared certain to be the first year in nearly eight decades that would show a trade deficit for the nation. Although the exact interrelatedness of all of these economic indicators might be debated, there were few experts, economic or political, who could put a good face to what was clearly a dangerous recessionary situation.

Through the middle of 1971, President Nixon pursued a "game plan" of going easy, hoping that the combination of inflationary and recessionary impulses could be dealt with by fairly conservative monetary and fiscal policy actions. However, the plan was clearly not working and, despite usually cheery talk from then Secretary of Treasury Connolly, the economy showed no inclination, or at least very little inclination, to pull out of its skid toward what many saw as an inevitable collapse. While pollsters indicated a general public approval for President Nixon's proposed phase-out from Vietnam, he now was threatened on his domestic economic flank with a serious economic downturn. And, although Americans had forgiven their presidents for blunders in foreign policy and war, they had almost never forgiven them, whatever their actual responsibility, for economic depressions.

By the last weeks of July 1971 the pressures growing within the economy combined with the potential political vulnerability of a president facing a re-election campaign within a year commanded a reassessment and a reversal in policy. What had been denied as possible only a few months before became necessary on the night of August 15th as President Nixon took to the people his new brand of economic policy for dealing with the nation's chronic economic problems. The plan of going easy, of biding time and awaiting a rebalancing of the market mechanism, reflecting an economic perspective that Nixon and many of his closest advisors had clearly believed all their lives whatever their actual appreciation of such an economic philosophy, was abandoned and replaced with a direct ninety-day wage-price freeze, proposals for business and personal income tax reduction, and an assault on the trade problem by means of tariff increases (the precise package and its later elaborations are discussed in Part V). With the exception of war or full-fledged economic collapse, it was reported these proposals were the most far-reaching and revolutionary interventions in the economy by government that had ever been attempted. Or, at least, at first blush, it seemed to many to appear that way. But, as the political shock wore off and later phases of the "new game plan" unfolded, it became possible to put the sudden presidential action in a more balanced perspective. And, on balance, little of his game plan was new and his program was more easily viewed as the logical extension of economic policy trends and general economic developments of the past decade or so. Only the plan's abruptness and the public concessions of economic crisis in the system, which the plan so clearly, if unconsciously, underlined, were startling. The "freeze," the "new game plan," "Nixonomics," or whatever the economic statement of August 15th and the policies devised thereafter would finally be known as, had deep roots in the historical evolution of government economic policy and at least carried in part the credentials of many leading neo-Keynesian theorists. While John K. Galbraith of the Americans for Democratic Action or Paul Samuelson, confidant and advisor to Democrats Kennedy and Johnson, could be expected to take issue with one part or another of Republican Nixon's version of the "new economics," there remained little difference in fact between what the president did and what these liberal economists had been calling for for some time. The shock of August 15th, it would seem, was more political and biographical than a calculated redirection or, as pundits exclaimed, "revolution," in national economic policy.

Nevertheless, the significance of August 15th and later should not be minimized, even if it was the only option left to the system. For, with all of the power and authority of his office, the president had struck down the official if unpracticed mythology of a "free enterprise" economy. For economists and historians the death of that myth had been acknowledged long before; August 15th was only the public funeral. The fact, however, that it was public was what made it significant. There could no longer be one set of values and perspectives that flourished in the arid atmosphere of economics seminar rooms and corporate and government councils and another for the citizen and voter on the street. What Mr. Nixon had done that Saturday night was to publicly state what a comparative few had grasped before—that there were no theoretical or practical limits to the actual use of state economic power for maintaining the present American economic system. There were no totems or taboos, however privately treasured and publicly praised, which would or could not fall as crisis dictated.

Despite official protestation about the "voluntary" nature of the new controls or their temporary nature until the "new prosperity" arrived, there was no way that Americans could evade the realization of the ultimate powers of the state in their economic and private lives. And that fact, perhaps more than anything else, augured the emergence of a new public consciousness, one which would be ultimately more sweeping and significant than the progressivism of the early twentieth-century decades or of FDR's New Deal. The power of the state in the economy was clearly revealed to everyone.

The final implication of that revelation and its full meaning in the lives of the American people and their eventual reaction to it go beyond the purpose of this essay. However, it is the object of this collection of readings, representing mainstream economic thought and radical critiques on the issue of state economic power, to lay open that question so that it may be examined by the student of economics. For now, though, our attention is focused only on presenting the actual dimensions and trends of the elaboration of state economic power in America.

Clearly, the dimensions of government in the economy can be measured in a number of different ways but the most obvious scheme and the least complex would be to examine the magnitude and direction of: (1) government spending changes as shown in GNP origination, (2) the direct and indirect employment functions of government, (3) the provision of social service and benefits and individual welfare transfers by the state, (4) the revenue or taxation functions of government, and (5) the operations of the state as the ultimate "rationalizer" of the forms and rules of market behavior. The following sections of this essay are offered only as a general description of magnitudes and trends in "government and the economy." More specific details and critiques will be found in the readings that follow.

I. Government Expenditures

The growth of government expenditures in the twentieth century has been, from any point of view, astounding. From a total of less than 7 per cent of GNP at the beginning of the century, federal, state, and local expenditures now constitute over 32 per cent of the nation's gross output. For the purpose of putting this enormous change in a useful perspective, we may view government expenditures in three ways: first, the long-term trend of government expenditures in dollars and as a percentage of Gross National Product (GNP); second, the division of government expenditures between the federal, state, and local governments and the nature of changes in these relationships;

TABLE I
Expenditures of All Governments (Federal, State, and Local): 1929–1970

Year	Governmental Expenditures (in Billions of Dollars)	Percentage of GNP
1902	1.7	7
1913	3.2	8
1922	9.3	13
1929	10.3	10
1932	10.6	18
1934	12.9	20
1936	16.1	20
1938	16.8	20
1940	18.4	19
1942	64.0	40
1944	103.0	49
1946	45.5	21
1948	50.3	22
1950	60.8	24
1952	93.7	27
1954	96.7	27
1956	104.1	25
1958	127.2	28
1960	136.1	27
1961	149.0	28
1962	159.9	29
1963	166.9	28
1964	175.4	28
1965	186.9	27
1966	212.3	28
1967	242.9	31
1968	270.7	31
1969	290.1	31
1970	313.0	32

SOURCE: Bureau of the Census, *U.S. Census of Governments: 1967, Historical Summary of Governmental Finances in the United States, 1967* and *Economic Report of the President, 1971.*

and, third, the nature of changes in the share of expenditures devoted to specific functions (i.e., defense, education, public welfare, etc.).

As indicated in Table I, total government expenditures in 1902 amounted to $1.6 billion while in 1970 this figure had risen to $313 billion. The dollar amount of government expenditures, except in a few post-World War II years, has grown steadily and rapidly upwards in the twentieth century. Government expenditures as a percentage of GNP illustrate even more precisely the changing relationship of government to the economy. Table I also shows that between 1902 and 1970 government expenditures as a percentage of GNP increased by over 450 per cent. The peak, as would be expected, came during World War II, when government expenditures accounted for 52 per cent of GNP. Although we have not returned to this level since the war, it is quite obvious that, taking into account the data for the present century as a whole, government expenditures as a percentage of GNP have risen significantly.

The division of government expenditures among federal, state, and local governments, however, indicates a more dramatic change in the nature of the state's role in the economy. Graph I indicates the changes, over time,

GRAPH I
Share of total expenditures by the level of government.

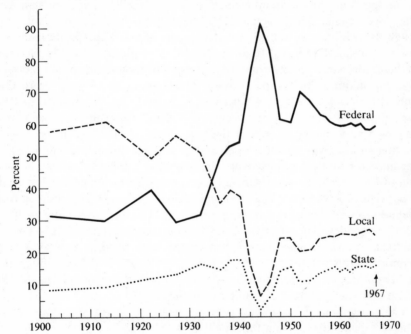

SOURCE: Data was derived from Bureau of the Census, *U.S. Census of Governments: 1967, Historical Survey of Government Finances in the United States, 1967.*

of the share of total government expenditures by each level of government. As might be expected with even a rudimentary understanding of American economic history, local government spending dominated at the beginning of the century. It was at the local level that essential urban and rural social services were provided, if they were provided at all. State spending remained slight until the automobile revolution of the 1920s began to produce massive state spending for highways and the depressionary 1930s added expanded state social outlays. Meanwhile, the federal share of state expenditures has risen significantly since the turn of the century, from 34 per cent of all government spending to almost 60 per cent.

This expansion of federal spending began of course during the 1930s as new public works and employment programs, with many functions taken over from local governments, produced a significant shift to federal expenditure sources. World War II's military demands ultimately centered more than 90 per cent of all state spending in federal hands by 1944.

It is evident from Graph I that during the late 1950s and the 1960s there has been a leveling off or even a general decline of federal expenditures as a percentage of total state expenditures. This is to be explained partially in the changing character of state and local revenues. Graph I excludes intergovernmental transfers from federal expenditures. These transfers (grants-in-aid to state and local governments) are counted as state and local expenditures. The purpose of this accounting method is to establish that it is state and local governments which actually purchase goods and services with this money. However, it is well known that grants-in-aid need specific and very closely scrutinized approval from the federal government. It would therefore not be inconsistent to say that the federal government essentially controls these expenditures. In the past twenty years, grants-in-aid have more than doubled (in 1948 they were 4.6 per cent of federal expenditures and in 1967 they accounted for 10.5 per cent of federal expenditures), and they are now a very significant part of the federal budget. To look at the transfer situation another way, of the 25 per cent of all government expenditures now accounted for by local governments, approximately 30 per cent came in some form of federal and state aid. Of state expenditures, which amounted to about 15 per cent of government spending, approximately 30 per cent resulted from revenue received from the federal government. This increase, more than accounts for the leveling off of the federal share mentioned above. The conclusion that control of expenditures has passed from local to federal, and to a minor extent to state government, is inescapable, as is the conclusion that the recent decline in the federal spending share radically understates the federal government's real expenditure significance.

A third method of examining government expenditures is to look at the share of expenditures from a functional point of view.

The reader should note that in 1948 expenditures on goods and services accounted for 57.2 per cent of all government expenditures. In a period when it has become fashionable to attack government for its extravagant transfer payments, it is interesting to note that transfers have played a relatively less important role in the budget, as the percentage of expenditures going for goods and services rose to over 70 per cent of all government spending by 1970. When we look at the data for expenditures for specific functions (Table II) the evidence is even more astounding. From 1902 to 1967 expenditures on public welfare increased by 1.2 per cent of all expenditures. Even when we look at the depression year 1936 expenditures on public welfare accounted for only 5.9 per cent of all expenditures. It can also be seen that although the relative share of expenditures on highways has declined in each year represented in Table II, expenditures on highways have been larger than expenditures on public welfare.

TABLE II
Government Expenditures by Specific Function as a Percentage of Total Expenditures

Year	National Defense and Space	Highways	Education	Public Welfare
1902	9.9	10.5	15.5	2.5
1922	9.4	13.9	18.4	1.4
1936	5.6	11.6	14.1	5.9
1944	77.8	1.1	2.6	1.0
1948	29.2	5.6	14.0	3.9
1954	44.3	5.0	10.1	2.8
1958	35.4	6.4	12.5	2.9
1960	34.2	6.7	12.4	2.9
1967	31.0	5.4	15.6	3.7

SOURCE: Data was derived from Bureau of the Census, *U.S. Census of Governments: 1967, Historical Survey of Government Finances in the United States, 1967.*

The reader should also note that despite the education boom of the late 1950s and early 1960s public expenditures on education have not changed significantly from the 1902 proportion.

The expenditure figures would also seem to support to a considerable degree the widely held conclusion that the military-space complex has come to play an increasingly important role in government and the economy. In 1902 defense expenditures accounted for 9.9 per cent of total expenditures while in 1967 expenditures on national defense and space programs accounted for 31.0 per cent of all expenditures. This, however, is not a recent development. When we take the relatively "peaceful" base year of 1958 we find that defense expenditures accounted for 35 per cent of total expenditures, a relatively higher share than 1967, a war year. Thus, although war and threats of war play a large part in determining the shares of government spending, the currently fashionable effort to single out this one item presents an unfair and unbalanced presentation of recent trends in government expenditures. All of this is not to underplay the importance of war, both to government and to the economy generally, but to put the contemporary debate about how much war itself has been the sole creator of government spending in a more critical perspective.

II. Government as an Employer

Another way to look at the dimensions of growth by the government sector in the economy is to examine its impact as a direct creator of employment, either through actual public sector jobs or through government's purchases of goods and services. In 1929, total employment of federal, state, and local employees, as well as of military personnel, stood at about 3.3 million or slightly over 6 per cent of the total labor force. As is illustrated in Table III, government employment proceeded to grow by slightly more than a million workers during the depression decade of the 1930s, about evenly divided between public sector expansion at the federal and at the state and local levels. Yet, this increase during the crisis of the 1930s still left all public sector employment at less than 8 per cent of the total labor force by 1939. Indeed, the war, and not the depression, became the chief initial stimulant to public employment. In 1945, nearly 17 million Americans, including 11.4 million under arms, were government employees. By 1945, with a cold war army of 1.6 million, total public employment still held at about 7.5 million or 12 per cent of the labor force; within the next two decades, this figure more than doubled, with government employment of all kinds constituting 18 per cent of the labor force. It is noteworthy, however, that the bulk of this growth took place at the state and local level where nearly 6 million jobs were added between 1949 and 1969. Particularly, the expansion of public education and the growth of a variety of social services, many of which are ultimately paid for by the federal government through transfers to the states, have accounted for much of this growth of state and local government employment.

At any rate, public sector employment of all kinds is now larger than employment in trade and rivals employment in manufacturing. There are almost five times as many public employees as farmers or construction workers and three times the number employed in transportation and public utilities.

TABLE III
Total Labor Force and Total Public Sector Employment, Selected Years 1929–1970 (in Thousands)

Year	Total Labor Force	Total Public Sector	Federal Government	State and Local Government	Military
1929	49,440	3,325	533	2,532	260
1939	55,600	4,365	905	3,090	370
1949	62,903	7,473	1,908	3,948	1,617
1959	70,921	10,735	2,333	5,850	2,552
1960	72,142	10,867	2,270	6,083	2,514
1961	73,031	11,166	2,279	6,315	2,572
1962	73,442	11,718	2,340	6,550	2,828
1963	74,571	11,964	2,358	6,868	2,738
1964	75,830	12,335	2,348	7,248	2,739
1965	77,178	12,797	2,378	7,696	2,723
1966	78,893	13,914	2,564	8,227	3,123
1967	80,793	14,844	2,719	8,697	3,446
1968	82,272	15,381	2,737	9,109	3,535
1969	84,239	15,710	2,758	9,446	3,506
1970	85,903	15,788	2,707	9,893	3,188

SOURCE: *President's Manpower Report, 1971.*

Impressive as these figures may be in asserting the persistent expansionary trend of government employment, they do not adequately measure the whole employment impact of expanded government. Tables IV and V, based upon a United States Department of Commerce study, illustrate the private sector gains directly attributed to government spending for goods and services since 1962.

While the average government-derived employment among the total labor force through the 1960s shows a gently rising consistency of between 25 to 28 per cent, marginal changes are more illustrative of the current trend. For instance, between the boom of the Vietnam build up, beginning in 1964, and the peaking out of 1969, government-generated jobs accounted for 48.5 per cent of the net increases in the total labor force and actually provided for more than 52 per cent of all of the net job gains the economy made (if we subtract out unemployment). Over the whole period 1962–1970, for those

TABLE IV

Year	Total Labor Force	Total Government-Generated Jobs	Government Employment*	Derived Private Employment
		(in millions)		
1962	73.4	18.3	12.2	6.1
1963	74.6	18.8	12.4	6.4
1964	75.8	19.2	12.8	6.4
1965	77.1	19.3	13.2	6.1
1966	78.9	20.8	14.5	6.3
1967	80.8	23.0	15.2	7.8
1968	82.3	24.0	15.7	8.3
1969	84.2	24.1	16.2	7.9
1970	85.9	23.5	16.2	7.3

SOURCE: *President's Manpower Report, 1971,* p. 327.
* Total includes federal employees, state and local employees, military personnel, and employees of state operated enterprises.

TABLE V
Government-Generated Jobs as a Percentage of Total Labor Force

Year	Percentage
1962	25.8
1963	25.2
1964	25.3
1965	25.0
1966	26.3
1967	28.4
1968	29.1
1969	28.6
1970	27.3

Derived from Table IV.

desiring a "more average margin," 41.6 per cent of the total labor force's growth was absorbed in direct government-generated jobs. Comparatively little of this trend is accounted for by direct military expansion. Indeed, the military grew by only 350,000 men between 1962 and 1970. However, a sizable portion can be attributed to private sector military and space spending. Of the nearly one and one-half million jobs created in the private sector by government purchases between 1964 and 1969, about one half were defense related.

Military spending, moreover, has had an especially concentrated effect upon certain firms and industries in the private sector. The 100 largest prime contractors provide about 67 per cent of all military sales, with the top ten alone doing more than 30 per cent of the war business. During the 1964–1969 Vietnam build up, the fifteen largest suppliers (each with over $1 billion in sales between 1962–1967) who were dependent upon government military purchases for more than half of their total income enjoyed an unprecedented boom as their employment grew by about 40 per cent. At the same time, while the entire economy prospered in the boom of the late 1960s, the civilian labor force grew by only 11 per cent. Looking at the data again somewhat differently, these fifteen firms accounted for more than 8 per cent of all private sector employment between 1964 and 1969.

The growing concern in the media and among certain politicians about a sprawling military-industrial complex is thus grounded on the obvious evidence of employment dependency upon military-space spending (see Part VII). Nor is this tendency explained away simply by the old, but thoughtless, radical rhetoric, which suggests that only capitalists benefit from wars and prospects of wars. American labor unions, at least through their official leaders, clearly recognized the benefits of increased government spending in the military-space hardware fields. The recent crisis of the SST and Boeing and the bankruptcy pinch at Lockheed not only prompted vigorous lobbying by the affected businesses and financial interests to aid the beleaguered companies but union leadership also fought for continued government spending and aid to these firms—not so much because workingmen really saw their interests as identical with ownership's but for the simple fact of maintaining jobs. Indeed, insofar as government spending constituted the real reason for the existence of these jobs, it must be understood that many workingmen found themselves, consciously or unconsciously, supporters of government fiscal subordination to the ends of private enterprise in general and to enhanced military procurement in particular.

It should be remembered, however, that defense-aero-space spending by government is not the sole generator of indirect employment by government purchases. For instance, "commerce and transportation" and "community development and housing" expenditures amounted to a figure nearly 18 per cent as large as defense and space outlays in 1970. Highway construction and urban renewal were thus a heavy stimulant to construction employment in the United States. The point is that the conjunction of private sector jobs and public spending is not narrowly limited to the "military-industrial complex" but penetrates many sectors of the economy. Moreover, government-generated employment of all types now plays a dominant and indispensible role in new job creation in the economy.

III. Social Services and Welfare Transfers

As late as 1932, in the face of a depression which had already seen GNP tumble by about 50 per cent in only three years time and national unemployment climb to nearly 24 per cent of the work force, the president of the United States, Herbert Hoover, could still argue publicly that social welfare payments to the unemployed were the domain of private charitable agencies or local government. Nor did Hoover stand alone on this position. His opponent in the autumn presidential election, Franklin Roosevelt, actually attacked some of the Hoover administration's modest efforts at providing a minimal social level for the depression's poor as wasteful and wrong. Moreover, it is probable that the vast majority of the disadvantaged themselves still were opposed, in principle at least, to the proposition that it was the federal government's obligation to provide social minimums.

The roots of such an outlook extended deeply into the American past. The frontier experience, the official ideology (if not practice) of *laissez-faire,* and the puritan tradition, among the many complementary forces, had served to produce a widely held belief in economic individualism among Americans of all social and economic classes. The myth of the self-made man, however wrongly it was used to protect the economically privileged, also served as a guidepost to the poor. To be sure, private charitable institutions had long worked in the slums and with the mentally and physically handicapped. Even local governments had provided minimal social transfers (not counting their extensive function in providing public education) through the dole or make-work jobs during "bad times." However, Americans, with few exceptions, at the coming of the Great Depression, still retained their earlier faith in economic individualism, and the nation lagged well behind European countries in the development and maintenance of a national social minimum. Workmen's compensation had only been introduced since 1910, with only about thirty states participating by 1930, and there were no state or federal unemployment insurance programs. Within four decades of the Great Crash, however, the United States developed an extensive, if often incoherent, state program for providing social transfers. Chart I on the following page illustrates the extent and pattern of the American program of social security which has evolved.

By 1967, federal, state, and local governments in the United States were spending more than $100 billion on their various social welfare programs (including education as well as social insurance and transfers). Of this total,

CHART I
Social Welfare Programs by Categories of Social Insurance and Public Charity

Social Insurance	Public Charity
Federal Programs	
Old age	Institutional care and welfare services in
Survivorship	federal jurisdictions
Permanent disability	
Hospital Costs for the Aged	Veterans' benefits
Supplementary medical costs for the aged	
Railroad employees	
Federal employees	
Federal-State Programs	
Unemployment	Welfare services
	Categorical assistance
	Old age
	Blindness
	Permanent total disability
	Dependent childhood
	Medical care for the medically indigent
	Food programs
	Housing programs
State and Local Programs	
Occupational injury and illness	Institutional care
Temporary disability	Welfare services
State and local employees	General assistance

SOURCE: Clair Wilcox, *Toward Social Welfare* (Homewood, Ill.: Irwin, 1969), p. 91.

it is estimated that approximately 45 per cent was grants or programs directly aimed at helping the poor. The change in the magnitude and direction of government social spending resulted from many pressures. First, the rising level of ouptut per capita made possible extensive social spending. Second, the real need for such spending was undeniable. The depression crushed out in many the last vestiges of belief in self-help, and the technological and structural displacement of many workers after World War II, even though average per capita income climbed, forced the extension of New Deal programs. The dual economies of a rich and increasingly affluent America contrasted with a smaller but still large bloc of poor and disadvantaged demanded the enlargement of social services, not just as a matter of reason, but to deal with mounting social and class friction. Thus, by 1965, President Johnson could call for a new and broadened agenda for social spending. As he put it:

> The President of the United States is President of all the people in every section of the country. But this office also holds a special responsibility to the distressed and disinherited, the hungry and the hopeless of this abundant nation.
>
> It is in pursuit of that special responsibility that I submit this message to you today.

The new program I propose is within our means. Its cost of $970 million is 1 percent of our national budget—and every dollar I am requesting for this program is already included in the budget I sent to Congress in January.

But we cannot measure its importance by its cost.

For it charts an entirely new course of hope for our people.

We are fully aware that this program will not eliminate all the poverty in America in a few months or a few years. Poverty is deeply rooted and its causes are many.

But this program will show the way to new opportunities for millions of our fellow citizens.

It will provide a lever with which we can begin to open the door to our prosperity for those who have been kept outside.

It will also give us the chance to test our weapons, to try our energy and ideas and imagination for the many battles yet to come. As conditions change, and as experience illuminates our difficulties, we will be prepared to modify our strategy.

And this program is much more than a beginning.

Rather, it is a commitment. It is a total commitment by this President, and this Congress, and this nation, to pursue victory over the most ancient of mankind's enemies.

On many historic occasions the President has requested from Congress the authority to move against forces which were endangering the well-being of our country.

This is such an occasion.[1]

Massive social programs, even if they never got beyond their initial stages of planning, were soon under fire. Increased social spending plus the war in Vietnam spelled inflation and higher taxes and, finally, by 1970, recession. Moreover, many of the programs demanded state and local participation and spending. And, of course, all such government spending programs were open to the old American criticism that government spending was wasteful and that the administration of such programs was brutally bureaucratic. Increasingly, taxpayers were understanding that "there ain't no such thing as a free lunch," as the burdens of local and state expenditures and the federal outlays for war and social spending cut deeper into paychecks. By the early 1970s, taxpayer revolts swept like wildfire through many states and communities, and, while some federal officials of the Nixon administration still talked hopefully about a guaranteed annual income for all Americans, it was apparent that the brief honeymoon with extensive social spending was over. The problem, of course, was just where to draw the line on essential and nonessential social outlays.

The decay of the cities, the unemployment plight of rural and urban blacks, white rural poverty, and the rising requests for educational spending and for

[1] "President Johnson's Message on Poverty and the Economic Opportunity Act of 1964," in Burton Weisbrod, *The Economics of Poverty* (Englewood Cliffs, N.J.: Prentice-Hall, Inc., 1965), pp. 111–12.

better health care could surely not be arrested by the decision to reduce such spending. The problems exist quite independently of the will or the capacity of the society to pay for them. While some Americans could still talk wistfully about hard work and self-help as solutions to the welfare and unemployment problems, no real solutions to the problems of poverty and income distribution seemed to be offered any longer in such homilies. The needs for social spending were apparent everywhere, whether it was a matter of keeping a fatherless family from starving or turning to crime or a question of building better public recreational facilities. Most Americans have now recognized such social needs as undeniable. It remains to be seen, however, to what degree and in what directions the state will now turn to satisfy these needs.

IV. Government as Tax Collector

At the turn of the century taxes played a relatively minor role in the lives of most Americans. Tariffs, the most important source of federal government revenue, had been a thorny political issue, but it was the more encompassing question of foreign markets rather than the specific issue of taxes that provoked the controversy. The federal income tax had not yet been enacted. Even the property tax at the state and local levels, the most important tax of all, accounted for only $706 million or $9 per capita in 1902. On the whole per capita taxation of federal, state, and local governments amounted, in 1902, to less than $18.

In the period from 1902 to the present both the scale and structure of the tax system have undergone great changes. In total dimensions, 1967 per capita taxes were more than $564, an increase of 3,300 per cent over the 1902 level. In 1902 local governments played the dominant role as tax collectors, collecting 51 per cent of all taxes, while in 1967 local taxes accounted for only 17 per cent of all taxes. The federal share of taxation, in the same period, went from 37 per cent to 65 per cent. Increasing federal control of tax collections at the expense of local control is the other side of the change discussed with respect to government expenditures. The federal individual income tax, which now accounts for 47 per cent of all federal tax collections, has been responsible for much of the federal increase. In recent years the income tax has become an increasingly utilized source of revenue for state governments, accounting for nearly 20 per cent of state revenues by 1971. State and local governments have also resorted to higher and higher sales taxes covering more items.

The changes in the dimensions and structure of the tax system have also been registered in an increasing professional and public awareness of the problems encountered in taxation. The economist's concern (and sometimes lack of it) with the effects of taxation on income distribution, the general concern (both public and professional) about the ability of tax policy to stimulate or depress the economy, and the middle- and low-income taxpayer's loud cries of disapproval and disgust with a tax system that seems to hit him

increasingly harder are all reflections of the changing dimensions and structure of the tax system. These changing economic and social dimensions of
taxation must form the framework for an analysis of the impact of taxation
on the economy, and these issues will be taken up in considerable detail in
Part IX of the readings and critiques.

V. Government as the Rule Setter of Market Behavior

The state's role in the creation and maintenance of market relations is probably the oldest of all of government's economic activities in the United States.
The American economic system, born as it was out of the wreckage of
English mercantilism, was committed from its beginnings to the utilization
of state power to regulate financial and commercial activity. Even as the peculiarly American mercantilism of the Federalist era gave way to Jacksonian
laissez-faire and ultimately to post-Civil War industrialization, the state continued to play a crucial role in setting the limits and the direction of market
behavior. The national and state subsidies to canal and railroad building, the
tariff, the National Banking Act, and certain state enactments affecting
finance, trade, and working conditions stand as only selective examples of
nineteenth-century "interferences" in the free functioning of market activity;
however, it remained for the twentieth century to experience the extensive
elaboration of state power in market regulation.

Quite simply "the market" had given way by the last decade of the century.
The rise of trusts, huge corporate consolidations, new forms of business integration and collusion, along with the largely speculative overbuilding of
American productive capacity, had dashed the economy on the rocks of a
long depression after the Panic of 1893. The traditional dependence upon
market forces to restore balance through market pricing and allocation clearly
no longer worked. Nor was the breakdown simply limited to the problem
of concentration and excess capacity on the production side. The rise and
increasingly militant organization of labor unions pointed toward the abolition
of "free labor" markets just as the closing of the frontier ended the dream
of free land.

In the first two decades of the twentieth century, the nation responded
with an elaborate, if not always integrated, program of Progressive legislation
aimed at restoring the market by means of extensive government intervention.
Although retaining the basic framework of market price determination and
resource allocation, controls over the trusts and business integration, over
the banking system, money supply, and certain commercial practices, as well
as the recognition and integration of labor unions into the regulated Progressive economy, characterized the growth of federal regulation of market affairs.
The collapse of the economy again in the 1930s produced extensive controls
over monopoly activities and the gradual development of fiscal and monetary
policy as instruments of control over aggregate economic performance.

World War II plus the wide acceptance of Lord Keynes' "new economics" further expanded the theoretical and practical perimeters of government activities in the manipulation and maintenance of general market stability through government taxing and spending programs and the regulation of the money supply.

Looking back over the system of state intervention in market activity since 1900, it is apparent that two themes have developed: first, in a microeconomic sense, the state, particularly the federal government, has enacted regulative devices to manipulate, on the supply side, both the production activities of corporations and the power of labor. Meanwhile, through certain consumer legislation efforts, it has similarly acted to rationalize the demand side of the market. Secondly, in a macroeconomic sense, the federal government has come to accept the necessary use of monetary and fiscal policies to maintain desired aggregate levels of supply and demand. All of this has been done, however, within the market framework. In other words, the state has sought to retain publicly the psychology of private incentives and behavior on both the individual and corporate levels of a market-oriented, private property system.

The past record of this elaboration of state interference with market activities would seem, on balance, highly effective through the past seven decades of this century. However, it has become increasingly evident in the past half decade or so that the American economic system has not evolved an unimpeachable system of minimal central regulation of market activity. Problems of monopoly power, indeed, seem to many as far from final resolution as they did at the time of the Northern Securities and Standard Oil cases. Conglomerate mergers have presented a type of business and financial integration with which existing antitrust regulation is simply unable to deal. Moreover, government regulative agencies, such as the ICC, the FTC, Food and Drug Administration, and others, have drawn increasing fire as having failed to properly represent the public's interest. Indeed, many critics see these agencies as acting largely on behalf of the industries they supposedly regulate. Similarly, labor legislation, supposedly created to balance corporate and union power, has been undercut by increasingly independent rank and file action and the huge growth of employment in the public sector where the traditional union powers are legally restricted by the state.

On top of these problems, the functioning of the market is challenged by other obstructions so complex that they can only be listed here: (1) the worsening international payments and dollar position of the United States, (2) the growth of foreign competition and the resulting export of United States capital, (3) a steady and eroding price inflation, (4) the reappearance of the old "bugaboo" of excess capacity in American industry, and (5) the growing public concern for the ecology problem and how to "pay for" the costs of reclaiming or at least halting the destruction of the environment. Moreover, the old self-assuredness of the "new economists," who believed that virtually any kind of aggregate market situation could be favorably resolved through some mix of monetary and fiscal policy, has been shaken by the effects of the war in Vietnam and the inexorable march of technology and structural change.

All of this is not to say that state efforts to supply balance and order to the market determination of prices, output, and resource allocation have failed. That particular question will be taken up in detail in Parts IV and V. It is clear, however, that Americans can expect more, not less, direct and indirect intervention in the operation of markets. The most obvious example of this trend is the acceptance of permanent "wage-price guidelines" and "incomes policy" among most leading economists and a growing number of political leaders. Depending upon how such a policy is finally developed and applied beyond the present tentative experiment, it would amount to the most sweeping and direct intervention in market relations yet undertaken by the American state.

At this point in our survey, the growth of government in the economy must certainly be seen as no accidental phenomenon, no mere "incident" to a rational and critical understanding of the American economy. Government, the state, plays a special and necessary role in American capitalism that must be admitted and understood. We shall now turn to taking up a study of the causes and effects of this "special condition" in the modern capitalist society.

PART ii

The Theory of the State: Conservative, Liberal, and Radical Perspectives

The proper role of the state in economic activity has always been an issue of particular interest to economists. The intense debate on this topic has not been confined to mere economic principles. Rather, economists have introduced their various ideological perspectives into the debate on an equal footing with the traditional economic notions of efficiency and equilibrium. In the six selections presented here we have attempted to outline the prevailing ideological views on the role of government in the economy.

The first two articles are representative of the modern conservative theory of the state. Adam Smith, writing in eighteenth-century England at the close of the mercantilist era, presents what has become the classic statement of the *laissez-faire* position on government intervention in the economy. The selection by Milton Friedman is from *Capitalism and Freedom* and is typical of contemporary conservative thought. The careful reader will note that both Smith and Friedman base their views on political as well as economic criteria.

The selections reflecting the modern liberal theory of the state are by J. M. Keynes and Walter Heller. Keynes, widely heralded as the father of the "new economics," examines in the first essay the goals of modern capitalist society and the means by which government can aid in the realization of these goals. Walter Heller, a former member of the Council of Economic Advisers under the Kennedy and Johnson administrations, proposes that through government we can achieve virtually any economic goal imaginable, regardless of the socioeconomic structure of society.

The radical view (as does the conservative) takes issue with the proposition that through government we can solve all our problems. The state is the product of class domination, with the dominant class organizing government in its interests. Therefore, in the radical view the state can solve only those problems which leave the existing class structure of society intact. The selections by Marx, Engels, and Sweezy examine the role of the state in a class-based society.

The discerning reader will note that the following selections of contrasting ideological views of the state clearly do not exhaust the possible range of perspectives on the state and the economy. This limitation is imposed both by problems of space and the logical need to lay out only what the authors feel are the most significant and cogent expressions of ideological diversity. Most certainly Friedman does not represent all of the modern market enthusiasm; nor is Walter Heller a perfect representative of all economists having a more or less modern liberal outlook; and it is equally true that a rather doctrinaire Marxist critique is not exhaustive of all contemporary radical analysis. These views are only broad archetypes. Selected writings later in the text will represent an ever-widening range of ideological and economic perspectives.

CONSERVATIVE VIEWS

The Functions of Government: The Laissez-Faire Position

ADAM SMITH

The first duty of the sovereign, that of protecting the society from the violence and invasion of other independent societies, can be performed only by means of a military force . . . .

The number of those who can go to war, in proportion to the whole number of the people, is necessarily much smaller in a civilized, than in a rude state of society. In a civilized society, as the soldiers are maintained altogether by the labour of those who are not soldiers, the number of the former can never exceed what the latter can maintain, over and above maintaining, in a manner suitable to their respective stations, both themselves and the other officers of government, and law, whom they are obliged to maintain. In the little agrarian states of ancient Greece, a fourth or a fifth part of the whole body of the people considered themselves as soldiers, and would sometimes, it is said, take the field. Among the civilized nations of modern Europe, it is commonly computed, that not more than one hundredth part of the inhabitants of any country can be employed as soldiers, without ruin to the country which pays the expence of their service.

The art of war in the progress of improvement necessarily becomes one of the most complicated of all arts. The state of the mechanical, as well as of some other arts, with which it is necessarily connected, determine the degree of perfection to which it is capable of being carried at any particular time. But in order to carry it to this degree of perfection, it is necessary that it should become the sole or principal occupation of a particular class of citizens, and the division of labour is as necessary for the improvement of this, as of every other art.

In these circumstances, there seem to be but two methods, by which the state can make any tolerable provision for the public defence.

It may either, first, by means of a very rigorous police, and in spite of the whole bent of the interest, genius and inclinations of the people, enforce the practice of military exercises, and oblige either all the citizens of the mili-

From Adam Smith, *The Wealth of Nations* (Edwin Cannan Edition, 1904).

tary age, or a certain number of them, to join in some measure the trade of a soldier to whatever other trade or profession they may happen to carry on.

Or secondly, by maintaining and employing a certain number of citizens in the constant practice of military exercises, it may render the trade of a soldier a particular trade, separate and distinct from all others.

If the state has recourse to the first of those two expedients, its military force is said to consist in a militia; if to the second, it is said to consist in a standing army. The practice of military exercises is the sole or principal occupation of the soldiers of a standing army, and the maintenance or pay which the state affords them is the principal and ordinary fund of their subsistence. The practice of military exercises is only the occasional occupation of the soldiers of a militia, and they derive the principal and ordinary fund of their subsistence from some other occupation. In a militia, the character of the labourer, artificer, or tradesman, predominates over that of the soldier: in a standing army, that of the soldier predominates over every other character; and in this distinction seems to consist the essential difference between those two different species of military force.

The first duty of the sovereign, that of defending the society from the violence and injustice of other independent societies, grows gradually more and more expensive, as the society advances in civilization. The military force of the society, which originally cost the sovereign no expense either in time of peace or in time of war, must, in the progress of improvement, first be maintained by him in time of war, and afterwards even in time of peace. . . .

The second duty of the sovereign, that of protecting, as far as possible, every member of the society from the injustice or oppression of every other member of it, or the duty of establishing an exact administration of justice requires two very different degrees of expense in the different periods of society.

Among nations of hunters, as there is scarce any property, or at least none that exceeds the value of two or three days' labour; so there is seldom any established magistrate or any regular administration of justice. Men who have no property can injure one another only in their persons or reputations. But when one man kills, wounds, beats, or defames another, though he to whom the injury is done suffers, he who does it receives no benefit. It is otherwise with the injuries to property. The benefit of the person who does the injury is often equal to the loss of him who suffers it. Envy, malice, or resentment, are the only passions which can prompt one man to injure another in his person or reputation. But the greater part of men are not very frequently under the influence of those passions; and the very worst men are so only occasionally. As their gratification too, how agreeable soever it may be to certain characters, is not attended with any real or permanent advantage, it is in the greater part of men commonly restrained by prudential considerations. Men may live together in society with some tolerable degree of security, though there is no civil magistrate to protect them from the injustice of those passions. But avarice and ambition in the rich, in the poor the hatred of labour and the love of present ease and enjoyment, are the passions which prompt to invade property, passions much more steady in their operation, and much more universal in their influence. Wherever there is great property, there is great inequality. For one very rich man, there must be at least five hundred poor, and the affluence of the few supposes the indigence of the many. The affluence of the rich excites the indignation of the poor, who are often both driven by want, and prompted by envy, to invade his possessions. It is only under the shelter of the civil magistrate that the owner of that valuable property, which is acquired by the labour of many years, or perhaps of many successive generations, can sleep a single night in security. The acquisition of valuable and extensive property, therefore, necessarily requires the establishment of civil government. . . .

The third and last duty of the sovereign or commonwealth is that of erecting and maintaining those public institutions and those public works, which, though they may be in the highest degree advantageous to a great society, are, however, of such a nature, that the profit could never repay the expense to any individual or small number of individuals, and which it therefore cannot be expected that any individual or small number of individuals should erect or maintain. . . .

The revenue which must defray, not only the expense of defending the society and of supporting the dignity of the chief magistrate, but all the other necessary expenses of government, for which the constitution of the state has not provided any particular revenue, may be drawn, either, first, from some fund which peculiarly belongs to the sovereign or commonwealth, and which is independent of the revenue of the people; or, secondly, from the revenue of the people.

I. The subjects of every state ought to contribute towards the support of the government, as nearly as possible, in proportion to their respective abilities; that is, in proportion to the revenue which they respectively enjoy under the protection of the state. The expense of government to the individuals of a great nation, is like the expense of management to the joint tenants of a great estate, who are all obliged to contribute in proportion to their respective interests in the estate. In the observation or neglect of this maxim consists, what is called the equality or inequality of taxation.

II. The tax which each individual is bound to pay ought to be certain, and not arbitrary. The time of payment, the manner of payment, the quantity to be paid, ought all to be clear and plain to the contributor, and to every other person. Where it is otherwise, every person subject to the tax is put more or less in the power of the taxgatherer, who can either aggravate the tax upon any obnoxious contributor, or extort, by the terror of such aggravation, some present or perquisite to himself.

III. Every tax ought to be levied at the time, or in the manner, in which it is most likely to be convenient for the contributor to pay it. A tax upon the rent of land or of houses, payable at the same term at which such rents are usually paid, is levied at the time when it is most likely to be convenient for the contributor to pay; or, when he is most likely to have wherewithal to pay. Taxes upon such consumable goods as are articles of luxury, are all finally paid by the consumer, and generally in a manner that is very convenient for him. He pays them by little and little, as he has occasion to buy the goods. As he is at liberty too, either to buy, or not to buy, as he pleases, it must be his own fault if he ever suffers any considerable inconveniency from such taxes.

IV. Every tax ought to be so contrived as both to take out and to keep out of the pockets of the people as little as possible, over and above what it brings into the public treasury of the state. A tax may either take out or keep out of the pockets of the people a great deal more than it brings into the public treasury, in the four following ways. First, the levying of it may require a great number of officers, whose salaries may eat up the greater part of the produce of the tax, and whose perquisites may impose another additional tax upon the people. Secondly, it may obstruct the industry of the people, and discourage them from applying to certain branches of business which might give maintenance and employment to great multitudes. While it obliges the people to pay, it may thus diminish, or perhaps destroy, some of the funds which might enable them more easily to do so. Thirdly, by the forfeitures and other penalties which those unfortunate individuals incur who attempt unsuccessfully to evade the tax, it may frequently ruin them, and thereby put an end to the benefit which the community might have received from the employment of their capitals. An injudicious tax offers a great temptation to smuggling. But the penalties of smuggling must rise in proportion to the temptation. The law, contrary to all the ordinary principles of justice, first creates the temptation, and then punishes those who yield to it; and it commonly enhances the punishment too in proportion to the very circumstance which ought certainly to alleviate it, the temptation to commit the crime. Fourthly, by subjecting the people to the frequent visits and the odious examination of the taxgatherers, it may expose them to much unnecessary trouble, vexation, and oppression; and though vexation is not, strictly speaking, expense, it is certainly equivalent to the expense at which every man would be willing to redeem himself from it. It is in some one or other of these four different ways that taxes are frequently so much more burdensome to the people than they are beneficial to the sovereign. . . .

Government in a Free Society: The Modern Conservative View

MILTON FRIEDMAN

In a much quoted passage in his inaugural address, President Kennedy said, "Ask not what your country can do for you—ask what you can do for your country." It is a striking sign of the temper of our times that the controversy about this passage centered on its origin and not on its content. Neither half of the statement expresses a relation between the citizen and his government that is worthy of the ideals of free men in a free society. The paternalistic "what your country can do for you" implies that government is the patron, the citizen the ward, a view that is at odds with the free man's belief in his own responsibility for his own destiny. The organismic, "what you can do for your country" implies that government is the master or the deity, the citizen, the servant or the votary. To the free man, the country is the collection of individuals who compose it, not something over and above them. He is proud of a common heritage and loyal to common traditions. But he regards government as a means, an instrumentality, neither a grantor of favors and gifts, nor a master or god to be blindly worshipped and served. He recognizes no national goal except as it is the consensus of the goals that the citizens severally serve. He recognizes no national purpose except as it is the consensus of the purposes for which the citizens severally strive.

The free man will ask neither what his country can do for him nor what he can do for his country. He will ask rather "What can I and my compatriots do through government" to help us discharge our individual responsibilities, to achieve our several goals and purposes, and above all, to protect our freedom? And he will accompany this question with another: How can we keep the government we create from becoming a Frankenstein that will destroy the very freedom we establish it to protect? Freedom is a rare and delicate plant. Our minds tell us, and history confirms, that the great threat to freedom is the concentration of power. Government is necessary to preserve our free-

From Milton Friedman, *Capitalism and Freedom* (Chicago: The University of Chicago Press, 1962), pp. 1–36. © 1962 by The University of Chicago. Reprinted by permission of the publisher and the author.

dom, it is an instrument through which we can exercise our freedom; yet by concentrating power in political hands, it is also a threat to freedom. Even though the men who wield this power initially be of good will and even though they be not corrupted by the power they exercise, the power will both attract and form men of a different stamp.

How can we benefit from the promise of government while avoiding the threat to freedom? Two broad principles embodied in our Constitution give an answer that has preserved our freedom so far, though they have been violated repeatedly in practice while proclaimed as precept.

First, the scope of government must be limited. Its major function must be to protect our freedom both from the enemies outside our gates and from our fellow-citizens: to preserve law and order, to enforce private contracts, to foster competitive markets. Beyond this major function, government may enable us at times to accomplish jointly what we would find it more difficult or expensive to accomplish severally. However, any such use of government is fraught with danger. We should not and cannot avoid using government in this way. But there should be a clear and large balance of advantages before we do. By relying primarily on voluntary co-operation and private enterprise, in both economic and other activities, we can insure that the private sector is a check on the powers of the governmental sector and an effective protection of freedom of speech, of religion, and of thought.

The second broad principle is that government power must be dispersed. If government is to exercise power, better in the county than in the state, better in the state than in Washington. If I do not like what my local community does, be it in sewage disposal, or zoning, or schools, I can move to another local community, and though few may take this step, the mere possibility acts as a check. If I do not like what my state does, I can move to another. If I do not like what Washington imposes, I have few alternatives in this world of jealous nations.

The very difficulty of avoiding the enactments of the federal government is of course the great attraction of centralization to many of its proponents. It will enable them more effectively, they believe, to legislate programs that—as they see it—are in the interest of the public, whether it be the transfer of income from the rich to the poor or from private to governmental purposes. They are in a sense right. But this coin has two sides. The power to do good is also the power to do harm; those who control the power today may not tomorrow; and, more important, what one man regards as good, another may regard as harm. The great tragedy of the drive to centralization, as of the drive to extend the scope of government in general, is that it is mostly led by men of good will who will be the first to rue its consequences.

The preservation of freedom is the protective reason for limiting and decentralizing governmental power. But there is also a constructive reason. The great advances of civilization, whether in architecture or painting, in science or literature, in industry or agriculture, have never come from centralized government. Columbus did not set out to seek a new route to China in response to a majority directive of a parliament, though he was partly financed by an absolute monarch. Newton and Leibnitz; Einstein and Bohr; Shakespeare, Milton, and Pasternak; Whitney, McCormick, Edison, and Ford; Jane Addams, Florence Nightingale, and Albert Schweitzer; no one of these opened new frontiers in human knowledge and understanding, in literature, in technical possibilities, or in the relief of human misery in response to governmental directives. Their achievements were the product of individual genius, of strongly held minority views, of a social climate permitting variety and diversity.

Government can never duplicate the variety and diversity of individual action. At any moment in time, by imposing uniform standards in housing, or nutrition, or clothing, government could undoubtedly improve the level of living of many individuals; by imposing uniform standards in schooling, road construction, or sanitation, central government could undoubtedly improve the level of performance in many local areas and perhaps even on the average of all communities. But in the process, government would replace progress by stagnation, it would substitute uniform mediocrity for the variety essential for that experimentation which can bring tomorrow's laggards above today's mean. . . .

It is widely believed that politics and economics are separate and largely unconnected; that individual freedom is a political problem and material welfare an economic problem; and that any kind of political arrangements can be combined with any kind of economic arrangements. . . .

The [thesis embodied here . . .] is that such a view is a delusion, that there is an intimate connection between economics and politics, that only certain combinations of political and economic arrangements are possible, and that in particular, a society which is socialist cannot also be democratic, in the sense of guaranteeing individual freedom.

Economic arrangements play a dual role in the promotion of a free society. On the one hand, freedom in economic arrangements is itself a component of freedom broadly understood, so economic freedom is an end in itself. In the second place, economic freedom is also an indispensable means toward the achievement of political freedom.

The first of these roles of economic freedom needs special emphasis because intellectuals in particular have a strong bias against regarding this aspect of freedom as important. They tend to express contempt for what they regard as material aspects of life, and to regard their own pursuit of allegedly higher values as on a different plane of significance and as deserving of special attention. For most citizens of the country, however, if not for the intellectual, the direct importance of economic freedom is at least comparable in significance to the indirect importance of economic freedom as a means to political freedom. . . .

Viewed as a means to the end of political freedom, economic arrangements are important because of their effect on the concentration or dispersion of power. The kind of economic organization that provides economic freedom directly, namely, competitive capitalism, also promotes political freedom because it separates economic power from political power and in this way enables the one to offset the other.

Historical evidence speaks with a single voice on the relation between political freedom and a free market. I know of no example in time or place of a society that has been marked by a large measure of political freedom, and that has not also used something comparable to a free market to organize the bulk of economic activity. . . .

From this standpoint, the role of the market, as already noted, is that it permits unanimity without conformity; that it is a system of effectively proportional representation. On the other hand, the characteristic feature of action through explicitly political channels is that it tends to require or to enforce substantial conformity. The typical issue must be decided "yes" or "no"; at most, provision can be made for a fairly limited number of alternatives. Even the use of proportional representation in its explicitly political form does not alter this conclusion. The number of separate groups that can in fact be represented is narrowly limited, enormously so by comparison with the proportional representation of the market. More important, the fact that the final outcome generally must be a law applicable to all groups, rather than separate legislative enactments for each "party" represented, means that proportional representation in its political version, far from permitting unanimity without conformity, tends toward ineffectiveness and fragmentation. It thereby operates to destroy any consensus on which unanimity with conformity can rest.

There are clearly some matters with respect to which effective proportional representation is impossible. I cannot get the amount of national defense I want and you, a different amount. With respect to such indivisible matters we can discuss, and argue, and vote. But having decided, we must conform. It is precisely the existence of such indivisible matters—protection of the individual and the nation from coercion are clearly the most basic—that prevents exclusive reliance on individual action through the market. It we are to use some of our resources for such indivisible items, we must employ political channels to reconcile differences.

The use of political channels, while inevitable, tends to strain the social cohesion essential for a stable society. The strain is least if agreement for joint action need be reached only on a limited range of issues on which people in any event have common views. Every extension of the range of issues for which explicit agreement is sought strains further the delicate threads that hold society together. If it goes so far as to touch an issue on which men feel deeply yet differently, it may well disrupt the society. Fundamental differences in basic values can seldom if ever be resolved at the ballot box; ultimately they can only be decided, though not resolved, by conflict. The religious and civil wars of history are a bloody testament to this judgment.

The widespread use of the market reduces the strain on the social fabric by rendering conformity unnecessary with respect to any activities it encompasses. The wider the range of activities covered by the market, the fewer are the issues on which explicitly political decisions are required and hence on which it is necessary to achieve agreement. In turn, the fewer the issues on which agreement is necessary, the greater is the likelihood of getting agreement while maintaining a free society.

Unanimity is, of course, an ideal. In practice, we can afford neither the time nor the effort that would be required to achieve complete unanimity on every issue. We must perforce accept something less. We are thus led to accept majority rule in one form or another as an expedient. That majority rule is an expedient rather than itself a basic principle is clearly shown by the fact that our willingness to resort to majority rule, and the size of the majority we require, themselves depend on the seriousness of the issue involved. If the matter is of little moment and the minority has no strong feelings about being overruled, a bare plurality will suffice. On the other hand, if the minority feels strongly about the issue involved, even a bare majority will not do. Few of us would be willing to have issues of free speech, for example, decided by a bare majority. Our legal structure is full of such distinctions among kinds of issues that require different kinds of majorities. At the extreme are those issues embodied in the Constitution. These are the principles that are so important that we are willing to make minimal concessions to expediency. Something like essential consensus was achieved initially in accepting them, and we require something like essential consensus for a change in them.

The self-denying ordinance to refrain from majority rule on certain kinds of issues that is embodied in our Constitution and in similar written or unwritten constitutions elsewhere, and the specific provisions in these constitutions or their equivalents prohibiting coercion of individuals, are themselves to be regarded as reached by free discussion and as reflecting essential unanimity about means. . . .

It is important to distinguish the day-to-day activities of people from the general customary and legal framework within which these take place. The day-to-day activities are like the actions of the participants in a game when they are playing it; the framework, like the rules of the game they play. And just as a good game requires acceptance by the players both of the rules and of the umpire to interpret and enforce them, so a good society requires that its members agree on the general conditions that will govern relations among them, on some means of arbitrating different interpretations of these conditions, and on some device for enforcing compliance with the generally accepted rules. As in games, so also in society, most of the general conditions are the unintended outcome of custom, accepted unthinkingly. At most, we consider explicitly only minor modifications in them, though the cumulative effect of a series of minor modifications may be a drastic alteration in the character of the game or of the society. In both games and society also, no set of rules can prevail unless most participants most of the time conform to them without external sanctions; unless that is, there is a broad underlying social consensus. But we cannot rely on custom or on this consensus alone to interpret and to enforce the rules; we need an umpire. These then are the basic roles of government in a free society: to provide a means whereby we can modify the rules, to mediate differences among us on the meaning of the rules, and to enforce compliance with the rules on the part of those few who would otherwise not play the game.

The need for government in these respects arises because absolute freedom is impossible. However attractive anarchy may be as a philosophy, it is not feasible in a world of imperfect men. Men's freedoms can conflict, and when they do, one man's freedom must be limited to preserve another's—as a Supreme Court Justice once put it, "My freedom to move my fist must be limited by the proximity of your chin."

The major problem in deciding the appropriate activities of government is how to resolve such conflicts among the freedoms of different individuals. In some cases, the answer is easy. There is little difficulty in attaining near unanimity to the proposition that one man's freedom to murder his neighbor must be sacrificed to preserve the freedom of the other man to live. In other cases, the answer is difficult. In the economic area, a major problem arises in respect of the conflict between freedom to combine and freedom to compete. What meaning is to be attributed to "free" as modifying "enterprise"? In the United States, "free" has been understood to mean that anyone is free to set up an enterprise, which means that existing enterprises are not free to keep out competitors except by selling a better product at the same price or the same product at a lower price. In the continental tradition, on the other hand, the meaning has generally been that enterprises are free to do what they want, including the fixing of prices, division of markets, and the adoption of other techniques to keep out potential competitors. Perhaps the most difficult specific problem in this area arises with respect to combinations among laborers, where the problem of freedom to combine and freedom to compete is particularly acute.

A still more basic economic area in which the answer is both difficult and important is the definition of property rights. The notion of property, as it has developed over centuries and as it is embodied in our legal codes, has become so much a part of us that we tend to take it for granted, and fail to recognize the extent to which just what constitutes property and what rights the ownership of property confers are complex social creations rather than self-evident propositions. Does my having title to land, for example, and my freedom to use my property as I wish, permit me to deny to someone else the right to fly over my land in his airplane? Or does his right to use his airplane take precedence? Or does this depend on how high he flies? Or how much noise he makes? Does voluntary exchange require that he pay me for the privilege of flying over my land? Or that I must pay him to refrain from flying over it? The mere mention of royalties, copyrights, patents; shares of stock in corporations; riparian rights, and the like, may perhaps emphasize the role of generally accepted social rules in the very definition of property. It may suggest also that, in many cases, the existence of a well specified and generally accepted definition of property is far more important than just what the definition is.

Another economic area that raises particularly difficult problems is the monetary system. Government responsibility for the monetary system has long been recognized. It is explicitly provided for in the constitutional provision which gives Congress the power "to coin money, regulate the value thereof, and of foreign coin." There is probably no other area of economic activity with respect to which government action has been so uniformly accepted. This habitual and by now almost unthinking acceptance of governmental responsibility makes thorough understanding of the grounds for such responsibility all the more necessary, since it enhances the danger that the scope of government will spread from activities that are, to those that are not, appropriate in a free society, from providing a monetary framework to determining the allocation of resources among individuals. . . .

In summary, the organization of economic activity through voluntary exchange presumes that we have provided, through government, for the maintenance of law and order to prevent coercion of one individual by another, the enforcement of contracts voluntarily entered into, the definition of the meaning of property rights, the interpretation and enforcement of such rights, and the provision of a monetary framework. . . .

A government which maintained law and order, defined property rights, served as a means whereby we could modify property rights and other rules of the economic game, adjudicated disputes about the interpretation of the rules, enforced contracts, promoted competition, provided a monetary framework, engaged in activities to counter technical monopolies and to overcome neighborhood effects widely regarded as sufficiently important to justify government intervention, and which supplemented private charity and the private family in protecting the irresponsible, whether madman or child—such a government would clearly have important functions to perform. . . .

Yet it is also true that such a government would have clearly limited functions and would refrain from a host of activities that are now undertaken by federal and state governments in the United States, and their counterparts in other Western countries. . . .

The End of Laissez-Faire

JOHN MAYNARD KEYNES

Let us clear from the ground the metaphysical or general principles upon which, from time to time, *laissez-faire* has been founded. It is *not* true that individuals possess a prescriptive "natural liberty" in their economic activities. There is *no* "compact" conferring perpetual rights on those who Have or on those who Acquire. The world is *not* so governed from above that private and social interest always coincide. It is *not* so managed here below that in practice they coincide. It is *not* a correct deduction from the Principles of Economics that enlightened self-interest always operates in the public interest. Nor is it true that self-interest generally *is* enlightened; more often individuals acting separately to promote their own ends are too ignorant or too weak to attain even these. Experience does *not* show that individuals, when they make up a social unit, are always less clear-sighted than when they act separately.

We cannot, therefore, settle on abstract grounds, but must handle on its merits in detail, what Burke termed "one of the finest problems in legislation, namely, to determine what the State ought to take upon itself to direct by the public wisdom, and what it ought to leave, with as little interference as possible, to individual exertion." We have to discriminate between what Bentham, in his forgotten but useful nomenclature, used to term *Agenda* and *Non-Agenda,* and to do this without Bentham's prior presumption that interference is, at the same time, "generally needless" and "generally pernicious."[1] Perhaps the chief task of Economists at this hour is to distinguish afresh the *Agenda* of Government from the *Non-Agenda;* and the companion task of Politics is to devise forms of Government within a Democracy which shall be capable of accomplishing the *Agenda.* I will illustrate what I have in mind by two examples.

1. I believe that in many cases the ideal size for the unit of control and

Reprinted from *Essays in Persuasion,* Norton Library Edition, 1963, by John Maynard Keynes. By permission of W. W. Norton & Company, Inc. Copyright All Rights Reserved by W. W. Norton & Company, Inc. Also by permission of the Royal Economic Society and Macmillan London and Basingstoke.

[1] Bentham's *Manual of Political Economy,* published posthumously, in Bowring's edition (1843).

organisation lies somewhere between the individual and the modern State. I suggest, therefore, that progress lies in the growth and the recognition of semi-autonomous bodies within the State—bodies whose criterion of action within their own field is solely the public good as they understand it, and from whose deliberations motives of private advantage are excluded, though some place it may still be necessary to leave, until the ambit of men's altruism grows wider, to the separate advantage of particular groups, classes, or faculties—bodies which in the ordinary course of affairs are mainly autonomous within their prescribed limitations, but are subject in the last resort to the sovereignty of the democracy expressed through Parliament.

I propose a return, it may be said, towards mediaeval conceptions of separate autonomies. But, in England at any rate, corporations are a mode of government which has never ceased to be important and is sympathetic to our institutions. It is easy to give examples, from what already exists, of separate autonomies which have attained or are approaching the mode I designate—the Universities, the Bank of England, the Port of London Authority, even perhaps the Railway Companies.

But more interesting than these is the trend of Joint Stock Institutions, when they have reached a certain age and size, to approximate to the status of public corporations rather than that of individualistic private enterprise. One of the most interesting and unnoticed developments of recent decades has been the tendency of big enterprise to socialise itself. A point arrives in the growth of a big institution—particularly a big railway or big public utility enterprise, but also a big bank or a big insurance company—at which the owners of the capital, i.e. the shareholders, are almost entirely dissociated from the management, with the result that the direct personal interest of the latter in the making of great profit becomes quite secondary. When this stage is reached, the general stability and reputation of the institution are more considered by the management than the maximum of profit for the shareholders. The shareholders must be satisfied by conventionally adequate dividends; but once this is secured, the direct interest of the management often consists in avoiding criticism from the public and from the customers of the concern. This is particularly the case if their great size or semi-monopolistic position renders them conspicuous in the public eye and vulnerable to public attack. The extreme instance, perhaps, of this tendency in the case of an institution, theoretically the unrestricted property of private persons, is the Bank of England. It is almost true to say that there is no class of persons in the Kingdom of whom the Governor of the Bank of England thinks less when he decides on his policy than of his shareholders. Their rights, in excess of their conventional dividend, have already sunk to the neighbourhood of zero. But the same thing is partly true of many other big institutions. They are, as time goes on, socialising themselves.

Not that this is unmixed gain. The same causes promote conservatism and a waning of enterprise. In fact, we already have in these cases many of the faults as well as the advantages of State Socialism. Nevertheless we see here, I think, a natural line of evolution. The battle of Socialism against unlimited private profit is being won in detail hour by hour. In these particular fields—it remains acute elsewhere—this is no longer the pressing problem. There is, for instance, no so-called important political question so really unimportant, so irrelevant to the reorganisation of the economic life of Great Britain, as the Nationalisation of the Railways.

It is true that many big undertakings, particularly Public Utility enterprises and other business requiring a large fixed capital, still need to be semi-socialised. But we must keep our minds flexible regarding the forms of this semi-socialism. We must take full advantage of the natural tendencies of the day, and we must probably prefer semi-autonomous corporations to organs of the Central Government for which Ministers of State are directly responsible.

I criticise doctrinaire State Socialism, not because it seeks to engage men's altruistic impulses in the service of Society, or because it departs from *laissez-faire,* or because it takes away from man's natural liberty to make a million, or because it has courage for bold experiments. All these things I applaud. I criticise it because it misses the significance of what is actually happening; because it is, in fact, little better than a dusty survival of a plan to meet the problems of fifty years ago, based on a misunderstanding of what some one said a hundred years ago. Nineteenth-century State Socialism sprang from Bentham, free competition, etc., and is in some respects a clearer, in some respects a more muddled, version of just the same philosophy as underlies nineteenth-century individualism. Both equally laid all their stress on freedom, the one negatively to avoid limitations on existing freedom, the other positively to destroy natural or acquired monopolies. They are different reactions to the same intellectual atmosphere.

2. I come next to a criterion of *Agenda* which is particularly relevant to what it is urgent and desirable to do in the near future. We must aim at separating those services which are *technically social* from those which are *technically individual.* The most important *Agenda* of the State relate not to those activities which private individuals are already fulfilling, but to those functions which fall outside the sphere of the individual, to those decisions which are made by *no one* if the State does not make them. The important thing for Government is not to do things which individuals are doing already, and to do them a little better or a little worse; but to do those things which at present are not done at all.

It is not within the scope of my purpose on this occasion to develop practical policies. I limit myself, therefore, to naming some instances of what I mean from amongst those problems about which I happen to have thought most.

Many of the greatest economic evils of our time are the fruits of risk, uncertainty, and ignorance. It is because particular individuals, fortunate in situation or in abilities, are able to take advantage of uncertainty and ignorance, and also because for the same reason big business is often a lottery, that great inequalities of wealth come about; and these same factors are also the cause of the Unemployment of Labour, or the disappointment of reasonable business expectations, and of the impairment of efficiency and production. Yet the cure lies outside the operations of individuals; it may even be to the interest of individuals to aggravate the disease. I believe that the cure for these things is partly to be sought in the deliberate control of the currency and of credit by a central institution, and partly in the collection and dissemination on a great scale of data relating to the business situation, including the full publicity, by law if necessary, of all business facts which it is useful to know. These measures would involve Society in exercising directive intelligence through some appropriate organ of action over many of the inner intricacies of private business, yet it would leave private initiative and enterprise unhindered. Even if these measures prove insufficient, nevertheless they will furnish us with better knowledge than we have now for taking the next step.

My second example relates to Savings and Investment. I believe that some co-ordinated act of intelligent judgment is required as to the scale on which it is desirable that the community as a whole should save, the scale on which these savings should go abroad in the form of foreign investments, and whether the present organisation of the investment market distributes savings along the most nationally productive channels. I do not think that these matters should be left entirely to the chances of private judgment and private profits, as they are at present.

My third example concerns Population. The time has already come when each country needs a considered national policy about what size of Population, whether larger or smaller than at present or the same, is most expedient. And having settled this policy, we must take steps to carry it into operation. The time may arrive a little later when the community as a whole must pay attention to the innate quality as well as to the mere numbers of its future members.

These reflections have been directed towards possible improvements in the technique of modern Capitalism by the agency of collective action. There is nothing in them which is seriously incompatible with what seems to me to be the essential characteristic of Capitalism, namely the dependence upon an intense appeal to the money-making and money-loving instincts of individuals as the main motive force of the economic machine. Nor must I, so near to my end, stray towards other fields. Nevertheless, I may do well to remind you, in conclusion, that the fiercest contests and the most deeply felt divisions of opinion are likely to be waged in the coming years not round technical questions, where the arguments on either side are mainly economic, but round those which, for want of better words, may be called psychological or, perhaps, moral.

In Europe, or at least in some parts of Europe—but not, I think, in the United States of America—there is a latent reaction, somewhat widespread, against basing Society to the extent that we do upon fostering, encouraging, and protecting the money-motives of individuals. A preference for arranging our affairs in such a way as to appeal to the money-motive as little as possible, rather than as much as possible, need not be entirely *a priori,* but may be based on the comparison of experiences. Different persons, according to their choice of profession, find the money-motive playing a large or a small part in their daily lives, and historians can tell us about other phases of social organisation in which this motive has played a much smaller part than it does now. Most religions and most philosophies deprecate, to say the least of it, a way of life mainly influenced by considerations of personal money profit. On the other hand, most men today reject ascetic notions and do not doubt the real advantages of wealth. Moreover it seems obvious to them that one cannot do without the money-motive, and that, apart from certain admitted abuses, it does its job well. In the result the average man averts his attention from the problem, and has no clear idea what he really thinks and feels about the whole confounded matter.

Confusion of thought and feeling leads to confusion of speech. Many people, who are really objecting to Capitalism as a way of life, argue as though they were objecting to it on the ground of its inefficiency in attaining its own objects. Contrariwise, devotees of Capitalism are often unduly conservative, and reject reforms in its technique, which might really strengthen and preserve it, for fear that they may prove to be first steps away from Capitalism itself. Nevertheless a time may be coming when we shall get clearer than at present as to when we are talking about Capitalism as an efficient or inefficient technique, and when we are talking about it as desirable or objectionable in itself. For my part, I think that Capitalism, wisely managed, can probably be made more efficient for attaining economic ends than any alternative system yet in sight, but that in itself it is in many ways extremely objectionable. Our problem is to work out a social organisation which shall be as efficient as possible without offending our notions of a satisfactory way of life.

The next step forward must come, not from political agitation or premature experiments, but from thought. We need by an effort of the mind to elucidate our own feelings. At present our sympathy and our judgment are liable to be on different sides, which is a painful and paralysing state of mind. In the field of action reformers will not be successful until they can steadily pursue a clear and definite object with their intellects and their feelings in tune. There is no party in the world at present which appears to me to be pursuing right aims by right methods. Material Poverty provides the incentive to change precisely in situations where there is very little margin for experiments. Material Prosperity removes the incentive just when it might be safe to take a chance. Europe lacks the means, America the will, to make a move. We need a new set of convictions which spring naturally from a candid examination of our own inner feelings in relation to the outside facts.

A Liberal Theory of
Public Expenditures

WALTER W. HELLER

What does the economist have to offer a perplexed public and its policymaking representatives on the theory of Government functions as they affect the budget? The cynic's offhand answer, "not much," may be close to the mark if one demands definitive rules of thumb for determining the precise scope of Government functions and level of Government expenditures. But if, instead, the demand is for economic guidelines to aid the budgetary decisionmaker (1) in blending rationally the service, stabilization, and income-transfer functions of Government, (2) in identifying those deficiencies in the private-market mechanism which call for Government budgetary action or, more broadly, those activities where Government use or control of resources promises greater returns than private use or control, and (3) in selecting the most efficient means of carrying out Government functions and activities (whether by Government production, contracts with private producers, transfer payments, loans, guaranties, tax concessions, and so forth)—if this is the nature of the demands on him, the economist is prepared to make a modest offering now and to work along lines that promise a greater contribution in the future.

In a sense, this paper is a progress report designed to show where the economist can already offer some useful counsel, to indicate some of the lines along which promising work is being done, and to suggest certain limitations or constraints within which the economic criteria for dividing resources between public and private use must be applied.

A Basic Framework

As a first step in the search for economic guideposts, we need to disentangle, classify, and define the basic objectives and functions of Government that shape its budgetary decisions. Fortunately, Prof. Richard A. Musgrave has developed a conceptual framework for this task in his "multiple theory of budget determination."

The component functions of the budget as he brings them into focus are: (1) The service, or want-satisfying, function: to provide for the satisfaction of those individual wants which the market mechanism cannot satisfy effec-

From testimony before Joint Congressional Economic Subcommittee, 1962.

tively (e.g., education and conservation) or is incapable of satisfying (e.g., defense and justice); (2) the income-transfer or distributional function: to make those corrections in the existing income distribution (by size, by occupational groups, by geographical area, etc.) which society desires; and (3) the stabilization function: to join with monetary policy and other measures to raise or lower the level of aggregate demand so as to maintain full employment and avoid inflation. The first function is of dominant interest [here] and the succeeding sections of the paper return to it. But several general implications of the Musgrave system as a whole deserve attention before turning to specifics.

Musgrave's formulation helps unclutter our thinking on the component parts of the budget decision. It drives home the significant point that our decisions on how much and what kind of want-satisfying services to provide by Government budgets need not be tied to our demands on the budget for correction of either the existing patterns of income distribution or the level of aggregate demand. If we prefer, we can have a small budget for services (financed by taxes levied on the benefit principle) combined with a big budget for redistributive transfers of income (financed by taxes levied on the ability principle), or vice versa; and either combination can be coupled with either a deficit to stimulate demand and employment or a surplus to reduce demand and check inflation. In this respect, it is reminiscent of Samuelson's "daring doctrine" that by appropriate fiscal-monetary policy "a community can have full employment, can at the same time have the rate of capital formation it wants, and can accomplish all this compatibly with the degree of income-redistributing taxation it ethically desires." Musgrave, in turn, points the way to achieving any combination of Government services, income redistribution, and economic redistribution, and economic stability we set our sights on. . . .

Economic Determinants of the Proper Sphere of Government Activity

Given a framework for straight thinking about budget functions, the economist is brought face to face with two questions that come closer to the central problem of the proper sphere of Government activity. First, where competitive bidding via the pricing mechanism is inapplicable, how are the preferences of voters for governmental services to be revealed, measured, and appropriately financed? Second, waiving the question of measurement of preferences, where would the line between public and private control over resources be drawn if economic efficiency were the only criterion to be implied?

On the first question, insofar as it relates to individual preferences for public goods, economists have agreed on the nature and difficulty of the problem, have made some intriguing suggestions as to its solution, and have concluded that it is next to insoluble. The key difficulty is that the voting process, unlike the pricing process, does not force the consumer of public goods to show his hand. The essence of preference measurement is the showing of how much of one good or service the consumer is willing to forgo as the price of acquiring another. But the amount of a public good or service (say, of defense, police protection, or schooling) available to the voter is independent of the amount he pays in taxes or the intensity of his demand for it. Unless and until we devise a reliable and reasonably accurate method of detecting specific voter preferences in some detail, our definition of the proper sphere of government activity will have to rely chiefly on the informed judgment and perception of those whom we vote into legislative and executive office.

This being the case, the economist's task is to contribute what he can to this informed judgment and perception. In effect, the economist's job becomes one of telling the voters and their representatives what their preferences as to governmental activities would be if they were guided by the principle of economic efficiency. In doing so, the economist is not proposing that decisions as to what kinds of activities should be assigned to government—what wants should be satisfied and resources should be redirected through government action—should be made on economic grounds alone. He is fully aware that values such as those of political and economic freedom play a vital role in these decisions. But he can perform the valuable service of identifying those deficiencies in the market mechanism and those inherent economic characteristics of government which make it economically advantageous to have certain services provided by government rather than by private initiative. In other words he can show where government intervention in resource allocation and use promises a greater return per unit of input than untrammeled private use.

The economist recognizes, of course, that there are areas in which he is necessarily mute, or at least should not speak unless spoken to. These are the areas of pure public goods, whose benefits are clearly indivisible and nonmarketable, and no amount of economic wisdom can determine the appropriate levels of output and expenditure. In the realm of defense, for example, one successful Russian earth satellite or intercontinental ballistics missile will (and should) outweigh 10,000 economists in determining the appropriate level of expenditures. At most, the economist stands ready to offer analysis and judgments as to the critical levels of defense expenditures beyond which they threaten serious inflation in the absence of drastic tax action or curtailment of civilian programs, or, given that action, threaten impairment of producer incentives and essential civilian programs.

A much more fruitful activity for the economist is to demonstrate the economic advantage offered by government intervention, budgetary and otherwise, in those intermediate service areas where benefits are at least partially divisible and marketable. A number of economists have made useful contributions on this front. In what situations does economic logic point to government intervention to correct the market mechanism's allocation of resources in the interests of greater efficiency in their use?

1. Where there are important third-party benefits [usually known as neigh-

borhood effects, external effects, or externalities] which accrue to others than the direct beneficiary of the service, as in the case of education, disease prevention, police and fire protection, the market price and demand schedules underestimate the marginal and total social benefits provided by the service in question. By and large, the direct beneficiaries are the only ones who enter the private market as buyers, with the result that the services would be undervalued, underpriced, and underproduced unless Government entered the transaction. Government is the instrument for representing the third-party beneficiaries and correcting the deficiency of the market place (though this is not to deny that private religious and philanthropic organizations, for example, also represent third-party beneficiaries and operate on budget rather than market principles).

2. Just as there may be indirect benefits not reflected in market demand, there may be indirect costs inflicted on society which do not enter the private producer's costs and therefore do not influence market supply. Classic examples are the costs of smog, water pollution, denuding of forests, and the like. In these areas, private output will exceed the optimum level unless government corrects the situation either by regulation or by a combination of expenditure and charge-backs to the private producers involved.

3. Where a service is best provided, for technical reasons, as a monopoly (e.g., postal service, electricity, railroad transportation), the Government is expected to step in either by regulation or operation to avoid costly duplication and improve the quality of service. Ideally, its function would also be to guide prices toward levels consistent with optimum output. Involved here is the problem of the decreasing cost industry, where efficient plant size is so large relative to total demand that average cost decreases as output increases, and the market solution of the output and price problem will not result in best use of the productive assets. To push production to a point representing an ideal use of resources may require, if not Government operation, a subsidy financed out of tax revenues.

4. Government may enjoy some advantages in production or distribution which make it an inherently more efficient producer of certain services. Here, the classic case is highways, streets, and sidewalks. By providing them free to all comers, Government effects substantial savings in costs of distribution since it does not have to meter the service and charge a price for each specific use. In this category we might also fit projects, such as the initial development of atomic energy, which involve such great risks and huge accumulations of capital that the private market does not have the financial tools to cope with them.

Alternative Means of Carrying Out Government Functions

Given the decisions as to the appropriate sphere of Government activity (on the basis not merely of considerations of greatest economic gain but also of value preferences), there remains the problem of choice among alternative methods to implement these decisions, to achieve given aims and satisfy expressed public wants. This choice will affect the budget in different ways. It may increase expenditures, decrease revenues, establish contingent liabilities, or perhaps have no effect on the budget at all (except for a small amount of administrative expenses involved in the supervisory and regulatory activities). Since the operational question is not merely what functions and activities Government should carry out, but what budgetary principles and expenditure levels these lead to, the problem of implementation must be included in any applied theory of public expenditures.

Here, the economist's role is to determine the most efficient method of providing the service or otherwise influencing resource allocation. He is concerned with minimizing costs, i.e, achieving the stated objective with a minimum expenditure of resources. Needless to say, other considerations will also influence the selection among alternative means, as even a brief consideration of the types of choices involved in the implementation process will make clear.

What are these choices? Take first the case of direct satisfaction of individuals' public wants. Should the Government produce the desired public goods or obtain them from private industry by purchase or contract? To accomplish redistributive ends, should the Government provide transfers in cash or transfers in kind? Should Government rely on public production of educational services, or should it consider private production combined with earmarked transfers of purchasing power to parents? Thus far, the choices all involve direct budgetary expenditures, the level of which differs, at least marginally, depending on the relative efficiency of the method chosen. But in making his choice, the policymaker must consider not merely the direct costs of providing the service but whether one method involves more or less disturbance of private market incentives and patterns of production than another, whether it involves more or less interference with individual freedom (which is largely a function of the extent of Government expenditures and intervention but certainly in part also a function of the form of that intervention), and so on.

Another set of choices may take the item off of the expenditure side of the budget entirely, or leave it there only contingently. Should such subsidies as those to promote oil and gas exploration, stimulate foreign investment, expand the merchant marine, promote low-cost housing, and increase the flow of strategic minerals take the form of (1) outright subsidies or above-market-price purchase programs, (2) Government loan programs, (3) Government guaranties, or (4) tax concessions? The choice will clearly involve quite different impacts on Government expenditures.

In many of these cases, the economist can be helpful with his efficiency criterion. But one would be naive to think that efficiency alone dictates the choice. The economist may show that a direct subsidy could stimulate a given amount of private direct investment abroad or a given amount of exploration for oil and gas, with a much smaller cost to the budget than is implicitly required in the tax concession method of achieving the same end. Yet, the costlier tax concession method may be preferred for two simple reasons: (1) it is virtually self-administering, involving no administrative hierarchy to substitute its authority for relatively free private decisions, and (2) it does not involve an increase in the expenditure side of the budget, a fact which has certain attractions to the Executive and Congress.

As yet, no clear boundary lines have been drawn among the various forms of Government intervention to mark off those that properly belong within the scope of public expenditure theory. But this illustrative review of the various choices makes clear that some forms of Government activity which are not reflected in expenditures at all (tax concessions) or only contingently (guaranties) are an integral part of such expenditure theory. In fact, there may be a stronger case for embracing these in expenditure theory than many Government activities which require budgetary outlays but are conducted on the pricing principle, i.e., Government enterprise activities.

Economists are conducting some provocative inquiries into questions of alternative methods of carrying out Government programs in areas where the answers had heretofore been taken for granted. For example, the transfer of schooling to a private production and Government transfer payment basis has been urged by Professor Milton Friedman as a more efficient means of providing the desired service. . . . Once fairly conclusive findings are devised as to the methods most likely to minimize costs, there remains the vital task of blending these findings with the nonmonetary values that would be gained or lost in the process of transferring from public to private production.

Some Constraints on the Application of Specific Economic Criteria

Repeatedly in this discussion, the note has been sounded that, in determining the level of Government activity, the policymaker cannot live by economics alone. More particularly, we need to guard against setting up our economic guides solely in terms of those considerations which lend themselves to sharp economic analysis and definition. In other words, the role of both economic and non-economic constraints must be given full weight.

The former include a host of considerations relating particularly to economic motivation in Government versus private undertakings. Government may, for example, have a decided edge in the efficiency of distribution or be able to achieve a better balancing of social costs and social benefits in a variety of fields. Yet, there may be important offsets to these economic advantages in terms of (1) bureaucracy, (2) lack of the profit criterion to gage the results of Government activities, and (3) undesigned or unintended (presumably adverse) economic effects of taxation.

The latter factor, in particular the fact that tax financing of public services involves breaking the link between an individual's cost of a given service and his benefit from it, may involve important offsets to economic advantages otherwise gained by Government expenditure. Thus far, to be sure, no dire consequences of the disincentive effects of taxation have been firmly proved, but changes in the form of private economic activity to minimize taxes are certainly a cost that must be weighed when netting out the balance of economic advantage in Government versus private performance of services.

Beyond the economic factors, one encounters an even more basic and less manageable constraint, namely that of freedom of choice. Thus, it is quite conceivable that following the kinds of economic criteria discussed earlier in the paper would take us considerably farther in the direction of Government spending and control over resource allocation than we would wish to go in terms of possible impairment of economic and political freedom. This consideration enters importantly not merely in decisions as to the proper range of Government activity but also in choosing among alternative methods of providing Government services.

This is not to imply that all value considerations run counter to the expansion of the Government sector of our economy. Such expansion may serve a number of social values, such as greater equality of income and opportunity, a more acceptable social environment, and so on.

To get all of these considerations into the decision-making equation on private versus public provision of a particular service, or on the choice among alternative forms of providing the service, requires a wisdom which goes well beyond the field of economics. Perhaps this explains why so few economists enter politics.

The State:
A Radical Critique

KARL MARX AND FREDERICK ENGELS

I. The State and Law

The Relation of State and Law to Property

The first form of property, in the ancient world as in the Middle Ages, is tribal property, determined with the Romans chiefly by war, with the Germans by the rearing of cattle. In the case of the ancient peoples, since several tribes live together in one town, the tribal property appears as State property, and the right of the individual to it as mere *"possession"* which, however, like tribal property as a whole, is confined to landed property only. Real private property began with the ancients, as with modern nations, with personal movable property—(slavery and community) (*dominium ex jure Quiritium*). In the case of the nations which grew out of the Middle Ages, tribal property evolved through various stages—feudal landed property, corporative movable property, manufacture-capital—to modern capital, determined by big industry and universal competition, i.e., pure private property, which has cast off all semblance of a communal institution and has shut out the State from any influence on the development of property. To this modern private property corresponds the modern State, which, purchased gradually by the owners of property by means of taxation, has fallen entirely into their hands through the national debt, and its existence has become wholly dependent on the commercial credit which the owners of property, the bourgeois, extend to it in the rise and fall of State funds on the stock exchange. By the mere fact that it is a *class* and no longer an *estate,* the bourgeoisie is forced to organize itself no longer locally, but nationally, and to give a general form to its mean average interest. Through the emancipation of private property from the community, the State has become a separate entity, beside and outside civil society; but it is nothing more than the form of organization which the bourgeois necessarily adopt both for internal and external purposes, for the mutual guarantee of their property and interests. The independence of the State is only found nowadays in those countries where the estates have not yet com-

From (I) Karl Marx and Frederick Engels, *The German Ideology* (written 1845–1846) and (II) Frederick Engels, "The Origin of the Family, Private Property, and the State" (published in 1844).

pletely developed into classes, where the estates, done away with in more advanced countries, still have a part to play, and where there exists a mixture; countries, that is to say in which no one section of the population can achieve dominance over the others. This is the case particularly in Germany. The most perfect example of the modern State is North America. The modern French, English and American writers all express the opinion that the State exists only for the sake of private property, so that this fact has penetrated into the consciousness of the normal man.

Since the State is the form in which the individuals of a ruling class assert their common interests, and in which the whole civil society of an epoch is epitomized, it follows that in the formation of all communal institutions the State acts as intermediary, that these institutions receive a political form. Hence the illusion that law is based on the will, and indeed on the will divorced from its real basis—on free will. Similarly, the theory of law is in its turn reduced to the actual laws.

Civil law develops simultaneously with private property out of the disintegration of the natural community. With the Romans the development of private property and civil law had no further industrial and commercial consequences, because their whole mode of production did not alter. With modern peoples, where the feudal community was disintegrated by industry and trade, there began with the rise of private property and civil law a new phase, which was capable of further development. The very first town which carried on an extensive trade in the Middle Ages, Amalfi, also developed maritime law. As soon as industry and trade developed private property further, first in Italy and later in other countries, Roman civil law was adopted again in a perfected form and raised to authority. When later the bourgeoisie had acquired so much power that the princes took up their interests in order to overthrow the feudal nobility by means of the bourgeoisie, there began in all countries—in France in the sixteenth century—the real development of law, which in all countries except England proceeded on the basis of the Roman Codex. In England too, Roman legal principles had to be introduced to further the development of civil law (especially in the case of personal movable property). It must not be forgotten that law has just as little an independent history as religion.

In civil law the existing property relationships are declared to be the result of the general will. The *jus utendi et abutendi* itself asserts on the one hand the fact that private property has become entirely independent of the community, and on the other the illusion that private property itself is based on the private will, the arbitrary disposal of the thing. In practice, the *abuti* has very definite economic limitations for the owner of private property, if he does not wish to see his property and hence his *jus abutendi* pass into other hands, since actually the thing, considered merely with reference to his will, is not a thing at all, but only becomes true property in intercourse, and independently of the right to the thing (a *relationship,* which the philosophers call an idea). This juridical illusion, which reduces law to the mere will, necessarily leads, in the further development of property relationships, to the position that a man may have a title to a thing without really having the thing. If, for instance, the income from a piece of land is lost owing to competition, then the proprietor has certainly his legal title to it along with the *jus utendi et abutendi*. But he can do nothing with it; he owns nothing as a landed proprietor if he has not enough capital besides to cultivate his ground. This illusion of the jurists also explains the fact that for them, as for every codex, it is altogether fortuitous that individuals enter into relationships among themselves (e.g., contracts); it explains why they consider that these relationships can be entered into or not at will, and that their content rests purely on the individual free will of the contracting parties. Whenever, through the development of industry and commerce, new forms of intercourse have been evolved (e.g., assurance companies, etc.), the law has always been compelled to admit them among the modes of acquiring property.

This crystallization of social activity, this consolidation of what we ourselves produce into an objective power above us, growing out of our control, thwarting our expectations, bringing to naught our calculations, is one of the chief factors in historical development up till now. And out of this very contradiction between the interest of the individual and that of the community the latter takes an independent form as the STATE, divorced from the real interests of individual and community, and at the same time as an illusory communal life, always based, however, on the real ties existing in every family and tribal conglomeration (such as flesh and blood, language, division of labour on a larger scale, and other interests) and especially, as we shall enlarge upon later, on the classes, already determined by the division of labour, which in every such mass of men separate out, and of which one dominates all the others. It follows from this that all struggles within the State, the struggle between democracy, aristocracy and monarchy, the struggle for the franchise, etc., etc., are merely the illusory forms in which the real struggles of the different classes are fought out among one another (of this the German theoreticians have not the faintest inkling, although they have received a sufficient introduction to the subject in *The German-French Annals* and *The Holy Family*).

II

The state is . . . by no means a power forced on society from without; just as little is it "the reality of the ethical idea," "the image and reality of reason," as Hegel maintains. Rather, it is a product of society at a certain stage of development; it is the admission that this society has become entangled in an insoluble contradiction with itself, that it is cleft into irreconcilable antagonisms which it is powerless to dispel. But in order that these antagonisms, classes with conflicting economic interests, might not consume themselves and society in sterile struggle, a power seemingly standing above society became necessary for the purpose of moderating the conflict, of keeping it within the bounds of "order"; and this power, arisen out of society, but placing itself above it, and increasingly alienating itself from it, is the state.

In contradistinction to the old gentile organization, the state, first, divides its subjects *according to territory*. As we have seen, the old gentile associations, built upon and held together by ties of blood, became inadequate, largely because they presupposed that the members were bound to a given territory, a bond which had long ceased to exist. The territory remained, but the people had become mobile. Hence, division according to territory was taken as the point of departure, and citizens were allowed to exercise their public rights and duties wherever they settled, irrespective of gens and tribe. This organization of citizens according to locality is a feature common to all states. That is why it seems natural to us; but we have seen what long and arduous struggles were needed before it could replace, in Athens and Rome, the old organization according to gentes.

The second is the establishment of a *public power* which no longer directly coincided with the population organizing itself as an armed force. This special public power is necessary, because a self-acting armed organization of the population has become impossible since the cleavage into classes. The slaves also belonged to the population; the 90,000 citizens of Athens formed only a privileged class as against the 365,000 slaves. The people's army of the Athenian democracy was an aristocratic public power against the slaves, whom it kept in check; however, a gendarmerie also became necessary to keep the citizens in check, as we related above. This public power exists in every state; it consists not merely of armed people but also of material adjuncts, prisons and institutions of coercion of all kinds, of which gentile society knew nothing. It may be very insignificant, almost infinitesimal, in societies where class antagonisms are still undeveloped and in out-of-the-way places as was the case at certain times and in certain regions in the United States of America. It grows stronger, however, in proportion as class antagonisms within the state become more acute, and as adjacent states become larger and more populated. We have only to look at our present-day Europe, where class struggle and rivalry in conquest have screwed up the public power to such a pitch that it threatens to devour the whole of society and even the state.

In order to maintain this public power, contributions from the citizens become necessary—*taxes*. These were absolutely unknown in gentile society; but we know enough about them today. As civilization advances, these taxes become inadequate; the state makes drafts on the future, contracts loans, *public debts*. Old Europe can tell a tale about these, too.

In possession of the public power and of the right to levy taxes, the officials, as organs of society, now stand *above* society. The free, voluntary respect that was accorded to the organs of the gentile constitution does not satisfy them, even if they could gain it; being the vehicles of a power that is becoming alien to society, respect for them must be enforced by means

of exceptional laws by virtue of which they enjoy special sanctity and in-
violability. The shabbiest police servant in the civilized state has more "authority" than all the organs of gentile society put together; but the most
powerful prince and the greatest statesman, or general, of civilization may
well envy the humblest gentile chief for the uncoerced and undisputed respect
that is paid to him. The one stands in the midst of society, the other is forced
to attempt to represent something outside and above it.

As the state arose from the need to hold class antagonisms in check, but
as it arose, at the same time, in the midst of the conflict of these classes,
it is, as a rule, the state of the most powerful, economically dominant class,
which, through the medium of the state, becomes also the politically dominant
class, and thus acquires new means of holding down and exploiting the oppressed class. Thus, the state of antiquity was above all the state of the slave
owners for the purpose of holding down the slaves, as the feudal state was
the organ of the nobility for holding down the peasant serfs and bondsmen,
and the modern representative state is an instrument of exploitation of wage
labour by capital. By way of exception, however, periods occur in which the
warring classes balance each other so nearly that the state power, as ostensible
mediator, acquires, for the moment, a certain degree of independence of both.
Such was the absolute monarchy of the seventeenth and eighteenth centuries,
which held the balance between the nobility and the class of burghers; such
was the Bonapartism of the First, and still more of the Second French Empire, which played off the proletariat against the bourgeoisie and the bourgeoisie against the proletariat. The latest performance of this kind, in which
ruler and ruled appear equally ridiculous, is the new German Empire of the
Bismarck nation: here capitalists and workers are balanced against each other
and equally cheated for the benefit of the impoverished Prussian cabbage
junkers.

In most of the historical states, the rights of citizens are, besides, apportioned according to their wealth, thus directly expressing the fact that the
state is an organization of the possessing class for its protection against the
non-possessing class. It was so already in the Athenian and Roman classification according to property. It was so in the mediaeval feudal state, in which
the alignment of political power was in conformity with the amount of land
owned. It is seen in the electoral qualifications of the modern representative
states. Yet this political recognition of property distinctions is by no means
essential. On the contrary, it marks a low stage of state development. The
highest form of the state, the democratic republic, which under our modern
conditions of society is more and more becoming an inevitable necessity, and
is the form of state in which alone the last decisive struggle between proletariat and bourgeoisie can be fought out—the democratic republic officially
knows nothing any more of property distinctions. In it wealth exercises its
power indirectly, but all the more surely. On the one hand, in the form of
the direct corruption of officials, of which America provides the classical example; on the other hand, in the form of an alliance between government

and Stock Exchange, which becomes the easier to achieve the more the public debt increases and the more joint-stock companies concentrate in their hands not only transport but also production itself, using the Stock Exchange as their centre. The latest French republic as well as the United States is a striking example of this; and good old Switzerland has contributed its share in this field. But that a democratic republic is not essential for this fraternal alliance between government and Stock Exchange is proved by England and also by the new German Empire, where one cannot tell who was elevated more by universal suffrage, Bismarck or Bleichröder. And lastly, the possessing class rules directly through the medium of universal suffrage. As long as the oppressed class, in our case, therefore, the proletariat, is not yet ripe to emancipate itself, it will in its majority regard the existing order of society as the only one possible and, politically, will form the tail of the capitalist class, its extreme Left wing. To the extent, however, that this class matures for its self-emancipation, it constitutes itself as its own party and elects its own representatives, and not those of the capitalists. Thus, universal suffrage is the gauge of the maturity of the working class. It cannot and never will be anything more in the present-day state; but that is sufficient. On the day the thermometer of universal suffrage registers boiling point among the workers, both they and the capitalists will know what to do.

The state, then, has not existed from all eternity. There have been societies that did without it, that had no conception of the state and state power. At a certain stage of economic development, which was necessarily bound up with the cleavage of society into classes, the state became a necessity owing to this cleavage. We are now rapidly approaching a stage in the development of production at which the existence of these classes not only will have ceased to be a necessity, but will become a positive hindrance to production. They will fall as inevitably as they arose at an earlier stage. Along with them the state will inevitably fall. The society that will organize production on the basis of a free and equal association of the producers will put the whole machinery of state where it will then belong: into the Museum of Antiquities, by the side of the spinning wheel and the bronze axe.

The State in Capitalist Society

PAUL M. SWEEZY

I. The State in Economic Theory

Probably few would deny that the state plays a vital role in the economic process. There are still many, however, who would argue that the state can and should be kept out of economic theorizing.

From one point of view, this is not difficult to understand. So long as economics is regarded as a science of the relations between man and nature in the manner of the modern school, the state requires consideration only at the level of application and not as a part of the subject matter of the science. There is no state on Robinson Crusoe's island, yet economics is as relevant to Robinson as it is to twentieth-century America. From this standpoint the state cannot logically be a concern of theoretical economics; it must be regarded as one of the factors which shape and limit the application of economic principles to any given set of actual conditions.

All this is changed when we take the position that economics is the science of the social relationships of production under historically determined conditions. Failure to include the state in the subject matter of economics then becomes an arbitrary and unjustifiable omission. In view of this, and after what has been said about Marx's fundamental approach to economics in earlier chapters, no further explanation seems required to justify the inclusion of a chapter on the state in our examination of Marxian economics. A word of caution is, however, necessary before we proceed.

As in the case of crises, Marx never worked out a systematic and formally complete theory of the state. That he originally intended to do so is clear. For example, he opens the Preface to the *Critique of Political Economy* with the following words:

> I consider the system of bourgeois economy in the following order: Capital, landed property, wage labor; state, foreign trade, world market . . . The first part of the first book, treating of capital, consists of the following chapters: 1. Commodity; 2. Money, or simple Circulation; 3. Capital in general. The first two chapters form the contents of the present

work . . . Systematic elaboration on the plan outlined above will depend upon circumstances.

The plan underwent substantial alterations in the course of time, as an examination of the three volumes of *Capital* makes clear, but the state always remained in the background and never received the "systematic elaboration" which Marx evidently had hoped to accord it. It follows that a neat summary of his views is out of the question. Instead we shall try to present a summary theoretical treatment of the state which is consistent with Marx's numerous and scattered remarks on the subject and which at the same time provides the necessary supplement to the main body of theoretical principles dealing with the development of the capitalist system.[1]

II. The Primary Function of the State

There is a tendency on the part of modern liberal theorists to interpret the state as an institution established in the interests of society as a whole for the purpose of mediating and reconciling the antagonisms to which social existence inevitably gives rise. This is a theory which avoids the pitfalls of political metaphysics and which serves to integrate in a tolerably satisfactory fashion a considerable body of observed fact. It contains, however, one basic shortcoming, the recognition of which leads to a theory essentially Marxian in its orientation. A critique of what may be called the class-mediation conception of the state is, therefore, perhaps the best way of introducing the Marxian theory.

The class-mediation theory assumes, usually implicitly, that the underlying class structure, or what comes to the same thing, the system of property relations is an immutable datum, in this respect like the order of nature itself. It then proceeds to ask what arrangements the various classes will make to get along with each other, and finds that an institution for mediating their conflicting interests is the logical and necessary answer. To this institution powers for maintaining order and settling quarrels are granted. In the real world what is called the state is identified as the counterpart of this theoretical construction.

The weakness of this theory is not difficult to discover. It lies in the assumption of an immutable and, so to speak, self-maintaining class structure of society. The superficiality of this assumption is indicated by the most cursory study of history.[2] The fact is that many forms of property relations with their concomitant class structures have come and gone in the past, and

---

[1] Among the most important Marxist writings on the state the following may be mentioned: Engels, *The Origin of the Family, Private Property and the State,* particularly Ch. IX; Lenin, *The State and Revolution;* Rosa Luxemburg, "Sozialreform oder Revolution?" *Gesammelte Werke,* Vol. III. An English translation of the latter work is available (*Reform or Revolution?,* Three Arrows Press, N.Y., 1937), but it is unfortunately not a very satisfactory one. A reasonably adequate survey of a large body of Marxist literature on the state is contained in S. H. M. Chang, *The Marxian Theory of the State* (1931).

[2] Many theorists recognize this up to a point, but they believe that what was true of past societies is not true of modern society. In other words, capitalism is regarded as the final end-product of social evolution.

there is no reason to assume that they will not continue to do so in the future. The class structure of society is no part of the natural order of things; it is the product of past social development, and it will change in the course of future social development.

Once this is recognized it becomes clear that the liberal theory goes wrong in the manner in which it initially poses the problem. We cannot ask: Given a certain class structure, how will the various classes, with their divergent and often conflicting interests, manage to get along together? We must ask: How did a particular class structure come into being and by what means is its continued existence guaranteed? As soon as an attempt is made to answer this question, it appears that the state has a function in society which is prior to and more fundamental than any which present-day liberals attribute to it. Let us examine this more closely.

A given set of property relations serves to define and demarcate the class structure of society. From any set of property relations one class or classes (the owners) reap material advantages; other classes (the owned and the non-owners) suffer material disadvantages. A special institution capable and willing to use force to whatever degree is required is an essential to the maintenance of such a set of property relations. Investigation shows that the state possesses this characteristic to the fullest degree, and that no other institution is or can be allowed to compete with it in this respect. This is usually expressed by saying that the state, and the state alone, exercises sovereignty over all those subject to its jurisdiction. It is, therefore, not difficult to identify the state as the guarantor of a given set of property relations.

If now we ask, where the state comes from, the answer is that it is the product of a long and arduous struggle in which the class which occupies what is for the time the key positions in the process of production gets the upper hand over its rivals and fashions a state which will enforce that set of property relations which is in its own interest. In other words any particular state is the child of the class or classes in society which benefit from the particular set of property relations which it is the state's obligation to enforce. A moment's reflection will carry the conviction that it could hardly be otherwise. As soon as we have dropped the historically untenable assumption that the class structure of society is in some way natural or self-enforcing, it is clear that any other outcome would lack the prerequisites of stability. If the disadvantaged classes were in possession of state power, they would attempt to use it to establish a social order more favorable to their own interests, while a sharing of state power among the various classes would merely shift the locale of conflict to the state itself.

That such conflicts within the state, corresponding to fundamental class struggles outside, have taken place in certain transitional historical periods is not denied. During those long periods, however, when a certain social order enjoys a relatively continuous and stable existence, the state power must be monopolized by the class or classes which are the chief beneficiaries.

As against the class-mediation theory of the state, we have here the underlying idea of what has been called the class-domination theory. The former takes the existence of a certain class structure for granted and sees in the state an institution for reconciling the conflicting interests of the various classes; the latter, on the other hand, recognizes that classes are the product of historical development and sees in the state an instrument in the hands of the ruling classes for enforcing and guaranteeing the stability of the class structure itself.

It is important to realize that, so far as capitalist society is concerned, "class domination" and "the protection of private property" are virtually synonymous expressions. Hence when we say with Engels that the highest purpose of the state is the protection of private property, we are also saying that the state is an instrument of class domination. This is doubtless insufficiently realized by critics of the Marxian theory who tend to see in the notion of class domination something darker and more sinister than "mere" protection of private property. In other words they tend to look upon class domination as something reprehensible and the protection of private property as something meritorious. Consequently, it does not occur to them to identify the two ideas. Frequently, no doubt, this is because they have in mind not capitalist property, but rather private property as it would be in a simple commodity-producing society where each producer owns and works with his own means of production. Under such conditions there are no classes at all and hence no class domination. Under capitalist relations, however, property has an altogether different significance, and its protection is easily shown to be identical with the preservation of class dominance. Capitalist private property does not consist in things—things exist independently of their ownership—but in a social relation between people. Property confers upon its owners freedom from labor and the disposal over the labor of others, and this is the essence of all social domination whatever form it may assume. It follows that the protection of property is fundamentally the assurance of social domination to owners over non-owners. And this, in turn, is precisely what is meant by class domination, which it is the primary function of the state to uphold.

The recognition that the defense of private property is the first duty of the state is the decisive factor in determining the attitude of genuine Marxist socialism towards the state. "The theory of the Communists," Marx and Engels wrote in the *Communist Manifesto,* "can be summed up in the single sentence: Abolition of private property." Since the state is first and foremost the protector of private property, it follows that the realization of this end cannot be achieved without a head-on collision between the forces of socialism and the state power.[3]

[3] The treatment of the relation between the state and property has of necessity been extremely sketchy. In order to avoid misunderstanding, the following note should be added. The idea that the state is an organization for the maintenance of private property was by no means an invention of Marx and Engels. On the contrary, it constituted the cornerstone of the whole previous development of political thought from the breakdown of feudalism and the origins of the modern state. Bodin, Hobbes, Locke, Rousseau, Adam Smith, Kant, and Hegel—to mention but a few outstanding thinkers of the period before Marx—clearly recognized this central function of the state. They believed private property to be the necessary condition for the full development of human potentialities, the *sine qua non* of genuine freedom. Marx and Engels added that freedom based on private property is freedom for an exploiting class, and

III. The State as an Economic Instrument

The fact that the first concern of the state is to protect the continued existence and stability of a given form of society does not mean that it performs no other functions of economic importance. On the contrary, the state has always been a very significant factor in the functioning of the economy within the framework of the system of property relations which it guarantees. This principle is generally implicitly recognized by Marxist writers whenever they analyse the operation of an actual economic system, but it has received little attention in discussions of the theory of the state. The reason for this is not difficult to discover. The theory of the state has usually been investigated with the problem of transition from one form of society to another in the foreground; in other words, what we have called the primary function of the state has been the subject of analysis. Lenin's *State and Revolution*—the title clearly indicates the center of interest—set a precedent which has been widely followed.[4] Consequently, the theory of the state as an economic instrument has been neglected, though evidently for our purposes it is necessary to have some idea of the essentials of Marx's thinking on the subject.

Fortunately Marx, in his chapter on the length of the working day, provides a compact and lucid analysis of the role of the state in relation to one very important problem of capitalist economy. By examining this chapter in some detail we can deduce the guiding principles of Marxist teaching on the role of the state within the framework of capitalist property relations.

The rate of surplus value, one of the key variables in Marx's system of theoretical economics, depends on three factors: the productivity of labor, the length of the working day and prevailing subsistence standards. It is therefore a matter of importance to discover the determinants of the length of the working day. This is clearly not a question of economic law in any narrow sense. As Marx put it,

> apart from extremely elastic bounds, the nature of exchange of commodities itself imposes no limits to the working day, no limit to surplus labor. The capitalist maintains his rights as a purchaser when he tries to make the working day as long as possible . . . On the other hand . . . the laborer maintains his right as a seller when he wishes to reduce the working day to one of definite normal duration. There is here, therefore, an antimony, right against right, both equally bearing the seal of the law of exchanges. Between equal rights force decides. Hence it is that in the history of capitalist production, the determination of what is a working day presents itself as the result of a struggle, a struggle between collective capital, i.e. the class of capitalists, and collective labor, i.e. the working class.

---

that freedom for *all* presupposes the abolition of private property, that is to say the achievement of a classless society. Nevertheless, Marx and Engels did not forget that the realization of a classless society (abolition of private property) is possible only on the basis of certain definite historical conditions; without the enormous increase in the productivity of labor which capitalism had brought about, a classless society would be no more than an empty Utopia.

[4] For example, Chang's book, cited above, follows Lenin's outline very closely.

After describing certain forms, both pre-capitalist and capitalist, of exploitation involving the duration of the working day, Marx examines "The Struggle for a Normal Working Day" in the historical development of English capitalism. The first phase of this struggle resulted in "Compulsory Laws for the Extension of the Working Day from the Middle of the 14th to the End of the 17th Century." Employers, straining to create a trained and disciplined proletariat out of the available pre-capitalist material, were frequently obliged to resort to the state for assistance. Laws extending the length of the working day were the result. For a long time, however, the extension of the working day was a very slow and gradual process. It was not until the rapid growth of the factory system in the second half of the eighteenth century that there began that process of prolonging hours of work which culminated in the notorious conditions of the early nineteenth century:

> After capital had taken centuries in extending the working day to its normal maximum length, and then beyond this to the limit of the natural day of 12 hours, there followed on the birth of machinism and modern industry in the last third of the 18th century a violent encroachment like that of an avalanche in its intensity and extent . . . As soon as the working class, stunned at first by the noise and turmoil of the new system of production, recovered in some measure its senses its resistance began.

The beginnings of working-class resistance ushered in the second phase of the development: "Compulsory Limitation by Law of the Working Time, The English Factory Acts, 1833 to 1864." In a series of sharp political struggles, the workers were able to wring one concession after another from their opponents. These concessions took the form of laws limiting hours of work for ever wider categories of labor, until by 1860 the principle of limitation of the working day was so firmly established that it could no longer be challenged. Thereafter progress pursued a smoother course.

The limitation of the working day was not simply a question of concessions by the ruling class in the face of a revolutionary threat, though this was undoubtedly the main factor. At least two other considerations of importance have to be taken into account. Marx noted that,

> Apart from the working class movement that daily grew more threatening, the limiting of factory labor was dictated by the same necessity which spread guano over the English fields. The same blind eagerness for plunder that in the one case exhausted the soil had, in the other, torn up by the roots the living forces of the nation.

Moreover, the question of factory legislation entered into the final phase of the struggle for political mastery between the landed aristocracy and the industrial capitalists:

> However much the individual manufacturer might give the rein to his old lust for gain, the spokesmen and political leaders of the manufacturing class ordered a change in front and of speech toward the workpeople. They had entered upon the contest for the repeal of the Corn Laws and needed the workers to help them to victory. They promised, therefore, not only a double-sized loaf of bread, but the enactment of the Ten Hours Bill in the Free Trade millennium . . .

And after repeal of the Corn Laws had gone through, the workers "found allies in the Tories panting for revenge." Thus factory legislation derived a certain amount of support from both sides to the great struggle over free trade.

Finally Marx concluded his treatment of the working day with the following statement:

> For "protection" against "the serpent of their agonies" the laborers must put their heads together and, as a class, compel the passing of a law, an all-powerful social barrier that shall prevent the very workers from selling, by voluntary contract with capital, themselves and their families into slavery and death. In place of the pompous catalogue of the "inalienable rights of man" comes the modest Magna Charta of a legally limited working day, which shall make clear "when the time which the worker sells is ended, and when his own begins." *Quantum mutatus ab illo!*

What general conclusions can be deduced from Marx's discussion of the working day? The principle of most general bearing was stated by Engels. Answering the charge that historical materialism neglects the political element in historical change, Engels cited the chapter on the working day "where legislation, which is surely a political act, has such a trenchant effect" and concluded that "force (that is, state power) is also an economic power" and hence is by no means excluded from the causal factors in historical change. Once this has been established, it is necessary to ask under what circumstances and in whose interest the economic power of the state will be brought into action. On both points the analysis of the working day is instructive.

First, the state power is invoked to solve problems which are posed by the economic development of the particular form of society under consideration, in this case capitalism. In the earlier period a shortage of labor power, in the later period over-exploitation of the laboring population were the subjects of state action. In each case the solution of the problem required state intervention. Many familiar examples of a similar character readily come to mind.

Second, we should naturally expect that the state power under capitalism would be used first and foremost in the interests of the capitalist class since the state is dedicated to the preservation of the structure of capitalism and must therefore be staffed by those who fully accept the postulates and objectives of this form of society. This is unquestionably true, but it is not inconsistent to say that state action may run counter to the immediate economic interests of some or even all of the capitalists provided only that the overriding aim of preserving the system intact is promoted. The legal limitation of the working day is a classic example of state action of this sort. The intensity of class antagonism engendered by over-exploitation of the labor force was such that it became imperative for the capitalist class to make concessions even at the cost of immediate economic advantages.[5] For the sake of preserving domestic peace and tranquility, blunting the edge of class antagonisms, and ultimately avoiding the dangers of violent revolution, the capitalist class is always prepared to make concessions through the medium of state action. It may, of course, happen that the occasion for the concessions is an actual materialization of the threat of revolution. In this case their purpose is to restore peace and order so that production and accumulation can once again go forward uninterruptedly.

Let us summarize the principles underlying the use of the state as an economic instrument within the framework of capitalism. In the first place, the state comes into action in the economic sphere in order to solve problems which are posed by the development of capitalism. In the second place, where the interests of the capitalist class are concerned, there is a strong predisposition to use the state power freely. And, finally, the state may be used to make concessions to the working class provided that the consequences of not doing so are sufficiently dangerous to the stability and functioning of the system as a whole.

[5] This example makes clear the concession character of state action favoring the working class, since it could not possibly be maintained that the workers had a share in state power in England at the time the main factory acts were passed. In this connection it is sufficient to recall that the Reform Act of 1832 contained high property qualifications for voting and it was not until 1867 that the franchise was next extended. By this time the most important victories in the struggle for factory legislation had already been won.

Questions for Discussion

1. What are the major ideological differences among the conservative, liberal, and radical views?
2. How is Adam Smith's emphasis on the division of labor similar to Milton Friedman's emphasis on the efficiency of competitive capitalism?
3. What does J. M. Keynes mean when he speaks of large industry socializing itself?
4. Paul Sweezy presents an analysis of the "actual role" government plays in the economy. How is this different from the liberal and conservative selections?

PART III

The Historical Development of Government in the Economy

Having examined the theoretical and ideological roots of the problem of the state and the economy, it is useful now to shift to an examination of differing historical analyses of exactly how and why the economic functions of government in the United States have developed to their present dimensions. Parenthetically, it might be added here that economics courses seem to have a general tendency to avoid institutional and historical analysis, and, in doing this, students are either left to develop the historical setting themselves or neglect it altogether. The point to be made here is: whatever one's ideological preferences on the question of state economic power, it did not just suddenly appear. It grew and developed from something to something and in a logically coherent, if not always agreeable, way. The point may seem elementary but it is a necessary one for students of the American economy to come to terms with in their own minds before proceeding to specific contemporary issues.

Four selections are offered below as representative insights to the historical relationship between government and the economy. The first is itself a historical document, written in 1791 and presented to the Congress by the then secretary of the treasury, Alexander Hamilton. In this report, Hamilton lays out his own neo-Mercantilist philosophy, in which government is to play a large and encouraging role in the stimulation of the nation's business and industry. It was from this position that the new nation began; and, despite the fact that Hamiltonian federalism was soon to falter politically and ultimately vanish, Hamilton's ideas on the role of government in the economy were never to be completely abandoned, neither by his arch-rival Jefferson nor by the *laissez-faire* philosophy of the Jacksonians.

59

The second article, by Michael Reagan, offers a contemporary "liberal" analysis of the growth of state power, linking government's more recent growth and elaboration to the alleged breakdown of *laissez-faire* capitalism. To Reagan, the development of state economic power is seen as an expression of a new democratic capitalism in which the state humanely and justly intervenes and regulates economic affairs on the behalf of the people.

The last two selections are harsh attacks on the growth of state economic power. The first of these is a radical analysis by one of the book's editors, arguing essentially that the use of state power has been directly detrimental to the nation and the people. While the essay is not strictly a Marxist analysis, it does attempt to lay bare the root economic causes, the basic crises of capitalism, as the reasons for the development and centralization of federal economic power and to connect these factors to present-day economic and social problems. The last article similarly attacks present trends, but this time from the political right. It might seem at first glance that there is here a kind of "convergence" between left and right. Mr. Rothbard's attack, however, is on behalf of an individualism he now sees beset by growing concentration of power in America. His argument is for a return to *laissez-faire*.

The Mercantilist Roots:
A Report on
Manufactures

ALEXANDER HAMILTON

Experience teaches that men are often so much governed by what they are accustomed to see and practice, that the simplest and most obvious improvements, in the most ordinary occupations, are adopted with hesitation, reluctance, and by slow gradations. The spontaneous transition to new pursuits, in a community long habituated to different ones, may be expected to be attended with proportionably greater difficulty. When former occupations ceased to yield a profit adequate to the subsistence of their followers, or when there was an absolute deficiency of employment in them, owing to the superabundance of hands, changes would ensue; but these changes would be likely to be more tardy than might consist with the interest either of individuals or of the society. In many cases they would not happen while a bare support could be insured by an adherence to ancient courses, though a resort to a more profitable employment might be practicable. To produce the desirable changes as early as may be expedient may therefore require the incitement and patronage of government.

The apprehension of failing in new attempts is, perhaps, a more serious impediment. There are dispositions apt to be attracted by the mere novelty of an undertaking; but these are not always the best calculated to give it success. To this it is of importance that the confidence of cautious, sagacious capitalists, both citizens and foreigners, should be excited. And to inspire this description of persons with confidence, it is essential that they should be made to see in any project which is new—and for that reason alone, if for no other, precarious—the prospect of such a degree of countenance and support from governments, as may be capable of overcoming the obstacles inseparable from first experiments.

The superiority antecedently enjoyed by nations who have preoccupied and perfected a branch of industry, constitutes a more formidable obstacle than either of those which have been mentioned, to the introduction of the same branch into a country in which it did not before exist. To maintain, between the recent establishments of one country, and the long-matured establishments

From Alexander Hamilton, "Report on Manufactures" (1791).

of another country, a competition upon equal terms, both as to quality and price, is, in most cases, impracticable. The disparity, in the one, or in the other, or in both, must necessarily be so considerable as to forbid a successful rivalship without the extraordinary aid and protection of government.

But the greatest obstacle of all to the successful prosecution of a new branch of industry in a country in which it was before unknown, consists, as far as the instances apply, in the bounties, premiums, and other aids which are granted, in a variety of cases, by the nations in which the establishments to be imitated are previously introduced. It is well known (and particular examples, in the course of this report, will be cited) that certain nations grant bounties on the exportation of particular commodities, to enable their own workmen to undersell and supplant all competitors in the countries to which those commodities are sent. Hence, the undertakers of a new manufacture have to contend not only with the natural disadvantages of a new undertaking, but with the gratuities and remunerations which other governments bestow. To be enabled to contend with success, it is evident that the interference and aid of their own governments are indispensable.

Combinations by those engaged in a particular branch of business in one country to frustrate the first efforts to introduce it into another, by temporary sacrifices, recompensed, perhaps, by extraordinary indemnifications of the government of such country, are believed to have·existed and are not to be regarded as destitute of probability. The existence or assurance of aid from the government of the country in which the business is to be introduced, may be essential to fortify adventurers against the dread of such combinations; to defeat their efforts, if formed; and to prevent their being formed, by demonstrating that they must in the end prove fruitless.

Whatever room there may be for an expectation that the industry of a people, under the direction of private interest, will, upon equal terms, find out the most beneficial employment for itself, there is none for a reliance that it will struggle against the force of unequal terms, or will, of itself, surmount all the adventitious barriers to a successful competition which may have been erected, either by the advantages naturally acquired from practice and previous possession of the ground, or by those which may have sprung from positive regulations and an artificial policy. . . .

. . . It is proper . . . to consider the means by which [the promotion of manufacturers in the United States] may be effected.

In order to obtain a better judgment of the means proper to be resorted to by the United States, it will be of use to advert to those which have been employed with success in other countries. The principal of these are:

1. *Protecting duties—or duties on those foreign articles which are the rivals of the domestic ones intended to be encouraged*

   Duties of this nature evidently amount to a virtual bounty on the domestic fabrics; since, by enhancing the charges on foreign articles, they enable the national manufacturers to undersell all their foreign competitors. The propriety of this species of encouragment need not be dwelt upon, as it is not only a clear result from the numerous topics which have been suggested, but is sanctioned by the laws of the United States, in a variety of instances; it has the additional recommendation of being a resource of revenue. Indeed, all the duties imposed on imported articles, though with an exclusive view to revenue, have the effect, in contemplation, and except where they fall on raw materials, wear a beneficent aspect toward the manufacturers of the country.

2. *Prohibitions of rival articles, or duties equivalent to prohibitions*

This is another and efficacious means of encouraging national manufacturers; but, in general, it is only fit to be employed when a manufacture has made such progress, and is in so many hands, as to insure a due competition, and an adequate supply on reasonable terms. . . .

Considering a monopoly of the domestic market to its own manufacturers as the reigning policy of manufacturing nations, a similar policy, on the part of the United States, in every proper instance, is dictated, it might almost be said, by the principles of distributive justice; certainly, by the duty of endeavoring to secure to their own citizens a reciprocity of advantages.

3. *Prohibitions of the exportation of the materials of manufactures*

The desire of securing a cheap and plentiful supply for the national workmen, and, where the article is either peculiar to the country, or of peculiar quality there, the jealousy of enabling foreign workmen to rival those of the nation with its own materials, are the leading motives to this species of regulation. It ought not to be affirmed that it is in no instance proper; but is, certainly, one which ought to be adopted with great circumspection, and only in very plain cases. It is seen at once that its immediate operation is to abridge the demand and keep down the price of the produce of some other branch of industry—generally speaking, of agriculture—to the prejudice of those who carry it on; and though, if it be really essential to the prosperity of any very important national manufacture, it may happen that those who are injured in the first instance, may be, eventually, indemnified by the superior steadiness of an extensive domestic market depending on that prosperity; yet, in a matter in which there is so much room for nice and difficult combinations, in which such opposite considerations combat each other, prudence seems to dictate that the expedient in question ought to be indulged with a sparing hand.

4. *Pecuniary bounties*

This has been found one of the most efficacious means of encouraging manufacturers, and is, in some views, the best. . . . Its advantages are these:

a. It is a species of encouragement more positive and direct than any other, and for that very reason has a more immediate tendency to stimulate and uphold new enterprises, increasing the chances of profit, and diminishing the risks of loss in the first attempts.

b. It avoids the inconvenience of a temporary augmentation of price, which is incident to some other modes; or it produces it to a lesser degree, either by making no addition to the charges on the rival foreign article, as in the case of protecting duties, or by making a smaller addition. . . .

c. Bounties have not, like high protecting duties, a tendency to produce scarcity. An increase of price is not always the immediate, though where the progress of a domestic manufacture does not counteract a rise it is commonly the ultimate, effect of an additional duty. In the interval between the laying of the duty and the proportional increase of price, it may discourage importation by the interfering with the profits to be expected from the sale of the article.

d. Bounties are, sometimes, not only the best but the only proper expedient for uniting the encouragement of a new object of agriculture with that of a new object of manufacture. It is the interest of the farmer to have the production of the raw material promoted by counteracting the interference of the foreign material of the same kind. It is the interest of the manufacturer to have the material abundant and cheap. If, prior to the domestic production of the material in sufficient quantity to supply the manufacturer on good terms, a duty be laid upon the importation of it from abroad, with a view to promote the raising of it at home, the interest both of the farmer and manufacturer will be disserved. . . .

5. Premiums
These are of a nature allied to bounties, though distinguishable from them in some important features.

Bounties are applicable to the whole quantity of an article produced, or manufactured, or exported, and involve a correspondent expense. Premiums serve to reward some particular excellence or superiority, some extraordinary exertion or skill, and are dispensed only in a small number of cases. But their effect is to stimulate general effort; contrived so as to be both honorary and lucrative, they address themselves to different passions—touching the chords, as well of emulation as of interest. They are, accordingly, a very economical means of exciting the enterprise of a whole community.

There are various societies, in different countries, whose object is the dispensation of premiums for the encouragement of agriculture, arts, manufactures, and commerce; and though they are, for the most part, voluntary associations, with comparatively slender funds, their utility has been immense. Much has been done, by this means, in Great Britain. Scotland, in particular, owes materially to it a prodigious amelioration of condition. From a similar establishment in the United States, supplied and supported by the government of the Union, vast benefits might, reasonably, be expected. . . .

6. The exemption of the material of manufactures from duty
The policy of that exemption, as a general rule, particularly in reference to new establishments, is obvious. It can hardly ever be advisable to add the obstructions of fiscal burdens to the difficulties which naturally embarrass a

new manufacture; and where it is matured, and in condition to become an object of revenue, it is, generally speaking, better that the fabric, than the material, should be the subject of taxation. Ideas of proportion between the quantum of the tax and the value of the article can be more easily adjusted in the former than the latter case. An argument for exemptions of this kind, in the United States, is to be derived from the practice, as far as their necessities have permitted, of those nations whom we are to meet as competitors in our own and in foreign markets. . . .

7. *Drawbacks of the duties which are imposed on the materials of manufactures*

. . . As a general rule . . . duties on those materials ought, with certain exceptions, to be forborne. Of these exceptions three cases occur which may serve as examples. One, where the material is itself an object of general or extensive consumption and a fit and productive source of revenue. Another, where a manufacture of a simpler kind, the competiton of which, with a like domestic article, is desired to be restrained, partakes of the nature of a raw material, from being capable, by a further process, to be converted into a manufacture of a different kind, the introduction or growth of which is desired to be encouraged. A third, where the material itself is a production of the country, and in sufficient abundance to furnish a cheap and plentiful supply to the national manufacturers. . . .

Where duties on the material of manufactures are not laid for the purpose of preventing a competition with some domestic production, the same reasons which recommend, as a general rule, the exemption of those materials from duties, would recommend, as a like general rule, the allowance of drawbacks in favor of the manufacturer. Accordingly, such drawbacks are familiar in countries which systematically pursue the business of manufactures, which furnishes an argument for the observance of a similar policy in the United States; and the idea has been adopted by the laws of the Union, in the instances of salt and molasses. It is believed that it will be found advantageous to extend it to some other articles.

8. *The encouragement of new inventions and discoveries at home, and of the introduction into the United States of such as may have been made in other countries; particularly those which relate to machinery*

This is among the most useful and unexceptionable of the aids which can be given to manufactures. The usual means of that encouragement are pecuniary rewards, and, for a time, exclusive privileges. The first must be employed according to the occasion and the utility of the invention or discovery. For the last, so far as respects "authors and inventors," provision has been made by law. But it is desirable, in regard to improvements and secrets of extraordinary value, to be able to extend the same benefit to introducers, as well as authors and inventors; a policy which has been practiced with advantage in other countries. Here, however, as in some other cases, there is cause to regret that the competency of the authority of the national government to the good which might be done, is not without a question. Many aids might be given to industry, many internal improvements of primary magnitude might be promoted by an authority operating throughout the Union, which cannot be effected as well, if at all, by an authority confined within the limits of a single state. . . .

9. *Judicious regulations for the inspection of manufactured commodities*

This is not among the least important of the means by which the prosperity of manufacturers may be promoted. It is, indeed, in many cases, one of the most essential. Contributing to prevent frauds upon consumers at home and exporters to foreign countries, to improve the quality and preserve the character of the national manufactures, it cannot fail to aid the expeditious and advantageous sale of them and to serve as a guard against successful competition from other quarters. The reputation of the flour and lumber of some states, and of the potash of others, has been established by an attention to this point. And the like good name might be procured for those articles, wheresoever produced, by a judicious and uniform system of inspection throughout the ports of the United States. A like system might also be extended with advantage to other commodities.

10. *The facilitating of pecuniary remittances from place to place*

Is a point of considerable moment to trade in general, and to manufacturers in particular, by rendering more easy the purchase of raw materials and provisions and the payment for manufactured supplies. A general circulation of bank paper, which is to be expected from the institution lately established, will be a most valuable means to this end. But much good would also accrue from some additional provisions respecting inland bills of exchange. If those drawn in one state, payable in another, were made negotiable everywhere, and interest and damages allowed in case of protest, it would greatly promote negotiations between the citizens of different states, by rendering them more secure, and with it the convenience and advantage of the merchants and manufacturers of each.

11. *The facilitating of the transportation of commodities*

Improvements favoring this object intimately concern all the domestic interests of a community; but they may, without impropriety, be mentioned as having an important relation to manufactures. There is, perhaps, scarcely anything which has been better calculated to assist the manufacturers of Great Britain than the melioration of the public roads of that kingdom, and the great progress which has been of late made in opening canals. Of the former, the United States stand much in need; for the latter, they present uncommon facilities.

The symptoms of attention to the improvement of inland navigation, which have lately appeared in some quarters, must fill with pleasure every breast warmed with a true zeal for the prosperity of the country. These examples, it is to be hoped, will stimulate the exertions of the government and citizens

of every state. There can certainly be no object more worthy of the cares
of the local administrations; and it were to be wished that there was no doubt
of the power of the national government to lend its direct aid on a comprehensive plan. This is one of those improvements which could be prosecuted
with more efficacy by the whole than by any part or parts of the Union. There
are cases in which the general interest will be in danger to be sacrificed to the
collision of some supposed local interests. Jealousies, in matters of this kind,
are as apt to exist as they are apt to be erroneous.

The Expanding
Economic Role of
Government—A
Liberal's View

MICHAEL D. REAGAN

The Myth of Laissez Faire

Perhaps the greatest American economic myth is the belief that private enterprise is self-sustaining, that the only political requirement for a healthy economy is a policy of laissez faire. It is small wonder, given this belief, that
every increase in the scope of governmental economic activity is met with
cries of alarm. Yet it is easily demonstrated that the freest economy imaginable would still require a considerable range of governmental actions and
institutions, supporting as well as regulatory. As Wilbert E. Moore has written, "competition without rules is a contradiction in terms," and social controls are necessary "not only to maintain order in an economy which is only
nominally self-regulating, but also to ensure the consistency of economic organization with such values as individual health and familial stability."

If government really left the economy alone, there would be no system
of competition but Hobbes's war of each against all. Without governmental
enforcement of contracts, business men would not dare to make them. If government did not protect property, each firm would have to hire its own police
force—or even an army. Without a money system backed by government,

From *The Managed Economy* by Michael D. Reagan. Copyright © 1963 by Oxford University
Press, Inc. Reprinted by permission.

we would be reduced to crude barter or constantly subjected to ruination by extreme fluctuations in the value of private money substitutes. Without governmental mechanisms for adjustment of disputes between employers and employees, our industrial relations would be patterned on the bloody model of the coal fields of 1900.

Government also provides organizational forms to fit business needs: proprietorships, partnerships, and the privilege of incorporation which vests the firm with immortality and the investor with limited liability. It develops procedures for bankruptcy and reorganizations, to minimize the economic and social losses of business failure. It rewards invention by giving it privileged economic status through the patent system. It collects and disseminates knowledge in support of business operations, as in research reports on technological developments and market opportunities, and it establishes standards essential to common exchange: weights and measures, grading, and labelling.

It is inconceivable that any economy could long endure in the absence of these governmentally provided supports. Certainly the modern, interdependent, complex industrialized economy could not. And businessmen recognize this, at least implicitly, for one does not hear them calling for repeal of the kinds of "intervention" mentioned to this point. What they object to is not intervention as such, but intervention which is regulatory rather than promotional. That is, it is not principle but self-interest which provides the rationale for their position.

The real question of government's role focuses on those activities which go beyond the provision of a legal framework. Undeniably, the extent of governmental involvement has vastly increased in this century. What are the causes of the more extensive role of government?

Why Government's Role Has Expanded

The reasons for expanding governmental economic activity are a mixture of circumstantial development, increased knowledge of how an economy functions, and changing community values, each related to and reinforcing the others.

The rise of industrialization and its social corollary, urbanization, represent the circumstantial development. Perhaps the broadest effect of industrialization has been to substitute formal social controls for the informal ones of earlier society and to create new controls to handle problems that did not exist in the simpler and less interdependent technology of agricultural society.

As an example of new formal controls, we have the pure food and drug statutes and the Federal Trade Commission replacing the old attitude of *caveat emptor*. When consumer goods were largely limited to food and fiber products, "let the buyer beware" was not an impossible rule, for the consumer could easily be as knowledgeable as the seller regarding the desirable qualities in a vegetable or a pair of trousers made of natural fibers. But when industrialization and technological progress introduced a new and vastly extended range of products, complex in their mechanism and often artificial in their materials, common knowledge became a poor basis for purchase. The informal control by consumer information then required supplementation by formal protection. The Pure Food and Drug Act established an agency and a set of rules to guard the hopeful and gullible consumer from harmful remedies and contaminated foods. Today we are moving toward additional protection: to ensure against the great economic waste and personal financial distress caused by purchase of products which are ineffective though innocuous, by requiring that the producer prove his remedy has beneficial effect. The Kefauver hearings on the drug industry, whatever they prove about profits, have certainly demonstrated the necessity to safeguard the consumer against medically meaningless though commercially profitable innovations in prescription and proprietary drugs. President Kennedy's 1962 consumer protection message to Congress and his establishment of a Consumer Advisory Council exemplify the increasing activities on the part of government in areas where lack of consumer knowledge needs to be compensated for by formal social control.

Or consider antimonopoly legislation. When production was agricultural and producers were many and small, the consumer was protected by the market mechanism itself, which enabled the retail distributor to have a choice of suppliers. With the rise of national markets and industrial producers, the maintenance of competition became a matter for conscious policy as concentration of production in a few firms came to typify the situation. It was not a change from no regulation to government regulation, but from market regulation to government regulation.

To illustrate the need for new controls where no controls previously existed, we can cite the development of traffic rules, motorcycle policemen, and traffic courts and, in quite another sphere, blue-sky laws and the Securities Exchange Commission. Also zoning and land-use regulations are the by-product of industrial urbanization, which makes my neighbor's use of his property a matter of economic, esthetic, and hygienic concern to me.

In addition to supplying the supporting framework for business, government in industrial society is also necessarily called upon to provide a supporting framework for individuals and families. This is not the result of an alleged loss of "moral fiber" in the people, but of the living pattern of urban culture and the specialization and interdependence of industrial employment. In the pre-industrial society, people were literally more self-sufficient than it is possible for them to be today: the farm family grew its own food, made some of its own clothing and built its own house and outbuildings. Families were large, and children contributed economically by working in the fields or the house at an early age. Because there was a minimum of exchange and minimal use of cash, there was not the dependence upon cash income that there is today. The grandparents could be cared for within the home, and usually could continue to be useful members of the family, not a drain on their children's resources. When industrialism began to make some headway, and a son went off to the city to become a factory worker, it was still possible for him to return to the family farm if he lost his city job or became ill. Family responsibility for each member was then more feasible than it can be today.

Contrast with this picture the situation today, and the underlying causes for the expansion of economic welfare activities by government become quickly apparent. Production and consumption are divorced. The man does not work on his own farm but for an organization. He does not produce his own food, let alone clothing and housing, but performs a specialized task for a cash income, which he then exchanges for all of his family's needs. Loss of cash thus means loss of all sustenance. The family farm is no longer there to fall back on in rough times, nor would the urban-raised man know how to do farm work if it were available. Children in the city are economically unproductive; they cannot perform small tasks on their father's assembly line or in his office, as they could on the farm. Urban housing and the concentrated living patterns of the city do not easily accommodate three generations under one roof, so the grandparents require separate housing at separate expense. Furthermore, industrial employment is subject to fluctuations against which no individual can protect himself. Given the consequences of unemployment, and this inability to guard against it, income-support programs by government, such as unemployment compensation, disability compensation, health insurance, and old age pensions, can be seen as simply the modern equivalent of protections once, but no longer, provided by the socio-economic system itself.

While agricultural societies had good and bad seasons, and incredible human suffering might be the price of the latter, they could still not have the complete collapse of economy that happened in 1933, when one-fourth of the work force was unemployed. The business cycle did not originate with industrialization, but its consequences were so vastly magnified that the price paid for a self-adjusting economy became intolerable. Hence changed circumstances called forth another whole area of governmental function: the stabilization of employment, production, and prices.

Yet it was not just changed circumstance, for when we say that a situation becomes intolerable we are making a value judgment, not just describing a situation. Community value changes were just as essential a part of the expanding economic role of government as changes in the objective situation. When unemployment was thought of, in Spencerian terms, as the justly deserved punishment of the shiftless and lazy, no one thought to provide governmental protection. When "the devil take the hindmost" and caveat emptor were the slogans of the day, the social and economic costs of the crude early brand of capitalism were ignored with good conscience—at least by those whose opinions counted politically. In short, when doctrines of individualism held a monopoly on the operative ideals of the community, collective economic action was by definition anathema. There were critics who posed more humane values—like Disraeli and Dickens in England, Lincoln Steffens and Ida M. Tarbell in the United States—but their impact was felt only belatedly.

Concepts of social justice began to receive more articulate support, and wider public awareness and acceptance around the turn of the century. The almost Marxian criticism of capitalism embedded in Pope Leo XIII's encyclical, *Rerum Novarum;* the growth of an industrial working class for whom the individualist precepts of the Horatio Alger literature had a distinctly hollow ring; the development of the Brandeis brief to break down with factual recitations of suffering and inequity the Supreme Court's dogmatic assumption of economic harmony under laissez faire; and the beginnings of sociological analysis of power relationships—all these were forces undermining the Spencerian-Darwinian scheme of values.

Simultaneous change in conditions and in values provided the elemental forces necessary for development of new governmental roles; the catalytic agent was often a crisis or a catastrophe. The Triangle Shirt Waist Company fire in New York in 1911, in which 146 workers died, led to much factory legislation in 1912–14; ship losses led to radio requirements and legislation; and the depression of 1929–39 led to a whole range of programmatic and institutional innovations patterned on an industrially oriented scheme of values: the Securities and Exchange Commission, Home Owner's Loan Corporation, Old Age and Survivors Insurance, and the Council of Economic Advisers—just to list a few.

Nor is the conflict of values over yet. Roughly speaking, what Galbraith called the conventional wisdom and what Barry Goldwater and the NAM preach in the name of individualism represent vestiges of pre-industrial thinking, which are still quite lively, unfortunately. Such thinking contends for the power to shape public policy with what may be called the liberal-labor ideology, which accepts industrialization and recognizes its social imperatives—indeed, it overstresses them, say conservatives. The recent and continuing conflict over the means test versus the social-insurance approach to publicly provided medical care is a perfect case in point. The means test philosophy dates back hundreds of years. Its view of man is that his dignity counts only when he is self-supporting; its view of the economy is that no one ever lacks adequate means of support except through his own shiftlessness or inadequacy. The social-insurance approach emphasizes the technical concept of risk-sharing, the ethical concept that dignity resides in all humans, not just the fortunate ones, and the economic concept that social costs and benefits are not synonymous with private costs and benefits as measured by the market. Pictures of the situation and systems of values are thus fused into total approaches to socio-economic problems, approaches with quite different implications for the range of public policy.

Two other developments were highly instrumental, and in some respects requisite, to expansion of government's economic role of social control. There was a recognition of social-economic institutions as man-made rather than divinely ordained, and, concurrently, the technical development of economic analysis as a social-scientific discipline. When social and economic systems were thought of as divinely ordained or as natural growths, it was popularly supposed that men neither could nor should make changes in the framework. If some men starved, it was regrettable; but nothing could be done in the face of "natural law." Although the early factory wage system reeked of injustice, one could not tamper with the "iron law of wages." Such crude doctrines of natural law, widely believed, for a long time effectively stopped social and economic reform measures, for "interference" with nature was immoral and, by definition, futile because "unnatural."

As the scientific spirit began to invade the sphere of moral philosophy and men began to doubt the finality of social institutions which showed great variation between cultures, it gradually came to be understood that social arrangements are what we make them, that within bounds set by resources and knowledge there are a great variety of ways in which goods production can be handled. And men began to demand that governments act as instigators of change to produce institutional patterns more in keeping with an enlightened humanist image of man. Although social science has become heavily self-conscious about its self-imposed role of analysis without prescription in recent years, its early growth came largely through men committed to engineering a better world. The draft of objectives circulated by Richard T. Ely in 1885 as a prospectus for an American Economics Association, for example, began with an explicit rejection of the laissez faire doctrine: "We regard the state as an educational and ethical agency whose positive aid is an indispensable condition of human progress. . . . We hold that the doctrine of laissez-faire is unsafe in politics and unsound in morals." Not all the economists of that time agreed with Ely, yet a milder version of this statement was incorporated into the original consitution of the Association. And some men would have made the Association's role even more activist. Simon Patten, for example, felt that the Association membership "should give in some specific form our attitude on all the leading questions where State intervention is needed."

Use of governmental power to achieve reform objectives was made socially feasible by the social scientists' demonstration that economic and other institutions were not the immutable creations of nature but the conscious and unconscious creations of man. What once had to be accepted, though regretted, could now be attacked: men could be blamed and held responsible; their behavior could be required to conform to standards other than those enshrined in the market mechanism; and institutions could be reformed to accord with humanistic aims.

The best will in the world will accomplish little, however, if objective analysis of the problem is faulty or techniques have not been developed for directing social forces toward the desired goal. Advances in economic theory and in techniques of measuring performance of the economy were therefore prerequisite to the translation of humane ideals into programs of public economic policy. Concretely, the Keynesian revolution provided an essential key to understanding the nature of the business cycle and the failure of conventional budget-balancing economics to pull the economy out of a slump once begun.

President Roosevelt's initial attempts to cut government spending are a leading example of the perils of action on the basis of faulty analysis. The development of the national income model and its accompanying analysis of the flow of funds and the relationships among savings, investment, and consumption are the intellectual basis for policies aimed at growth and full employment. While our understanding of economic behavior still appears to lag far behind our understanding of the physical world, and our institutional arrangements for using economic knowledge are about as well adapted to our needs as the old wagon trail would be to a high-speed automobile, we do know enough now to avoid the grosser fluctuations of the business cycle. In fact, these and similar technical developments in economic science have probably been themselves a causative factor in the change in values from acceptance of adversity as God-given to community demands that the economy be controlled in the interests of the general public.

For all of these reasons then, the economic role of government has been enlarged many times over in our day. The ubiquity of this development in all economically advanced or advancing nations is sufficient proof against the unenlightened conservative's easy explanation that it is all the fault of "that man in the White House," whether Roosevelt, Truman, Eisenhower, or Kennedy. And the nature of the forces catalogued suggests that the limits of essential intervention have not yet been reached.

The Crisis of the 1890's and the Shaping of Twentieth Century America—A Radical Analysis

ROBERT B. CARSON

Although the afterglow of later achievements has tended to obscure the fact, the United States entered the twentieth century with the spectre of chaos hanging heavy over the land. The closing decades of the nineteenth century had been marked by a series of social and economic ruptures which to many contemporary observers seemed to augur not only the demise of the old political and social system, but the ultimate collapse of order in general. The threats seemed to come from all sides. For one thing, the values men lived by for so very long seemed not to work in an increasingly complex urbanized and industrialized society. New consumer products, new communications media, new types of jobs and working conditions, new immigrants, and wild, new ideologies dizzied the head of anyone steeped in the traditions of an earlier, predominantly agrarian, way of life. While these external threats generated an atmosphere pregnant with anxiety and concern, the real threat to order lay within the system itself, in its obvious inability to function well.

The country's economic performance, despite the vaunted growth of new industries, such as railroads, steel, and oil, and the steady westward expansion of the nation, was simply quite disappointing. Between the close of the Civil War and the end of the century, the economy had suffered five major depressions and during 23 of these 35 years, the United States found itself in straitened economic conditions.[1] Successively, the economic crises appeared to be deeper and more protracted as the economy seemed to show an ever-accelerating tendency toward stagnation.

By the 1890's, the incipient decline had begun to produce great rifts in the social system and could no longer be dismissed as the familiar boom-

From David DeGrood, Dale Riepe, and John Somerville, eds., *Radical Currents in Contemporary Philosophy* (St. Louis: Warren H. Green, 1971), pp. 117–32, 138–39. Reprinted by permission of the publisher.

[1] Herman E. Krooss, *American Economic Development* (Englewood Cliffs: Prentice-Hall, 1966), p. 11.

bust-boom rhythm of a capitalist economy. In the face of the rising crisis, the traditional philosophy of economic and political liberalism seemed wholly incapable of dealing with the growing disenchantment with American institutions and values.

In agricultural areas, the brushfires of populism were raging out of control, producing a radicalism heretofore unique among American farmers. Farmers were urged to "raise more hell and less corn," to fight against the railroad, farm machinery, and marketing combinations which seemed to be the cause of their depressed prices and high costs.[2] In industry, as wages tumbled and short work-weeks grew more common in the 1890's, the labor movement, which had been characterized by a growing radicalism and commitment to industrial violence since the 1870's, adopted increasingly militant postures. Throughout 1892, 1893, and 1894, a rash of violent strikes staggered the economy. At Homestead, Pennsylvania, Cour d'Alene, Idaho, Buffalo, New York, and Pullman, Illinois, it was necessary to call in military units to put down the strikes, and, successively, the strikes seemed to be worsening.[3] Whereas, only 8,000 Pennsylvania National Guardsmen had been needed to force the Carnegie steelworkers back to their jobs at Homestead, the implied power of the entire United States Army had to be employed by President Cleveland in 1894 to break the back of the Pullman strike and boycott. Meanwhile, by early spring of 1894, an army of unemployed men were marching from a number of points about the country toward Washington to demand that the government create a $500 million program of public works to provide jobs.[4] Although Coxey's army disintegrated rather timidly at the Capitol steps when its leaders were arrested for trespassing, the spectacle of Washington under siege was not to be passed off lightly.

The loss of faith in the American economic system was by no means limited to laboring groups. As business failures mounted after the panic of July, 1893, the normal optimism of the business community, which usually prevailed even in the worst of economic conditions, began to vanish. A few men, like J. P. Morgan, who was appalled by the fact that more than one-third of the American railroad network lay in bankruptcy and that steel and other industries were similarly threatened, talked openly about the need to reform American economic institutions so that they were no longer vulnerable to the economic fluctuations associated with a *laissez faire* market organization.[5] To this end, Morgan set the pattern for other business and financial leaders and for other industries by attempting to establish a banker hegemony over American railroads which would have replaced the usual excessive competition and periodic instability with central direction and control.

Confused and incredulous at the wave of events, the dyspeptic Henry Adams managed to be relevant for once and probably spoke for many of

---

[2] See J. D. Hicks, *The Populist Revolt* (New York: 1931).

[3] Ray Ginger, *Eugene V. Debs: A Biography* (New York: Collier, 1962), pp. 101–167.

[4] See D. L. Murray, *Coxey's Army* (New York: 1929); and Thorstein Veblen, "Army of Commonweel," *Journal of Political Economy*, Vol. II (1894), pp. 456–71.

[5] Frederick Lewis Allen, *The Great Pierpont Morgan* (New York: Bantam, 1956), pp. 62–76.

his countrymen, both intellectuals and ordinary people, as he observed to a friend in 1894:

> We don't know what is the matter with us, yet we all admit that we have had a terrific shock of some sort. We see no reason at all for assuming that the causes, whatever they are, which have brought about the prostration, have ceased, or will cease, to act. On the contrary, as far as we can see, if anything is radically wrong, it must grow worse, for it must be in our system itself, and at the bottom of all modern society. If we are diseased, so is all the world. Everyone is discussing, disputing, doubting, economizing, going into bankruptcy, waiting for the storm to pass, but no sign of agreement is visible as to what has upset us, or whether we can cure the disease. That the trouble is quite different from any previous experience, pretty much everyone seems to admit; but nobody diagnoses it. . . . We want to know what is wrong with the world that it should suddenly go to smash without visible cause or possible advantage. Here in this young, rich continent, capable of supporting three times its population with ease, we have had a million men out of employment for nearly a year, and the situation growing worse rather than better.[6]

The depiction of anxiety and despair in American life became the persistent theme in American literature after the early nineties. A generation of writers, from Howells and Mark Twain to Dos Passos and Sinclair Lewis repeated Henry Adams' lamentations about the aimlessness and drift of American life, as the old values and the old ways became incredibly irrelevant in actual practice. As Ray Ginger has pointed out in his *Age of Excess,* repeatedly the novels of the nineties dealt with the emotional disorientation of individuals, and, strikingly, this disorganization all too frequently terminated in suicide.[7] America was a land of dreams, but the dreams were being smashed; and, like Dreiser's Sister Carrie, America "had learned that in this world, as in her own present state, was not happiness. Though often disillusioned, she was still waiting for that halcyon day when she could be led forth among dreams become real."[8] But real conviction in the belief that the society could rebuild itself was usually lacking. As Twain observed to Howells, "we all belong to the nasty stinking little human race. . . . Oh, we are a nasty lot— and to think that there are people who would like to save us and continue us. It won't happen if I have any influence."[9]

However, the apparent disorder and chaos invoked by the crisis of the 1890's did not always produce despair. While the old order of social relations

[6] Letters of Henry Adams to Charles Gaskell, April 28, 1894, in W. C. Ford, ed., *Letters of Henry Adams, 1892–1918* (Boston: Houghton Mifflin, 1938), pp. 46–47.

[7] Ray Ginger, *Age of Excess* (New York: Macmillan, 1965), p. 304.

[8] Theodore Dreiser, *Sister Carrie* (New York: Modern Library, 1900), p. 557.

[9] Letter of Mark Twain to William Dean Howells, April 2, 1899, in H. N. Smith and W. M. Gibson, eds., *Mark Twain-Howells Letters* (Cambridge: Belknap Press, 1960), Vol. II, p. 692.

no longer worked, this only pointed out to some men the necessity of creating a new order, one that would prove less fragile and more adaptable. One among many of different pursuits and talents who labored on this problem was Harvard University philosopher William James. To James, the answer was to jettison all of the old philosophies and political theories which supported the image of a world in which there were unchanging truths and values. Men were instead to determine their own truths as the test of performance proved them successful or "practical." In short, James argued for an activist's philosophy in which men could, in fact, manage and manipulate their own lives and institutions for their own improvement. Writing in the *New York Times* some years after his pragmatic philosophy, or "radical empiricism" as he preferred, had gained wide appeal, James outlined his creed:

> Our minds are not here simply to copy a reality that is already complete. They are here to complete it, to add to its importance by their own remodeling of it, to decant its contents over, so to speak, into a more significant shape. In point of fact the use of most of our thinking is to help us *change* the world. . . . Thus we seem set free to use our theoretical as well as our practical faculties . . . to get the world into a better shape, and all with a good conscience. The only restriction is that the world resists some lines of attack on our part and opens herself to others so that we must go with the grain of her willingness, to play fairly. Hence, the *sursum corda* of pragmatism's message.[10]

Not all James' words were always to be remembered, and the "tough-mindedness" he referred to was to be replaced by some practitioners of pragmatism with simple hard-headedness, but his call for activism and experimentation and his faith in progress was appealing for it seemed to offer a way out of the desperation of the 1890's.

The political and economic analogue to James' pragmatism was, of course, "progressivism." Although the term usually is applied rather narrowly to a specific political philosophy or movement falling within the time period roughly bounded by the presidential administrations of Theodore Roosevelt and Woodrow Wilson, progressivism has been more than just a relatively short-lived category of political thought or period in American history.[11] Progressivism was a new way to look at the problems of political economy. It was both a method of analysis and a policy. Moreover, it was, in terms of analysis and policy, the dominant theme in twentieth century American politics, not simply an ideology narrowly associated with any one particular political party or special group of reformers. While it has been handy to use the term "progressive" in contrast to "conservative" in our simplistic categorization of American politics, this has only obscured the fact that few real differences in political philosophy ever developed in American politics in this

---

[10] *New York Times,* November 3, 1907.
[11] For representative writings of these years, see Otis Pease, ed., *The Progressive Years* (New York: Braziller, 1962).

century and that the whole corpus of theory and policy as it developed was essentially progressive.

In the same way that James' pragmatism sought to restore order and meaning to fields of philosophic inquiry, progressivism, in all its various forms, attempted to reconstruct the American economic and political order so as to provide purpose and rationality to social relations and institutions. Progressivism at the minimum required only an unshakable belief that the American social system could be manipulated to maintain a steady economic development with its attendant general happiness, without a radical reconstruction of the institutional arrangements or ideology of the society. Lest such a definition of progressivism be considered so amorphous as to be meaningless, it should be pointed out that one of the striking characteristics of American political thought in this century has been the general agreement among its leaders on means by which economic and social progress was to be attained. Moreover, it has been this inclination to study only the relatively minor differences in political theory and policy and the tendency to expand these differences out of all sense of proportion that has confounded serious attempts to study and explain modern American history. Progressivism in one form or another pervaded all layers of American society and politics. It made Republicans and Democrats or labor leaders and businessmen more alike than different on the really crucial questions of how the society should be organized and governed.

This consensus on goals and means doubtless contributed to the quite remarkable political continuity and economic stability of the nation in the twentieth century. The consensus was also self-supporting. As stability and continuity seemed to be the by-products of a progressive system, it was possible to accept as a fundamental dogma of American political thought the euphoric belief that the system could not really have any unsolvable problems. As social and economic difficulties inevitably arose, it was understood that any and all could be resolved without radically altering the social system.

While at the very minimum progressivism demanded a belief in the pragmatic manipulation of American institutions, there were more rigorous articles of faith. In particular, progressivism presumed that traditional values of economic individualism and private property relations were to be preserved. As Professor William Appleman Williams has observed:

> Only the anarchists and a few doctrinaire laissez faire spokesmen seemed willing to accept the possibility of chaos. Arguing that it was both necessary and possible, most Americans reformulated and reasserted their traditional confidence in their ability to choose and control their fate . . . given a consensus on the sanctity of private property, and confronted by the increasingly obvious failure of laissez faire, this faith could be verified only by controlling the marketplace.[12]

[12] William Appleman Williams, *The Contours of American History* (New York: World, 1961), p. 356.

The system that eventually developed along these lines was a regulated capitalist economy which has been given a variety of names. To Williams, it was "corporate capitalism." Others have labeled it variously, "political capitalism," "the mixed economy," "corporate liberalism" and a sundry collection of other terms.[13] But terms or labels are really of little importance; the fact remains that the economic and political system as it was understood in the 1890's needed to be reordered, and it was, but along lines consistent with traditional economic and political beliefs.

In simplest terms, the fundamental flaw in the old political and economic organization which had been discovered in the crisis of the 1890's was the system's capacity to produce more than it was able to consume. This led, in turn, to chronic fluctuations in prices and employment, diminished assurity of markets and profits for business ventures, and the prospect, and to some degree, the reality, of social and political collapse which Marx had brilliantly postulated as the attendant manifestations of the later stages of capitalist disintegration.

On the burning question of what to do about the problem of excess productive capacity, two lines of policy gradually developed. First, industrial competition, which excess capacity too frequently triggered, was to be replaced by monopolistic or oligopolistic market arrangements. Through industry regulation, the periodic price wars and diminished profits were to be eliminated. At first, regulation was largely of a private nature with businessmen expected to act, according to J. P. Morgan, "ably and with wisdom and restraint."[14] But, when private regulation proved incapable of controlling private profit-seeking motives, it was gradually understood that federal regulatory machinery would be erected and employed to correct market imperfections. Moreover, this concept of regulation was eventually expanded to mean not only rational decision-making and cooperation between firms, but also the construction of a rational and regulated relationship between business and its traditional protagonist, labor.

The second technique for eliminating excess capacity problems was to expand the market. By the mid and late 1890's, this was accepted by practically all American economic groups to mean expansion of world markets. Professor Frederick Jackson Turner had proclaimed in 1894 that ". . . now, four centuries from the discovery of America, at the end of one hundred years of life under the constitution, the frontier has gone, and with its going has closed the first period in American history."[15] Turner's words were a threat or provocation as much as a statement of fact. To a nation whose economy had always seemed to depend on the constant expansion of the market, the closing of the frontier and the economic difficulties of the 1890's appeared to be connected events, and during the 1890's, a growing number of business,

[13] See Gabriel Kolko, *The Triumph of Conservatism* (New York: Free Press, 1963).

[14] Lewis Corey, *The House of Morgan* (New York: Grosset & Dunlap, 1930), p. 145.

[15] Frederick Jackson Turner, *The Frontier in American History* (New York: 1947), p. 38.

agricultural and labor leaders urged that America's new economic frontier should be the world.[16]

The always sanguine Theodore Roosevelt spoke more directly to the question of American expansion than did most of his contemporaries. To Roosevelt, opportunities were there for those strong and courageous enough to pick them up. For America, facing "very serious social problems" at home, it was essential that opportunities to develop foreign markets and overseas economic penetration be seized and exploited. "America," he noted, "has only just begun to assume that commanding position in the international business world which we believe will more and more be hers."[17]

It is noteworthy that both of these basic themes in twentieth century American development have generally been misrepresented or neglected by conventional historical writing. The rationalization of a highly regulated domestic economy has been wrongly depicted as a victorious struggle by progressive or liberal elements, who sought to curb the power of financial or business interests, over willful, self-centered groups bent on exploiting the rest of society. America's emergence as a world power similarly has been misinterpreted, viewed as the position taken by a nation reluctantly thrust into international leadership.[18]

The twin progressive policies of market regulation and market expansion, of course, did not suddenly emerge as full-blown and complete programs. Consensus on both the means and goals was by no means total by the turn of the century, and serious differences of opinion existed into the early years of the twentieth century; but, to emphasize the diversity among men and ideas and the apparent inconsistency of many actual policies undertaken is misleading. There was substantial agreement on the broad outlines of these two programs by virtually all important economic and political groups, and a pattern for consensus was being laid down which would be the framework of American action and thought for the next half-century or more.

To obtain this consensus, serious contradictions in American economic and political theory and practice had to be resolved. Regulation and expansion presupposed the centralization and nationalization of economic and political power. For a society which broadly acclaimed the principles of individualism and which had not been noted in the nineteenth century for its singlemindedness and unity, the fairly speedy acceptance of uniformity and strong methods of internal control might have seemed impossible. However, Americans proved themselves equal to the task, and centralization and control became not only attributes of public affairs, but nationalization pervaded all levels of American life, so that the society created not only strong national markets

[16] See Walter LaFeber, *The New Empire* (Ithaca, N.Y.: Cornell University Press, 1963), pp. 153–196.

[17] President Roosevelt's Annual Message to Congress, December 3, 1901; in William Appleman Williams, ed., *The Shaping of American Diplomacy* (Chicago: Rand McNally, 1956), pp. 486–487.

[18] Representative of this view, see Arthur Schlesinger, Jr., *The Vital Center* (Boston: Houghton Mifflin, 1949), pp. 219–242.

and federal agencies, but also a national culture and national tastes and values. Most important, this nationalization was accomplished without admitting that the older values now stood as irrelevancies. After 1900, the public and private rhetoric in praise of individualism and freedom never wavered and, if anything, became louder and more ponderous, while the actual practice of politics, economics, and everyday life evidenced greater control and conformity. In a process of massive, national self-deception, Americans constructed for themselves illusory institutions and ideologies to create the effect but not the substance of a democratic society.

The progressive administration of Theodore Roosevelt set the pattern of pretense for twentieth century domestic politics. While arguing for reform to protect consumers, small businessmen, farmers, and laborers, economic and political power was steadily centralized into instruments over which these groups had no effective control. The Meat Inspection Act and the Pure Food and Drug Act of 1906, while ostensibly attacking such ills as those pointed out in Upton Sinclair's *The Jungle,* in reality were devices used for the elimination of small food processors whose competitive zeal had posed a threat to market stability. The cleaning up of conditions of meat and food preparation was really only a guise to effectively control these producers. Meanwhile, the whole point of Sinclair's muckraking, the work conditions of the employees of the meat plants, was ignored.[19] Similarly, the Elkins and Hepburn Acts, frequently cited as progressive attempts to strengthen Interstate Commerce Commission control over the railroads, in fact, provided the rate setting stability and non-competitiveness for the rail industry which it had never been able to obtain by itself. Even Roosevelt's reputation as a "trustbuster" was a pose, for he did not halt the steady acceleration in mergers nor did his forty-four anti-trust indictments interfere with his tennis playing with banker friends or their continued financial contributions to the Republican Party. In fact, Roosevelt's dependence upon the financial oligarchy was made quite apparent when he had to seek out the leadership of J. P. Morgan to solve a major banking crisis in 1907.[20]

No administration after Roosevelt radically altered this pattern of business-government relations. Disagreements occasionally raged over the selection of means, but the proposition that it was government's and business's responsibility to maintain a strong, centrally-managed economy was not seriously challenged. The Wilson administration, with all its posturing for a "New Freedom" for the ordinary citizen, defined that freedom only as a by-product of a strong, business-dominated economy. The creation of such agencies as the Federal Reserve System and the Federal Trade Commission, popular mythology notwithstanding, was with the general concurrence of business, for they were understood as attempts to replace market instability with rational guidelines for banking and business behavior.[21] The Republican years

[19] Kolko, *op. cit.,* p. 107.
[20] *Ibid.,* pp. 153–158.
[21] *Ibid.,* p. 273.

of the 1920's further demonstrated the non-partisan appeal of the progressive ideology. Coolidge's apt observation that the "business of America is business" was translated into policy at the Department of Commerce by a man both political parties had considered for the presidency in 1920. For all his well-known belief in the tonic of a philosophy of "rugged individualism," Herbert Clark Hoover, as Secretary of Commerce and as President, saw no inconsistency with making all of the machinery of government available for business's use.[22] "Business organization," he noted, "is moving strongly toward cooperation. There are in this cooperation great hopes that we can even gain in individuality . . . and, at the same time, reduce many of the great wastes of over-reckless competition in production and distribution."[23] To Hoover, any cooperation which government might encourage would thus strengthen business, and, thereby, strengthen America.

The crisis of the 1930's, rather than producing a serious reappraisal of the directions of American political economy, only pointed up the need for further tightening of central control. Franklin Roosevelt's early New Deal programs, such as the National Industrial Recovery Act, the Public Works Administration, and the use of the Reconstruction Finance Corporation were devices to give direct aid to business. In fact, the short-lived NIRA virtually suspended anti-trust legislation in allowing price-setting and output collusion. Meanwhile, the WPA, the Social Security Act and legislation giving unions broader powers served to blunt any popular radical assault upon the system.[24]

The depression also brought forth an important addition to orthodox economic theory. In the writings of British economist, John Maynard Keynes, there seemed to be a way to forestall economic depressions and recessions.[25] According to Keynesian economics, the chronic instability of capitalism, quite as Marx had pointed out sixty years before, was the natural tendency of the economic system. To Keynes, it could only be eliminated by central government actions which would maintain high levels of consumer and investment demand for goods and services. Keynes called for new roles to be played by the government through its monetary and fiscal policy to stimulate and maintain high levels of demand and offset the system's basic tendency for production capacity to outrun consumption. While supporters of the older, more conventional, economic theories were initially uncomfortable with Keynes' direct appeal for greater government control and direction of the economy, it was gradually understood that there was little in Keynesian economics which attacked established property relations and concentrations of economic power. Indeed, it was a brilliant move to protect these arrangements.

Much of the opposition to the vast expansion of federal economic control

[22] See Joseph Brandes, *Herbert Hoover and Economic Diplomacy* (Pittsburgh: University of Pittsburgh Press, 1962).

[23] Herbert Hoover, *American Individualism* (New York: 1922), p. 44.

[24] Williams, *Contours*, pp. 439–440.

[25] See John M. Keynes, *The General Theory of Employment, Interest, and Money* (New York: Harcourt, 1935).

necessitated by the Great Depression and legitimated by Keynesian economics was erased during World War II and the post-war years. First of all, the war required virtually complete control of the nation's economy by the government. Secondly, with the coming of peace in 1945, many economic and political leaders feared a return to the depression conditions of the thirties, and, as a testament to their belief that *laissez faire* was now dead, the Congress enacted the Employment Act of 1946, committing to governmental responsibility the maintenance of high levels of employment, stable prices, and economic growth.

Although the acceptance of Keynesian devices for managing the economy were at first only haltingly tried and frequently challenged by dissenters, the "new economics" was victorious by the 1960's. The 1964 presidential election had in some respects been a referendum on this issue, and it had seen large numbers of business leaders desert their traditional party in support of the clearly Keynesian economic policies of the Johnson Administration. Indeed, consensus on the proper economic policy seemed so broad that the President's Council of Economic Advisers could confidently report in 1965:

> The role of the Federal Government changed in the New Deal of the 1930's, and in World War II. The Government accepted responsibility for assuring a minimum of economic well-being for most individuals, for many special groups, industries, and agriculture. It undertook the task of stabilizing the economy against the destructive power of the business cycle. . . . After years of ideological controversy, we have grown used to the new relationship among Government, householder, business, labor, and agriculture. The tired slogans that made constructive discourse difficult have lost their meaning for most Americans.
>
> It has become abundantly clear that our society wants neither to turn backward the clock of history nor to discuss our present problems in a partisan spirit.[26]

The Annual Report of the council then proceeded to enumerate the unfinished economic problems facing the society—urban decay, inadequate education, poor health, poverty, and inequality of economic opportunity. It was a measure of the self-deceptiveness of American political and economic thought that no one seemed to see the irony or contradiction in such a bombastic pronouncement of the victory of progressive ideas on the one hand, and the tacit admission of failure on the other. The "success" of a political philosophy obviously did not depend on whether it really worked.

The victory of the progressive program for an integrated and controlled domestic economy was complemented by the political acceptance of the necessity to expand and protect overseas markets. And again, the process of self-deception was important. Expansion was couched in terms of duties and responsibilities as well as economic necessity when it was initially discussed in the 1890's. It took on a strong moral and religious flavor, becoming

[26] *The Economic Report of the President, 1965,* p. 145.

a way of doing the Lord's work as well as America's. To Rev. Josiah Strong, that indefatigable proponent of picking up the white man's burden, it was nothing short of a God-given responsibility for the "Anglo-Saxon," of which the United States was the only strong representative, ". . . to exercise the commanding influence in the world's future."[27] Senator Albert Beveridge meanwhile intoned that "God has not been preparing the English-speaking and Teutonic peoples . . . for nothing. . . . He made us the master organizers of the world to establish a system where chaos reigns . . . that we administer government among savages and senile peoples."[28]

The pattern for American overseas expansion, what William Appleman Williams has called "Imperial Anti-Colonialism," had been laid down in Secretary of State Hay's Open Door notes of 1899.[29] While the notes seemed specifically addressed to the problem of keeping China open to trade and halting the growth of European spheres of economic interest on the China mainland, the real thrust was to state America's intention to keep all world markets open to free commerce, meaning our commerce as well as anybody else's. The Open Door became the basic theme of American foreign policy in the twentieth century. America never really sought to acquire an empire in the eighteenth or nineteenth century meaning of the word and what overseas possessions we had always proved embarrassing to us. America eschewed taking others' land in favor of the real or imagined benefits of penetrating their markets, and the nation would go to any lengths to keep world markets open to American products and investment.

The internationalism of Theodore Roosevelt, Taft, and Wilson, with its erection of a virtual hegemony over the Caribbean, economic penetration into South American, Asian, and even European markets, and eventual involvement in World War I (which Wilson justified largely in terms of freedom of the seas and freedom for commerce) is a well-known tale, hardly needing recounting. However, this period of vigorous, often ruthless, overseas expansion is sometimes depicted as an exception to later developments. The twenties and the thirties are frequently shown as "isolationistic" and the post-World War II period as humanitarian internationalism. In viewing themselves in this way, Americans have come to think of their country as a reluctant internationalist thrust into the world for the world's sake. The facts reveal, however, quite a different story.

First of all, America never was isolationist except in the irrelevant domestic political poses of the 1920's and 1930's, which were sheer self-deception. From a theretofore all time high of $2.4 billion in exports in 1913, the United States exported $4.9 billion in 1925 and $5.2 billion by 1929. Between 1920 and 1933, overseas United States private investment grew by more than $10 billion and income on these investments averaged about two percent of the

[27] Josiah Strong, *Our Country* (New York: The Home Missionary Society, 1885), p. 168.
[28] Senator Albert Beveridge (1899), in Williams, ed., *The Shaping of American Diplomacy*, pp. 433–434.
[29] William Appleman Williams, *The Tragedy of American Diplomacy* (New York: Delta, 1962), p. 16.

gross national product, perhaps not an awesome figure by itself, but enough to make the difference between profit and loss for many firms.[30]

The rejection of the Treaty of Versailles and the League of Nations did not indicate a withdrawal from the world, but the assertion that America should remain free to act without the possible interference of a super-government it might not yet have been able to dominate. As the world's leading creditor and industrial power, America perceived few benefits in such an organization. Meanwhile, at the newly organized Department of Commerce, Herbert Hoover labored to induce American businessmen to tap foreign markets. His agency produced a flood of propaganda publications through the twenties, broadcasting the potential return on foreign investment. It published detailed analyses of the economic and political conditions of possible investment areas and unmistakably hinted that the full political and military power of the nation would be utilized to protect wisely undertaken investment.[31]

The international economic collapse during the thirties and World War II clearly illustrated the weaknesses of attempting to maintain the "open door" through our own individually initiated arrangements. Moreover, the war cleared away any remaining sympathy for a "little America" line of policy and induced practically all Americans to accept what most businessmen and all twentieth century presidents had understood since the turn of the century—that America must, for its own sake and that of the world, act as the dominant international power. The United Nations seemed to be the device by which the "open door" would become the basis for post-war international arrangements. By the logic of its charter and by the fact that America dominated the Allied wartime alliance, it seemed that American principles would have to prevail.

But, as the war closed, Soviet Russian Communism failed to collapse as many supposed, and its implied threat of world revolution raised a new spectre which had to be dealt with. The world was to be divided between the free half which was dominated by American economic and political power and the communist half which was understood as a constant threat to any sensible man's concept of freedom. Through the 1950's, America, by a maze of confusing economic and military alliances, tied the "free world" to herself. The "free world," of course, was that which had institutions or held political views which opened it to our commerce or our political leadership, that part which subscribed to the "Open Door." Communist nations, with their anti-capitalist ideology, by definition were threats to the international capitalist economic apparatus that the United States conceived as essential for its and the "free world's" continuation. Most Americans, meanwhile, understood the cold war treaties and aid programs not as devices to expand and strengthen the business economy, a justification which might have had dubious appeal by itself, but as necessary means to halt the spread of anti-democratic communism, a way to protect our freedom as well as other people's. Meanwhile, the gov-

[30] U.S. Department of Commerce Publications.
[31] Brandes, *op. cit.*, pp. 151–169.

ernment poured more than $120 billion in aid into receptive countries and business accumulated $70 billion in overseas investment by 1969.[32] That this overseas investment for the sake of freedom did not always produce freedom for the people of the recipient nations, or that American business penetration generally produced greater economic dependency rather than growth or self-sufficiency was usually overlooked. The simple arithmetic which showed that America returned in profits about two dollars for every one directly invested abroad during the 1950's and 1960's was rarely seen as connected with the rising tide of social revolution and its growing anti-American bias.

The illusion of world markets and their relation to the domestic economic security of America became the reality of garrisoning the "free world" and intervening in the affairs of both weak and strong nations.

In 1898, Senator Albert Beveridge had observed:

> The rule of liberty that all just government derives its authority from the consent of the governed, applied only to those who are capable of self-government. We govern the Indians without their consent, we govern our territories without their consent, we govern our children without their consent. . . . We cannot fly from our world duties: it is ours to execute the purpose of a fate that has driven us to be greater than our small intentions. We cannot retreat from any soil where Providence has unfurled our banner; it is ours to save that soil for liberty and civilization.

The tragedy of America's relations with the rest of the world lay in the fact that such an outlook more aptly described American foreign policy in the 1970's than it had at the beginning of the century. . . .

Looking back over more than seven decades, the progressive resolution of the crisis posed in the 1890's must be considered, in terms of specific goals, successful—but at the price of creating a kind of Frankenstein monster. In the world, the United States by the 1970's has found both markets and highly profitable sources of investment; but, it also has emerged as the chief supporter of political and economic reaction, attempting always to head off truly revolutionary social movements by use of its enormous wealth, its notorious support of friendly repressive regimes, and, when all else fails, its willingness to commit its vast resources and young men in wars of opposition to radical social change, even when such efforts are threats to its own economic well-being. At home, the material abundance, easily attributed to the successful development of a carefully rationalized and directed market system, can be seen everywhere. But, equally obvious is the evidence that for all its abundance, the society has not provided, nor shows much sympathy for providing, solutions to many crucial problems. The gross inequities of being black in white America, which have built a lengthening legacy of civil disobedience and disorder, the scarred and disfigured countryside, with its polluted water

---

[32] U.S. Department of Commerce, Office of Business Economics, *Balance of Payments* and *Survey of Current Business.*

and air, the ugly cities and the uglier suburbs are also outgrowths of the internal system Americans created. . . .

In the reconstruction of the American political economy after the crisis of the 1890's, Americans had chosen not to question the traditional property relations and power arrangements of their society. Rather than viewing the crisis of the system as basic to the organization of the society itself, as Marx and some home-grown heretics had argued, Americans decided only to reform their social and economic institutions by doing everything possible to strengthen them. By concluding that crisis in America could be headed off only through the construction of a regulated capitalist-type economy, Americans had never come to grips with the question of what kind of life-style to build. The "quality of life" for the society, therefore, could never be a seriously pursued line of inquiry so long as all discussions started from the proposition that the American system was necessarily committed to maintaining essentially capitalist economic, political and social institutions. The quality of life was really the by-product of whatever was necessary to keep such a system going, and, to keep it going, it became necessary to be increasingly expansionistic in the world and ever more tightly controlled at home.

There was never any serious challenge to this line of policy after the 1890's. Radical interpretations of American development simply never gained any serious attention. Indeed, this lack of a radical tradition or theme in American thought and politics makes the present-day crisis all the more difficult to understand and to deal with. America had deceived itself into believing that the traditionally cherished values of individual freedom and identity depended upon the continuation of a capitalist social system and it had, indeed, become a wealthy and strong nation. However, in the 1970's this wealth and power seems to threaten both the lives of its citizens and the rest of the world. The new American crisis now lies in resolving this paradox, for very much as Engels had once observed while traveling by train through the countryside of his native Germany, "What a lovely land, if only one could live in it!"[33]

[33] In Edmund Wilson, *To the Finland Station* (New York: Doubleday, 1940), p. 337.

The Great Society:
A Libertarian Critique

MURRAY ROTHBARD

The Great Society is the lineal descendant and the intensification of those other pretentiously named polities of twentieth-century America: the Square Deal, the New Freedom, the New Era, the New Deal, the Fair Deal, and the New Frontier. All of these assorted Deals constitute a basic and fundamental shift in American life—a shift from a relatively laissez-faire economy and minimal state to a society in which the state is unquestionably king.[1] In the previous century, the government could safely have been ignored by almost everyone; now we have become a country in which the government is the great and unending source of power and privilege. Once a country in which each man could by and large make the decisions for his own life, we have become a land where the state holds and exercises life-and-death power over every person, group, and institution. The great Moloch government, once confined and cabined, has burst its feeble bonds to dominate us all.

The basic reason for this development is not difficult to fathom. It was best summed up by the great German sociologist Franz Oppenheimer; Oppenheimer wrote that there were fundamentally two, and only two, paths to the acquisition of wealth. One route is the production of a good or service and its voluntary exchange for the goods or services produced by others. This method—the method of the free market—Oppenheimer termed "the economic means" to wealth. The other path, which avoids the necessity for production and exchange, is for one or more persons to seize other people's products by the use of physical force. This method of robbing the fruits of another man's production was shrewdly named by Oppenheimer the "political means." Throughout history, men have been tempted to employ the "political means" of seizing wealth rather than expend effort in production and exchange. It should be clear that while the market process multiplies production, the political, exploitative means is parasitic and, as with all parasitic

[1] Recent triumphal disclosures by economic historians that pure laissez faire did not exist in nineteenth century America are beside the point; no one ever claimed that it did. The point is that state power in society was minimal, relative to other times and countries, and that the general locus of decision making resided therefore in the individuals making up society rather than in the State. Cf. Robert Lively, "The American System," *Business History Review,* XXIX (1955), pp. 81–96.

action, discourages and drains off production and output in society. To regularize and order a permanent system of predatory exploitation, men have created the state, which Oppenheimer brilliantly defined as "the organization of the political means."[2]

Every act of the state is necessarily an occasion for inflicting burdens and assigning subsidies and privileges. By seizing revenue by means of coercion and assigning rewards as it disburses the funds, the state creates ruling and ruled "classes" or "castes"; for one example, classes of what Calhoun discerned as net "taxpayers" and "tax-consumers," those who live off taxation.[3] And since by its nature, predation can only be supported out of the surplus of production above subsistence, the ruling class must constitute a minority of the citizenry.

Since the state, nakedly observed, is a mighty engine of organized predation, state rule, throughout its many millennia of recorded history, could be preserved only by persuading the bulk of the public that its rule has not really been exploitative: that, on the contrary, it has been necessary, beneficent, even, as in the Oriental despotisms, divine. Promoting this ideology among the masses has ever been a prime function of intellectuals, a function that has created the basis for co-opting a corps of intellectuals into a secure and permanent berth in the state apparatus. In former centuries, these intellectuals formed a priestly caste that was able to wrap a cloak of mystery and quasi-divinity about the actions of the state for a credulous public; nowadays, the apologia for the state takes on more subtle and seemingly scientific forms. The process remains essentially the same.[4]

In the United States, a strong libertarian and antistatist tradition prevented the process of statization from taking hold at a very rapid pace. The major force in its propulsion has been that favorite theater of state expansionism, brilliantly identified by Randolph Bourne as "the health of the state": namely, war. For although in wartime various states find themselves in danger from one another, every state has found war a fertile field for spreading the myth among its subjects that they are the ones in deadly danger, from which their state is protecting them. In this way states have been able to dragoon their subjects into fighting and dying to save them under the pretext that the sub-

[2] Franz Oppenheimer, *The State* (New York: 1926), pp. 24–27. Or, as Albert Jay Nock, heavily influenced by Oppenheimer's analysis, concluded: "The state claims and exercises the monopoly of crime" in its territorial area. Albert Jay Nock, *On Doing the Right Thing, and Other Essays* (New York: 1928), p. 143.

[3] See John C. Calhoun, *Disquisition on Government* . . . (Columbia, S.C.: 1850). On the distinction between this and the Marxian concept of the ruling class, see Ludwig von Mises, *Theory and History* (New Haven, Conn.: 1957), pp. 112 ff. Perhaps the earliest users of this kind of class analysis were the French libertarian writers of the Restoration period of the early nineteenth century, Charles Comte and Charles Dunoyer. Cf. Elie Halévy, *The Era of Tyrannies* (Garden City, N.Y.: 1965), pp. 23–34.

[4] On various aspects of the alliance between intellectuals and the State, see George B. de Huszar, ed., *The Intellectuals* (Glencoe, Ill.: 1960); Joseph A. Schumpeter, *Capitalism, Socialism, and Democracy* (New York: 1942), pp. 143–55; Karl A. Wittfogel, *Oriental Despotism* (New Haven, Conn.: 1957); Howard K. Beale, "The Professional Historian: His Theory and Practice," *The Pacific Historical Review* (August, 1953), pp. 227–55; Martin Nicolaus, "The Professor, The Policemen and the Peasant," *Viet-Report* (June–July, 1966), pp. 15–19.

jects were being saved from the dread Foreign Enemy. In the United States, the process of statization began in earnest under cover of the Civil War (conscription, military rule, income tax, excise taxes, high tariffs, national banking and credit expansion for favored businesses, paper money, land grants to railroads), and reached full flower as a result of World Wars I and II, to finally culminate in the Great Society.

The recently emerging group of "libertarian conservatives" in the United States have grasped a part of the recent picture of accelerated statism, but their analysis suffers from several fatal blind spots. One is their complete failure to realize that war, culminating in the present garrison state and military–industrial economy, has been the royal road to aggravated statism in America. On the contrary, the surge of reverent patriotism that war brings to conservative hearts, coupled with their eagerness to don buckler and armor against the "international Communist conspiracy," has made the conservatives the most eager and enthusiastic partisans of the Cold War. Hence their inability to see the enormous distortions and interventions imposed upon the economy by the enormous system of war contracts.[5]

Another conservative blind spot is their failure to identify which groups have been responsible for the burgeoning of statism in the United States. In the conservative demonology, the responsibility belongs only to liberal intellectuals, aided and abetted by trade unions and farmers. Big businessmen, on the other hand, are curiously exempt from blame (farmers are small enough businessmen, apparently, to be fair game for censure). How, then, do conservatives deal with the glaringly evident onrush of big businessmen to embrace Lyndon Johnson and the Great Society? Either by mass stupidity (failure to read the works of free-market economists), subversion by liberal intellectuals (e.g., the education of the Rockefeller brothers at Lincoln School), or craven cowardice (the failure to stand foursquare for free market principles in the face of governmental powers). Almost never is interest pinpointed as an overriding reason for statism among businessmen. This failure is all the more curious in the light of the fact that the laissez-faire liberals of the eighteenth and nineteenth centuries (e.g., the Philosophical Radicals in England, the Jacksonians in the United States) were never bashful about identifying and attacking the web of special privileges granted to businessmen in the mercantilism of their day.

In fact, one of the main driving forces of the statist dynamic of twentieth century America has been big businessmen, and this long before the Great Society. Gabriel Kolko, in his path-breaking *Triumph of Conservatism,*[6] has shown that the shift toward statism in the Progressive period was impelled by the very big business groups who were supposed, in the liberal mythology,

---

[5] Thus, cf. H. L. Nieburg, *In the Name of Science* (Chicago: 1966); Seymour Melman, *Our Depleted Society* (New York: 1965); C. Wright Mills, *The Power Elite* (New York: 1956).
[6] (New York: 1963). Also see Kolko's *Railroads and Regulation* (Princeton, N. J.: 1965). The laudatory reviews of the latter book by George W. Hilton (*American Economic Review*) and George W. Wilson (*Journal of Political Economy*) symbolize a potential alliance between "new left" and free-market historiography.

to be defeated and regulated by the Progressive and New Freedom measures. Rather than a "people's movement" to check big business, the drive for regulatory measures, Kolko shows, stemmed from big businessmen whose attempts at monopoly had been defeated by the competitive market, and who then turned to the federal government as a device for compulsory cartellization. This drive for cartellization through government accelerated during the New Era of the 1920s and reached its apex in Franklin Roosevelt's NRA. Significantly, this exercise in cartellizing collectivism was put over by organized big business; after Herbert Hoover, who had done much to organize and cartellize the economy, had balked at an NRA as going too far toward an outright fascist economy, the U.S. Chamber of Commerce won a promise from FDR that he would adopt such a system. The original inspiration was the corporate state of Mussolini's Italy.[7]

The formal corporation of the NRA is long gone, but the Great Society retains much of its essence. The locus of social power has been emphatically assumed by the state apparatus. Furthermore, that apparatus is permanently governed by a coalition of big business, big labor groupings, groups that use the state to operate and manage the national economy. The usual tripartite rapprochement of big business, big unions, and big government symbolizes the organization of society by blocs, syndics, and corporations, regulated and privileged by the federal, state, and local governments. What this all amounts to in essence is the "corporate state," which during the 1920s served as a beacon light for big businessmen, big unions, and many liberal intellectuals as the economic system proper to a twentieth century industrial society.[8]

The indispensable intellectual role of engineering popular consent for state rule is played, for the Great Society, by the liberal intelligentsia, who provide the rationale of "general welfare," "humanity," and the "common good" (just as the conservative intellectuals work the other side of the Great Society street by offering the rationale of "national security" and "national interest"). The liberals, in short, push the "welfare" part of our omnipresent welfare-warfare state, while the conservatives stress the warfare side of the pie. This analysis of the role of the liberal intellectuals puts into more sophisticated perspective the seeming "sellout" of these intellectuals as compared to their role during the 1930s. Thus, among numerous other examples, there is the seemingly anomaly of A. A. Berle and David Lilienthal, cheered and damned as flaming progressives in the thirties, now writing tomes hailing the new reign of big business. Actually, their basic views have not changed in the least. In the thirties, these theoreticians of the New Deal were concerned with condemning as "reactionaries" those big businessmen who clung to older in-

---

[7] The National Recovery Administration, one of the most important creations of the early New Deal, was established by the National Industrial Recovery Act of June, 1933. It prescribed and imposed codes of "fair competition" upon industry. It was declared unconstitutional by the Supreme Court in 1935. For an analysis of the inception of the NRA, see my *America's Great Depression* (Princeton, N. J.: 1963).

[8] Part of this story has been told in John P. Diggins, "Flirtation with Fascism: American Pragmatic Liberals and Mussolini's Italy," *American Historical Review*, LXXI (January, 1966), pp. 487–506.

dividualist ideals and failed to understand or adhere to the new monopoly system of the corporate state. But now, in the 1950s and 1960s, this battle has been won, big businessmen are all eager to be privileged monopolists in the new dispensation, and hence they can now be welcomed by such theorists as Berle and Lilienthal as "responsible" and "enlightened," their "selfish" individualism a relic of the past.

The cruellest myth fostered by the liberals is that the Great Society functions as a great boon and benefit to the poor; in reality, when we cut through the frothy appearances to the cold reality underneath, the poor are the major victims of the welfare state. The poor are the ones to be conscripted to fight and die at literally slave wages in the Great Society's imperial war. The poor are the ones to lose their homes to the bulldozer of urban renewal, that bulldozer that operates for the benefit of real estate and construction interests to pulverize available low-cost housing.[9] All this, of course, in the name of "clearing the slums" and helping the aesthetics of housing. The poor are the welfare clientele whose homes are unconstitutionally but regularly invaded by government agents to ferret out sin in the middle of the night. The poor (e.g., Negroes in the South) are the ones disemployed by rising minimum wage floors, put in for the benefit of employers and unions in higher-wage areas (e.g., the North) to prevent industry from moving to the low-wage areas. The poor are cruelly victimized by an income tax that left and right alike misconstrue as an egalitarian program to soak the rich; actually, various tricks and exemptions insure that it is the poor and the middle classes who are hit the hardest.[10] The poor are victimized too by a welfare state of which the cardinal macro-economic tenet is perpetual if controlled inflation. The inflation and the heavy government spending favor the business of the military–industrial complex, while the poor and the retired, those on fixed pensions or Social Security, are hit the hardest. (Liberals have often scoffed at the anti-inflationists' stress on the "widows and orphans" as major victims of inflation, but these remain major victims nevertheless.) And the burgeoning of compulsory mass public education forces millions of unwilling youth off the labor market for many years, and into schools that serve more as houses of detention than as genuine centers of education.[11] Farm programs that supposedly aid poor farmers actually serve the large wealthy farmers at the expense of sharecropper and consumer alike; and commissions that regulate industry serve to cartellize it. The mass of workers is forced by governmental measures into trade unions that tame and integrate the labor force into the toils of the accelerating corporate state, there to be subjected to arbitrary wage "guidelines" and ultimate compulsory arbitration.

The role of the liberal intellectual and of liberal rhetoric is even more stark in foreign economic policy. Ostensibly designed to "help the underdeveloped

---

[9] See Martin Anderson, *The Federal Bulldozer* (Cambridge, Mass.: 1964).

[10] Thus, see Gabriel Kolko, *Wealth and Power in America* (New York: 1962).

[11] Thus, see Paul Goodman, *Compulsory Mis-Education and The Community of Scholars* (New York: Vintage Books, 1966).

countries," foreign aid has served as a gigantic subsidy by the American tax-payer of American export firms, a similar subsidy to American foreign invest-ment through guarantees and subsidized government loans, an engine of infla-tion for the recipient country, and a form of massive subsidy to the friends and clients of U.S. imperialism in the recipient country.

The symbiosis between liberal intellectuals and despotic statism at home and abroad is, furthermore, no accident; for at the heart of the welfarist men-tality is an enormous desire to "do good to" the mass of other people, and since people don't usually wish to be done good to, since they have their own ideas of what they wish to do, the liberal welfarist inevitably ends by reaching for the big stick with which to push the ungrateful masses around. Hence, the liberal ethos itself provides a powerful stimulant for the intellec-tuals to seek state power and ally themselves with the other rulers of the corporate state. The liberals thus become what Harry Elmer Barnes has aptly termed "totalitarian liberals." Or, as Isabel Paterson put it a generation ago:

> The humanitarian wishes to be a prime mover in the lives of others. He cannot admit either the divine or the natural order, by which men have the power to help themselves. The humanitarian puts himself in the place of God.
> But he is confronted by two awkward facts; first, that the competent do not need his assistance; and second, that the majority of people . . . positively do not want to be "done good" by the humanitarian. . . . Of course, what the humanitarian actually proposes is that he shall do what he thinks is good for everybody. It is at this point that the humanitarian sets up the guillotine.[12]

The rhetorical role of welfarism in pushing people around may be seen clearly in the Vietnam War, where American liberal planning for alleged Viet-namese welfare has been particularly prominent, e.g., in the plans and actions of Wolf Ladejinsky, Joseph Buttinger, and the Michigan State group. And the result has been very much of an American-operated "guillotine" for the Vietnamese people, North and South.[13] And even *Fortune* magazine invokes the spirit of humanitarian "idealism" as the justification for the United States' falling "heir to the onerous task of policing these shattered colonies" of West-ern Europe, and exerting its might all over the world. The will to make this exertion to the uttermost, especially in Vietnam and perhaps China, consti-tutes for *Fortune,* "the unending test of American idealism."[14] This lib-eral–welfarist syndrome may also be seen in the very different area of civil rights, in the terribly pained indignation of white liberals at the recent deter-mination of Negroes to take the lead in helping themselves, rather than to keep deferring to the Lords and Ladies Bountiful of white liberalism.

[12] Isabel Paterson, *The God of the Machine* (New York: 1943), p. 241.

[13] See John McDermott, "Welfare Imperialism in Vietnam," *The Nation* (July 25, 1966), pp. 76–88.

[14] *Fortune* (August, 1965). As the right wing of the Great Society Establishment, *Fortune* presumably passes the Berle–Lilienthal test as spokesman for "enlightened" as opposed to narrowly "selfish" capitalism.

In sum, the most important fact about the Great Society under which we live is the enormous disparity between rhetoric and content. In rhetoric, America is the land of the free and the generous, enjoying the fused blessings of a free market tempered by and joined to accelerating social welfare, bountifully distributing its unstinting largesse to the less fortunate in the world. In actual practice, the free economy is virtually gone, replaced by an imperial corporate state Leviathan that organizes, commands, exploits the rest of society and, indeed, the rest of the world, for its own power and pelf. We have experienced, as Garet Garrett keenly pointed out over a decade ago, a "revolution within the form."[15] The old limited republic has been replaced by Empire, within and without our borders.

[15] Garet Garrett, *The People's Pottage* (Caldwell, Idaho: 1953).

Questions for Discussion

1. What seem to be the chief political-economic intentions of Hamilton's report? What kind of economic relationship does he seek between government and the market?

2. Would you say that Hamilton's ideas have had a long-run influence or not?

3. According to Michael Reagan, what were the chief reasons for the recent historical enlargement of government power in the marketplace? Does Reagan oppose or support such actions? Why?

4. The Carson article argues that the Progressive era has been misinterpreted, as have succeeding expansions of government economic power. In what way, according to the author, were elaborations of power justified and what in fact were their effects?

5. In what ways can it be argued that the new capitalism of the twentieth century was the same old capitalism simply clad in new clothes? Do you agree or disagree with Carson's conclusion about where the new capitalism was to lead?

6. On the surface, Rothbard's critique seems to parallel and agree with the previous article. Is this really true? What are the basic ideological differences in perspective?

PART IV

Government and Levels of Economic Activity: Indirect Controls

This section of the readings takes up the matter of government's actions in maintaining levels of economic activity through the use of monetary and fiscal policy. Some question may be raised in the reader's mind by the suggestion that such controls are "indirect" but this is only used to differentiate this section on neo-Keynesian policy from the following section on incomes policies and price controls—policies which are indeed quite direct.

The reader may initially find it profitable to go back to Part II to review the broad policy outlines of Keynesian economics before going on to these readings since the debate in this section largely turns on the issues and the interpretations set out by Lord Keynes. The first two articles, "Mainstream Documents," are drawn from the President's Council of Economic Advisors' Reports for 1962 and 1970. They are instructive in two ways. First, the documents represent the policy development of neo-Keynesian analysis. Secondly, the differences in concern and thrust in the two reports reflect certain important changes in theory and conception of economic problems over an eight-year period. A reader can hardly fail to be struck by the comparison of the optimism in the first report with the guarded concern in the second.

The third article, by a former member of the President's Council of Economic Advisors, is offered as a liberal, or "conventional wisdom," balance sheet on which the fiscal and monetary policy debates and practices of the 1960s were produced. Given the events of the past year or more, much of this resumé may now seem to be irrelevant; however, as a representative document it remains important.

The last two articles represent two left critiques. The first is a long but important elaboration of the Marxian concept of economic surplus and a study of how government spending policy is essential to the utilization or absorption of this surplus. Indeed, it is argued here, if the consistent elaboration of government spending were not possible, economic stagnation would have been the outcome. However, the argument goes beyond this point, which is after all very similar to Keynes, and attempts to study the composition and effects of government fiscal activity—the class basis of taxes and transfers, the role of war spending, the evasion of social needs, and so on. To Baran and Sweezy, such a study of government utilization of the surplus reveals the inner contradictions of a capitalist, even a modified capitalist, economy. The last article attacks modern income theory for its value biases and its maintenance that it is a "value-free" theory.

Mainstream Documents: Policies for Maximum Employment and Production

PRESIDENT'S COUNCIL OF
ECONOMIC ADVISERS

In Part I of this chapter, the progress of the economy in 1961 and the prospect for further progress in 1962 were reviewed in terms of the objectives of maximum employment, production, and purchasing power. Part II describes more fully and specifically how government policy can, does, and will promote progress toward these goals. Two major kinds of government policy are involved: measures for economic stabilization, which influence the total volume of spending; and measures to reduce structural unemployment and underemployment by better mutual adaptation between available jobs and available workers.

Economic Stabilization

Insufficient demand means unemployment, idle capacity, and lost production. Excessive demand means inflation—general increases in prices and money incomes, bringing forth little or no gains in output and real income. The objective of stabilization policies is to minimize these deviations, i.e., to keep over-all demand in step with the basic production potential of the economy.

Stabilization does not mean a mere leveling off of peaks and troughs in production and employment. It does not mean trying to hold overall demand for goods and services stable. It means minimizing deviations from a rising trend, not from an unchanging average. In a growing economy, demand must grow in order to maintain full employment of labor and full utilization of capacity at stable prices. The economy is not performing satisfactorily unless it is almost continuously setting new records of production, income, and employment. Indeed, unless production grows as fast as its potential, unemploy-

From the *President's Council of Economic Advisers Report, 1962.*

ment and idle capacity will also grow. And when the economy starts from a position well below potential, output must for a time grow even faster than potential to achieve full utilization.

The Postwar Record

Despite the recessions of recent years and the inflationary excesses of the early postwar years, the postwar record of economic stabilization is incomparably better than the prewar. The economy fluctuated violently in 1919–21 and operated disastrously far below potential from 1930 to 1942. The 1929 level of GNP, in constant prices, was not exceeded, except briefly in 1937, until 1939. The difference between the 17 percent unemployment of 1939 and the 3 percent rate 10 years earlier is a dramatic measure of the growth of labor force and productivity even during depression. Since the war, the economy's detours from the path of full employment growth have been shorter in both time and distance. There have been four recessions, but none of them has gotten out of hand, as did the decline of 1929–33. All of the declines have been reversed within 13 months, before unemployment reached 8 percent of the labor force. For this improved performance there are several reasons.

First, the war and preceding depression left business firms and households starved for goods. Further, wartime earnings coupled with scarcities of civilian goods, rationing, and price control, saturated business firms and consumers with liquid assets. For these legacies of depression and war, the economy paid a price in the inflations of 1946–48 and 1950, with delayed effects throughout the past decade.

Second, the structure of the economy was reformed after 1933 in ways which substantially increased its resistance to economic fluctuations. The manner in which government tax revenues and income maintenance programs serve as automatic or "built-in" economic stabilizers is described below. The New Deal strengthened and reformed the Nation's banking and financial system with the help of new governmental credit institutions, deposit insurance, and loan and guarantee programs. These have virtually eliminated the possibility that economic declines will be aggravated by bank failures, foreclosures, and epidemic illiquidity.

Third, there is a significantly improved understanding of the manner in which government fiscal and monetary tools can be used to promote economic stability. Under the Employment Act and the climate of opinion which it symbolizes, the Government has been expected to assume, and has assumed, greater responsibility for economic stabilization.

Finally, businessmen and consumers no longer regard prolonged and deep depression as a serious possibility. They generally expect recessions to end quickly; they anticipate a long-term upward trend in the economy; and they spend and invest accordingly. This stability of expectations is in part the result of stability achieved in fact, and reflects general understanding of the structural changes which have contributed to it. But expectations of stability are also a cause of stability—nothing succeeds like success.

Achieving Greater Stability

While our postwar performance is a great advance over that of prewar years, it is still far from satisfactory. We have had no great depression, but we have had four recessions. Even the relatively short and mild recessions of the postwar period have been costly. In the last decade, the Nation has lost an estimated $175 billion of GNP (in 1961 prices) by operating the economy below potential. Industrial production has been below its previous peak nearly half the time since 1946.

There is general agreement that economic fluctuations in the United States are intensified by—if not always caused by—a rhythm in inventory investment, alternating between periods in which stocks are accumulating at an excessively high rate and periods in which they are being liquidated. But it is not beyond hope that stabilization measures, both automatic and discretionary, can be strengthened in force and improved in timing so as to compensate for inventory swings better than has been true in the past. If this is done the swings themselves will be dampened.

The possible gains from improved economic stabilization are impressive. Losses of production, employment, and consumption will be cut. More saving and investment will be realized, contributing steadily to the long-run growth of production potential. Business, consumer, and labor decisions will allocate resources more efficiently when they respond less to cyclical prospects and more to long-run developments. There will be less need and less justification for restrictive practices which are now designed to provide sheltered positions in markets periodically hit by recession.

It is true that an economy operating steadily at a high level of employment, with only limited excess plant capacity, is more subject to the risks of price increases than an economy with heavy unemployment and large unused capacity. However, the dampening of economic fluctuations may itself help to counter this tendency. Cyclical fluctuations have been exerting a "ratchet effect" on prices; costs and prices have been relatively inflexible downward in recessions but have been responsive to increases in demand during recoveries. Cyclical swings in total spending also tend to be accompanied by sharp and transitory shifts in the composition of spending. Because prices and costs respond more readily to upswings than to downswings, these rapid changes in the composition of demand impart an upward bias to the whole price level. These sources of upward price bias will tend to be reduced as a more even pace of advance is achieved.

To capitalize on the potential gains of stabilization requires skillful use of all economic policy, particularly budgetary and monetary policy.

The Federal Budget and Economic Stability

Federal expenditures and taxes affect total employment and production by influencing the total volume of spending for goods and services. Direct Federal purchases of goods and services are themselves part of total demand for national output. In addition, the Federal Government makes "transfer payments" to individuals, for which no current services are rendered in return. Examples are social security and unemployment insurance benefits, and veterans compensation and pension benefits. Both purchases of goods and services and transfer payments add to private incomes and thereby stimulate consumption and investment. Federal taxes, on the other hand, reduce disposable personal and business incomes, and restrain private spending.

By increasing the flow of spending, additional Federal outlays—with tax rates unchanged—have expansionary effects on the economy. Whether an expansion in spending—government or private—leads mainly to more output or mainly to higher prices depends on the degree of slack in the economy. Under conditions of widespread unemployment and excess capacity, businessmen respond to higher demand by increasing production; under conditions of full employment, prices rise instead. In the slack economy of 1961, for example, additional demand from both private and public sources was readily converted into increased production.

Built into the Federal fiscal system are several automatic defenses against recession and inflation. Given the tax rates, tax revenues move up and down with economic activity, since most taxes are levied on private incomes or sales. Indeed, tax revenues change proportionally more than GNP. Furthermore, certain Federal expenditures, such as unemployment compensation payments, are automatically affected by the state of the economy. Economic fluctuations, therefore, result in substantial changes in Federal expenditures and revenues, even when basic expenditure programs and tax rates remain unchanged. With the present system of tax rates and unemployment compensation payments, a one-dollar reduction in GNP means a reduction in Federal tax receipts and an increase in transfer payments totaling about 30 cents. Therefore, private incomes after Federal taxes fall by only 70 cents for each reduction of one dollar in GNP. For this reason, any initial decline in spending and output is transmitted with diminished force to other sectors of the economy.

These automatic or built-in stabilizers moderate the severity of cyclical swings in the economy. If the forces causing a downturn in economic activity are weak and transient, the automatic stabilizers cushion the severity of the decline and give the basic recuperative powers in the private economy a better opportunity to produce a prompt and full recovery.

But if the forces causing the downturn are strong and persistent, the built-in stabilizers may not suffice to prevent a large and prolonged recession. Furthermore, they are blindly symmetrical in their effects. When economic activity quickens after a slump, the rise in Federal revenues begins immediately and slows the recovery in employment and incomes. For these reasons, the task of economic stabilization cannot be left entirely to built-in stabilizers. Discretionary budget policy, e.g., changes in tax rates or expenditure programs, is indispensable—sometimes to reinforce, sometimes to offset, the effects of the stabilizers.

To be effective, discretionary budget policy should be flexible. In order to promote economic stability, the Government should be able to change quickly tax rates or expenditure programs, and equally able to reverse its actions as circumstances change. Failure to arrest quickly a downturn in income, production, and employment may shake the faith of firms and households in prompt recovery and thereby lead to a cumulative decline. Delay in countering inflationary pressures may permit the development of a self-propelling speculative boom, with disruptive consequences to the domestic economy and the balance of payments. If moderate fiscal action can be taken quickly and can be speedily reversed when circumstances warrant, the dangers of overstimulating or overrestricting the economy are much smaller than if fiscal responses are sluggish and difficult to reverse.

Fiscal policy can be made a more flexible and more powerful tool of economic stabilization by means that do not change the basic structure and level of taxation or the long-run size and composition of Federal expenditure programs. Changes in the basic structure and level of taxation should be made by the Congress with full deliberation in the light of the many relevant considerations, including the long-run revenue needs of the Government, equity among individuals and groups, and the effects of various taxes on economic efficiency and growth. Similarly, changes in the magnitude and content of government expenditures should represent the considered judgment of the people and the Congress on national priorities. For purposes of economic stabilization all that is needed of tax policy is temporary variation in the general level of tax rates within the existing structure, and all that is required of government outlays is timing of certain expenditures so that they bolster employment and purchasing power when the economy needs stimulus and taper off as it approaches full employment. In both cases, the form of action required for purposes of stabilization and the procedure for taking timely action can be agreed upon in advance. . . .

Monetary and Credit Policies and Economic Stability

The second major instrument of the Government for economic stabilization is monetary and credit policy, interpreted in the broadest sense to encompass all governmental actions affecting the liquidity of the economy and the availability and cost of credit. Here the Federal Government has broad and inescapable responsibilities, stemming basically from the sovereign right of Congress "to coin money, regulate the value thereof. . . ." The Government's influence is exercised in several ways—principally through Federal Reserve control of the total volume of bank reserves, but also through Treasury management of the public debt and through the administration of a variety of government lending and credit guarantee programs. These powers can significantly affect the flow of funds into business investment, capital expenditures of State and local governments, residential construction, and purchases of consumer durable goods. Monetary and credit policies can be flexible, responding at short notice to changes in economic circumstances and prospects.

In an important sense, the private economy of the United States contains automatic or "built-in" monetary stabilizers. Unless the Government acts to make compensating changes in the monetary base, expansion of general economic activity, accompanied by increased demands for liquid balances and for investment funds, will tend to tighten interest rates and restrict the availability of credit. Similarly, a recession of business activity will normally lead to lower rates, easier terms, and less stringent rationing by lenders. Like fiscal stabilizers, the monetary stabilizers are often useful built-in defenses against recessions or against inflationary excesses of demand. But these defenses may not be strong enough. Being automatic stabilizers, they can only moderate unfavorable developments; they cannot prevent or reverse them. And at other times, unless the monetary authorities offset their effects, they can operate counter to basic policy objectives, braking expansions short of full employment. Discretionary policy is essential, sometimes to reinforce, sometimes to mitigate or overcome, the monetary consequences of short-run fluctuations of economic activity. In addition, discretionary policy must provide the base for expanding liquidity and credit in line with the growing production potential of the economy. For these reasons, the Federal Reserve System is continuously making and executing discretionary monetary policy.

The proper degree of general "tightness" or "easiness" of monetary policy, and the techniques by which the various governmental authorities can appropriately seek to achieve it, depend on the state of the domestic economy, on the fiscal policies of the Government, and on the international economic position. When the economy is in recession or beset by high unemployment and excess capacity, monetary policy should clearly be expansionary. How expansionary it should be depends very much upon the extent of the stimulus that the government budget is, and will be, giving to over-all demand. When demand is threatening to outrun the economy's production potential, monetary policy should be restrictive. How restrictive it should be depends, again, upon how much of the job of containing inflation is assumed by fiscal policy. There is, in principle, a variety of mixtures of fiscal and monetary policies which can accomplish a given stabilization objective. Choice among them depends upon other objectives and constraints. The relation of this choice to economic growth was noted above; the stabilization of demand at full employment levels by a budget surplus compensated by an expansionary monetary policy is favorable to growth. On the other hand, monetary policy may in some circumstances be constrained by the balance of payments. If low interest rates encourage foreign borrowing in the United States and a large outflow of funds seeking higher yields abroad, monetary policy may have to be more restrictive than domestic economic objectives alone would dictate. The first line of defense is to try to adapt the techniques of monetary control, so that policy can serve both masters at once. Even so, difficult decisions of balance between conflicting objectives may sometimes be unavoidable.

Monetary Policy and Debt Management

At the beginning of 1960, monetary policy was restrictive and interest rates were generally at postwar peaks. Despite bullish expectations about the economy, interest rates soon began a slow decline that lasted seven or eight months, aided by a gradual reversal of Federal Reserve policy beginning in March and furthered by the recession starting in May.

However, the Federal Reserve's anti-recession policy, for the first time since the early 1930's, was constrained by a serious balance of payments situation. Through its choice of expansionary monetary techniques, the Federal Reserve sought to avoid adding to the already large outflow of short-term capital. The 3-month Treasury bill rate did not fall below 2 percent. Long-term interest rates declined from their peaks but remained considerably above their previous cyclical troughs. This was a matter of serious concern because of the importance of long-term interest rates for business capital investment, residential construction, and State and local governmental spending on public facilities. And neither the money supply nor long-term private financing responded as promptly as in previous periods of monetary ease.

The new Administration faced in January 1961 both economic recession and a crisis of confidence in the dollar that threatened to limit sharply the use of expansionary monetary policy for economic recovery and growth. The Administration's forthright attack on the balance of payments problem restored confidence in the dollar. The resulting reduction in the discount on the dollar in the forward markets for foreign exchange eliminated any significant advantage in sending short-term funds abroad and helped to make it possible for monetary policy to support domestic expansion. . . .

Monetary Expansion and Recovery

As the economy advances toward full employment, it will need more liquidity. Throughout the postwar period, and particularly in the three previous economic recoveries, the growth in liquidity has fallen considerably short of the growth in GNP. The economy had to work off the excess liquidity inherited from the war, interest rates were generally rising, and expectations of higher prices were spreading. These factors worked to reduce the liquidity requirements of the economy relative to GNP. And the growth in nonmonetary liquid assets diminished even more the needed growth in the money supply (bank deposits and currency). Business firms, government units, and individuals learned, to their advantage, how to minimize holdings of cash.

For each 1 per cent rise in GNP in the three past economic recoveries, commercial bank deposits and currency increased by only about one-third of 1 per cent, while liquid assets, more broadly measured, increased by about two-fifths to three-fifths of 1 per cent. If these relationships should hold in the current economic recovery, and if gross national product rises to full employment levels by the middle of 1963—an increase of more than 20 per cent from the trough in the first quarter of 1961—commercial bank deposits and currency would grow over the same period by 7–8 per cent and liquid assets by 11–12 per cent.

In the current recovery, however, the factors that served to limit liquidity requirements in the earlier recoveries may well be less important. In particular, interest rates may appropriately be more stable, for reasons already explained. Thus, these estimates of needed liquidity are probably conservative. The appropriate expansion of liquidity will depend upon the strength of private demands, on the tightness of fiscal policy, and on the balance of payments position.

Mainstream Documents: The Stabilization Problem in the Longer Run

PRESIDENT'S COUNCIL OF
ECONOMIC ADVISERS

The main lesson of stabilization policy in 1969 was the importance of avoiding in the future the kind of inflationary situation and pervasive inflation-mindedness that had built up by the end of 1968. Starting from that situation a major change in the behavior of the economy and in expectations was required, a change that would run against the current of strong ongoing forces. No one could tell how fast that change could be successfully accomplished or the degree of monetary and fiscal restraint required to accomplish it.

The objective of stabilization policy in 1970 will be to move us toward a position where the main goal can be continuity. That position will have been reached when inflation has been brought down to a significantly slower

From the *President's Council of Economic Advisers Report, 1970.*

rate, and real output is growing at about its potential rate. At that point growth of the GNP in current dollars at a steady and moderate rate, such as 6 percent per year, would serve to support steady growth of output at its potential rate with a far better performance of the price level than has been experienced in recent years.

The problem then will be threefold:

1. To stabilize the rate of growth of money GNP as far as feasible at a pace that will permit the economy to produce at its potential;
2. To adapt the economy so that it lives better with whatever remaining instability may develop; and
3. To press on with measures to reduce both inflation and unemployment further.

Stabilizing the Growth of GNP

To stabilize the growth of GNP will require avoiding destabilizing moves in fiscal and monetary policies and instead using these policies to offset, or at least constrain, destabilizing forces arising in the private economy. One difficulty is that the attempt to use fiscal and monetary policies to counter fluctuations arising in the private economy may itself be destabilizing, if moves are not made in the right amounts and at the right times.

Stabilization by Fiscal Policy

Fiscal policy should avoid large destabilizing swings occurring at random or contrary to the clear requirements of the economy. The big upsurge of Federal spending (nondefense as well as defense spending) after mid-1965, which was unmatched by any general tax increase for 3 years, is a major example of such a destabilizing movement.

The likelihood of achieving economic stability would not be greatly affected by the size of the surplus or deficit, within a reasonable range, if that size were itself stable or changing only slowly, and if the effects on liquidity resulting from secular increases or decreases in the Federal debt were offset by monetary policy. Therefore, it should be possible to decide on the desired full-employment surplus or deficit on grounds other than stability, and without sacrificing stability if the target itself is kept reasonably stable. If the budget position changes sharply in the short run in the absence of marked shifts in private demand, the adaptation of the private economy and the compensatory force of monetary policy may not come into play quickly enough to prevent large swings in overall economic activity. This is a major lesson for the 1970's.

. . . Except as a result of a national emergency, there is probably no reason for this decision to change in a way that would radically alter, from year to year, the size of the surplus or deficit that would be the objective under conditions of high employment.

If the surplus or deficit position of the budget that would be yielded by a steadily growing, full-employment GNP were kept stable, the actual figure would, of course, automatically respond to changes in the pace of the economy. If the economy were to grow unusually slowly in any year, receipts would rise slowly also, and the surplus would be below normal (or the deficit would be enlarged further). These variations in the size of the surplus or deficit would tend to stabilize the growth rate of the GNP. The question is in what circumstances and how to go beyond this and vary expenditure programs and tax rates to offset fluctuations in the private economy. There is now abundant experience with the obstacles to effective and flexible use of tax changes for this purpose. Moreover, recent experience and analysis suggest that the stabilizing power of temporary income tax changes may not be as great as had been hoped, and it might become less if they were used frequently, because people would tend to adjust their behavior to what they regard as the normal rate of taxation. Nevertheless, there will be situations in which tax rates must be changed in order to maintain the desired longrun deficit or surplus position and there may also be circumstances in which the effort should be made to use a temporary tax change to offset destabilizing shifts in private demand.

The possibility of varying the rate of increase of Federal spending in the interest of stability is somewhat greater though still limited. Although tax and expenditure decisions are both politically sensitive, the fact that the President has some discretion to adjust the timing of expenditures within the limits of legislation avoids some of the complications that beset tax changes. Moreover, the effect of expenditure changes on economic activity can probably be more reliably foreseen than the effect of temporary tax changes. It is true that the part of the total expenditures that is open to deliberate variation is small, because of legal and implied commitments. Nevertheless, some variations can, in fact, be made, as they were in 1969, and it would be unwise to rule out the attempt to do more of this when the economic necessity is clear. Furthermore, it is possible to broaden the "automatic stabilizers" in Federal expenditure, as the Administration has proposed in the Manpower Training Act and Employment Security Amendments mentioned earlier.

The possibility of using debt management as an instrument of stabilization policy has been severely inhibited by the $4\frac{1}{4}$-percent interest rate ceiling on Government bonds. This ceiling has forced the Federal Government to sell only short or intermediate securities since 1965. Raising the ceiling to realistic levels, or eliminating it, would provide the Federal Government with a desirable degree of latitude in conducting its financial operations.

Stabilization by Monetary Policy

Monetary policy can be devoted somewhat more singlemindedly to maintaining stability than can fiscal policy. Nevertheless, there are a number of difficulties in its use. Apparently the effects of changes in monetary policy are felt in the economy with widely varying and often long lags. Therefore, if policy that is intended to have a restrictive effect is continued until the effect is visible, the lagged consequences of what has been done may show up in excessive contraction. The attempt to counter this by a sharp reversal in policy to an expansive posture may, after a while, generate inflationary rates of expansion. In the present state of knowledge there is no ideal solution for this problem. Prudence, therefore, suggests the desirability of not allowing monetary policy to stray widely from the steady posture that is likely on the average to be consistent with long-term economic growth, even though forecasts at particular times may seem to call for a sharp variation in one direction or another.

The suggestion that monetary policy might well be steady, or at least steadier than it has been, raises the question of the terms in which this stability is to be measured. There is abundant evidence that the steadiness of monetary policy cannot be measured by the steadiness of interest rates. Interest rates will tend to rise when business is booming and inflation is present or expected; they will tend to decline in the opposite circumstances. Better results might be obtained by concentrating more on the steadiness of the main monetary aggregates, such as the supply of money, of money plus time deposits, and of total bank credit. This still leaves questions of policy to be resolved when these aggregates are tending to move in different directions, or at different rates of change, as they often do. There is no substitute for trying to understand in particular cases what the significance of the divergences is and what they indicate about the underlying behavior of the supply of liquidity.

Improving Our Economic Data

Since the Federal Government has the responsibility for keeping the economy on a noninflationary growth path with high employment, it must have at its disposal the tools for accurately measuring on a timely basis the performance of the economy at the national level. The Government now publishes a broad array of economic statistics that serve this purpose. These statistics, particularly those relating to economic activity in the short run, have grown over the years in volume and quality and have served the Nation well. But our demands for economic data of high quality keep outrunning the supply. The Federal Government is not alone in requiring better statistics, since to an increasing extent businesses have been making use of economic data for planning their own operations. Indeed, never before have so many businesses watched so closely the economic indicators that appear each month or quarter.

More accurate measurement of economic performance would improve the management of policy in a number of ways. It would tell us more certainly where we have been. Elementary as this may sound, it is of crucial importance. Too often this is a fundamental problem for the policymaker. The economy, or some important part of it, may be on a somewhat different course from that indicated by the data. Or economic series that purport to measure the same thing, or almost the same thing, may move in contradictory directions. Sometimes a series that moves in one direction one month moves in the opposite direction when revised the following month. The first requirement for making judgments about where the economy is going or what policies are needed is an accurate picture of where we have been.

Accurate data are also needed in order to help analyze the past and find relationships that have some degree of stability. Accomplishing this aim is obviously only partly a question of statistics; the economy is, of course, more than a mechanism. For example, swings in sentiment and attitudes in our affluent economy have a powerful effect on the inclinations of consumers and businesses to spend. Consumer behavior has been especially difficult to predict in recent years, and may be more complex than had been thought previously. Business decisionmaking is equally complex. Yet economic analysis is a continuing search for patterns of regularity that can be helpful in forming judgments about the economy. And the first requirement for this search is reliable basic data. The Administration has proposed substantial improvements in many of the key economic statistics, including, for example, those relating to retail sales, construction, the service industries, international prices, and job vacancies.

Having data on a timely basis is also important for the policymaker. This is particularly important if there is reason to think that the economy may be shifting its course. This Nation probably has more timely statistics than any other economy, but clearly much improvement is in order here. Early in 1969 the President directed the Director of the Bureau of the Budget to take action that would secure prompter issuance of monthly and quarterly statistical series by Federal agencies. The Bureau of the Budget issued a set of guidelines governing release of major economic indicators, and the statistical agencies have already achieved a considerable speedup. Further progress depends heavily on obtaining prompter reporting from the business community.

Living with Instability

If the American people assign sufficient priority to doing so, they should be able to enjoy a higher degree of economic stability than in the past. Still, some instability will remain, and this emphasizes the importance of improving the operation of the economy so that the remaining instability will cause less pain and inefficiency. The most obvious and probably most important step in this direction is improvement of the unemployment compensation system. Proposals of the Administration to accomplish this have been discussed earlier in this chapter. Improvement of labor markets—through better provision for retraining and movement of workers—would also help to prevent the concentration of unemployment on a small group of workers who are substantially injured by it.

On the inflation side, also, some useful steps can be taken. The distortions introduced into the economy by the presence of interest rate ceilings of various kinds—on savings deposits and shares, on guaranteed and insured mortgages, on loans generally under State usury laws—have become evident in this inflationary period. When market interest rates rise certain uses of credit are shrunk disproportionately because of these ceilings. . . .

The construction industry has experienced much greater fluctuations in conjunction with general economic instability than most other industries. This has been painful to the workers and contractors in the industry and harmful to the growth of its productivity. . . .

The Continuing Problems of Inflation and Unemployment

The present anti-inflation effort should reduce the rate of inflation substantially and demote inflation from its position as the Nation's most important economic problem. Still the problem of getting the inflation rate down further, while at the same time maintaining high employment, will probably remain. This will require persistent efforts to reduce the inflation that occurs when demand is growing sufficiently to keep employment high. One of the most hopeful lines of attack will be to improve the adaptation of the labor force—in skills and location—to the pattern of demand for labor. This will shorten the interval of job-search for persons losing or leaving old jobs or entering the labor force, in given conditions of the labor market. It will permit an increasingly high rate of employment to be attained without so strong a pressure of demand as to cause inflation. Manpower programs to move in this direction by better training programs, application of computer technology to job placement and general overhaul of the Nation's job exchange system, have already been discussed. Evaluation of experience with them should permit further development of improved methods. Measures to improve the competitiveness of product markets to assure that business policies will freely and flexibly adapt to changes in market demand will also contribute to reducing the average rate of inflation that accompanies high employment. . . .

There is no inherent reason why a high employment economy must be an inflationary economy—even a mildly inflationary economy. After the series of inflationary episodes since World War II, the transition to a stable condition of high employment without inflation will come slowly. But with persistent attention and effort it is attainable.

The Economics of the 1960s—A Backward Look

OTTO ECKSTEIN

The 1960s are behind us. What have we learned? And what should we forget? Regretfully, there still is little study of the history of economic policy. Historians record the minutiae of foreign affairs and domestic politics, but the successes and failures of economic policy, which affect the lives of the people more directly than the struggles of personalities for power, are still not the subject of serious study. The books by Arthur Schlesinger and Eric Goldman on the Kennedy and Johnson administrations give short shrift to economic management.

This essay cannot fill that void. It presents only the reflections of a brief participant in the economic policies of the 1960s, and a partial assessment of that decade in the area of domestic policy.

In 1959 the Joint Economic Committee studies on *Employment, Growth, and Price Levels* expressed concern about the slow growth of the economy in the 1950s, the rising unemployment, and the increasing frequency of recessions. All these were blamed on the restrictive policies in the management of aggregate demand, a low rate of increase in the money supply of only 1.9 per cent for 1953 to 1959, and a destabilizing fiscal policy because of the gyrations of the defense budget. The Committee issued reports about the dimensions of poverty and the inadequacy of health care, but it implicitly argued that if the economic growth rate was increased, poverty would be reduced and the resources would be created to help solve all our problems. Economic growth, then, was the major issue as we entered the 1960s.

The critics of the 1950s maintained that the "natural" growth of the American economy was substantially higher than the performance. By "natural" growth they meant the performance that is possible, given advancing technology, the institutional arrangements (e.g., sector distributions) of the economy, and full utilization of this potential. Leon Keyserling, who made economic growth a major issue, argued that the economy was capable of growing at a full 5 per cent a year. James Knowles, in his pioneer aggregate

From Otto Eckstein, "The Economics of the 1960s—A Backward Look," *The Public Interest,* No. 19 (Spring 1970), pp. 86–97. Copyright © National Affairs, Inc., 1970. Reprinted by permission of the author and publisher.

production function study for *Employment, Growth, and Price Levels,* produced a medium estimate of 3.9 per cent, with a half per cent on either side for low or high growth policies. In reply to these voices, Edward F. Denison, in his famous study *Sources of Economic Growth,* concluded that the natural rate of growth was only 3 per cent, implying that the policy of the 1950s was not in error, and that even major changes in investment in physical and human capital would accelerate the rate of growth by only a few small decimals. If 1 per cent sounds like a quibble, we should realize that an additional 1 per cent of economic growth during the decade is $85 billion of extra output by 1969.

Actually, the economy grew at an annual average of 4.6 per cent during the decade 1959 to 1969. To obtain the natural rate of growth one must correct for the gap of 4 per cent between actual and potential GNP in 1959 and for an overfull employment of 2 per cent of potential in 1969. Thus, the apparent growth of potential GNP was 4 per cent for the decade; James Knowles was right.

Where did Denison go wrong? The depression of the 1930s did more harm to the economy than the Denison analysis indicated. The loss in capital formation, and perhaps the lost technology and innovations as well, were not fully made up when World War II brought full employment. High employment has raised potential growth above prewar standards.

How was the high growth rate achieved in the 1960s? Economic measures enacted in 1962 stimulated the rate of growth of the economy's potential through the investment credit and more liberal depreciation allowances. The neoclassical school of investment analysts, led by Dale Jorgenson, assigns great weight to this stimulus, though other equations can probably explain the historical record as well. Without doubt, these measures helped accelerate capital goods spending by mid-1963. They led to certain abuses, including an excessive growth of leasing. But the investment credit idea has not obtained a firm place in our institutional structure and is about to disappear.

The central feature of economics in the 1960s was the triumph of modern fiscal policy. It was a victory slow in coming. Six years passed from the time in 1958 when many economists, Arthur Burns as well as the Keynesians, saw the need for a tax cut until the needed policy prevailed. Why did it take so long to take the commonsense step of reducing an excessive burden of taxation, so obviously in the interest of politicians and their constituencies? It is a dramatic example of the power of established prejudices over self-interest, even of ideas that were quite wrong.

First, even Keynesian economists forgot the lesson of their master, that an economy could remain at underemployment equilibrium. Public and scientific opinion had come to accept the necessity of government deficits when the economy was sliding into recession. But the classical view of the natural tendency to return to full employment remained deeply ingrained. At the bottom of the 1958 recession, the leading indicators established that the lower turning point had been reached and tax reduction was ruled out. The Samuelson task force to president-elect Kennedy concluded that the economy was in an upswing, and therefore did not endorse immediate tax reduction. Even this sophisticated group fell into the classical trap. (Or was it political realism?) Recovery proceeded, and by 1962 unemployment had fallen to 5.5 per cent. But then the economy stalled. Months dragged by as a good set of figures would raise hopes of renewed advance and the next month would dash them. Only gradually was it recognized that the tax burden was excessive and that the economy was going nowhere. In this respect, the Council of Economic Advisers understood the issue long before its academic allies.

Second, the concept of the annually balanced budget and the fear of debt still held many persons in its grip. Few outside the government believed that a tax cut would pay for itself—as it did—and so it appeared that the initial impact of tax reduction would be an enlargement of the budget deficit.

Third, the structuralists, with a following both in the Federal Reserve Board and the Department of Labor, argued that the high unemployment was the outcome of an imbalance between the new, technologically advanced jobs and the supply of unskilled, disadvantaged workers. The structuralists had a legitimate point in advocating an upgrading of a portion of the labor force. But in overstating their case they were obstructionists to modern fiscal policy. When the economy finally approached full employment after 1964, the job gains of the unskilled and of the disadvantaged greatly exceeded the gains of the more skilled; we discovered the social power of a tight labor market.

Fourth, Professor Galbraith's voice, carrying from Delhi to Washington, argued that tax reduction would permanently lower the government's ability to command resources. He favored the traditional Keynesian route of stimulating the economy through expenditures. Whatever the merits of greater public spending, the simple fact was that the Congress of the early 1960s would not go that route.

Fifth, advocates of tax reform felt that tax reduction offered them the only opportunity to put together a political package which would make the Congress accept the closing of loopholes. The theory was that Congress would give the President some tax reform in exchange for the privilege of cutting taxes. Actually it was the President and his advisors who wanted tax reduction, while tax reform was a millstone around fiscal policy.

Sixth, the monetary school of economists argued that tax reduction was a minor element in economic policy, and that what was really needed to stimulate the economy was a more suitable increase in the money supply. At the time of the great fiscal debate, however, the monetary school had little influence and cannot be said to have been a significant factor in the delay.

After six years the taxes were cut. By July 1965, before defense contracts began to rise, unemployment was down to 4.5 per cent and falling rapidly, the economy was growing at over 5 per cent a year, and wholesale prices were still stable and no higher than five years earlier. The economy had shown, at least for 18 happy months, that it could prosper without war with sensible, modern economic management; doubts about fiscal policy were wiped out, and for a year or two economists rode high indeed.

Then came the Vietnam war and the end, for a period at least, of modern fiscal policy. The budget underestimated defense spending by $10 billion for fiscal 1967 and $5 billion for fiscal 1968. The impact on the economy was underestimated by larger amounts because of the greater jumps in defense contracts. If the economic impact of the war had been known, the excise taxes would not have been cut in the summer of 1965. In early 1966 there should have been a broad across-the-board tax increase. But taxes were not increased because the President could not get the American people to pay for the war. In the end, the war paralyzed the political process, producing the surrealistic debate over the tax surcharge from mid-1967 to mid-1968. International financial crises followed one on another. Demand became excessive. The tax surcharge of mid-1968, which Congress voted, finally restored some fiscal order.

The impact of the federal budget on the economy in the 1960s can be measured crudely by the high employment budget surplus—an estimate of the surplus that the budget would produce if the economy were at full employment and producing revenues accordingly. The excessively restrictive policies of the 1950s had raised the full employment budget surplus to about $13 billion in 1960. Increased expenditures to fight recession, the military buildup over the Berlin crisis, and the investment credit and depreciation reform lowered the surplus to about $6.5 billion in 1962. Delay in tax reduction and a slowdown in expenditure increases raised the surplus once more, reaching an $11 billion peak at the end of 1963.

The tax cuts, and the increases in spending, caused an enormous swing in the federal budget. By the beginning of 1967, the full employment budget showed a deficit of $12 billion—a welcome stimulus during the slowdown; but its deepening to $15 billion by mid-1968 was a disaster. Once the tax surcharge was passed and expenditure restraint became effective, the swing in the opposite direction was equally massive. By the second quarter of 1969 the high employment surplus approached $10 billion again. No wonder that the economy got rather out of hand, and now faces a period of slow growth.

What judgment can be passed about discretionary policy in the light of this record?

First, while the necessary alternative model simulations have not been done, and so answers must remain qualitative at best, the record of the 1960s seems to repeat the verdict of the 1950s. Discretionary policy did harm as well as good. The policy proposed by the Committee for Economic Development in 1947, if it had been followed, would have done better. The CED recommended that the government maintain a small full employment surplus in its budget, and normally eschew the attempt to pursue a more ambitious, discretionary stabilization policy. The CED policy would have avoided the excessive full employment surpluses in the late 1950s and the early 1960s, the swings which led to the reemergence of a very large surplus in 1963, and it would have forced the financing of the Vietnam war by current taxes. The Great Society programs still could have been financed out of the increase in full employment revenues during a period of rapid growth.

Second, it is evident that the major movements in the full employment surplus were not the result of deliberate stabilization policy. The big swings were due to exogenous events: i.e., the Vietnam war and the inability of the political process to make revenues respond to swings in expenditures. Even if the government had abandoned discretionary policy altogether, and sought to maintain a steady full employment balance of small surplus, the same political difficulties would have gotten in the way. Taxes would have had to be raised. It is likely that the political process would have failed to execute the CED policy, just as it failed to carry out a rational discretionary policy.

In the 1960s, expenditures by government rose at a substantially higher rate than the gross national product. The total outlays (on national income account) of all levels of government were 27.1 per cent on the GNP in 1960; by 1969, the figure rose to 31.4 per cent. The outlays of states and localities rose from 9.9 per cent to 13.1 per cent of GNP; federal outlays rose from 18.5 to 20.5 per cent.

This increase in part represents the Vietnam war, which absorbed about 3 per cent of GNP, some of it at the expense of other defense outlays. Most of the remainder was due to the growth of public activities in response to a rising population and to slow productivity growth of government service activities. But a major reason for the rise of government spending was the Great Society programs enacted from 1964 to 1966.

It is important to understand how this change in the public-private mix came about. So long as the issue was posed in Galbraithian terms—public versus private spending—the Congress did not respond. The Great Society programs were made possible by the large spurt in the growth rate from 1964 to 1966. Public spending came out of economic growth, not out of private spending.

These are the summary figures: in 1964, before the Great Society programs, the federal government collected $113 billion and spent $119 billion, producing a $6 billion deficit. By 1968, following the substantial tax reductions, revenues were up to $154 billion, a rise of $41 billion, expenditures were up to $179 billion, a rise of $60 billion. As a result, the $6 billion budget deficit rose to $25 billion. What happened is clear enough: military spending, mainly for Vietnam, rose by $27 billion. Spending on education at the federal level rose from $2 to $7 billion; on health, from $2 to $10 billion; and the total of all other fields, including Social Security, agriculture, urban affairs, and the old-line programs, went up from $61 to $81 billion.

Thus, during the period of the Great Society legislation, there was plenty of spending for old and new programs, civilian and military. Economic growth produced the revenues, though in the end we did stumble into an enormous deficit.

Because human beings are fallible and policy-makers all over Washington are subject to common tides of opinion and politics, the record of monetary policy has similarities to fiscal policy. Until 1965, monetary policy accommodated the gradual recovery to full employment, while interest rates remained fairly stable. One might argue that interest rates should have risen as the economy moved toward full employment, but one should also remember that interest rates were already high at the beginning of the decade because of the excessively restrictive monetary policies of 1959.

The monetary school of economists, led by Milton Friedman, claims that the recovery to full employment was really due to a good expansion of the money supply, perhaps prompted by the need to finance the budget deficits. The theoretical debate about the relative importance of fiscal and monetary policy is not likely to be settled here; but one can observe a striking contrast for the period under review. The rhythm of the economy seemed to respond to changes in fiscal policy. Unemployment stayed high so long as the budget aimed for large high employment surpluses. It fell after the tax cut of 1964. The increase in the broad money supply was fairly steady, both in the period of high level stagnation and during full recovery. If easy money alone sufficed, full employment should have come more quickly.[1]

From 1965 on, the Federal Reserve Board no longer fully accommodated the economic growth, and interest rates began to rise. With the benefit of hindsight about the war, the federal deficit, the capital goods boom, and the inflation, it is now evident that monetary policy should have become tougher earlier. Further monetary policy was too aggressive during the 1967 slowdown, and if ever there was a case of overkill, the antirecession fiscal and monetary policies of 1967 were an example. In the summer of 1968, monetary policy eased too quickly after the passage of the tax surcharge, and the authorities have been struggling ever since to bring the banking system and inflation under control.

The monetary theorists sing a siren song which says that if money supply is expanded at a constant rate, we would free ourselves of the fallibility of human judgment about the timing of restricting or loosening the amount of money in response to the economic cycle. There is little doubt that we have overmanaged money, perhaps never more so than during the extreme restraint of 1969–70. But there are hurdles on the way to a more stable policy: if it really is the money supply that is to be regulated, there had better be agreement on the figures. The record of the money supply for the first half of 1969 has been rewritten, as it was for several other crucial periods. Who would rest a policy on so weak a statistical reed? Further, it is difficult to define a "neutral" policy. Structural changes in the financial system give different growth trends to the various monetary magnitudes.

---

[1] For the statistically inclined reader, let me add a few regression results on this point. For the period 1961 to 1965, correlations of quarterly data, utilizing poly-nomial distributed lags of third degree, four quarters, constrained to zero at the remote end show the following: the unemployment rate on the Full Employment Surplus: .82; on the rate of increase of the money supply: .64. The results are not as clear cut for other periods; but the first half of the 1960's does seem to have been fiscal policy's day.

There has been little study of the quantitative relationships between the various monetary measures, explaining the differences in the growth of such variables as unborrowed reserves, the narrow money supply, the broad money supply, the monetary base, total bank credit, bank loans, total credit in the economy, etc. Until this work is done, adoption of any rule applicable to one concept will simply convert the present disputes into a quarrel about the selection and care of statistics.

The level of interest rates is also an indicator of monetary policy, and to me still the most unambiguous. But it is evident from experience that a stable interest rate is not a neutral policy. Interest rates should rise and fall with the business cycle. Indeed, a stable interest rate policy is probably significantly destabilizing for the economy. Thus, while interest movements are a useful gauge, they do not provide a simple rule which policy can follow.

By the end of the 1950s the need to reconcile full employment and price stability was widely recognized. The new administration, building on earlier *Economic Reports,* established "Guideposts for Wage-Price Stability." At first the guideposts only asserted some rather bland principles about price and wage behavior which a competitive economy would achieve on its own. It reminded labor that wage increases beyond productivity served mainly to raise prices; it reminded business that price increases beyond trend costs raised profits only temporarily. But until January 1966, when the guideposts were breached by the New York subway settlement, the administration had pursued an active policy of seeking to hold settlements close to the productivity rate.

The guidepost policies must be understood in the context of their day. The economy was moving toward full employment; industrial operating rates were rising. Productivity was advancing rapidly and wage demands were predicated on stable consumer prices. The longer the stable costs and prices could be preserved, the closer the economy could come to full employment without stumbling into the inflationary difficulties which had haunted us in the mid-1950s.

In their heyday, in 1964 to 1966, the guideposts were a major element of government policy. Government spending programs, fair labor standards proposals, minerals stockpile policy, civil service pay, agricultural policy, and protective measures for specific industries both internal and at the frontier, were examined, at the president's direction, for their effect on cost-price stability. This probably was the first time in history that an administration examined its policy proposals fully from the objective of price stability.

In addition, the guideposts partially reoriented the usual government interventions in collective bargaining. Settlement of industrial conflicts was not an objective by itself but was coordinate with cost stability. For some time, at least, a Democratic government modified its traditional role of urging management to settle for large increases in order to restore industrial harmony. On the price side, presidential intervention slowed down the increases of some highly visible basic materials and a few final products.

Did these policies have any effect? Wage equations which explain other years of the postwar period fail during the guidepost years. To be sure, other explanations have been found for the extraordinarily low wage increases of 1963 to 1966, but they are not totally convincing. Without claiming statistical proof, I would evaluate the episode as prolonging the virtuous circle of high productivity growth, stable costs, and stable price expectations by some months, and slowing the pickup of the price-wage spiral.

The guidepost policies were politically very difficult. Every time the president reduced a government program, intervened in a labor dispute, rolled back a price, let goods in from abroad, or made a release from the stockpile, he trod on sensitive toes. In due time, the affected industries sought retribution through the political process. Only a president elected by an enormous majority and commanding firm control over the Congress could withstand the politicking of industries, which President Johnson did.

As the Vietnam war escalated and the president's popularity began to fade, the authority of the guidepost policies shrank. When the president lost his command over the Congress in the 1966 elections, the most active phase of guidepost policies drew to a close, though there were some successful interventions as late as the summer of 1968.

There has been criticism of the guideposts as violating the principles of a free market economy. These criticisms are misplaced. The markets in our economy are relatively free compared to other economies; but many industries benefit from government programs, from government purchases, government-enforced production controls, import restrictions and tariff, artificial reductions of supply through stockpile policies, and so on. Similarly, the strength of labor unions is immensely aided not only by the basic laws which redress the balance between employer and worker, but also by the Davis-Bacon Act which strengthens the grip of the construction unions, Walsh-Healey, and so on. We saw in the opening months of 1969 that the government cannot shelve all its powers to influence wage and price decisions. The absence of guidepost policies does not make the government neutral.

The guidepost episode and the recent inflationary explosion leave a nagging question: is the inflationary bias of the economy excessive at a 4 per cent unemployment rate, and does the rate of inflation inevitably worsen at full employment? The United States has never had uninterrupted prosperity before. Now that we have unlocked the secret, are we unable to use it because we do not know how to live with full employment?

What should we have learned? What mistakes have we no right to repeat? And where is the new ground that should be broken? A review of the predictions made at the beginning of this decade indicates that one cannot anticipate what will be the dominant problems. In 1960 no one thought about the Vietnam war or appreciated that the inequality of economic opportunity and disparities between black and white would become the central social problem. The impact of an advancing economy on the physical environment was not totally a surprise, but was far down the agenda of the decade. Even such traditional items as the deterioration of the cities, the improvement of health and education, housing, and rural opportunity had little specificity ten years ago. So don't expect much help here in pinpointing the major problems of the 1970s even within the area of economic performance.

Nonetheless we owe it to ourselves to attempt to distill a few points from the review of the past period.

1. The natural rate of growth of the economy for the 1970s exceeds 4 per cent and we should judge economic performance accordingly. The growth of the labor force accelerated in the mid-1960s and will remain at a high rate. The advance of technology gives every sign of remaining very rapid. The current high rate of growth of the capital stock indicates the prospect of a natural rate of growth at least as great as in the 1960s. We will begin the decade with a very slow growth year. The overfull employment of recent months will be converted into a small gap between actual and potential output in 1970. If we focus economic policy exclusively on fighting inflation, and if the fight on inflation is confined to the strictly classical medicine, we condemn ourselves to several years of slow growth and the development of a considerable gap between actual and potential output.

2. The economy still seems unable to reconcile full employment with price stability. The need for structural changes to improve the competitiveness and flexibility of markets and to minimize the harm of government protectionist policies remains as strong as ever. Government machinery could be strengthened for these pursuits.

3. The trend cycle in the private economy will be in an upswing phase at the beginning of the decade. While government policy may temporarily slow the conversion of fundamental strength into economic activity, rapid family formation with the resultant need for housing and durables will keep the underlying tone of the private economy strong. This is in sharp contrast to the beginnings of the 1960s.

4. Fiscal and monetary policies should avoid the extreme swings which have characterized them in the last 20 years. Very full employment surpluses and deficits have been mistakes without exception. Periods of extreme advance or no advance in the money supply have been mistakes without exception.

5. The informed public finally understands the question of priorities of resource use. The searching examination of our military budget and the attempt to determine the economic costs of our foreign policy commitments contain the promise of a more rational approach to resource allocation in the public sector.

6. Economic performance is increasingly judged by its ability to meet the social and environmental goals of the society. The 1960s have shown that good macro-performance is a necessary but not a sufficient condition for adequate social progress. The realization that the resources are

available may well have heightened the impatience of the black and the young with our halting efforts. The systematic changes in the private and public sector necessary to assure adequate social progress and halt deterioration of the environment appear to be the main challenges to economic policy for the 1970s. But then again, the main tasks may prove to be something else; by 1980 we will know.

The Economic Surplus
and Its Absorption
by Government

PAUL BARAN AND
PAUL M. SWEEZY

Our essay-sketch makes no pretense to comprehensiveness. It is organized around and attains its essential unity from one central theme: the generation and absorption of the surplus under conditions of monopoly capitalism.[1]

We believe that this is the most useful and enlightening way to analyze the purely economic functioning of the system. But, no less important, we also believe that the modes of utilization of surplus constitute the indispensable mechanism linking the economic foundation of society with what Marxists call its political, cultural, and ideological superstructure. In some societies this mechanism is relatively simple and its effects easily accessible to analysis. In a true feudal society, for example, the surplus is forcibly extracted by feudal lords from the labor of serfs and directly consumed by the lords and their retainers without significant mediation of traders and other types of middlemen. Under these circumstances, the determinants of the size of the surplus, the way it is used, and the relation between these matters and the politics and culture of the society are readily understandable. In other

From Paul Baran and Paul M. Sweezy, *Monopoly Capital* (New York: Monthly Review Press, 1966), pp. 8–10, 142–151. Copyright © 1966 by Paul M. Sweezy; reprinted by permission of Monthly Review Press.
[1] For a discussion of the concept of the economic surplus, see Paul A. Baran, *The Political Economy of Growth,* Chapter 2.

societies the connecting mechanism between economic and noneconomic phenomena is vastly more complicated and may come to play an important role in the functioning of both the foundation and the superstructure. We believe that monopoly capitalism is a society of the latter type and that any attempt to understand it which omits or slights the modes of utilization of surplus is bound to fail. . . .

The economic surplus, in the briefest possible definition, is the difference between what a society produces and the costs of producing it. The size of the surplus is an index of productivity and wealth, of how much freedom a society has to accomplish whatever goals it may set for itself. The composition of the surplus shows how it uses that freedom: how much it invests in expanding its productive capacity, how much it consumes in various forms, how much it wastes and in what ways. It would obviously be highly desirable to have a full statistical record of the development of each country's surplus over as long a period as possible. Unfortunately, to the best of our knowledge, no such record exists for any country, even for a short period of time. There are various reasons for this, of which perhaps the most obvious are lack of familiarity with the surplus concept and the absence of reliable statistics. But even where, as in the United States, a reasonably large body of statistical material does exist, it is very difficult to arrive at accurate estimates of the magnitude of the surplus and its various components.

To attempt a full explanation of these difficulties would be to anticipate. Suffice it to say at this point that in a highly developed monopoly capitalist society, the surplus assumes many forms and disguises. . . .[2]

The Absorption of Surplus:
Civilian Government

. . . The purpose of this and the following chapters is twofold: to demonstrate, first, that government plays a similar role but on a larger scale; and second, that the uses to which government puts the surplus which it absorbs are narrowly circumscribed by the nature of monopoly capitalist society and as time goes on become more and more irrational and destructive.

In the older theories—and here we include Marxian as well as classical and neoclassical economics—it was normally taken for granted that the economy was operating its plant and equipment at full capacity so that anything government might take from total output of society would necessarily be at

---

[2] It is for this reason that we prefer the concept "surplus" to the traditional Marxian "surplus value," since the latter is probably identified in the minds of most people familiar with Marxian economic theory as equal to the sum of profits + interest + rent. It is true that Marx demonstrates—in scattered passages of *Capital* and *Theories of Surplus Value*—that surplus value also comprises other items such as the revenues of state and church, the expenses of transforming commodities into money, and the wages of unproductive workers. In general, however, he treated these as secondary factors and excluded them from his basic theoretical schema. It is our contention that under monopoly capitalism this procedure is no longer justified, and we hope that a change in terminology will help to effect the needed shift in theoretical position.

the expense of some or all of its members.[3] When to this was added the assumption that real wages are fixed at a conventional subsistence minimum and are hence for all practical purposes irreducible, it followed that the burden of financing government must fall on the surplus-receiving classes: part of what they would otherwise consume or add to their capital goes to the state through taxation for the support of officials, police, armed forces, poor relief, etc. This was the core of the classical theory of public finance, and for obvious reasons it acted as a powerful bulwark of the principle that the best government is that which governs least. The interests of the rich and powerful, it seemed clear, were best served by limiting government, as nearly as possible, to the role of policeman—a limitation which was likewise justified, ostensibly for the good of society as a whole, by the theory of self-adjusting competitive markets.

Under monopoly capitalism, matters are very different. Here the normal condition is less than capacity production. The system simply does not generate enough "effective demand" (to use the Keynesian term) to insure full utilization of either labor or productive facilities. If these idle resources can be put to work, they can produce not only necessary means of subsistence for the producers but also additional amounts of surplus. Hence if government creates more effective demand, it can increase its command over goods and services without encroaching on the incomes of its citizens. This creation of effective demand can take the form of direct government purchases of goods and services, or of "transfer payments" to groups which can somehow make good their claims for special treatment (subsidies to businessmen and farmers, doles to the unemployed, pensions to the aged, and so on).

Thanks largely to the work of Keynes and his followers, these possibilities first began to be understood during the depression of the 1930's. For some time it was widely believed, however, even among economists, that government could create additional demand only if it spent more than it took in and made up the difference by such forms of "deficit financing" as printing more money or borrowing from the banks. The theory held that the total increment in demand (government plus private) would be some multiple of the government deficit. The strength of the government stimulus was therefore believed to be proportional not to the level of government spending as such but to the magnitude of the deficit. Thus no amount of government spending could exercise an expansionary effect on total demand if it was matched by an equivalent amount of taxation.

This view is now generally recognized to be wrong. Where there is unemployed labor and unutilized plant, government can create additional demand even with a balanced budget. A simple numerical example will illustrate the point, without omitting any of the essential factors. Suppose that total demand (= Gross National Product, GNP) is represented by the figure 100. Suppose that the government share of this is 10, which is exactly matched by taxation

---

[3] In the Marxian theory, unemployment (the "industrial reserve army" or "relative surplus population") was assumed to be normal and to play a key role in regulating the wage rate. In the absence of idle plant and equipment, however, the unemployed could not be put to work to produce additional surplus.

of 10. Government now decides to increase its purchases of goods and services—say, for a larger army and more munitions—by another 10 and to collect additional taxes of the same amount. The increased spending will add 10 to total demand and (since there is idle labor and plant available) to total output as well. The other side of the coin is an increase of income by 10, the equivalent of which can be drained into the public treasury through taxation without affecting the level of private spending. The net result is an expansion of GNP by 10, the exact amount of the increase in the government's balanced budget. In this case the "multiplier" is equal to 1: the increased taxation cuts off any secondary expansion of private demand.

Suppose now that a further expansion of government spending by 2 is decided upon but that this time no additional taxes are to be collected, the entire amount thus representing a deficit.[4] As government pays out this new money, private incomes are raised and part of the increase is spent, and so on. Since the increments to private spending become negligibly small after a few rounds, the amount of the aggregate addition to private spending can be calculated if the proportion of each increment spent is known. Assume, for example, that this aggregate addition is 3. Then the overall expansion of demand attributable to the deficit comes to 5 (2 government and 3 private). In this case, therefore, the multiplier is 2.5.

Looking now at the whole economy we see that, compared to the initial state, GNP has risen from 100 to 115, private spending from 90 to 93, government spending from 10 to 22, and the government is running a deficit of 2. Clearly this situation will last only as long as the government continues to run the deficit. Assume that a decision is made to balance the budget again. If spending were reduced by 2 to wipe out the deficit, the multiplier would work in reverse and GNP would sink to 110. If instead spending were maintained and taxes raised by 2, the private increment would be cut off and GNP would stabilize at 112.

These highly simplified examples could be qualified and refined.[5] The main principles, however, would not be affected. They can be summarized as follows: (1) The influence of government on the level of effective demand is a function of both the size of the deficit and the absolute level of government spending. (2) A temporary deficit has temporary effects. (3) Even a persistent deficit, unless it grows steadily larger, will not cumulatively raise effective demand.

Since the focus of our attention is the economy of the United States, and since American fiscal history has not been characterized by persistent and steadily mounting deficits, we can concentrate on changes in the level of government spending. It has been through changes in the overall total of spending that government has exercised its greatest influence on the magnitude of effective demand and hence on the process of surplus absorption.

---

[4] For this result, some reduction in tax rates would of course be necessary.

[5] See, for example, Daniel Hamberg, *Principles of a Growing Economy,* New York, 1961, Chapters 12 and 17.

What has actually happened to government spending during the monopoly capitalist period?[6] Official statistics for both government spending (state and local as well as federal) and GNP go back only as far as 1929, and available data for earlier years are neither strictly comparable nor very accurate. Nevertheless enough is known to leave no doubt about the orders of magnitude involved and hence about the overall trend. Table 1 presents figures for selected non-war years going back to the beginning of the century.

TABLE I
Government Spending, 1903–1959 (Billions of Dollars)

	Gross National Product (GNP)	Total Government Spending (GS)	GS as Percent of GNP
1903	23.0	1.7	7.4
1913	40.0	3.1	7.7
1929	104.4	10.2	9.8
1939	91.1	17.5	19.2
1949	258.1	59.5	23.1
1959	482.1	131.6	27.3
1961	518.7	149.3	28.8

SOURCES: For 1903 and 1913, Paolo Sylos Labini, *Oligopoly and Technical Progress,* Cambridge, Massachusetts, 1962, p. 181. For later years, Council of Economic Advisers, *1962 Supplement to Economic Indicators,* Washington, 1962, p. 3.

The trend of government spending, both absolutely and as a percentage of GNP, has been uninterruptedly upward throughout the present century. Until 1929 the rise was slow—from 7.4 per cent of GNP in 1903 to 9.8 per cent in 1929. Since 1929 it has been much faster, the ratio now being well over one quarter. The rise in this ratio can be considered an approximate index of the extent to which government's role as a creator of effective demand and absorber of surplus has grown during the monopoly capitalist era.[7]

This trend to more and more government spending of course tells us nothing whatever about the desirability or undesirability of the developments that underlie it. Such judgments can be formed only when due account is taken of the forms assumed by government-absorbed surplus—a subject we have not yet reached. In the meantime it should be noted that the trend toward

[6] The relevant figure here is total government spending including transfer payments, not only "government purchases of goods and services" which constitute the government component of GNP in the official statistics. As seen above, government generates effective demand by transferring purchasing power to individuals and business firms as well as by direct purchases of goods and services. In the official GNP estimates, however, transfer payments are excluded from the government component and go to swell the personal and business components. This procedure, statistically necessary to avoid double counting, should not be allowed to obscure the true magnitude of government's role as a creator of effective demand.

[7] The United States is by no means an extreme case in respect to the role of government as a creator of effective demand. Here are figures showing the percentage of total government spending to GNP in selected recent years for six advanced capitalist countries: United Kingdom (1953), 35.7 per cent; Belgium (1952), 31.2 per cent; West Germany (1953), 30.8 per cent; Canada (1953), 26.6 per cent; Sweden (1952), 25.9 per cent; United States (1957), 25.5 per cent. F. M. Bator, *The Question of Government Spending,* New York, 1960, p. 157.

larger government absorption of surplus, both absolutely and relative to society's total output, is not peculiar to monopoly capitalism. It is apparently a feature of most expanding economic systems. In a rationally ordered socialist society with productive potential comparable to that of the United States, the amount and proportion of surplus absorbed by the state for the satisfaction of the collective wants and needs of the people would certainly be larger, not smaller, than the amount and proportion absorbed by government in this country today.

To return to our main theme: the vast and growing amounts of surplus absorbed by government in recent decades are not, we repeat, deductions from what would otherwise be available to corporations and individuals for their private purposes. The structure of the monopoly capitalist economy is such that a continually mounting volume of surplus simply could not be absorbed through private channels; if no other outlets were available, it would not be produced at all. What government absorbs is in addition to, not subtracted from, private surplus. Even more: since a larger volume of government spending pushes the economy nearer to capacity operation, and since up to this point surplus grows more rapidly than effective demand as a whole, it follows that both the government and the private segments of surplus can and indeed typically do grow simultaneously. It is only when government absorption continues to expand even after full utilization has been reached, as during the later years of the Second World War, that private surplus is encroached upon.

These relationships can be illustrated by what has happened to corporate profits before and after taxes in recent decades. Before the Second World War, taxation of corporate incomes was rather low. During the war, rates were sharply increased, were raised again during the Korean War, and have remained high ever since. This change in the level of corporate taxation, however, has not meant any reduction in profits after taxes. On the contrary, the amount of profits after taxes increased as the economy expanded, and remained at about the same proportion of national income during the 1950's as during the 1920's.

Table 2 shows clearly that what impairs the after-tax profitability of cor-

TABLE 2
Share of Corporate Profits in National Income
(Per Cent)

	Before Taxes	After Taxes
1919-1928	8.4	6.7
1929-1938	4.3	2.8
1939-1948	11.9	6.0
1949-1957	12.8	6.3

SOURCE: Irving B. Kravis, "Relative Income Shares in Fact and Theory," *American Economic Review,* December 1959, p. 931. The figures after 1929 are official Department of Commerce data; those for 1919–1928 are Kuznet's data adjusted by Kravis.

porations, absolutely and relative to the rest of the economy, is not high taxation, and certainly not high government spending, but depression.[8] What the government takes in taxes is in addition to, not a subtraction from, private surplus. Moreover, since large-scale government spending enables the economy to operate much closer to capacity, the net effect on the magnitude of private surplus is both positive and large.

The American ruling class, at any rate its leading echelon of managers of giant corporations, has learned these lessons through the rich experience of three decades of depression, war, and Cold War. And its attitude toward taxation and government spending has undergone a fundamental change. The older hostility to any expansion of government activities has not of course disappeared. In the realm of ideology, deeply rooted attitudes never disappear quickly. Moreover, in some sections of the ruling class—especially rentiers and smaller businessmen—hatred of the tax collector dominates feelings about the role of government. But the modern Big Businessman, though he sometimes speaks the traditional language, no longer takes it so seriously as his ancestors. To him, government spending means more effective demand, and he senses that he can shift most of the associated taxes forward onto consumers or backward onto workers.[9] In addition—and this point is of great importance in understanding the subjective attitudes of Big Businessmen—the intricacies of the tax system, specially tailored to fit the needs of all sorts of special interests, open up endless opportunities for speculative and windfall gains.[10] All in all, the decisive sector of the American ruling class is well on the way to becoming a convinced believer in the beneficent nature of government spending.

What about workers and other lower-income groups? Since the big corporations shift their tax burdens, is not the increased absorption of surplus by government in the last analysis squeezed out of what Veblen called the underlying population? This question has already been answered, at least by implication. If what government takes would otherwise not have been produced at all, it cannot be said to have been squeezed out of anybody. Govern-

[8] One other injurious factor should be mentioned: price controls. The poorer showing of the 40's as compared with either the 20's or the 50's is most plausibly explained by wartime controls. This factor was also present, to a lesser extent, during the Korean War and hence affected the record of the 50's. In addition, the creeping stagnation of the 50's was of course reflected in a downdrift of the corporate profit share both before and after taxes.

[9] As Professor Boulding says, "the relative stability of profits after taxes is evidence that the corporation profits tax is in effect almost entirely shifted; the government simply uses the corporation as a tax collector." K. E. Boulding, *The Organizational Revolution,* New York, 1953, p. 277.

[10] An article in the *Harvard Law Review* begins as follows: "The genesis of this paper is the casual remark of a Washington lawyer who asked, 'What is the point of litigating a tax case when we can have the statute amended for the same outlay of time and money?' Probably his statement was inaccurate, and certainly it was extreme, but it comes as no surprise to sophisticated counsel daily studying the tax services to identify new patchwork stitched upon the internal revenue quilt. Whether their efforts take the form of new sections, or euphemistically called 'technical changes,' there is today an accelerating tendency away from uniformity and toward preferential treatment." William L. Cary, "Pressure Groups and the Revenue Code: A Requiem in Honor of the Departing Uniformity of the Tax Laws,"*Harvard Law Review,* March 1955.

ment spending and taxing, which used to be primarily a mechanism for transferring income, have become in large measure a mechanism for creating income by bringing idle capital and labor into production. This is not to say that no one gets hurt in the process. Those with relatively fixed incomes (rentiers, pensioners, some groups of unorganized workers) certainly do suffer as taxes rise and are shifted by the corporate sector. But the losses of these groups are of secondary magnitude and importance compared to the gains of that large proportion of the workers which owes its employment, directly or indirectly, to government spending. Furthermore, the bargaining power of the working class as a whole, hence its ability to defend or improve its standard of living, is of course greater the lower the level of unemployment. Thus, within the framework of monopoly capitalism, the lower-income classes taken as a whole are better off with higher government spending and higher taxes. This explains why, despite the wails of some traditionalists, there has never been any really effective political opposition to the steady rise of government spending and taxing which has characterized recent decades. Given the inability of monopoly capitalism to provide private uses for the surplus which it can easily generate, there can be no doubt that it is to the interest of all classes—though not of all elements within them—that government should steadily increase its spending and its taxing.

We must therefore reject decisively the widely accepted notion that massive private interests are opposed to this trend. Not only is the viability of the system as a whole dependent on its continuation but likewise the individual welfare of a great majority of its members. The big question, therefore, is not whether there will be more and more government spending, but on what. And here private interests come into their own as the controlling factor.

Scientific and Ideological Elements in the Economic Theory of Government Policy—A Radical Critique

JAMES O'CONNOR

The purpose of macroeconomic, or income theory, is to analyze the determinants of aggregate or total spending on commodities. The elementary concept is the utility of objects for individuals; the general relation is the principle of maximization of utility for individuals and returns (profits) for firms. A million light years, however, separate individual utility and demand for commodities from aggregate demand for commodities, and in macroeconomic theorizing, individual utility is ordinarily lost sight of. This means that macroeconomics in no sense can be considered pure economic theory.

In the most simple macroeconomic model total income, or the value of total production (Y), is constituted by consumption spending (C), investment spending (I), and government spending (G), $(Y = C + I + G)$. The level of employment is determined by the level of income or production $(E = E(Y))$. The price level (P) is assumed to be unchanged up to the point of full employment. When full employment is reached, the price level is determined by the level of spending.

Macro-theory does not independently investigate the determinants of consumption, which is made to depend on income via the "marginal propensity to consume" (MPC). The simplest form of the consumption function is $C = a + bY$, where a is the volume of consumption when income is zero, and b is the propensity to consume, or the proportion of income consumed. Income itself, and hence employment and prices, are thus determined by investment spending and government spending.

There are almost as many theories of investment as there are investment theorists. The original Keynesian theory, a simple one, views investment as

From *Science and Society*, Vol. 33, No. 4 (1969), pp. 396–405. Reprinted by permission of the publisher.

depending on the anticipated rate of profit (p), the money supply (M), and society's preference for holding assets in liquid (cash) form (LP). Government spending is determined by the political authorities and is not subject to economic laws.

The elementary functional relations of the system are: (1) The higher the MPC, the higher the level of income and employment; (2) The greater the stock of money, the lower the rate of interest, the higher the volume of investment, and the higher the level of income and employment; and (3) The weaker the preference for holding assets in the form of cash, the greater the demand for bonds, the higher the price of bonds, the lower the rate of interest, and the greater the level of investment, income, and employment.

The system is said to be in equilibrium when the volume of production at current prices equals consumption, government spending, and intended investment. Actual investment equals intended investment when inventories of commodities are no lower or greater today than capitalists expected them to be yesterday, i.e., when today's sales equal yesterday's production. In this event, the market is cleared; there is no excess demand or supply. The peculiar characteristic of the Keynesian model is that the system may be in equilibrium even though there may be a sizeable amount of unemployment (or, alternatively, inflation).

Thus to increase employment, income must be increased. Income may be increased directly by raising the propensity to consume (for example, by deflating the economy and increasing the real value of savings, and hence liberating savings for consumption), by raising investment (e.g., by subsidies to capitalists), and by government spending or tax reductions. Income may be increased indirectly by increasing the supply of money, lowering the rate of interest, and hence raising the level of investment.

It should be obvious from this discussion that macro-theory was formulated with an eye to macro-policy—that in no sense can macro-theory be considered pure theory, or value-free theory. The orientation of macro-theory is toward the *control* of income, employment, and prices via state economic policy. Thus macro-theory, fiscal theory (the analysis of the effects of government spending, taxation, and borrowing), and fiscal policy (applied fiscal theory) all boil down to fundamentally the same phenomenon—how to make capitalism a viable economic and social system by keeping unemployment and inflation within reasonable bounds.

It should also be obvious that macro-theory (like microeconomic) is not a *social* science. It does not analyze the relations between men, but rather the relations between abstractions such as total income, the price level, etc.

Macro-theory of the type discussed above (i.e., theory which places primary emphasis on demand) has been popular during two historical eras— during the late mercantilist period and today, the epoch of monopoly capitalism. In both periods the state plays a central role in the economy. During the era of laissez faire, income theory was banished by the classical and neoclassical economists. Brought to life by Keynes, today it dominates economic thought in the advanced capitalist countries.

The main point is that macro-theory is at one and the same time the science and ideology of the ruling class—or, more precisely, the dominant stratum of the ruling class, the corporate oligarchy. The corporate oligarchy has long ago accepted the inevitability and desirability of economic self-regulation—or what is euphemistically called government intervention in the economy. What is more, the corporate oligarchy is the only segment of the ruling class which is in a position to effectively *control* macro-fiscal policy. I do not think that this assertion requires elaborate proof. There is a growing historical literature which describes the sources and development of a class consciousness on the part of the corporate rich, and there is a sociological literature which describes the modes of control by the corporations of the quasi-private planning and policy organizations such as CED, and the process of ideology formation in which these organizations play a decisive role. Even if such a literature did not exist, it is easy to understand why fiscal policy *must* be formulated in the interests of the hundred or so dominant corporations, because the health of the economy depends almost exclusively on the health of these giants.

Income theory, then, is a *technical* science to the degree that it has practical value to the corporations. To put it another way, income theory is scientific insofar as it is useful to preserve and extend monopoly capitalism as a system and perpetuate class divisions and class rule. On this criterion, for example, neo-Keynesian theory is more scientific than Keynes' original doctrines. A fiscal policy for growth is more practical than one for economic stabilization because of its bias in favor of investment, and hence profits.

On the other hand, income theory is not a *critical* science because it constitutes itself on the given economic and legal foundations of capitalism. It fails to make the foundations of capitalism themselves a subject for analysis. At best, then, income theory offers only a description of the *mechanics of operation* of advanced capitalist economies. A critical science is not a science of mechanics, but of real causes, historical causes; the variables are not abstractions such as the interest rate, or supply of money, but rather they are *human* agents.

Thus over the past 30 years there has developed an elaborate analysis of the determinants of income, employment, and production—an analysis which has proven to have great practical value in helping the state underwrite business investments and business losses—or to use the long-current euphemism, in helping the government to stabilize the economy and encourage it to grow. What is more, its practical value to the corporations and business in general is greatly enhanced by the fact that business increasingly takes it for granted that income theory *is* an accurate description of the economy.

On the other hand, few would place much confidence in the explanations of the ultimate causes of fluctuation and growth which are integral to income theory. These explanations run in terms of individual psychological motivations and responses and abstract completely from the ever-changing, concrete socioeconomic setting which decisively conditions consumer and business behavior. The concepts of "propensities," "preferences," "anticipations and expectations" seem to Marxist economists to be very fragile foundations for such an elaborate structure as income theory. The alternative, and correct, path, in my view, is to submit consumption, investment, and government spending to a *structural* determination; that is, to deduce the implications for the volume of and changes in investment (or consumption) in the context of the *actual* behavior of large corporations operating in oligopolistic markets.

Perhaps an analogy will be useful at this stage. A good one is the relationship between medicine, on the one hand, and biochemistry, biophysics and other sciences which attempt to understand the body as a whole, on the other. To a surprising degree, there is frequently a great gulf separating medicine from the body sciences. The diagnosis and treatment of some diseases—a good example is mental illness—often remain unchanged when the body scientists advance their understanding of the causes of illness, for the simple reason that medicine remains an excellent description of the mechanics of the body. In fact, it is well known that in psychotherapy a priori statements about which technique will produce results with any given patient are very hard to come by. Often, the therapist is not even aware of why he has achieved results. One could make the same statement about some economic policymakers.

Income theory is neither right nor wrong—in the sense of being close to or distant from the real causes of economic change—because income theory does not pretend to investigate real causes. It is only more or less useful— more useful if the mechanics of operation of the economy are accurately specified, less useful if not. The main criterion of success is *results*.

Income theory can achieve good results even though its theoretical foundations may be weak. But it could get better results if it were scientifically based on real causes, as we will suggest below. The point which needs emphasis, however, is that it is impossible for an economic theory which exists to maintain capitalism and class rule to be based on real causes. The reason is that a causal science is a critical science, one which subjects the foundations of capitalism—as well as the transitory economic manifestations of these foundations—to analysis. Clearly, a theory which is designed to perpetuate the social and economic relations (and indirectly the taboos and superstitions) of capitalism will be of little value to anyone who wishes to question these relations and taboos and superstitions.

If the economic theory questioned its own assumptions, it would negate itself; and since income theory is first and foremost ruling-class theory, a critical theory would imply that the ruling class would have to question itself, its own right to rule, or negate itself. Let me illustrate with a simple example in the form of a hypothesis: suppose that inflation is caused by the groups or classes which benefit from inflation; suppose further that anti-inflation policy is in the hands of those who caused the inflation. The anti-inflation policy will leave some groups or classes worse off and some better off. Among those who will be better off, will be the group which was the prime mover behind the inflation, the original beneficiaries. Now suppose that the ruling class employs economists to study inflation—indeed, not only study inflation, but find acceptable ways to cause inflation. Clearly, a critical science of inflation would require that economists study not only their employers but themselves.

The economics profession adamantly refuses to do this—to consider itself a part of the experimental field. But it is obvious that economics as a technical science is a *social* phenomenon—and it may be true that only economists are in a position to comprehend their own social role. In fact, we believe it can be shown that the economist's tools have made it possible to have a little unemployment and a little inflation, an optimal situation for the corporations. For example, two famous economists, Paul Samuelson and Robert Solow, wrote an article entitled, "Our Menu of Policy Choices," in which "we" are given the "choice" of a little unemployment and a little inflation, or, alternatively, a little inflation and a little unemployment! Abolishing both unemployment and inflation is impossible given the fact (for bourgeois economists, the eternal fact) that employment depends on the growth of income, which in turn depends on investment, which in turn requires at least a slight profit inflation (that is, prices rising faster than money wages).

In short, income theory does not seek to remove the extremes of society—unemployment and inflation (and capital and labor, rich and poor, privileged and underprivileged, rulers and ruled)—but rather, to quote Marx, it attempts to "weaken their antagonisms and transform them into a harmonious whole," Marxists believe this to be impossible. And hence a critical bourgeois social science, including income theory, is for this reason impossible.

Let us now turn to the treatment which public finance affords the relationship between budgetary policy and economic growth. "Growth models in their present form," Peacock and Wiseman write, "cannot be treated as anything more than exercises in a technique of arrangement." The basic reason that income and growth theory is unrealistic is the failure to include a theory of state expenditures. Evsey Domar once noted that government expenditures can be dealt with in one of three ways: they can be assumed to be "exogenous" to the system, they can be merged with consumption expenditures, or they can be assumed "away altogether." The latter alternative is completely unsatisfactory, and to assume that government expenditures are determined by "outside" forces is tantamount to an admission that they are beyond the realm of comprehension. Merging all government spending with private consumption merely substitutes fiction for fact.

Paradoxically, government spending is increasingly placed in the middle of discussions of growth and stagnation. Most economists view the state as a kind of *deus ex machina* and assume that government spending not only can but should make up the difference between the actual volume of private expenditures and the level of spending which will keep unemployment down to a politically tolerable minimum. State expenditures in this way are incorporated into models of fluctuations and growth. However, the *actual* determinants of government spending are not considered; rather, what is considered is the volume of spending and taxation necessary to achieve certain goals given certain assumptions and characteristics of the given model.

The reason why economists do not know the actual determinants of government expenditure is not hard to find. There are no markets for most goods and services provided by the state, and hence it is not possible to lean on the doctrine of revealed preferences. Thus a theory of state expenditures requires an examination of the forces influencing and conditioning demand. But utility theory forbids any inquiry into these forces—putting aside statistical explanations such as the age-mix of the population, climatic conditions, and the like.

This line of thinking leads to the conclusion that before fiscal theory can lay claim to being a critical science, the laws which govern the determination of the volume and composition of state expenditures, and the relation between expenditures and taxes, must be uncovered. This means that fiscal theory must have a clear notion of the character of the state under monopoly capitalism—fiscal theory is then a branch of the theory of the state.

Space does not permit any but the briefest discussion of the elements which truly scientific fiscal theory must contain.

First of all, a clear distinction must be made between socially necessary costs and economic surplus—a distinction between the value of total output and the costs of producing that output. The concept of "necessary costs" is value-free in the sense that it has meaning independently of any given economic system. Necessary costs are outlays required to maintain the economy's productive capacity and labor force in their given state of productivity or efficiency. The difference between total output and necessary costs constitutes economic surplus. Further, a distinction must be made between what may be called discretionary uses of the surplus by the state, and nondiscretionary spending. Without these distinctions, it is not possible to evaluate the role of state expenditure in the determination of aggregate demand and economic growth.

To the degree that state expenditure constitutes necessary costs, state outlays merely substitute for private outlays; hence, do not have any independent effect on aggregate demand. The only difference is that taxpayers as a whole, rather than as a specific industry or branch of the economy, are charged with the costs. An example is education outlays required to maintain the labor force in its given state of productivity.

To the degree that state expenditures comprise economic surplus, and to the degree that the surplus consists of nondiscretionary spending (e.g., education outlays required to raise the skill level of a labor force in accordance with advancing technology), state outlays again substitute for private spending—and aggregate demand remains unchanged. In our view, nondiscretionary spending is made up of two main categories: first, a large part of collective consumption—expenditures on social amenities laid out more or less voluntarily by residents in a given community; second, what might be called complementary investments, a special form of private investment the costs of which are borne by the taxpayer, and without which private investment would be unprofitable. Water investments in agricultural districts would be a good example.

Additional demand, and hence economic surplus, *is* generated, first, by wasteful and destructive outlays (the main example being military spending) and, second, discretionary investments, or state investments made to encourage future private accumulation (e.g., industrial development parks). In this case, there is an increment to demand and surplus because private capital would otherwise not have made the expenditure. Here the rise in government spending will be financed largely out of taxes and thus at the expense of private consumption. The state will in this event create more surplus (or savings) than it absorbs.

Finally, transfer payments (e.g., debt interest and farm payments) generate more surplus than they absorb because they alter the distribution of personal income in the direction of greater inequality.

Whether or not fiscal policy can be a viable instrument for maintaining a respectable volume of demand depends on whether or not total state spending generates more surplus than it absorbs. If so, then the state budget must continuously increase for the economy to remain in the same place. If not, then state expenditures cannot be considered in any sense autonomous, and correspondingly, the state cannot be considered to be able to act independently of the specific interests of specific firms, industries, or other segments of the ruling class. Of course, the truth lies somewhere in between these extremes—exactly where we do not know. But often it is more scientific to admit to an area of ignorance than to confidently predict that capitalism can or cannot save itself by the utilization of budgetary policy.

Questions for Discussion

1. How do you account for the difference in tone in the 1962 and the 1970 Council of Economic Advisers Reports?
2. What particular changes in policy emphasis have taken place?
3. Overall, is Eckstein critical or supportive of the economic policies of the 1960s?
4. Do you agree with Eckstein's analysis for the 1970s?
5. What is the concept of "the economic surplus" as used by Baran and Sweezy?
6. Contrast Baran and Sweezy's analysis of government economic activity with that of Eckstein. In what basic analytical and theoretical ways do they differ, even though they are looking at the same phenomenon?
7. Do you agree or disagree with O'Connor's contention that modern employment theory is not neutral but heavily loaded with specific ideological judgments?

V

Government and Levels of Economic Activity: Direct Controls

According to the report of Lyndon Johnson's Council of Economic Advisers for 1968 (p. 119),

> The most obvious—and least desirable—way of attempting to stabilize prices is to impose mandatory controls on prices and wages. While such controls may be necessary under conditions of an all-out war, it would be folly to consider them as a solution to the inflationary pressures that accompany high employment under any other circumstance. They distort resource allocation; they require reliance either on necessarily clumsy and arbitrary rules or the inevitably imperfect decisions of Government officials; they offer countless temptations to evasion or violation; they require a vast administrative apparatus. All these reasons make them repugnant. Although such controls may be unfortunately popular when they are not in effect, their appeal quickly disappears once people live under them.

How then did we arrive at August 15, 1971, and President Nixon's speech reprinted here in which the president ordered a ninety-day freeze on wages and prices to be followed by the Wage-Price Stabilization Board? Is it not paradoxical that the "liberal" Lyndon Johnson did not impose such controls despite the insistence of liberal economists like John K. Galbraith while the "conservative" Richard Nixon did so despite the opposition of conservative economists like Milton Friedman?

This was not, of course, America's first experience with such controls. Prices and wages had been strictly regulated in much of the economy during

World War II. That experience, however, left little reason to believe that controls would achieve their purpose to any great degree in any but the most crisis-laden circumstances.

As Clair Wilcox puts it,

> The wartime controls were supported by patriotism. They were tolerated as temporary. But, even so, they encountered serious obstacles. Price control, in particular, was subjected to continuous political attack. Congress, in response to such pressures, acted repeatedly to handicap the Office of Price Administration by denying it necessary powers.[1]

These "political attacks" were, of course, partly a function of the length of the period of control, three years. It is possible that in the current case the president expected to destroy inflationary momentum with the ninety-day freeze so that even the stabilization board would not be needed, and that "political attacks" would not have time to develop.

In this respect, it is clearly too early to make a final judgment on the current controls. Whether or not the walkout by four of the most powerful labor leaders on the pay board will lead to a prolonged and more open political battle probably depends on the country's experience with inflation and unemployment over the next few months. If what is left of the board does not find it necessary to impose a significant degree of control, the board and the president will surely be less assailed. If, on the other hand, inflationary pressures continue to have force without employment responding favorably, the controls will be more hotly debated, and their imposers more critically discussed.

The articles included in this section following President Nixon's address represent the preliminary reactions of three sources to the controls.

The first of these readings, by the American Institute for Economic Research, chides Paul W. McCracken, chairman of the President's Council of Economic Advisors, for "abandonment of economic principles" for his role in the freeze because he had earlier criticized J. K. Galbraith for suggesting just such controls. More than anything else this short article is probably indicative of the shocks felt among professional economists at the president's sudden decision.

Robert Lekachman's article is more a critique of the present state of the study of economics than of the controls of Phase I or Phase II. He interprets the policies themselves and the battle over wage and price decisions taking place as a result of the Wage-Price Board as indicative of the kind of power struggles that make up economic activity. Thus the free-market equilibrating mechanisms common to economic theory are not the sole important determinants of, for example, the levels of wages and prices.

The final article by Frank Ackerman and Arthur MacEwan contains a more

---

[1] Clair Wilcox, *Public Policies Toward Business* (Homewood, Ill.: Irwin, 1971), p. 813.

detailed analysis of both the substance and, from a radical point of view, the explanation of the new policies. Ackerman and McEwan see the economic trends of the past few years, both domestically and internationally, as indicative of the underlying building crisis of capitalist society. One important conclusion of the authors' is that "the new controls will remain a recurrent if not quite permanent, feature of American capitalism."

A New Economic Policy

RICHARD M. NIXON

America today has the best opportunity in this century to achieve two of its greatest ideals: to bring about a full generation of peace and to create a new prosperity without war.

This not only requires bold leadership ready to take bold action; it calls for the greatness in a great people.

Prosperity without war requires action on three fronts. We must create more and better jobs; we must stop the rise in the cost of living; we must protect the dollar from the attacks of international money speculators.

We are going to take that action—not timidly, not halfheartedly and not in piecemeal fashion. We are going to move forward to the new prosperity without war as befits a great people, all together and along a broad front.

New Economic Policy

The time has come for a new economic policy for the United States. Its targets are unemployment, inflation and international speculation, and this is how we are going to attack those targets:

First, on the subject of jobs. We all know why we have an unemployment problem. Two million workers have been released from the armed forces and defense plants because of our success in winding down the war in Vietnam. Putting those people back to work is one of the challenges of peace, and we have begun to make progress. Our unemployment rate today is below the average of the four peacetime years of the 1960s, but we can and we must do better than that.

The time has come for American industry, which has produced more jobs at higher real wages than any other industrial system in history, to embark on a bold program of new investment of production for peace. To give that system a powerful new stimulus I shall ask the Congress when it reconvenes after its summer recess to consider as its first priority the enactment of the Job Development Act of 1971.

I will propose to provide the strongest short-term incentive in our history

From President Nixon's address to the nation of August 15, 1971, reprinted in *The New York Times*, August 16, 1971.

to invest in new machinery and equipment that will create new jobs for Americans: a 10 per cent job development credit for one year effective as of today with a 5 per cent credit after August 15, 1972.

This tax credit for investment in new equipment will not only generate new jobs. It will raise productivity; it will make our goods more competitive in the years ahead.

Second, I will propose to repeal the 7 per cent excise tax on automobiles effective today. This will mean a reduction in price of about $200 per car.

I shall insist that the American auto industry pass this tax reduction on to the nearly 8 million customers who are buying automobiles this year. Lower prices will mean that more people will be able to afford new cars, and every additional 100,000 cars sold means 25,000 new jobs.

Third, I propose to speed up the personal-income-tax exemptions scheduled for January 1, 1973, to January 1, 1972, so that taxpayers can deduct an extra $50 for each exemption one year earlier than planned.

This increase in consumer spending power will provide a strong boost to the economy in general and to employment in particular.

The tax reductions I am recommending, together with this broad upturn of the economy, which has taken place in the first half of this year, will move us strongly forward toward a goal this nation has not reached since 1956, fifteen years ago: prosperity with full employment in peacetime.

Looking to the future, I have directed the Secretary of the Treasury to recommend to the Congress in January new tax proposals for simulating research and development of new industries and new techniques to help provide the 20 million new jobs that America needs for the young people who will be coming into the job market in the next decade.

To offset the loss of revenue from these tax cuts, which directly stimulate new jobs, I have ordered today a $4.7 billion cut in Federal spending.

Tax cuts to stimulate employment must be matched by spending cuts to restrain inflation. To check the rise in the cost of government I have ordered a postponement of pay raises and a 5 per cent cut in Government personnel.

I have ordered a 10 per cent cut in foreign economic aid. In addition, since the Congress has already delayed action on two of the great initiatives of this Administration, I will ask Congress to amend my proposals to postpone the implementation of revenue sharing for three months and welfare reform for one year.

Priorities Reordered

In this way, I am reordering our budget priorities so as to concentrate more on achieving our goal of full employment.

The second indispensable element of the new prosperity is to stop the rise in the cost of living. One of the cruelest legacies of the artificial prosperity produced by war is inflation. Inflation robs every American, every one of you. The 20 million who are retired and living on fixed incomes—they are particularly hard hit. Homemakers find it harder than ever to balance the family budget. And 80 million American wage earners have been on a treadmill.

For example, in the four war years between 1965 and 1969, your wage increases were completely eaten up by price increases. Your paychecks were higher, but you were no better off. We have made progress against the rise in the cost of living. From the high point of 6 per cent a year in 1969, the rise in consumer prices has been cut to 4 per cent in the first half of 1971. But just as is the case in our fight against unemployment, we can and we must do better than that. The time has come for decisive action—action that will break the vicious circle of spiraling prices and costs.

I am today ordering a freeze on all prices and wages throughout the United States for a period of 90 days.

In addition I call upon corporations to extend the wage-price freeze to all dividends. I have today appointed a Cost-of-Living Council within the government. I have directed this council to work with leaders of labor and business to set up the proper mechanism for achieving continued price and wage stability after the 90-day freeze is over.

Let me emphasize two characteristics of this action. First, it is temporary. To put the strong vigorous American economy into a permanent straitjacket would lock in unfairness; it would stifle the expansion of our free-enterprise system, and second, while the wage-price freeze will be backed by government sanction, if necessary, it will not be accompanied by the establishment of a huge price-control bureaucracy.

For Voluntary Cooperation

I am relying on the voluntary cooperation of all Americans—each one of you workers, employers, consumers—to make this freeze work. Working together, we will break the back of inflation, and we will do it without the mandatory wage and price controls that crush economic and personal freedom.

The third indispensable element in building the new prosperity is closely related to creating new jobs and halting inflation. We must protect the position of the American dollar as a pillar of monetary stability around the world.

In the past seven years, there's been an average of one international monetary crisis every year. Now who gains from these crises? Not the working man, not the investor, not the real producers of wealth. The gainers are the international money speculators: because they thrive on crises, they help to create them.

In recent weeks, the speculators have been waging an all-out war on the American dollar. The strength of a nation's currency is based on the strength of that nation's economy, and the American economy is by far the strongest in the world.

Accordingly, I have directed the Secretary of the Treasury to take the action necessary to defend the dollar against the speculators.

I directed Secretary Connally to suspend temporarily the convertibility of the dollar into gold or other reserve assets except in amounts and conditions determined to be in the interest of monetary stability and in the best interests of the United States.

Now what is this action—which is very technical—what does it mean to you? Let me lay to rest the bugaboo of what is called "devaluation." If you want to buy a foreign car or take a trip abroad, market conditions may cause your dollar to buy slightly less.

But, if you are among the overwhelming majority of Americans who buy American-made products, in America, your dollar will be worth just as much tomorrow as it is today.

The effect of this action, in other words, will be to stabilize the dollar. Now this action will not win us any friends among the international money traders. But our primary concern is with the American workers, and with their competition around the world.

To our friends abroad, including the many responsible members of the international banking community who are dedicated to stability in the flow of trade, I give this assurance: The United States has always been and will continue to be a forward-looking and trustworthy trading partner.

New Monetary System

In full cooperation with the International Monetary Fund and those who trade with us, we will press for the necessary reforms to set up an urgently needed new international monetary system. Stability and equal treatment is in everybody's best interest. I am determined that the American dollar must never again be a hostage in the hands of international speculators.

I am taking one further step to protect the dollar, to improve our balance of payments and to increase jobs for Americans. As a temporary measure I am today imposing an additional tax of 10 per cent on goods imported into the United States.

This is a better solution for international trade than direct controls on the amount of imports. This import tax is a temporary action. It isn't directed against any other country. It's an action to make certain that American products will not be at a disadvantage because of unfair exchange rates.

When the unfair treatment is ended, the import tax will end as well. As a result of these actions the product of American labor will be more competitive and the unfair edge that some of our foreign competition has will be removed.

This is a major reason why our trade balance has eroded over the past 15 years.

At the end of World War II, the economies of the major industrial nations of Europe and Asia were shattered. To help them get on their feet and to protect their freedom, the United States has provided over the past 25 years $143 billion in foreign aid.

That was the right thing for us to do. Today, largely with our help, they have regained their vitality. They have become our strong competitors, and we welcome their success.

But now that other nations are economically strong, the time has come for them to bear their fair share of the burden of defending freedom around the world. The time has come for exchange rates to be set straight, and for the major nations to compete as equals.

There is no longer any need for the United States to compete with one hand tied behind her back.

The range of actions I have taken and proposed tonight on the job front, on the inflation front, on the monetary front, is the most comprehensive new economic policy to be undertaken in this nation in four decades.

We are fortunate to live in a nation with an economic system capable of producing for its people the highest standard of living in the world, a system flexible enough to change its ways dramatically when circumstances call for change, and, most important, a system resourceful enough to produce prosperity with freedom and opportunity unmatched in the history of nations.

The purposes of the government actions I have announced tonight are to lay the basis for renewed confidence, to make it possible for us to compete fairly with the rest of the world, to open the door to new prosperity.

But government with all of its powers does not hold the key to the success of a people. That key, my fellow Americans, is in your hands. A nation, like a person, has to have a certain inner drive in order to succeed. In economic affairs that inner drive is called the competitive spirit.

Every action I have taken tonight is designed to nurture and stimulate that competitive spirit, to help us snap out of the self-doubt, the self-disparagement that saps our energy and erodes our confidence in ourselves.

Whether this nation stays number one in the world's economy or resigns itself to second, third or fourth place, whether we as a people have faith in ourselves or lose that faith, whether we hold fast to the strength that makes peace and freedom possible in this world or lose our grip—all that depends on you.

All that depends on you, on your competitive spirit, your sense of personal destiny, your pride in your country and in yourself.

We can be certain of this: As the threat of war recedes, the challenge of peaceful competition in the world will greatly increase. And we welcome competition, because America is at her greatest when she is called on to compete.

Voices Will Be Heard

As there has always been in our history, there will be voices urging us to shrink from that challenge of competition, to build a protective wall around ourselves, to crawl into a shell as the rest of the world moves ahead.

Two hundred years ago a man wrote in his diary these words: "Many thinking people believe America has seen its best days." That was written in 1775, just before the American Revolution, the dawn of the most exciting era in the history of man.

And today we hear the echoes of those voices preaching a gospel of gloom and defeat, saying the same thing: We have seen our best days. I say, "Let Americans reply, 'Our best days lie ahead.'" As we move into a generation of peace, as we blaze the trail toward the new prosperity, I say to every American: Let us raise our spirits, let us raise our sights, let all of us contribute all we can to this great and good country that has contributed so much to the progress of mankind. Let us invest in our nation's future. And let us revitalize that faith in ourselves that built a great nation in the past and will shape the world of the future.

Dr. McCracken on Price-Wage Controls

AMERICAN INSTITUTE FOR
ECONOMIC RESEARCH

Last July 28 *The Washington Post* published an article by Dr. Paul W. Mc-Cracken, Chairman of the President's Council of Economic Advisers, entitled "Galbraith and Price-Wage Controls." In that article Dr. McCracken described the economic benefits that result from changes in prices of things in the markets and the undesirable consequences of price and wage controls. The editors of the *Monthly Economic Letter,* which is published by the First National City Bank, wrote that the article "explains clearly and persuasively why the Administration has consistently resisted proposals for price-wage controls, and we feel it merits the attention of our readers." The article was reprinted in the August issue of the *Monthly Economic Letter.*

We, too, believe that Dr. McCracken's article is useful for furthering understanding of the consequences of such controls, and, therefore, on August 20 we requested his permission to reprint it in these reports. He replied that the article "is now so obsolete that I doubt if there is any real point in pursuing the matter further." Although Dr. McCracken has chosen to suppress further dissemination of his comments, we believe that they are important enough to warrant describing them below.

From *Economic Education Bulletin,* Vol. XII, No. 1 (January 1972), pp. 1–2. Reprinted by permission of the publisher.

Dr. McCracken began his article by reporting that the noted economist John Kenneth Galbraith recently had advocated, in testimony before the Joint Economic Committee of Congress, the adoption of wage and price controls. Dr. McCracken observed that such advocacy was logical within the limits of Dr. Galbraith's peculiar view of the economic system in the United States. Dr. McCracken noted that Dr. Galbraith has ridiculed for at least two decades the idea that prices indicate to processors what consumers want. The former also noted that, inasmuch as Dr. Galbraith believes that prices are arbitrarily set solely for the purpose of extracting income from consumers, he believes that prices should be controlled.

Dr. McCracken observed that these beliefs about prices and about the means for keeping them from being "too high" are not unusual and are widely held among uneducated persons. He noted that what is unusual is that these beliefs are held by the president-elect of the American Economic Association (Dr. Galbraith). The latter, Dr. McCracken asserted, advocated a wage-price freeze followed by permanent Government control of pricing by large corporations and of union wages.

Although Dr. McCracken described the temptation to undertake such action as great, he wrote that it must be resisted for several reasons, which he listed as follows:

1. Changes in prices in the markets contribute to efficient processing and satisfaction of consumers' desires. Attempts by U.S. Government authorities to control prices generally during wartime and to a lesser extent in regulated industries have reduced consumer satisfaction. Attempts by authorities of other countries have had a similar result and have led to increased reliance on market prices in some European countries.
2. General control of prices and wages would seriously threaten individual freedom. Many journalists who zealously defend freedom of the press apparently do not recognize the implications of Government control of all incomes in the Nation. Such control might violate the Constitutional prohibition of involuntary servitude.
3. The popular image of wage and price controls is that a small group of dedicated and objective men in Washington would prevent leaders of large corporations and unions from exploiting citizens. The fact is that all citizens would be controlled, not by wise men but by politicians and bureaucrats such as those who operate other Government agencies.
4. The notion that all wages and prices can be frozen is an illusion. Contracts of millions of workers include provisions for future wage increases. Such increases will force many employers to increase prices in order to maintain already small profit margins, which will force further increases in wages governed by escalator clauses. Attempts to establish "equitable" increases in wages and prices may increase, rather than reduce, inflationary expectations.
5. Various kinds of restraint of wages and prices have been proposed to-

gether with expansionist policies, such as tax reductions or increased spending, in order to stimulate economic activity. The expansionist policies are easy and popular, but the restraint would be neither. When officials of the Johnson Administration adopted wage-price guideposts for restraint and fiscal policies for expansion, the restraint failed and the expansionary policies overstimulated economic activity.

In concluding his article, Dr. McCracken wrote that he and other Administration officials believe that the relative freedom of the price system was a factor of major importance in the high standard of living in the United States, and that they were determined to preserve this system.

As most people know, the freedom of American citizens to agree on prices of things, including labor, that they exchange in the markets was suspended for 90 days by Presidential decree on August 15. Subsequently, Administration officials, including Dr. McCracken and Secretary of Commerce Maurice H. Stans, implied that some form of control of prices and wages would be continued by the Federal Government after the 90-day period has elapsed.

Almost exactly a month after describing the advantages of a free price system and the disadvantages of controlling prices and wages, Dr. McCracken pronounced his description "obsolete." In testimony before the Joint Economic Committee of Congress on August 30, he asserted that "I think that some kind of quantitative guidance is productive." He also asserted that some sort of Government control of prices and wages would be continued so that the existing price-wage freeze does not "merely pile up ammunition for an explosion of wages and prices." We cannot imagine a more candid acknowledgment that the freeze will not solve the problem.

We regard Dr. McCracken's abandonment of economic principles expressed so forthrightly only a month before as a shocking compromise of integrity. Such action can be expected by a professional politician whose overriding objective is to remain in office. That it has been taken by an allegedly professional economist, who is the chief economic adviser to the President and who helps to formulate economic policies of the United States, is discouraging and frightening.

Phase II: Casting Light on Economic Power

ROBERT LEKACHMAN

When President Nixon on August 15 stunned his countrymen with an array of government wage and price controls unmatched since the Korean War, he took pains to reassure his TV audience that "every action I have taken tonight is designed to nurture and stimulate the competitive spirit." His address was plentifully strewn with such inspirational phrases as the "challenge of competition," "inner drive" and "economic and personal freedom." And administration spokesmen have since reiterated their desire to shuck controls and return, so runs the implication, to a status quo ante of unbridled competition.

Presumably, a substantial number of ordinary Americans accept this official view of the American economy, namely, that it is, most of the time, an engine powered by uncoerced, inner-motivated decisions of legions of ardently competing businessmen and hordes of their customers; such, indeed, is the thrust of conventional economic thought in the United States. Its profoundly conservative perspective intimates that success is ultimately related to individual merit and application—that economic power and income gravitate toward those who, like successful quarterbacks and attorneys, mingle grit and determination with superior mental or physical attributes. If ability is distributed in the manner of income, why then, according to this perspective, shouldn't the affluent 5 per cent at the top of the heap receive their customary 20 per cent of the national income? Conversely, poverty is seen as representing the inadequacies of the poor. So why shouldn't the bottom 20 per cent get only 5 per cent of the national income?

However, one need not be an economist—it may even help to be formally ignorant of the glum science—to perceive that in big business, at least, competitive acumen and zeal are hardly the only determinants of money-making. In fact, in industry after major industry—oil, shipping, airlines, communications, farming, utilities, and broadcasting, for a start—the decisions of regula-

From the *Saturday Review*, January 22, 1972, pp. 40, 45, a special issue produced in co-operation with the Committee for Economic Development. Copyright 1972 Saturday Review, Inc.

tory agencies, Congress, and the White House have more impact upon sales and profits than either old-fashioned competition among the sellers or spontaneous demand by the customers.

Thus, far from its being a temporary departure from unbridled competition as the American way of economic life, Phase II does represent an acting out of something much closer to our real economics. Above all, Phase II is a struggle over public power affecting the distribution of income; so is much of our regular economic activity. The elements in the Phase II struggle, however, are more visible and less deniable than counterparts in the "free" economy extolled by Mr. Nixon. Phase II and its difficulties therefore provide some particularly revealing reflections on much of our economic machinery and how it really runs.

Gladiatorial contests between President Nixon and George Meany in the public arena provided by Phase II, assorted quarrels among the contending pay board blocks, and other such divertisements are adornments to serious arguments over who is to have power to set wage rates and how the sales dollar is ultimately to be divided between wages and profits.

Phase II's pay board and the price commission, in their daily labors, must cope with a large collection of individual demands by employees for pay increases and by businessmen for price increases, the second often occasioned in whole or in part by the first. All too often what the applicants seek far exceeds the guidelines. The wisdom of Solomon frequently is required to deal justly with workers inequitably situated by comparison with like groups, or with industries that face bankruptcy unless generous price relief is rapidly forthcoming, or with militant unions that threaten protracted (and potentially inflationary) strikes unless their (inflationary) demands are met.

Nevertheless, all is well so long as high wage awards are balanced by low ones affecting equal numbers of workers and, on the price front, the big advances are offset by small ones or even rollbacks of similar significance to the price indexes. It's the averages that matter in containing inflation, not the overplump individual benefits to corporations or employees. Then why doesn't the whole affair proceed more smoothly? If the intent of the controls is to leave management and unions in approximately the same relative position, why should either party complain?

One reason, of course, is the suspicion by both contestants that the outcome of the control process is likely to be not the status quo but a shift of relative income and power to either the business or the labor community. On the whole, labor has been more wary than business, and with some cause. To begin with, business has been generally receptive to the President's controls (a reason all by itself for the AFL-CIO to take the opposite position) and to Mr. Nixon himself. In fact, the President has enjoyed business support, financial and political, unexampled since Barry Goldwater frightened businessmen into the embrace of Lyndon Johnson in 1964. And whatever public criticism of specific administration actions corporate spokesmen may utter, business—and labor—has good reason to esteem the President as business's great friend in Washington. Indulgent tax policies, pro-business appointments to the regulatory agencies, preservation of oil quotas, and extraction from the protesting Japanese of textile quotas all bespeak such a friendship.

From labor's point of view, Presidential appointments to the pay board confirm their suspicions. Of the five public members of the board, who hold the balance between labor and management representatives, a Republican judge appointed by Dwight Eisenhower was named chairman, and the others named included a former administration official fresh from an important post in the Office of Management and Budget, a former vice president for industrial relations of Inland Steel, and an ex-member of the Council of Economic Advisers during the Eisenhower administration.

Nothing is perfect, and businessmen too have had their grievances, notably over the price commission's stubborn reluctance to automatically allow price hikes substantial enough to cover the largest pay awards. If a general pattern of such behavior should occur, business's profit margins would shrink and income nationally would undergo some redistribution in the direction of workers, both organized and unorganized.

But the likelihood is that no such pattern will be sustained, and in terms of the distribution of income the unions fear and say they detect an opposite direction. In George Meany's colorful rhetoric:

"Today's political cliché—'reordering national priorities'—has been applied with a vengeance by President Nixon. But he applied it in reverse.

"Unprecedented and unhealthy tax relief to corporations would be the ultimate effect of the keystone of the President's new economic program. It would reverse progress in America. The government of compassion, which many believed had come into being, would be halted. Corporate profit-and-loss charts—not the public need—would have first priority. The poor, the cities and states, federal employees, wage and salary earners—all would foot the bill, and the sole beneficiaries would be the wealthy and the corporations."

That the bulk of the tax breaks was going to businessmen instead of ordinary working stiffs was quite enough to mobilize the Meany ire, no meager emotion. As labor saw it, wages seemed likely to be more tightly regulated than rent, profits, dividends, and interest, all of which were either exempted entirely or restrained much more loosely and much less publicly than wages. The investment tax credit, now dubbed the job development credit, was a way of adding to corporate cash flow without lifting apparent profits. Accelerated depreciation has a similar effect. From these attractive devices, stockholders who held on could anticipate rising securities prices and ultimate capital gains, taxed at soothingly low rates. The combination of tax concessions, accounting changes, indulgent controls over property income, and outright exemption promised (or, according to taste, threatened) a substantial shift in the distribution of income away from labor and toward capital. Rightly or wrongly (I believe on the whole rightly), labor spokesmen have consistently so interpreted Nixon policies and control devices.

All of this is sufficient to explain the bitter struggles over the payment of retroactive wage gains and the validity of contracts signed before controls were imposed. For unions as for their employers, money is itself important. But still more vital is the sanctity of collective bargaining agreements. Unions derive their influence over increasingly restive memberships from their capacity to negotiate contract gains that stick. Any intimation that these gains are subject to the pleasures of a not necessarily sympathetic national administration, in which employers exercise inordinate influence, necessarily impairs the credibility of union officials with ordinary members, diminishes their ability to negotiate contracts acceptable to the membership, and increases wage-earner dependence upon politicians in place of leaders who cannot deliver.

Such considerations are weighed in an old and continuing pattern of embattlement that has little to do with conventional economic notions about competition. At the plant level, local officials struggle hard over job definitions, work rules, the introduction of new processes, retimings of old ones, and the minutiae of rest breaks, lockerroom facilities, sick leaves, and vacation schedules. At contract renewal time, national negotiators struggle with equal vehemence over the division of the sales dollar. Time and again, friendly or hostile Presidents pleasantly or painfully influence the course of negotiation. An armory of federal statutes awaits the selective enforcement of Secretaries of Labor and the Department of Justice. Often Congress is impelled to intervene. As these external battles ebb and flow, private intra-union clashes between old and young, blacks and whites, newcomers and veterans, skilled and unskilled operatives, and male and female workers must somehow be, if not resolved, at least cooled.

Probably in the end what workers in general can get is in a large way related to productivity, just as economists assert. But hardened unionists ought to be pardoned if they interpret the negotiating process at all levels and, on occasions far removed from Phase II, as an exercise in the uses of power. The union model of reality, in fact, focuses upon politics and power rather than upon competitive markets and marginal productivity. Like all other models of the world, it contains distortions and oversimplifications. Still, when unions argue that income and wealth are generated by private and public power as well as by more conventional economic processes, then unions have come to terms with an essential aspect of American experience.

This praise of union realism has as a corollary an implicit criticism of economic theory. The brutal fact is that economists cherish an intellectually splendid explanation of how free, reasonably competitive markets operate to maximize producer efficiency and consumer gratification. The only difficulty is in locating out there the markets the economists talk about. The profession lacks a generally accepted doctrine of the way in which powerful economic organizations, above all the giant corporation, exercise sovereignty.

Lacking a doctrine to explain events in other than competitive markets, economists are tempted to believe that, with all their empirical imperfections, existing markets do allocate resources with reasonable efficiency. They are similarly inclined to the judgment that, despite even graver institutional flaws, the existing arrangements for income distribution do roughly measure collective market judgments upon the comparative contributions of assorted human beings and varied nonhuman resources.

Until economists grapple rather more seriously than any but a radical fringe has thus far attempted to do with the realities of the concentration of economic power and until the profession recovers from its two-century-old romance with free competition, economists are unlikely to have anything very useful to add as theorists to the comprehension of such economic adventures as a conservative President's unanticipated conversion to *dirigisme*.

I make no forecast here of the success or failure of Phase II or the identity of the winners and losers in the continuing contest for pay, profit, and power. Of one thing I am unfortunately certain: Economists have lamentably failed in their duty of rationally explaining the nature of the contest and its relationship to American economic patterns in general. If one of the unexpected consequences of August 15 and after is stimulus to the construction of a persuasive explanation of power and influence in the economy, Mr. Nixon will have done economists and the public an unexpected favor.

Inflation, Recession, and Crisis, or Would You Buy a New Car from This Man?

FRANK ACKERMAN AND
ARTHUR MacEWAN

Economic policies of a capitalist government are aimed at maintaining the stability or "smooth functioning" of the system. That is, the government works to protect and extend the operation of fundamental institutions of the system—the labor and capital markets, and private ownership and control of the means of production. It is primarily through the workings of these institutions that exploitation takes place and power is exercised in capitalist

Reprinted by permission from the *Review of Radical Political Economics*, Vol. IV, No. 3 (August 1972). The original version of this paper appears in issue No. 3 of *Upstart*, a radical socialist journal, available from the authors.

society. By insuring the smooth functioning of these institutions, rather than by favoritism to particular groups or by corruption, the state guarantees the expansion of opportunities for profit.

Nixon's new policies, as well as the more traditional economic policies that were used throughout the Kennedy-Johnson era, are a good illustration of the government assuring profits through stabilization of the economy. The switch to new kinds of policies, involving considerable political risk, is evidence that the changed economic and political situation has rendered the traditional policies far less effective than they were in the early 1960's. . . .

I. The Domestic Economy

. . . By comparison with earlier periods, the economy has grown quite steadily and rapidly in the postwar years. Since 1946 the real gross national product has increased at an average annual rate of more than 3.5 per cent, and real per capita income has grown by almost 60 per cent.

During the 1950s, however, recessions caused recurrent minor interruptions in growth. In 1958, for example, unemployment reached 6.8 per cent, the highest level of the postwar period, and real national income fell by 1 per cent. Popular resentment at the "Republican recessions" doubtless played a major part in bringing the Democrats to power in 1960.

The Kennedy administration was committed to active government regulation of the economy and took several steps to counter the 1960–61 recession. Government spending, especially military spending, was increased, thus raising the total demand for goods and services. Tax cuts in 1962 and 1964 increased the after-tax incomes and, therefore, the spending of business and consumers. Interest rates on long-term loans were kept low to encourage borrowing for industrial investment, mortgages and home construction, and installment purchases. The policies seemed effective: annual growth of GNP averaged more than 5.5 per cent from 1962 through 1965 and unemployment dropped, though slowly, from 6.7 per cent in 1961 to 4.5 per cent in 1965.

Low inflation combined with persistent unemployment provided the necessary framework for the effectiveness of the government's policy in the early 1960s. Prices rose by less than 2 per cent a year until 1966; unemployment, while declining, did not drop below 5 per cent until after 1964. The low inflation removed any concern about the inflationary effects of deficit spending, and assured the stability necessary for corporate planning.

High unemployment made labor's bargaining power in wage negotiations weak, and therefore business could respond to the government's expansion of demand without worrying about high wage bills cutting into profits. In fact, as usual in the expansion out of a recession, profits did rise faster than wages. While the real value of total wages and salaries rose by 27 per cent from 1960 to 1965, the real value of profits rose by 64 per cent. That is, both capital and labor gained in *absolute* terms, but capital gained in *relative* terms as well; the share of national income going to profits rose from 8.4

per cent to 10.6 per cent, while the share going to wages and salaries fell from 73.8 per cent to 72.2 per cent.

The combination of low inflation and high unemployment that characterized the early 1960s, as well as most earlier recessions, has not been repeated in the current period. We shall see below that the simultaneous high unemployment and high inflation of 1970–71 created contradictory pressures upon the government that could not be resolved within the framework of traditional policy.

The situation of the early 1960s was politically as well as economically favorable to government stimulation of the economy. In the decade between the end of the Korean War and beginning of the Vietnam war buildup, immediate political and military demands on the government were at a remarkably low level. There were political and economic conflicts—over tax cuts and steel prices, for instance—but they were far less serious than the clashes of a few years later. In the early 1960s there were no strong domestic reform movements. There was no "hot" war going on. And the cold war required an indefinite, that is an easily manipulable, level of military expenditure.

Thus the Kennedy-Johnson administration faced almost uniquely favorable economic and political circumstances for its intervention in the economy. The situation was not only unique: it was also quite brief. By 1965–66, the government was confronted with near-full employment, more rapid inflation, a war in Asia, and rising domestic opposition. In the new situation the government's economic policies were pathetically but necessarily inept.

The War Overkills the Economy

With the expansion of the war in Indochina, the Johnson administration encountered serious difficulties in financing its military operations. In past wars, increased taxes and cutbacks in nonmilitary government programs had provided major sources of finance. Both of these sources were largely unavailable, however, because of the unpopularity of the Vietnam war. Major tax increases or significant curtailment of popular government programs would have directly increased opposition to the war, and would have hindered Johnson's effort to hide the whole issue. Thus the government was forced to rely on expansion of deficit spending, with unfortunate consequences for the economy.

In a period of high unemployment, deficit spending, by expanding demand, can create more jobs, lead to rising incomes, and generate more economic growth. In a period of low unemployment, however, the expansion of demand cannot readily be met by expansion of output. Thus, the government simply competes with the private sector for the available goods and services. The result is a rise in prices, that is, inflation. This is exactly what happened: beginning in 1966, war financing required increased deficit spending just as the economy was reaching near-full employment, and the result was rapid inflation.

The claim that the Vietnam war would be short may have led the Johnson administration to underestimate the inflationary effects of war deficits. United States war makers kept seeing the light at the end of the tunnel and suggesting that they were about to win. Johnson's economic policy makers probably worked on this assumption, even if the Pentagon and the State Department knew it was not true.

In 1965, at the beginning of the major escalation of the war, unemployment, though declining, was still over 4 per cent. Johnson's economic advisors may have hoped that a short spurt of war spending would only bring the economy to a slightly lower unemployment level without creating further inflationary pressures. This hope could conceivably have been realized if the war had ended by 1967, but the struggle of the Vietnamese people was not so easily suppressed.

Inflation, Employment, and the Role of the Government

The inflation and low unemployment after 1966 posed a number of problems for the United States government. In general, the role of the government in the economy is to maintain the "smooth functioning" of the system. In addition to the international complications dealt with below, the economic conditions of the late 1960s disrupted corporate planning and labor supply.

Modern capitalism very much depends on large corporations being able to make long-run plans. A uniform and predictable level of inflation can be compatible with planning; except for the problems of foreign trade, it is not crucial whether businesses know whether prices will increase by 0, 3, or 10 per cent a year, as long as they know which it will be. But the inflation of the late 1960s involved a significant departure from the past and was thus neither uniform nor predictable.[1]

The smooth functioning of capitalism also depends on business having a readily available supply of labor at its command. We have seen how the rapid expansion of the economy in the early 1960s was based on the availability of labor: the expansion of government demand in a time of high unemployment permitted rapidly rising profits. But in the late 1960s unemployment rates became exceptionally low. The period 1966 through 1969 was the only four-year period since World War II in which unemployment remained below 4 per cent.

Such conditions enhance the economic power of labor. With high employment levels workers are able to demand wage increases. Often having other family members working or having ready access to part-time and second jobs, workers hold a strong bargaining position. The bargaining power of employ-

---

[1] For some Latin American countries, for instance, annual price increases of 10–15 per cent are normal and expected; but for the United States in the 1960s, price increases as high as 5–6 per cent a year seriously hampered corporate planning since they were quite unexpected. Unexpected inflation can initially yield gains for business, because at the outset prices can often be raised more quickly than wages. But with the labor market conditions in the United States (see following paragraphs) any initial gains to capital due to the inflation were soon eliminated.

ers is weakened, since they cannot turn to the unemployed as an alternative source of labor. So unless employers can maintain very rapid increases in productivity (to make output grow faster than wages), a period of protracted full employment allows labor to improve its relative, as well as absolute, income position.

In fact, during the late 1960s, the share of national income going to labor rose, and the share going to corporate profits fell. Total wages and salaries, which were down (in relative terms) to 72.2 per cent of national income in 1965–66, climbed to 76.3 per cent of national income by 1969. Corporate profits, on the other hand, were up (in relative terms) to 10.6 per cent of national income in 1965–66, but then fell to 8.2 per cent of national income in 1969.

It is well-known that workers' average real take-home pay has remained roughly constant since 1965.[2] Increases in money wages were quickly eroded by inflation and rising taxes. Nonetheless, the rapid expansion in the number of people employed meant that working people as a class were receiving a higher share of national income, as well as a higher total income in absolute terms. From 1965 to 1969 the real value of total wages and salaries rose by over 17 per cent. Average family incomes, especially those of poor families, rose rapidly with more family members working; per-capita consumption continued to rise throughout the 1960s.

Corporate profits, on the other hand, rose slightly from 1965 to 1966, and then actually declined in real value. From 1965 to 1969, the real value of corporate profits declined by 14 per cent.

These figures show the crisis in which American business found itself at the beginning of the 1970s. The deteriorating state of business profits alone would certainly be enough to prompt the government to take strong actions. Also important, however, inflation meant that workers did not feel that their position was improving.

While total labor income had risen since 1965, both absolutely and as a share of national income, inflation limited any positive feeling that workers might have derived from this increase in income. The increase had come through more work, rather than through higher real wages per worker; family incomes were rising only because, on the average, more family members were now working. Furthermore, workers constantly saw any gains they made eaten up by higher prices, a generally disconcerting situation. Thus government action to deal with inflation had popular, as well as business, support.

---

[2] The oft-quoted average, however, obscures the real picture. First, government and agriculture workers are excluded from the figure. Second, and probably more important, since the composition of the work force has shifted with higher employment rates to include more low paid workers—e.g., blacks and women—it is possible that everyone's wage could rise while the average remained constant. Imagine an economy with one man working with a wage of $100/week and one woman working with a wage of $50/week in 1965. The average wage would be $75. In 1969 there are two women and one man. The man gets $110/week, each woman gets $55/week, and the average is $73.33. The average goes down while everyone's wage goes up. Something like this actually was happening in the United States economy during these years.

The Limitations on the Government's Options

The Nixon administration initially tried to solve the economic problems of the late 1960s in the traditional manner: causing a contraction of demand, by eliminating the government deficit (raising taxes or lowering government spending), and by raising interest rates. Such actions were designed to curtail economic activity, raise unemployment, and thereby slow down wage increases. Eventually business, in response to the lessened wage pressures and declining consumer spending, would stop raising prices, and inflation would slow down.

It all worked according to plan except for the slowing down of inflation. Unemployment was indeed raised, ushering in the 1970–71 recession. Inflation, however, continued unabated. Rather than the "either-or" choice between inflation and unemployment which faced previous administrations—the famous "trade-off"—the Nixon government found itself enjoying the worst of both.

From the above account of the 1960s, it should be clear how the trade-off between unemployment and inflation operates. Beginning with high unemployment, as the economy expands unemployed workers can be drawn into production and no inflation occurs. But as unemployment falls the continuing rise in demand causes price and wage increases because different industries reach bottlenecks and cannot readily expand output, because of the increasing labor scarcity.

If the trade-off worked equally well in reverse, Nixon's initial attempts to control the economy would have most likely worked. However, once inflation becomes serious, as it did in the late 1960s, it tends to become self-perpetuating and continues after the original inflationary pressures have been eliminated. Having experienced inflation, employers and workers alike expect there to be more, raise their prices and wages accordingly, and their collective actions fulfill their expectations in spite of the government's reduction of demand. In a more competitive economy such a process would be inhibited, because a decline in demand would quickly force price reductions. But monopolistic elements in the United States economy can resist the pressures and maintain their prices.

So in the summer of 1971 Nixon and United States capitalists found themselves in a predicament. Unemployment rates had again risen to around 6 per cent. Traditional policies of the "new economics" would call for an expansion of government spending. But an expansion of government spending would exacerbate the inflation, already close to 6 per cent.

Either the Nixon administration had to simply wait out the present situation—that is, live with the high level of unemployment until the inflation subsided—and then stimulate the economy, or it had to find some new means by which to intervene in the economy. If the elections had been further away and if the international monetary crisis could have been forestalled, the first alternative might have been feasible. But the elections were a fact, and, as we shall argue below, the international situation could not be forestalled because it could not be separated from the domestic events. Nixon had to act.

II. Origins of the International Crisis

As a result of the two world wars, the United States became the unchallenged, leading power among capitalist nations. In the late 1940s and early 1950s United States business rapidly spread its overseas activity. It made inroads to areas that had previously been dominated, formally or informally, by Western Europe and Japan. In parts of the world where before 1914 United States business had been one of many competing foreign groups—Brazil or Argentina, for example—it moved to undisputed dominance by the 1950s.

Economic expansion was accompanied by spreading military and political activity. The Pentagon extended its network of bases and advisors around the globe. United States diplomatic missions replaced former colonial offices as the real seats of power in much of the Third World. This power had its costs, as well as its benefits, to the United States. When rebellions break out in the Third World, the United States pays the bills for suppressing them, whether it is done with United States or with puppet troops. As we will point out below, the costs of the major United States intervention of the 1960s, in Indochina, played an important role in causing the current economic crisis.

But of course the extension of United States political and economic power was not confined to underdeveloped areas. The Marshall Plan, the suppression of rebellion in Greece, and the maintenance of the United States military presence in Germany provided a foundation for the rapid expansion of United States business activity in Europe.

The postwar expansion of foreign trade and investment depended, among other things, on the establishment of a new set of international monetary institutions. The key factor in the new monetary arrangements, created at the 1944 Bretton Woods conference, was that the dollar became, along with gold, the basis of international transactions. The governments of countries taking part in the system (developed capitalist nations) agreed to maintain a fixed exchange rate between their currencies and the dollar. The United States government agreed, in turn, to maintain a fixed value of the dollar in terms of gold—$35 an ounce.

The postwar system of dollar based exchange rates provided a stable basis for trade beneficial to business in all capitalist nations. Furthermore, the system had other aspects which, by causing the accumulation of dollar reserves around the world, serve the particular interests of United States capitalism.

. . . Other countries, increasing their reserves, have a continuing need to accumulate dollars. The United States, providing these dollars, can therefore spend more abroad than it receives. The foreign need for dollar reserves, in effect, finances part of the United States balance of payments deficit.

What has happened, in short, is that the total dominance of the United States in the international capitalist economy after World War II led to the creation of a system—partly formal and partly *de facto*—that further enhanced the relative position of the United States.

Reconstruction and Competition

United States leadership of the capitalist world after 1945 was a natural consequence of the long-run balance of power. But the extent of United States predominance immediately after the war was unusually great, and clearly temporary. All the other major industrial nations had been ravaged by the war, while the United States economy had benefited immensely from the stimulus of war production. With the return of peace and gradual reconstruction, European and Japanese competition with the United States was sure to reappear.

The United States furthermore was caught in a situation that impelled it to hasten the decline of its relative power. First, the military and strategic imperatives of the cold war required that the United States build up the economies of all developed capitalist countries, including its recent enemies as well as allies. Second, the expansion of the United States economy was dependent on the revitalization of world trade and the reopening of opportunities for foreign investment, and this also required rebuilding the economies of Western Europe and Japan.

Even though it was clear that the relative dominance of the United States had to decline, the timing and the extent of that decline remained unclear. Several counterforces operated to preserve the United States position. United States economic strength at the end of World War II led, as we have pointed out above, to an international financial system that continually favored United States interests. Also, while United States economic dominance could be challenged, the military might of the United States was less assailable. And so long as military hegemony could be maintained, the economic power of the United States would have a firm support.

Finally, the rise of socialism greatly affected the question of conflict and unity among capitalist nations. The military challenge and social threat of socialism would certainly force a certain solidarity among capitalists even with a decline in United States economic power; indeed, the situation might force the lesser powers into greater reliance on United States political and military leadership.

Genesis of the Current Crisis

It is tempting to identify the current United States balance of payments crisis as the natural result of foreign competition and declining United States economic predominance. Closer examination of the facts, however, suggests that more emphasis should be placed on direct and indirect effects of the war in Vietnam, and less on European and Japanese competition, than is commonly recognized. We can trace the changes in the United States international position in three major components of the balance of payments—trade, costs of empire, and long-term investments—and in the secondary effects of short-term investment.

Trade and Wages

Throughout the twentieth century the United States has had a trade surplus—exports have exceeded imports each year until 1971. The existence of a United States trade surplus may seem paradoxical. After all, wages are higher in the United States than in all other parts of the world. How could United States industry, paying such high wages, continue to compete with low wage producers elsewhere?

The answer is, of course, that United States industry could compete so long as its higher paid labor produced sufficiently more than other countries' lower paid labor. Having more education (imparting both skills and discipline), better nourishment, more industrial and organizational experience, and better equipment to work with, United States labor has been the most productive labor in the world, as well as the highest paid. Although some industries—e.g., textiles and shoes—requiring large amounts of relatively unskilled labor have long been hurt by competition from low-wage foreign industry, such cases are not typical of most United States industry throughout the postwar period.

The high wages of United States labor would become a fetter on industry only when foreign capitalists were more successful than United States capitalists in keeping productivity increases ahead of wage increases. This might be the case, especially in industries with strong United States unions but weak foreign unions. The growth of multinational corporations may accelerate the entrance of foreign labor into effective competition with United States labor. A United States based multinational enterprise can use its advanced technology, organizational skills, marketing power, and highly trained skilled labor along with cheap foreign unskilled labor.

Such forces undoubtedly have great significance over the long run. But the crucial question, for understanding any concrete, immediate situation, is: How long is the long run? Should we expect foreign competition to challenge United States trade in twenty years after World War II, or in forty? And when it happens, will the challenge be felt abruptly, or gradually?

Obviously there is no *a priori* basis on which to decide how soon to expect the United States would face serious trade competition. But there is some *a priori* basis for expecting the effects of foreign competition to be felt rather gradually. There is no one uniform level of productivity throughout industry, in the United States or in any other industrial country. Similarly there is no uniform productivity differential between, say, American and Japanese industry as a whole, but rather a wide spectrum of differentials in various industries. Thus, it should take different lengths of time for Japan to reach the level of the United States in different industries, and Japanese competition, all other things being equal, should cut a little further into the United States trade surplus each year.

But in the real world all other things never are equal. This "pure model" of gradually intensifying competition may be assumed to provide a background against which short and medium-run effects can be seen, . . . but it cannot explain the rapid fluctuations experienced by the United States trade balance in the 1960s.

. . . From 1964 to 1968, the United States went from a "net" trade surplus (the trade balance excluding aid-financed exports) of $4 billion to a "net" deficit of more than $1 billion—a drop of over $5 billion in four years. The contrast between United States trade performance in 1960–64 and 1964–68 seems far too abrupt to be explained by any likely pattern of productivity changes in Europe and Japan. Fortunately, a better explanation is available, which distinguishes sharply between the two four-year periods: differences in the rates of inflation.

From 1960 to 1964, the United States and other industrial countries had similarly low rates of inflation: United States export prices rose only 2 per cent over the four-year period, compared to a 3 per cent rise in the average of all industrial countries' export prices. . . . But from 1964 to 1968, United States export prices rose 10 per cent, while the average for all industrial countries rose only 3 per cent. It is hard to avoid the conclusion that war-related inflation made United States goods higher priced and less competitive with foreign goods, both at home and abroad.

Costs of Empire

A second component of United States international economic accounts that has caused balance of payments difficulties is the costs of empire. These are the costs of the military and "aid" operations of the United States government that provide a necessary support for multinational corporate activities.

The costs of empire do not result from mistaken or extravagant overseas activity; they flow directly from the requirements of the capitalist system. Economic activity cannot exist in a political vacuum; it requires the active support of the state. The significant form of this support is not graft or short-run favoritism to particular businesses (though such favoritism is recurrent), but rather long-run programs designed to maintain the "smooth functioning" of the system, internationally as well as domestically.

The United States government, for instance, played a leading role in establishing international monetary institutions and negotiating trade agreements. Similarly, the United States provides economic aid to friendly, weak governments and employs a military strategy designed to keep the world safe for capitalist activity.

Aid and military operations can be costly. From 1960 to 1965, United States spending abroad on costs of empire averaged $5.5 billion a year. When major spending for the Vietnam war began, the costs of empire increased, averaging $6.9 billion a year from 1966 to 1971. The burden of war spending was greater than these figures suggest: the increase in costs of empire was held down to $1.4 billion a year only through cutbacks in aid and military programs in the rest of the world, which partially offset rising spending in Indochina. . . .

Short-Run Capital Flows: Precipitating the Crisis

While trade problems and costs of empire lie at the roots of the crisis, the international movements of short-term capital investments affected its timing. The importance of these short-term movements should not be ignored. They reflect the increasing integration of international capital markets, and the present crisis illustrates how that integration can hamper the activity of a national government attempting to regulate "its own" economy.

The balance of payments difficulties attributable to trade and costs of empire began to appear in 1966 and became substantially more serious in 1967–69. . . . However, rising interest rates in the United States accompanied by economic difficulties in Europe resulted in a large inflow of short-term investments—that is, investments in short-term bonds and securities—into the United States. This forestalled for a few years the coming balance of payments problem.

By 1970, the increasing severity of the recession in the United States led the government to push down interest rates to stimulate investment in productive activity. Instead of inducing investment, the lower interest rates, along with more stable conditions and higher interest rates in Europe, resulted in a huge flight of short-term capital from the United States. Short-term capital flows, which amounted to a $9.6 billion inflow to the United States in 1969, plummeted to a $5.8 billion outflow in 1970—an unprecedented change of more than $15 billion in one year. Further declines in the United States interest rate and continuing better conditions in Europe led to a further outflow of capital: in early 1971 the balance of payments deficit from short-term investment flows was running at an annual rate of over $10 billion. . . . It was these dramatic shifts which brought the balance of payments crisis to a head in 1971 rather than 1969 or 1973.

Beyond the effect on the timing of the crisis, the importance of short-term capital flows is twofold. First, the increasing internationalization of capital markets will from now on force all major capitalist countries to maintain near-identical interest rates: any country which sets its interest rate significantly below the world rates will be faced with huge short-run capital outflows. Manipulation of the interest rate, one of the government's traditional instruments of domestic economic policy, must now be used to stabilize international capital markets. This limits the ability of government to counter recession or inflation.

Second, Nixon and the mass media are probably wrong in attributing these movements of short-term investment to "international speculators." More likely the culprits are not the stereotyped scheming individuals—the "gnomes of Zurich"—but rather the treasurers of United States-based multinational corporations. These treasurers are responsible for the tremendous cash balances maintained by their companies; they would be remiss in their profit-maximizing duties if they failed to use their cash wherever it provided the highest quick returns. . . .

Thus the internationalization of capital markets, and the use made of those markets by large corporations, limits the freedom of individual governments to regulate their economies, illustrating the contradiction that arises in advanced capitalism between international integration and nationalism.

Balance of Payments: A Summary

. . . The trade deterioration of the late 1960s, apparently resulting from war-related inflation, and the rising costs of empire during the Vietnam war, seem to be the principal factors causing the long-term balance-of-payments deficit. This theory, unlike theories which place primary emphasis on the longest-term factors, can provide an easy explanation of the abrupt reversals in the United States balance of payments in the mid-1960s. We are not denying that gradually rising foreign competition intensified the 1971 balance of payments crisis and spurred the government to more dramatic action than would have been taken otherwise. Nonetheless, we see little evidence that the longest-term factors played more than a secondary, background role in causing the recent crisis.

War and inflation, we should emphasize, are fundamental and recurrent features of the present world capitalist system. Thus, it should be clear that we are not treating the balance of payments problem as a passing aberration.

One major contradiction of post-World War II United States capitalism is that the United States, through aid, trade, and investment, was compelled to rebuild its economic rivals in Europe and Japan, eventually undermining the United States trade position. Another major contradiction is that the United States is compelled to play a counterrevolutionary role throughout the Third World, which can entail substantial economic strains in the United States; combined with domestic opposition as during the Vietnam war, these strains can cause serious disruption. Both of these contradictions must be incorporated in any complete theory of modern capitalism. It is our judgment of the empirical evidence, however, that the latter is far more important than the former in causing the recent crisis.[3]

III. Nixon's Program and Where It Is Leading

The seriousness of the international monetary crisis, coupled with the mounting pressure in the domestic economy and the impending election, left the Nixon administration little choice but to take strong economic action. Fur-

---

[3] This conclusion about the recent past should not be confused with a prediction about the future. It would be consistent with our position to argue that in the coming years the failure of the United States to "handle" the Third World and the resulting difficulties could exacerbate the contradictions among advanced capitalist nations.

thermore, having chosen to act, Nixon had no general alternative to the policy he has pursued.

To succeed the government policy must achieve expansion without inflation, and it must at least show signs of progress in this direction before the 1972 election—sooner than inflation could have been controlled without direct price controls. While the incomes policy of Phase II permits gradual increases of wages and prices, the government maintains the existence of controls established during the freeze. Such controls, together with expansionary policies, were the only option Nixon possessed.

The program had to be one that would hold down everything but profits. (Only in a situation of total crisis, such as World War II, can business be expected to tolerate a "profit freeze" of any sort; and even during that war, business did not do so badly.) Many opponents of the government's program responded by calling for a "profits freeze." The discussion of a "profits freeze" reflects a basic misunderstanding of capitalism. That is the way capitalism works. Within the capitalist system the controls on wages and prices, but not profits, are rational; more "humane" or "equitable" alternatives were not possible.

To call for a profits freeze, or to join the liberals in carping at the especially blatant aspects of the program, is to encourage the idea that the economy's problems could be solved by a liberal administration. But a liberal government, no less than a conservative one, would have to maintain the smooth functioning of the system. At most the talk about a profits freeze might lead a Democratic administration to a trivial increase in the corporation income tax rate, to create a pretense that business, also, is suffering from austerity. And, beyond the profits freeze issue, most liberal politicians have only minor criticisms of Nixon's program. It is what they would have done themselves.

The Meaning of Direct Intervention

It is quite significant that United States capitalism has come to a point where there is no alternative to direct government intervention in the determination of wages and prices. Although many European capitalist governments have pursued these sorts of policies for years, United States government and business alike have shied away from such programs. Indeed the prerogative to make price, wage, and production decisions without government interference has long been seen by United States business as the foundation of economic success.

When United States business leaders welcomed the wage-price freeze and the controls of Phase II, they saw the program as an escape from crisis, not necessarily as a permanent new order. They will use the program as best they can, but if the circumstances change they may exert pressure for a return to old, indirect forms of government policy.

But are the circumstances producing the freeze so ephemeral? The current crisis, in both its international and its domestic aspects, results in large part from the war in Vietnam. Even though military action on the scale of the late 1960s is probably not a permanent state, United States intervention in Southeast Asia is not about to end, and there will no doubt be other wars in the future.

Furthermore, our analysis has suggested that the traditional policies work well only when the economy is free of serious wage-price spirals and when the government is free of strong domestic and international political constraints on its budget. The political limitations should be stressed: the stronger the opposition facing the United States government at home and abroad, the greater the need for direct controls on the economy. In addition, the onset of the present crisis marks the end of United States hegemony in the capitalist world; accordingly, United States policy is subject to greater constraints of all kinds.[4]

Thus there are dim prospects for a long-lasting reversion to the old system of indirect controls. The new controls will remain a recurrent, if not quite permanent, feature of American capitalism.

Will the New Policies Work?

But the question remains, will the new policies succeed where the old ones failed? There is little doubt that the policies can have initial success in at least one area—reducing inflation. From the time of the introduction of Nixon's new policy to the date of this writing (April 1972), inflation has proceeded at an annual rate of 2.7 per cent; a lower rate for an entire year has not been achieved since 1965. If we are correct in our analysis of the current inflation as a wage-price spiral set in motion by forces no longer active, breaking the spiral may reduce inflation for a considerable period of time.

As to moving the economy out of recession again, at least in the short run, the program has stimulated the growth of output, but has failed to reduce unemployment. Gross national product has risen (albeit not too dramatically), and the standard economic indicators—the industrial production index, new housing starts—have shown continuing gains.

We should emphasize that even this limited growth is not a result of new, direct controls alone, but of controls plus the traditional Keynesian antidote to a recession—large government deficits. In 1970 the deficit reached $13.6 billion, the largest since World War II. Yet in 1971, the deficit rose to $23.8 billion, and is expected to be even larger in 1972. These deficits in the absence of direct controls would greatly exacerbate the inflation of the late 1960s. And certainly the controls without the deficits would have done relatively little to make the economy grow. The lesson seems relatively clear:

---

[4] Even in otherwise ideal circumstances, the scope of indirect government policy is now more limited than it used to be: as pointed out above, international movements of short-term investments force all capitalist countries to adopt nearly the same interest rates, removing one traditional policy instrument from the hands of national government.

the United States economy is still dependent on large injections of government spending in order to grow.

While there has been growth since August 1971, that growth has not been matched by a decline in the unemployment rate. The first three months of 1972 have shown no marked departure from 1971, when the unemployment rate fluctuated around 6.0 per cent. If we are to judge from the experience of the early 1960s, it would require at least another year of expansion to bring the unemployment rate down significantly.

From the point of view of business, the failure of the policies to reduce unemployment is not an unmitigated loss. Of course businesses do not advocate recession; but neither do they enjoy the very low unemployment rates (i.e., the scarcity of labor) which characterized the late 1960s. The four-year period, 1966 to 1969, when the unemployment rate stayed below 4 per cent, was bad for profits. Businesses can be expected to encourage government policies that, while promoting economic growth, stop short of unpleasantly full employment.

A solution to the domestic crisis would go a long way toward solving the balance of payments problem as well. Effective control of inflation would eventually increase the competitiveness of United States goods in world markets, thereby increasing the United States trade surplus. Be that as it may, the international effects of domestic expansion are slow in coming, and the fourth quarter of 1971 showed a further decline in the United States trade position.

But there are other issues in the international situation beyond simply the competitiveness of United States goods. The real question is this: will the United States be able to establish a new set of stable political and economic relations to replace the earlier arrangements from the period of unchallenged United States hegemony? On a formal level, there has certainly been progress. The seemingly intransigent position of the United States in the late summer of 1971 was transformed into agreements which, while they involved United States compromise, were by no means a defeat for the United States.

Formal arrangements, however, are only formal arrangements. A workable set of new international financial arrangements depends on the establishment of a stable power relationship among the advanced capitalist nations. Over the past twenty-five years such stability has been based on United States hegemony. In the absence of United States hegemony, it remains to be seen whether the leading powers can maintain stable relationships among themselves.

On the one hand, if one simply projects the trends that led to the crisis of 1971, increasing conflict among the capitalist powers would seem to be most likely. Not only has there been the rising economic challenge to the United States posed by Japan and Europe, but a shift in the balance of military power is also developing. The inability of the United States to handle its empire militarily, combined with its long-run international economic problems, has led it to share the costs of "free world defense." But it is not possible to share costs without sharing power. Furthermore, changes in power relations carry with them reinforcing ideological changes—a redevelopment of nationalism and assertions of independence from United States control.

On the other hand, while the United States is no longer hegemonic it is still dominant, both in terms of economic and military power. In addition, while there are strong protectionist and nationalist forces at work within the United States, the leading sectors of United States capital have interests strongly opposed to a movement away from continuing integration of the capitalist world. The United States-based multinational firms will exert strong influence towards the establishment of a stable working arrangement that will allow smooth functioning of international economic activity. While the international scene will definitely be characterized by more intracapitalist conflict than in the preceding twenty-five years, we are inclined to believe that the interests of internationally oriented capital will tend to prevail over the more nationalist elements. . . .

Questions for Discussion

1. President Nixon's speech focuses on the international repercussions of his new policies. Why?
2. How right is Lekachman in his criticism of economics? Is power ignored by supply-demand models?
3. Do you agree with the prediction of Ackerman and MacEwan that direct controls are here to stay?
4. Did President Nixon make the correct choice of policy in the current crisis? What choices were available to him?

PART VI

Corporate
Capital and the
State

It is widely believed that the years of the Progressive era and the Great Depression produced sweeping changes in the relationship between the state and
the growing corporate sector. While virtually no social scientist would disagree with this proposition, there is considerable disagreement on the nature
of the changes that took place during these periods.

Liberals have argued that these changes constituted a great leap forward
for American capitalism and democracy. The general public was now able
to exert political control over the huge corporate monster that was emerging
in the United States. Through the agencies of government the people could
now realize goals that were beyond the tenets of the competitive phase of
capitalism. The business cycle would be eliminated, full employment would
be restored, and all Americans would share in the benefits of modern capitalism; the monopoly power of the corporation would be tamed, and we
would all stroll down the path to the affluent society with a minimum of
conflict and the help of government.

Radicals, on the other hand, have taken an extremely pessimistic view of
this interpretation. They contend that, while the extent of government-business
relations has greatly increased, the nature of the system has remained essentially the same. Radicals believe that both before and after the systematic
introduction of government control of the economy the state still serves as
a committee of the ruling class. The subtle way in which government serves
this function is one of the main issues taken up in this section.

These two points of view imply a widely divergent analysis of the problems
of the modern state. The liberal view implies that the problems of modern
America could be solved if only we would elect good officials who would
see their moral duty and use all the tools of government to create a great
society. On the other hand, the radical views government as a product of
the power relationships of the capitalist system. Only by changing the politi-

cal-economic system will we achieve what William Appleman Williams calls the ethical-equitable community.

The first article in this section by Clair Wilcox lays out rather clearly the liberal view of the relationship between government and business. It emphasizes the pluralistic nature of American democracy.

The second article, by William Appleman Williams, is a radical historical analysis of the growth of government control of business and the social and political aspects of the Progressive and depression years. Readers who wish to find more articles on the historical development of government and business relations are referred to Part III, "The Historical Development of Government in the Economy," and to the bibliography at the end of this text.

The third article in this section is excerpted from James O'Connor's excellent essay, "The Fiscal Crisis of the State." While the article may pose some difficulty for the reader, it is well worth the trouble. O'Connor not only lays out a framework for a radical analysis of the budget, but also presents a great amount of data in support of his argument. We only regret that we have had to cut a major portion of the article and with it much of his supporting information.

The last two articles deal with the nature of the modern corporation and government. The first is an excerpt from J. K. Galbraith's noted book, *The New Industrial State.* In it he expresses the view that the technology of modern production has substantially altered the character of American capitalism. Contrary to popular belief the modern corporation is highly efficient and we must not sacrifice this efficiency in the name of competition. What we need are stronger public controls to alleviate the abuses of modern capitalism. The other article (a review of *The New Industrial State,* by Ralph Miliband) takes issue with Galbraith and his thesis. Miliband says that the modern corporation is not a substantially different institution, or is government any different. They are still the product of a class-based society and more and better government will not solve this problem.

These articles should give the reader a base from which to analyze critically the relationship between government and business in modern America.

Public Control of Business: The Liberal View

CLAIR WILCOX

Business, in the United States, is affected in many ways by the activities of government. Indeed, it is government that provides the institutional foundation upon which business rests, the legal framework within which it functions, and many of the instruments through which its activities are carried on. Government establishes the status of the business unit, grants the privilege of incorporation, and makes the laws that control bankruptcy and reorganization. It defines and maintains the rights of ownership, enforces private contracts, and provides for the adjudication of disputes. It coins money, issues currency, controls credit, and regulates banking, thus freeing business from barter and providing it with a medium of exchange. It establishes standards of weight and measurement, sets up systems for grading commodities, inspects shipments, and regulates central markets, thus facilitating the processes of trade. It directs traffic on streets and highways, maintains police forces and fire departments, builds dams and dikes, inspects ships and aircraft, issues warnings of coming storms, operates lighthouses, and patrols the coasts, thus affording protection against the loss of life and property.

Government also renders valuable services to business, extends to it various forms of public assistance, and promotes its activities in many ways. It collects and disseminates data that provide businessmen with information on the availability of productive resources, credit, and investment funds, on methods and costs of production and distribution, on trends of business activity, on present market conditions and future market prospects. It engages in fundamental research relating to the problems of agriculture, industry, and public health, tests the properties of materials and the effectiveness of productive processes, contributes to the advancement of technology, and makes its discoveries available for general use. Through its system of public education, government trains the labor force and cultivates consumer demand. Through its consular service, it assists business in finding markets abroad. Through

Reprinted with permission from Clair Wilcox, *Public Policies Toward Business* (4th ed.; Homewood, Ill.: Richard D. Irwin, Inc.), pp. 3–17.

its diplomatic service, it seeks to protect investments made in other lands. Government offers technical advice to small business and makes loans to finance productive activities. It supports transport, agriculture, and mining, in some measure, by providing public subsidies. In all of these matters, business leans heavily on government.

The economic system within which business functions is shaped by government; the character of its performance depends upon decisions that are made by government. The demand for the products of business and the nature of its costs are influenced by public regulations, by the character of public expenditures, and by the types of taxes that are used in raising public revenues. Its expectations—of stability or instability, of prosperity or depression, of profit or loss—depend upon the policies adopted by central banking authorities in controlling the volume of credit and on those pursued by government in balancing its budget, accumulating a surplus, or running a deficit. Its daily operations must be carried on within the limits that are fixed by a variety of public controls. . . .

The Nature of Controls

What, then, is "control"? Business is influenced, inevitably, by all of the activities of government. But many of them are not to be included in the concept of control. This is true, for instance, of such services as police and fire protection, public health and education, and national defense. It is true, too, of those activities that create the general environment within which business may be carried on, such as the provision of legal status for the business unit, the establishment of a monetary system, and the enforcement of contracts. The meaning of "control," as the word is used here, is confined to the deliberate adoption, by government, of measures designed to cause the policies of business managements to differ, in material respects, from those that they would voluntarily pursue. Control thus comprehends a great variety of measures that differ in purpose, method, and effect. Their common feature is modification of the behavior of business in response to pressures applied through government. . . .

The Long History of Control

The control of business is not a new departure in public policy. Government has always regulated business in the United States. Even before specific statutes were enacted, the practices of business were subject to decisions of the courts under the rules of common law: agreements to restrain trade were held to be unenforceable, unfair methods of competition were enjoined, enterprises affected with a public interest were required to serve all comers—adequately, speedily, continuously, and without discrimination—and persons who sustained injury at the hands of business were awarded damages. The enactment of state laws requiring safe and sanitary conditions of employment dates back to 1877; laws forbidding the misrepresentation of securities to 1911; laws insuring workers against industrial accidents and laws establishing maximum hours and minimum wages for women to 1911 and 1912. Commissions set up by the states have regulated banking since 1838, railroads since 1844, insurance companies since 1854, and public utilities since 1907. Intervention by the federal government, in the form of the restrictive tariff and the patent system, is as old as our national history. Federal regulation of the railroads goes back to the first administration of Grover Cleveland in 1887, and the Sherman Antitrust Act to the administration of Benjamin Harrison in 1890. The Pure Food and Drug Law was enacted under Theodore Roosevelt in 1906, the Clayton and Federal Trade Commission Acts under Woodrow Wilson in 1914. The first conservation laws date from the seventies; the first law controlling the methods used in producing oil and gas was passed in Texas in 1919. A number of regulatory agencies, set up under Franklin D. Roosevelt in the early years of the New Deal, have now seen more than three decades of service. Regulation of business in the public interest is by no means alien to American tradition. It is an outgrowth· of generations of experience.

The Growth of Control

The scope of public regulation has grown steadily with the passage of time. A century ago controls were few and simple. In the economy of that day they were all that seemed to be required. In relation to its great resources the population of the country was small. There were still free lands to be occupied, virgin forests to be cut, and deposits of minerals waiting to be tapped. Productive activity centered in agriculture, in the extractive industries, in handicrafts and small manufactures, and in petty trade. Enterprises were organized, in the main, as individual proprietorships or partnerships. They were managed by their owners; employers dealt directly with employees. The scale of industrial operations was small; the production of goods and services was scattered among many firms. Economic independence was the general rule.

Now all of these conditions have changed. The population has grown; the land has been settled, and its natural wealth exploited. Agriculture has declined in relative importance; manufacturing, transport, and the public utilities have grown. The individual proprietorship and the partnership have given way, in many fields, to the modern corporation. Ownership has been divorced from management, and labor has been organized. Technology has advanced: new products, new materials, new machines, and new methods have been introduced. The scale of industrial operations has grown; production, in many industries, has come to be concentrated in the hands of a few large firms. Economic relationships have steadily grown in complexity. Interdependence, rather than independence, has come to be the rule.

These changes have brought with them a host of new problems, and as these problems have arisen solutions have been sought through the extension of public controls. New laws have been enacted, new agencies established, and new methods of regulation devised. But the process of adapting political institutions to economic change has not been a steady one. Public sentiment has swung from radicalism to conservatism and back again, and legislation has come in spurts as abuses have become so evident as to call for reform. But even during the conservative administration of President Eisenhower, control was extended to the labeling of furs, textiles, and hazardous substances, to the sale of flammable fabrics, and to the pricing of natural gas at the wellhead; the minimum wage was raised, insurance benefits were provided to the totally disabled, old-age benefits were extended to millions of additional workers, and the level of these benefits was raised. Controls have been extended most rapidly when deep depression has emphasized the need for individual security and in periods when preparation for the nation's defense has placed a heavy burden on the whole economy. These controls have generally been abandoned when the emergency has passed. But other controls, once adopted, have usually been retained. Regulation often advances; it seldom retreats. . . .

Private Enterprise and the Public Interest

The behavior of business is not a matter that affects business alone. A single enterprise may use the savings of thousands of investors, employ other thousands of workers, and serve still other thousands of customers. The opportunity that it affords and the security that it provides for investment and employment, the income that it distributes in the form of wages, salaries, interest, and dividends, the quantity and quality of the goods and services that it produces, and the prices at which it sells may influence the well-being of thousands on thousands of citizens. If it possesses a monopoly, suppliers may have no alternative but to sell to it and consumers no alternative but to buy from it. If it competes with other concerns, the methods it employs may affect everyone who invests in, works for, or buys from, its competitors. If it engages in the exploitation of exhaustible resources, the methods it uses may threaten the nation's security and do damage to generations yet to come. If the products that it supplies are not pure, if the working conditions that it provides are not safe, if its wastes go down the stream and up the flue, polluting the water and the air, it may impair the health of the whole community. The behavior of business inescapably affects the general welfare; it is properly a matter of public concern.

It is not always safe to leave business to its own devices; experience has shown that its freedom will sometimes be abused. Investors have been defrauded by promoters, corporate insiders, and market manipulators. Men, women, and children have been put to work under needless hazards, amid unhealthful surroundings, for long hours, at low pay, and without assurance of future security. Competitors have been harassed by malicious and predatory tactics, handicapped by discrimination, excluded from markets and sources of supply, and subjected to intimidation, coercion, and physical violence. Consumers have been victimized by short weights and measures, by adulteration, and by misrepresentation of quality and price; they have been forced to contribute to the profits of monopoly. Water and air have been polluted with the wastes of industry; the nation's resources have been dissipated through extravagant methods of exploitation. These abuses have not characterized all business at all times, but they have occurred with sufficient frequency to justify the imposition of controls. Regulation is clearly required, not only to protect the investor, the worker, the consumer, and the community at large against the unscrupulous businessman, but also to protect the honest businessman against his dishonest competitor.

The Origin of Controls

When government moves to extend its controls, it does not act of its own volition. Government, in the United States, is not an independent entity; it does not possess a will of its own; it is not animated by purposes that are alien to the desires of its citizens. The American government is a creature of the American people; it responds to the pressures that they bring to bear upon it; its policies and its programs, wise or unwise, find their origin in organized demand and depend for their survival upon popular sufferance. If government regulates the securities markets and the stock exchanges, it is because investors demand protection. If it establishes maximum hours and minimum wages, requires collective bargaining, and sets up a system of social insurance, it is because labor demands protection. If it outlaws unfair methods of competition and curbs discrimination in the prices that are quoted to competing firms, it is because competitors demand protection. If it prohibits the sale of impure foods and drugs, if it forbids falsehood in advertising, if it enforces competition in one industry and regulates monopoly in another, it is because consumers demand protection. If it seeks to conserve the nation's resources, it is because a substantial body of public opinion insists that it do so. Government does not willfully interfere with business. It intervenes only when it is forced to intervene. It acts reluctantly, deliberately, and tardily, in response to overwhelming pressures. Criticism of public intervention is criticism, not of dictatorship, but of the results of the democratic process.

It must be noted, moreover, that many of the laws that now regulate business have been enacted, not in the face of business opposition, but at the urgent solicitation of business itself. There are tariffs that prevent businessmen from buying goods abroad, statutes that prevent them from doing business across state lines, and ordinances that exclude them from local markets. There are patents that keep businessmen from competing with the patentees, and licensing requirements that deny them entry into sheltered trades. There are regulations that prevent businessmen from reducing the costs of production, from introducing new methods, and from employing new materials. There are laws that handicap the efficient businessman and laws that subsidize the inefficient one. There are laws that prevent the businessman from increasing his output and laws that prevent him from reducing his price. None of these are measures which an aggressive government has forced upon a reluctant business community. All of them are measures which government has adopted at the behest of business itself. If government is interfering with business, it is largely because business has invited it to interfere. . . .

The Need for Control

The case for private enterprise, as it was developed by economists and expounded by teachers of economics for a century and a half, was based upon the assumption that competition would prevail. Businessmen were selfish; they would seek to maximize their profit by paying too little and charging too much. But their competitors, though equally selfish, would prevent them from doing so by paying more and charging less. Competition would thus harness selfishness and make it serve the common weal.

With the growth of big business, in later years, it has appeared to many observers that competition has declined. If this were true, the selfishness of the businessman was no longer held in check. A new defense of private enterprise was thus required. One was found in the doctrine of social responsibility. This is the view that recent changes in the structure of the corporation, the character of management, and the environment of enterprise have so transformed the motivation of businessmen that they seek, now, to serve the general interest.

In this view, social responsibility is assumed voluntarily; it is not compelled. Another theory rests upon a new form of compulsion—countervailing power. According to this theory, protection against the selfishness of big business is afforded, not by the competition of other enterprises on the same side of the market, but by the emergence of equally large units on the other side of the market. Big sellers thus find themselves confronted by big buyers, and vice versa, so that neither one can take advantage of the other.

Each of these theories argues that business will serve the general interest, whether through the discipline of competition, the assumption of social responsibility, or the force of countervailing power. What need is there, then, for the imposition of public controls?

The Rationale of Competition

Private enterprise is justified, in the defense long offered by economists, by the service it renders to people in their capacity as consumer. Private enterprise seeks profit. But, to obtain profit, it must serve consumers, for this is the only way to profit that competition will allow. It is thus on the foundation of competition that the case for private enterprise is built.

Human wants are many and growing; the productive resources through which they can be satisfied—land, labor, capital, materials, and power—are scarce. The central problem of economics is to determine how these resources shall be allocated; to decide what goods shall be produced. The goods produced by private enterprise, in a market economy, will be those that the consumer demands. In such an economy, the consumer exercises sovereign power. Each time he spends a dollar he casts a vote for the production of the thing he buys. His dollar votes, recorded in his purchases, express the character of his demands. Where his demand for a commodity declines, its price will fall. Where demand increases, price will rise. When producers, in their turn, compete against each other to obtain resources, those with products where demand is weak will find themselves outbid by those with products where demand is strong. Resources will be diverted from the one field to the other, away from producing goods that are wanted less and toward producing goods that are wanted more. Competition is thus the regulator that compels producers to follow the guidance of consumer choice.

Competition serves the consumer in other ways. It operates negatively to protect him against extortion. If the quality of the product offered by one producer is low, the quality of that offered by another may be high. If the price charged by one producer is high, that asked by another may be low. The consumer is not at the mercy of the one as long as he has the alternative of buying from the other. More than this, competition operates affirmatively to enhance quality and reduce price. The producer who wishes to enlarge his profits must increase his sales. To do so, he must offer the consumer more goods for less money. As he adds to quality and subtracts from price, his rivals are compelled to do the same. The changes which he initiates soon spread throughout the trade. Every consumer of its products gets more and pays less. Competition also makes for efficiency. It leads some producers to eliminate wastes and cut costs so that they may undersell others. It compels others to adopt similar measures in order that they may survive. It weeds out those whose costs remain high and thus operates to put production in the hands of those whose costs are low. As the former are superseded by the latter, the general level of industrial efficiency is accordingly enhanced. Competition is congenial to material progress. It keeps the door open to new blood and new ideas. It communicates to all producers the improvements made by any one of them. Competition is cumulative in its effects. When competitors cut their prices, consumers buy more goods, output increases, and unit costs may decline. The lower prices compel producers to seek still further means of cutting costs. The resulting gains in efficiency open the way to still lower prices. Goods are turned out in increasing volume, and the general plane of living is raised.

Competition is thus held to be a stern disciplinarian. It has long been recognized, however, that there still is need, in a competitive economy, for public controls. The existence of competition is not always assured. Many firms may agree among themselves that they will not compete. Two or more firms may combine to make a single unit. One or a few firms may come to dominate an industry, through the employment of unfair methods or through the enjoyment of special advantages. If the consumer is to reap the benefits of competition, government must make sure that competition is maintained.

Opposite to the benefits of competition are the evils of monopoly. Monopoly prevents the allocation of resources in accordance with the pattern of consumer choice. The monopolist is likely to increase his profit by raising his price. He will then limit his output to the quantity that the market will take at the price that he has fixed. Consumers who would be willing to purchase larger quantities of his product at a lower price are left, instead, to buy goods that are wanted less. Resources are thus diverted from those things which the community prefers to those which are, at best, a second choice. The resources that are excluded from the superior occupation compete with others for employment in inferior ones and their productivity declines. Monopoly, moreover, affords the consumer no protection against extortion. The monopolist may persist in offering inferior quality at a high price, since the purchasers of his product lack the alternative of turning to other sources of supply. He may obtain his profit, not by serving the community, but by refusing to serve it. Monopoly inflicts no penalty on inefficiency. The monopolist may eliminate wastes and cut costs, but he is under no compulsion to do so. Through inertia, he may cling to accustomed techniques. His hold upon the market is assured. Monopoly, as such, is not conducive to progress. The large firm may engage in research and invent new products, materials, methods, and machines. But when it possesses a monopoly, it will be reluctant to make use of these inventions if they would compel it to scrap existing equipment or if it believes that their ultimate profitability is in doubt. The monopolist may introduce innovations and cut costs, but instead of moving goods by reducing prices he is prone to spend large sums on alternative methods of promoting sales. His refusal to cut prices deprives the community of any gain. Monopoly impedes the improvement of levels of living. Because it does not compel the enhancement of quality or the reduction of price, because it fails to penalize inefficiency, because it is not conducive to progress, it makes the total output of goods and services smaller than it otherwise would be.

The maintenance of competition protects the community against the evils of monopoly. But this is not enough, for harm may also be done by the behavior of competitors. Competing sellers and competing buyers may not be equally well informed, and those who possess information may take advantage of those who lack it. Sellers and buyers may not be equally able to bargain, and those who are strong may impose upon those who are weak. Sellers seeking present profits and buyers seeking present satisfactions may waste scarce natural resources, thus impairing the well-being of future generations. Government must therefore be concerned, not only with the preservation of competition, but also with the ways in which men compete. It must act to equip traders with accurate information, to protect the weak against the strong, and to safeguard future needs against present wastes. Public control is thus required to facilitate the operation of competitive markets and to protect them against abuse. . . .

Forms of Control

The purposes for which government applies controls to business are many: maintenance of internal order, defense against external aggression, preservation of individual freedom, reduction of inequality of income, assurance of economic stability and social security, and improvement of consumer welfare. It is only with measures adopted for the last of these purposes, and with those related to them and affecting them, that the present volume is concerned.

To promote the welfare of consumers, levels of living must be raised; men must be given more leisure in which to enjoy more goods and services. To this end, waste must be reduced, efficiency increased, and costs cut; innovation must be encouraged, new methods developed, and new products introduced; quality must be improved and prices cut. The oldest and most comprehensive form of control applied to business for this purpose is that of maintaining competition. In particular industries, however, policy has substituted administrative control of enterprise as a regulator, or substituted public for private enterprise. In important fields, moreover, controls have modified competition in a variety of other ways.

Controlling Monopoly

Government has sought, in general, to maintain competition. It has preserved freedom of entry into markets, forbidden agreements to curtail production or fix prices, broken up existing combinations and prevented the formation of new ones, and outlawed competitive methods that would destroy competition and make for monopoly. . . .

In a few industries, notably those providing transport and public utility services, government has accepted monopoly as unavoidable, and has substituted administrative regulation for competition as a method of control. This has involved control of entry and abandonment, of securities and accounts, of the quality of service and the level of the structure of rates. In transport, this type of control has been retained even though the field has grown increasingly competitive. In the case of radio and television, regulation is necessitated by the shortage of desirable channels; it has to do with problems of organization, technology, and service that are incidental to the allocation of airspace. . . .

In industries where monopoly is inevitable, public enterprise affords an alternative to administrative regulation. Its present scope, in the United

States, is small. In a few fields, such as the postal service, public enterprise is traditional. In others, it is largely an outgrowth of depression and war. The case in which it is at issue today is electric power. . . .

Controlling Competition

Honesty in business dealings must be assured. Consumers must not be cheated, investors swindled, or tradesmen deprived of sales by the crookedness of their competitors. Government has therefore sought to raise the plane of competition by preventing fraud. To this end, it has established standards, forbidden adulteration and misrepresentation, required publicity, inspected business operations, and regulated organized exchanges. It is also necessary, in the interest of future generations, to prevent competitive enterprises from employing wasteful methods in the exploitation of natural resources. For this reason, government requires observance of conservation practices. . . .

Competition has been moderated, finally, as a means of promoting the development of new industries, relieving the distress of declining industries, preserving small enterprises, and increasing the profits of organized producing groups. To these ends, government has limited entry to the market, controlled output, fixed prices, and provided other sorts of subsidies.

The Evolution of the Corporate Liberal State: A Radical Critique

WILLIAM APPLEMAN WILLIAMS

The triumph of the corporation, and the creation of an oligarchy of firms within each sector of the economy, was a natural outcome of the principles of possessive individualism operating in a competitive marketplace. Such a marketplace has an ecology of its own, and that largely explains why businessmen found Darwinism such a useful ideology at the end of the nineteenth

Reprinted by permission of Quadrangle Books from *The Great Evasion* by William Appleman Williams, copyright © 1964 by William Appleman Williams.

century. The analogy with nature is more helpful, however, if it is made on a less grandiose scale than that employed by the Social Darwinists. The ecological balance of the marketplace is predicated upon a coincidence between the interest and the need of the giants to accumulate capital and the desire of the defeated entrepreneurs to retain, and of the would-be businessman to attain, some measure of citizenship in the capitalist society. This convergence of interest and need produced what Marx called the modern joint-stock company, usually referred to as the corporation.

In recent years, largely as part of the propaganda battle with the Soviet Union, this broad process has been praised as People's Capitalism. The slogan has not generated much enthusiasm because most people realize that the average purchase of stock does not buy any significant share in the decision-making process of the system. Indeed, the campaign to sell the idea of People's Capitalism offers one of the more plaintive examples of the general failure of American capitalism to create a true community.

But it is true that capitalist principles operating in and through the corporation have served to impose a new and extensive rationality on the marketplace, and to boost the material output of the system far beyond anything previously attained. Marx himself seemed to stand in awe of what he called "the stupendous productive power" of corporation capitalism. Clearly enough, it has created—even without the final rationalization of cybernated production—the possibility of material affluence. . . .

Marx did not live long enough to speak explicitly about the national class created by the corporation, or about corporation capitalism's own particular expression of the phenomenon he called feudal socialism and bourgeois socialism when it appeared in the earlier eras of capitalism. It is not particularly difficult, however, to make the appropriate extrapolation of his central ideas. Corporation capitalism has clearly produced such a national class in the persons of the large corporation's directors, administrators, experts, and an associated group of politicians and intellectuals.

This contemporary system is far closer, in both the structural sense and in the nature of its national class, to the capitalism created during the age of mercantilism than to the society of nineteenth-century entrepreneurial capitalism. These similarities offer, indeed, a helpful insight into the essential difficulties confronted by modern American capitalism. On the one hand, the productive power of the corporation offers the means whereby the secular part of the outlook of mercantilism might be translated into action. But, on the other hand, the functioning of capitalism since the era of mercantilism has severely weakened—if not effectively destroyed—the inclusive social and moral conception of society that was an integral part of mercantilism; and it has, in addition, produced so many changes in the non-Metropolitan areas of the world that it is impossible any longer to sustain the imperial aspects of mercantilism.

Contemporary American corporation capitalism is comparable to the mercantilist system, not only in the sense that stockholding of consequence is highly concentrated in a tiny fraction of the adult population, but also in the more significant respect that wealth and participation in the decision-making process of the entire political economy are likewise consolidated within a very small group. Although some of their superficial reactions might indicate otherwise, Americans do not suffer in ignorance of these truths that their society is structured by and around the corporation, or that its affairs are generally managed by a small and powerful community composed of the leaders of the economic, the political, and the military sectors of the system.

The lack of any sustained, excited public criticism and opposition to the existing situation, however, is based on the performance of the national class as well as upon the dearth of well-defined and vigorously advocated alternatives, and upon the great difficulty of changing the central features of the system. This national class has a defensible record, for example, if capitalism (or socialism, for that matter) is defined in a loose and general way as an institutional arrangement for providing increasing access to a greater range of material goods and services. And that is precisely the primary way that the principles of capitalism do define achievement. When the resulting pattern of production and consumer credit is furthermore linked, as it always is, with the successful defense of the nation in two wars and one cold war, the argument obscures the costs and consequences of the performance—and even many of the outright failures—with the emotion of nationalism. This chain of reasoning results in a superficially impressive balance account that camouflages the elementary truth: if capitalism did its narrow economic cost accounting in the same way it does its general social cost accounting, the system would have gone bankrupt within two generations.

It nevertheless remains true that the national class of corporation capitalism, particularly as it has been influenced by the reformers that Marx might have called the corporation socialists, has in some respects performed in keeping with the ideals and the tradition of responsibility associated with mercantilism. This became more noticeable after it began, at the time of World War I, to absorb and integrate many of its critics within its own community of power. It of course used force against such heretics as Eugene Debs whenever they seemed to be winning significant support for a challenge to the system. But the critics who operated within the limits of capitalism have gradually been accepted as participating advisors (and even subordinate administrators), or effectively weakened by using their ideas while ignoring their persons. Coupled with the pressure exerted by such critics, this strategy employed by the national class ultimately created a framework of regulatory and compensatory legislation that included ground rules for the corporation and various kinds of minimum (and still insufficient) support and assistance for the sizable number of citizens not taken care of by the normal functioning of the system.

Most of these administrative and welfare provisions emerged as a result of the Great Depression, and have been sustained as part of the response to the more general challenge to the system manifested by the social and colonial revolutions which erupted in full force at the end of World War II. But the process itself began during the era of President William McKinley, Marcus Hanna, and the National Civic Federation at the turn of the century.

McKinley and Hanna were conservatives who perceived the need to create and maintain a consensus including all segments of the new corporation order, and to offer all such elements a minimum share of the benefits of the new system. They understood that the corporation was so powerful that it would destroy the social fabric if it operated unchecked in the fashion of the giant entrepreneurs of the nineteenth century. They were not reformers, and they undoubtedly erred in the direction of preserving what to them seemed the essential freedom of the corporation. But they did hold and act on the basic features of the broader view that was essential to the creation of a national class.

The National Civic Federation was an indirect outgrowth of the early efforts by corporation socialists to reform the system. In its early stages, at any rate, it was a catholic organization which included such labor leaders as Samuel Gompers, and such aristocrats with a tradition of *noblesse oblige* as young Franklin Delano Roosevelt, as well as corporation executives. Though it played a significant role in establishing the idea and the existence of a national class, it ultimately became a narrowly conservative organization. As this happened, the more perceptive members of the national class itself, as well as the reformers, attempted to achieve their objectives by operating in and through the Progressive movement.

As a coalition including nineteenth-century bourgeois reformers and men who accepted the order created by the corporation, the Progressive movement fluctuated between trying to protect the traditional entrepreneur and endeavoring to rationalize and reform the new system. The early result of this divided effort was a hodgepodge of legislation. While in some respects appropriate to both objectives, it did not culminate in any single coherent pattern. Part of it flowed from the leadership provided by strong presidents like Theodore Roosevelt and Woodrow Wilson. Other laws emerged from the initiative manifested (and the compromises reached) within state legislatures and the Congress. And still other parts of this legislation, including some of the most important laws, represented the efforts of the leaders of the corporation's national class to check the more militant critics by accepting—and managing—some rational reforms.

Prior to the Great Depression, the creation of the Federal Reserve System was probably the single most important achievement of the coalition of the national class and the reformers. Further legislation of a comparable nature was passed during the New Deal era. While sometimes spoken of as a revolution, the New Deal was in reality the culmination of the Progressive movement and represented an operating consensus among the most astute members of the national corporation class and the reformers (or corporation socialists). It saved rather than changed the system, and thus can fairly be considered the finest performance of the national class and its associated reformers.

While it warrants high praise within its own framework and limits, this effort did not overcome the structural economic difficulties of the system, it did not initiate institutional and policy reforms that evolved into solutions of such problems, it did not revitalize the capitalist conception of citizenship and representative government, and it did not transform corporation capitalism into an ethical and equitable community. These failures had been anticipated, moreover, by a few members of the national class, as well as by critics who analyzed the situation from a vantage point outside the coalition of corporation spokesmen and reformers. The reformers concentrated their attention on the conservatives and the radicals, and hence did not contribute as much as they might have to raising and answering the fundamental questions.

One of the most striking evaluations of the weaknesses of the system was offered during the 1920's by Herbert Clark Hoover. This facet of Hoover's performance as a member of the national class is usually overlooked, and he is seldom thought of as a social commentator along with such figures as Brooks Adams, Herbert Croly, or Walter Lippmann. The neglect is understandable in view of his far more active career as an economic and government leader, and his ill-deserved reputation as both the cause of the Great Depression and as the man who failed to stop it immediately. But the negligence obscures his several important insights into the failure of corporation capitalism to create a true community.

Hoover not only understood the nature of the problems which confronted the national class, but astutely recognized the dangers involved in the new corporation order. Provoked by his concern that no incisive, sustained effort was being made to control the inherent propensities of the system, he projected three possible avenues of devolution. If left to themselves to provide the membership and the policies of the national class, Hoover feared that the corporation leaders would produce an American form of fascism. If labor became predominant, on the other hand, the result would be socialism or some willy-nilly variation thereof that would be equally undesirable. If each broad interest group in the economy continued its evolving attitude of viewing the government as a marketplace in which to compete for its share of the gross wealth, then the system would ultimately be dominated by a state bureaucracy which would lack even the distinguishing characteristic of a positive ideology. And wars engendered by struggles for predominance in the world marketplace threatened to produce a tyranny of even graver proportions because of the increased role and influence of the military.

Wherever it came from, perhaps his Quaker family background and his education at Stanford, Hoover enjoyed a clear insight into the crucial importance of reinvigorating and strengthening the social, co-operative half of man if capitalism was to survive economically and create a true community. He did not propose to destroy the traditional capitalist definition of the ego in terms of possessive individualism in the competitive marketplace, but he did want to delimit and balance it by reasserting the social definition of man as an ethical, co-operative being. He thus proposed, as he tried to explain in a misleadingly titled and generally misread essay called *American Individual-*

ism, that American capitalism should cope with its economic problems by voluntaristic but nevertheless organized co-operation within and between each major sector of the economy. This would in turn revitalize social life and representative government.

As he made explicitly clear as early as 1919, Hoover was consciously trying to balance "the immutable human qualities" of "selfishness" and "altruism" through the use of man's will power and intelligence, and through a broad program of education. He faced the issue posed by the capitalist marketplace more directly than most of his contemporaries—or successors. If the system could not be made to work through self-control and "by cooperation," Hoover concluded at the end of World War I, then it would be "better that we accept German domination and confess the failure of our political ideas, acquiesce in the superiority of the German conception and send for the Germans to instruct us in its use." Having arrived at this estimate of the alternatives, Hoover committed himself to the proposition that the co-operative ideal could be realized in practice.

Hoover's failure to accomplish this gargantuan task was due less to the depression per se, or even to his own inability to act because of his deep-seated fears of driving the system into one of the cul-de-sacs he had spotted in advance, than to the inherent nature of the undertaking itself. Despite the austere nature of his style and personality, which seem to belie the very idea, Hoover was actually proposing to socialize capitalism without socializing the economic system. Whether this was really a contradiction in terms, and therefore an unrealizable vision, can be left a moot question; it is enough to point out that it would have been a Herculean task under the very best of circumstances. It was in effect an attempt to do under corporation capitalism what the mercantilists such as John Quincy Adams had tried, and ultimately failed, to do in the seventeenth and eighteenth centuries.

Unfortunately, neither Hoover nor others who shared the same general objective have been able to realize the goal. But a good many of the attempts to accomplish it, which are usually associated with President Franklin Delano Roosevelt and the New Deal (and subsequent variations thereon), have been derived from Hoover's own efforts. One of these, which has lately returned to favor, involves his persistent campaign to persuade American farmers to establish themselves as the equals of the industrial corporation (and the labor unions) by organizing co-operatives through which they could control their production and manage their marketing operations.

Another illustration of Hoover's foresight is offered by his militant opposition in the 1920's to turning the atmosphere, which he considered social property in the most elementary sense, over to the corporations as an arena in which they could stage a free-for-all over profits to the suffering of the citizen radio (and later television) listener. Hoover instituted strong restrictions on the radio industry while he was Secretary of Commerce; so strong, indeed, that they were overruled by the Attorney General after sustained protests from the corporations. The law substituted by the Congress was considerably less effective. But however weak and ineffective they have been in limiting the abuses of the industry, or in improving the quality of its product, the Federal Radio Commission and the later Federal Communications Commission owe their existence to Hoover's original willingness to act upon a broad conception of social responsibility. Similar actions initiated by Hoover, including the effort to establish good neighbor relations with Latin America, were expanded by later administrations which received most, if not all, of the credit for whatever successes they produced.

Hoover's most pertinent and trenchant criticism has been generally ignored by members of the national class, and even more noticeably by the reformers. The reason for this is that both groups have attempted to sustain the system by following the precise course of action that Hoover judged most severely as being inequitable and ultimately unsuccessful. This strategy of saving the system was initiated by some industrialists and reformers before World War I, and then agitated militantly by the farm bloc in the 1920's. Its central theme was that the government should give direct and indirect subsidies to sustain various functional groups of entrepreneurs in the marketplace, such funds to be provided by the taxpayers present and future.

Hoover assailed and fought such proposals on several grounds. They subjected the citizen to double payments for goods and services, since in addition to the price paid over the counter, the consumer-taxpayer contributed to the same firms through the internal revenue service. Such subsidies also opened the door to, and actually legalized, wholesale raids on the federal treasury— meaning the pocketbook of the public. And they would, at least in Hoover's mind, lead to the kind of bureaucratic state capitalism that he considered so dangerous because it pointed toward fascism or some variation thereof. Hoover insisted that saving capitalism by juggling subsidies drawn from the taxpayer would ultimately "lead to the destruction of self-government," because as the government became so intimately involved in the system the citizen would lose his ability to act independently. His own self-interest would become so intimately bound to the government-corporation complex that the alternatives he was offered would concern only means rather than ends.

Hoover's analysis and warnings were lost or discounted as the subsidy approach was adopted and institutionalized during the crisis of the depression. It may have been impossible for corporation capitalism to have sustained itself in any other fashion, but the results nevertheless make it necessary to evaluate the system's material achievements in the light of its general inability to create an ethical and equitable community. *This failure evolved from the decision to shore up the corporation political economy by using the government to accumulate social capital from the taxpayer. This capital was then used to maintain the existing pattern of private control over the system. The government thus adapted the corporation's technique of accumulating capital from individual entrepreneurs without offering or providing such investors any significant share in making basic decisions.* Instead of socializing the system without socializing property, the result was to socialize the accumulation of capital without socializing control of the capital.

Confronted with the threatened demise of the system itself in the Great Depression, the coalition of the national class and the reformers undertook to save and rationalize the existing order through a further expansion of the marketplace and a vastly enlarged collection and use of taxes. The United States became a tax state in the fullest sense: the rules for collecting the funds, and the budget by which they were allocated, became in effect the X-ray photographs of the structure of the system and the priorities by which it operated.

In thus socializing the accumulation of capital, however, the New Deal did not socialize either the decisions concerning the allocation of that capital or the distribution of wealth in the United States. Even moderately heavy taxation of the upper class, for example, did not come during the reform period of the New Deal, but only as the nation prepared to enter World War II. And as that action was undertaken, moreover, the New Deal also extended the income tax to the middle and lower income classes on a retrogressive basis. The national class clearly had vastly more to say about the allocation of these funds than the citizens who paid them; and, since the funds had by definition to be used primarily for sustaining the key productive elements in the established order, the industrial corporation, the giant agricultural units, and other large operators received fantastically greater returns on their investment in taxes than the individual or small entrepreneur.

This expansion of the tax base occurred between 1939, when four million units were liable to pay, through 1941, when 17.6 million were obligated, to 1944, when the number so bound reached 42.4 million. The retrogressive nature of the resulting system is revealed in many ways. The tax paid in 1957 by the average family in the poorest fifth of the population, which was 3.3 per cent, for example, was clearly a greater burden than the 13.7 per cent paid by the average family in the richest fifth of the society. The tax ratio between poor and wealthy was 1:4, whereas the income ratio was approximately 1:11.

Another indication of the nature of the system is provided by comparing the taxes collected from Americans who earn between $1 and $4,000 with the amount spent by the federal government on welfare programs. The sum collected from the poor during 1958 was $6.037 billion. The government spent a total of $4.509 billion on all its public assistance programs, its public health operations, its aid to education, and all other welfare programs. That sum includes, furthermore, half the cost of farm supports and half the total spent on housing programs. It is thus apparent that the poorest people are not only paying their own way on welfare, but are providing part of the public assistance for the middle- and upper-class citizens.

The high income groups are of course entitled to those benefits. The issue here is how the tax system instituted by the New Deal and sustained by later reform administrations is skewed to favor the higher income groups. This can be seen even more directly from figures for the top 20 per cent of the income earners. They received 45.7 per cent of all personal income before taxes in 1959, and still had 43.8 per cent of it after taxes. And when the vast sums deducted from gross incomes as business expenses, including entertainment as well as depreciation, are considered, the imbalance becomes even greater and more obvious. In the central area of tax collection and allocation, therefore, corporation capitalism has failed even to approximate an ethical and equitable system.

It has done little better in dealing with the problem of poverty. There is no conceivable ethical justification, or support in equity, for either the kind or the extent of poverty that exists today in the United States. It is a blot not only upon American society per se, but a standing monument to the inability of corporation capitalism to include everyone in its economic benefits, even though everyone contributes through taxes (and even voluntary welfare and medical gifts) to its operating capital. It is a system and a government which has *by its actions* given a higher priority to putting machines into space than to sustaining life within its own boundaries.

Even as subsidized, moreover, corporation capitalism has failed to sustain a viable economy. Significant and persistent unemployment continues, and many existing jobs will be destroyed or downgraded (and thereby dehumanized) if cybernation continues within the existing framework. The programs to cope with these current difficulties—let alone the problems clearly on the horizon—are inadequate in conception and insufficient in extent. The same judgment is warranted in connection with slum clearance (which has notoriously benefited the middle class and the wealthy rather than the poor), with metropolitan and continental transportation, with care of the sick and invalided, with programs for the young and aged alike, and with education in general.

Perhaps this failure of corporation capitalism to meet either the narrow economic or the broader social needs and challenges of contemporary America is most aptly typified in the almost obsessive concern with the growth rate of the system. Now the economy obviously has to grow if only to keep pace with population increases. But this definition of the problem is not really to the point, anymore than a discussion of the growth rate in terms of the current or projected Russian figure confronts the real issue. For the *existing* capacity of the established order is capable of producing enough to relegate the contemporary growth discussion to a secondary level. The real problems concern how to use that capacity, and how to initiate and sustain a dialogue about the further growth of what, for what, at what cost, and decided by whom through what process. Yet there is almost no candid debate about those matters which lie at the very heart of creating an ethical and equitable community.

By defining any and all changes needed to meet these and similar issues as being dangerous to the existing order, the leaders of the system are forced to make such alterations behind the scenes, if they make them at all. This extends the already extensive centralization of power within the national class and within the government per se. The result may well be the disappearance of the existing pattern of private control over social production and its replacement by a system of administrative control over bureaucratic production. This would most certainly not be socialism. It would not even be fascism, at least not of the kind evolved in Italy and Germany during the 1920's and 1930's. It would be a kind of eerie and distorted verification of Herbert Hoover's fear that the government in becoming the marketplace would also become the corporation to end all corporations. It would be a corporation, furthermore, controlled by inside administrators only fitfully checked or directed by the citizen through the political process.

All this serves to dramatize the extent to which representative government has already broken down under corporation capitalism. The logic of possessive individualism operating in a competitive marketplace is presently creating a system in which neither the entrepreneur nor the wage earner has a fulcrum upon which to rest his political lever. Political units no longer coincide even roughly with economic and social reality. Issues are of necessity cast, and men elected, within a framework that has a steadily *decreasing* relevance to the nature of problems, simply because the existing political ground rules require a multiple distortion of the issues in order to piece together the required number of electoral votes to win access to the top executive and administrative offices.

Though it presents a very serious problem that will not be solved simply through continued urbanization and industrialization, the issue of political organization per se is actually secondary. The heart of the problem lies in the question facing both major parties concerning the formulation of relevant alternatives within the limits of capitalist ideology. The corporation, as Marx pointed out, represents "private production without the control of private property." The stockholders do not formulate or choose between alternatives. Neither do the labor unions. And most certainly the taxpaying citizens do not. Marx was essentially correct: the corporation itself, and the political economy it dominates, rests upon the "command of social capital" through the "appropriation of social property" by the small decision-making community which makes up the national class of the system.

In theory, at any rate, this leadership community could involve the citizen in the decisions affecting the allocation of the social capital. In order to do so, however, the decision-makers would first have to admit candidly that the system operates on the basis of the appropriation of social capital from the taxpayer as well as from the individual investor. Then the national class would have to formulate its internal differences into competing programs and policies, and reorganize the political system around such groups. Then the citizen would have an opportunity to choose between the rival segments of the national class. This would be an improvement over the existing situation, to be sure, but it would still represent a very low order of representative government. For the citizen who supplies the capital would still be denied any significant part in formulating the choices.

Even this first step in rationalizing the existing system would require an open admission that the reality of the system has little if any relationshp to the ideology of the system. It would involve an acknowledgement that private property no longer provides the individual with any significant leverage upon the central decisions of the political economy. And to say that is to say that the individual no longer attains freedom through exercising his right to alienate part of himself as labor in a competitive marketplace. For the property he thereby acquires does not affect the marketplace, either directly or indirectly.

The principles of capitalism have produced a reality in which the principles no longer hold true. Man does not become human and free by acting within the axioms of possessive individualism and the competitive marketplace. Instead, he becomes alienated. He is free to choose only among alternatives, and on issues, which no longer effect the nature of the society. He is becoming a mere consumer of politics as well as a mere consumer of goods. The sharing of profits is mistaken for the sharing of direction and control of the enterprise itself, just as the sharing of the leader's charisma is mistaken for the sharing of power.

This process is the negative side of what Marx had in mind when he spoke of the "socialization from within" brought on by the corporation. The corporation has socialized the accumulation of capital: directly through the substitution of money rights for property (or control) rights, and indirectly by effecting a liaison through its national class with the government of the tax state. The system relies on social accumulation but tries to operate on the classical capitalist principle of private control. It is unable on this basis either to sustain efficient economic operation or to create an ethical and equitable community.

The Fiscal Crisis
of the State

JAMES O'CONNOR

The relations of production in capitalist society are antagonistic. Marx demonstrated that the antagonism springs from the basic contradiction of capitalism; on the one hand, capitalist production is intrinsically social in character; on the other hand, the means of production are privately owned—that is, production is for profit, not for use. This contradiction gives rise to the class struggle.

For Marx, the class struggle was conducted by the industrial working class

Reprinted from *Socialist Revolution*, I, 1, 2, January–February and March–April, 1970. By permission.

against the capitalist class at the point of direct production (and politically, as well) over the division of the social product into wages and profits. Since Marx wrote *Das Kapital* the world capitalist system has undergone a tremendous advance in the development of the forces of production and important changes in the relations of production, some of them foreseen by Marx, others not.

On the one side, production has become much more social; there has developed an incredibly complex world network of economic interdependency. The advanced social character of production in turn has led to higher forms of social integration—for example, the modern corporation integrates labor power drawn from dozens of different countries, and applied to thousands of specific tasks. On the other side, the means of production have become concentrated in fewer and fewer hands; small-scale industrial capital and medium-scale finance capital have merged into large-scale corporate capital. The basic contradiction of capitalism has therefore intensified; and since this contradiction gives rise to class struggle, class struggle has also intensified.

World capitalism has undergone other changes, changes in the arenas in which the class struggle is fought, and changes in the forms of struggle. In short, the class struggle has been diffused, fragmented, and displaced. The reason that the class struggle has been displaced is the higher form of social integration which has accompanied the intensified social character of production. . . .

The present article takes up the question of the growing movement of employees of the state, clients of the state, and others who must look to the state for that which they cannot provide for themselves, and which private capital cannot provide. Its major thesis is that the fusion of economic base and political superstructure in the current era has extended the class struggle from the sphere of direct production to the sphere of state administration, and transformed the forms of struggle. . . .

Progressively tighter budgets, falling real wages and salaries of state employees, and declining welfare expenditures and social services in general have unleashed a torrent of criticism against the state by employees, dependents, and others. Public employee unions grow by leaps and bounds. The American Federation of State, County and Municipal Employees grew from 150,000 members in 1950 to 400,000 today. Unions are calling more strikes, and strikes are fought for longer periods: in 1953 there were only thirty strikes against state and local governments; in 1966 and 1967, 152 and 181 strikes, respectively. In 1967–1968 the American Federation of Teachers alone conducted thirty-two major walkouts and mini-strikes which involved nearly 100,000 teachers.[1] In Massachusetts, state employees have created an organization which cuts across occupational and agency lines, and which has mounted a demand for a twenty percent wage and salary increase. In New York twenty-five percent of the city's union membership are public employees. In the past few years, whole towns and cities have been brought to a standstill as a result of general strikes of municipal employees.

[1] *American Teacher*, 52, 10, June, 1968.

Practical criticism of the state has not been confined to local general strikes, nor still less to traditional labor union activity. State clients and dependents have been compelled to conduct their struggles around budgetary issues in highly unorthodox ways. Today, there are few sectors of the state economy which remain unorganized. Welfare recipients have organized hundreds of welfare rights groups; student organizations have conducted militant struggles in small or large part over the control of the state budget for minority studies programs, student activities, and so on; blacks are struggling in countless ways to force the state to intervene on their behalf; public health workers, doctors, probation officers, prisoners, even patients in public mental hospitals have organized themselves, and seek better work facilities or better treatment and more finances and resources for themselves and the people whom they serve. And in New York there is growing collaboration between state workers and clients in the form of common, militant action against the state by welfare workers and welfare recipients.

On the other side, there is developing a serious revolt against high taxation. The forms of the present tax revolt are many and varied; the core cities are demanding that suburban commuters pay their "fair share" of city expenditures, and the suburbanites are resisting attempts to organize their communities into metropolitan governments; working class residential districts organize tax referendums against downtown business interests; and property owners vote into office politicians who promise to reduce property tax burdens.

All of these activities—the demands mounted by state workers and dependents, on the one hand, and the tax revolt, on the other—both reflect and deepen the fiscal crisis of the state, or the contradiction between expenditures and taxation. Yet, by and large, these struggles have not been fought along class lines, and therefore do not necessarily pose a revolutionary challenge to the United States ruling class. In fact, the popular struggle for the control of state expenditures has been led by liberal forces, and, to a much lesser degree, by militant black and radical forces. And the tax revolt has been all but monopolized by the right wing. . . .

Government Expenditures: A Political Analysis

The developing economic struggles against the state are rooted in the structural contradictions of United States capitalism. Full comprehension and evaluation of these struggles requires a political framework for an analysis of the state budget. Budgetary theory is a branch of the theory of the state, and thus a brief sketch of the nature of state power is needed.

How do the main production relations in the United States express themselves politically? In the first place, the state is the economic instrument of the dominant stratum of the ruling class—the owners and controllers of the large corporations, who have organized themselves along both interest group and class lines.

Interest group organization, activity, and participation in the state have been studied by McConnell, Hamilton, Kolko, Engler, and others.[2] In Hamilton's words, "there are currently associations of manufacturers, of distributors, and of retailers; there are organizations which take all commerce as their province; and there are federations of local clubs of businessmen with tentacles which reach into the smaller urban centers and market towns. All such organizations are active instruments in the creation of attitudes, in the dissemination of sound opinion, and in the promotion of practices which may become widespread."[3]

In essence, these organizations are self-regulatory private associations which are ordinarily organized along industry, rather than regional or other lines, owing to the national character of commodity markets. More often than not, these industry groups use the state to mediate between their members, as well as to provide needed credits, subsidies, technical aid, and general support. Some of the key industry and interest groups are the highway lobby (automobiles, oil, rubber, glass, branches of construction, etc.), the military lobby, oil, cotton textiles, railroads, airlines, radio and television, public utilities, banking and brokerage. In agriculture, wheat, cotton, sugar, and other growers, together with cattlemen, are also organized into industry associations.

These and other interest groups have appropriated numerous small pieces of state power through a "multiplicity of intimate contacts with the government."[4] They dominate most of the so-called regulatory agencies at the Federal, State, and local levels. Many bureaus within the Departments of Agriculture and Interior, the Bureau of Highways, and a number of Congressional committees. Their specific interests are reflected in the partial or full range of policies of hundreds of national and State government agencies, for example, the Interstate Commerce Commission and other regulatory bodies, Department of Defense, Corps of Engineers, United States Tariff Commission, and the Federal Reserve Bank. "What emerges as the most important political reality," McConnell writes in a summary of the politics of interest groups, "is an array of relatively separated political systems, each with a number of elements. These typically include: (1) a federal administrative agency within the executive branch; (2) a heavily committed group of Congressmen and Senators, usually members of a particular committee or subcommittee; (3) a private (or quasi-private) association representing the agency clientele; (4) a quite homogeneous constituency usually composed of local elites. Where dramatic conflicts over policy have occurred, they have appeared as rivalries among the public administrative agencies, but the conflicts are more conspicuous and less important than the agreements among these systems. The most frequent solution to conflict is jurisdictional demarcation and establishment

[2] Grand McConnell, *Private Power and American Democracy,* New York, 1966; Walton Hamilton, *The Politics of Industry,* New York, 1957; Gabriel Kolko, *Railroads and Regulation, 1877–1916,* Princeton (N.J.), 1965; Robert Engler, *The Politics of Oil,* New York, 1961.
[3] Hamilton, op. cit., p. 9.
[4] McConnell, op. cit., p. 279.

of spheres of influence. Logrolling, rather than compromise, is the normal pattern of relationship."[5]

By itself, interest group politics is inconsistent with the survival and expansion of capitalism. For one thing, "the interests which keep [the interest groups] going," Hamilton writes, "are too disparate, and the least common denominator of action is too passive to bring into being a completely cohesive union."[6] For another, interest consciousness obviously leads to contradictory policies; enduring interest groups require a sense of "responsibility"—that is, class consciousness. For example, the attempt by regulatory agencies to maintain profitable conditions in a particular industry tends to freeze the pattern of resource allocation, establish monopoly conditions, and so on, which in turn retards capital accumulation and expansion in the economy as a whole. Foreign economic expansion thus becomes increasingly important, as a key mode of economic growth and as a way to transform interest group conflict into interest group harmony. And foreign expansion clearly requires a class conscious political directorate.

The *class* organization of corporate capital—both its private activity and participation in the state—have been studied by Williams, Weinstein, Kolko, Domhoff, Eakins, and others.[7] These writers have shown that increasing instability and inefficiency attendant upon capitalist production increased investment risk and uncertainty, contributed to crises and depressions, and led to a deficiency of aggregate demand. By the turn of the century, and especially during the New Deal, it was apparent to the vanguard corporate leaders that some form of rationalization of the economy was necessary. And as the twentieth century wore on, the owners of corporate capital generated the financial ability, learned the organizational skills, and developed the ideas necessary for their self-regulation as a class.

Thus, it was a class conscious corporate directorate which controlled the War Industry Board during World War I, parts of the NRA and AAA, and the Office of War Mobilization, the last of the World War II planning agencies. Class conscious corporate capital today profoundly influences or controls the Department of Defense, agencies within the Department of Commerce and State, Treasury Department, Council of Economic Advisers, and Bureau of the Budget. Owing to the necessity of reconciling and compromising conflicts within the corporate ruling class and to the complex and wide-ranging nature of the interests of this class, policy is not dictated by a single directorate but rather a multitude of private, quasi-public, and public agencies.

[5] Ibid., p. 244.

[6] Hamilton, op. cit., p. 9.

[7] William Appleman Williams, *The Contours of American History*, New York, 1961; James Weinstein, *The Corporate Ideal in the Liberal State, 1900–1918*, Boston, 1968; Gabriel Kolko, *The Triumph of Conservatism, 1900–1916*, Glencoe (Ill.), 1963; William Domhoff, *Who Rules America?* Englewood Cliffs (N.J.), 1967; David Eakins, "The Development of Corporate Liberal Policy Research 1885–1965," Ph.D. dissertation, University of Wisconsin, 1966.

The theoretical issues in the analysis of ruling class, interest groups, and power elite are discussed in: W. Wesolowski, "Class Domination and the Power of Interest Groups," *Polish Sociological Bulletin*, No. 3–4, 1962; "Ruling Class and Power Elite," *Polish Sociological Bulletin*, No. 1, 1965.

Policy is formulated within the highly influential Business Advisory Council, in key ruling class universities and policy planning agencies such as the Foreign Policy Association and the Committee for Economic Development, and by the corporate dominated political parties, and translated into law through legislation written and introduced by the Federal executive. The President and his key aides thus have the supreme task of interpreting corporate ruling class interests, and translating these interests into action, not only in terms of immediate economic and political needs, but also in terms of the relations between corporate capital on the one side, and labor and small capital, on the other.

This is the second way the production relations are expressed politically—the regulation of the social relations between classes in the interests of maintaining the social order as a whole. Around the turn of the century, labor, socialist, and populist forces posed a potentially serious threat to American capitalism. In a series of political moves designed to prevent popular movements from "removing the extremes of society"—capital and wage labor—the corporate leaders and the political directorate sought "to weaken their antagonisms and transform them into a harmonious whole." In Lelio Basso's words, "capitalism can function only thanks to the permanent intervention of the state to organize the markets and ensure the process of accumulation."[8] The political meaning of this "permanent intervention" is that all elements of the population must be integrated into a coherent system, not rejected by it. Far and away the most important element is organized labor, which was taught a responsible attitude toward corporate capital, and society as a whole. Specifically, this required regular cooperation between the leaders of organized labor, the corporations, and the state to head off mass social movements, transform collective bargaining into an instrument of corporate planning, guarantee a high level of employment and wages commensurate with productivity advances, and maintain labor's reproductive powers, not only with regard to the level of private consumption, but also social insurance, health, education, and general welfare.

Class conflict is thus bureaucratized, encapsulated, administered; qualitative demands originating on the shop floor are transformed by union leaders into quantitative demands which do not threaten "managerial prerogatives;" contradictions between labor and capital at the point of production are displaced or deflected into other spheres. Corporate capital's agencies for regulating the relations between labor and themselves are numerous—the National Labor Relations Board, National Mediation Board, Federal Mediation and Conciliation Service, Department of Labor, Social Security Administration, Department of Health, Education, and Welfare, Congressional committees and subcommittees, and State Employment agencies are some of the most important.

The state also regulates the relations between big capital and small capital,

[8] Lelio Basso, "State and Revolution Reconsidered," *International Socialist Journal*, February, 1968, p. 82.

between capital based in different regions, and between capital in expanding sectors of the economy and capital in contracting sectors. Corporate capital requires the political support of local and regional capital for its national and international programs, and thus cannot afford to antagonize the latter needlessly; subsidies must be granted to declining industries and to capital in underdeveloping regions. Deeply involved in managing relations within the ruling class as a whole, and permanently engaged in financing small capital support for corporate capital are, among other agencies, the Department of Agriculture, the Department of Commerce, many Congressional committees, and Federal grant-in-aid programs.[9]

These aspects of state power, which are not unique to monopoly capitalism, but which have taken special forms in the twentieth century, are many of them extremely expensive. Further, excepting interest group economic needs, to which the elected branch is highly responsive, the new functions of the state require a strong executive branch, and executive control of the state budget, because they require over-all planning. The growth of the executive branch, the multiplication of its functions, the decline of Congressional-initiated legislation, the growth of bureaucratically managed governments at the State and local levels, the development of city manager governments, and the spread of the giant supra-municipal authorities—that is, the major trend of our times which signifies the removal of decision-making from politics and the substitution of bureaucratic and administrative rule—is a familiar story. . . .

In the late nineteenth and twentieth centuries, technological innovations in production and the need to harmonize and stabilize production relations again revolutionized the state finances and the budgetary principles on which they were based. The development of science and organized technology, the accumulation of large blocks of capital, and the concentration and integration of the work force needed to be regulated and controlled. As state capitalism and monopolistic industry developed, the budgetary principles of the liberal state were gradually discarded.

One change was the substitution of direct for indirect taxation; another was the surrender of the principle of balanced budgets; still another was the acceptance of an inconvertible paper monetary standard and a new role for loan finance. But most important, there was a steady expansion of state expenditures and an increase in the number and variety of state economic functions.

A brief review of the changing relationships between the representative and executive branches of the state is needed to fully comprehend the charac-

---

[9] There is a final aspect of state power, the financial dependence of the state on the banks and other financial institutions whose cooperation is necessary to float the state debt. Only in times of national emergency has this dependence dissolved; for example, during World War II when the Treasury compelled the Federal Reserve system to support Federal bond prices. At the State and local level, the dependence of the state on finance capital for capital funds is total, for reasons to be taken up below.

ter and significance of the revolutionary change in the budget principles of monopoly capitalism. It will be recalled that the budget was transformed into an instrument of the financial control of the Crown by the rising middle classes in Britain during their struggle for political representation and, finally, political dominance. In the United States, revolutionary warfare eliminated the Crown, removing any analogous development. From the very beginning, there existed a certain harmony between Congress and the executive because both represented more or less perfectly the interests of local and regional capital. The budget was from the start the expression of the material interests of the planter and merchant classes and, later, the farmers, and was always a source of private profit. By the late nineteenth century, the ascendancy of national capital and the giant regional interest groups began to drive a wedge between the representative and executive branches of the Federal government. In general, the latter finally became the instrument of national capital while the former never ceased to represent small, regional and local capital. Congress, which had not found it necessary to jealously guard its own interests and power, compared with the British Parliament, became increasingly unable to exercise its prerogatives and actually helped to transfer them to the executive. Especially since the turn of the century, the control exercised by the representative body over appropriations has become increasingly imperfect. The ways in which Congress has disabled itself include the establishment of revolving funds, the creation of government corporations, the refusal to prohibit transfers between appropriations, the authorization of the use of departmental receipts without limitation of amount, and the voting of lump-sum appropriations.[10] Attempts to reestablish control by way of large numbers of specific appropriations "far from securing to Congress that completeness of financial control which is . . . its constitutional birthright, has served only to make the law less certain and to satisfy Congress with the name, rather than the substance of power."[11] Congressional control after funds have been appropriated has been equally imperfect. It is instructive to compare the situation in the United States with that in Britain, where parliamentary control after appropriations is relatively secure and the House of Commons is able to ensure that its policies are carried out "accurately, faithfully, and efficiently."[12]

Meanwhile the executive branch of the Federal government has been eager to transform the budget into an instrument of national economic planning in accordance with the needs of national capital. With this aim in mind, the executive has hurried along the consolidation of its own financial powers by mingling appropriations, bringing forward the unexpended balance of former appropriations and backward the anticipated balance of future appropriations, and by incurring coercive deficiencies.[13]

---

[10] Lucius Wilmerding, Jr., *The Spending Power, a History of the Efforts of Congress to Control Expenditures*, New Haven, 1943, p. 193.

[11] Ibid., p. 195.

[12] Basil Chubb, *The Control of Public Expenditures*, London, 1952, p. 1.

[13] Wilmerding, op. cit., p. 194.

Changes in the formal character of the state budget, however, have been the major steps toward executive financial control. At least three budgetary changes deserve mention. The first was the introduction of the "administrative budget," which coordinates expenditures proposed by the executive, and the creation of the Bureau of the Budget by the Budget and Accounting Act of 1920. The administrative budget is the basic instrument which coordinates the various activities of the Congressional committees which in turn are responsive to the specific industrial, regional, and other interests of private capital. It is the chief mode of "management and control by the Executive and Congress over activities financed with federal funds . . . which (once approved) becomes a tool of Executive control over the spending of the various departments, agencies, and government corporations."[14] In effect, the Act took the initiative away from Congress and gave it to the President. The class conscious, corporate dominated Institute for Government Research led the way. Many decades passed before the Congress was willing to support the idea of coordinated executive expenditure proposals, and historically the individual executive departments had dealt directly with the specific congressional committees. Thus it was not until well into the twentieth century (putting aside the post-Revolutionary War period) that the state was sufficiently independent of specific private interests to begin to impose its own discipline, or the discipline of private capital as a whole, on the private economy.

The second change in the increasing executive domination of the budget is the gradual substitution of "line-time" budgets with "program" budgets. Line-time budgets are the net result of many specific competing forces, and classify expenditures in terms of the items to be purchased, while program budgets classify outlays on the basis of outputs and the resources necessary to yield certain outputs, and hence require some measure of resource costs—that is, some planning. The idea of program budgeting was first put forth in 1912 by the Taft Commission on Economy and Efficiency and the first applications were made by the Tennessee Valley Authority and the Navy Department. Beginning in 1961, program budgeting was introduced in the Department of Defense. For fiscal year 1968, twenty-three major departments and agencies were instructed to prepare program budgets, and many other departments were encouraged to do so.[15]

From an administrative point of view, program budgeting lays the basis for the application of marginal analysis and hence is attractive to many economists. Smithies, for example, writes that "budgeting is essentially an economic problem in solving as it does the allocation of scarce resources among almost insatiable and competing demands."[16] In supporting program budgeting, this school of thought denies that budgetary issues are political issues and sees little or no difference between the allocation of resources by the household

[14] David J. Ott and Attiat F. Ott, *Federal Budget Policy*, Washington, 1965, p. 6.
[15] David Novick, editor, *Program Budgeting—Program Analysis and the Federal Budget*, Cambridge (Mass.), 1965, passim.
[16] Arthur Smithies, *The Budgetary Process in the United States*, New York, 1955, pp. xiv–xv.

or business firm, on the one hand, and the state, on the other. Critical analysis of the state and the state budget per se is replaced by an implicit acceptance of the given balance of private interests as reflected in the given composition of the budget. As one defender of program budgeting writes, "marginal analysis points to the need for continual reassessment of the pattern of expenditure *at the margin,* rather than being beguiled by arguments concerning the over-all 'necessity' of a particular program."[17] Other economists, however, clearly understand that the real significance of program budgeting is that it strengthens the executive office of the president not only in relation to the federal agencies but also to the Congress. The program budget, according to Burkhead, "becomes a technique, not for management at the operating level, but for the centralization of administrative authority."[18]

The third step toward executive control of the state finances was taken in 1963 when for the first time the budget contained an analysis of expenditures and receipts on a national income accounting basis. The national income budget is a more perfect measure of the impact of federal spending on general economic activity because it excludes purely financial credit transactions and accounts for receipts and expenditures at the time of their economic impact rather than when cash receipts and payments are actually made. The national income budget represents an explicit recognition of the integral relation between the budget and the private economy and is a necessary pre-condition for over-all fiscal planning.

In Congress there is no immediate sense of a loss of power. Congressional procedures for appropriating federal funds have remained unchanged for decades and the budget is still viewed by the representative branch as a set of individual and unrelated parts. It remains true that "taxes and expenditures are decided separately by the separate committees in each house, and although the bills on taxes and appropriations are passed by vote of the whole House and whole Senate, there is little evidence that the two groups of bills are related closely to each other when they are considered."[19] Similarly, the benefits and costs of the programs authorized in the specific appropriations bills are never analyzed or judged in relation to each other. Nor are the bills discussed or studied in detail by the full committees, and full house debate is rare. Each subcommittee of the House Appropriations Committee, for example, is still concerned with a different division of the government and "it is quite natural that a group of men familiar with a particular division of the executive branch will be inclined to take a parochial interest in its welfare."[20] In any event, only about thirty percent of Federal expenditures is within Congressional discretion to change from year to year. Finally, in recent years the military budget and weapons policies have been determined by the

[17] James R. Schlesinger, *The Political Economy of National Security,* New York, 1960, p. 109.
[18] Jesse Burkhead, *American Economic Review,* LVI, No. 4, September, 1966, p. 943, review of Novick, op. cit.
[19] Ott and Ott, op. cit., p. 36.
[20] Schlesinger, op. cit., p. 111.

Department of Defense and the Armed Services Committees without any critical examination by the Congress. In 1968, only two witnesses at the House Armed Services Committee hearings on the military budget were not Pentagon employees.

In one sense, Congress still effectively "represents" the various parochial interests. But the executive increasingly interprets and coordinates these interests. This is an extremely subtle process and has few formal expressions, even though informal control is substantial. We have already reviewed the major techniques of control, and here we can do no more than sketch some of the more obvious informal control mechanisms. For one thing, any bill initiated by an individual congressman without "legislative clearance" from the Budget Bureau faces enormous obstacles. The Bureau has considerable control over the direction and timing of federal obligations incurred because it is the apportioning authority, hence augmenting its powers even more. During the Kennedy years, the Bureau, the Treasury, and the Council of Economic Advisors were organized into an informal group with the responsibility for overall fiscal planning, and began to exercise a powerful influence on the budget and general fiscal decisions. Thus increasingly budget policy is formulated by the executive without any attempt to revolutionize or "modernize" the appropriations process in the Congress itself. The effect of this shift in financial control to the executive has been succinctly described by Schlesinger: "The Congress, secure in its belief that the basic legislation has established policy, may view its annual consideration of the budget formulated by the experts simply from the standpoint of assuring the most economical attainment of legislative goals. Thus policy formulation, which is so intimately connected with the appropriations levels, may slip into organizational limbo and finally be unconsciously seized by the Bureau of the Budget—the one organization that, in theory, should be concerned with economy and efficiency, and should be divorced entirely from policy formulation." The general result is that budget issues cease to be political issues, and the budget becomes a more perfect planning instrument by the executive. In the past two decades, no major program introduced during previous administrations has been eliminated. The Republican administration in the 1950's even failed to reverse the upward trend of federal spending, including the expansion of outlays in the health, education, and welfare fields. In the contemporary period, only the executive can interpret the needs of private capital and private interests as a whole, and effectively act on these interpretations. So far as the operation of bourgeois democratic institutions is concerned, there is no need to add anything to the conclusion of one economist: "The relationship between the legislative and executive branches largely determines the success or failure of democratic government. Hence, the budget, because it is at the same time the most important instrument of legislative control and executive management, is at the very core of democratic government." . . .[21]

---

[21] Harold D. Smith, "The Budget as an Instrument of Legislative Control and Executive Management," *Public Administration Review,* 4, No. 3, Summer, 1944, p. 181.

Government and Business:
The Political Economy of the Budget

In specific, the budget reflects the particular and general economic needs of corporate capital, on the one hand, and the general political needs of the ruling class as a whole, on the other. Preliminary to an investigation of these needs, and their budgetary reflections, it should be stressed that there are no specific budgetary items which mirror *exclusively* any particular or general need. There are no hard and fast theoretical categories applicable to the analysis of the budget because there are no precise, real, historical budgetary categories. Individual expenditure items do not reflect with absolute precision any particular interest; quite the contrary, a particular item may express imperfectly a multitude of interests. To cite one outstanding example, state financed railroad construction in the nineteenth century was determined by a combination of related economic and political factors. The predominant motive for the nationalization and consolidation of the transcontinental railroads by the Canadian government in the 1920's was the necessity to underwrite business losses owing to a decline in profitability. The primary motives for the first United States transcontinental railroad were the opening of new markets, new sources of raw material supply, and the settlement of new lands. Railroads were built in the great majority of export economies very simply to get raw materials out of the country. Yet in India, "really large-scale [railroad] construction began . . . only after the popular uprising of 1857–59, when the colonialists fully grasped the significance of communication lines to maintain their domination."[22] Railroad construction in Russia bore a similar thrust, beginning in earnest in the 1860's after the Crimean War had revealed the military importance of good land transportation. Yet the decision to build the Trans-Siberian Railway was made only in 1891 when it became apparent that Britain was seeking to penetrate the markets of South Manchuria.

Today, there are few state expenditures which fail to serve a number of different, although related ends. Johnson's War on Poverty aimed simultaneously to insure social peace, upgrade labor skills, subsidize labor training for the corporations, and help finance local governments. Highway expenditures complement private investments in manufacturing and distribution facilities, encourage new private investments, link up the major metropolitan centers in accordance with the needs of the Department of Defense, facilitate the mobility of labor, and provide a kind of social consumption—or goods and services consumed in common. Outlays on other forms of transport, communications, water supplies, utilities, and the like also simultaneously provide inputs to private capital and services to the working class. Nevertheless, it is useful to categorize specific expenditures into four major groups, not for purposes of exposition, but rather because there is always a preponderant

[22] A. I. Letovsky, *Capitalism in India: Basic Trends in Its Development*, Bombay, 1966, p. 46.

set of social forces determining the amount, type, and location of the particular facility.

The first major category of expenditures consists of facilities which are valuable to a specific industry, or group of related industries. These are projects which are useful to specific interests and whose financial needs are so large that they exceed the resources of the interests affected. They also consist of projects in which the financial outcome is subject to so much uncertainty that they exceed the risk-taking propensities of the interests involved. Finally, these are projects which realize external economies and economies of large-scale production for the particular industries.

These projects fall into two sub-categories: first, *complementary* investments; second, *discretionary* investments. Both types of investments, like private investments, increase the stock of tangible or intangible capital. But the first consists of facilities without which private projects would be unprofitable.[23] Complementary investments are determined completely by the rhythm of private capital accumulation, or by the spheres that private capital has chosen to expand and by the technical relations or coefficients between private investment and complementary activities. Complementary investments are thus a special form of private investment: their determination rests squarely on the determination of private commodity production and accumulation. And since private accumulation is increasingly social—since the economy is increasingly interdependent—there is no economic or technical limit on state expenditures for facilities which complement private facilities. The most dramatic example of complementary investments are infrastructure projects in backward capitalist economies which specialize in the production of one or two primary commodities for export. The relationship between state and private capital is here seen in its pure form. Private investments in agriculture and mining completely determine the location, scale, function, and degree of flexibility of infrastructure projects. Railroads, ports, roads, communication and power facilities are oriented to serve one or two industries making up the export sector.

The purpose of the second type of state investment is to provide incentives for private accumulation. In practice, there is no hard line drawn between complementary and discretionary investments; highway extensions, for example, facilitate the movement of goods and also encourage new investments. While complementary investments are part of the normal rhythm of capital accumulation, discretionary investments are ordinarily made during times of crisis—when profitable opportunities for capital as a whole are lacking, or in the event that declining industries depress certain regions. Both kinds of investments are oriented by profit, although the latter may or may not raise the rate of profit. . . .

---

[23] A further distinction can be made between state investments required to maintain or augment the production system at the current rate of profit, and state investments required to maintain the distribution system. These distinctions are not academic, but extremely important in the analysis of the generation and absorption of the economic surplus. The author is engaged in research in this area, which goes beyond the subject of the present essay.

The second major determinant of state expenditures stems from the immediate economic interests of corporate capital as a whole. The budgetary
expression of these interests takes many forms—economic infrastructure
investments, expenditures on education, general business subsidies, credit guarantees and insurance, social consumption, and so on. In the United States,
most of these forms appeared or developed fully only in the twentieth century,
although in Europe state capitalism emerged in an earlier period—in France,
during the First Empire, generalized state promotion buoyed the private economy; in Germany, state economic policy received great impetus from political
unification and war; in Italy, laissez-faire principles did not prevent the state
from actively financing and promoting accumulation in the major spheres of
heavy industry; and everywhere liberal notions of small, balanced budgets
and indirect taxation came face to face with the fiscal realities of wartime
economies.

In the United States, the budget remained small throughout the nineteenth
century; transportation investments were chiefly private, and natural resource,
conservation, public health, education and related outlays were insignificant.
The state served the economic needs of capital as a whole mainly in non-fiscal
ways—land tenure, monetary, immigration, tariff, and patent policies all
"represented and strengthened the particular legal framework within which
private business was organized,"[24] State subsidies to capital as a whole were
confined to the State government and local levels and were largely the product
of mercantile, rather than industrial capital, impulses.[25]

In the twentieth century, however, corporate capital has combined with
state capital to create a new organic whole. Corporate capital is not subordinated to state capital, or vice versa, but rather they are synthesized into a
qualitatively new phenomenon, rooted in the development of the productive
forces and the concentration and centralization of capital.[26] More specifically,
the rapid advance of technology has increased the pace of general economic
change, the risk of capital investments, and the amount of uncontrollable
overhead costs. Further, capital equipment is subject to more rapid obsolescence, and there exists a longer lead time before the typical investment is
in full operation and thus is able to pay for itself.[27] The development of the
production relations has also compelled corporate capital to employ state
power in its economic interests as a whole, and socialize production costs.
The struggles of the labor movement have reinforced the general tendency
for the rate of profit to decline and have thus compelled corporate capital

[24] Henry W. Broude, "The Role of the State in American Economic Development, 1820–1890,"
in Harry N. Scheiber, editor, *United States Economic History: Selected Readings,* New York,
1964.
[25] Louis Hartz, *Economic Policy and Democratic Thought: Pennsylvania, 1776–1860,* Cambridge (Mass.), 1948, pp. 290–291.
[26] This synthesis of corporate and state capital has profound implications for the generation
and absorption of the economic surplus, and therefore indirectly for the fiscal crisis. Following up this line of analysis, however, would lead us too far away from the framework of
the present article.
[27] Good general discussions of these tendencies can be found in: Shonfield, op. cit., p. 192
and John Kenneth Galbraith, *The New Industrial State,* Boston, 1967, passim.

to use the state to mobilize capital funds from the liquid savings of the general population. And, finally, the onset of general realization crises have forced large-scale business to use the budget to subsidize the demand for commodities. . . .

Another rising expense facing corporate capital as a whole consists of investments in economic infra-structure—plant and equipment for education and research; water, power, and similar projects; and harbor, air, and other transportation facilities. Specific industries or groups of related industries normally do not provide the political impetus for these expenditures, but rather regional or corporate capital as a whole does. These kinds of economic infra-structure ordinarily serve a wide variety of industries, either precede or coincide with private capital accumulation, and generate many-sided, long-term, economic effects. They are also capital-intensive projects that are characterized by large "indivisibilities"; they require large original capital outlays and normally are constructed in large, discrete units. To cite one example, the Boeing 747 jetliner will make most existing air terminal facilities obsolete, and will require the construction of entirely new airports, rather than a gradual modernization of existing facilities.

These projects place a growing burden on the state budget for three reasons: first, their absolute size is increasingly large, owing to their capital-intensive and "indivisible" character; second, corporate capital needs more economic infra-structure, due to the increased complexity and interdependence of production; and, third, state and local governments seeking to attract branch-plants of large corporations by subsidizing infra-structure projects tend to produce an over-supply of projects. For all these reasons, federal outlays and grants-in-aid and state and local bond issues for "capital improvements" will continue to expand.

Still another fiscal burden heaped on the state by corporate capital are the *expenses of selling*. The need for state programs to expand individual commodity demand springs from the rapid development of the productive forces that have reached the stage at which most individual economic needs—needs formed by goods production itself—can be easily satisfied. As a result the corporate bourgeoisie is compelled to lay out larger and larger portions of profits on selling expenses—for packaging, advertising, model and style changes, product differentiation, and forced commodity obsolescence—in order to discourage savings and maintain and expand the volume of consumption.[28]

The corporate ruling class has learned to use the state budget to subsidize commodity demand by reinforcing and accelerating the production of waste. Government "full employment" policies lead to a large volume of waste production. Safety laws, truth-in-lending, truth-in-packaging, food and drug laws, and other forms of "consumer protection" are designed to buoy up the market

[28] Paul Baran and Paul Sweezy, *Monopoly Capital,* New York, 1966.

by officially sanctioning particular commodity lines. Highway expenditures increase the demand for automobiles and contribute to urban and suburban sprawl. They indirectly expand the demand not only for consumer durable goods needed in private dwellings, but also for social consumption expenditures in the suburbs. Owing to the extreme individualistic character of the suburbanization process—single-unit dwellings, and the increased separation of places of work, residence, and recreation—the burden on local budgets arising from the need for more education, recreational, and similar facilities continues to mount.

The corporate ruling class has also learned to use the state and federal colleges and universities as proving grounds for new marketing ideas, new products, and new brands of full employment economics. The activities of these "marketing departments" of the coporate ruling class range from market research courses, home economics departments and seminars in Keynesian economics to the art and industrial design schools that train, mobilize, and apply creative talent to the latest problems of product design and packaging.

The state also underwrites consumer credit—the process of borrowing purchasing power from the future to realize surplus value in the present—in many fields; in particular, housing. The state guarantees and subsidizes private, single-unit-housing in order to expand the demand for residential construction, automobiles, appliances, and other consumer durable goods. Partly for this reason, mortgage debt on non-farm residential properties has risen from about $25 billion during World War II to roughly $250 billion in 1968, when there was an outstanding $50 billion in FHA-insured mortgage loans, and another $34 billion in VA-guaranteed mortgages.

From a theoretical standpoint, the need for state spending destined to underwrite private commodity demand is limitless. Capital "accumulates or dies" and in the absence of regular increases in private commodity demand, which in the current era require fresh state subsidies, accumulation comes to a halt. Moreover, a few particular commodities receive the greatest share of state subsidies. Highways and education receive the most direct subsidies and private suburban housing and development receive the greatest indirect subsidies. Politically, it is difficult for the state to shift resources from highway construction to other modes of transportation, from suburban residential development to urban housing, and from social consumption in the suburbs to social consumption in the cities. This introduces an element of *inflexibility* in the budget, and tends to intensify the overall fiscal crisis.

The uncontrolled expansion of production by corporate capital as a whole creates still another fiscal burden on the state in the form of outlays required to meet the *social costs of private production* (as contrasted with the socialization of private costs of production, which we have discussed above). Motor transportation is an important source of social costs in the consumption of oxygen, the production of crop- and animal-destroying smog, the pollution of rivers and oceans by lead additives to gasoline, the construction of freeways that foul the land, and the generation of urban sprawl. These costs do not enter into the accounts of the automobile industry, which is compelled to minimize its own costs and maximize production and sales. Corporate capital is unwilling to treat toxic chemical waste or to develop substitute sources of energy for fossil-fuels that pollute the air. (There are exceptions to this general rule. In Pittsburgh, for example, the Mellon interests reduced air pollution produced by its steel mills in order to preserve the values of its downtown real estate.) And corporate farming—the production of agricultural commodities for exchange alone—generates still more social costs by minimizing crop losses (and thus costs) through the unlimited use of DDT and other chemicals that are harmful to crops, animals, water purity and human life itself.

By and large, private capital refuses to bear the costs of reducing or eliminating air and water pollution, lowering highway and air accidents, easing traffic jams, preserving forests, wilderness areas, and wildlife sanctuaries, and conserving the soils. In the past these costs were largely ignored. Today, owing to the increasingly social character of production, these costs are damaging not only the ecological structure, but also profitable accumulation itself, particularly in real estate, recreation, agriculture, and other branches of the economy in which land, water, and air are valuable resources to capital. The portion of the state budget devoted to reducing social costs has therefore begun to mount.[29] In the future, the automobile industry can be expected to receive large-scale subsidies to help finance the transition to the electric or fuel-cell car. Capital as a whole will receive more subsidies in the form of new public transportation systems. Subsidies to public utilities to finance the transition to solar, nuclear, or sea energy will expand. Corporate farmers will insist on being "compensated" for crop losses arising from bans on the use of DDT and other harmful chemicals. And more Federal funds will be poured into the states to help regulate outdoor advertising, alleviate conditions in recreational areas, finance the costs of land purchase or condemnation, and landscaping and roadside develmpment, and otherwise meet the costs of "aesthetic pollution."

Some local and national leaders are seeking to reduce pressures on the budget arising from these social costs by attempting to shift the burden to private capital. For example, the State of Illinois is attempting to force the airlines using Chicago's airports to install air-pollution control devices on their aircraft. Former Secretary of the Interior Udall has stated that "waste treatment is a proper business cost." And the Water Quality Act of 1965—introduced into Congress by the Federal executive—requires State governments to establish and enforce water purity levels for interstate waterways within their boundaries.

---

[29] These and other costs of maintaining the social order have been estimated at roughly $109 billions (Alexander L. Crosby, "The Price of Utopia," *Monthly Review*, May, 1968). Private capital attempts to profit from the environmental conditions it has produced itself. For example, one corporation advertises private solutions to the social problem of pollution in the form of eye drops.

Law suits, legislation and moral suasion cannot be expected to provide a *total* solution to the problem of social costs. Total environmental planning is needed to socialize the costs of protecting the natural environment while simultaneously avoiding sharp financial pressures on the specific corporation or industry interests involved. No one corporate farmer can afford the costs of conserving soils, water and plant, animal, and human life. No single manufacturer can bear the expense of manufacturing automobiles that do not pollute the air. No airline alone can meet the expenses of "sound pollution" or by itself modernize air traffic facilities and control. These facts are understood by the Congress, which represents the interests of specific capitals and local business interests, and which continues to vote more state subsidies to specific industries and local and state governments.[30]

The third major category of state expenditures consists of the expenses of stabilizing the world capitalist social order: the costs of creating a safe political environment for profitable investment and trade. These expenditures include the costs of politically containing the proletariat at home and abroad, the costs of keeping small-scale, local, and regional capital at home, safely within the ruling corporate liberal consensus, and the costs of maintaining the comprador ruling classes abroad.

These political expenses take the form of income transfers and direct or indirect subsidies, and are attributable fundamentally to the unplanned and anarchic character of capitalist development. Unrestrained capital accumulation and technological change creates three broad, related economic and social imbalances. First, capitalist development forces great stresses and strains on local and regional economies; second, capitalist growth generates imbalances between various industries and sectors of the economy; third, accumulation and technical change reproduce inequalities in the distribution of wealth and income and generate poverty. The imbalances—described by Eric Hobsbawm as "the rhythm of social disruption"—not only are integral to capitalist development, but also are considered by the ruling class to be a sign of "healthy growth and change." What is more, the forces of the marketplace, far from ameliorating the imbalances, in fact magnify them by the multiplier effects of changes in demand on production. The decline of coal mining in Appalachia, for example, compelled other businesses and able-bodied workers to abandon the region, reinforcing tendencies toward economic stagnation and social impoverishment. . . .

The political containment of the proletariat requires the expense of maintaining corporate liberal ideological hegemony, and, where that fails, the cost

---

[30] For example, Senator Muskie, Chairman of a Senate Public Works subcommittee, said: "Just ordering a city or an industry to stop polluting isn't the answer. The costs of treatment are simply overwhelming. If we mean it when we say our national policy is to enhance the quality of our water resources, then we've got to be willing to put up the money to get the job done; and the present spending level doesn't begin to reflect the magnitude of the problem." Quoted in the *Wall Street Journal*, June 23, 1966.

of physically repressing populations in revolt. In the first category are the expenses of medicare, unemployment, old age, and other social insurance, a portion of education expenditures, the welfare budget, the anti-poverty programs, non-military "foreign aid," and the administrative costs of maintaining corporate liberalism at home and the imperalist system abroad—the expenses incurred by the National Labor Relations Board, Office of Economic Opportunity, Agency for International Development, and similar organizations. . . .

The second major cost of politically containing the proletariat at home and abroad (including the proletariat in the socialist world) consists of police and military expenditures required to suppress sections of the world proletariat in revolt. These expenditures place the single greatest drain on the state budget. . . .

The final expense of stabilizing the world capitalist social order consists of the funds needed to keep local and regional capital securely within the corporate liberal political consensus at home and the costs of maintaining the comprador ruling classes abroad. The latter take the form of foreign aid: in particular, balance-of-payments assistance through the International Monetary Fund; infra-structure loans by the World Bank and AID that economically strengthen export industries in the Third World and politically harden the rule of local bourgeoisies whose economic interests are based on export production, processing, and trade; and outright military and non-military grants-in-aid.

At home, corporate capital must make alliances with traditional agricultural interests (especially those of the Southern oligarchy) and small-scale capital. In the Congress, the votes of Southern and Midwest farm legislators and other representatives bound to local and regional economic interests, for example, shipping, soft coal mining, and the fishing industry, are indispensible for the legislative victories of corporate liberal policies. Support for Federal programs in the areas of urban renewal, education, health, housing, and transportation by state legislators, municipal governments, and local newspapers, TV stations, and other "opinion-makers" is equally important.

The political support of small businessmen, farmers, and other local and regional interests is extremely costly. Billions of dollars of direct and indirect subsidies are required by the farmers, especially the large growers who dominate the farm associations and many local and state governments. The first New Deal farm plan—the so-called domestic allotment plan—was introduced to quell a farm revolt organized in the Midwest.[31] Since the 1930s, price support, acreage restriction, credit, soil conservation, and rural redevelopment and rehabilitation programs—all designed with the aim of politically con-

---

[31] This revolt was led by the Farm Holiday Association over the issues of foreclosures and low farm prices. See John L. Shover, *Cornbelt Rebellion: The Farmer's Holiday Association*, Urbana (Ill.), 1955.

servatizing the farmers—have proliferated. "It was soon discovered that these programs were, on the whole, more helpful to the 'top third' of the farmers than they were to the 'lower two-thirds' . . . The small landowners, tenants, sharecroppers, wage hands, and migrant workers who composed the majority of the farm population received only indirect benefits and, in some cases, were actually harmed by these programs."[32] Today, the large, commercial farmers make up less than 15 per cent of the farm population, but receive an estimated 63 per cent of farm subsidies. . . .[33]

In the preceding sections, we have attempted to analyze state expenditures in terms of the development of the forces and relations of production. We have seen that the increasingly social character of production requires the organization and distribution of production by the state. In effect, neo-capitalism fuses the "base" and "super-structure"—the economic and political systems—and thus places an enormous fiscal burden on the state budget.

[32] Willard Range, "The Land and the Landless: Georgia Agriculture, 1920–1940," in Harry N. Scheiber, editor, *United States Economic History: Selected Readings,* New York, 1964, pp. 466–67.
[33] James O'Keefe, "The Effects of Price Support Programs on Low Income Farmers," manuscript.

The New Industrial State

JOHN KENNETH GALBRAITH

A curiosity of modern economic life is the role of change. It is imagined to be very great; to list its forms or emphasize its extent is to show a reassuring grasp of the commonplace. Yet not much is supposed to change. The economic system of the United States is praised on all occasions of public ceremony as a largely perfect structure. This is so elsewhere also. It is not easy to perfect what has been perfected. There is massive change but, except as the output of goods increases, all remains as before.

As to the change there is no doubt. The innovations and alterations in economic life in the last seventy years, and more especially since the beginning of World War II, have, by any calculation, been great. The most visible has been the application of increasingly intricate and sophisticated technology to the production of things. Machines have replaced crude manpower. And increasingly, as they are used to instruct other machines, they replace the cruder forms of human intelligence.

Seventy years ago the corporation was still confined to those industries—railroading, steamboating, steel-making, petroleum recovery and refining, some mining—where, it seemed, production had to be on a large scale. Now it also sells groceries, mills grain, publishes newspapers and provides public entertainment, all activities that were once the province of the individual proprietor or the insignificant firm. The largest firms deploy billions of dollars' worth of equipment and hundreds of thousands of men in scores of locations to produce hundreds of products. The five hundred largest corporations produce close to half of all the goods and services that are available annually in the United States.

Seventy years ago the corporation was the instrument of its owners and a projection of their personalities. The names of these principals—Carnegie, Rockefeller, Harriman, Mellon, Guggenheim, Ford—were known across the land. They are still known, but for the art galleries and philanthropic foundations they established and their descendants who are in politics. The men who now head the great corporations are unknown. . . .

Equally it is a commonplace that the relation of the state to the economy has changed. The services of Federal, state and local governments now account for between a fifth and a quarter of all economic activity. In 1929 it was about eight per cent. This far exceeds the government share in such an avowedly socialist state as India, considerably exceeds that in the anciently social democratic kingdoms of Sweden and Norway, and is not wholly incommensurate with the share in Poland, a Communist country . . .

Additionally, in the wake of what is now called the Keynesian Revolution, the state undertakes to regulate the total income available for the purchase of goods and services in the economy. It seeks to insure sufficient purchasing power to buy whatever the current labor force can produce. And, more tentatively and with considerably less sanction in public attitudes, it seeks, given the resulting high employment, to keep wages from shoving up prices and prices from forcing up wages in a persistent upward spiral. Perhaps as a result of these arrangements, and perhaps only to test man's capacity for feckless optimism, the production of goods in modern times has been notably high and remarkably reliable. . . .

Three further changes are less intimately a part of the established litany of accomplishment. First, there has been a further massive growth in the apparatus of persuasion and exhortation that is associated with the sale of goods. In its cost and in the talent it commands, this activity is coming increasingly to rival the effort devoted to the production of goods. Measurement of the exposure, and susceptibility, of human beings to this persuasion is itself a flourishing science.

Second, there has been the beginning of the decline of the trade union. Union membership in the United States reached a peak in 1956. Since then employment has continued to grow; union membership in the main has gone down. Friends of the labor movement, and those who depend on it for a livelihood, picture this downturn as temporary or cyclical. Quite a few others have not noticed it. There is a strong presumption that it is deeply rooted in related and deeper change.

Finally, there has been a large expansion in enrollment for higher education together with a somewhat more modest increase in the means for providing it. This has been attributed to a new and penetrating concern for popular enlightenment. As with the fall in union membership, it has deeper roots. Had the economic system need only for millions of unlettered proletarians, these, very plausibly, are what would be provided.

The Significance of Change

These changes or most of them have been much discussed. But to view them in isolation from each other, the usual practice, is greatly to minimize their effect. They are related to each other as cause to consequence. All are part of a yet larger matrix of change. In its effect on economic society this matrix has been more than the sum of its parts.

Thus mention has been made of machines and sophisticated technology. These require, in turn, heavy investment of capital. They are designed and guided by technically sophisticated men. They involve, also, a greatly increased elapse of time between any decision to produce and the emergence of a salable product.

From these changes come the need and the opportunity for the large business organization. It alone can deploy the requisite capital; it alone can mobilize the requisite skills. It can also do more. The large commitment of capital and organization well in advance of result requires that there be foresight and also that all feasible steps be taken to insure that what is foreseen will transpire. It can hardly be doubted that General Motors will be better able to influence the world around it—the prices and wages at which it buys and the prices at which it sells—than a man in suits and cloaks.

Nor is this all. The high production and income which are the fruits of advanced technology and expansive organization remove a very large part of the population from the compulsions and pressures of physical want. In consequence their economic behavior becomes in some measure malleable. No hungry man who is also sober can be persuaded to use his last dollar for anything but food. But a well-fed, well-clad, well-sheltered and otherwise well-tended person can be persuaded as between an electric razor and an electric toothbrush. Along with prices and costs, consumer demand becomes subject to management. This adds an important further element of control over environment.

When investment in technological development is very high, a wrong technical judgment or a failure in persuading consumers to buy the product can be extremely expensive. The cost and associated risk can be greatly reduced if the state pays for more exalted technical development or guarantees a market for the technically advanced product. Suitable justification—national defense, the needs of national prestige, support to indispensable industries such as supersonic travel—can readily be found. Modern technology thus defines a growing function of the modern state.

And technology and associated requirements in capital and time lead even more directly to the regulation of demand by the state. A corporation, contemplating an automobile of revised aspect, must be able to persuade people to buy it. It is equally important that people be able to do so. This is vital where heavy advance commitments of time and money must be made and where the product could as easily come to market in a time of depression as of prosperity. So there must be stabilization of overall demand.

Affluence adds to the need for such stabilization of aggregate demand. A man who lives close to the margin of subsistence must spend to exist and what he earns is spent. A man with ample income can save, and there is no assurance that what he saves will be offset by the spending or investment of others. Moreover, a rich society owes its productivity and income, at least in part, to large-scale organization—to the corporation. Corporations also have the option of retaining or saving from earnings—and can exercise it with the unique sense of righteousness of men who are imposing thrift on others. There is no guarantee that this corporate saving will be offset by spending. In consequence, in a community of high well-being, spending and hence demand are less reliable than in a poor one. They lose their reliability precisely when high costs and the long period of gestation imposed by modern technology require greater certainty of markets. The Keynesian Revolution occurred at the moment in history when other change had made it indispensable. Like the other changes with which this chapter began, it is intimately a cause and consequence of yet other change.

In economics, unlike fiction and the theater, there is no harm in a premature disclosure of the plot: it is to see the changes just mentioned and others as an interlocked whole. I venture to think that modern economic life is seen much more clearly when, as here, there is effort to see it whole.

I am also concerned to show how, in this larger context of change, the forces inducing human effort have changed. This assaults the most majestic of all economic assumptions, namely that man in his economic activities is subject to the authority of the market. Instead, we have an economic system which, whatever its formal ideological billing, is in substantial part a planned economy. The initiative in deciding what is to be produced comes not from the sovereign consumer who, through the market, issues the instructions that bend the productive mechanism to his ultimate will. Rather it comes from the great producing organization which reaches forward to control the markets that it is presumed to serve and, beyond, to bend the customer to its needs. . . .

The Imperatives of Technology

Nearly all of the consequences of technology, and much of the shape of modern industry, derive from this need to divide and subdivide tasks and from the further need to bring knowledge to bear on these fractions and from the final need to combine the finished elements of the task into the finished product as a whole. Six consequences are of immediate importance.

First. An increasing span of time separates the beginning from the completion of any task. Knowledge is brought to bear on the ultimate microfraction of the task; then on that in combination with some other fraction; then on some further combination and thus on to final completion. The process stretches back in time as the root system of a plant goes down into the ground. The longest of the filaments determines the total time required in production. The more thoroughgoing the application of technology—in common or at least frequent language, the more sophisticated the production process—the farther back the application of knowledge will be carried. The longer, accordingly, will be the time between the initiation and completion of the task. . . .

Second. There is an increase in the capital that is committed to production aside from that occasioned by increased output. The increased time, and therewith the increased investment in goods in process, costs money. So does the knowledge which is applied to the various elements of the task. The application of knowledge to an element of a manufacturing problem will also typically involve the development of a machine for performing the function. (The word technology brings to mind machines; this is not surprising for machinery is one of its most visible manifestations.) This too involves investment as does equipment for integrating the various elements of the task into the final product. . . .

Third. With increasing technology the commitment of time and money tends to be made ever more inflexibly to the performance of a particular task. That task must be precisely defined before it is divided and subdivided into its component parts. Knowledge and equipment are then brought to bear on these fractions and they are useful only for the task as it was initially defined. If that task is changed, new knowledge and new equipment will have to be brought to bear. . . .

Fourth. Technology requires specialized manpower. This will be evident. Organized knowledge can be brought to bear, not surprisingly, only by those who possess it. However, technology does not make the only claim on manpower; planning, to be mentioned in a moment, also requires a comparatively high level of specialized talent. To foresee the future in all its dimensions and to design the appropriate action does not necessarily require high scientific qualification. It does require ability to organize and employ information, or capacity to react intuitively to relevant experience. . . .

Fifth. The inevitable counterpart of specialization is organization. This is what brings the work of specialists to a coherent result. If there are many specialists, this coordination will be a major task. So complex, indeed, will

be the job of organizing specialists that there will be specialists on organization. More even than machinery, massive and complex business organizations
are the tangible manifestation of advanced technology.

Sixth. From the time and capital that must be committed, the inflexibility
of this commitment, the needs of large organization and the problems of
market performance under conditions of advanced technology, comes the
necessity for planning. Tasks must be performed so that they are right not
for the present but for that time in the future when, companion and related
work having also been done, the whole job is completed. And the amount
of capital that, meanwhile, will have been committed adds urgency to this
need to be right. So conditions at the time of completion of the whole task
must be foreseen as must developments along the way. And steps must be
taken to prevent, offset or otherwise neutralize the effect of adverse developments, and to insure that what is ultimately foreseen eventuates in fact. . . .

The Technostructure

The need to draw on, and appraise, the information of numerous individuals
in modern industrial decision-making has three principal points of origin. It
derives, first, from the technological requirements of modern industry. It is
not that these are always inordinately sophisticated; a man of moderate genius
could, quite conceivably, provide himself with the knowledge of the various
branches of metallurgy and chemistry, and of engineering, procurement,
production management, quality control, labor relations, styling and
merchandising which are involved in the development of a modern motor
car. But even moderate genius is in unpredictable supply, and to keep abreast
of all these branches of science, engineering and art would be time-consuming
even for a genius. The elementary solution, which allows of the use of far
more common talent and with far greater predictability of result, is to have
men who are appropriately qualified or experienced in each limited area of
specialized knowledge or art. Their information is then combined for carrying
out the design and production of the vehicle. It is a common public impression, not discouraged by scientists, engineers and industrialists, that modern
scientific, engineering and industrial achievements are the work of a new and
quite remarkable race of men. This is pure vanity; were it so, there would
be few such achievements. The real accomplishment of modern science and
technology consists in taking ordinary men, informing them narrowly and
deeply and then, through appropriate organization, arranging to have their
knowledge combined with that of other specialized but equally ordinary men.
This dispenses with the need for genius. The resulting performance, though
less inspiring, is far more predictable.

The second factor requiring the combination of specialized talent derives
from advanced technology, the associated use of capital, and the resulting
need for planning with its accompanying control of environment. The market
is, in remarkable degree, an intellectually undemanding institution. The Wis-

consin farmer, aforementioned, need not anticipate his requirements for fertilizers, pesticides or even machine parts; the market stocks and supplies them. The cost of these is substantially the same for the man of intelligence and for his neighbor who, under medical examination, shows daylight in either ear. And the farmer need have no price or selling strategy; the market takes all his milk at the ruling price. Much of the appeal of the market, to economists at least, has been from the way it seems to simplify life. Better orderly error than complex truth.

For complexity enters with planning and is endemic thereto. The manufacturer of missiles, space vehicles or modern aircraft must foresee the requirements for specialized plant, specialized manpower, exotic materials and intricate components and take steps to insure their availability when they are needed. For procuring such things, we have seen, the market is either unreliable or unavailable. And there is no open market for the finished product. Everything here depends on the care and skill with which contracts are sought and nurtured in Washington or in Whitehall or Paris.

The same foresight and responding action are required, in lesser degree, from manufacturers of automobiles, processed foods and detergents. They too must foresee requirements and manage markets. Planning, in short, requires a great variety of information. It requires variously informed men and men who are suitably specialized in obtaining the requisite information. There must be men whose knowledge allows them to foresee need and to insure a supply of labor, materials and other production requirements; those who have knowledge to plan price strategies and see that customers are suitably persuaded to buy at these prices; those who, at higher levels of technology, are so informed that they can work effectively with the state to see that it is suitably guided; and those who can organize the flow of information that the above tasks and many others require. Thus, to the requirements of technology for specialized technical and scientific talent are added the very large further requirements of the planning that technology makes necessary.

Finally, following from the need for this variety of specialized talent, is the need for its coordination. Talent must be brought to bear on the common purpose. More specifically, on large and small matters, information must be extracted from the various specialists, tested for its reliability and relevance, and made to yield a decision. This process, which is much misunderstood, requires a special word.

The modern business organization, or that part which has to do with guidance and direction, consists of numerous individuals who are engaged, at any given time, in obtaining, digesting or exchanging and testing information. A very large part of the exchange and testing of information is by word-of-mouth—a discussion in an office, at lunch or over the telephone. But the most typical procedure is through the committee and the committee meeting. . . .

Nor should it be supposed that this is an inefficient procedure. On the contrary it is, normally, the only efficient procedure. Association in a committee enables each member to come to know the intellectual resources and the reliability of his colleagues. Committee discussion enables members to pool information under circumstances which allow, also, of immediate probing to assess the relevance and reliability of the information offered. Uncertainty about one's information or error is revealed as in no other way. There is also, no doubt, considerable stimulus to mental effort from such association. One may enjoy the luxury of torpor in private but not so comfortably in public at least during working hours. . . .

Thus decision in the modern business enterprise is the product not of individuals but of groups. The groups are numerous, as often informal as formal, and subject to constant change in composition. Each contains the men possessed of the information, or with access to the information, that bears on the particular decision together with those whose skill consists in extracting and testing this information and obtaining a conclusion. This is how men act successfully on matters where no single one, however exalted or intelligent, has more than a fraction of the necessary knowledge. It is what makes modern business possible, and in other contexts it is what makes modern government possible. It is fortunate that men of limited knowledge are so constituted that they can work together in this way. Were it otherwise, business and government, at any given moment, would be at a standstill awaiting the appearance of a man with the requisite breadth of knowledge to resolve the problem presently at hand.

In the past, leadership in business organization was identified with the entrepreneur—the individual who united ownership or control of capital with capacity for organizing the other factors of production and, in most contexts, with a further capacity for innovation. With the rise of the modern corporation, the emergence of the organization required by modern technology and planning and the divorce of the owner of the capital from control of the enterprise, the entrepreneur no longer exists as an individual person in the mature industrial enterprise. Everyday discourse, except in the economics textbooks, recognizes this change. It replaces the entrepreneurs, as the directing force of the enterprise, with management. This is a collective and imperfectly defined entity; in the large corporation it embraces chairman, president, those vice presidents with important staff or departmental responsibility, occupants of other major staff positions and, perhaps, division or department heads not included above. It includes, however, only a small proportion of those who, as participants, contribute information to group decisions. This latter group is very large; it extends from the most senior officials of the corporation to where it meets, at the outer perimeter, the white and blue collar workers whose function is to conform more or less mechanically to instruction or routine. It embraces all who bring specialized knowledge, talent or experience to group decision-making. This, not the management, is the guiding intelligence—the brain—of the enterprise. There is no name for all who participate in group decision-making or the organization which they form. I propose to call this organization the Technostructure.

Professor Galbraith and American Capitalism

RALPH MILIBAND

The intellectual defence of capitalism has long ceased to be confined to the simple celebration of its virtues; or even to the argument that, whatever might be said against it, it was still a much better system, on economic, social and political grounds, than any conceivable alternative to it. Such arguments are of course still extensively used. But they belong to an older school of apologetics; and for some considerable time now, many people, who see themselves as part of the "democratic left," as liberal and even radical critics of the existing social order, and as anything but its apologists have argued that the question of alternatives to capitalism had been rendered obsolete by the internal developments of the system itself; capitalism, the argument goes, has been so thoroughly transformed in the last few decades that the need to abolish it has conveniently disappeared. The job, for all practical purposes, has been done by the "logic of industrialization," which is well on the way to erasing all meaningful differences between "industrial systems," whatever misleading labels they may choose to pin upon themselves.

The New Industrial State is a further version of this by now familiar thesis. Professor Galbraith, however, does not conceal his belief that he is here unrolling a map of American capitalism (or of "what is commonly called capitalism") which is entirely new, and immeasurably more accurate than any previous one. The former claim is rather exaggerated, but it is perfectly true that there is much in his essay which is indeed new. The question, however, is whether what is new is also true, and whether the combination of old and new really does provide an accurate, reliable map of American economic life. The answer, as I propose to argue in this review, is that it does not; and that much more interesting than the revelation which it purports to bring about the true nature of American capitalism is what it reveals of the confusion and bafflement of the latter-day liberalism which Professor Galbraith represents, in regard to an "industrial system" which it approaches with a mixture of admiration and distaste, and whose basic irrationality, some

From *The Socialist Register* (London: Merlin Press Ltd., 1968). Reprinted by permission of the publisher.

aspects which it perceives, it is either unable or unwilling to locate and
transcend. It is not surprising that Professor Galbraith should sometimes be
seen as a critic of the system and sometimes as its defender. For he is both,
at one moment belabouring conservative economists, yet echoing, in more
elegant language, their own vulgar apologetics, at another trembling on the
brink of radical criticism, yet unable to jump. The famous style of exposition
itself, the laboured humour, the straining after ironic effect, the attempt at
cool wit, all testify to the ideological tension. Professor Galbraith perceives
that an advanced industrial system *requires* the transcendence of private appropriation and much of his book is in fact a documented though seemingly
unconscious comment on Marx's prediction that, with the development of
capitalism, "centralization of the means of production and socialization of
labour at last reach a point where they become incompatible with their capitalist integument." But the central point of the book, which is also its central
weakness, is that the "industrial system" has actually *solved* the problem,
and that whatever adjustments it further requires can be achieved within its
present framework, and without, perish the thought, the invocation of the
old socialist gods. The tone is critical and so is the intent, but the result is
all the same profoundly apologetic.

In *American Capitalism: The Concept of Countervailing Power,* first published in 1952, Professor Galbraith advanced the notion that, while the growing concentration of economic enterprise might appear to entail a dangerous
increase in the power of business, traditional liberal, not to speak of socialist,
fears on this score were really misconceived: for the power of business was,
he argued, effectively balanced and checked by a variety of forces and
agencies, such as organized labour, other economic interests, the state, the
consumer, and so forth. This notion of "countervailing power," coming as
it did in the early days of an ideological, political and military struggle which
counterposed power-diffused democracy to monolithic communism was an
exceptionally useful ideological weapon; and it served as one of the foundations of a theory of political pluralism which has since greatly prospered,
to the point of becoming the dominant orthodoxy of Western political and
social theories of power in capitalist societies: in these societies, a plurality
of "interests" (classes being rather *vieux jeu*) compete under the watchful
eye of a democratic state, and achieve, as a result of that competition, a rough
equilibrium in which everybody has some power and no one has, or can have,
too much.

In *The New Industrial State,* Professor Galbraith has now come to discard
the notion of "countervailing power." Unions, he now believes, are a declining
force, consumers are the manipulated prisoners of induced demand, the state
serves the goals of the "industrial system," and there is no "interest" remotely
comparable in importance to the five or six hundred large corporations which
are "the heartland of the modern economy." Professor Galbraith writes,

> Nothing so characterizes the industrial system as the scale of the
> modern corporate enterprise. In 1962 the five largest industrial corporations

in the United States, with combined assets in excess of $36 billion, possessed over 12 per cent of all assets used in manufacturing. The fifty largest corporations had over a third of all manufacturing assets. The 500 largest had well over two-thirds. Corporations with assets in excess of $10,000,000, some 2,000 in all, accounted for about 80 per cent of all the resources used in manufacturing in the United States. In the mid nineteen-fifties, 28 corporations provided approximately 10 per cent of all employment in manufacturing, mining and retail and wholesale trade. Twenty-three corporations provided 15 per cent of all employment in manufacturing. In the first half of the decade (June 1950–June 1956) a hundred firms received two-thirds by value of all defence contracts; ten firms received one-third. In 1960 four corporations accounted for an estimated 22 per cent of all industrial research and development expenditure. Three hundred and eighty-four corporations employing 5,000 or more workers accounted for 55 per cent of these expenditures; 260,000 firms employing fewer than 1,000 accounted for only 7 per cent.

This is, indeed, impressive and Professor Galbraith is certainly right to place this formidable complex at the centre of the picture, since those who control it might also reasonably be thought to concentrate in their hands a vast amount of power, not only economic but political and cultural as well.

Not so at all, Professor Galbraith hastens to reassure us. For while *resources* are concentrated, *power* is not. Power, in the "industrial system" is not in the hands of the old-style owner-capitalist, who has, he suggests, all but disappeared; nor of course is it held by essentially passive shareholders; nor even by that managerial élite which had long been claimed to have inherited the power of both. The people to whom corporate power *has* passed, Professor Galbraith insists again and again, is an entirely different element, so far overlooked by all other toilers in this field, namely "the technostructure." On this, it is necessary to quote Professor Galbraith at some length, firstly because much of his thesis rests on this discovery, and secondly because it will be argued here that the "technostructure" as the new repository of corporate power is unmitigated nonsense.

The "technostructure" comprises a "very large" group of people who "contribute information to group decisions" and who "extend from the most senior officials of the corporation to where it meets, at the outer perimeter, the white and blue collar workers whose function is to conform more or less mechanically to instructions or routine. It embraces all who bring specialized knowledge, talent or experience to group decision-making." "It will be evident that nearly all powers—initiative, character of development, rejection or acceptance—are exercised deep in the company. It is not the managers who decide. Effective power of decision is lodged deeply in the technical, planning and other specialized staff." Indeed, Professor Galbraith, later in the book, goes even further. For, he tells us, "distinctions between those who make decisions and those who carry them out, and between employer and employee, are obscured by the technicians, scientists, market analysts, computer programmers, industrial stylists and other specialists who do, or are both. A continuum thus exists between the centre of the technostructure and the more routine white-collar workers on the fringe."

On this view, the demon Power has once again been exorcized, without the help of "countervailing power": for the "technostructure" is very large, and the power which accrues to it is therefore diffuse, shared—indeed, why not say it? democratic.

In examining this remarkable argument, it may, to begin with, be noted that much of it rests on the by now well-entrenched notion of the separation of ownership from control, which Professor Galbraith pushes to its furthest limits: for him, those who control the corporations are now virtually owner-less, and ownership is in any event wholly irrelevant to corporate policy.

A considerable amount of evidence and argument, which Professor Galbraith does not discuss, has been produced over the years to rebut or at least to qualify this thesis; and some interesting further evidence against it has recently appeared in *Fortune* magazine.

In an article entitled "Proprietors in the World of Big Business," and concerned with ownership and control in the 500 largest corporations in the United States, Mr. Robert Sheehan writes that "in approximately 150 companies on the current *Fortune* list (i.e. of the 500 largest industrial corporations) controlling ownership rests in the hands of an individual or of the members of a single family"; and, he adds, "the evidence that 30 per cent of the 500 largest industrials are clearly controlled by identifiable individuals, or by family groups . . . suggests that the demise of the traditional American proprietor has been slightly exaggerated and that the much-advertised triumph of the organization is far from total." Mr. Sheehan, it should be explained, also notes that he has used a very conservative criterion of control, i.e., that his list only includes companies in which the largest individual stockholder owns 10 per cent or more of the voting stock or in which the largest block of shares—representing 10 per cent or more of the total votes—is held by members of a single family. This, he points out, leaves out "coalitions" which may assure working control for small groups of associates in many companies; and also businessmen known to wield great influence with holdings of less than 10 per cent. Even so, "at least 10 family-controlled companies rank among the top 100, and several of these are actively owner-managed"; and "approximately seventy family-named companies among the 500 are still controlled by the founding family."

Even if these pretty severe qualifications to the thesis of the disappearance of the owner-controller are ignored (and Professor Galbraith was in no position to consider them, since they appeared after he had written his book) the question remains as to the managerial élite's relation to ownership. Professor Galbraith, as noted, wholeheartedly endorses the thesis of managerial ownerlessness. Thus: "stock holdings by management are small and often non-existent"; "even the small stock interest of the top officers is no longer the rule"; and so on.

This, too, however, is rather extreme. For, as one writer among many has noted, "the managerial class is the largest single group in the stockholding population, and a greater proportion of this class owns stock than any other." Another writer notes that "a recent study by the National Industrial Conference Board shows that 73 per cent of 215 top executives during the period 1950–1960 gained at least 50,000 dollars through the use of stock options, that 32 per cent gained 250,000 dollars, and that 8 per cent gained at least 1,000,000 dollars"; and by 1957, it may also be noted, option plans for the purchase of stock had been instituted by 77 per cent of the manufacturing corporations listed in the New York or American Stock Exchange. Managers, the evidence shows, are by no means as ownerless as Professor Galbraith, following many others, maintains.

On the other hand, how often ownership determines control is a rather more complex question. That it does not has of course been an article of faith with managerial revolutionists ever since Berle and Means claimed in 1932 that "ownership is so widely distributed that no individual or small group has been a minority interest large enough to dominate the affairs of the company." This too has long been held to be far too categorical. There is dispersal of ownership (though even this should not be exaggerated) but, as Mr. Clive Bede of the University of Melbourne has recently argued, the method used by Berle and Means "is unable to separate ownership from control because it does not establish empirically the proportion of votes needed for control in the real as distinct from the legal company situation . . . since ownership is very widely dispersed (among different names) in management controlled companies, either it could mean, with Berle and Means, that no one individual or small group could gain sufficient votes for control, or, contradicting Berle and Means, that only a few percent of votes was required for control."

Various such percentages have at one time or another been advanced. As Mr. Sheehan suggests, 1 per cent is a very conservative estimate. Mr. Villarejo took 5 per cent as the amount of stock required to control a corporation whose stock is widely dispersed, and found that in at least 76 of the 232 largest United States corporations, ownership on boards of directors was sufficient to ensure working control; and Mr. Bede also notes that Professor Gordon's 1945 study, *Business Leadership in the Large Corporations,* on which Professor Galbraith greatly relies, held that 3 per cent ultimate ownership might exercise control. In fact, as Mr. Bede suggests, "the possibility of *'any percentage'* control does exist." And where it does, that control-through-ownership is most likely to be in the hands of top managers. Moreover, one place where it is *not* likely to be lodged is in Professor Galbraith's "technostructure." For it is scarcely to be thought that "the technical planning and other specialized staff" in which, according to him, "the effective power of decision is lodged" ("deeply") are to be counted among the "large owners" of corporate stock.

This, however, is by no means the main reason for thinking that the claim is invalid. For even if it is assumed—which is obviously often the case—that top managers do not exercise control through ownership, the notion that they do not exercise control *at all,* and that the men at the top of the corporate structure are, as Professor Galbraith claims, virtually powerless and ceremonial figures, whose function within the corporation is "to give the equivalent of the royal assent to agreements, contracts and indentures"—this notion too must invite complete disbelief, the more so since Professor Galbraith provides no concrete evidence whatever to buttress his claim.

That claim, in fact, would appear to rest on an extreme "technocratic" view of the degree of influence which hierarchically subordinate technical experts of one sort or another (and the corporation is of course a highly hierarchical, and hierarchy-conscious organization) may wield with men upon whom the power of managerial decision rests. There may be "mature corporations" where the top men are *rois fainéants* or constitutional monarchs. But hard evidence to that effect is lacking. Professor Galbraith claims that the expert influence in the corporation is decisive. There is every reason to think that, here as in government, it is nothing of the kind. The expert does not decide policy: he works out how best to carry it out. In that role, he may well affect policy, but this is hardly synonymous with the dramatic reversal of roles—the experts on top, the managers on tap—which Professor Galbraith claims to be the present reality of the "industrial system."

Having lodged the "effective power of decision" in the "technostructure," Professor Galbraith proceeds to discuss the latter's "motivations." Since there is no good evidence to suggest that the "technostructure" does have such power, it might seem superfluous to follow him in this exercise. But since much that he has to say about the motivations of the "technostructure" also concerns wider issues of corporate policy, it is worthwhile persevering.

Theories of motivation have been closely linked with the thesis of ownerless management. That thesis was not, it may be surmised, so passionately embraced by so many writers because of its irresistible conceptual beauty. Ideology came into it as well. For from the view that the new class of managers neither owned the resources it controlled, nor was the subject to the control of owners, it was but the shortest step, which was eagerly taken, to the claim that managers were, in their running of the corporation, moved by impulses altogether different from those of old-style capitalist owner-entrepreneurs, or from those of passive shareholders, and that these impulses were not only different, but *better,* less "selfish," more "socially responsible." It was this notion which Professor Carl Kaysen once epitomized in the phrase "the soulful corporation." "No longer the agent of proprietorship seeking to maximize return on investment," he claimed, "management sees itself as responsible to stockholders, employees, customers, the general public, and perhaps most important, the firm itself as an institution . . . there is no display of greed and graspingness; there is no attempt to push off onto the workers or the community at large part of the social costs of the enterprise. The modern corporation is a soulful corporation." This, incidentally, was also the view of Mr. C. A. R. Crosland, who wrote in *The Conservative Enemy* that "now perhaps most typical amongst very large firms, is the company which pursues rapid growth and high profits—but subject to its sense of social responsibility and its desire for good labour and public relations. . . . Its goals are a 'fair' rather than a maximum profit, reasonably rapid growth and the warm glow which comes from a sense of public duty." Much the same view, it may be recalled, also found expression in a major Labour Party policy document, which proclaimed that "under increasingly professional management, large firms are as a whole serving the nation well."

This notion of soulful managerialism has often been challenged on two different grounds. Firstly, on the ground that top managers do, as "large owners," often have a direct financial interest in "profit maximization." Thus, Mr. Sheehan, in the article quoted earlier, notes that "Chairman Frederic C. Donner, for example, owns only 0.017 per cent of G.M.'s outstanding stock, but it was worth about $3,917,000 recently. Chairman Lynn A. Town-send owns 0.117 per cent of Chrysler, worth about $2,380,000. Their interest in the earnings of those investments is hardly an impersonal one." And Professor Kolko also notes that "in early 1957, 25 General Motors officers owned an average of 11,500 shares each. Collectively their holdings would have been inconsequential if they had chosen to try and obtain control of G.M. through their stocks. Yet each of these men had a personal share of roughly half a million dollars in the company. . . ." The largest part of managerial income may not be derived from ownership, or depend upon such ownership, but managers are hardly likely, all the same, to ignore their share-holdings in their view of what their firms ought to be about. As indeed why should they?

The second and more important reason why managers *are* concerned with "profit maximization" has been well put by Baran and Sweezy: "The primary objectives of corporate policy," they write, "—which are at the same time and inevitably the personal objectives of the corporate managers—are thus strength, rate of growth and size. There is no general formula for quantifying or combining these objectives—nor is there any need for one. For they are reducible to the single common denominator of profitability. Profits provide the internal funds for expansion. Profits are the sinews and muscle of strength, which in turn gives access to outside funds if and when they are needed. . . . Thus profits, even though not the ultimate goal, are the neces-sary means to all ultimate goals. As such, they become the immediate, unique, unifying, quantitative aim of corporate policies, the touchstone of corporate rationality, the measure of corporate success."

As it happens, the inventor of the "soulful corporation" himself concedes a good deal to this view. "It may be argued," Professor Kaysen writes "that all this (i.e. the managers' multiple responsibilities) amounts to no more than long-run profit maximization, and thus that management in the modern cor-poration does no more than business management has always tried to do, allowing for changed circumstances"; furthermore "only the ability to continue to earn a substantial surplus over costs makes possible a variety of expenditures whose benefits are broad, uncertain and distant." This is also Mr. Sheehan's conclusion: "Very few executives argue that the managers of a widely held company run their business any differently from the proprietors of a closely held company"; "it is unrealistic to assume that because a manager holds only a small fraction of his company's stock he lacks the incentive to drive up the profits." Indeed, Professor James Earley has even gone further and suggested, very plausibly, that the modern manager may be better placed to pursue profit than the old-style entrepreneur, because with "the rapidly growing use of economists, market analysis, other types of specialists and management consultants by our larger businesses . . . profit-oriented rationality is likely to be more and more representative of business behaviour."

For his part, Professor Galbraith will have none of this. Profit maximization, he holds, excludes other goals. But this can only be true if "profit-maximization" is taken to mean, as Professor Galbraith appears to mean, a reckless and wholly irrational pursuit of immediately realizable profit, regardless of any longer term consideration. And this is a purely arbitrary definition, which is applicable neither to corporate management, nor, for that matter, to owner-entrepreneurs.

In any case it is not the motivation of managers, but of the "technostructure" which, in Professor Galbraith's view, is what matters. The professional and salaried staff who mainly compose it are, he insists, even less concerned with "profit-maximization" than top managers. This may well be the case, but would only be significant if one were to accept the view that the corporation "as an instrument of power" is used "to serve the deeper interests and goals of the technostructure." And there are no good grounds, as I have suggested, for accepting this view.

Even so, it may be worth examining what, according to Professor Galbraith, these "goals" of the "technostructure" are, since his discussion illustrates so well the extreme difficulty of finding a rationale for corporate enterprise clearly distinct from financial reward.

Despite solemn announcements of motivational revelations, the motives and goals which Professor Galbraith ascribes to the "technostructure" (purely on the basis of supposition and inference) turn out, upon examination, to be no different from the goals which have often been ascribed to top management—the survival of the firm, its growth, its independence from outside control. But these are precisely the kinds of issues which the technical and professional staffs within the corporation are least likely to be called upon to decide.

Nor is Professor Galbraith at all successful in locating the larger "social" goals which, he claims, move the "technostructure." "The individual," he tells us, "will identify himself with the goals of the corporation only if the corporation is identified with, *as the individual sees it,* some significant social goal." On the other hand, "the individual," he also tells us, "serves organization because of the possibility of accommodating its goals more closely to his own." But *then,* we also find that "he will normally think that the goals he seeks have social purpose," "for individuals have a well-marked capacity to attach high social purpose to whatever—more scientific research, better zoning laws, manufacture of the lethal weapons just mentioned—*serves their personal interest.*" Moreover, it does not appear to matter in the least *what* the corporation produces, whether "life saving drugs" or "an exotic missile fuel, or a better trigger for a nuclear warhead."

What this amounts to is that whatever "goals" members of the "technostructure" may have will be seen, *by them,* as having a "social purpose"; and whatever the corporation produces will be deemed, *by them,* to have an equally "social purpose." As Professor Galbraith puts it, "what counts here is what is believed." But this surely renders the discussion of "goals" quite meaningless. For why should we accept the "goals" of the "technostructure" as having a "social purpose" simply because its members happen to believe this to be the case?

In any case, Professor Galbraith himself is compelled to attribute more importance to "pecuniary compensation" than many of his formulations would tend to suggest. For it appears that other "goals" only operate *after* a certain level of income has been achieved; it is only "above a certain level" that other motivations "may operate independently of income" "the participants are well compensated" and "few regard their compensation with disinterest." On one page, "pecuniary compensation, as an explanation of effort, has now a much diminished role"; twenty pages later, "pecuniary compensation is an extremely important stimulus to individual members of the technostructure up to a point. If they are not paid this acceptable and expected salary, they will not work." As a "general theory of motivation," these extraordinary contortions may be thought to leave something to be desired.

One of Professor Galbraith's most insistent themes is that modern economic life requires planning. But this requirement, it would appear, is already largely met in the American "industrial system": for the United States, *mirabile dictu,* is "a largely planned economy." This remarkable assertion rests on the notion that the "mature corporation" is able to plan because it is no longer subject to the vagaries of a market which it controls, or to the cold winds of competition; and its planning is the more secure in that the state controls aggregate demand: "the firm is the basic planning unit in the western economies. In the Soviet system it is still the state." This is surely pushing "convergence" beyond the bounds of sense. For whatever may be thought of Soviet planning, it is hardly to be assimilated to the "planning" of which Professor Galbraith speaks. Even if one leaves aside his dubious elimination of the market and of competition from the "industrial system," and his no less dubious assurance that the state has perfected its mechanism of control of aggregate demand (i.e. that depression is now not only unlikely but impossible), the planning in which individual corporations engage bears no relation to, and is in fact the opposite of, any meaningful concept of national planning. Professor Galbraith may *wish* to overcome the anarchy of production characteristic of his "industrial system"; but the wish ought not be taken for a fact.

As for "state intervention," Professor Galbraith clearly sees that what he calls "the public sector," i.e. government expenditure, is the "fulcrum" for the regulation of demand. And he also notes that "plainly military expenditures are the pivot on which the fulcrum rests." This he finds regrettable. But all he has to offer, concretely, as an alternative to military expenditure is expenditure on space competition. "In relation to the needs of the industrial system, the space competition is nearly ideal." He is then moved to ask: "Are there no better uses for the resources so employed?" And he answers, in a remarkable and revealing phrase: "There is no rational answer to these questions as there is none to a query as to why negotiated disarmament is inherently more dangerous than a continuance of the weapons competition. *Truth in both instances is subordinate to need and the needed belief.* But this does not affect the value of the space competition in meeting the needs of the industrial system in a comparatively harmless instead of an extremely dangerous competition."

This would do very well as a satire on the "industrial system," of the kind presented, deliberately or unwittingly, by *Report from Iron Mountain.* But Professor Galbraith is not here, to all appearances, in the least satirical. And his prescription therefore betokens, in the face of genuine human need, an illuminating willingness to sacrifice reason so as to meet the "need and the needed belief" of the "industrial system."

But what, in any case, if armaments expenditure is not simply produced by a deluded view, as Professor Galbraith suggests, of the "Soviet threat"? What if it is the inevitable expression of the determination to maintain the largest possible area of the globe open to the "industrial system," and to a consequent determination to counter by every means, including military means, all attempts to resist that penetration? What, in other words, if military expenditure is the necessary concomitant of the expansionist needs of the "industrial system" itself? Professor Galbraith has not a word to say about *this* aspect of the "industrial system," of its relation to the world, of its imperialist urges; and it is only by ignoring it, and by ignoring the supreme irrationality of his prescription, that he is able to urge "space competition" as an alternative to armaments.

In a sense, his default is all the greater in that he does see that the system generally ignores or holds as unimportant those services of the state which are not closely related to the system's needs; and that a state attuned to capitalist purposes therefore neglects those services.

Yet even here, there is a typical disregard of the *scale* of the human needs which are left unfulfilled. Professor Galbraith is of course concerned with poverty. But in *The New Industrial State* as in *The Affluent Society,* he treats it as an all but marginal, "special" problem. The latter book rendered an immense service to the "industrial system" by helping to popularize the notion that capitalism had all but eliminated poverty, or that it had at least reduced it to marginal, "minority" proportions. In *The Affluent Society,* he described poverty as mainly confined to "special" sections of the population: either "some quality peculiar to the individual or family involved—mental deficiency, bad health, inability to adapt to the discipline of modern economic life, excessive procreation, alcohol, insufficient education, or perhaps a combination of several of these handicaps—has kept these individuals from participating in the *general* well-being" (the notion that these are qualities "peculiar to the individual" is distinctly odd, but let it pass); or, alternatively poverty was an "insular" phenomenon, which had "something to do with the desire of a comparatively large number of people to spend their lives at or near the place of their birth." In either case, his readers, presumably mentally alert, healthy, disciplined, sexually sophisticated, non-alcoholic, educated and mobile, were given to understand, for this was the theme of the whole book, that here *was* a special problem, which might be thought to involve, since Professor Galbraith did not venture figures, a quite easily manageable minority. Poverty might be a "disgrace" to an "affluent society"; but the very idea of the affluent society exiled the poor to its outer fringes, and greatly helped to obscure them from view.

It was not long after the publication of *The Affluent Society* that poverty was rediscovered in the United States (and in Britain), not as a marginal and special phenomenon, on the way to eradication in "post-capitalist" societies, but as a literally massive phenomenon, of quite gruesome proportions. Harry Magdoff has summarized thus, to take but one example, the findings of an impeccably official Conference on Economic Progress which reported in April 1962: "The simple summary of the Conference Report on the 1960 income situation in the U.S. is as follows: 34 million people in families and 4 million unattached individuals (that is, unattached economically to a family unit) lived in poverty; 37 million people in families and 2 million unattached individuals lived in deprivation. The total of 77 million comprised two-fifths of the U.S. population in 1960." This is not, as Professor Galbraith had it, "private affluence and public squalor," but public squalor *and* private poverty.

There is nothing in *The New Industrial State* to suggest that Professor Galbriath has taken note of such findings, nothing to qualify his view of poverty as a special, marginal and easily soluble "problem." Certain "tasks"—"the care of the ill, aged and physically or mentally infirm, the provision of health services in general, the provision of parks and many other services"—"are badly performed to the general public's discomfort or worse. Were it recognized that they require planning, and in the context of a largely planned economy [*sic*] have been left unplanned, there would be no hesitation or apology in the use of all the necessary instruments for planning. Performance would be much better." In fact, nothing is more certain than that it would require much more than "recognition" for performance to be much better. Here is not simply optimism but blindness to the reality which Professor Galbraith so insistently claims, throughout his book, to portray; and it is a blindness induced by the wish to see all "problems" of the "industrial system" as readily soluble within its framework, and without the need to look beyond it.

The final question raised by Professor Galbraith's modest discontents with the "industrial system" concerns the likely agencies of its reform. Not labour, certainly; for in that system, "everything is more benign. Compulsion will have receded. In consequence, there is little or no alienation; the way is open for the worker to accept the goals of the organization"; interests that were once radically opposed are now much more nearly in harmony." Demand for change cannot, clearly, be expected from the happy industrial family which Professor Galbraith has conjured up; where, but fifteen short years ago, there were large reserves of countervailing power, there is now un-alienated integration. But all hope is not lost, for there remains, in growing numbers and strength, the "educational and scientific estate." "It is possible," Professor Galbraith suggests, "that the educational and scientific estate requires only a strongly creative political hand to become a decisive instrument of political power." "A decisive instrument of political power" is pitching it rather high, and the notion of people as "an instrument" of political power, decisive or otherwise, is ambiguous and unattractive. Still, there is everything to be said for the stress on the responsibility and possible power of intellectuals. But the question then arises—political power for what? Professor Galbraith has no serious answer to that question. In fact, his whole soothingly complacent view of the "industrial system" and of American society precludes him from providing such an answer. For all the verbal iconoclasm, and the seeming dismissal of "conventional wisdom" and orthodox economics, there is too much here of apologetics and obfuscation, too little genuine probing, too ready an acceptance of the "logic" of the system, too cramped a view of its contradictions, too much underlying intellectual and political timidity, notwithstanding the self-conscious *enfant terrible* posturings, for Professor Galbraith to speak seriously to the American condition, or to those who seriously seek to change it. For such people, *The New Industrial State* has little to offer, either by way of diagnosis, or of prescription. What it does offer is a further demonstration of the limitations, both in diagnosis and in prescription, of a type of liberalism which constitutes not an alternative but a variant of that conservatism which Professor Galbraith claims to condemn.

Questions for Discussion

1. Compare the functions of government listed by Clair Wilcox with James O'Connor's notion of the "socialization of investments."

2. If government is a committee of the ruling class, how do you explain the fact that it provides billions of dollars in welfare payments to the poor?

3. Is America characterized by harmony and equilibrium as the liberal view implies or is it better described as a society in intense conflict?

4. What does Galbraith's argument about the control of the modern corporation imply about the economics of profit maximization? Do you agree with Galbraith?

5. Radicals insist that the important relationships in capitalist societies are power relationships. What kinds of power are there, and how does the power manifest itself?

VII

The Government-Military-Industrial Complex

The importance of defense expenditures in total government outlays documented in the introductory section of this volume and in some of the following articles is sufficient reason to require a section devoted solely to military spending. The effects of the government approval or disapproval of any proposed contract on the firms and their employees are obviously of tremendous proportion. When one adds the region where a potential supplier is located and the various alternative subcontractors it is clear that the final decision of the government on any given contract will have important influences on the personal and spatial distribution of income and wealth as well as on the very structure of industry. Despite these facts, rarely is military spending given more than cursory examination in economics texts or courses.

The principal issues raised in this section concern the origins and purposes of the military-industrial complex, so christened by Dwight D. Eisenhower in his farewell address.

The first article, however, by Charles Hitch and Ronald McKean, neither confirms nor denies the existence of the military-industrial complex, but is included here as an example of the work carried out at the now famous (or infamous) Rand Corporation, and of the way the question of military spending is dealt with, when at all, in the works of economists *qua* economists. Hitch and McKean argue that technological developments in weaponry and the spread of that technology have required an entirely new approach to defense planning. Their principal conclusion is that the country must not rely on its overall industrial superiority as an effective means of defense in the nuclear age, but that sufficient resources be "effectively diverted to security purposes before war starts."

The succeeding essays deal more specifically with the question of the military-industrial complex.

The first article, by the Ad Hoc Committee on the Economy and the War of the Union of Radical Political Economists, attempts to "detail the operations and consequences" of the military-industrial complex and concludes that the military-industrial complex is not "just a conspiracy against the public interest or an isolated bureaucratic phenomenon" but that it "is deeply rooted in the U.S. economic and political system."

The third selection, by Seymour Melman, while agreeing on the existence of the military-industrial complex, denies that it is necessary to the development of industrial capitalism, arguing that it is the result of misguided policies and a misinterpretation or misrepresentation of Keynesian analysis along with a fanatical fear of Communist aggression. Melman has been perhaps the most popular chronicler of the military-industrial complex and his point of view is therefore an important one.

Walter Adams, in the fourth article, also argues that the military-industrial complex has arisen because of mistaken policies but focuses on such specific policies as contracting procedures as an explanation. His article was written as a case study in critique of the argument by John Kenneth Galbraith (see Galbraith's selection in Part VI of this book) that bigness in business has evolved primarily because of technological necessity and, therefore, by implication suggests that the development of the military-industrial complex is not integral to our capitalistic system.

The last article, by James Cypher, questions this last hypothesis. Writing in review of Melman, Cypher claims the United States economy could not survive for long without the demand generated by government's military expenditures.

The careless reader will find this section repetitive of Part IV, but it clearly deals with a different issue. If defense spending were needed only to increase aggregate demand sufficiently to keep the economy relatively prosperous this goal could be achieved in the long run by any form of government spending, or at least less environmental damage could be obtained by later destroying the products without war.

Defense Against What?

CHARLES J. HITCH AND
ROLAND N. McKEAN

During the last decade or so the development and accumulation of nuclear weapons—first by the United States, then by the USSR and finally by other nations—have revolutionized the problems of national security. No comparable technological revolution in weapons has ever before occurred in history. The analogy of gunpowder is frequently suggested, but the substitution of gunpowder took place gradually over a period of centuries; and, like the weapons it replaced, gunpowder was used almost exclusively in a circumscribed area known as the battlefield. Nuclear weapons, a few years after their invention, have made it feasible—indeed, cheap and easy—to destroy economies and populations. They will not necessarily be used for this purpose; but the fact that they can be so used profoundly influences the character of the security that is attainable, as well as the policies by which we must seek it. Today, or next year, or within ten years, any one of several nations can unilaterally destroy the major cities of the others, and the latter, if they are prepared and respond quickly, can make the destruction mutual. In these circumstances, problems which once dominated our thinking about defense become unimportant. And while other problems assume new importance, we have scarcely had time to learn what they are, let alone how to think about them.

Because the weapons environment critically influences choice of policy, this chapter will first describe and project the weapon developments themselves, and then attempt to trace their implications for the kinds of war that our policies should be designed to prepare for or prevent. At this point we shall be concerned with the technological possibilities in the absence of any agreement to disarm or adopt significant limitations on the use of weapons.

Weapon Developments

Enough is known concerning the development and production of nuclear weapons and the means of delivering them—both here and in the USSR—for

Reprinted by permission of the publishers from Charles J. Hitch and Roland N. McKean, *The Economics of Defense in the Nuclear Age* (Cambridge, Mass.: Harvard University Press, Copyright, 1960, by The Rand Corporation).

a general consideration of medium- and long-term policies. For this purpose we can collapse the next decade or so to the present point in time. Exact estimates of present or near-future capabilities of both the United States and the USSR in terms of thermonuclear weapons and carriers are not here required. The significant facts are plain enough to informed public opinion throughout the world. They may be summarized as follows:

1. The number of urban centers which account for most of the economic strength of a major military power like the United States or Russia is small—certainly not more than a few hundred. Fifty-four United States metropolitan areas contain sixty per cent of the nation's manufacturing industry. Their population of well over 65,000,000, while only forty per cent of the national total, includes a much larger proportion of the nation's highly skilled technical, scientific, and managerial personnel. The 170 metropolitan areas listed by the Census Bureau contain seventy-five per cent of manufacturing industry and fifty-five per cent of the nation's population.[1] The concentration of industry in Russian urban centers appears to be roughly the same as in the United States, although the centers themselves tend to be more compact and therefore easier targets. While the total Russian population is less concentrated than that of the United States (almost half live on farms), the concentration of industrial and skilled labor and management is at least as great. Britain, Germany, and other industrial countries present even fewer targets.

   The elimination of fewer than 200 metropolitan areas in either the United States or the USSR (still fewer elsewhere) would therefore, as a direct effect, reduce industrial capital by 75 per cent and the most valuable human resources by about as much. This, in itself, would demote a first-class power to third class, but to the direct effects must be added indirect ones. Because of the interdependence in a modern industrial economy, the productivity of the surviving unbalanced economic resources would be reduced, perhaps disastrously. Radioactive fallout would be likely to inflict serious casualties on populations outside the target cities.

2. How many bombs would be required to "eliminate" a metropolitan area? It depends, of course, upon the size and shape of the area and the size of the bomb as well as upon other factors. But we were told by the Chairman of the Atomic Energy Commission after one test in the Pacific that a thermonuclear explosion could destroy any city on

---

[1] The metropolitan area concept as defined by the Census Bureau is, unfortunately, not a perfectly satisfactory measure of urbanization—because its definition is primarily on a county unit basis. The figures above include, therefore, some capital and population which may be sufficiently far from presumed city targets as not to be vulnerable to the direct effects of urban bombing, except fallout. On the other hand, the arbitrary legal boundaries of cities are much too restricted and even less satisfactory for our purposes.

earth.[2] We know that very much smaller bombs will destroy small cities, as the first primitive 20 kiloton atomic bomb destroyed Hiroshima, a city of 250,000, killing a third of its population; that thermonuclear weapons have been made in the multi-megaton "yield" range; and that the area of destruction from blast increases as the two-thirds power of the yield (thus, a ten megaton bomb would devastate an area approximately sixty times as great as that devastated by a twenty kiloton bomb). We have also been told that the area of intense radioactive fall-out from the Bikini shot was 7,000 square miles—that is, an area fifteen times the size of Los Angeles or approximately equal to the total land area of New Jersey.

About the long-term radiation hazards from such fission products as strontium-90 and cesium-137 we know less. The dangers resulting from a large-scale attack would be significant, though they may not affect the number of weapons that "rational" attackers would be willing to dispatch.

In any event, we are clearly entering a one-bomb-to-one-large-city era, which means usually one, perhaps occasionally two or three, bombs per metropolitan area. Barring large-scale passive defenses, total bomb-on-target requirements to destroy urban concentrations in the United States appear to be in the low hundreds, even allowing some to be assigned to economic targets outside cities. A larger number of bombs would have to be dispatched if delivered by missiles with low accuracy or reliability. Against a very effective air defense the number dispatched might have to be several times the number required on target—but we are told that no completely effective air defense is in existence and, as we shall see, it is questionable how effective air defense can be made against surprise attack.

3. Nuclear weapons of the same kind or in their small, light, "tactical" guise[3] may revolutionize war on the ground and at sea as drastically as the strategic air war. Less is evident about "requirements" for nuclear weapons against military targets: the number needed to destroy some highly dispersed and "hardened" military forces could be very large. What is evident is (1) that tactical forces armed with even moderate numbers of nuclear weapons and the means of delivering them can easily and quickly defeat forces which do not possess them; (2) that both the United States and Russia can use such weapons, and (3) that ground, naval, or tactical air forces that have not adapted their deployment and tactics to the new weapons will be hopelessly vulnerable to nuclear attack.

[2] *New York Times,* April 1, 1954. Mr. Strauss was not using "destroy" in a literal physical sense, and he was undoubtedly implicitly assuming no large-scale expensive passive defense measures to reduce vulnerability.

[3] The largest "strategic" thermonuclear weapons may be even more effective against some military targets, e.g., by making huge areas uninhabitable for long periods.

4. While Russia's weapon technology and nuclear stockpile *may* still lag behind ours, it would be rash indeed to expect any such lags to widen. As to technology, the Russians have obviously made tremendous progress in rocket engines and missiles, and quite possibly have more first-rate scientists working on their programs than the United States has in its programs. As to nuclear stockpiles, increases in production rates on both sides depend mainly on a willingness to invest in additional productive capacity. No one believes any longer that a shortage of some crucial specific resource like uranium ore will conveniently (for us) inhibit Soviet production. The Soviet Union is compelled by the strongest of motives to match or surpass the United States programs, and has not hesitated in the past to undertake very large investment programs (for example, in steel) to meet security objectives.

Several implications of these weapon developments for the relative strengths of offense and defense have become fairly clear. These implications may be summarized in the following way.

1. The game is loaded against the defense when small-scale (by World War II standards) sudden attacks can cause catastrophic and perhaps irreparable damage.
2. Responsible officials of the Air Force and of the North American Air Defense Command have told us repeatedly that a leak-proof defense is not now attainable. Under some, not too unlikely, circumstances of surprise attack, we could fare very badly.[4]

   While air defenses can undoubtedly be vastly improved over the next few years, the offense is likely to improve concomitantly. Ballistic missiles present formidable problems for air defense.
3. The superiority of the offense does not necessarily imply that either side can eliminate the enemy's ability to retaliate in force; still less that either side can *guarantee* such elimination. A strategic bombing force is much easier to protect by active and passive measures and by mobility and concealment than are economic and population targets. Such developments as nuclear-powered submarines armed with Polaris and train-mobile Minuteman missiles are offensive weapons with revolutionary implications. Moreover, the development of thermonuclear weapons, by greatly reducing the number of bombs on target required to cause massive damage to economic and population targets, has enhanced the retaliatory capability of whatever portion of one's striking force manages to escape surprise enemy attack. Unless the attacker is extremely successful, he may fail to prevent effective retaliation.
4. Similar considerations apply to tactical engagements, on the ground and at sea. Nuclear weapons and modern delivery systems give an attacker the ability to compress a devastating attack in space and time. Again

---

[4] We could of course do much better against a *small* attacking force *if we had adequate warning* than we could in less favorable circumstances.

we appear to have made much greater progress in offensive missiles than in missile defenses. And here, as in the strategic war, it is hard for the attacker to insure against effective counterattack.

That the superiority of the offense will persist is, of course, not certain. Judgments about the future rarely are. The revolution in military technology which began with the atomic bomb is a continuing, even perhaps an accelerating, one and will certainly take unexpected, unpredictable turns. And the fact that the odds favor the offense by no means implies that attempts to provide any defense are a foolish waste of resources. On the contrary, some kinds of defense measures are essential and integral components of a strategy of deterrence. But the prospects are poor that we will ever again be able to rely on such defenses to prevent great destruction if deterrence fails and an attack is launched.

Implications for Kind of War

The weapon developments that have been described could conceivably influence the character of warfare in either of two directions, neither of which can be ignored in our plans. They could increase the violence of war, or they could limit it.

All-out Thermonuclear War and
Limited Local Conflicts

Most obviously, these developments could make war "total" to a degree never before experienced. And all-out thermonuclear war involving nations like the United States and the Soviet Union could easily destroy either or both, at least as powers of any consequence, in a matter of days or perhaps even hours.

There is increasing recognition, however, that the dangers implicit in participation in all-out thermonuclear war may result in a stalemate. In the words of Sir Winston Churchill, a "balance of terror" may replace the balance of power. Nations may become too fearful and cautious to use or even threaten to use their ultimate weapons, except for direct self-protection. This would mean, assuming no change in the objectives of Russia or Red China, a continuation of the cold war, with the Russians and Chinese attempting to win uncommitted areas by political and economic warfare, by subversion, and by limited, local military aggression. To avoid piecemeal surrender, we might determine to engage in defensive or counter-military actions also limited in character.[5]

These military actions, or limited, local wars, may flare up as a result—indeed as an extension—of international negotiation, of internal revolution, or

[5] See Henry A. Kissinger, *Nuclear Weapons and Foreign Policy*, Harper and Bros., New York, 1957, Chapter 5 and *passim*, for an extreme but persuasive statement of this argument.

of pawn moves by major powers to test or exploit a weakness. They are the late twentieth century "balance of terror" counterpart of the limited-scale, limited-objectives wars of the "balance of power" century between Waterloo and World War I. We have seen many of these limited wars in recent years: the contest in the Formosa Straits, the Indo-China War, the Korean War (small only in comparison with World War II), the Greek-Albanian-Yugoslav conflicts, the Chinese Civil War, the Indonesian revolutions, the Suez invasion, the Lebanon crisis, and others. While some of these were not of primary concern to the major powers, most of them were. Challenges (or opportunities) like Greece, Korea, and Suez will continue to present themselves. The recent history of restraint in the use of nuclear weapons,[6] of attempts to confine these conflicts, of negotiated armistices, of ability to swallow frustration where the outcome was completely adverse (as for us in Indo-China and for the USSR in Greece)—all these are significant indications that the war of limited scale and limited objectives is here to stay.

But so is the danger of thermonuclear war, despite its recognized suicidal threat. There are many ways in which all-out war could be triggered by accident or misunderstanding. Either side may resort to a thermonuclear strike to protect some presumed vital interest (for example, on our side, Western Europe), or in frustration or desperation (for example, if the cold war appears to be going hopelessly against it), gambling upon the very great advantages accruing from a surprise first strike. Finally, the very fearsomeness of the threat is an invitation to a calculating, ruthless power to remove it by force if any happy circumstance presents itself—as, for example, the temporary impotence or vulnerability of the opposing strategic air force; or his own temporary invulnerability resulting from, say, a breakthrough in air defense technology. Moreover, in considering the prospects of some power initiating thermonuclear war, we cannot confine ourselves to the Soviet Union and the United States. Within the next ten to twenty years (not too long a period for the weighing of some military economic policies) several nations in addition to the United States and the USSR are likely to acquire a substantial thermonuclear capability. Quite apart from specifically military atomic programs, the widespread use of reactors for power will result in stocks of nuclear materials that may find their way into weapons.

It appears then that in our national security planning we must consider at least two kinds of war—all-out thermonuclear war on the one hand, and limited, local actions of a holding or counteroffensive character on the other.

The relative probabilities of these two kinds of war occurring will depend in part on the policies we pursue. If we prepare to deal with only one, we invite defeat, indeed destruction, by the other. The number of kinds of war which we must consider cannot, therefore, be reduced below two.

---

[6] We would by no means rule out the use of tactical atomic weapons in local wars; in fact, there have been numerous authoritative statements that the U.S. will so use them. But past restraint must be explained in part by the fear that their use would make it more difficult to limit the scale and objectives of the conflict.

War Calling for Prolonged Mobilization

Does the number have to be increased to three? Is there a third kind of war, besides total and local wars, for which we must prepare? It has sometimes been suggested that a third possibility is a large-scale and long war, like World War II, in which strategic bombing of cities is either withheld or, if attempted, is ineffective *on both sides*.[7] Let us call this the World War II type war, although it might differ from World War II in such important military aspects as the widespread use of atomic weapons against military targets.

The question whether this World War II type of war is likely enough or dangerous enough to justify extensive preparations is, as will be seen, a crucial one for economic mobilization policy. We will simply state our views, because to defend them would carry the discussion far beyond its intended scope.

The contingency that strategic bombing would be attempted but ineffective *on both sides* seems to be extremely unlikely, for reasons already explained.

Mutual withholding of strategic attacks on cities for fear of retaliation is a somewhat more serious possibility—but only if the withholding is combined with quite limited war objectives: If the apparent winner presses on for anything like "unconditional surrender," the apparent loser would convert the limited war to a total one. But a limited objectives war would be unlikely to be large-scale and long, like World War II. Mutual withholding plus limited objectives define what is essentially a local action.[8]

If a war of this kind did occur, we would have time to mobilize our industrial potential and ought to "win" eventually, just as we did in World War I and World War II, even if we were relatively unprepared at its beginning.[9]

In short, this kind of war appears so far to be the least likely (of the three) and least important in our preparations. It might become most important if atomic disarmament is achieved. But this has not looked very promising, and effectively controlled atomic disarmament (the only kind that United States policy has contemplated) may no longer be feasible unless completely new ideas for inspection and enforcement are conceived and accepted.[10]

Some British writers have suggested that the contestants might fight a lengthy "broken-back war" to a conclusion on the ground *after* successful strategic bombing on both sides. This would be Phase II of an all-out thermonuclear war. We should not completely ignore it in our planning, yet it is obviously not too important if Phase I is completely successful on both sides, or if one side falls substantially shorter of complete success than the other.

---

[7] If ineffective on only one side, the strategic bombing would be decisive and the war short.

[8] There are other difficulties associated with mutual withholding of city bombing in any war transcending a local action. There may be no practicable way to delimit the restriction: we know that many "strictly military" targets are separated from large centers of population by less than the lethal radius of large bombs.

[9] This is almost a *reductio ad absurdum*. Russia would not allow us to win complete victory while she possessed a nuclear stockpile.

[10] See Eugene Rabinowitch, "Living with H-Bombs," *Bulletin of the Atomic Scientists*, Vol. XI, No. 1, January 1955, pp. 5–8.

Implications for the Importance of Economic Strength

Declining Importance of Economic War Potential in its Conventional Sense

The term "economic war potential" has usually meant the maximum *fully mobilized* capability of an economy to supply the men and materials required to fight a war. There are two objections to this concept. The first is its vagueness. What constitutes a "maximum" diversion of resources to war depends importantly upon (a) political and morale factors which in all countries fluctuate with circumstances, and (b) the time allowed for conversion to war production: the longer the mobilization period, the greater the peak war output. There is no single number or simple set of numbers which can represent "the" economic war potential of a nation.

Second, and more important, recent and prospective technological developments associated with nuclear weapons have greatly reduced the significance of economic war potential in the sense of maximum fully mobilized capacity for war production. Before the development of nuclear weapons and the means of delivering them on distant targets, the military power of the United States could be fairly well measured by its economic potential. Geography afforded us the time we needed, if pressed, to translate most of our potential into power.[11] Because we were the wealthiest nation in the world with the largest steel and machinery industries, we were also the most powerful militarily.

The development of nuclear and especially of thermonuclear weapons represents a momentous turning point in the cost of acquiring military capabilities. Destructive power has now become so cheap that wars can be won or economies destroyed before there is time for mobilization.

In an all-out thermonuclear war the superior economic war potential of the United States is important only to the extent that it has been effectively diverted to security purposes before war starts. This is true for all our forces, offensive or defensive. It is particularly and most obviously true for our strategic air offensive forces and air defense. For preparedness for full thermonuclear war the United States must learn to rely on forces in being —not as cadres about which much larger, newly mobilized forces will be organized, but as *the* important forces.

Economic war potential also appears to be less than decisive in fighting local wars (Viet Minh could defeat France in the jungles of Northern Indo-China), and of even less importance, as potential, in countering assaults by infiltration, subversion, civil war, and astute diplomacy. In limited wars, too, forces in being seem likely to play a crucial role, useful reserves being mainly those that can be mobilized promptly. Once hostilities have begun, industrial

---

[11] Even before the development of nuclear weapons, geography proved an inadequate defense for European countries against Blitzkrieg tactics based on aircraft and tanks.

potential cannot be brought to bear soon enough. Even in World War II, the industrial potential of the allies did not save France or count for much in the first two or three years.[12] More recently, in the Korean War, industrial potential was not the force that saved the port of Pusan or shaped the course of the conflict. In all such actions—limited in objectives, means, and scope—full industrial mobilization is not approached, and economic war potential never comes into play.

In consequence the significance of economic war potential in its usual meaning has been degraded. The nation which can maintain the most formidable forces in being is not necessarily the wealthiest. In peacetime the proportion of national resources that can be diverted to national security purposes is by no means constant among nations. Both in peacetime and in fighting limited wars, countries with less economic war *potential* may support larger military budgets and forces. Russia, for example, a much poorer country than the United States, has supported a larger peacetime military program.

This situation is a particularly dangerous one for the United States. Shielded by geography, we have traditionally (before the Korean War) maintained very small forces in peacetime, and have regarded them as cadres rather than as integrated fighting units in a state of readiness. There is a strong tendency for nations (like individuals) to persist in policies which have been successful long after the external conditions essential to success have vanished, especially when they are pleasant and cheap like this one. The United States will probably maintain a substantial industrial lead over possible enemies for many years, but if we rely upon it as mobilization potential as we did before World War II, we will be inviting irrevocable disaster.

The Importance of Economic Strength Before the Outbreak of War

Without doubt, then, "the nostalgic idea that our industrial power is our greatest military asset could ruin our military planning."[13] This does not mean, however, that economic strength will be any less important in the pursuit of national objectives in the future than in the past. Military power is derived from economic strength, and foreign policy is based on both. Economic strength that is used for national security purposes *in time* is the embodiment of military power. Using it in time demands a new approach to national security problems—which to some extent we have already made.

The essential contribution of economic strength is that it enables us to do more of the numerous things which are desirable from the point of view of national security, but which, in their fullness, not even the wealthiest nation can afford.

[12] See C. J. Hitch, *America's Economic Strength*, Oxford University Press, London, 1941, pp. 60–73, 95–110.

[13] Thomas K. Finletter, *Power and Policy*, Harcourt, Brace and Company, New York, 1954, p. 256.

What are these desirable things in a thermonuclear era—that is, things that have positive payoffs and that we would like to have if resources were unlimited?

1. Preparations for and deterrence of thermonuclear war. These would include strategic air forces, warning networks, active air defenses, and passive defenses of various kinds including perhaps dispersal, shelters, and large-scale stockpiling of both weapons and industrial commodities. It appears desirable not only to do all these things but to do them in style—to confront the Soviet Union with a variety of strategic air threats, each absolutely invulnerable to any conceivable weapon which might be used against it; to erect a continental air defense system embodying all the latest and most expensive equipment of which any scientist has dreamed; and to buy enough passive defense of all kinds to insure our survival if by any chance an enemy attack still gets through.

2. Preparations for local and limited wars also appear desirable: challenges to fight such wars are almost certain to occur, and it would be comforting to be able to accept such challenges, or to make counterchallenges, if we want to. Sometimes it is argued that limited wars can be handled without ground forces or tactical air power simply by threatening massive retaliation against any and all provocations. If this were true, conventional military forces would be superfluous. The trouble is that the enemy might not believe our threat to launch a thermonuclear attack in the event of minor provocations.[14] Moreover, he might be correct in disbelieving, for we are probably not willing to use H-bombs to cope with minor aggressions—partly to avoid inhumane destruction, partly to retain allies, but mostly to escape the H-bombs that could in turn descend on us. Consequently, without conventional forces, we might have nothing with which to counter local aggressions and be wide open to "nibbling" tactics by the enemy. The net result might also be a heightened probability of thermonuclear war.

Preparation in style also seems desirable. Local, limited wars have taken many forms and have occurred in many places in recent history; future possibilities are even more numerous. We might have to fight in Southeast Asia, the Middle East, or the Balkans, with or without atomic bombs, with native help of varying qualities. We should like to have heavy matériel stocks pre-positioned and, in addition, a large capacity for moving men and matériel rapidly by sea and by air to the theater of action. To back up our ready forces for such wars it would be desirable to have trained reserves and facilities for quickly expanding the production of matériel.

3. It would be desirable too (if resources were unlimited) to prepare to

---

[14] For a discussion of these issues, see Bernard Brodie, "Unlimited Weapons and Limited War," *The Reporter,* November 18, 1954, pp. 16–21; and William Kaufmann, "Limited Warfare," in W. Kaufman (ed.), *Military Policy and National Security,* Princeton University Press, Princeton, N.J., 1956, pp. 102–36.

fight a World War II type of war. Even though this sort of conflict seems unlikely, it might conceivably occur. Preparations would call for ready forces to fight a holding action (these might do double duty for local wars), and measures to enlarge the mobilization base and to increase its security and the speed with which it can be converted. The accumulation of raw material stockpiles from overseas sources would be desirable, for example, in addition to securing the sea lanes. Construction of new capacity in industries that might "bottleneck" the expansion of war production, support of multiple sources of supply by expensive splitting of procurement contracts, and the training and maintenance of large reserve forces might be undertaken.

4. Cutting across all these areas, it would clearly be desirable to support a very large research and development effort. We are in an era in which a single technological mutation (as in the past, the development of radar and the atomic bomb) can far outweigh in military importance our substantial resource advantage. There are conceivable future mutations of equal importance—invulnerable long-range ballistic missiles, perhaps a high-confidence defense against nuclear weapons. Research and development is most obviously desirable in the context of thermonuclear wars: here certain kinds of technological slippage could break the stalemate, blunt deterrence, and place us at the mercy of the Kremlin. But it is also possible to conceive of developments which would, for example, greatly improve the capability of the United States to fight small engagements in out-of-the-way places. Development is cheap only by contrast with the procurement and maintenance of ready forces. If we tried to develop everything interesting (and possibly significant and therefore "desirable"), we could use all the potential as well as all the actual scientific and engineering resources of the country.

5. Finally, there are substantial opportunities to use economic strength in the cold war itself. Economic warfare, whether waged against our enemies or for our friends, can be expensive. It is widely believed that the Marshall Plan saved Western Europe from collapsing into chaos and perhaps Communism between 1947 and 1950, but at a cost of about 10 billion dollars. The United States is now spending roughly a billion dollars a year on economic aid to friendly and neutral countries; and the Soviet Union is lending over half a billion dollars annually, partly to its satellites and partly to other countries. Britain and Western Europe might spend many billions of dollars "uneconomically" on nuclear power plants to reduce their economic dependence on Middle Eastern oil, which is vulnerable both to Arab nationalism and to Soviet power. Economic strength permits a nation to wage the cold war more effectively, to reduce its vulnerability to hostile moves, and to improve its position and power by extending its influence.

These, then, are the desirable things—the things it would be nice to do from the point of view of national security. In the aggregate they far exceed our economic capabilities, so that hard choices must be made. But the greater our economic strength, the more desirable things we can do, and the better we can do them. We cannot prepare for all kinds of wars, but maybe we can prepare for more than one. We cannot develop every technological idea of promise, but maybe with three times Russia's economic strength we can develop enough more than she to keep ahead in the race for technological leadership. We cannot buy perfect protection against thermonuclear attack by any combination of active and passive defenses, but perhaps we can afford enough defense to reduce Russian confidence of complete success to the point where she is deterred from striking. Perhaps on top of all this, we can afford a positive economic foreign policy which will preserve our alliances and increase our influence on developments in the uncommitted parts of the world.

At the least, the possession of greater economic strength enables us to do more of these things than we otherwise could do. But it does so if, and only if, we use the strength now, during the cold war, before a hot war starts. For that reason the term "economic war potential" will not be used in the present study. The timely translation of economic strength into military power, the proportion of that strength so translated, and the efficiency of the forces in being, have become of critical importance—as opposed to some theoretical maximum potential which could be translated into military force at some later date. While the traditional concept of the mobilization base is not yet fully obsolete and may even justify a limited expenditure of budget, it is no longer the shield of the Republic.

Political Power and Military Spending

AD HOC COMMITTEE ON
THE ECONOMY AND THE
WAR

The Vietnam war must be viewed in the wider context of U.S. military expenditures since World War II for two reasons:

1. the heavy joint-costs in modern military technology make isolation of the costs (i.e., those directly incurred by the Department of Defense) of Vietnam difficult and arbitrary.
2. there is a dynamic within the system of determining military spending

From the *Review of Radical Political Economics*, special issue, Vol. 2, No. 3 (Summer 1971), pp. 29–40. Reprinted by permission of the publisher.

which operates so as to consolidate past levels of expenditure and pushes continually for increases therein: as a consequence, the pursuit of U.S. power interests results in a ratchet effect[1] in the level of defense spending.

Vietnam is to a large extent a substitute for other military outlays which can be expected to replace it if the war ends, given the current system of allocating funds to the military. As a corollary, there need be little fear that ending the war will lead to a recession, as there are several military programs likely to get the go-ahead when Vietnam finishes. The war should be treated merely as an upward aberration along a strongly growing trend in military spending.

The basis for this proposition is the existence of what is commonly known as the Military Industrial Complex (MIC), a coalition of interests and influences which has come to control so sizeable a portion of the political and economic process that its preferences for a high and rising level of arms spending can be translated into reality through a variety of means. Whether or not such a development was inevitable within a capitalist economy will not be considered—this paper will merely detail its operations and consequences.

Facts About Military Expenditures[2]

Defense spending is currently running at just over $80 billion a year, just under 9 per cent of GNP; this employs about 10 per cent of the labor force, which is about 7–8 million jobs. The proportion of output and employment which depends indirectly on military spending is not included here.

This level of spending amounts, with interest on previous war loans and veterans payments, to well over half of Federal expenditures on *everything*. Federal expenditures on health and education are less than one-fourth of direct military spending; all public spending on education and manpower training amounts to only three-fifths of military spending.

Defense spending amounts to over $360 per capita in the U.S., which represents a total of about $1500 per annum for a family of four.

Direct defense spending, at $80 billion per annum, is nearly sufficient by itself to absorb the whole yield of the personal income tax ($90.5 billion in 1969).

Since Korea, the proportion of GNP going to defense has fluctuated but little; from 8 per cent to 11 per cent. Given an upward trend in GNP, this means an upward trend in arms spending. Since 1948, there have been only two interruptions in this upward trend—moderate declines in the two years after Korea, and a one-year fall in 1965 before Vietnam really built up.

---

[1] Defense-related spending rises sharply during war, then declines after hostilities, but steadies at a plateau considerably higher than before the war. See *The Costs of American Governments*, Mosher and Poland, 1964, p. 26.

[2] *The Economic Report of the President*, 1970, contains all the data used here.

Neither of these reductions amounted to more than 10 per cent of the previous peak level of military outlays. No other predictions of imminent decreases in the military budget within the period have been translated into reality.[3]

The civilian Apollo space program, a prime target in the "national priorities" controversy, never cost more than 10.4 per cent of the defense budget.

Explanation of Trends in Military Spending

To secure such an enormous level of spending, there must have been both strong forces pushing for it and weak forces opposing it. This situation can be traced to the growth of the military industrial complex as a cohesive and powerful force advocating and rationalizing a high level of military outlays.

Elements of the Military Industrial Complex

1. The Pentagon: With over 1 million civilian employees and a net worth of at least $300 billion,[4] it disposes of contracts of value of over $40 billion per annum.[5] It is the center of the military industrial complex, and its phenomenal growth over the last 25 years has been the core of the problem.
2. The industrial contractors (22,000) and subcontractors (100,000) who compete in various fashions for the annual Pentagon business. These include many of the top corporations.
3. The Congressional defense lobby, including the important Armed Services Committee and many Congressmen with varying degrees of interest in and approval of heavy military spending.

This is the central triangle within the military industrial complex, and it constitutes the most sizeable domestic lobby and interest-group ever known.[6] It draws support also from several liaison and propaganda bodies such as the American Ordnance Association and the American Security Council. It subsidizes more sophisticated bodies such as private research groups, think-tanks and the like.

Cohesion Within the Military Industrial Complex

Before the interlocking elements within the military industrial complex are outlined, the factors favorable to its existence and growth will be detailed:

1. The U.S. view of its role in the world and the choice of a high level of military spending as the means to the end. This is to some extent

---

[3] See Baran and Sweezy, *Monopoly Capital* (New York: Monthly Review Press, 1966).

[4] S. Lens, *The Military-Industrial Complex*, p. 12. The Pentagon estimate of $200 billion is too low.

[5] Lens, op. cit., p. 12.

[6] "The Department of Defense dominates the budget. There is uncritical acceptance by the Committees of what the Defense Department wants to do." Eugene Skolnikoff, Professor of Political Science at M.I.T., as quoted in the *Wall Street Journal*, June 11, 1969, p. 1.

partly a result of the activities of those with an interest in arms spending, in fostering scares about Red aggression, missile gaps, hopes for
nuclear superiority and "victory," etc.

2. The nature of modern armaments technology, requiring a high degree
   of cooperation between buyer and seller, fostering the growth of liaison
   bodies and close connections between the Pentagon and industry. As
   Admiral J. M. Lyle put it, "If we didn't have a military industrial complex, we would have to invent one, for the design and production and
   maintenance of today's complicated weapons necessarily entails the
   closest cooperation between the military . . . and industry . . . ."[7]

3. The prestige of the military after the successes of World War II, remaining more or less unshaken until the reverses of Vietnam.

There remain the conscious actions taken within the defense/military interest to consolidate and extend their coalition. The essential strategy here has
been to create and stimulate a feeling of need for heavy military spending
for security and the defense of "freedom," and the use of funds voted in
response to such appeals to secure support for further increased appeals for
funds.

The central connection is that between the *Pentagon and industry,* for a
cohesive unit here is fairly sure of sufficient influence in Congress (although
the ABM vote proved a near squeak). Personnel move freely back and forth
between these firms and the military and defense establishment. Such interlocking effects are reflected in the 2,072 retired senior officers employed by
the top 100 defense contractors (Proxmire report), the employment of such
defense contractors as David Packard (Undersecretary) in the Pentagon,[8] the
commissioning of reports on future defense strategy and needs from major
suppliers.[9] The Pentagon takes care to cement the alliance of interest well
by making defense contracting a very special kind of business. Aspects of
defense contracting include:

a. Absence of competition in the allocation of the bulk of contracts. According to the Proxmire Committee, in 1968 formally advertised competitive contracts accounted for only 11.5 per cent of all contract dollars.
   Negotiated procurement in which more than one corporation was so-
   licited for bids accounted for an additional 30.6 per cent. Contracts
   negotiated with a single company chosen in advance accounted for
   57.9 per cent of all awards.

b. Even where nominal competition exists, the Department of Defense
   (DOD) can choose a contractor on the basis of "expected performance"

---

[7] Quoted by Lens, op. cit., p. 15.

[8] R. Lapp, *The Weapons Culture,* (Pelican edition, 1969), p. 11. Packard owns 3½M shares
in Hewlett-Packard. Problems of potential conflict of interest were resolved in Packard's
favor, as selling his stock would have broken the market.

[9] Lens, op. cit., p. 54, quotes a Douglas Aircraft study for the DOD, on world political patterns until 1985. It concluded that the U.S. "is not an imperialistic nation," although it has
"acquired imperial responsibilities": A neat rationale for arms spending in defense of freedom.

rather than price. More important, in many cases the idea for a new weapon does not originate with the Pentagon but rather with the prospective contractor.[10] The Pentagon closely guards its methods for awarding contracts. This leaves great latitude for political or personal friendship influences on decisions.

These practices conspire to make military procurement highly concentrated. According to Proxmire, in 1968 the 100 largest contractors secured two-thirds of the contracts. Also, the large contractors hold entrenched positions and can reasonably expect not to be abandoned by the government, which avows its interest in maintaining a strong defense industry.

The defense industry is the beneficiary of a number of practices which, according to the Proxmire report, sanction inefficiency and amount to concealed subsidies to industry. These include:

1. Government supply of capital to contractors,[11] in the form of publicly owned plant and equipment, and of "progress payments" which often completely cover the vast working capital needs of the industry. This amounts to a heavy subsidy (interest-free loans) to favored large firms.
2. Complete patenting rights over discoveries resulting from DOD-financed research.
3. Waiving of and noncompliance with the Truth-in-Negotiations Act. Proxmire found substantial overcharging as the result of DOD failure to investigate contractor costs.
4. Use of specification changes as a way of repricing contracts once they have been secured. This is called "contract nourishment."

Proxmire found the result of such practices to be a combination of inefficiency and high profits. Weapons systems were usually subject to large cost overruns (an average of 300–700 per cent in the 1950's), late deliveries (2 years on average) and faulty performance. The Weidenbaum study of the large defense-based firms and their counterparts in civilian markets revealed that between 1962 and 1965 the former had a rate of return on investment of 17.5 per cent as against 10.6 per cent for the latter.[12]

Galbraith asserts that industry likes the military business because of its low-risk, cost-push, high-return[13] and advanced technology aspects.[14] This

---

[10] The importance of this can hardly be exaggerated in view of the facts that (a) Congress has never refused to fund a major weapons system proposed to it, and (b) Many growth-oriented contractors such as Lockheed, General Dynamics, and McDonnell Douglas depend heavily on their federal sales. A vested interest in heavy arms competition ensues.

[11] An amount of $13.3B during fiscal year 1968 in the hands of private contractors, Proxmire reported.

[12] Lens, op: cit., p. 8 gives other evidence of fat profits in defense work. See also, M. Wiedenbaum, The Modern Public Sector, 1970, p. 56.

[13] Robert Heilbroner in The Limits of American Capitalism (1966) asserts on p. 36 that Western Electric made a 31 per cent profit on its Nike production and that Douglas Aircraft made a 44 per cent profit on its defense contracts.

[14] J. K. Galbraith, The New Industrial State, Chap. 29. Wiedenbaum, op. cit., p. 72.

seems to be borne out by these considerations:

1. Among the top 100 firms, according to the *Fortune* listing, 65 are significantly involved in the military market. All but five of the top twenty-five industrial corporations were among the 100 largest contractors for the Defense Department.
2. By 1966, 93 out of the *Fortune* top 500 corporations had diversified into defense work from primary interests outside it—a rate which probably exceeds the one which would be expected from the recent trend toward business diversification.[15]

These facts may be taken as implicating more than just a small enclave of industry in the Military Industrial Complex.

Such, however, is only part of the story. As will be outlined below, the unholy alliance of military and business has gone out of its way to ensure that this good business is also a growing business.

The second important connection is that between this *Military Industrial Complex and the legislature and executive.* This is what secures the funds and sanction for the Military Industrial Complex's activities. The basic facts are that:

1. The Pentagon employs 339 lobbyists; there were 5 in 1945. This requires a budget of $4.1 million—largely for hospitality to friendly legislators.[16]
2. Fifty-nine Congressmen carry officer rank in the Forces[17] and most are receptive to Pentagon overtures. It seems that marginal voters are offered upgradings to secure their favor. On top of this there is an unknown amount of stock held by Congressmen in the defense industries, which may be presumed to influence their voting behavior.
3. The Armed Services Committees are headed by conservative aging Southerners (Russell, Stennis, Mahon, and Rivers); their hearings on such projects as ABM have been blatantly one-sided[18] and have tended to rubber-stamp Pentagon funds requests. It has been left to the Joint Economic Committee to investigate waste.
4. Favorable Congressional response has been assured by political manipulation in the allocation of Armed Forces bases, facilities, contracts, and subcontracts—a patronage currently worth 45 billion dollars per annum and hence the subject of substantial local competition for its employment-generating effects. Stalwart Pentagon supporters are rewarded with lush defense awards to their States. It is not easy to tell what the natural location of defense activities would be, but it is clear that places such as Georgia and South Carolina have been favored beyond the merits of their natural endowments. Defense contractors create constituencies

[15] The *New York Times,* June 22, 1969.
[16] Lens, op. cit., p. 42.
[17] The *New York Times,* May 11, 1970, p. 14.
[18] Lens, op. cit., p. 43.

for themselves where they locate. For example, by settling in Washington State, the Boeing Company ensured itself two votes in the Senate. Defense spending has been crucial to the post-war development of Southern California, eastern Massachusetts, and, more recently, Texas, among others. Even the most dovish Senator will vigorously protest the closing of a defense facility in his home state.[19] Defense industry workers are aware that their skills are highly specific and that if they were laid off they would be unable to find jobs with prestige and salaries comparable to what they currently enjoy.[20] Programs to train defense personnel or to direct defense-oriented firms into civilian applications have proved notoriously unsuccessful.[21]

In addition to such factors, there is the problem of how the Military Industrial Complex uses *patriotism* and the *cold war ideology* to win the adherence of those who cannot or need not be bought, and to affirm the correctness of the self-interest of the beneficiaries of the "pork-barrel." This will be considered now.

Uses of the Power of the Military Industrial Complex

I. To maintain and increase the level of military spending. On the above analysis, the power of the Military Industrial Complex rests mainly on the use of previously secured funds to secure increases in defense allocations where possible. The means to this end have included:

A. Insistence upon the ever-present communist threat—even in this period of Russian offers of peaceful coexistence and defensive postures in foreign policy the Cold War is aggravated by the various liaison and publicity groups loosely associated with the Pentagon.[22] The threat to the American Way of Life is as strong as ever, especially from Chinese aggressiveness. This is no doubt believed by many, especially the followers. For the molders of opinion, the doubt cast on their sincerity or judgment by this combination of self-interest and prescription is reinforced by more concrete evidence.

B. To maintain an artificially high level of arms consumption, artificiality must be introduced into estimates of supply of and need for advanced weapon systems. These two aspects are not independent, as, in nuclear strategy, supply of a new weapon has tended to create the demand for it—through fear of enemy adoption if one ignores it. However, there is evidence of excessive *searching for new weapons* even when Russian technology was lagging behind. More damning is the tendency of the Pentagon to push through pro-

---

[19] Most notably, Javits and Goodell whom the *New York Daily News* of October 29, 1969 reported released "a joint statement [saying] too many New York State bases are on Laird's list compared with other states."

[20] S. Melman, *Our Depleted Society*, Chap. 6, gives examples of how defense contracts have paid high salaries in order to attract top scientists and engineers.

[21] Wiedenbaum, op. cit., p. 70. See also, *The Economy of Death*, Richard Barnet, 1969, p. 152.

[22] Lens, op. cit., Chap. 3.

grams that are in fact superfluous or obsolete—so that not only is there waste in the execution of approved programs but also many programs have been unnecessary from the point of view of their contribution to national security.[23] The whole attempt to press home missile superiority by piling up overkill capacity falls into this category. If a second-strike deterrence capability were all that was required, most of the 1,000 ICBM's and 41 Polaris submarines built up under Kennedy would be redundant, given the extreme difficulty of destroying Polaris in a first-strike. The overwhelming U.S. bomber forces are currently being added to with the AMSA (Advanced Manned Strategic Aircraft) in an age when bombers are redundant. An early-warning system (SAGE) against enemy bombers was underway when it was found that it was vulnerable to low-flying bombers.[24] It did not matter that the Soviets showed no interest in such forms of attack; $18 billion was spent at first and then more on modifications so that it might deter the Russians from developing such bombers. Similarly, Poseidon was developed when its initial rationale was found to be false. The technique of smallish initial commitments mushrooming into irreversible programs was one reason for the unprecedented opposition to the ABM program. These cases of systems being developed for their own sake illustrate the self-extending nature of the Military Industrial Complex. Although new systems create their own demand to a certain extent, the Military Industrial Complex still finds it convenient to *"stimulate" demand* for more and more of existing arms—using real or artificial hopes of "victory" by survival in war, so as to justify more and more overkill. Evidence for this view is not hard to find; the most damning is the series of "gaps" in U.S. strategic forces since the war:

1. "A 'bomber gap' was therefore made to order for competitive-minded people," says Lapp of the mid-50's scare, which resulted in the building of a "vast armada of strategic aircraft."[25]
2. In his first year of office, Kennedy secured greatly increased military appropriations on the strength of his "missile gap"—the "combination of pork and patriotism" which helped elect him—*which he then knew to be a fiction* on the basis of overflight intelligence.[26]
3. The conventional forces gap of 1963 and the current Soviet SS-9 threat (justifying ABM) fall into the same category of specious claims about Soviet or Chinese powers by men whose aim is to create a need for expensive weapon systems in a vapid chase for "superiority."[27]

Such are the artificialities used to ensure a high level of defense spending. (Often learned institutions are employed to give sophisticated rationales for such extravaganzas.)

C. Use of public funds for public relations and propaganda. Activities

---

[23] See *American Militarism in 1970*, (1969), p. 86.
[24] All references are to Lens, op. cit., pp. 96–7.
[25] Lapp, op. cit., pp. 68–9, 136–7.
[26] Lapp, op. cit., p. 38. *ABM, MIRV and the Arms Race*, 1969, p. 69.
[27] Lapp, op. cit., Preface to Pelican edition—on ABM decision.

under this heading range from warnings of imminent Soviet missile superiority in "Ordnance" magazine, through learned volumes by strategy "experts" (often in contractor companies) to heavy subsidy of such favorable films as "The Green Berets."[28] One of the most revealing cases is the way ABM was "sold" with public funds; when a political row blew up, the campaign was left to private and "spontaneous" organizations such as the Citizen's Committee for Peace and Security. This organization placed wholly misleading ads about ABM; among its signatories were 11 key officials of eight firms holding more than $150 million in ABM contracts—and hoping for more. Such is the "software" end of the trade. In 1951, it was revealed that the Pentagon employed 3,000 PR men[29]—one wonders how many worked on ABM.

II. Spread military uniformity in society and enable a rapid mobilization of the armed forces to meet "brushfire wars," as with the extended and expensive campaign to secure Universal Military Training. This was paid for with public funds and lasted from 1944 to 1955.[30] It resulted in a compromise—the Selective Service System. The peacetime draft gave the President the power to raise an army without the express consent of Congress, a power that was crucial to the escalation in Vietnam.

III. Extend Pentagon influence into spheres of foreign policy, labor, riot control, and even (the ultimate irony if it ever gets beyond the proposal stage) social action.[31]

These are the ways in which the Military Industrial Complex has used its power and extended the resources of which it disposes.

Opposition to the Military Industrial Complex

The phenomenal success of this lobby/complex since 1945 has also depended upon the weak and isolated nature of the forces opposing it. The main aspects of this problem are:

1. The lack of a private lobby or coalition to oppose government spending on the military. This frees the Pentagon from the forces that have operated to hold down public spending on health, river valley development, and public housing.[32]

2. The success of the Military Industrial Complex in identifying its own interest with the national interest, offering quick political capital to those who go along with it (as the vice-president of Ling-Temco-Vought put it, "you can't sell Harlem or Watts, but you can sell self-preservation . . . ; we are going to increase defense budgets as long as those

[28] Lens, op. cit., Chap. 3.
[29] Lens, op. cit., p. 53.
[30] Lens, op. cit., pp. 35–7.
[31] Lens, op. cit., Chap. 4 gives details.
[32] Baran and Sweezy, op. cit., Chaps. 5 and 6.
[33] Quoted in Lapp, op. cit., p. 13.

bastards in Russia are ahead of us").[33] Also, the willingness of public opinion to leave complex weapons decisions to the experts—viz., the Military Industrial Complex. The above shows the folly of such attitudes.

3. The sabre-rattling of the "liberal" administrations of the 1960's, who completely fell in with the "arms beyond doubt" policy. It is important to discount the noises made about disarmament in this period; some idea of the relative priorities of these Administrations is given by the fact that in 1964 the Arms Control and Disarmament Agency had a staff of 166; as against this, the American Battle Monuments Commission had a staff of 413. Moreover, the staff and advisory committee of the ACDA were mainly military-men and hard-liners.[34]

Conclusions

1. By a combination of largess, patriotism, and claims to be the bastion of freedom around the world, the Military Industrial Complex has built up a formidable position of power in the allocation of Federal funds (apart from its influence on the size of the Budget).

2. It is doubtful whether the end of the Vietnam War will greatly influence trends in military spending, as

(a) Present U.S. military commitments appear likely to generate similar situations and the Military Industrial Complex will provide strong pressures for a similar response to that in Vietnam.

(b) The Military Industrial Complex is adept at using current power to build up future power, as shown above. The strength of the Military Industrial Complex depends greatly on a large military budget—at least in the first instance.

3. Care must be taken not to conclude that the Military Industrial Complex is just a conspiracy against the public interest or an isolated bureaucratic phenomenon. It is deeply rooted in the U.S. economic and political system. It has shown itself capable of vigorous expansion to absorb all funds available to it. This paper has confined itself to outlining the mechanisms by which this expansion could take place.

[34] I. F. Stone, Melman, op. cit., p. 175; Lapp, op. cit., p. 52.

Can the State-
Management
Be Stopped?

SEYMOUR MELMAN

Is the growth of the Pentagon and its state-management a necessary condition of industrial capitalism or can industrial capitalism evolve without priority to such a war-oriented institution? There are two main elements in this issue. The first concerns the use of government: does industrial capitalism have to use government as a necessary instrument for its operation? The second element concerns war-making and war priority. With or without the use of government as an instrument of economic control, can industrial capitalism prosper without recourse to military production on a large scale?

Throughout the world, government has been used as an instrument of production decision-making in industrial capitalist societies. In the older capitalist nations, government was made an important center of economic decision-making since the Great Depression, when the theories of John Maynard Keynes showed how government could be used as a regulator of economies. Government initiative was thereafter used with increasing confidence to restrict fluctuations of industrial capitalist economies and to produce significant expansion and contraction of economic activity. In the newer lands of industrial capitalism, including state-centered capitalism (socialism), government has often been used from the very first as a center of economic initiative and management. Clearly, the use of government as an instrument of production decision-making is characteristic of both private and state capitalism, of both older private capitalist and the newer "socialist" economies.

Is war production essential for the viability of the capitalist state? This part of the theoretical problem proposed here has to be examined in light of the particular experience of the United States and of other countries, especially since the Second World War. During the 1950's and 1960's, the outstanding industrial growth performer in the world was Japan, with almost no military establishment (1 per cent of the Gross National Product for military purposes in 1966), followed closely by West Germany, with its limited military capability (4.1 per cent of GNP in 1966). Also, the data of western

European countries allied to the United States indicate that they have done very well economically from 1945 to 1969, while using substantially smaller parts of their GNP's for military purposes than the United States. The case of the Scandinavian countries is outstanding in this respect. Sweden, in particular, is a land of economic well-being and economic growth, a land where poverty has been virtually eradicated; it also spends 4.3 per cent of its GNP for military purposes.

All this suggests that countries with military budgets ranging from almost 0 to 4 per cent of Gross National Product as compared with 8 to 10 per cent in the United States, have been prospering in an outstanding fashion, while operating burgeoning industrial capitalist economies. The following data portray intensity of spending on arms and rate of growth in output per employee. If there were a necessary and positive relation between large arms budgets and economic growth in capitalist economies, then the countries of most intense military spending would show greatest economic growth rate. That is not confirmed by the following data:

	Military Spending, Per Cent of GNP 1966	Per Cent Growth Rate in Output Per Employee 1950-1965
United States	8.5	2.4
West German Federal Republic	4.1	5.3
Japan	1.0	7.7

SOURCE: U.S. Arms Control and Disarmament Agency, *World Military Expenditures 1966–67*, Research Report 68–52, Washington, D.C., 1968, pp. 9 ff.; U.S. Department of Commerce, *Statistical Abstract of the U.S.: 1968*, Washington, D.C., 1968, p. 842.

While government has been widely used as an instrument of economic decision-making, economic growth in viable capitalist economies has been possible without large-scale military activity.

The Second World War peace settlements contributed importantly to the subsequent low level of German and Japanese armed forces. In conventional wisdom that should have been associated with capitalist economic lethargy in those countries—which was not the case at all. Nor can it be said that these countries have prospered as they have because they are economic satellites of the United States, operating under control of either private American industry and finance or U.S. government control. Japan is an example of a nation that has made investment by foreigners in its economic system a very difficult affair. From 1960 to 1964, Japan's annual rate of growth in output per employee reached 9.8 per cent.

Some people may respond intuitively with the comment that Japan's high growth rate reflects the low level of economic activity from which Japan started after the Second World War. True, United States bombers wrecked major parts of Japan's cities and industry. Still, that economy produced a great navy and air fleet, including thousands of the formidable Zero fighter planes, before the military debacle. This was no industrially underdeveloped country. The 1950–1965 Japanese growth rate had something to do with the concentration on productive economic growth. If Japan had gone the U.S. (and U.S.S.R.) route after the Second World War, then priority to parasitic growth would have restrained economic development there as well.

On the other hand, if the United States were to change priorities in favor of productive growth, then the repair of depletion in many spheres of life would require spending about $76 billion per year for these purposes. Serious U.S. participation in world economic development would cost about $22 billion per year (see my book *The Peace Race*). Almost $100 billion of new, productive activity would give the United States annual growth rates in the range of 8 to 10 per cent—comparable to Japan.

Do capitalist nations require military production as a priority economic activity—because they are capitalist? The available evidence says "no."

How, then, can we account for the priority attention that has been given to military expenditure and military organization in the United States during the last decades? If that is not assignable to a generally necessary, inherent feature of capitalism, what special conditions of American economy or society account for this development? I think an explanation must begin with the Great Depression. At that time, the civilian government in Washington was unable to extricate the nation from the economic depression by civilian economic policy as then practiced. With hindsight, many people have held that a more aggressive policy of government economic investment would have turned the trick, but at the time there was not enough confidence and general agreement in the pursuit of Keynesian-type economic intervention. The result was that the American Great Depression was terminated as the United States became involved in war production, and finally, in the Second World War itself. Since the war involved full mobilization of U.S. resources, this terminated unemployment for millions of Americans and brought many others into the greatly enlarged labor force. The result was an unprecedented outpouring of goods of every kind, with a parallel increase in the level of living. All this occurred with massive output of military matériel—enough for wars in Europe and the Pacific. This experience led many Americans to believe that military production and organization was the occasion of economic prosperity and that this nation could have both guns and butter.

Nevertheless, from a 1945 military budget of $80.5 billion, there was a reduction to $13.3 billion by 1950. With the beginning of the Korean war in mid-1950, the American government and population became convinced that a military containment policy directed toward Stalin's Russia was required for American security. From that time on, military budgets underwent substantial general expansion, particularly for constructing and operating a considerable nuclear delivery system that would be competent for "massive retaliation."

The Kennedy administration introduced a major innovation. It formulated the requirement that United States armed forces must be suited for fighting three wars at once: a NATO war, a Southeast Asia war; and a smaller military engagement in Latin America. All this was paralleled by the organization of the state-management institution in the Department of Defense. The combined effects of these decisions included military priorities, the Vietnam wars program, and general depletion of American society. . . .

Evidently, the state-management in the United States is the result of a nationally and politically specific set of developments. This does not detract from the importance of the institution, but it does tell us that the operation and formation of this institution is not necessarily intrinsic to industrial capitalism itself. Knowing this is significant for an assessment of possible options within American society concerning the state-management and its operation. Since the future of the state-management is not determined by a built-in economic necessity of industrial capitalism, this leaves the future of the institution as a political issue. The issue is clearly political because the Congress has the key regulatory power by its control over the state-management's capital. Just as the Congress can enlarge the state-management by appropriating more money, the same mechanism could enable the Congress to check or diminish the state-management's power.

Who needs the state-management, and who opposes it? Here is an enumeration of principal groups within American society that have supported the state-management (by backing its policies), despite the contradictions and depletions that have arisen from its operations:

The administrative staff of the state-management,
Career men, military and civilian, in the armed forces,
People employed in military industry,
People working in the military research-and-development establishment,
Communities and parts of communities dependent on military industry and bases,
Many members of Congress representing areas of high military activity,
Believers in a world Communist conspiracy against the United States,
People of strongly authoritarian personality, who identify with martial leadership.

The directorate of the state-management is committed to its professional role not only because it is there, but also because military organization is the purest hierarchical organizational form and therefore its enlargement produces a maximum extension of decision-power over the people directly involved.

The men and women accounted for by these categories are appreciable in number, even discounting the last two categories of political belief. But the 8 million persons directly employed in military work, and those indirectly connected to military work, who may be three to five times as many, are still not a majority of the American population. The importance of these groups, however, is not accounted for simply by numbers. The various "think tanks"—research establishments supported by the military—include about 12,000 employees. Research activity carried on within universities for the Pentagon accounts for the full-time professional work of about 20,000 people. Taken together, this is a relatively small group of people in a society of 200 million. But their influence is considerable, since they are a part of those institutions upon which the whole society depends for the creation of new knowledge and teaching of the young.

The Congress has been a crucial supporter of the state-management, since the Congress must vote the capital funds without which the Pentagon could not function. Beyond that, however, many members of Congress are actively involved in securing industrial contracts for firms located in their districts or states. In some areas, groups of Congressmen have formed regular committees, with designated persons to look after these matters of liaison with the Department of Defense. These relationships are, in part, facilitated by the large staff of liaison officers which the Department of Defense deploys in the halls of Congress. Further, many Congressmen get involved in efforts to locate and continue the operation of military bases in their districts or states. In part, this is viewed as a continuation of a classic sort of "pork-barreling"—efforts by energetic Congressmen to secure government-financed public works for their districts. Finally, many Congressmen belong to the military reserve.

On the other hand, there are definable groups in America that constitute the state-management's potential opposition, whether from interested or disinterested motives:

The more educated part of the population,
Education and health professionals,
A major part of the clergy,
Part of the management and labor force of civilian business and finance,
Parts of the racial underclasses,
People with strong commitment to values of humanism and personal
    freedom,
Opponents of the Vietnam war and its conduct.

During the 1960's, public opinion polls repeatedly disclosed that the degree of criticism of government policies concerning Vietnam and similar matters was correlated with educational level. The most intense criticism of militarist policies was found in the college-educated part of the population. In 1968, about 30 per cent of the American population was attending schools, and over 6 million were students in American colleges and universities. University enrollments have increased by about 70 per cent from 1960 to 1968, promising to almost double by 1985.

Neither of the defined groups of fairly committed Americans comprise a clear majority of American society. Other factors, notably the impact of Pentagon operations on American society, as well as ideology and belief, are significant in determining the balance of political forces in the United States.

The Pentagon's military failure in Vietnam shattered the major myth of its military invincibility. The political and moral criticism of the war, including the outcry against U.S. casualties, exposed the Pentagon to opposition that cut through occupational-class lines. The failure of the "guns and butter" promise, plus rapid price inflation produced disillusion with the morality of government, even among those hitherto committed to patriotic acquiescence to government policy. These considerations, cutting across occupational, class, and political lines, could lead to a national majority rejecting the Pentagon, and its parasitism at home and abroad, as the dominant institution of government.

If the state-management institution and its priorities are continued, then the following may be expected: increased international competition in nuclear weapons and delivery systems, with emphasis on shorter response time and, hence, more reliance on mechanisms and greater probability of nuclear war by accident; continuation of the Vietnam wars program elsewhere; acceleration of domestic depletion as a consequence of greatly enlarged Department of Defense budgets; decline in the international value of the dollar as a consequence of unacceptable accumulation of dollars abroad owing to world-wide United States military spending. Even in the absence of society-destroying nuclear war, these effects would, in turn, greatly aggravate the race problems in the United States, for domestic economic development would be foreclosed. The same depletion process would produce increasing rebellion against the authority of government and its allies. Altogether, these would be profoundly destabilizing effects in society, possibly including mass violence and civil war mainly along racial lines.

These consequences from the continued operation of the state-management and its priorities would be forestalled only in the measure that declining support for the state-management is translated into political action that is competent to substantially reduce its decision-power. The critical test of this is either a drastic reduction in money allotted to the Pentagon by the Congress or significant withdrawal of popular readiness to implement Pentagon decisions, or both.

Despite the fact that the state-management operates with durable bases of support in nation-wide management and production systems, even that base is substantially weakened by the growing contradiction between ideology and performance. Thus, the contrast between Pentagon-supporting theory and visible reality . . . weakens the self-assurance even of the state-management staff and supporters—an essential ingredient to continued operation of the system.

Until now, the most durable source of support for sustaining and enlarging the operation of the state-management has been the pattern of antagonistic cooperation between the U.S. state-management and its Soviet counterpart. On each side, there is an appeal to the respective society to grant resources necessary for attaining superiority in particular weapons systems—qualitatively and numerically. On both sides, the appeal is similar—that the competitor is proceeding along lines that must be matched or exceeded under penalty of being disadvantaged. These appeals continue, successfully thus far, despite the fact that neither state-management is able to break through the limits on "defense" and military "superiority" that were imposed by the application of nuclear weapons to offensive military purposes. Despite this, the mutual appeal to fear—pointing to the hostile behavior of the antagonist—has become the single most powerful ingredient making for sustained build-up of the state-managements and their military organizations on each side.

On the American side this pattern is likely to continue until two things are perceived: first, that military priority imposes an unbearably high cost in the form of a depletion process, while the military cannot deliver on their promises of military advantage or a defensive shield; and second, that a politically vigorous part of the population has to marshal a cross-population coalition to compel the Congress to suppress the Pentagon and its society-destroying programs. . . .

The power of the state-management derives from the readiness of millions of people to accept and execute the orders issued by the Department of Defense, as well as from the formal political authority and financial power inherent in it. Thus, the power of the state-management in the area of research performed in the universities is not only derived from the funds offered and orders issued, but from the acceptance of these funds and the compliance with these orders by professors and students within the universities. That is, the strength of the institution rests in large measure on at least the tacit support of a large part of the population.

The economic characteristics of the state-management are usually glossed over by the ordinary folk wisdom that a dollar spent is a dollar spent and that military spending puts money into circulation and thereby adds to national income. But spending of dollars by the state-management has characteristics without counterpart in a private firm's operation. Thus, a private management usually attempts to enlarge the scope and intensity of its decision-making by investing capital, recovering the money that has been invested through the sale of products, thereby having profits in hand for further investment. Extension of control or the enlargement of decision-making by management is made possible by the profit that this cycle of investment, recovery, and re-investment brings.

In the case of the state-management, the process is altogether different. There, capital is invested, but in the form of funds appropriated by Congress—a proportion of the national income of the society. These funds, and the material resources they represent, once "invested," give direct returns in extension of control, taking the form of military power. There is a return, an enlargement of economic as well as military decision-power, but no return of money from applied capital. No profit-yielding market transaction is involved in the direct use of capital funds by the state-management to acquire military matériel and organizations, the direct manifestation of enlarged decision-power. In the absence of a profit accumulation process, and with one-half the federal taxes as a source of funds, there is little incentive in the state-management to conserve cost in its operations. Characteristically, the theory of the cost-minimizing firm is inapplicable to understanding the operations of the state-management or its subdivisions. While the state-management itself earns no profit, selected submanagements, are granted capital funds—in excess of costs—by the central office. These capital grants are termed "profit" in the conventional accounts of the subfirms, although this "profit" is surely not the entrepreneur's reward for risk-taking.

The capital of the state-management is obtained by alleging the existence of external "threats." This word implies both imminent dangers and the promise of future danger. Pentagon spokesmen typically evoke fear by alluding to some "threat" from the outside. Thus, the justification for Pentagon budgets is imperiled by the possibility, not to mention the actuality, of a workable détente between the great powers.

The state-management has to obtain resources from a society that can sustain full employment through generally accepted civilian public policies. The attempt to preempt resources from a high employment economy for economically parasitic growth places great pressure on the relation between currency in circulation and the supply of goods, thereby generating unacceptable price inflation at home. Sustained high military expenditures threaten the value of the dollar at home and abroad. However, the state-management is not itself endangered by a diminution in the value of the dollar, whether from domestic or external causes. For whatever the relative value of the dollar may be, the state-management receives the goods and the services these dollars purchase, and for its purpose that is sufficient.

Civilian economy and civilian management, financial and industrial, all have a clear interest in a currency of stable (predictable) value and in having an economy that functions within predictable and acceptable limits of variation. The state-management needs neither condition in order to function or in order to expand its decision-power.

The military-industrial complex of President Eisenhower's generation was superseded by the state-management. That complex was still essentially a market operation, a network of relations between buyers and sellers. One could not easily abolish the market that was the military-industrial complex. But the operations of the state-management might, for example, be legislated against, since its operation is contingent on a budget passed by the Congress each year. Control of that budget would bring control over the state-management.

The state-management has a propensity for virtually unlimited extension of its decision-power. This is reflected in its budgets, hardware, and political planning. In December, 1968, the Pentagon leaked to the press the fact that it was going to ask for a budget of $100 to $110 billion for the next year. Included in this budget, besides funds for items and organizations already existing, were requests for funds for a new series of enterprises and weapons systems. Among the new items were an enlarged antiballistic missile system, a new strategic bomber, a larger successor to the Minuteman missile, a larger successor to the Polaris missile carried by the submarines, a new continental air defense system, an altogether new intercontinental ballistic missile system—far larger than any of those now in hand, a new type of "quiet" submarine—to cost $150 to $200 million each, and on and on. In response to alleged external "threats," Congressional committees are asked to vote astronomical funds. Rarely do they get an answer to the crucial question: "Does the system as it exists, or as proposed, actually constitute a true defense for the United States?" It is reasonable to suppose that most citizens approve of large allocations for the Department of Defense on the understanding that they are buying an effective shield against external attack.

The state-management's mode of operation has had the effect of enmeshing an ever-widening part of society. For example: consider the political significance of Texas having been transformed between 1965–1968 into a state with the second-largest military industry in the country. Following this change, is this state likely to dispatch Representatives and Senators to Washington who would be critical of the state-management? In a similar vein, would an anti-DuPont candidate be elected in Wilmington, Delaware? Evidently, the state-management's industrial operations produce effects that are in the manner of a closed-loop growth system—automatically reinforcing and enlarging its operation. . . .

For all its immense resources and access to high-grade personnel for its planning and operations management, the state-management has come to be a fundamentally fantasy-oriented organization. Its strategic military plans are oriented to nuclear supremacy, but the mutual attainment of overkill frustrates all ambitions of this sort. Its "conventional war" plans are oriented to winning guerrilla wars with immense firepower superiority, when the Vietnam war has shown this expectation to be only a Pentagon illusion. The Pentagon calculated that with superior military power, world political development could be substantially controlled, but American hegemony in critical places—as in much of Western Europe—has been leaking at the seams, just as Soviet hegemony has frayed in many parts of the world. Above all, the state-management has promised that, through its operations, the United States could be defended, and that is precisely what they have not been able to do. It took the Cuban missile crisis to produce the moment of truth: there is no shield when nation-states confront each other with great nuclear forces.

Structurally, the military economy is cross-class, that is, it represents a vertical slice of society, not simply a modern version of the celebrated "merchants of death" of the First World War vintage. While the top echelon of the state-management does the crucial planning and decision-making, its power depends upon the support and energetic participation of sub-managers, scientists, engineers, and trade union members in the great array of bases, research and development establishments, and weapons-manufacturing industries. One effect of this has been to produce a cross-class lobby for the Pentagon and its budgets. This cross-class bloc depletes the rest of the society.

There has been a similar pattern of cross political-ideological support for the operation of the state-management. Obviously, most conservatives have supported military budgets without limit in the name of defense against Communism. But an important bloc of support for the state-management is composed of moderates, political liberals, and leftists, whose ideology favors more authority for central government. Characteristically, this is justified by the proposition that central government alone has the capacity for regulating economic behavior and for planning and executing the economic amelioration which many liberals and leftists profess to desire. In the name of these ends, ever-increasing budgets for the federal government are supported, even though these growing budgets are for predominantly military purposes. Thus, pro-big-government liberals and leftists, often critical of certain Pentagon policies, function as the loyal left opposition for the state-management.

The highly structured Pentagon, with its state-management, immense funds, collateral organizations in government and in industrial and other spheres of life, and its decisive influence on national and international affairs has become a true "state within a state," a para-state.

The normal operation and expansion of the para-state and its state-management has been based upon the wholesale selling of fear—fear of nuclear war, fear of Communism (even after the post-Stalin thaw)—as a lever for prying more and more support from the public and Congress for ever-larger military budgets.

The Military-Industrial Complex and the New Industrial State

WALTER ADAMS

I

My hypothesis—the obverse of Galbraith's—holds that industrial concentration is not the inevitable outgrowth of economic and technical forces, nor the product of spontaneous generation or natural selection. In this era of big government, concentration is often the result of unwise, man-made, discrimi-

From *American Economic Review,* Vol. LVIII, No. 2 (May 1968), pp. 652–65. Reprinted by permission of the author and the American Economic Association.

natory, privilege-creating governmental action. Defense contracts, R and D support, patent policy, tax privileges, stockpiling arrangements, tariffs and quotas, subsidies, etc., have far from a neutral effect on our industrial structure. In all these institutional arrangements, government plays a crucial, if not decisive, role [1].[1] Government, working through and in alliance with "private enterprise," becomes the keystone in an edifice of neomercantilism and industrial feudalism. In the process, the institutional fabric of society is transformed from economic capitalism to political capitalism.

My hypothesis is best explained in Schumpeterian power terms. According to Schumpeter, the capitalist process was rooted, not in classical price competition, but rather "the competition from the new commodity, the new technology, the new source of supply, the new type of organization—competition which commands a decisive cost or quality advantage and which strikes not at the margin of the profits and outputs of existing firms but at their very foundations and their very lives" [11, p. 84]. The very essence of capitalism, according to Schumpeter, was the "perennial gale of creative destruction" in which existing power positions and entrenched advantage were constantly displaced by new organizations and new power complexes. This gale of creative destruction was to be not only the harbinger of progress but also the built-in safeguard against the vices of monopoly and privilege.

What was obvious to Schumpeter and other analysts of economic power was also apparent to those who might suffer from the gales of change. They quickly and instinctively understood that storm shelters had to be built to protect themselves against this destructive force. The mechanism which was of undoubted public benefit carried with it exorbitant private costs. And, since private storm shelters in the form of cartels and monopolies were either unlawful, unfeasible, or inadequate, they turned increasingly to government for succor and support. By manipulation of the state for private ends, the possessors of entrenched power found the most felicitous instrument for insulating themselves against, and immunizing themselves from, the Schumpeterian gale. . . . A case in point is the military-industrial complex. . . .

Here government not only permits and facilitates the entrenchment of private power but serves as its fountainhead. It creates and institutionalizes power concentrations which tend to breed on themselves and to defy public control. The scenario of events should be familiar. The "mad momentum" of an international weapons race militates toward large defense expenditures (currently at an annual rate of $75 billion). This generates a demand, not only for traditional, commercial, shelf items like food, clothing, fuel, and ammunition, but also for the development and production of sophisticated weaponry. Lacking a network of government-owned arsenals, such as produced the shot and cannot in the days of American innocence, or having dismantled the arsenals it did have, the government is forced to buy what it no longer can make. It becomes a monopsonistic buyer of products which are not yet designed or for which production experience is lacking. It buys

[1] Numbers in brackets refer to the list of references at the end of this article.

at prices for which there is little precedent and hardly any yardsticks. It deals with contractors, a large percentage of whose business is locked into supplying defense, space, or atomic energy needs. It confronts powerful oligopolists in a market where technical capability rather than price is the controlling variable—in an atmosphere shrouded by multilateral uncertainty and constant warnings about imminent aggression. In the process, government becomes almost totally dependent on the chosen instruments, i.e., creatures of its own making, for effectuating public policy [4] [8] [9]. Lacking any viable in-house capabilities, competitive yardsticks, or the potential for institutional competition, the government becomes—in the extreme—subservient to the private and special interests whose entrenched power bears the governmental seal.

This unique buyer-seller relationship, which defies analysis by conventional economic tools, lies at the root of the military-industrial complex and the new power configurations generated by it. The complex is not a conspiracy between the "merchants of death" and a band of lusty generals, but a natural coalition of interest groups with an economic, political, or professional stake in defense and space. It includes the armed services, the industrial contractors who produce for them, the labor unions that represent their workers, the lobbyists who tout their wares in the name of "free enterprise" and "national security," and the legislators who, for reasons of pork or patriotism, vote the sizable funds to underwrite the show. Every time the Congress authorizes a military appropriation, it creates a new constituency (i.e., propaganda machine) with a vested interest in its perpetuation and aggrandizement. Thus, the current proposal for an anti-ballistic-missile system, the "thin" variety of which would cost $5 billion and the "thick" variety $40 billion, and which would probably be obsolete by the time it was completed, has been estimated to involve 28 private contractors, with plants located in 42 states (i.e., 84 senators), and 172 congressional districts. Given the political reality of such situations and the economic power of the constituencies involved, there is little hope that an interaction of special interest groups will somehow cancel each other out and that there will emerge some compromise which serves the public interest. There is little assurance that the corporal's guard of auditors in the General Accounting Office or Galbraith's scientific-professional elite or a handful of distinterested university analysts will constitute a dependable and adequate force of countervailing power. The danger remains that the "conjunction of an immense military establishment and a large arms industry," against which President Eisenhower warned, will become a Frankenstein threatening to control the contract state which brought it into being. The danger persists that power will be coalescing, not countervailing—that the political cloakroom will displace the economic market place.

It would be facile to conclude that the military-industrial complex and the new industrial state represent a price which society must pay—and inevitably so—because of national defense considerations or because of technological inexorability. But this would be to miss the point—to ignore the crucial political component in the institutional arrangements at issue. The military-industrial complex is only a special case illustrating the power problems inherent in the new industrial state. Both are created, protected, privileged, and subsidized by the state. Both represent a form of private socialism—a type of social planning through fragmented, special-interest chosen instruments operating in the "private" sector. Both represent a blending of private economic power and public political power. Both are reminiscent of the Elizabethan monopoly system and its abuse, corruption, favoritism, waste, and inefficiency—an *imperium in imperio,* without demonstrable public benefits, and without any built-in safeguards for the public interest. In sum, to the extent that they are creatures of political power and not the product of natural evolution, there is nothing inevitable about their survival and nothing inevitable about the public policies which spawn and preserve them.

II

Let us examine these public policies which lie at the base of the new industrial state, and particularly the military-industrial complex.

Defense and Space Contracts

These contracts, typically awarded on a negotiated rather than a competitive bid basis and as much the result of political as economic bargaining, convert the private contractor into a quasi-governmental, mercantilist corporation, maintained in a privileged position by "royal" franchise. The attendant abuses, especially the creation of entrenched power positions, are not inconsiderable.

In 1965, the U.S. Comptroller General, an Eisenhower appointee, highlighted the following characteristics of the contract system before a congressional committee:

1. excessive prices in relation to available pricing information,
2. acceptance and payment by the government for defective equipment,
3. charges to the government for costs applicable to contractors' commercial work,
4. contractors' use of government-owned facilities for commercial work for extended periods without payment of rent to the government,
5. duplicate billings to the government,
6. unreasonable or excessive costs, and
7. excessive progress payments held by contractors without payment of interest thereon [12, p. 46].

To this list could be added the procurement of items that were not needed, or in adequate supply elsewhere in the armed services, or were in fact being sold as surplus by the buying agency; indirect procurement through the prime contractor rather than direct purchase from the actual manufacturer—at far lower prices and without the pyramiding of overhead and profits; awarding of sole-source contracts for which the contractor had no special competency; the refusal by firms with overall systems responsibility to break out components for competitive bidding, or to furnish specifications for such bidding [12] [13]; and finally, according to the Comptroller General, "excessive prices resulting from the failure of the agencies to request, or the contractors to furnish, current, accurate, and complete pricing data or from the failure to adequately evaluate such data when negotiating prices" [12, p. 46]. In quantitative terms, according to a summary of GAO studies covering the period from May, 1963, to May, 1964, there was ascertainable waste of $500 million in a 5 percent sample of procurements [9, p. 269].

Perhaps it is unavoidable that in the procurement of complicated weapons systems, where uncertainty is pervasive and precedents are unavailable, cost estimates will be unduly inflated. As Peck and Scherer found in their study of twelve major weapon system development programs, actual costs exceeded predicted costs by 3.2 times on the average, with a range of actual versus predicted costs of from 70 to 700 percent [10, pp. 19–25]. Recent prediction errors in the F-111 and Apollo programs, Scherer reports, are of the same order of magnitude.

One can sympathize with the contracting officers negotiating for complex and sophisticated weapons technology and still agree with the McClellan Committee's conclusion that the government should not abdicate its responsibilities for program management, nor delegate these responsibilities to private contractors, if it wants to avoid avoidable abuses and flagrant overcharges: "Even the most reputable and ethical contractor is placed in the conflicting position of managing a program where the feasibility, technical, and economic decisions which should be made by the customer-Government are made by the producer-contractor," the Committee observed with charitable understatement. "The absence of competition, coupled with the urgency to get the program underway, removes normal safeguards against large profits and weakens the Government's negotiating position" [16, p. 141].

On the other hand, one must understand the reluctance to endanger the national security because of excessive delays caused by punctilious bookkeeping. As Charles G. Dawes told a congressional committee investigating World War I procurement scandals:

> Sure we paid. We didn't dicker. Why, man alive, we had to win the war. We would have paid horse prices for sheep if sheep could have pulled artillery to the front. Oh, it's all right now to say we bought too much vinegar and too many cold chisels, but we saved the civilization of the world. Damn it all, the business of an army is to win the war, not to quibble around with a lot of cheap buying. Hell and Maria, we weren't trying to keep a set of books, we were trying to win the war! [8, pp. 53–54.]

Government R and D and Patents

The awarding of government R and D contracts—and the disposition of patent rights thereunder—is another technique of creating, privileging, subsidizing, and entrenching private power. Again, this is a matter of man-made policy, not institutional inevitability.

The importance of federal policy in this area derives from a number of characteristics of federally financed research. Since World War II, the government has generally paid for roughly 65 per cent of the nation's research and development, but performed only 15 per cent of the work. Two agencies, the Department of Defense and NASA, account for about 80 per cent of the government's R and D outlays. The lion's share of these outlays is concentrated in a few industries, notably aerospace, electronics, and communications. The concentration of R and D contracts is even greater than that of production contracts. There is high correlation between companies receiving R and D contracts and those receiving production contracts. Finally, the benefits of military R and D tend to spill over into civilian markets [3, pp. 71–90].

The typical R and D contract, it should be noted, is a riskless cost-plus-fixed-fee venture. It usually protects the contractor against increases in labor and materials costs; it provides him with working capital in the form of periodic progress payments; it allows him to use government plant and equipment; in addition, it guarantees him a fee up to 15 per cent of the estimated cost. Nevertheless, some contractors demand additional incentives. With the arrogance characteristic of all privilege recipients, they want to extend and compound such privilege. "We recognize," says the vice-president of the Electronics Industries Association, a prime beneficiary of government-financed R and D, "that the ownership of a patent is a valuable property right entitled to protection against seizure by the Government without just compensation" [17, p. 132]. In this view, the patent is a right, not a privilege voluntarily bestowed by the government to effectuate a public purpose. By a curious perversion of logic, it becomes a vested privilege to which the private contractor is entitled and of which he is not supposed to be deprived without "just" compensation.

Characteristically, both the Department of Defense and NASA have accepted this argument for privilege creation and made it the cornerstone of their patent policies. The principle at issue requires little adumbration. Allowing a contractor to retain patents on research financed by and performed for the government, as Wassily Leontief points out, "is no more reasonable or economically sound than to bestow on contractors, who build a road financed by public funds, the right to collect tolls from the cars that will eventually use it" [17, p. 234]—or the right to close the road altogether. It is tantamount to socializing the financial support for research while permitting private monopolization of its benefits. Moreover, as Admiral Rickover observed, firms receiving R and D contracts "are relatively few huge corporate entities already possessing great concentrated economic power. They are not ailing segments of the economy in need of public aid or subsidy. Nor are there any real reasons to offer patent give-aways in order to induce them to accept Defense Department research grants or contracts. . . . To claim that agencies cannot get firms to sign such contracts unless patent rights are given away strikes me as fanciful nonsense" [9, p. 294].

Stockpiling of Strategic and Critical Materials

This is an "ever normal granary" program, ostensibly designed to enable the United States to fight a war of specified duration, determined by the strategic assumptions of the Joint Chiefs of Staff. In reality, it is a price support program, the details of which are buried in secret government files and the "primary purpose" of which is to subsidize selected mining interests in the name of national security [14, p. 36–45]. That, at least, was the conclusion of the exhaustive hearings conducted by the Symington Subcommittee of the Senate Armed Services Committee which examined the origin and growth of the national stockpile, the Defense Production Act inventory, and supplemental stockpile, which by 1961 had involved the expenditure $8.9 billion [14, p. 4].

These were the specific findings of the Symington Subcommittee:

1. Stockpile objectives were constantly manipulated to increase purchases regardless of national security needs. Thus, starting in 1954, "to justify further purchases of lead and zinc, when use of the old formula or requirements versus supplies did not permit additional buying, basic strategic assumptions were changed, and two objectives for each material were established. Under this new concept, the basic objective was determined under the usual method, but a new objective—the maximum objective—was arrived at by disallowing all supplies of a material from overseas. This had the effect, in many instances, of doubling the amount of a material that had to be stockpiled. It was then discovered, however, that even this new system would not permit additional purchases of lead and zinc in the amounts needed to maintain higher prices for lead and zinc. Resort was then had to the arbitrary one-year rule. Under this rule objectives were set at one year's consumption of the total national economy during a normal year without regard to what our requirements and supplies were" [14, pp. 4–5]. In the case of some ores and minerals, an arbitrary six-month rule was adopted.

2. The buying programs to develop a domestic supply of certain ores, said the Committee, "can only be described as a failure. . . . Much of the material purchased was not needed. A substantial part of these ores did not meet the specifications of the stockpile. Nor was any domestic mobilization base established by these purchases as is indicated by the

fact that when the purchases stopped production stopped as well" [14, pp. 8–9, 66]. Moreover, contrary to expectations, most of the expenditures did not go to small business but to well-established mining companies; 86.7 per cent of the tungsten purchases, for example, were made from the ten largest producers.

3. The price support level of some materials, like tungsten, e.g., were set two or three times above world prices, thus allowing the contractors windfall profits by buying at low world prices and supplying the stockpile at artificially exorbitant prices [14, pp. 69–71].

4. Premium prices were often paid to contractors on the assumption that it would be necessary for the contractor to incur substantial capital expenditures to perform under the contract. Yet the government was denied the right under these contracts to check whether the capital expenditures had in fact been made, or to inspect the contractor's book to ascertain his production costs, or to renegotiate the price if the anticipated high costs were not realized [14, pp. 68–69].

5. When market prices for some materials, like copper, e.g., rose above the contractual stockpile price, producers were permitted to divert deliveries from the stockpile to private industry—without sharing this windfall with the government [14, pp. 49–54].

6. When the Joint Chiefs of Staff changed their strategic assumptions from a five-year war to a three-year war, the stockpile administrators waited for two years before implementing the change. Felix Wormser, Assistant Secretary of the Interior for Minerals Resources, who before and after his government service was vice-president of the nation's largest lead producer (St. Joseph Lead Co.), protested that such a change would constitute "a breach of faith with the mining industry" [14, p. 25].

7. Disposals of excess supplies were resisted strenuously, and only in tin and rubber were any large-scale sales made. "It is significant," the Symington Committee noted wryly, "that there are no producers of natural rubber and tin in the United States and this could well account for the fact that the only two large disposals have been in these materials" [14, p. 28].

The point need not be belabored. The rules for operating the national stockpiles as articulated by the industries concerned and their protagonists in government are fairly simple: The government must accumulate reserves against the most unthinkable eventualities. It must buy these materials at prices industry considers remunerative, regardless of world market conditions. This subsidy must be adequate to enable industry to operate profitably until such time as its services are required for mobilization in time of war. Finally, regardless of the available stocks, no disposal must ever be made from the stockpile. Such sales would not only endanger national security but also disturb market conditions and hence constitute unwarranted government interference with free enterprise.

Alienation of the Public Domain

To achieve or solidify their control over prices and markets, the giants of American industry cannot rely on the imperatives of modern technology. On the contrary, they must live in constant fear of the "creative destruction" wrought by new technology; and they must always be alert to the potential competition of substitute products and processes. Even more important, they must fight to contain, neutralize, and sterilize the "institutional" competition of the public domain which threatens to impose an intolerable regulatory yardstick on their operations. TVA is an embarrassment to the electric power monopoly, the communication satellite to AT&T dominance, navy shipyards to the shipbuilding cartel, and the Army's Redstone Arsenal and Jet Propulsion Laboratory to the condottieri of aerospace. Pressure must be exerted, therefore, to dismantle such operations, or to circumscribe their competitive viability, or to sell their facilities to private enterprise—in a manner which does not disturb the existing power structure and indeed might even entrench it more solidly. Here, again, governmental cooperation is required for implementation of this grand strategy, and this is a matter of political decision, not technological or economic inevitability.

The disposal of government-owned plants at the end of World War II underscores the nature of the power struggle and the availability of public policy alternatives [1, pp. 117–41]. In aluminum, the disposal program was a qualified success; Alcoa's prewar monopoly was broken, Kaiser and Reynolds sprung like Minerva from Jupiter's brow, and the aluminum industry was converted into a triopoly. Synthetic nitrogen production was also deconcentrated by the infusion of additional sellers. In steel, by contrast, the disposal program served to entrench and extend oligopoly dominance; the Geneva Steel plant, built at a cost of $202.4 million, was sold to the United States Steel Corporation for $47.5 million, and enabled U.S. Steel to increase its regional control over the Pacific Coast and Mountain States market from 17.3 to a commanding 39 per cent. In synthetic rubber, the wartime operation of the government plants gave a handful of large firms enormous patent and know-how advantages for the postwar period, and the subsequent disposal program resulted in the sale of twenty-five plants to three firms controlling 47 per cent of the industry's capacity.

More recent is the controversy over the disposition of the government's oil shale lands, located in the Rocky Mountain States, and estimated to contain two trillion barrels of oil (i.e., six times the known oil reserves of the entire world) [19, pp. 106–07]. It illustrates the public policy options which are available to influence the structure of markets and to cope with existing power concentrations. At issue are the ground rules to be established for the control and development of a resource valued at $2.5 to $3.5 trillion [19, pp. 403, 407].

The petroleum industry's plan, according to one of its spokesmen, is to create "an economic climate equivalent to that provided [for] crude oil."

Under its plan, the oil companies would be allowed to carve out homestead-like leases from the public lands and would be eligible for the customary subsidy of 27½ depletion allowance in return for their development efforts. Shell Oil has already proposed to lease a "homestead" that would cover its refining requirements (at present rates) for the next 660 years; Sinclair has entered its more modest request for a tract that would fill its needs for 226 years; Humble's request would provide for the next 54 years; and Continental's for the next 27 years [19, p. 455]. The desire to gain control of a potentially competitive resource is not coupled with any guarantee to produce from it; and if production should take place, it would be subject to the oligopolistic rationality of the oil majors, restrained from undue competitiveness by government proration regulations.

Opponents of this plan, notably John K. Galbraith, argue that this "would be a free ride to monopoly for the big companies. Unless safeguards . . . are carefully spelled out what would happen is that few of the majors would get these reserves as their reward. An eventual position in the basins would be their payoff. This would be in addition to the lands that they already own in most cases. Were there development, the processes for recovering the shale would then presumably be patented by them and reserved to them" [19, p. 22]. Obviously there are policy alternatives, including *inter alia* TVA- and COMSAT-like arrangements. "Certainly," as Senator Hart, chairman of the Senate Antitrust Subcommittee put it, "the development of oil shale reserves should offer a unique opportunity for new sources of competition to penetrate the petroleum industry. And that opportunity depends substantially on Government policy" [19, p. 3].

International Trade Barriers

No system based on protection, privilege, and subsidy is safe without barriers to foreign competition. Its beneficiaries recognize the rough validity of the Mancunian assumption that "free international trade is the best antimonopoly policy and the best guarantee for the maintenance of a healthy degree of free competition." Action is, therefore, necessary to protect domestic restrictionism against erosion and subversion from abroad. And governmental action is the most reliable technique available.

The steel industry, in its current clamor for tariffs and/or quotas, illustrates the rationale of (what *Barron's* calls) the "protection racket" (Oct. 18, 1967). Roger Blough, congenitally unable to resist the ludicrous, observes that "obviously there are many things in life that should and must be protected. For example, millions of our people—and a number of government agencies—are laudably striving to protect certain vanishing forms of wildlife that are threatened with extinction; and one may reasonably wonder, I suppose, how far down the road to oblivion some of our major industries must go before they are deemed to merit similar concern" [5]. To this, the president of the American Iron & Steel Institutes adds the ominous warning that "a first-class power with global responsibilities cannot afford to rely for any important part of its needs on overseas sources of steel thousands of miles away. There is the constant danger that these sources may be cut off at a critical moment" [15, p. 830]. Finally, the United Steel Workers of America, upon whom Galbraith once relied as a source of countervailing power, and not to be outdone in their concern for the public interest and national security, lend their voice and not inconsiderable political influence to the fight for a quota law to limit steel imports [15, pp. 888–96].

What is at stake, of course, is the steel industry's right to preserve its administered price structure, to remain the catalyst of seller's inflation, to impose periodic price squeezes on independent fabricators, to price itself out of world export markets, to encourage the growth of substitute materials, and to persist in its technological lethargy [15, pp. 846–88]. Specifically, the industry needs government help to validate its investment in "40 million tons of the wrong capacity—the open hearth furnace" which it built in the 1950's. This capacity, as *Fortune* points out, was "obsolete when it was built" and the industry by installing it "prepared itself for dying" [15, p. 855]. This is the $800 million blunder, the cost of which the industry would like to shift to the public by obtaining government protection from foreign competition.

The point need not be stressed. Tariffs, quotas, "anti-dumping" statutes, "Buy American" regulations, and similar devices are not only a tax on domestic consumers and a subsidy to sheltered industries, but the capstone of any policy to protect entrenched economic power. They are a crucial facet of the *Realpolitik* designed to preserve the discipline of a nation's *Ordnungswirtschaft*.

III

In conclusion, we may note that the problem at hand is not one of technological determinism which would militate toward fatalistic acceptance of the *status quo*. Nor is it rooted in the ineffectiveness of what Galbraith calls the charade of antitrust. Instead, it is largely a political problem of governmental creation, protection, and subsidization of private privilege. If this diagnosis is indeed correct, then public policy alternatives are available and a reasonably competitive market is more than a utopian policy objective.

Let me offer two general policy recommendations:

1. Most important is government noninterference in markets which in the absence of such interference would be workably competitive. In the words of Adam Smith, it may be difficult to "prevent people of the same trade from sometimes assembling together," but government "ought to do nothing to facilitate such assemblies; much less to render them necessary." While assuring effective enforcement of the antitrust laws, government should abjure the role of the mercantilist state in sanctioning and legitimizing private privilege. One can only speculate on the quantitative benefits of such measures as the abolition of tariffs in con-

centrated industries, the deregulation of surface transportation from ICC control, or the elimination of the honeycomb of governmental supports for the petroleum price and power structure.

2. In those areas where competition cannot be allowed full sway or where government cannot avoid active participation in the economic game, the basic guidelines point to preserving the maximum amount of power decentralization feasible. This may require positive encouragement of institutional competition from whatever source available and, at the very least, the preservation of effective yardsticks by which to measure and control monopoly performance. In the national defense sector, for example, government must rebuild and preserve its in-house competence for R and D, systems engineering and management, and contract evaluation. As the Bell Report of 1962 concluded, "there are certain [management] functions which should under no circumstances be contracted out" [4, p. 213]. Basic policy and program decisions respecting the research and development effort—relating to "the types of work to be undertaken, when, by whom, and at what cost—must be made by full-time Government officials. Such officials must also be able to supervise the execution of work undertaken, and to evaluate the results" [4, pp. 214–15]. In short, the government cannot surrender the yardsticks essential for the discharge of its responsibilities to the public [9, pp. 334–50]. And the public must recognize that the servants of the military-industrial state cannot be allowed to become its masters—either in the name of "free enterprise" or under the guise of promoting the "national security."

What I have said here is not likely to please those who rationalize the *status quo* by invoking some deterministic inevitability. I do not claim that what I have said is particularly new or startling. I do believe, however, that it is true and that, as Dr. Johnson said, men need not so much to be informed as reminded.

References

1. Walter Adams and Horace M. Gray, *Monopoly in America: The Government as Promoter* (New York, 1955).
2. Morris A. Adelman, "Efficiency of Resource Use in Crude Petroleum: Abstract," *A.E.R.*, May, 1964.
3. Richard J. Barber, *The Politics of Research* (Washington, 1966).
4. David E. Bell, "Report to the President on Government R&D Contracting," Apr., 1962, printed in House Committee on Government Operations, *Systems Development and Management, Hearings,* Part 1, Appendix I, 87th Cong., 2d Sess., 1962, pp. 191–337.
5. Roger M. Blough, "Progress Is Not Our Most Imported Product," Address at the Annual Meeting of the Indiana Manufacturers Association, Indianapolis, Nov. 16, 1967.

6. Milton Friedman, "Oil and the Middle East," *Newsweek,* June 26, 1967.

7. John K. Galbraith, *The New Industrial State* (Boston, 1967).

8. Clark R. Mollenhoff, *The Pentagon* (New York, 1967).

9. H. L. Nieburg, *In the Name of Science* (Chicago, 1966).

10. Merton J. Peck and Frederic M. Scherer, *The Weapons Acquisition Process: An Economic Analysis* (Harvard Bus. Sch. Div. of Res., 1962).

11. Joseph A. Schumpeter, *Capitalism, Socialism, and Democracy* (New York, 1942).

12. U.S. House Committee on Government Operations, *Comptroller General Reports to Congress on Audits of Defense Contracts, Hearings,* 89th Cong., 1st Sess., 1965.

13. U.S. Joint Economic Committee, *Background Materials on Economic Impact of Federal Procurement,* Washington, various years 1964–67; appendices contain lists and digests of General Accounting Office reports on defense activities to Congress.

14. U.S. Senate Committee on Armed Services, Draft Report of the National Stockpile and Naval Petroleum Reserves Subcommittee, *Inquiry into the Strategic and Critical Material Stockpiles of the United States,* 88th Cong., 1st Sess., 1963.

15. U.S. Senate Committee on Finance, *Import Quota Legislation, Hearings,* Part 2, 90th Cong., 1st Sess., 1967.

16. U.S. Senate Committee on Government Operations, *Pyramiding of Profits and Costs in the Missile Procurement Program, Report No. 970,* 88th Cong., 2d Sess., 1964.

17. U.S. Senate Committee on Small Business, *Economic Aspects of Government Patent Policies, Hearings,* 88th Cong., 1st Sess., 1963.

18. U.S. Senate Select Committee on Small Business, *Planning, Regulation, and Competition, Hearings,* 90th Cong., 1st Sess., 1967.

19. U.S. Senate Subcommittee on Antitrust and Monopoly, *Competitive Aspects of Oil Shale Development, Hearings,* Part 1, 90th Cong., 1st Sess., 1967.

20. U.S. Senate Subcommittee on Antitrust and Monopoly, *Economic Concentration, Hearings,* Parts 3 and 6, Washington, 1965 and 1967.

The Liberals Discover Militarism

JAMES M. CYPHER

Just as the Liberals "discovered" poverty in the United States in the early 1960's, so too the Liberals have "discovered" the existence of militarism in the United States in the 1970's. Militarism now appears to be the "in" topic.

There exists an unfortunate analogy between the "poverty books" of the 1960's and the "military-industrial books" of the 1970's. The prevailing methodology adopted in the poverty books is similar to that adopted in the book here under review by Seymour Melman. The approach, in both cases, is to treat the problem in *isolation* from the dynamics of the capitalist system. As such, the poverty books never succeeded in theoretically relating the causes of poverty to the functioning of the U.S. economy.[1] Likewise, Seymour Melman fails to relate militarism to the underlying needs of the mature capitalist economy.

Outside of a new Galbraithian term—"The State-Management" and the application of a Berle-Means type hypothesis to the concept of the "State-Management," *Pentagon Capitalism* contributes a surprisingly meager addition to our understanding of the Warfare State.

What exactly does Melman mean by the term, "State-Management?" According to Melman, this term is intended to convey the idea that the Pentagon is firmly in control of the private capitalistic institutions which accept military contracts. And, that the Pentagon not only wields controlling power over the military contractors, but also over the Congress which willingly submits to any and all budgetary requests made by the Pentagon. Thus, in the place of C. Wright Mills' theory of factionalized elite of Big Business, Big Government, and The Military, Melman argues that the "industrial system" is firmly controlled by the men of the Pentagon—"The New State-Management." Thus, Melman states that:

> My purpose here . . . is to underscore not convergence but the managerial primacy of the new managerial control institution in the Department of

From the *Review of Radical Political Economics*, Vol. 4, No. 1 (Winter 1972), pp. 109–16. Reprinted by permission of the publisher. A review of Seymour Melman, *Pentagon Capitalism* (New York: McGraw-Hill, 1970).

[1] Michael Harrington's *The Other America* (Baltimore, 1963) came closer to treating poverty within the context of the political-economic system than subsequent writers.

Defense, and the consequences for the character of American economy (sic) and society that flow from this. [p. 13]
The state-management decides on which submanagements [military contractor—J.M.C.] in the Pentagon industrial empire get work orders. The state-management also decides which firms shall undergo the greatest expansion. These are the controlling production decisions and they are made at the state-management level. [p. 176]

So much for the hypothesis, but what about the evidence? Melman offers a great deal of data on production and engineering specifications as well as hard data concerning the purchase of capital goods by the Pentagon for the private use of the military contractors. (Ostensibly these capital goods are used *only* for the production of military goods.) In the process the reader is introduced to the Defense Supply Agency (DSA) and the Armed Service Procurement Regulations (ASPR) which, according to Melman, offer through their existence sufficient evidence to indicate that because the military has the legal right to closely regulate the development and production of military goods it also *controls* these firms. No one, I suppose, would question the fact that the military *does* have an exhaustive set of technical-engineering specifications, that it is concerned with and defines the nature of quality control, and that it generates needless amounts of progress reports, bureaucratic forms, etc. The point, however, is not that the Pentagon has the power to control the nature of its contracted work, but why that work should be undertaken in the first place. In other words, while the Pentagon controls the technical specifications of military contracting, who controls the military?

Melman never takes up this question as it is his assumption that the "State-Management" is *the* controlling factor in the economy. Yet, if that is the case why does the Pentagon ". . . act to restore financial 'responsibility' . . ." [p. 54] for major military contractors who are in danger of going under due to their own blunders? Melman states that the Pentagon has acted to help the Douglas Aircraft Co., the General Dynamics Co., and the Lockheed Co., out of various financial predicaments, that total military waste from May 1963 to May 1964 amounted to an estimated $10 billion [p. 64] and that cost overruns have become a "normal" part of the system. Recently a newspaper scribe suggested that the reason for appropriating more money for Boeing's SST contract was to "bail Boeing out of Puget Sound." Under these conditions, who is controlling whom? If the "State-Management" is actually in control, why should they care to "save" any of the military contractors? Indeed, it would serve merely to jeopardize their assumed hegemony of power to continually engage in the various overrun fiascos. And in addition, if the Pentagon has so much control over their contractors, why should there be overruns? Melman has no satisfactory answers for these questions, nor do they make any sense in the Melman schema. But, if one assumes that the sequence runs the other way, from the contractors to the Pentagon, and if one assumes that the contractors can in fact influence the procurement priorities of the Pentagon, *then* the above questions are easily answered.

The existence of the Defense Industry Advisory Council (now the Industry Advisory Council) would tend to support a revised sequence.[2] The Defense Industry Advisory Council (a non-government group composed of high level Pentagon officials *and* representatives of the large military contractors) is concerned with setting up procurement and policy goals through the interaction of the military-oriented industries with the Pentagon. It appears that the military-oriented firms are very active partners in the determination of military expenditure levels—rather than the silent, docile state-firms that Melman would have us envisage. Thus, outright waste, cost overruns and the "bailing out" of specific firms make a great deal of sense to the military contractors. To the extent that they have power over the Pentagon this is to be the expected behavioral pattern of the profit maximizing firm.

In further defining the "State-Management," Melman makes use of the Berle-Means hypothesis of the separation of ownership and control. Unaware, apparently, of the heavy criticism that Berle and Means have received on the part of many economists,[3] Melman argues that while the military contractors own their firms, the Pentagon is the true source of control. Further, like any managerially controlled firm, the Pentagon has an "objective function" (or behavioral set of goals) which includes maximum growth through greater "sales," i.e., "Defense" budgets. While it is probably true that the Pentagon, like any other institution, public or private, has survival and therefore growth as a goal, it does not follow from this that the *Pentagon* has any unique role to play in the set of socio-economic forces which drive the system toward ever greater levels of military expenditure. This is not to deny that the Pentagon has a great facility for gaining funds from the Congress. Rather, it is to point out that the Congress is more than willing to do the bidding of the Pentagon, and that in most cases the *ideas* for new weapons systems have been developed by and *sold* to the Pentagon by private military contractors.[4]

This introduces the final, and most important issue, which *Pentagon Capitalism* skirts. In Melman's words, "Do capitalist nations require military production as a priority (sic) economic activity—because they are capitalist?" [p. 210] After a facile comparison of economic growth rates and levels of

[2] A more detailed statement can be found in: Hearing of the Subcommittee on Economy in Government, *Economics of Military Procurement*, Part I (Washington, 1968), pp. 127–34.

[3] See, Paul Baran and Paul Sweezy, *Monopoly Capital* (New York, 1966), particularly Chapter 2. And, Ferdinand Lundberg, *The Rich and the Super-Rich* (New York, 1968), particularly Chapter 6.

[4] Some evidence of a sales effort on the part of the military contractors is contained in the following account of industry's efforts to sell the concept of the Fast Deployment Logistics Ship to the Congress:

> A number of key congressmen are listed under the heading "completed action and results" followed by the individuals who visited them to discuss the FDL program. The paper notes that "Mr. Dan Houghton (Lockheed) talked to Senator Russell. The Senator was not responsive. Direct contact by Navy personnel required." Senator Kennedy and Congressman Burke were "contacted by Mr. Roger Lewis (General Dynamics), who explained the overall merits of the program. Follow-up briefing required." Derek Shearer, "The Pentagon Propaganda Machine," in L. S. Rodberg and D. Shearer, *The Pentagon Watchers* (New York, 1970), p. 131.

military expenditures by "capitalist" West Germany and Japan, Melman argues that there is no evidence supporting this view. It should be obvious that Melman proves nothing by his spurious correlation. Simple economic theory would suggest that any country which has its partially obsolete capital stock destroyed, while maintaining its "human capital," should show rapid economic growth if the capital stock is replaced—especially with *new* capital. Indeed, just as the German economy showed spectacular economic growth from 1870 to 1910 by avoiding the "penalty of taking the lead"[5] (i.e., by borrowing advanced technological ideas and incorporating them into the capital stock), one would expect that with the addition of a technically trained labor force, Germany and Japan would show, in the post-World War II period, rapid economic growth. Moreover, Melman seems to forget that the gold drain which he worries about (created by military expenditures abroad) has directly boosted both of these countries' economies.

Can the U.S. economy do without the military? Melman seems to feel that it can. He realizes that there would be severe reallocation problems since most military-specialized capital equipment, managerial talent, and labor (including scientific and research labor) cannot be quickly converted to productive employment. To achieve such an end he puts his faith in some vague coalition of individuals which would protest the predatory military expenditures. The relative ineffectiveness of the vocal anti-war movement in the U.S. during the past five years would call into question this sort of naive hopefulness. (Marginal changes such as the withdrawal of troops in S. Vietnam can probably be attributed, in part, to the anti-war people—but *militarism,* alas, remains.)

The military is an undeniably large part of the U.S. economy. The most conservative estimate of its *direct* quantitative importance is that the military employed 9.2% of the labor force[6] and accounted for 9.2% of the G.N.P.[7] in 1967. After adding the indirect or "multiplier" effects of military expenditures it becomes clear that the war machine plays a significant role in the U.S. economy. A conservative multiplier effect of one (1) would suggest that 18–19% of the economy is dependent upon military expenditures.[8] Removal of the military component of aggregate demand would thrust the economy into "Great Depression" levels of unemployment unless one could assume some neoclassical offset. However, the facts of limited feasible reconversion of military resources to peace-time type production coupled with the fact that some of the military money returned to individuals would not be spent would indicate a disastrous depression. The need for planned, prolonged reconversion is admitted by all informed critics.

[5] See, Thorstein Veblen, *Imperial Germany* (New York, 1915).
[6] Richard P. Oliver, "The Employment Effects of Defense Expenditures," *Monthly Labor Review* (September, 1967), p. 9.
[7] Council of Economic Advisors, *Economic Report of the President, 1969* (Washington, 1969), p. 227.
[8] The Editors, "Review of the Month: Economic Stagnation and the Stagnation of Economics," *Monthly Review* (April, 1971), p. 9.

Finally, Melman seems oblivious of the fact that American capitalism was unable to generate adequate aggregate demand to maintain sustained economic growth after 1928—until World War II. Returning to such a world would undoubtedly bring the Stagnationist models out of the economist's closet. There is little reason to believe that personal consumption is adequate, in the absence of the military, to keep the growth rate of G.N.P. above 3% per year. Indeed, if such were the case, the reduction in military outlays expressed as a percentage of G.N.P. in 1970–1971 would have promoted expansion. Instead, G.N.P. has declined relative to 1969 (after stagnating in 1969) and "official" unemployment is greater than 6% of the labor force. Thus the Stagnationist model, which assumes a low growth rate of personal consumption, a low growth rate of population, limited technical change, and reticence on the part of investors to start new projects, would appear all too real in the absence of a dynamic military-government sector. Melman, like many a good neoclassical economist, ignores all this. It is a crucial mistake. Moreover, Melman ignores the fact that fiscal expenditures are not malleable. What is not spent on the military space program probably will not be spent elsewhere. If the public does not have a sufficient desire to consume, what will Melman do with the resources which are currently being consumed by the military? Aside from pyramid building, every conceivable activity except military-space expenditures would put the government into competition against some very powerful capitalist interests. Indeed this argument is carefully developed by Paul Baran and Paul Sweezy[9] and there is no need to labor the point here.

But Melman appears to have missed the point. Unless he can show how the economy is going to proceed without military expenditures, he is engaging in wishful thinking. . . .

Melman consistently (albeit implicitly) assumes that the military can be examined in isolation from the other sectors of the economy and in isolation from the historical needs of the economic system. It is not surprising, then, that writers who think otherwise have been excluded from this book of readings.

In conclusion it appears that Melman has remained true to the dictates of bourgeois scholarship. Rather than clarifying the relationship between the military and the larger economy, he has obscured this relationship. Melman's obscurantism is a result of the liberal assumptions that problems can be treated in isolation, ahistorically, and without a socio-economic theory of change or power. Melman's failure to deal with the interrelationships between the Pentagon, the Congress, and private military contractors is a result of his methodology. The phenomenal size of the U.S. military is no historical accident. Rather, it is the "logical" result of modern Keynesianism. Before

---

[9] Paul Baran and Paul Sweezy, *op. cit.,* pp. 142–77. Also, see the excellent article by: Michael Reich and David Finkelhor, "Capitalism and the 'Military-Industrial Complex': The Obstacles to 'Conversion,' " *Review of Radical Political Economics* (Fall, 1970). pp. 1–25.

we can do anything about militarism, we must be able to understand it. Melman, in spite of his humanistic intentions, is not much help.

Questions for Discussion

1. Should the kind of analysis found in Hitch and McKean be carried on in universities or does it belong in organizations like the Rand Corporation?
2. Is there a military-industrial complex? If so, is it necessary? If so, how should it be regulated or controlled, if at all?
3. Are universities part of the military-industrial complex?
4. Do you find Melman's, Adams', or Cypher's view of the explanation of the military-industrial complex more compelling? Why?

PART **VIII**

Government and the Labor Force

Government's direct relations to the labor force may be seen in at least three distinct ways: (1) through its relations with labor unions, (2) through its manpower development policies, and (3) through its actions affecting income distribution and maintenance. The latter relationship will be examined in the next section and our attention in this unit is focused upon union and manpower policies.

Successively, by legislative action, court decision, and bargaining practice, a special arrangement has evolved governing union-government affairs. First, beginning with the Clayton Act (1914), unions have been formally and legally integrated into the functional apparatus of the American economy. Secondly, government has steadily enlarged its role as the arbiter in the traditional struggles between labor and management. As a result of the latter development, government has actually replaced business as the agency with which unions must deal on matters of wages, work conditions, and so on. There is no need here to call the roll of landmark enactments and decisions that have elaborated this policy, but clearly government has insinuated itself as the final and most powerful force in settling union-management disputes. Such a development necessarily compels us to rethink the older explanation of how wages and work conditions are actually determined, to jettison the simpleminded notion that these issues are to be resolved by some tug-of-war between giant unions and industrial giants. Although unions do not represent all workers, patterns established in union industries set or affect wage-work policies among nonunion labor as well; thus, governmental actions in the area of union-management bargaining reach out much farther than is immediately apparent.

The first of the following articles offers a fairly conventional study of the development of collective bargaining, finally arguing on behalf of greater governmental authority in controlling both wages and prices and hence asserting the need for greater control of both union and management's choices of action. The selection is clearly consistent with the philosophy of wage-price stabilization which has emerged since mid-1971.

The next two readings are radical assaults upon government-union relations. The first asserts that unions have become "sellouts," having thoughtlessly allowed themselves to be absorbed by government (and, by implication, by management), thus failing to lead battles on behalf of workers' welfare. The second article contends that unions must be seen as part of the basic apparatus of the "corporate state" in America. Using the case of unions and American foreign policy, Ronald Radosh argues that unions have become truly counterrevolutionary instruments of state power.

The second area of government's direct relations to the work force is that of manpower and manpower development policies. Although it is popular to see manpower policies as a comparatively recent assertion of state power—really an outgrowth of the experimental 1960s—this is not true. At least since the turn of the century, government has asserted its power and acted with much firmness in determining both the quantity and quality of the available labor force. The fourth article surveys the development of governmental manpower policies, explicitly defending such actions as "humane," "progressive," and in the furtherance of American economic development. The last section, by one of this book's editors, offers a contrary analysis, emphasizing the pragmatic and exploitative nature of government manpower policies (in this case the author looks only at the problem of youthful labor). Moreover, he argues that attempts to rationalize the corporate capitalist system, with its basic propensity toward unemployment, are now confronted with imminent failure.

The Problems of
Collective Bargaining

JOHN T. DUNLOP

The American public does not well understand the role of collective bargaining. It is dangerous for a society to distort and misconceive so widely the purposes, operations and limitations of so basic an institution. It is no less inimical to the future of organized labor and management. John Mitchell, the great leader of the miners at the turn of the century, wrote: "In the long run, the success or failure of trade unions will depend upon the intelligent judgment of the American people." Alfred Marshall concluded his analysis of trade unions in the early 1890s: "Public opinion, based on sound economic and just morality, will, it may be hoped, become ever more and more the arbiter of the conditions of industry." These judgments are no less relevant today in shaping the future of collective bargaining and highlighting the decisive role of public opinion.

The social utility of collective bargaining, or any institution for that matter, is to be appraised fundamentally by reference to alternative ways of performing the same functions in the society. What are the central purposes of collective bargaining? What are the major alternatives in our industrial society for achieving these purposes? How is collective bargaining to be judged in comparison to other institutions which involve conflicting interest of individuals and groups, such as local governments, the press, medical care, universities, and Congress?

Purposes and Alternatives

In our industrial relations system, collective bargaining purports to accomplish three major functions: (a) it is a system to establish, revise and administer many of the rules of the work place; (b) it is a procedure to determine the compensation of employees and to influence the distribution of the economic pie; (c) it is a method for dispute settlement during the life of agreements and on their expiration or reopening, before or after, resort to the

John T. Dunlop, "The Social Utility of Collective Bargaining" from Lloyd Ulman, Editor, *Challenges to Collective Bargaining* © 1967 by The American Assembly, Columbia University, New York, New York. Reprinted by permission of Prentice-Hall, Inc., Englewood Cliffs, New Jersey.

strike or lockout. These are basic purposes which every industrial society and economy must somehow perform.

The major competitors to collective bargaining are three: these decisions may be made unilaterally and posted by management subject to competitive and political limitations; they may be imposed by a labor organization which specifies the conditions on which it will furnish or maintain labor services; they may be decided in one form or another by governmental fiat. Even when decisions are made unilaterally, they are influenced by a variety of constraints: managements must accommodate within limits to the labor market, and government decrees must meet the tests of acceptability and the market within limits in order to survive. There are various combinations or compromises among these three broad alternatives, and our present system of collective bargaining is one.

There is no doubt a role today as always for the prophet wailing against the evils of the system and the reformer who reminds us how far our institutions fall short of perfection. Every conspicuous strike brings forth a rash of editorials and articles. Wrote A. H. Raskin in 1959:

> The steel companies and the United Steelworkers of America have become standard bearers in what amounts to an outbreak of class warfare—low-voltage, non-violent, but none the less destructive in its implications for industrial democracy and an economy calculated to serve the consuming public, as well as its dominant power blocs . . . And these potential explosions are merely the most dramatic in a series of equally dismaying indications that something is seriously awry in the system of collective bargaining that is our main reliance in keeping labor disputes from wrecking our free economy.

There is much in contemporary collective bargaining, as in other aspects of American life, which generates frustration, alarm and disenchantment. But we would do well to concentrate upon the hard questions of the alternatives, the realistic choices, for major changes or for continuing tinkering with our system of industrial relations.

The Debate: Pro's and Con's

The popular debate about collective bargaining has been conducted with reference to five main issues, or five groups of charges and defenses:

1. *Strife vs. Peace*—The charge is made that collective bargaining exhausts the parties and the community in strife and conflict. Unions are depicted as the most powerful organizations in the community in that they, and they alone, can deprive the community of essential goods and services.

The defense is made that the extent of strife in collective bargaining is declining, and there is even talk of the withering away of the strike. The average level of strike activity in the six years 1960–65, as a percentage of working time, was one-half the level of the preceding decade. The extent of violence in labor disputes has been very materially reduced over the past generation. The occasional withdrawal of services or a lockout is said to be inherent in the free market, a refusal to buy or sell. In fact, the community has never been seriously hurt by a work stoppage. The alternatives to collective bargaining are likely to prove of greater mischief to the community.

2. *Economic Distortion vs. Standardized Competition*—The detractors of collective bargaining contend that it leads to labor and management combining against the public interest. Producers combine to push up wages and prices against the interests of the consumer. Moreover, the allocation of resources in the economy is distorted so that there are too few workers at too high wages in organized sectors and too many workers at too low wages in sectors without collective bargaining. The national product for everyone is lower as a result.

The defenders argue that collective bargaining "takes wages out of competition" and compels employers to compete among each other on the basis of managerial efficiency rather than on their capacity to depress wage rates. It places competing employers on an equal basis and assures that competitors are confronted with the same price for labor services.

3. *Disruptive Inflation vs. Plea of Not Guilty*—Charles E. Lindblom wrote that "Unionism is not disruptive simply because it causes inflation and unemployment, for these are problems in a non-union economy as well. Rather it is disruptive because it will cause an amount of lasting unemployment or a degree of continuing inflation which will become so serious that the competitive price system will be abandoned in the search for remedies." The experience with incomes policies in Western countries suggests that free collective bargaining, full employment and a reasonable degree of price stability are incompatible.

The proponents of collective bargaining plead not guilty to the charge of constituting a significant independent influence creating inflation. The finger should be pointed rather to monetary or fiscal policy of governments or to high profits which may appropriately stimulate larger wage demands. The relative stability of labor costs in manufacturing over the past five or six years is cited to support this defense.

4. *Stifle vs. Stimulate Management*—The indictment is made that collective bargaining constricts management with a variety of artificial rules leading to excessive manning, inefficient operations and loss of prerogatives essential for an enterprise to grow and adapt in a dynamic economy. In the absence of collective bargaining management would be more efficient and productivity would grow faster. On the other hand, according to the late Sumner Slichter,

> Unions have greatly improved the management of American enterprises by accelerating the shift from personal management to management based upon policies and rules, and they have given the workers in industries the equivalent of civil rights. The strong upward pressure of unions on wages has been an important influence stimulating technological change and raising real wages—though other influences have been even more important.

Collective bargaining procedures facilitate orderly introduction of change.

5. *Union Dictatorship vs. Industrial Democracy*—The advent of the union at the work place is seen by its critics as installing an arbitrary union boss over the members to replace the management boss over the employees. The union officer is depicted as having vast powers over the member in disposing of grievances and setting wages and other conditions of work.

Collective bargaining is described, in contrast, as the introduction of industrial democracy at the work place. Through elected representatives, the individual worker participates in the determination of wages and working conditions. Our labor organizations are among the most democratic of institutions in the society; indeed, they may be much too responsive to the immediate wishes of the rank and file on wage and technological displacement issues. The Landrum-Griffin law has accentuated these problems by making union officers even less willing to take unpopular positions with the rank and file.

These conflicting views on collective bargaining are not readily reconciled. There are no doubt individual collective bargaining relationships which can be found to fit each of the above conflicting categories. In a large country with more than 150,000 agreements diversity should not be surprising. Some of these pro's and con's arise from inherent conflicting tendencies within collective bargaining. Some tension and inner conflict is normal to institutions as well as to personalities. Some of these opposing appraisals involve appeals to contending social and economic values—price stability, economic growth, full employment, industrial peace, union democracy, distributional equity and freedom from government regulation. These goals are scarcely entirely compatible, and a degree of one can be achieved only at the price of giving up a degree of another. Finally, some of the popular views sketched in opposition are simply in error or are gross oversimplifications.

It is perhaps foolhardy for anyone to state an over-all appraisal in capsule form. Professor Slichter once put it this way:

> Our system . . . gives the American worker better protection of his day-to-day interests than is received by workers anywhere else; it puts American employers under greater pressure than the employers of any other country to raise productivity; and, though it gives unions a wonderful opportunity to whipsaw employers, it gives employers a freedom to bargain which they like and for which they seem willing to pay a big price. Hence, we seem justified in being grateful that we have been favored by fortune and perhaps also in taking modest pride that we have pursued opportunist policies with considerable flexibility and good sense.

My own summary appraisal would state that our collective bargaining system must be classified as one of the more successful distinctive American institutions along with the family farm, our higher educational system and constitutional government of checks and balances. The industrial working class has been assimilated into the mainstream of the community, and has altered to a degree the values and direction of the community, without disruptive conflict or alienation and with a stimulus to economic efficiency. This is no mean achievement in an industrial society.

The Future of Collective Bargaining

In recent years the community has placed new obligations on collective bargaining, and recent public criticism of collective bargaining basically involves the issue whether still additional constraints and obligations are to be imposed upon this institution. Beyond the central purposes of collective bargaining noted at the outset of this paper—rule making at the work place, compensation setting, and disputes settlement—an expectation is being developed for imposing four new qualities of performance and new purposes on collective bargaining:

(a) Collective bargaining is now to be conducted by labor organizations which are expected to adhere to new standards of democratic procedures to insure more immediate response of officers to the rank-and-file.

(b) The results of collective bargaining are expected to meet new standards of efficient performance. The test of long-term market survival is not enough; regardless of the preference or power of workers and their unions, excessive manning and inefficiencies are to be rooted out. As Professor Taylor has commented: "Featherbedding, which once upon a time had such happy connotations, has been remade into a general call to arms not simply against preferred treatment but for denial to labor of some kinds of leisure and job security which is treasured by so many of us in managements and the professions."

(c) The results of collective bargaining are to conform further to stabilization guideposts promulgated by government without consultation and without labor and management assent.

(d) Not only should the public health and safety be protected in industrial conflict, but the public convenience should not be disrupted. The reaction to recent airline and newspaper stoppages is illustrative.

A central question is whether these new expectations can reasonably be achieved by collective bargaining or whether such new social purposes can be attained only through other institutions. Can collective bargaining stand the additional stresses and strains? What changes would be required in collective bargaining? If these new standards prove to be incompatible with collective bargaining as it has been operative, how much of each shall we give up? It is important to be clear that such questions are concerned with the long-run adaptability of collective bargaining, with institutional changes in managements and employer associations, in labor organizations, in the mechanisms of bargaining as well as in public policy.

While the history of collective bargaining impresses one with its viability and adaptability, public regulation of collective bargaining agreements which sets aside terms and conditions mutually agreeable to the parties has not been very successful even in the face of strong regulatory measures. A number of provisions of the Taft-Hartley Act concerning payments for services not performed, hot cargo clauses and union security are illustrative. The new expectations for collective bargaining, particularly those relating to stabilization, efficiency and public convenience, may be largely unattainable if the community pursues policies of full employment so vital to the disadvantaged, foreign aid, military operations and maintains the price of gold. This is not to say that collective bargaining results in gross inefficiency, rampant inflation or widespread serious inconvenience. In my view this is not so. But the new expectations may be so high as to be unattainable except under stringent government regulation which is itself also unacceptable except in all-out war. Drastic changes imposed on collective bargaining to meet these new standards may well make the institution impotent to perform those functions it now does so well.

The community needs to be clearer about the limitations of collective bargaining; one may admire or condemn an institution without regarding it as a cure-all. It is not primarily an institution to cure the poverty problem; it may make a small contribution but it also can make the problem worse. It is not primarily effective to treat the issues of civil rights, although it may also make a contribution. It is not primarily an instrument to treat the problems of unemployment, although there are some interrelations. H. A. Turner and H. Zoeteweij have said: "The public interest in over-all economic stability is not a consideration that can be expected to play an important role in the work of wage negotiators, especially where the bargaining unit is small . . . or even in industry-wide bargaining. . . ." The public debate on collective bargaining would benefit from recognizing what the institution does well and what is beyond its range.

Tough Choice

In the inter-relations between collective bargaining and the community, not all of the adjustments are on the side of collective bargaining. The community has some tough choices to make. The community must learn that it cannot expect all good things; it must learn to give up desired, but second ranked, objectives. Free collective bargaining, democratic unions, industrial peace, full employment, improvement in the position of the disadvantaged, price stability, balance in the international accounts, the present price of gold, freedom from governmental controls, etc. are simply not fully compatible. The relative priorities and preferences the community assigns to these objectives will be crucial for the future of collective bargaining. For example, the British government had to choose in 1966 between a degree of devaluation and a measure of stern controls over collective bargaining. There are a growing number of economists in this country who would advocate a floating dollar in international money markets. The abandonment of our present international money policy would provide collective bargaining with more elbow room.

No doubt there are many different scales of preferences. It is my estimate, however, that the dominant view of the American community, as expressed in the political process, is that a degree of freedom in collective bargaining and in the setting of both wages and prices at the margin is more expendable than a closer approach to full employment, more jobs and higher incomes for Negroes, a degree of price stability, the Vietnam expenditures and the price of gold.

My own preferences would be to give up first some of the exaggerated views of union democracy expressed in the spirit of the Landrum-Griffin statute. Among other steps, international union officers should be expressly authorized, with the approval of the international union executive board, to sign collective bargaining agreements without ratification of the employees directly affected. This practice is now used in some unions, but the expression of public approval of a greater degree of international union control would help to have some constraining influence. Changes in the structure of bargaining in many industries would also help. My preferences would then be to give up some of our present commitment to exchange dollars and gold at a fixed price. Even should limited steps be taken in these two directions, my view is that our economy operating at a level of activity yielding 3 per cent unemployment or so is likely to require appreciable changes in the institutions which make wage and price decisions, including collective bargaining, in order to keep price increases within limits deemed to be tolerable by the political processes of the community.

In making such choices it is imperative the community understand and appreciate much better both the functions and limitations of collective bargaining.

What Can We Expect from the Unions?—A Radical Lament

PAUL JACOBS

Historically it has been a basic premise for socialists that because the trade union constituency is composed of workers, unions must play a progressive role in society. This assumption was rarely challenged, especially since unions for many years did exercise their power in ways that benefited masses of people who had no other spokesmen.

And so American radicals have always dreamed of the role unions might perform in our society. Even today, men with a deep commitment to basic social change believe that the civil rights movement, for example, must depend on an alliance with the trade unions in order to succeed. But with rare exceptions the vision of the union role has always remained only that. Throughout their history American unions have stubbornly resisted the call that they become more than the instrument of a special, although very large and important, interest group operating only within the confines of the social order rather than seeking to break through those borders.

One of the inescapable facts about the American trade unions is that it seems to make little difference what set of ideas a union leader brings to the bargaining table: inexorably the process of negotiation within the system endows the *contractual* relationship with primary importance. Contract becomes king and, as a result, nearly all unions are indistinguishable from each other, at least in their relationship to the employer.

Without the contract the union is powerless, as power is viewed in America. Thus it is understandable why the first demand made by unions in achieving status is for their recognition by the employer as an agency capable of negotiating a collective contract on behalf of individual members. The union demands of the employer what the employer is capable, most easily, of giving to the union—changes for the better in wages, working conditions, and future status of the workers. In an assembly line factory, for exam-

From Paul Jacobs, "What Can We Expect from the Unions?" in Irving Howe, ed., *The Radical Papers* (New York: Doubleday, 1966), pp. 262–267, 268–272. Reprinted by permission of *Dissent*.

ple, a union might insist that the wages paid workers on the line be increased continually, that future pension rates be reasonable ones, and that the union be allowed to exercise some degree of control over how fast the lines move. But the union does not demand that the employer abolish the assembly line itself.

Union acceptance of welfare capitalism and union use of its collective power to achieve benefits for its members within that economic order have had inevitable consequences. The notion of contract implies a recognition by the union of *its* responsibilities for enforcement of the agreement it has negotiated with the employer, thus sometimes placing the union in the seemingly anomalous position of having to act against its own members when they violate the contract. The price the union must pay for the benefits it gets for its members is that it becomes part of the productive system, able to help modify but not change in any basic way the nature of that system.

And the unions have no class identity, for a fundamental assumption of American life is that we are already a classless society: a society in which every man can achieve some substantial measure of material success. On this premise, then, the union is only one among a range of agencies by which an individual can better his lot. So it is that very few union members view a fellow worker as "betraying" his class if he leaves the ranks of the union to become a foreman or supervisor. Indeed, such a line of progression is considered eminently reasonable.

Without a class self-concept, unions inevitably become the instrument of an interest group, thus fitting admirably into the pluralist view of American society. But then, because fundamentally they are no more than an interest group, their stated social objectives frequently conflict with their objectives as representatives of their specific constituency. Thus on two domestic issues today—the anti-poverty program and the race crisis—the trade unions are confronted with a serious dilemma. At the national level they are committed to a course which often meets with strong opposition from their local organizations and, frequently, they must defend local action or inaction which runs contrary to their stated policies. One of the grave difficulties the anti-poverty programs have encountered at the municipal level is that the unions are frequently aligned with the conservative elements in the society, both because they believe their economic interests may be menaced by some aspect of the poverty program and because their political alliances tend to be with those groups whom the new advocates of participation by the poor must confront.

On the race question, too, the unions have encountered serious internal difficulties. The militant posture of Negroes toward unions in the past decade has forced the union leaders into a defensive position, especially because the national leadership often feels incapable of forcing more progressive policies on its constituent bodies if those policies may endanger intraunion relationships. Even though they may have the best intentions (which not all of them have), few national union leaders have exerted the kind of forceful leadership which could educate the members to harmonious relationships even at some cost to their re-election possibilities.

As a result, not all the American workers are among the best treated and best paid in the world: Negroes, Indians, Puerto Ricans, Mexican-Americans, and a few million whites, too, are outside the union constituency and so deprived of its benefits. They are the farm workers, the laundry workers, the hospital workers, the car washers, the domestics, the menials of America, the millions of unemployed and underemployed workers. They are closed off from union membership by either fierce employer resistance, union indifference, or active bars to membership, and while automation and technology rapidly erode some of the traditional bases for union membership, the unions seem incapable of attracting the new techno-collar work force, or of recruiting from the activist youth generation which has played so prominent a role in the civil-rights and student movements. Indeed, the basic reason why this generation views unions as being no different from any other institution of society is the unions' refusal to assume an active role in those issues which are of importance to the youth.

On domestic issues, the radical posture toward unions is a rather difficult one to define and carry out. With some notable exceptions, I am convinced that many unions respond to the Negroes' demand for equality in direct relationship to the pressure exerted upon them: the more pressure, the more unions have moved. There is no doubt in my mind that if it had not been for the persistent attacks upon the AFL-CIO's segregationist practices made by Herbert Hill of the NAACP's Labor Department, Negroes would still be barred from admission to those unions which, reluctantly, have opened a crack in the door to them, and would still not have access to equal opportunities at promotion in many others.[1]

I believe, too, it could not be otherwise. When the demands of the Negroes for equality are expressed in a march on Selma, Alabama, some AFL-CIO leaders and some AFL-CIO staff members join them singing, "We Shall Overcome"; but when the demands of the Negroes for equality are expressed in a mass picket line stopping a construction job, the AFL-CIO leaders try feverishly to get the picket line called off. I do not underestimate the difficulties faced by those union leaders who participate in civil rights marches; I know they are subject to severe attack from their membership. But that's what being a leader is all about anyway, so I see no reason to single out union leaders as deserving of any special sympathy in such situations.

It would be foolish for radicals to expect much more from the unions than a kind of generalized support for anti-poverty programs. I was not deeply disappointed at the strong support given to the extension of the *bracero* program by the Teamsters' Union in California. That union was convinced that

[1] For a detailed analysis of the NAACP's grievances against the AFL-CIO, see the *Congressional Record*, House, January 31, 1963, pp. 1496–99, testimony of Herbert Hill; see also "Racial Practices of Organized Labor in the Age of Gompers and After," by Herbert Hill, in *Employment, Race and Poverty*, edited by Arthur M. Ross with Herbert Hill (New York: Harcourt, Brace, 1966).

without *bracero*s the growers could not harvest a tomato crop and if there were no tomatoes its members in the canneries would suffer from lack of work. To protect the specific interests of their members they will sacrifice the larger good of society, just as for years the specific interests of the agricultural workers in California were regularly exchanged in the state legislature for benefits given to the industrial workers whose dues paid the salaries of the state AFL lobbyists.

I cannot get terribly indignant, either, when a union representative on the Mayor's Economic Opportunity Council in San Francisco uses his power to veto a suggestion that unemployed teenagers be used as runners in the public libraries because, for some years, the unions have been attempting to bring these jobs under union jurisdiction. A genuine conflict of economic interests may exist between the poor, seeking work at any wage, and the unions, whose function it is to keep wages high.

But there is no need to recite again the dreary roster of union failures. The critics of unions have made their points repeatedly and with the exception of a few troglodytes there is a growing awareness among union leaders that something is amiss in the house of labor. They recognize that some of the problems they confront today cannot be solved by traditional methods of collective bargaining, and even though they pay very little attention to their critics the current rumblings among union members certainly make them consider their own positions. The downfalls, with the help of the Landrum-Griffin law, of such union presidential stalwarts as Carey of the IUE, McDonald of steel, and Knight of OACW, has forced other union leaders to look at their own positions. It is certainly possible that without these provisions of the law, which now give union members certain minimal protections against election frauds, Carey might still be president of the IUE and McDonald still head of the steelworkers. And in the case of McDonald, at least, no one doubts that the most important reason for his defeat was the members' dissatisfaction with the kind of personal, top-level bargaining relationship McDonald had developed with steel management. But no one ought to have any illusion that the successors to McDonald and Carey will try to lead the unions in markedly different directions from that in which they have been going.

Indeed, if there is any hope at all for a change from within the union structure it will come from groups which most unions seem incapable, thus far, of either attracting or organizing: the professionals, such as the teachers and engineers, the techno-collar workers in the automated industries, and the unskilled workers to whom a few unions have begun to turn their attention. . . .

Perhaps one key to getting a higher degree of membership participation in union activities lies in giving the decision-making function significant effect on the lives of the individuals involved. Obviously if the members believe, correctly, that what they have to say is of no value in making decisions that affect themselves, they will not say it. My own experience as a union representative convinced me that when important issues affecting the members did come up in a situation where they could exercise effective control, participation increased very rapidly.

No precise blueprint showing in detail how to increase membership participation can be drawn up. What is required is a willingness to experiment with new forms, even at the risk of inefficiency. But it would be foolish to assume that the leadership of most unions will undertake such experiments if the cost might be the loss of their own power. If a movement to experiment with such devices does occur, it will come either through the challenging of leaders by other leaders or by pressure from the membership. Ironically, too, such challenges can now be made more effectively only because the government is legally in a position to make some judgments about how union elections are conducted, as the Labor Department did in the case of the battle between Carey and Jennings in the IUE.

Another hopeful sign is the successful split of twenty thousand West Coast paper workers from a union which they believed, with justice, was not representing them properly. At present the group is operating independently of the AFL-CIO but with the co-operation of local unions in Oregon and Washington. Indeed, because of this split it is possible that the Western paper industry will now face, for the first time, a united group of paper, lumber, and sawmill workers, cooperating in their bargaining instead of fighting among themselves as they have in the past.

From the outside, however, pressure could be exerted for allowing such movements to take their natural course through the life of a union. One of the great needs of the day is simply a vehicle for the exchange of information, if nothing else, so that the union members in the West Coast paper industry, fighting a brave battle against their leadership, might have the benefit of the knowledge gained by the New York City painters struggling to gain control of their own destiny. . . .

In general, I think the posture of the radical toward the unions must be a severely critical one. But it should not be uncivil. Let Meany and other union leaders question the motives of those with whom they disagree; let us assume that their motives are good and that they are honorable men. But we should speak out openly and firmly.

Let us move on now to the unions' role in matters outside their specific concern with wages and working conditions. On one of the most important international questions confronting the world today, American foreign policy, almost every union and union leader repeats only the official U.S. position.

George Meany's description of the serious academic critics of the President's foreign policy as those "who are either a little woozy upstairs or who are victims of Communist propaganda" is a typical representation of the AFL-CIO position. So, too, is Meany's dictum that "it is up to all of us, on affairs outside the boundaries of this nation, to have one policy. We can disagree in here but we cannot disagree outside the boundaries of the nation and have an effective foreign policy."

The torpid tenth anniversary convention of the AFL-CIO in December, 1965, provided the most recent and nauseating demonstration of the attitude taken by union officials towards those who disagree with the administration position on the war in Vietnam. Not only were the protestors thrown out of the convention hall, but the pickets outside the convention hall had their signs torn away from them. And with the exception of Emil Mazey, who attempted to defend only the right of dissent, not one union leader publicly attacked these actions of Meany or his supporters. It was only in the bars or in their hotel rooms, where they couldn't be overheard, that some of the old CIO leaders expressed their indignation over the federation's completely jingoistic posture. Indeed, if the new generation of radicals needed verification of their belief that "liberal" union leaders are indistinguishable from "reactionary" ones, this convention gave it.

But it can be argued, fairly, the AFL-CIO isn't just Meany, Jay Lovestone, and the rubber-stamp Executive Board speaking out on foreign policy; it's all the international unions too. Agreed. And what do they have to say about this question which so engrosses the nation today? Generally, nothing; and if they do speak it is usually to duplicate, in less vulgar terms, what Meany says. The spectrum of official international union statements on foreign policy ranges from complete silence to denunciation of those who question the Administration and includes a few somewhat more apologetic statements which still end up by justifying the present policies.

And in discussing the position of the AFL-CIO on foreign policy we are not talking about mere resolutions passed at conventions and board meetings or editorials in official newspapers. In the case of foreign affairs, at least, the AFL-CIO policy *is* translated into action: the federation maintains an active international staff which, under the direction of the still Bolshevik ex-Bolshevik Lovestone, aggressively conducts its own international operations in true Bolshevik style. (Indeed, the time is long overdue for a full-length analysis, from the radical viewpoint, of how Lovestone has conducted a private war, using union funds, against his former comrades and all others of whose politics he disapproves.) [2]

The notion of George Meany speaking as an authority on foreign policy illustrates one basic dilemma of the radical's relationship to the unions: they are a powerful and accepted pressure group, committed in rhetoric and frequently in action to many worthy though limited social objectives, especially on the domestic scene, while simultaneously acquiescing in a foreign policy that, most charitably, can only be described as reactionary.

The unions' position vis-à-vis American foreign policy is derived from their commitment to the national anti-communist consensus and their specific economic interests, which are tied to the military economy. Thus unions do not question the current belief that the defeat of communism can be accomplished by continually increasing military power. And individual international unions

[2] For a very good short study of this question, see Sidney Lens's "American Labor Abroad: Lovestone Diplomacy" in *The Nation,* July 5, 1965.

must vie with each other in order to protect the jobs of their own members: a union representing missile workers insists that a larger missile program is required while the shipyard workers speak out in favor of a larger fleet.

And so I view the notion of an alliance between the civil rights movement and the trade unions with great skepticism. At the practical level, very little would be accomplished by it: such an alliance would necessarily limit the action of civil rights groups that might need to be directed against unions and, even worse, it could draw the civil rights movement into the kind of support the trade unions now give almost unquestionably to the Johnson administration on other issues.

Since welfare capitalism, in the American model, is incapable of dealing with its internal and external problems, no institution which is committed to working only inside that system can be effective in making the kind of radical changes that are needed today. Nevertheless, I am convinced that unions and unions alone are responsible for whatever industrial justice prevails for workers in America now. And in some places where no such justice exists, some unions are still trying, even heroically, to bring workers the benefits they ought to receive.

But on balance I remain deeply dissatisfied. With all the good they have done and all the good they are doing, the trade unions are no longer sufficiently alert to the new and different problems faced by workers and society. As a radical I find them wanting and I believe that unless they make fundamental changes of direction time will pass them by, leaving them as bystanders rather than participants in our history.

Nor do I believe that the presence of new and younger men on the AFL-CIO Executive Council will have any serious effect on the federation. The one or two men among the new Council members who might once have spoken out on issues have been silent because they were afraid of antagonizing Meany and losing his support for their candidacy; now that they are on the board, they will be just as silent as their predecessors.

Taken as a whole, I believe that trade unions today continue to lag rather than lead in any movement to change society for the better whenever that movement requires a serious attack upon the status quo.

Unions as Part of the Corporate Liberal State—A Radical Critique of Labor and American Foreign Policy

RONALD RADOSH

Cooperation between organized labor and the federal government in foreign policy matters has become an aspect of American politics questioned only by radicals and right-wingers.[1] The labor statesman has become such an accepted part of our way of life that all postwar administrations have received unswerving loyalty from the leadership of the American Federation of Labor and the Congress of Industrial Organizations. Indeed, the virtually universal acceptance of cold war diplomacy in American political life has been made possible by the active support at home and abroad of the American labor movement. This was not always the case. Not until the period of the First World War was labor's support in foreign policy matters actively sought by the government, and concessions offered in exchange.

From World War I to the present era of Cold War, the leaders of organized labor have willingly offered their support to incumbent administrations, and have aided the Department of State in its pursuit of foreign policy objectives. . . . Before beginning, it is necessary to raise a basic question. What are the factors which motivated American labor leaders to develop a close identification with State Department policy? Workers, after all, formed the trade union movement in order to better the economic position of wage earners. No apparent relationship existed between the ability to attain their desired goal and American foreign policy. Union leaders, however, not only supported Administration foreign policy; they became the most vociferous

From *American Labor and United States Foreign Policy* by Ronald Radosh. Copyright © 1969 by Ronald Radosh. Reprinted by permission of Random House, Inc. and by Ronald Radosh, c/o International Famous Agency.

[1] Criticisms from the Left of labor's foreign policy role include: Henry W. Berger, "American Labor Overseas," *The Nation,* January 16, 1967; Sidney Lens, "American Labor Abroad: Lovestone Diplomacy," *The Nation,* July 5, 1965; George Morris, *CIA and American Labor* (New York, 1967). Criticism from the far Right is presented in Hilaire Du Berrier, *Labor's International Network* (New Orleans, 1962).

advocates of a firm stand on behalf of State Department goals. A token gesture was dubbed insufficient. Often labor leaders saved their most militant posture for diatribes against Administration "enemies" abroad.

A recent example is the AFL-CIO Executive Council's offer of total support to President Lyndon B. Johnson's position in Vietnam. Criticism of the war, George Meany and his associates proclaimed in August 1966, "can only pollute and poison the bloodstream of our democracy." In adopting this position, the labor leaders remained true to an analysis and outlook held since 1914. Like its early predecessors, the contemporary AFL-CIO Executive Council spends much of its time and money on behalf of Administration foreign policy. A provocative answer as to why labor leaders have engaged in such activity was provided by one observer of the labor scene in the late 1920's. In that era, the union movement supported what it called "the new unionism." Labor leaders stressed the need to cooperate with corporations to attain a high degree of efficiency and productivity, out of which the employers would gain enough profits to pay labor adequate and even high wages. Unions, Arthur W. Calhoun wrote, emphasized productivity and labor leaders spoke about the "ways and means of increasing output." Calhoun was not enamored of this conservative approach. But he saw no alternative "but for organized labor to go along with triumphant American capitalism in its conquest of the world." Better to be a "side-partner to American business in its march toward the enslavement of the world," he sarcastically commented, "than to take poor chances in a battle with the employers." Calhoun knew that such a course would prove advantageous to the labor leaders, because American capitalism could "easily afford to hand out a continual stream of material benefits" to organized labor "so that social solidarity might be maintained in the face of an unfriendly foreign world." Calhoun accurately predicted that the corporate system would hand out tangible benefits to organized labor "as the price of loyalty."[2]

Calhoun was wrong in one respect. The adoption by labor leaders of an expansionist course abroad begun during the period of the Spanish-American War. Samuel Gompers, president of the American Federation of Labor between 1886 and 1924 (with the exception of one year's term), conceived of the trade union movement as an aid to the corporations. "If the devil's advocates had the slightest regard for fact," Gompers wrote, "the development of the past few years would seal their lips and put an end to the baseless assaults upon unionism." It had been proven that American labor was the cheapest in the world, in spite of higher wages prevailing within the United States. American labor was the "most efficient, intelligent, alert, conscientious and productive." American manufacturers "have conquered the markets of the world and have defeated their competitors on the latter's own ground," Gompers boasted. "American supremacy as an exporter of manufactured goods is certain and inevitable. Already all Europe is alarmed and earnestly

[2] Arthur W. Calhoun, "Labor's New Economic Policy," in J. B. S. Hardman, ed., *American Labor Dynamics* (New York, 1928), pp. 320–26.

considering the ways and means of checking the advance of the United States as an exporter. In accounting for American success in foreign trade every competent student pays high tribute to labor." Gompers agreed with major corporate leaders that industry and labor could both share the fruits of foreign expansion. "Never was labor better organized and more alive to its interests than now," wrote Gompers in 1901, "and never was America's foreign trade so stupendous as now. If unions are fudamentally injurious, where are the evidences, the manifestations of the harm done by them?"[3]

Success for unionism was tied up with the view that all economic groups would benefit from extension of the export trade, and from the growth of an American-style, noncolonial, informal empire. From 1898 on, Gompers continually reiterated that the American Federation of Labor did not "oppose the development of our industry, the expansion of our commerce, nor the power and influence which the United States may exert upon the destinies of the nations of the world."[4] This commitment to trade expansion paralleled the need of the business community to find and develop new markets abroad.

It was not until World War I, however, that Gompers and the AFL saw the policy begin to pay off. The war created an abnormal demand for labor. After four million men entered the armed services, the eight-hour day and forty-hour week became standard in many war industries. It was the entry into the World War, Joseph Rayback writes, that "provided organized labor with a fortuitous opportunity for advancement." The Wilson Administration "fostered a spirit which encouraged increases in wages, decreases in hours, and better working conditions."[5]

The *raison d'être* behind the Administration's attitude toward organized labor was clear. Military victory depended on increased production and the avoidance of domestic labor disputes. The war created a favorable situation in which organized labor could act to obtain basic demands. Since labor was regarded as an uncertain link in the preparedness chain, the Administration was prepared to offer some reforms. Once Samuel Gompers showed his willingness to support Administration foreign policy, Woodrow Wilson acted to give the AFL general recognition. . . .

Union leaders soon found that wartime conditions provided them with the opportunity to gain union victories. Large clothing contracts were being awarded by the Administration to firms that were hostile to organized labor, that refused to bargain collectively and used their power to force laborers to work under substandard conditions. The government, Hillman wrote to Newton D. Baker, could not "permit conditions to continue which make for the breaking down of the standards of labor established in our industry through many sacrifices and bitter struggles." Workers had to be protected from the greed of employers who tried to enrich themselves through the war.

[3] Samuel Gompers, "American Labor Cheapest Because Most Efficient," *American Federationist*, VIII (1901), 261–62.

[4] Samuel Gompers, speech before the National Committee of the Chicago Peace Jubilee, October 18, 1898, *American Federationist*, V (1898), 182.

[5] Joseph Rayback, *A History of American Labor* (New York, 1966), pp. 273–75.

While they could stop such practices by striking, Hillman noted that the Amalgamated preferred "not [to] do anything that might hinder our government." Hillman stressed that he had "entered negotiations . . . in a spirit of cooperation" and had done nothing "that might possibly interfere with the actual manufacture of clothing" or that would "arouse public sentiment against the government." At union meetings he pleaded with the rank-and-file to be patient, but needy workers were arguing that the Administration was "encouraging non-union employers" and was causing unemployment among union labor. Hillman asked that the Government not "directly or indirectly lend its authority to the misconduct of union hating employers."[6]

Hillman's cooperative efforts were successful. In August 1917 Secretary of War Baker established a Board of Control to govern the award of army contracts. Recipient firms had to prove that they respected sound industrial and sanitary conditions, that they had abandoned sweatshops, that they would engage in collective bargaining, and that they would honor an eight-hour day. As a result of the Board's requirements, thousands of new workers joined the Amalgamated Clothing Workers. Within one year the bulk of the men's clothing industry was successfully organized.

While the negotiations were going on with Newton D. Baker, the union leadership was given reason to believe that the Administration did not appreciate the Amalgamated's anti-war position. Editors of the *Advance,* the official union newspaper, complained of facing considerable difficulty from the Post Office in securing second-class mailing privileges.[7] Sidney Hillman himself heard "some rumors that the 'Advance' is being investigated by the Post Office authorities" because of its anti-war stand. If news of this got out, Hillman warned, it might do "a great deal of damage" to the "standing of our organization."[8]

Although editor Joseph Schlossberg called Hillman's story only a rumor,[9] the union leadership took steps to curb the expression of anti-war views. Amalgamated executive Frank Rosenblum wrote to Jacob Potofsky in June 1917 that the paper had "overdone itself in its criticism of the government." While Rosenblum agreed that the war was unjust, he felt that criticism of the war could not be given "the space and prominence it has until now." The union simply could not, Rosenblum advised, "do anything which will antagonize anyone." To Rosenblum it was "all a question of expediency." To attack the war meant to provide an opening for those who wanted to harm the union, and there were "enough forces in and out of the labor movement seeking to destroy the Amalgamated without getting the U.S. Government on the job to assist them." If it kept asserting its anti-war position, Rosenblum asserted, the union would "lose friends which it might need in

[6] Hillman to Baker, October 6, 1917, Sidney Hillman MSS, Amalgamated Clothing Workers Headquarters, New York City.

[7] Joseph Schlossberg to Fiorello La Guardia, March 6, 1917, *ibid.*

[8] Hillman to Schlossberg, May 14, 1917, *ibid.*

[9] Schlossberg to Hillman, May 16, 1917, *ibid.*

the future."[10] The Amalgamated did not undertake further criticism that would antagonize the Administration. As a result, it got an official agreement which afforded the union its great opportunity to complete organization of the men's clothing industry.

The policy pursued by men like Samuel Gompers and Sidney Hillman during the 1920's set the stage for the labor policy followed during the New Deal and thereafter. In the 1940's, war production would once again give a new union movement, the Congress of Industrial Organizations, a massive opportunity. CIO leaders sat on war production boards alongside industrialists and Administration leaders, helping to run the corporate system from the top. Like Gompers before World War I, Sidney Hillman became the government's favored labor leader. Franklin D. Roosevelt appointed Hillman to a post on the National Defense Advisory Commission in May of 1940. Hillman worked closely with men like William S. Knudsen, president of General Motors, and the noted corporation lawyer Edward Stettinius, Jr. . . . .

The idea was a compromise between the union movement's desire to extend the union shop and management's opposition. It represented a major advance for unions in the mass production industries, where they had originally enjoyed bargaining rights only for their own membership. As a result, no strong challenges to union recognition took place during the wartime era. "Maintenance of membership," Brooks commented, "helped to dovetail the 'New Unionism' into the new corporatism. What unionists envisaged as "industrial democracy,' sophisticated management came to view as a practical means for the handling of personnel problems within a company structure that had become too unwieldy for the old-fashioned face-to-face relationship to work with equity or satisfaction. Collective bargaining, in this light, became a system for drawing up the rules for employment; and the unions became agencies for enforcing these rules."[11]

Once the rules were drawn up, the union leaders pledged to abide by them, and to urge the work force to produce efficiently and to work with a cooperative spirit. If individual workers failed to toe the line, the union, not the employer, would then act as the disciplinary agent. This scheme convinced sophisticated corporate employers that unions were indeed responsible, conservative institutions, useful in terms of guaranteeing continuous uninterrupted production. The union leader could show his rank-and-file that they had obtained recognition and collective bargaining rights, and could argue that responsible behavior and increased productivity would keep the employer favorable to the same unionism that had produced direct benefits for the worker. Together with men from the corporation community, the union leader worked with government spokesmen and made the key decisions that kept corporate capitalism intact.

[10] Rosenblum to Schlossberg, June 2, 1917, *ibid.* Rosenblum evidently learned from this early experience. In the 1960's, he was one of the few established labor leaders to protest publicly the war in Vietnam, and to urge adoption of a new foreign policy by the labor movement.
[11] Thomas R. Brooks, *Toil and Trouble: A History of American Labor* (New York, 1965).

Basic to the ability to create such an informal working arrangement was the explicit support for United States foreign policy that was offered by the labor leadership. Had men like Gompers during World War I or Hillman during World War II opposed the fundamental assumptions of policy, or even the byproducts of the assumptions, labor–management cooperation would not have existed. Domestic friction would have been the result had Gompers condemned Woodrow Wilson's declaration of war and proceeded to defend the civil liberties of persecuted anti-war Socialists and revolutionary workers in the IWW. Eventually strikes that would have interfered with wartime production would have taken place, and the unions might have issued demands judged to be revolutionary by the corporations and the Administration.

These options, however, were never presented to the rank-and-file for consideration. Whether they would have insisted on waging a fight for the eight-hour day in 1918, even if it meant breaking with the Wilson Administration, is a point only for conjecture. The basic fact is that the union leadership operated in the realm of foreign policy without consulting, and without obtaining the consent of, those rank-and-file workers who paid the steady flow of union dues. The union membership, for its part, looked only at whether the union was bringing them more of the pie; not at how such an achievement was gained. Their leadership did not let them know that the opportunities existed to gain more benefits, if a different course was chosen.

The conservative policy followed by the labor leadership had other ironic overtones. During World War I, the path taken by Samuel Gompers and the AFL leadership was so conservative that Gompers ended up aiding those social groups in Europe who opposed the most moderate social democratic brand of unionism. Gompers' efforts on behalf of a rigid-anti-revolutionary policy provided strength for rightist European conservatives, and weakened Woodrow Wilson's liberal capitalist allies among the European left. This part of the story, and the arduous work done by Gompers in his fight against world social revolution, will be taken up in the following pages.

The reactionary program of post-World War II trade union leaders follows along the path charted originally by Samuel Gompers, with similar effects on the international scene. Rather than identifying with forces of social change in Europe, Latin America, and Asia, the AFL and CIO union leaders have offered their suport to any type of anti-Communist regime. Often AFL agents have helped local dictators establish the very machinery they later used to crush independent trade union movements. The AFL-CIO would then propagate the myth that the remaining shadow union—controlled by the local power elites—was a legitimate anti-Communist force that represented the workers' true interests.

In Latin America especially, AFL-CIO unions worked to curb social revolution. Direct agents of American unions helped to overthrow the democratically elected Socialist government of Cheddi Jagan in Guyana (formerly British Guiana), and worked with the most conservative aristocrats in the Dominican Republic against the moderate social democrat Juan Bosch.

After Bosch was deposed by the military junta, the AFL-CIO supported intervention by the United States Marines and backed the junta while dubbing the nationalists as Communists. The AFL-CIO leaders opposed cooperation with those workers who sought to end control of their countries by local oligarchies. Instead, George Meany and his associates backed the most reactionary social groups and echoed their propaganda claims. By pursuing such a policy, the AFL-CIO contributed its share to hindering the efforts of non-Communist nationalists who sought a native radical alternative to control by the oligarchs. AFL-CIO activity confirmed the validity of the arguments forcefully presented by Latin American revolutionaries.

By the 1960's, American labor's foreign policy had traveled a complete circle. Samuel Gompers started with the assumption that domestic progress coincided with the growth of an informal American empire. As the export trade grew, American labor would find more jobs and enter into harmonious relationships with the corporations. Domestic progress, Gompers assumed, depended upon continued expansion abroad.

As the union movement grew, its leaders accepted the existing corporate political economy, in return for a minor share in the decision-making process and increasing economic rewards for union members. Its leaders developed organized labor into an institution that functioned to integrate workers into the existing political economy, rather than as a lever for changing it. It was the labor leaders' desire, C. Wright Mills explained, to "join with owners and managers in running the corporate enterprise system and influencing decisively the political economy as a whole." The result was a "kind of 'procapitalist syndicalism from the top.' "[12]

Holding such a conception of unionism, the union leaders understood that a viable movement would aid a statist government to assure the cooperation of a relatively docile labor force. The postwar era, with the Korean war, increased defense spending, a new Cold War, and eventually Vietnam, accelerated the development of a highly bureaucratic and statist corporate capitalist machinery. To keep such a machine functioning smoothly, the corporate national class required the aid of a state-regulated and approved movement. Such a brand of unionism would help the corporations maintain their hegemonic control over American society.

It was essentially for this reason that Franklin D. Roosevelt's administration had aided in the development of the CIO. The new industrial union federation served as a government-created instrument that enabled sophisticated corporate leaders to overcome the resistance to change of both old-style laissez faire capitalists and the old-line craft unions that refused to accept a statist structure. Organized labor could not be integrated into the system via the old craft unions, which were insufficiently structured to aid unskilled labor. Thus the National Recovery Administration turned unionism into a semi-public institution whose organization was part of an official government

---

[12] C. Wright Mills, "The Labor Leaders and the Power Elite," in A. Kornhauser, R. Dubin and A. Ross, eds., *Roots of Industrial Conflict* (New York, 1954), pp. 144–52.

program. As Benjamin Stolberg wrote in 1933, "in short, the socialist unions, whose militancy has been kept alive these last few years by an inner left wing opposition, fitted very easily into the drift towards state capitalism, which characterizes the New Deal."[13]

In the mid-1950's, both the AFL and CIO mended their fences and merged. The new federation symbolized the attainment of a new consensus. The old AFL had accepted the permanence of an informal corporate state, and it was ready to join with the CIO to centralize control over the American working class. It was not accidental that unity was attained only after the CIO unions had approved the bipartisan Cold War consensus, and had taken the necessary steps to purge their own internal left-wing opposition. The AFL-CIO has since played the role of a "labor front" for the American-style corporate state, and has worked to keep the laborer wedded to the system. As late as the 1968 presidential election, the joint federation did its best to curb any labor sentiment on behalf of a rational foreign policy. The Administration program was endorsed, as was its favored candidate, Hubert Humphrey. The labor leaders failed to express even the moderate criticism of the war advanced by Eugene McCarthy, while many workers were considering support of the populist demagogue George Wallace.

The problem for the unions is whether the time-honored formula criticized by Arthur Calhoun in the 1920's is going to be workable in the future. Calhoun, we recall, had predicted labor support for an expansionist foreign policy, since the system would be able to give labor material benefits in exchange for its support of an imperialist program. It is becoming increasingly possible that American unionism may become as impotent as the Fascist unions were in Nazi Germany. The willingness of George Meany to place stringent maxima upon wage increases, at the behest of the Johnson Administration, is a case in point. According to the Administration's proposed "guidelines," wage increases were to be aligned with a small productivity increase. They were not to be geared to the larger general price rise or to the basic rise in the cost of living.

American corporate leaders have been committed to the warfare-welfare state as the best means for stabilizing corporate capitalism. Domestic consensus has depended upon gains being made for all major groups in the economy, within a context of continuous expansion abroad. Today, the basis for such a consensus has begun to collapse. It becomes increasingly difficult to maintain a steady growth rate for the economy. Acute competition develops with European capitalist nations, while at the same time the system's leaders find themselves unable to cope with the upsurge of revolutionary nationalism in the underdeveloped world. The Johnson Administration tried to cope with

---

[13] Benjamin Stolberg, "A Government in Search of a Labor Movement," *Scribner's,* December 1933, pp. 345–50. For elaboration on the above point, see Ronald Radosh, "The Development of the Corporate Ideology of American Labor Leaders, 1914–1933" (unpublished Ph.D. dissertation, University of Wisconsin, 1967), pp. 254–313. The writer is indebted to the analysis presented by the anarchist writer Weiner in *Ethics and American Unionism* (New York, 1958).

domestic turmoil by calling for sacrifices to curb inflation—and the brunt of the effort was to be made by the workers who would adhere to government "guidelines" beyond which wages would not be raised. With a productivity increase of 3.2 per cent a year, and prices rising at a rate of 3.3 per cent, wages would have had to increase by 6.5 per cent to equalize the laborer's condition. But the administration asked that wages increase no more than 3.2 per cent, which in effect asked workers to take no increase in a period when corporate profits were setting all-time highs.[14]

The direction in which the system's leaders were and are moving is toward an administered corporate system in which the power of the state is directly tied to the needs of the large corporations. The new business collectivism, initiated during the presidency of Woodrow Wilson, has come to resemble the type of business-government alliance established by Benito Mussolini in Fascist Italy. In place of old-style collective bargaining, which depended upon the relative strength of the contending functional economic units, more and more corporate spokesmen are moving toward a system of administered wages and prices. As long as the AFL-CIO leadership accepts working within this context, they have actually departed from the traditional standards of Gompers-style business unionism, which was based on labor's use of its economic power to gain demands. And as long as the AFL-CIO leaders favor advances within the context of wage increases that fall behind both price and productivity increases, the only possible result can be the growing alienation of the union rank-and-file from their own national leadership. The future holds out the possibility of massive contract rejections by rank-and-file workers, who are dissatisfied with the advances which their leadership tells them have been made. It should be no surprise that many blue collar workers, out of frustration caused by their inability to control their own destinies, toyed with the idea of giving their support to George Wallace, who made a strong point of promising true advances to union workers.

When such a breakdown occurs, the gains achieved by support of government foreign policy may then prove to not be worth the game. But the labor leaders' approval of a foreign policy designed to bolster the international status quo is *not* a position in itself contrary to the goals of corporate unionism. Rather, labor's foreign policy stems from the conservative union movement as it has been fashioned by the AFL-CIO leaders. In their eyes, labor unions are meant to function as junior partners of the large corporations, and the leaders naturally seek only those gains that are acceptable to the system's top men, men from the corporate community who depend for their profits on the continuation of Cold War politics; the union leaders see the chance for limited gains disappearing if they offer challenges to corporate foreign policy. Just as American foreign policy in general reflects the domestic organization of the political economy—and the idea that domestic progress depends upon foreign expansion—so does the labor leaders' foreign policy

[14] Marvin Gettleman and David Mermelstein, eds., *The Great Society Reader* (New York, 1967), p. 120.

reflect the type of corporate unionism that has developed in the United States.

Today the AFL-CIO leaders support waging the Cold War; they favor a vast armaments program, and they approve the use of military force to crush social revolution, be it in the Dominican Republic, Guyana, or Vietnam, Espousal of this reactionary foreign policy reflects the integrative function which American unions fulfill. Unless the entire conception of trade unionism changes, it will be impossible to get the labor leadership to move away from a rigid Cold War position. Since the days of the revolutionary Industrial Workers of the World, there has been no independent union movement controlled by its own rank-and-file and not tied to the machinery of the state. Only with such a union movement, however, will workers be able to mold a democratic movement that will develop leaders who move beyond limited aims that fail to challenge the hegemony of the corporations. When such a new movement is fashioned, American workers will begin a long overdue assessment of the assumptions behind adoption of a backward and reactionary foreign policy.

Toward a More Productive Use of Our Labor Force—The Conventional View from the Mid-1960s

PRESIDENT'S COUNCIL OF
ECONOMIC ADVISERS

America's great productive capability is due to a highly productive labor force. It reflects the health, education, skill, mobility, and motivation of the people, as well as the Nation's capital stock and advanced state of technology. If the contribution of the labor force is to continue growing, our human resources must be further strengthened and the effectiveness of our labor markets must be improved. Only then will each worker find the employment in which his potential productivity is greatest.

A labor market that efficiently matches workers and job opportunities also

From the *President's Council of Economic Advisers Report, 1965*.

serves other objectives of economic policy. It permits raising the sights of our employment targets without risking inflation, thereby helping to reconcile two vital policy objectives, full employment and price stability. It plays a key role in restoring to a productive life workers displaced by technological change and in guiding new workers into areas of expanding job opportunities.

The American economy has traditionally been characterized by an adaptable and highly mobile labor force. Members of this labor force—generally better educated and trained than those of any other country in the world—have filled the jobs created by advancing technology and have responded to shifting patterns of final demand.

The changes that have occurred have been enormous. Some have taken place so smoothly that we have barely been aware of them. This has been the case, particularly, when the total number of jobs was sufficient—when the market had enough jobs to allocate. Other adjustments have been more difficult, leaving in their wake high unemployment rates and poverty for some groups. Government must focus its effort on those changes which the market cannot carry through without personal hardship, even in a high-employment environment.

The task of economic analysis is to identify both those changes that the market cannot carry through effectively on its own and those that can and should be left to market forces.

Changes in the Composition of Employment Opportunities and of the Labor Force

Changes in the over-all pattern of employment in this century have been substantial (Table 1). The amazing rise of productivity in agriculture and the slower growth of demand for its products reduced the percentage of the work force in farm occupations steadily and continuously, from almost 40 per cent at the turn of the century to only 5 per cent today. The revolution in management and marketing techniques and the growth of service industries and professions increased the share of white-collar employment from 18 per cent to 44 per cent during the same period. The share of employment accounted for by blue-collar occupations has been generally steady, but the amount of unskilled work has declined sharply as mechanical and electrical power have replaced human energy.

The employment changes have resulted from shifting patterns of demand for labor—as the techniques of production and the nature of the final products have changed—in combination with the rising educational attainment of the labor force. In 1900, 6 per cent of the high school age population received secondary school diplomas; today this figure exceeds 70 per cent. The percentage of the college age population enrolled in college increased from approximately 4 per cent to 36 per cent. As shown in Table 2, median years of schooling among the civilian labor force, aged 18 to 64, rose by one-third between April 1940 and March 1964—from 9.1 to 12.2 years.

TABLE 1
Distribution of the Economically Active Civilian Population, by Major Occupation Group, Selected Years, 1900–64 [Per Cent]

Major Occupation Group	1900	1920	1940	1960	1964[1]
Total	100.0	100.0	100.0	100.0	100
White-collar workers	17.6	24.9	31.1	42.3	44
Professional, technical, and kindred workers	4.3	5.4	7.5	11.4	12
Managers, officials, and proprietors except farm	5.8	6.6	7.3	8.5	9
Clerical and kindred workers	3.0	8.0	9.6	14.9	16
Salesworkers	4.5	4.9	6.7	7.4	7
Blue-collar workers	35.8	40.2	39.8	39.6	39
Skilled workers[2]	10.5	13.0	12.0	14.3	14
Semiskilled workers[3]	12.8	15.6	18.4	19.9	20
Unskilled laborers[4]	12.5	11.6	9.4	5.5	5
Service workers	9.0	7.8	11.7	11.7	13
Private household workers	5.4	3.3	4.7	2.8	3
Service workers, except private household	3.6	4.5	7.1	8.9	10
Farm workers[5]	37.5	27.0	17.4	6.3	5

[1] Estimated from Monthly Labor Force Survey data, using 1960 Census data as benchmark.
[2] Craftsmen, foremen, and kindred workers.
[3] Operatives and kindred workers.
[4] Laborers, except farm and mine.
[5] Farmers, farm managers, farm foremen, and farm laborers.
NOTE—Data relate to June 1900, January 1920, and April for the years 1940, 1960, and 1964. Detail will not necessarily add to totals because of rounding.
SOURCE: Department of Commerce.

TABLE 2
Distribution of Civilian Labor Force 18 to 64 Years of Age, by Educational Attainment, 1940, 1952, and 1964

Years of School Completed	April 1940	October 1952	March 1964
	Per Cent		
Total, 18 to 64 years of age	100.0	100.0	100.0
Less than 5 years	9.2	6.8	3.4
5–8 years	40.4	29.6	20.0
9–11 years	18.4	19.1	19.4
12 years	19.7	27.8	35.4
13–15 years	6.5	8.5	10.7
16 years or more	5.7	8.1	11.2
Median school year completed	9.1	11.1	12.2

NOTE—Detail will not necessarily add to totals because of rounding.
SOURCES: Department of Commerce and Department of Labor.

The portion of the work force with eight years or less of education—that is, the group particularly ill suited to work under conditions of modern technology—declined in a generation, from 50 per cent of the labor force to 23 per cent. Today this group consists primarily of people beyond the age of 45, and its number is shrinking rapidly.

Labor Market Adjustment

The effectiveness of labor markets in adjusting to change will receive one of its severest tests in the next few years. The composition of demand for labor will continue its gradual shift toward higher skill levels. But the more dramatic changes will come on the supply side of the market as the size of the labor force expands rapidly and its composition is substantially altered.

The degree of flexibility in the network of labor markets is not the same for different groups or different types of adjustment. This is illustrated below in two ways. First, some major long-run trends in supply and demand for labor are presented to illustrate how the economy has been adjusting to change. Employment and unemployment among female, Negro, teenage, and part-time workers show a variety of responses to the changes in labor market conditions. Second, the adequacy of the balance of skills demanded and supplied is examined: years of education, occupational skills, and industrial attachment play an important part in this balance.

Women Resuming Job Careers

The response of the labor force to rapidly increasing job opportunities is most clearly demonstrated by the growth of the female labor force. Both the number of women seeking work and the number of jobs open to them rose sharply in the postwar period. Women constituted only a quarter of the labor force in 1947, but between 1947 and 1964 they provided 58 per cent of the growth in the labor force and 64 per cent of the increase in employment.

Of the total of 9.5 million additional women in the labor force, half was due to the growth of the female population and half was due to the rising percentage of women looking for jobs. Women between 45 and 64 particularly became more active job-seekers. In 1947, 29 per cent chose to be in the labor force; by 1964 the figure had risen to 47 per cent. Most of these women moved into the rapidly growing employment opportunities in trade and service sectors of the economy. The flexibility of the labor market is shown by the fact that the unemployment rate for older women has fallen relative to the total female unemployment rate despite the much more rapid growth of the numbers of older women seeking work. These women still constitute a sizable reservoir of talent—some highly trained—available to respond to further expansion of demand for their services.

Negroes Seeking Employment Opportunities

The adjustment powers of the labor market have been least adequate for Negroes. During the postwar recessions, a disproportionately large number of Negroes lost their jobs; when recovery came, many of them were not reemployed. Part of this was due to inadequate training, part to job discrimination. In addition, the Negro labor force grew somewhat faster than the white, particularly in urban areas where migration from farm to city was a major element. In both 1950 and 1964, the unemployment rate for whites was 4.6 per cent, but the rate for Negroes rose from 8.5 per cent in 1950 to 9.8 per cent in 1964. Despite a reduction during the past year, Negro unemployment is more than twice that for whites. The ultimate elimination of this difference must be a key goal of our manpower policies.

Teenagers Entering the Labor Force

The great increase in the number of young, inexperienced workers constitutes the most important change in the labor force during this decade. Recent increases in teenage employment, cited in Chapter 1, are an encouraging sign of the labor market's ability to absorb inexperienced workers when total employment rises rapidly. Yet relatively high teenage unemployment rates, 15 per cent in 1964, make it clear that an insufficient number of jobs is channeled to this group.

Future increases in the number of teenagers will provide an even more severe test of the adaptability of the labor market. Because of the low birthrates during the Great Depression and World War II, the number of teenagers in the labor force actually declined through the mid-1950's. It then began to rise and by 1960, there were 5.8 million persons aged 14–19 in the labor force; by 1964, the number had increased to 6.5 million; and by 1966 it is expected to be 7.5 million. Thereafter the rate of increase will slow appreciably. Without specific policy measures aimed to improve the access of teenagers to job opportunities, their unemployment rates will continue to be high under any except labor shortage conditions. The successful absorption of these new workers into high-productivity jobs is the greatest test now confronting our labor market and our general economic and manpower policies.

Teenagers and Women Seeking Part-Time Employment

Increases in part-time employment are closely related to the larger number of females and teenagers in the labor force. Many women and teenagers seek part-time jobs that will permit them to keep house or go to school but still provide opportunities to supplement family income. Between May 1957 and May 1964, the part-time labor force increased by 3 million, to a total of 8.8 million. Adult women (20 years of age and above) and teenagers of both sexes accounted for most of the increase.

During this period, part-time employment rose by 2.7 million, resulting in an increase in the rate of part-time unemployment paralleling the rise in the full-time rate. The continuous expansion of the female and teenage population groups will cause the part-time labor force to increase further.

Every major industry increased its proportion of part-time workers, with the most significant increases occurring in wholesale and retail trade and in services and finance. These two industries not only provided the bulk of the private economy's employment gains, they also provided most of the increase in part-time employment. Manufacturing industries offered relatively less part-time work because of the difficulty of adjusting production schedules.

Balance of Labor Skills and Requirements

Unemployment rates for skilled occupations are well below average rates, but show two rather different trends. The rates for craftsmen and foremen have fallen recently relative to the total rate, while those for professional and technical workers have risen. In 1964, the unemployment rate for craftsmen and foremen was 4.2 per cent, the lowest since 1956. The rate for professional and technical workers was 1.7 percent in 1964, substantially above levels in the mid-1950's (Table 3).

The relative decline of unemployment for craftsmen and foremen may be due to an increase in the relative demand for skilled workers or to the effect of an extended period of high unemployment on the supply of this type of

TABLE 3
Unemployment Rates by Major Occupation Group, 1957–64 [Per Cent[1]]

Major Occupation Group	1957	1959	1962	1964
Total	4.3	5.5	5.6	5.2
White-collar workers:				
Professional, technical, and kindred workers	1.2	1.7	1.7	1.7
Managers, officials, and proprietors, except farm	1.0	1.3	1.5	1.4
Clerical and kindred workers	2.8	3.7	3.9	3.7
Sales workers	2.6	3.7	4.1	3.4
Blue-collar workers:				
Craftsmen, foremen, and kindred workers	3.8	5.3	5.1	4.2
Operatives and kindred workers	6.3	7.6	7.5	6.5
Laborers, except farm and mine	9.4	12.4	12.4	10.6
Service workers:				
Private household workers	3.7	4.8	4.9	4.9
Service workers except private household	5.1	6.4	6.4	6.1
Farm workers:				
Farmers and farm managers	.3	.3	.3	.5
Farm laborers and foremen	3.7	5.1	4.3	5.8

[1] Unemployment as per cent of civilian labor force in group.
SOURCE: Department of Labor.

labor. Since much of the training for skilled workers is acquired in apprenticeship and other on-the-job training programs, this particular labor force grows very slowly during a period of high unemployment. Few new workers are hired, workers laid off may go to the other industries, older workers retire, and the number of people admitted to apprenticeship programs falls. When job expansion resumes, the labor force is smaller, and the unemployment rate drops quickly.

Increases in the unemployment rate for professional and technical workers since 1959 are partly linked to unemployment among those individuals who have college training (Table 4). Increased flows of young college graduates into the labor force in the past several years have eased shortages that may have been felt earlier in this particular segment of the labor market. Shifts in defense production have also reduced the demand for these classes of workers.

TABLE 4
Unemployment Rates of Males 18 Years of Age and Over, by Educational Attainment, Selected Dates, 1952–64 [Per Cent[1]]

Years of School Completed	1952	1957	1959	1962	1964
Total	1.5	4.1	6.3	6.0	5.2
Less than 8 years	2.3	6.9	9.8	9.2	8.4
8 years	1.4	4.4	7.3	7.5	6.9
9–11 years	1.6	4.7	8.1	7.8	6.6
12 years	1.1	3.0	4.9	4.8	4.1
13–15 years	1.1	2.7	3.3	4.0	3.8
16 years or more	.4	.6	1.4	1.4	1.5

[1] Unemployment as per cent of civilian labor force in group.
NOTE—Data relate to March of all years except 1952. Data for 1952 relate to October.
SOURCE: Department of Labor.

Employment trends for less skilled labor, persisting since the Korean war, have recently been reversed. During the period in which the gap between actual and potential output developed, employment of semiskilled factory operatives, for example, expanded at a much slower rate than total employment. As a result their unemployment rate rose. But the acceleration of economic expansion in 1964 was felt particularly in the Nation's factories, creating many employment opportunities for operatives. Between 1962 and 1964, when total employment increased by 4 per cent, employment of operatives rose by more than 7 per cent. This has reduced the unemployment rate from 7.5 to 6.5 per cent (Table 3).

With an expanding economy, the employment situation for those with less education has improved. As shown in recent years, an adequate rate of growth expands employment opportunities in industries and occupations where semiskilled and unskilled workers can find jobs. If growth is not ade quate, the unskilled and semiskilled are the ones who find jobs most difficult to locate. Furthermore, rapid and sustained expansion facilitates the adjustment to changing skill requirements by providing continuing opportunities for acquisition of new skills on the job.

Unemployment in Durable Goods Industries

Looking at the balance of skills and workers by industry rather than by occupation reveals that the employment opportunities in durable goods manufacturing have risen particularly sharply with the accelerated rate of growth of the past few years. With an unemployment rate of 4 per cent by the end of 1964, the pool of unemployed workers in durable goods manufacturing was smaller than in any year since the Korean war. During the years of high unemployment, the labor force of this industry group shrank, as some workers switched to other industries and those who retired or died were not replaced. The continuing growth of durable goods production will test the ease with which the durable goods labor force can be expanded once again. A combination of job opportunities and high wages will attract labor to these industries, but firms will have to train these workers instead of relying on the recall of unemployed skilled workers. This would be a return to the historic role of these industries of drawing in the unskilled young workers and workers from rural areas and training them on the job. To channel some of the greatly increasing number of new workers into the durable goods industries will be one of the great challenges to private and public manpower policies. Today, teenagers account for 9 per cent of the labor force, but only 3 per cent of workers in durable good industries.

Manpower Policy

An active manpower policy—sensitive both to the strengths and the limitations of the labor market—must develop our manpower resources to give everyone the opportunity to make the best use of his abilities, and must improve the organization of the labor market to provide the best possible matching of people and jobs, with regard to race, creed, sex, or age.

Creating Jobs

Between now and 1970, about 1.5 million new jobs a year will be needed to absorb the growing labor force and to reduce unemployment to a 4 per cent level. Furthermore, output, income, and jobs will have to expand to offset normal increases in output per man-hour. Even more jobs and lower unemployment can be achieved through effective policies.

Major responsibility for achieving our employment objectives must rest with fiscal and monetary policies. In addition, we shall need policies aimed at developing our manpower resources, increasing the efficiency with which labor markets adjust to changes in the demand for and supply of labor, and revitalizing depressed areas. This combination of policies will reduce the likelihood that inflation will impede the pursuit of full employment and will ameliorate the human costs incident to a changing job market.

Developing Manpower Resources

Our system of general education is the foundation upon which specific occupational and professional skills are built. It provides an adaptability to change that pays dividends throughout an individual's work life. . . .

Occupational competence is obtained in many ways, including on-the-job training organized by employers; apprenticeship and union-sponsored training programs; private technical institutes; trade and business schools; the Armed Services training programs; and Federal, State, and local government programs.

The Department of Labor has studied the ways in which labor force participants with less than three years of college education acquired their occupational and professional training. As shown in Table 5, about one-third of those interviewed had formal training (in schools, apprenticeship programs, or the armed forces) to prepare them for their vocation; only 7 per cent of laborers, but 65 per cent of professional and technical workers, had this kind of preparation. Among skilled workers and foremen, 41 per cent had formal training. All but a few of the least-skilled categories contained high percentages with on-the-job training. Casual methods were important for all categories.

Public policy is increasingly focused on the needs of the young and the disadvantaged. Our rapidly growing teenage labor force must be enabled to acquire the skills required in today's world. Negroes must be prepared for the skilled jobs that will become increasingly available to them as discriminatory barriers are removed. And older workers displaced by technological change must be reequipped for new jobs.

Vocational education is an important type of formal training to prepare youth for skilled jobs. Yet experience with training programs in recent years has revealed the limited scope and obsolescence of some of our public vocational education. High school programs that include generous amounts of general education and concentrate on skills relevant to clusters of occupations are most likely to provide students with the flexibility to adapt to future occupational changes. The Vocational Education Act of 1963 was designed to meet that objective. In cooperation with State and local educational systems, the Act provides programs for all age groups, from high school students and dropouts to adults who can profit from training or upgrading or who need specialized training to become reemployed. It also calls for systematic review of the curriculum of the programs.

Apprenticeship is another important system for training youth to be skilled workers. About two-thirds of apprentices are in programs registered under

TABLE 5
Training Taken by Persons in Civilian Labor Force[1]

Current Occupational Group	Per Cent Reporting Job Learned By—			Per Cent Reporting No Training Needed
	Formal Training[2]	On-the-job Training[3]	Casual Methods[4]	
Total	30.2	56.2	45.4	7.5
White-collar workers:				
Professional, technical, and kindred workers	64.6	66.7	33.2	2.1
Managers, officials, and proprietors, except farm.	36.2	57.1	55.7	4.0
Clerical and kindred workers	53.6	71.4	29.5	2.0
Sales workers	23.4	60.2	47.4	7.5
Blue-collar workers:				
Craftsmen, foremen, and kindred workers	40.6	64.8	47.5	1.8
Operatives and kindred workers . .	12.9	61.8	42.6	8.6
Laborers, except farm and mine.	6.9	40.0	50.5	18.1
Service workers:				
Private household workers.	10.3	9.3	56.4	27.9
Service workers, except private household	24.6	45.5	42.7	13.5
Farm workers:				
Farmers and farm managers	20.6	17.6	79.7	8.4
Farm laborers and foremen	11.1	19.2	64.8	17.7

[1] Data relate to survey taken in April 1963.
[2] Includes training obtained in schools of all kinds (company training schools as well, where training was full-time and lasted at least 6 weeks), apprenticeship, and armed forces.
[3] Includes on-the-job training by supervisors, company training courses (part-time, or full-time for less than 6 weeks), and "worked way up by promotion."
[4] Includes learning from a relative or friend, "just picked it up," and other such methods.
NOTE—Since about one-third of the respondents indicated more than one way, the sums of the percentages exceed 100. These figures include all civilian labor force participants aged 22 to 64 with less than 3 years of college. For the unemployed, data relate to the last job held.
SOURCE: Department of Labor.

the Department of Labor. The remaining one-third are mainly in unregistered courses run by large employers. Small firms have been generally inhibited by the cost of training and by their inability to insure that trained workers would remain with the firm. Recently, these costs have been lessened by funds made available under the Manpower Development and Training Act (MDTA) for pre-apprenticeship and on-the-job training programs. The extent of the apprenticeship training programs depends on the current and anticipated need for trained labor. Therefore, prosperity encourages on-the-job training. However, employers cannot recover the full benefits of such programs, since workers trained at their expense may move to other employers. Thus, cooperative programs by groups of employers should be encouraged.

Three Government programs started in recent years have been directed at helping those in especially unfavorable circumstances to acquire the attitudes and skills that will enable them to attain, or regain, employment.

The Area Redevelopment Administration (ARA), established in 1961, has provided training and training allowances for unemployed and underemployed persons in depressed areas. Training has been provided for more than 40,000 workers, about 70 per cent of whom have found jobs.

MDTA programs were established in 1962 to offer training for unemployed and underemployed workers with previous work experience. Training allowances were provided for a period of up to 52 weeks. Training, mostly in institutional programs, has been authorized for more than 350,000 persons. Machine operation and auto repair work have been the most common courses for men, and clerical and nursing courses for women.

The Economic Opportunity (Anti-Poverty) Act will emphasize work and training for youth through such programs as the Neighborhood Youth Corps, the Job Corps, and the Work-Study Program. . . .

Improving the Functioning of the Labor Market

For the labor market to operate efficiently, job opportunities must be open to all qualified individuals; workers must have knowledge of alternative employment opportunities; and employers must have a means of making their manpower needs known. It is therefore important that unions and professional and business organizations avoid restrictions on entry and hiring designed to enhance the incomes and employment opportunities of the restricted group. Such restrictions can be as injurious as monopoly in the sale of goods.

About three-quarters of all jobs are now filled without the use of any placement agency, public or private. But the way in which the remaining jobs and workers are matched may spell the difference between an efficient and an inefficient labor market. The 1,900 State employment service offices affiliated with the U.S. employment Service are designed to fulfill this task.

Many of the young teenage labor force entrants need testing and counseling if they are to make wise vocational choices. The State employment services, in cooperation with the schools, now provide testing services to approximately one-half of the Nation's high schools. Counseling and testing are provided for about one-fifth of the new applicants at employment service offices.

The employment service should be available to all workers, regardless of occupation or current employment status. Greater separation of unemployment insurance activities from other employment service functions is desirable to strengthen counseling, training, referral, and placement activities. In large metropolitan areas, employment service offices that specialize by industry can provide better services to both employers and workers in those industries than can be supplied by offices that try to cover the whole range of industries. Specialized offices are now in operation in 41 of the 56 largest metropolitan areas.

In addition, special services are required for those who are at a competitive disadvantage in the labor market—the inexperienced, the undereducated, the unskilled, older workers, the handicapped, and minority groups. Some special services for these groups are now being provided—including those related to ARA, MDTA, and anti-poverty programs. During the coming year, emphasis will be placed on employment services for younger persons. The services will include exploratory interviews, counseling, and testing; referral to community agencies for diagnostic and remedial assistance; and strengthening of placement efforts, including those directed at rapidly expanding part-time employment opportunities.

An effective manpower policy also will require better information on the current and future structure of supply and demand in local labor markets. Experimental surveys of job vacancies during the coming year will help to fill an important gap in manpower statistics.

The employment service can become an important aid to geographic mobility in our dynamic economy. An increase in interarea exchange of job information can contribute to this goal. The current experimental program in the use of relocation allowances, revised and expanded as necessary, can help to translate this interarea information into effective placements.

The Nation's flexible labor markets have enabled us to adapt to dramatic changes in labor supply and demand. They provide a solid foundation upon which to build an effective manpower policy that can both increase the efficiency of the labor market and open up new opportunities for those burdened by past disadvantages or faced with exceptionally difficult shifts in market supply or demand.

A manpower policy that is geared to steady employment for all who seek work, that deals responsively with the income, training, and placement needs of the unemployed, and that meets the special problems of distressed areas and groups will reinforce the ability of our economy to grow and will facilitate adjustment to change.

Youthful Labor Surplus in Disaccumulationist Capitalism

ROBERT B. CARSON

Despite the mounting external evidence that the heart of orthodox Keynesianism and neo-Keynesianism no longer offers many solutions to the dilemmas of the modern warfare-welfare state, bourgeois economists and policy makers tenaciously hold to the view that somewhere the "new economics" tool box contains the proper mix of fiscal and monetary instruments to produce desired full-employment policies. Tragically, however, many Left political-economic critiques in recent years have tended to adopt exactly the same position. Indeed, the American Left seems woefully unprepared to accept the increasingly obvious possibility that the traditional employment problems within capitalism are again resurfacing, and in ways that bear a greater resemblance to the old Marxist critique than many radicals could have expected only a couple of years ago. Radicals have, by and large, avoided a systematic and thorough analysis of the changing structure of employment and unemployment in advanced monopoly capitalism and, therefore, have overlooked the possible effect of these employment shifts in generating a class-based socialist movement in America.

The Left has not challenged bourgeois economics on its own grounds. This is not to say that it has not challenged the system in terms of its behavior and its effect upon people, but this has largely been done in emphasizing matters of life style only rather than looking beyond these apparent contradictions to their roots in the structure and organization of the economy proper. Herbert Gintis, in what is still a most useful and instructive article, tells us:

> The basic "contradiction" that capitalism faces, then, is the following: Economic growth is a prerequisite to social stability; yet men have essentially satisfiable material needs, satisfiable in the sense that further increase in material goods and services plays a minor part in securing their welfare

First printed in *Socialist Revolution*, No. 9 (May–June, 1972), pp. 15–20, 22–23, 23–24. Reprinted by permission of the publisher.

independent of whether they think it will or not; economic growth leads to the capacity for satisfaction of these needs; hence economic growth, the prerequisite for stability, leads to instability.[1]

Whether Gintis is right or wrong about the basic contradiction (and in a way I think he is right) is not the point. The problem is that there is no analysis beyond the assertion of the superficial contradiction itself. In no way is the full-employment argument taken up except to argue the increased irrationality of work and its object, consumption. Without recognizing it or admitting it, Gintis' analysis and many like it unconsciously and unnecessarily concede the economics of full employment as essentially correct. The struggle then is unavoidably shifted off into a narrowly qualitative realm, a struggle for abstractly reasonable social goals triumphing over irrational private ones. But such approaches are dangerously moralistic and are an idealization of Marx's critique of capitalism.

The argument laid out below will attempt to examine the full-employment crisis of modern capitalism. In this study, however, only one segment of the American work force will be examined in detail—youthful labor. The study argues: (1) that advanced monopoly capitalism has continuously faced the chronic unemployment crisis foreseen by Marx, (2) that this crisis has been avoided only by the most skillful manipulation of labor demand and labor supply, and (3) that young people have been one of the crucial safety valves in balancing labor supply and demand (however, it is of course obvious to this writer that other vulnerable laboring groups—blacks and women for instance—have played their own equally important role in maintaining labor market rationality). A final point, which is in need of further examination but may be helpful to the reader at the outset, is that I believe—as Gintis does (although for other reasons)—that youth can no longer be counted as a safety valve for the system but are a growing revolutionary force within it.

The Process of Disaccumulation

The dwindling capacity of the economy to create new productive jobs in proportion to national income expansion is a distinctive feature of advanced monopoly capitalism, traceable to its origins in the closing decades of the nineteenth century. In his groundbreaking study of this process of disaccumulation in advanced capitalism Martin Sklar states:

> . . . in a society undergoing capital accumulation in the course of industrialization, the expansion of manufactured goods-production entails the expansion of the labor force in the production and operation of the means of production in manufacturing. At the point where there is no such increased employment of labor-power in the production and operation

[1] Herbert Gintis, "The New Working Class and Revolutionary Youth," *Socialist Revolution* Vol. 1, No. 3 (May–June, 1970), p. 42.

of the means of production, that is, where the production and operation of the means of production results in expanding production of goods without the expansion of such employment of labor-power, capital accumulation has entered the process of transformation to disaccumulation.[2]

In theory, and initially in practice, the expanded expulsion of labor from goods production raised the Marxian spectre of an army of unemployed, but, as Sklar goes on to note, the emerging Progressive or "Corporate-Liberal" adjustment to the process successfully set aside the crisis, at least for the time being. While workers were no longer needed in large numbers in direct production tasks, they were absorbed increasingly in sales promotion and in what might be called the "general servicing" of the disaccumulationist capitalist system. Those readjustments in the traditional economic order were, according to Sklar, manifested in (1) the extension of monopolistic capitalist domination over the whole labor system, (2) the shift in production to waste and underutilization of resources, especially labor, and (3) the implementation of an elaborate state apparatus by capitalists to enforce "this system of labor domination, this system of restricted and perverted production."[3] To be more precise, "This system of restricted and perverted production" meant the direction of labor toward nonproduction employment as well as the creation of useless, inferior or destructive goods production (and hence jobs) to avoid the classic capitalist unemployment dilemma.

The disaccumulationist tendencies of American capitalism can and have been traced down in a number of lines of related inquiry and study: their effects upon the changing quality and meaning of work itself, the increasingly antisocial nature of production, the consumeristic organization, direction and division of working class people, etc. Whether one reads the initial editorial statement of *Socialist Revolution,* or the works of Paul Baran and Paul Sweezy,[4] or any number of other radical writers who have dealt with the problem, disaccumulation (or "absorbing the surplus" in Baran and Sweezy's terms) translates into progressive elementality and irrationality in the economic and social choices that the economy must make with regard to the production of things and the concomitant utilization of its own human and natural resources, as well as the world's.[5]

The irrationality was, however, by no means self-evident in the early decades of the twentieth century. Assuming that the system could somehow provide the markets, at home or overseas, for its vastly increasing output and at the same time eliminate the old capitalist anarchy of production by

[2] Martin Sklar, "On the Proletarian Revolution and the End of Political Economic Society," *Radical America,* III, No. 3 (May–June, 1969), p. 9.

[3] *Ibid.,* p. 12.

[4] In particular *Monopoly Capital* (New York: Monthly Review Press, 1966) or Baran, *The Political Economy of Growth* (New York: Monthly Review Press, 1957).

[5] Although it must be admitted as a possible deficiency in the following paper, no attempt is made here to develop a connection between employment relations in America and the special role of American imperialism. The decision to avoid such a study was made only in terms of simplifying the argument which, this writer sees, is not substantially altered by an extensive study of imperialism's special effects.

means of official monopoly controls, the process of disaccumulation could be understood and represented as a positive boon to the society. The rising ability of the economy to sustain a growing proportion of its people (even at higher levels of real income) with less of its population involved in manufactured goods production, could be translated into direct human benefits. It was a measure of a greatly increasing productive capacity, in Baran's appropriation of Marx, "a rising potential surplus." The greater the real output per worker, the greater was the possible surplus and the greater the possibility of completely retiring some members from the work force. Given the enormous productivity of American labor, the possibility of releasing real productive labor has in this century been steadily enhanced. Thus, the potential for more humane lives became a technical possibility as accumulationist capitalism came to an end. It facilitated the shortening of the work week, the official recognition and ideological absorption of labor unions, and the extension for the first time in America of leisure and recreational activities among all strata of the population, as well as the "seeding" of a consumeristic social philosophy which would later produce strange but economically profitable fruit. More important, it provided a temporary mantle of "humaneness" and "reform" beneath which the emerging corporate liberal philosophy could hide its true nature, could camouflage its own destructive organization of labor and production.

The true nature of the corporate liberal order, however, was bound to assert itself for there was no way under a capitalist system, where the social distribution of the surplus was to be determined by the capitalist class, to permanently resolve the surplus problem. At best, the system could only paper over its basic flaws. Given that the progressive or corporate liberal position early recognized the social dynamite of a large and rising unemployment (which within an unregulated capitalism was the other side of rising productivity), disaccumulationist capitalism had to stabilize the sagging demand for real productive labor, but in ways that did not undercut the economic order or blatantly reveal the intrinsic class content of social and productive relations within the system. The shift of much employment toward useless or socially wasteful labor was one alternative that Marx himself had anticipated. . . .[6]

The direction of labor, however, to nonproductive pursuits could only be a partial solution because of the potential magnitude of the labor surplus and because of the consistent disemployment effect of technological and capital advances in all areas of disaccumulationist capitalism. Quite simply, the economic system faced a perpetual problem of having more and more potential workers to absorb. Therefore, it became important to develop and elaborate techniques of limitation and control on the labor force itself. Only by being able to exercise controls over the raw quantity and intensity of labor supply could monopoly capitalism adjust that supply rationally to both cyclical and

[6] See Martin Nicolaus, "Proletariat and Middle Class in Marx," *Studies on Left*, Vol. VII, No. 1 (January–February, 1967).

long-run production and social demands. Thus, to summarize the employment situation in disaccumulationist capitalism, it became at one and the same time *possible* to introduce reductions in real labor time among certain labor sources (most of which has been represented by bourgeois social scientists as "humane" progress), and it became *necessary,* from the point of view of maintaining the social and economic order, to reorder the labor force so as to eliminate the historic capitalist tendency toward chronic unemployment. It should be understood, of course, that this labor policy did not emerge suddenly, full-blown and complete. On the contrary it was and is a matter of consistent elaboration and development. Nor was it foisted, as a subtle conspiracy, upon the worker by the ruling class. Indeed, the corporate liberal elaboration of a labor policy for disaccumulationist capitalism necessitated and successfully received (for reasons taken up below) the general support of the American people; but that, of course, was and is the object of Progressivism or Corporate Liberalism. In any case, the point to be made here is that advanced American capitalism early recognized the need to control labor supply and participation and only when the economy tended to go entirely out of control, such as in the 1930s and perhaps at the present, has Corporate Liberalism been unable to integrate a rational labor policy with its general economic goals. Employment was not left as just a *mere* dependent variable of national income and growth. . . .

The Outline of the Proposed Study

The special vulnerability of the young in America to the chronic capitalist employment problem has not attracted anything like the attention it deserves. There are several reasons for this. In the past, radical scholarship rarely distinguished between young and old workers. Moreover, the young were often difficult to identify and measure. Useful statistical data was usually absent and the existence of any profound cultural disimilarities between age groups, which the Left in particular has made much of recently, went largely ignored; but, corporate liberal policy makers from the time of the Progressive era have been profoundly concerned with the problems of absorbing the young, either productively or unproductively, into the American social system. Nevertheless, the system sometimes failed to make the needed adjustments and the young often became a dangerous surplus on labor markets. This was of course to be a more obvious situation among blacks but here at least some efforts have been made to lay bare the historical relations of the black worker to disaccumulationist capitalism.[7] The special problems of women in the work force have also begun to attract more attention.

On the other hand, most recent radical scholarship on youth in general has tended to emphasize only the potential cultural revolutionary content of their struggle and to dwell merely on the life style dimensions of their prob-

[7] See Harold Baron's fine piece "The Demand for Black Labor, Historical Notes on the Political Economy of Racism," *Radical America,* Vol. 5, No. 2 (March–April, 1971), pp. 1–46.

lems. This has too often meant skimming over the top of the youthful labor problem without admitting and reexamining the basic fact that young workers, black and white, male and female, face a special employment problem as a group, that the unemployment and the organized and unorganized nonparticipation in the labor force by youth is a basic structural problem of modern monopoly capitalism. This understanding should precede an examination of the marginality and powerlessness of the young. Indeed, conventional economists show a much acuter understanding of this dilemma as a threat to bourgeois full-employment theories than do most radicals. The pages of the *Wall Street Journal, Business Week,* and *Fortune* as well as the Department of Labor's *Monthly Review* are filled with references to the matter. However, the bourgeois analysis fails, of course, to see the issue as part of a trend and a chronic condition of advanced monopoly capitalism. The current 15 per cent unemployment among returning Vietnam veterans, the raging heroin problem among youth, and even the dropping out or "greening" of the college young as well as the long-standing decay of the ghetto youth are presented as mere problems, as partial and technical deviations, to be solved by some new pragmatic tinkering here or there.

The Evolution of Youthful Labor Policies

The record of monopoly capitalism in its attempts to bring order to domestic labor markets, however inept its grasp of the total and long-run performance of the system, has, nevertheless, been a "success" through most of the disaccumulationist epoch. Although the closing decade of the nineteenth century has been examined in considerable detail by radical and revisionist historians as the "crisis of the 1890s"—a period of domestic economic difficulties and a time of confused and groping economic and political efforts to restore stability and order to a sagging economy—the decade nevertheless managed to produce a 37 per cent increase in real Gross National Product.[8] While there can be no denying that the crisis of the 1890s reflected a significant slowing of economic growth in the United States, at least temporarily, the decade as a whole did not compare too unfavorably with the years that followed (see Table 1). The early epoch of swift growth under accumulationist capitalism was now over, and the system, except in the general crisis of the 1930s, adapted to a slower rate of growth with a comparatively high level of employment (or low level of unemployment depending on how you look at this). The realities of the bitter labor strife after 1893, the revolt on the farms, the unemployment estimates of 18 to 20 per cent for 1894–5, and the spectacle of Coxey's army of unemployed marching on the nation's capital to demand jobs or the dole were not to be quickly forgotten. From the point of view of maintaining the capitalist system, it was essential that the unemploy-

[8] *The Statistical History of the United States* (Stamford, Conn.: Fairfield Publishers, 1965), p. 139.

TABLE 1
Estimated Average Growth of GNP and Estimated Average Unemployment by 10-year periods

Year	GNP Growth	Unemployment Average
1869–1879	55%	8–10%(?)
1879–1889	60%	4 (?)
1889–1899	37%	10
1899–1909	45%	4
1909–1919	34%	5
1919–1929	40%	5
1929–1939	3%	18
1939–1949	55%	5
1949–1959	46%	5
1959–1969	53%	5

SOURCES: *The Statistical History of the United States* (Stamford, Conn.: Fairfield Publishers, 1965), p. 139, and Lebergott, *Manpower in Economic Growth* (New York: McGraw-Hill, 1964), p. 189.

ment problem of the nineties never reappear, that order be created and maintained in labor markets.

The Progressive era policy of imposing limits (both upward and downward as required by the market situation) on the size of the available labor force and the simultaneous direction of some workers into less-productive or marginal tasks was applied differentially within the society in the decades immediately following the collapse of the 1890s. First, the more or less systematic exclusion of black workers from industrial labor continued as it had since the Civil War, with the exception of the brief rise in black factory labor during the special demands of World War I. By and large blacks remained southern, rural, and the most marginal of all agrarians, with the few in the cities taking up the lowest paid and dirtiest service jobs. Within the system blacks generally retained a *lumpenproletarian* position not yet integrated into the American work force.

Second, America closed its doors to the apparently unlimited flood of European immigrants, first by the war in 1914 and by official action after 1920. Here much of the pressure for reducing the supply of immigrant labor doubtless emanated from unions in particular and native labor in general; however, the old accumulationist capitalist demand for cheap labor, heard on and off since the beginning of the nineteenth century, was no longer a widely used argument among business leaders. Among the articulators of progressive political and social philosophy, both intellectuals and men of business, the maintenance of open immigration drew increasing attack.[9] Often masked behind protestations that the "American way" was threatened by a new cultural diffusion or behind more vehement objections to the importation of European

[9] For a recent study of the supporters of exclusion see Thomas L. Hartshorne, *The Distorted Image* (Cleveland: Case Western Reserve University Press, 1968), pp. 35–58. It is noteworthy that progressives were often among the most vehement exclusionists: these included Herbert Croly, Senator Beveridge, Charlotte Perkins Gilman, Jane Addams, Henry Cabot Lodge, and John R. Commons.

socialist and radical philosophies stood the obvious economic fact that a cheap, unskilled labor supply was no longer an essential requisite to American capitalist expansion. In fact, its oversupply was a direct threat to the social order.

Third, women were phased out of certain traditionally feminine occupations and industries by a combination of machine development and the general adoption of "humane" female labor legislation. Female labor force participation, however, was not reduced but actually expanded.[10] Women were systematically redirected into special kinds of employment and their labor force participation, both personally and from the view of aggregate production developed a specifically marginal or "insignificant" connotation. A sexist differentiation of the work force despite the large number of women's rights advocates associated with the progressive philosophy was clearly an outcome of this reorientation of female labor after the 1890s.[11]

In the case of the young and especially the very young, the Progressive approach was systematically to exclude them from the labor force—and by so doing to considerably reduce the pressure of labor supply upon labor demand. What Adam Smith had seen as individually desirable and personally uplifting, what Ricardo and Malthus had deemed as absolutely essential, and what Dickens had blanched at was now ended. Child labor was the requirement of an early and primitive capitalist epoch. Sending urchins to work at man-killing jobs picking coal or tending the machines was no longer needed, just as it was socially and economically no longer possible. The reformists, of course, struggled long and bitterly with capitalist exploiters before the child labor issue was resolved to their favor; but reform *was now possible,* not just from a moral position but from an economic perspective as well. And,

[10] An indication of the general upward trend in female labor participation can be obtained from the following data:

Year	Female Civilian Labor Force (in millions)	Male Civilian Labor Force
1890	3.7	18.1
1900	4.9	22.6
1920	8.2	32.0
1930	10.3	37.0
1940	13.0	40.3
1944	18.4	35.8
1947	16.6	42.5
1955	21.0	44.4
1960	22.2	46.3
1965	26.1	48.2
1970	31.5	51.1

An intensive study of the relative occupational or skill distribution between men and women would of course be more revealing than the above data. It is also useful to note the great increase in employed married women. In 1900 only about one out of 20 were employed (though many of course were hardworking farm wives). Today about one in three have some manner of part or full-time employment. See Seymour Wolfbein, *Work in American Society* (Glenview, Ill.: Scott, Foresman, 1971), p. 23.

[11] It is interesting that few if any of the leading feminists realized the real sexist threat of Progressive positions on education for women and restrictive female work rules. However, to this writer's knowledge, a study of this problem remains still to be done. For a useful and related analysis, although from a different emphasis than the above paper, see M. J. Buhle, A. G. Gordon, and N. Schrom, "Women in American Society: An Historical Contribution," *Radical America,* Vol. 5, No. 4 (July–August, 1971), pp. 3–66.

because of the eventual victory of the reformists, many came to see the system as all the more durable and humane. Forgotten was the fact that child labor no longer was a crucial labor necessity. Thus, while reformers won their victories, it was really the corporate liberal philosophy which emerged victorious.

In the decade prior to 1899, at least twenty-eight states enacted some type of child labor protection; but, typically, these laws "remained limited in scope to children employed in manufacturing, set a minimum age of twelve years, fixed maximum hours at ten per day, contained some sketchy requirements as to school attendance and literacy, and accepted the affidavit of the parent as proof that the child had reached the legal minimum age."[12] Obviously such legislation served as only the most minimum type of official restraint on child labor. However, beginning in 1904, the National Child Labor Committee nurtured and staffed by Rooseveltian progressives initiated a broad national campaign to bring child labor under uniform federal regulation. In 1916, Congress finally passed the Palmer-Owen Bill by an overwhelming vote. This act forbade the interstate shipment of goods from mines or quarries produced by children under fourteen years of age or who worked more than an eight-hour day.[13] Although this and several successive pieces of related legislation were eventually declared unconstitutional by a strict constructionist Supreme Court, most states individually passed stronger child labor regulations between 1915 and 1920. Only in the South, where exploitative child labor remained characteristic until the 1930s, was there any serious opposition to such regulation.

Federal and state agencies complemented the official reduction in unskilled child labor by enlarging and enhancing public school attendance. The object was at once to remove the unskilled child, who eventually became the unskilled youth, from labor ranks and to return teenagers to the labor force with the requisite skills for an increasingly technical and machine oriented type of labor. Nor was the traditional "little red school house" approach to the three "R's" to be the vehicle for the elaborate educational needs of the new work force. Much more than merely reading and writing was demanded. Schools were to provide vocational direction and training, in short, channeling of the young potential workers. Following the models of a number of states that inaugurated vocational training programs aimed especially at low income youth, the federal government introduced a broad channeling system with the Smith-Hughes Vocational Act of 1917. This legislation provided payments to states offering educational programs in agricultural subjects, industrial arts, and home economics.[14]

The inclusion of home economics in the vocational schools should not be

---

[12] Harold U. Faulkner, *The Decline of Laissez Faire, 1897–1917* (New York: Holt Rinehart and Winston, 1962), p. 259.

[13] *Ibid.,* pp. 529–60.

[14] *Ibid.,* p. 266. Two "classic" studies of the application of machine and business techniques and needs to education are: Raymond E. Callahan, *Education and the Cult of Efficiency* (Chicago: University of Chicago Press, 1962), and Lawrence A. Cremin, *The Transformation of the School* (New York: Knopf, 1961).

overlooked or underestimated. Again, it was no long-run victory for women's rights and reform but amounted to a successful, if not yet fully understood, effort to get young girls off the labor market and into the kitchen, or, at least, to assert ever more firmly the primacy of male productive labor.[15]

This assault on increasingly superfluous child labor, whatever the "humaneness" involved, was effective by the 1920s in limiting the entrance age of the average young worker to fifteen or sixteen years and in training these potential workers so that they might be more useful and adaptive productive labor once entering the work force. Moreover, it deterred the extensive entrance of young women into the force, or at least shifted them to skills and industries not generally competitive with male workers. This established women as willingly underpaid workers, often conscious of themselves as mere subordinates to their husbands' "breadwinner" status. The effect of this secondary or "surplus" role for women's labor was temporarily altered during World Wars I and II, but its long-run effect was to make the family dependent on the male wage-earner and thus, by rendering the greater economic and vocational gains to the male, to integrate him more firmly into the established economic order. Regardless of how important the wife's or even the children's earnings might be in obtaining the incremental consumer benefits of advanced capitalism, men were established, by youthful training and hiring practices, as central to the labor force. Women have been a long time comprehending the effects and significance of this element of Progressive labor philosophy.

These, then were the essential contours of the Progressive response to the potential problem of youthful labor surplus, and they have remained, except during the special labor circumstances between 1930 and 1945, the basic rationale for youthful labor policies.

The gathering depression after 1929 of course meant the collapse of stability among the youthful labor force. By 1933, national unemployment stood at 25 per cent of the civilian labor force and about 40 per cent among the nonagricultural workers. Not only were the vocational and general public educational programs reduced initially as government revenue sources dried up, but there were obviously no jobs to be had, however skilled the young worker. Although data is inadequate, it is probable that fully 75 per cent of those under 24 years of age and wanting work were without jobs or only obtained periodic employment. Perhaps as many as a million young men and women were "on the road" by 1934. Moreover, these unemployed young constituted fully 40 per cent of national unemployment.[16]

A gauge of the official concern for the depth and the implications of such a radical increase in labor surplus among the young may be seen in the speed and effectiveness with which the federal government acted to deal with the problem. Beginning with the Civilian Conservation Corps in 1933 and the National Youth Administration in 1936, as well as makeshift appendages to

---

[15] Courses in sewing, cooking, and homemaking skills were also useful to girls entering clothing factories or service as domestics. As late as 1940, 2.5 million women were still employed as "family servants."

[16] Lebergott, *op. cit.*, pp. 523–527.

other programs such as the WPA, the administration of Franklin Roosevelt largely succeeded in absorbing the youthful labor surplus.[17] Young people were put to work in the forests, on the roads, on irrigation and reclamation projects, and, on occasion, lent out to businessmen for government paid on-the-job-training programs. As late as 1940, 1.3 million 18–24 year old would-be-workers, or almost 10 per cent of the total 18–24 year old population of the country, were on government work-relief programs.[18]

While the situation of young workers during the depression and the federal response to their plight has yet to receive adequate attention from radical scholars, a few observations are nonetheless possible.[19] First of all, the potential proletarianization of the young, that is their self-conscious realization of their employment or nonemployment relations to the capitalist system, was largely avoided, for the time being anyway, by the makeshift creation of jobs and the regular payment of a small but nevertheless personally important dole.[20] Secondly, both the CCC and NYA, despite their occasionally criticized political ineptness and wasteful planning, usually enjoyed broad bipartisan congressional support during their life spans. The NYA alone received nearly $750,000,000 in appropriations between 1936 and 1941.[21] Despite the military appearance which the CCC projected, it consistently represented itself as teaching basic American values. Certainly few business leaders would contest the picture created by two official apologists of the program. According to these defenders:

> It [the CCC] provided these youth with a healthful environment, trained them to respond to orders, know the meaning of a day's work. It taught many of them specific skills—often simple in character but also often varied and useful. It taught some of the enrollees how to go about getting a job and explored with them the problem of holding the job once it had been obtained.[22]

[17] In 1938, the following was the distribution of 16–25 year olds among federal youth programs:

	Total	Male	Female
WPA under 25	242,615	202,525	39,790
CCC	273,681	273,681	......
NYA	768,337	402,034	366,303
Total	1,284,633	878,540	406,093

From Lewis Lorwin, *Youth Work Programs* (Washington: American Council on Education, 1941), p. 26.

[18] By 1938, 17-year-olds comprised 52 per ·cent of CCC members. Kenneth Holland and Frank E. Hill, *Youth in the CCC* (Washington: American Council on Education, 1942), p. 244.

[19] The only recent study of the CCC for instance is the competent but uncritical work of John Salmond. *The Civilian Conservation Corps, 1933–1942* (Durham, N.C.: Duke University Press, 1967).

[20] In the CCC, this amounted to $30 per month plus room and lodging. It was expected that a boy would send $25 of this home to his family.

[21] *The CCC, the National Youth Administration and the Public Schools* (Washington: National Educational Association, 1941), p. 21.

[22] Holland and Hill, *op. cit.,* pp. 243–244.

The possible benefits from a docile and trained young work force, especially one that accepted its place unquestioningly within the corporate order, were surely not lost on business leaders.

The youth relief programs were conspicuously aimed at young white males, who, when good times would return, would likely take their normal place in the labor force. Nearly twice as many boys as girls were involved in the various federal programs that perhaps reached as many as 5 million young people in one form or another during the thirties. Blacks, meanwhile, were almost systematically excluded from CCC and NYA activities in the South and border states and enjoyed only token participation in the North.[23] As one southern CCC administrator observed, the $25 allotment permitted families of CCC enrollees was just more cash income than Negro families needed.[24]

The coming of World War II quickly put an end to the labor crisis of the 1930s. By 1945, 11.5 million men and women, mostly young, were in the armed forces, and reported national unemployment was under 2 per cent of a civilian labor force about equal to that of 1938. This subtraction of 11 million workers had been made possible largely by tapping the heretofore dormant labor supply of blacks, women, and some of the young. The youth of the thirties who had earlier been mobilized into a number of relief programs now found themselves in the factory, on the farm, or in the army.[25] In fact, the CCC boys, who had been under a quasi-military command anyway during their enrollment, were among the earliest drafted, and draft boards meticulously snatched up the unemployed young men before taking those with jobs.[26]

The extraordinary output demands of World War II had produced significant changes in labor force composition and participation which, of course, demanded immediate adjustment upon the conclusion of hostilities in 1945. First, nearly 5.5 million women had replaced men in the civilian labor force and a large portion of these had entered direct production work in factories.[27] These women had to be phased out of traditional male jobs and into the home or into lower paying or less useful work. Second, the great influx of black workers into the nothern war plants demanded a redefining of the blacks' productive role. By 1945, black wages nationally had climbed to 58 per cent of white average wages, and in some industrial states, such as Michigan, they were fully 85 per cent of white wages.[28] Systematically through the 1950s and 1960s the white-black wage differentials widened as blacks lost their wartime gains in crafts and semiskilled positions. It should be noted

[23] Salmond, pp. 87–91.

[24] *Ibid.*, p. 90.

[25] In the last year of the NYA, 1941–42, more than 500,000 unemployed young people were placed in critical defense jobs by that agency.

[26] At least as late as early 1943, having a job, virtually any kind of full-time job, was a fairly certain cause for draft exemption.

[27] *Economic Report of the President, 1971*, pp. 221–228.

[28] Herman Miller, *Rich Man, Poor Man* (New York: Crowell, 1964), pp. 84–124.

that these trends were quietly supported, if not in some cases actually initiated, by some corporate liberal unions.

The war had also produced an extraordinary increase in the demand for certain labor skills that carried over into a peacetime economy which soon began a long and sustained upward drive (despite the expectations of many bourgeois economists, such as Paul Samuelson, who anticipated a return to depression conditions). The extensive introduction of highly technical machine production in factories (automation) and beginning of the computer revolution (cybernation) were direct outgrowths of wartime production and procurement program developments. The returning veterans and the normal new youthful entrants to the labor force were the natural source for these new, more highly skilled workers. In the half-dozen years after World War II, the Veterans Administration and a number of state and federal programs established a wide variety of training programs supporting everything from the learning of more sophisticated industrial arts skills to college degrees in business administration or engineering. By 1953 more than 3,000,000 veterans had taken advantage of G.I. higher educational benefits.[20]

Programs offered to veterans provided two direct benefits in the required adjustment of the postwar work force. First, they led to the temporary voluntary withdrawal from the work force of many who sought new educational opportunities; and, second, they provided a better trained work force from which ever greater productivity gains could be expected, one which could adjust to the new employment demands of highly developed disaccumulationist capitalism. However, the output advances could, in the long run, only serve to produce the classic labor surplus problem unless the new potential workers were either induced to extend their periods of nonproductivity or shifted into new types of jobs which may be essential from a view of the system's overall functioning but tended to be increasingly wasteful and irrelevant in terms of individuals' or the society's actual progress. This was the only way that labor demand could be maintained as disaccumulation produced expanded expulsion of labor from direct goods production.

The experience with veteran's education was soon extended generally to the young by means of building an extensive higher education system during the postwar years. The withdrawal of the young from the labor force by means of providing college degrees was a long step from the earlier passage of child labor laws, but the outcome was substantially the same, with the added benefit that the education itself prepared and integrated the workers-to-be for both the special jobs and the personal consumeristic role expected of them in advanced capitalism. While the education and the jobs remained essential from the point of view of the corporations and the state, their elementality and marginality could not be permanently hidden behind the allegation that education necessarily produced a worthwhile "payout."

College enrollments grew by 406 per cent between 1940 and 1970 with more than two-thirds of this increase resulting from the expansion of public educational facilities. From absorbing a mere five per cent of 18–21 year old

[29] Clair Wilcox, *Toward Social Welfare* (Homewood, Ill.: Richard D. Irwin, 1969), p. 176.

population in higher education in 1900, the system was able to take in about 50 per cent by 1970. Moreover, in the decade after Sputnik more than $28 billion of capital investment went into higher education, with again the federal government and states providing directly at least two-thirds of the costs of building the massive higher educational plant.[30] By 1970, current higher educational expenditures were running over $12 billion per year; and more than 525,000 professionals were employed in higher educational institutions, which along with the 2,200,000 public school teachers, accounted for about 4 per cent of the total nonagricultural workers of the nation and a figure fully 14 per cent of the total workers engaged in all manufacturing jobs in the United States.[31] Until this educational bubble began to burst in 1969–70, aided certainly by the pressure of college youth's cultural and political disaffection with "conventional" values and symbols, educational as well as political leaders seemed to see no end to the "absorption" that was possible by educational expansion.

Besides the incredible growth in higher education, military enlistment served as the next largest device for taking young men out of the civilian labor force. After an initial demobilization which reduced military personnel to a comparative low (by wartime standards) of 1.5 million men under arms in 1948, the Korean War–cold war–Vietnam war years averaged slightly more than 3 million men in the military. About two-thirds of these were in the ages 16–24. In fact, by 1968, fully 13 per cent of all males in these age categories were on active duty.[32]

The Breakdown in Labor Force Rationality Among the Young

Neither the elaboration of educational facilities nor the cold war were sufficient, however, by the late 1960s to absorb the potential labor surplus among the young. While national employment rates remain about the same when comparing the roughly similar boom years of 1952–3 and 1969, unemployment for 16–19 year olds has almost doubled. By 1970 teenage unemployment stood at 15.3 per cent, more than three times the national average.[33] Nor did these figures really measure the extent of youthful labor unemployment. By 1970, there were more than a half million young men and women (16–19 years of age) neither in school nor "actively looking" for jobs. Doubtless, many of these were teenage blacks long ago accustomed to the reality of permanent unemployment but many also were white youth from affluent homes, who either did not want or did not need employment in the usual sense.

Taking the case of young (16–19 aged) male workers in particular, the

[30] See *ibid.*, pp. 171–178 for a detailed breakdown of federally sponsored aid to education bills during the Kennedy-Johnson administrations.

[31] *Projections of Educational Statistics* (Washington: USGPO, 1969), pp. 23 and 55.

[32] Calculated from *Economic Report of the President, 1971*, and *Manpower Report of the President, 1970*.

[33] *Economic Report of the President, 1971*, p. 225.

data in Table 2 reveals the phenomenal collapse of youthful employment markets and the dimensions of voluntary and involuntary labor nonparticipation among the young.[34]

As Table 2 shows, the regaining of prosperity in the late 1960s did not mean a proportional rise of job opportunities among young male workers. The trends become somewhat more apparent when the prosperous Korean War year of 1953 is compared with the prosperous Vietnam war year of 1969 (indeed, the most prosperous year since 1953 in terms of employment).

TABLE 2
Selected Employment Data on 16–19 Year Old Males, 1947–1970 and National Unemployment Averages

Year	Military Service (000 omitted)	Nonlabor Force (000 omitted)	Unemployment (000 omitted)	Total Nonproducers (000 omitted)	Nonparticipation Rate (a)	Ratio of Nonproducers to Labor Force (b)	Unemployment Rate of 16–19 Year Old Males	National Unemployment Rate (all ages)
1947	565	1527	270	2362	.516	.774	10.9	3.9
1948	402	1479	255	2136	.477	.712	9.8	3.8
1949	422	1469	352	2243	.514	.774	14.2	5.9
1950	317	1459	318	2094	.489	.742	12.7	5.3
1951	519	1379	191	2089	.492	.729	8.1	3.3
1952	501	1457	205	2163	.507	.769	8.9	3.0
1953	458	1504	184	2146	.502	.774	7.9	2.9
1954	429	1658	310	2397	.547	.879	13.5	5.5
1955	443	1654	274	2371	.531	.843	11.6	4.4
1956	513	1587	269	2369	.522	.804	11.1	4.1
1957	568	1667	299	2534	.545	.849	12.4	4.3
1958	523	1864	416	2803	.582	.950	17.3	6.8
1959	444	2056	398	2898	.568	.953	15.3	5.5
1960	398	2178	425	3001	.560	.943	15.3	5.5
1961	436	2319	479	3234	.583	1.002	17.2	6.7
1962	483	2381	407	3271	.581	1.006	14.7	5.5
1963	499	2590	500	3589	.599	1.054	17.2	5.7
1964	501	2793	487	3781	.594	1.058	15.8	5.2
1965	434	2921	479	3834	.568	1.001	14.1	4.5
1966	439	2974	432	3845	.542	.933	11.7	3.8
1967	580	2905	448	3933	.552	.933	12.3	3.8
1968	524	3002	427	3953	.549	.942	11.6	3.6
1969	411	3059	441	3911	.533	.913	11.4	3.5
1970	390	3136	599	4125	.547	.938	14.9	4.9

(a) Shows percentage of 16–19 age male population who are not producers (Military Service, Nonlabor Force, and Unemployed)

(b) This is simply a ratio of nonproducers to total labor force among 16–19 year old males.

SOURCE: Data for this table and all data in this study is derived from *Manpower Report of the President, 1971* (Washington: USGPO, March 1971).

[34] The decision to select 16–19 year old males was arbitrary but seemed to avoid the special problems of teenage female work force enumeration.

In both cases, war was a considerable spur to employment and production, and there was a moderately uncomfortable price inflation. In both years a significant proportion of young men were in the armed services—again, a *necessary* but wasteful utilization of the young in maintaining the imperial policies of advanced capitalism. Nevertheless, the ratio of young male non-producers to the total young male labor force stood at 0.774 in 1953 and at 0.913 in 1969.

Such an increase in labor nonparticipation reflected at least two important developments: first, a decided weakening of job markets for the young male worker, and, second, a marked increase in decisions to stay in school rather than join the labor force. In comparing other trends between 1953 and 1969, these developments come into sharper focus and clearly are not just a special case for young men. For instance, between these years, the 16–19 year old population of males and females grew by a little over 70 per cent. However, unemployment for both sexes expanded by 175 per cent and the voluntary non-labor force category grew by about 78 per cent, the latter reflecting the fact that school enrollment shot up from a total of 54 per cent of the 16–19 population in 1953 to 71 per cent in 1969. Put a different way, 16–19 year olds accounted for 16 per cent of all unemployment in 1953; by 1969, they accounted for over 30 per cent of the nation's unemployed. In 1953, they were 9 per cent of the total population who were voluntary nonparticipants in the labor force; by 1969, they were 15 per cent of that total.

At this point, it is perhaps wise to place post-World War II attempts to regulate youthful labor supply in the setting of our general argument and to ask how well the corporate liberal effort to maintain balance in labor demand and labor supply has worked during the most recent period. First, there was a clear effort to simultaneously reduce labor supply and upgrade it through extended education—a modern day expression of child labor law social philosophy. To the extent that this reduced youthful labor participation rates from what they might otherwise have been, this program succeeded. But the alleged "payout" to individuals and the society for formal educational attainments is highly questionable despite an extensive professional literature in the 1950s on "education as social capital investment" and the temporary empirical experience of individuals with higher education as a real step upward in occupational and income movement.[35] Individual gains from educational achievement were short-lived. For instance, it is noteworthy that the age groups which might be expected to have reaped the greatest educational gains over the last four or five years, 20–24 year old white males, have actually had continually rising unemployment rates since 1966. Indeed, they have been the *only* sex-age category whose job position has consistently worsened over this period.

A second element of corporate liberal "full employment" policy making

---

[35] For a classic expression of the "Social Investment" thesis see: Theodore W. Schultz, "Rise in Capital Stock Represented by Education in the United States, 1900–1957," in Selma J. Mushkin, ed., *Economics of Higher Education* (Washington: USGPO, 1962), pp. 93–101.

was to maintain labor demand at least high enough to approximately equal the regulated supply. This has simply failed in the case of the young, whatever the effectiveness of programs at general unemployment stabilization. As Table 2 indicates teenage unemployment among males has been consistently high and unresponsive to either general increases in national output or to elaborate programs of retraining and retooling. Over the past seven or eight years more than 4 million persons, mostly young, have had the benefit of extensive job training benefits at a cost of nearly $4 billion to administer. Nevertheless, 1970 unemployment for teenage males stood at about 15 per cent or three times higher than the national average, and for young, urban blacks the unemployment rate ranged around 50 per cent.

The corporate liberal efforts to deal with the dilemma of chronic labor surplus among the young in disaccumulationist capitalism surely cannot be counted presently as a success nor should reasonable men believe that the trend examined above will be arrested or turned back. Absorption of the labor surplus is increasingly difficult. Since 1960, the state's direct and indirect spending has accounted for the creation of more than half of all new jobs in America. This should not be seen as unconnected to the official efforts to absorb the young through higher educational expansion and retraining programs. The taxpayer revolts of 1970 and 1971 easily point to the eventual end of the "free lunch" lie, as taxpayers, both productive and nonproductive workers themselves, see that it is the people who pay the cost of maintaining the capitalist order—not the businesses nor some abstraction like the state.[36] The educational bubble which took so many of the young out of the labor force has now collapsed—in part because the youth themselves, as Herbert Gintis has pointed out, reject the pointlessness of their education and vocational choices; but, *primarily,* the scheme fails because it simply cannot be paid for in the growing fiscal crisis of the state. At bottom it will not be alienation and life style issues which will bring the university to its knees but the simple economic fact that working people, all other things being equal, simply cannot pay the burden demanded to keep the youthful labor supply at acceptably low levels. At least they cannot be expected to pay it without reaction or under the pressure of coercion. Nor is there the slightest possibility of absorbing all these college graduates into the labor force after completion of their degrees. In a slightly different context Ernest Mandel has observed:

> It is obvious that there are not 6,000,000 jobs for capitalists in con-
> temporary American society: neither for capitalists or self-employed pro-
> fessionals or for agents of capitalism. Thus, a great number of present-day
> students are not future capitalists at all, but future salary-earners, in teach-
> ing, public administration and at various technical levels in industry and

---

[36] A particularly valuable insight to the fiscal dilemma of the state set in disaccumulationist analysis but one that demands further elaboration is James O'Connor "The Fiscal Crisis of the State," *Socialist Revolution,* Vol. I, Nos. 1 and 2 (January–February and March–April, 1969).

the economy. Their status will be nearer that of the industrial worker than that of management. For meanwhile, as a result of automation, the difference of status between the technician and the skilled worker is rapidly diminishing. U.S. society is moving towards a situation in which most of the skilled workers for whom there remain jobs in industry will have to have a higher or semi-higher education.[37]

The educational expansion that Mandel here cites even understates the growing job crisis for the young. Beyond the question of merely channeling or tracking college students (and especially those in the growing two-year state institutions and public arts and science colleges) into wage-earner status as intellectual proletarians is a much larger question: can they be absorbed at all in the labor force, whatever their education and skills? Seymour Wolfbein, in projecting work force supply and demand into the mid-1970s, sees the following trends for American workers by age category:

TABLE 3
Employment Distribution and Labor Force Distribution by Age in 1975

Age	Labor Force in 1975	Employment in 1975 Assuming Present Employment Patterns
Total	100%	100%
14–19	9.7	7.6
20–24	13.5	10.5
25–34	22.4	19.5
14–34 Total	45.6	37.6
35–44	17.5	23.2
45–54	19.5	21.4
55–64	13.9	13.4
65 and over	3.9	4.1

SOURCE: Seymour Wolfbein, *Work in American Society* (Glenview, Ill.: Scott, Foresman, 1971), p. 122.

We can easily see, in this forecast by a respectable and competent bourgeois economist, the anticipation of a continued tightening of employment opportunities for the young.[38] Thus, it is more than just the problem of there not being jobs for 6–7 million capitalists, as Mandel says, but jobs of any kind for the college graduate, a reality the class of 1971 has already discovered.

Of course, what has been and is happening to the young potential workers, and has been absorbed by blacks for a much longer time and to a deeper extent, is really an object lesson to the entire American labor force. As youth and blacks cease to be the disemployment safety valve, other sectors of the labor force will begin to pay the bills of economic contraction that are the

[37] Ernest Mandel, "Where Is America Going?," *New Left Review,* No. 54 (March–April, 1969), pp. 5–6.
[38] Wolfbein is a well-known labor economist and is currently Dean of the School of Business Administration at Temple University.

ultimate end to which disaccumulation points. Initially, the struggles may not take the form of vast unemployment. They may be shifted to comparative wage losses through inflation, taxes, or "wage-price guideline" deceptions. There is also the possibility of pitting worker against worker or worker against nonworker (welfare payer versus welfare payee). But these can only be short-run and diversionary tactics. They cannot hide the increasingly obvious fact that capitalism cannot find jobs for its people, productive or unproductive jobs, without paying either a cost that ultimately abolishes the capitalist system or calls for further repression and quantitative exploitation of its citizens—and, so far as American imperialism remains vital, the world.

All this is not to say that future struggles within American capitalism will not have an important qualitative dimension with increased irrationality in production, consumption, and life style. But, as this study of the problems of the youthful labor force has tried to indicate, the classic employment crisis, the more or less orthodox quantitative critique of the capitalist system, has not been evaded by the historic shift of American capitalism to disaccumulation. In other words, there is no need for the Left to give ground to the conventional economics of the full employment theorists and therefore to dwell needlessly and dangerously on exotic but self-serving prophesies emphasizing only the moral and psychological imperatives of building a socialist revolution in America, for, to a greater extent than many on the Left might care to admit, we have adopted only the politics and sociology of Marx and Lenin while accepting, for ourselves, in our country at least, the economics of Keynes. We must come to realize that despite its resiliency and adaptability, disaccumulationist capitalism has not and cannot perpetually avoid the fatal internal contradictions of a production for private profit economy.

Questions for Discussion

1. What is actually meant by collective bargaining?
2. What are the arguments for and against the extension of collective bargaining procedures?
3. How do you react to Dunlop's view of the future of collective bargaining—especially in light of the past two years' experimentation with government wage-setting policies?
4. Why is Jacobs critical of the unions' abilities to act in the workers' interests? Do you agree with him? Why or why not?
5. Do you believe that labor unions' support for American foreign policy has been in labor's interest? What assumptions are necessary to answer this affirmatively? Negatively?
6. What do you consider to be the most important contemporary manpower problem?
7. What is meant by "disaccumulationist capitalism?" How, according to Carson, is disaccumulation related to manpower policies of the government?
8. Will education "solve" the problem of youthful labor surplus?

PART IX

Government and the Question of Equality

In a typical course in basic economics the student learns early that the distribution of income in a capitalist economy is determined by the so-called market mechanism. Later the student will be introduced to the effects of the tax and transfer functions of the state on the distribution of income. While recognizing that government exerts a significant influence on the distribution of income, the analysis usually falls short of the explicit realization that, to a large extent, the distribution of income in the United States is determined not in the market, but by action of the state. In addition, these courses usually treat topics such as government-business relations and government expenditures on goods and services as somehow unrelated to the distribution of income.

The effect of this type of presentation is to constrain the student's outlook. He or she is led to focus on the "economic" and moral aspects of income inequality, rather than engaging in a serious analysis of how power (both political and economic) manifests itself in modern capitalist society. Thus, the unequal distribution of income becomes the product of bad government (which can be changed if only the people would realize their moral duty to provide everyone with a decent income) rather than of an economic system that is based on inequality.

In this section a number of readings have been assembled that deal, in a critical way, with the effects of government on equality. The readings focus on the question of power and how the social relations of production determine the structure of power in American society.

The first essay, by Frank Ackerman, Howard Birnbaum, James Wetzler, and Andrew Zimbalist, sketches the general dimensions of income inequality in the United States. They calculate the distribution of income by economic status, race, and sex and find that, contrary to popular belief, the inequality of income in the United States is not diminishing.

The next three selections deal with the effects of taxation on the distribution of income. The first article is a liberal analysis of the aggregate effects of taxation (at state, local, and federal levels) on the distribution of income. This essay by Joseph Pechman contains a great deal of useful information on the tax system and deserves the careful attention of the student. The second selection is part of a book review written by John Gurley on Pechman's book, *Federal Tax Policy,* of which the preceding article is a synthesis. Gurley feels that, although Pechman has broken some important ground in his study, he has viewed the working of the tax system from much too narrow a perspective. Gurley suggests that the tax system must be examined from the broad perspective of a class analysis of the society in which we live. The third selection is an excerpt from *The Rich and the Super-Rich* by Ferdinand Lundberg, which provides the student with an understanding of the importance of some of the loopholes in our tax law that benefit the rich.

The last two articles deal with two particular problems of inequality in the modern capitalist economy. Samuel Bowles presents an excellent treatment of the class nature of the modern educational system. Setting his analysis in historical perspective, he concludes that inequality of education is tied to the existence of modern capitalism. Only by transforming our political-economic society will we be able to provide equal educational opportunities for all. The last selection is a small part of Harold M. Baron's fine essay "The Demand for Black Labor: Historical Notes on the Political Economy of Racism." In this excerpt Baron examines the present economic conditions of blacks in America as well as the changes in American capitalism that led blacks to where they are now. The careful reader will be able to discern the part that the state has played in these changes.

An important point that we have neglected in this section is the effect of government expenditures on the distribution of income. This neglect reflects the general disregard for this problem by most economists. There simply are no good articles dealing with this aspect of government policy. The reader who wishes to explore this issue should read carefully the two selections by James O'Connor and the section on the military-industrial complex. This reading should give the interested student an idea of how to proceed with such an analysis.

Income Distribution
in the United States

FRANK ACKERMAN,
HOWARD BIRNBAUM,
JAMES WETZLER, AND
ANDREW ZIMBALIST

The persistence of income inequality in America is well-known. Affluence in the suburbs contrasts starkly with the slums of any major city or the numerous "pockets" of rural poverty. This inequality is embarrassing in a democracy. Perhaps for this reason, income distribution is rarely an explicit political issue in the United States. The prevailing ideology seems to be that inequality is needed for economic growth and that soon the economy will be so prosperous that even the relatively poor will have a high standard of living. This argument gains some apparent plausibility from the history of Western Europe and North America: in these areas capitalism, with its great inequality, has been the agent of economic development.

For several reasons, we reject this neglect of distributional issues and its implicit toleration of existing inequality. First, it would require many decades of growth without redistribution to eliminate poverty, and there is no reason to assume that past rates of growth can be maintained this long. Economic growth is having increasingly intolerable ecological effects: either resources will be diverted to improve the environment or ecologically expensive production will be reduced. American growth, moreover, depends on consuming a disproportionate share of the world's natural resources: if currently underdeveloped countries ever begin to grow, America's share will be reduced.[1]

Second, the need for inequality to promote growth arises in our society

From the *Review of Radical Political Economics,* Vol. 3, No. 3 (Summer 1971), pp. 207–218. Reprinted by permission of the publisher.

[1] In 1968, North America, with less than 9% of the world's population, had the following percentages of total world consumption of energy:

natural and imported gases	67.5%
liquid fuel	38.6%
total energy	37.5%

In the same year the United States, with approximately 6% of the world's population, had the following percentages of total world consumption of

steel	26%
rubber	42%
tin	35%
fertilizer (nitrogenous, potash, and phosphate)	26%

SOURCE: United Nations, *Statistical Yearbook,* 1969.

because people are socialized to respond only to material incentives. Such responses are neither attractive nor unchangeable, and we can envision a society in which production takes place with little, if any, inequality.

Third, there are several human objections to inequality. Meaningful democracy is impossible in a society where political resources, such as wealth, are unequally distributed. Inequality is wasteful since, after elemental needs have been satisfied, people consume partly to emulate others; as a result, total social welfare (including our unhappiness over our rival's goods) increases more slowly than income. Finally, differences in material conditions tend to conceal more fundamental human qualities and pervert interpersonal relations.

The first section of this paper is an overview of inequality. We examine the distribution of income among people and its stability over time, the effect of taxes and government spending, the distribution of wealth, and the definition and extent of poverty. The second section focuses on income differences between particular categories of people. We consider inequalities by class, race, sex, education, and family background.

The Distribution of Income

Personal Income Before Taxes

The best measure of ability to purchase goods and services is after-tax income. Appropriate data exist, however, only for the distribution of before-tax income, so we must look at that first and consider the tax structure separately. A good way to illustrate the income distribution is to rank the population by income and measure what percentage of total personal income accrues to the richest 20% of the population, the second richest 20%, and so forth (richest here meaning highest income). The more income going to the richest 20% and the less going to the poorest 20%, the more unequal is the distribution of income.

Table 1 shows that in the U.S. during the postwar period, the poorest 20% of all families have consistently received less than 6% of total personal income, while the richest 20% have gotten over 40%. In 1969, the richest

TABLE 1
Distribution of Before-Tax Family Income

	1969	1964	1960	1956	1950	1947
Poorest fifth	5.6%	5.2%	4.9%	5.0%	4.5%	5.0%
Second fifth	12.3%	12.0%	12.0%	12.4%	12.0%	11.8%
Middle fifth	17.6%	17.7%	17.6%	17.8%	17.4%	17.0%
Fourth fifth	23.4%	24.0%	23.6%	23.7%	23.5%	23.1%
Richest fifth	41.0%	41.1%	42.0%	41.2%	42.6%	43.0%
Richest 5%	14.7%	15.7%	16.8%	16.3%	17.0%	17.2%

SOURCE: U.S. Census Bureau, *Current Population Reports*, Series P–60, No. 75, Table 11, p. 26.

TABLE 2
The Distribution of Income of Unrelated Individuals, 1969

Poorest fifth	3.4%
Second fifth	7.7%
Middle fifth	13.7%
Fourth fifth	24.3%
Richest fifth	50.9%
Richest 5%	21.0%

SOURCE: U.S. Census Bureau, *Current Population Reports*, Series P–60, No. 75, Table 11, p. 26.

5% of all families received over 14% of total family income, or over twice as much as the entire bottom 20%. Moreover, Table 1 understates inequality since income received by people not in families (see Table 2) is much more unequally distributed than family income.[2]

The improvement in the relative position of the poorest fifth in 1969 is probably due to the reduction in unemployment during the Vietnam escalation (see the discussion of black incomes and unemployment, below). The apparent decline in the share of the top income groups results entirely from the exclusion from Census Bureau income data of capital gains—that is, of the increase in the value of assets such as corporate stocks. *If capital gains are included, the share of the top fifth has been constant over the past twenty years.*[3] We conclude that the entire distribution has not really changed since World War II.

[2] For the family distribution in 1968, a family was in the top 5% if it had income exceeding approximately $23,000; in the top 20% with income over about $13,000; and in the bottom 20% with income under about $4,600.

[3] See Edward C. Budd, *American Economic Review*, May, 1970; and John Gorman, "The Relationship Between Personal Income and Taxable Income." *Survey of Current Business*, May, 1970. Because fully one-half of capital gains and only a portion of dividends are tax-exempt, individual stockholders generally prefer capital gains to dividends; corporations now systematically retain earnings rather than pay them out in dividends, so capital gains are a customary, almost predictable source of income for many rich people. A complete picture of money income distribution should include capital gains.

The following table is a rough adjustment of the share of the top 20% to include estimated capital gains.

Year	Share of Top Fifth Without Capital Gains (From Table 1)	Total Reported Capital Gains As a Percent of Total Personal Income	Share of Top Fifth With Capital Gains
1947	43.0%	2.2%	44.2%
1950	42.6%	2.6%	44.1%
1956	41.2%	2.8%	42.8%
1960	42.0%	2.6%	43.5%
1964	41.3%	3.2%	43.1%
1968	40.6%	5.2%	43.5%

Reported capital gains are two times taxable capital gains, since Federal income tax laws consider only half of long-term capital gains as taxable income. Data on taxable capital gains are in Gorman. We are assuming that all capital gains are long-term and go to the richest 20%, which is approximately true.

Taxes and Government Spending

In theory, Federal income taxes take a much higher percentage of income from the rich than from the poor. If this were true, the distribution of income after taxes would be much more equal than the distribution before the income tax. In reality, the effect of the income tax is rather modest, as is seen in Table 3.

TABLE 3
Income Distribution Before and After the Federal Income Tax, 1962

	Poorest Fifth	Second Fifth	Middle Fifth	Fourth Fifth	Richest Fifth	Richest 5%
Before tax	4.6%	10.9%	16.3%	22.7%	45.5%	19.6%
After tax	4.9%	11.5%	16.8%	23.1%	43.7%	17.7%

SOURCE: Edward C. Budd, *Inequality and Poverty*, 1967, pp. xiii, xvi.

In 1962, as in all years since World War II for which data are available, the share of the top 20% of the population is only about two percentage points lower after the income tax than before it. The Federal income tax laws have nominal tax rates that increase sharply with income, but they are vitiated by various deductions which reduce *taxable* incomes of the rich below their actual incomes. Thus, the rich gain the political advantages of high nominal rates and the economic advantages of low effective rates.

But if the Federal income tax takes only a small step toward improving the income distribution, the overall tax structure takes a much smaller step. Less than 40% of all taxes are individual income taxes; an almost equal amount is collected in property and sales taxes (see Table 4). Most studies of property and sales taxes have concluded that they take a larger percentage of income from the poor than from the rich. There is an involved, and still

TABLE 4
Distribution of Tax Revenue by Type of Tax, Fiscal Year 1966–67

	All Levels of Government	Federal Government	State and Local Governments
All taxes	100.0%	100.0%	100.0%
Property and sales taxes	35.7	13.7	80.2
Individual income tax	38.2	53.4	9.6
Corporation income tax	20.6	29.5	3.7
Miscellaneous taxes	4.4	3.3	6.7

SOURCES: U.S. Bureau of the Census, *Census of Governments*, 1967, Vol. 4, No. 5; *Compendium of Government Finances*, Table 5. Motor vehicle license fees, 1.3% of all taxes, are combined with property and sales taxes.

unsettled, academic debate over how completely corporations shift their income taxes onto consumers by raising prices. If the corporation income tax is shifted, it could be considered similar to a sales tax. We might tentatively conclude that taxes other than individual income taxes do not reduce, and probably increase, income inequality.

It is sometimes argued that the government improves the income distribution through its spending policies. We believe that military spending, accounting for nearly one-third of government spending (federal, state, and local), disproportionately benefits the wealthy. Many other programs appear to be of little benefit to the poor: foreign aid, space, police, interest on public debt (largely paying for past military spending), and highways which, combined with military spending, amounted to one-half of all government spending in 1966. By comparison, spending of the traditional welfare-state variety, on schools, parks and recreation, health and hospitals, and welfare, amounted to just over one-fourth of government spending, and it is by no means obvious that these programs are primarily beneficial to the poor.

Wealth

Income distribution approximates the distribution of economic welfare because consumption is usually limited by income. By temporarily enabling some people to consume more than their income, personal wealth is a second source of economic well-being. More important, wealth is a principal source of power in our society, especially political power. It is their superior wealth that enables managements to outlast strikes. The wealthy control virtually all mass media and thus have a disproportionate influence over public opinion. They finance political campaigns and lobby in the legislature. Above all they own and control the giant corporations that make many important decisions about allocation of resources and distribution of income. For instance, corporations influence state and local governments (as well as foreign governments) by their ability to locate their businesses only in places where a favorable political environment exists. We must consider, then, the distribution of various types of wealth, particularly corporate stock.

The best recent data on distribution of personal wealth are in a government-sponsored survey of over 2,500 households.[4] Ranking households by wealth, Table 5 shows the wealthiest 1% own 31% of total wealth and 61% of corporate stock.

Apologists for American capitalism often refer to the statistic that over 30 million people own corporate stock, implying that this form of wealth is widely distributed. This is clearly nonsense: many people do own a little stock, but the vast bulk of corporate stock is owned by a very few people. Ownership of unincorporated businesses and professions is only slightly more

[4] Dorothy S. Projector and Gertrude Weiss, *Survey of Financial Characteristics of Consumers*, Federal Reserve System, 1966.

TABLE 5
Distribution of Various Types of Personal Wealth, 1962

	Wealthiest 20 Per Cent	Top 5 Per Cent	Top 1 Per Cent
Total wealth	76%	50%	31%
Corporate stock	96%	83%	61%
Businesses & professions	89%	62%	39%
Homes	52%	19%	6%

SOURCES: Projector and Weiss, *Survey of Financial Characteristics of Consumers,* pp. 110–114, 151; and Irwin Friend, Jean Crockett and Marshall Blume, *Mutual Funds and Other Institutional Investors: A New Perspective,* p. 113.

equally distributed than is corporate stock. The types of wealth that are relatively more equally distributed are such things as autos and homes, which are not sources of power as is ownership of businesses and corporations.

Personal wealth, of course, does not tell the whole story. Wealth is also held by pension funds and charitable foundations. The foundations are largely formed by the wealthy, but many pension funds exist for workers. In 1969, total pension fund assets were $238 billion, less than 10% of national wealth.[5] In 1968, private non-insured pension funds held only 9.7% of the corporate stock held by domestic individuals, personal trusts, and private non-insured pension funds. So, including individuals' shares of pension fund assets probably raises slightly the share of the poorest 80% but does not alter the basic pattern of great inequality. The pension funds, moreover, are usually managed by either banks or the government, so their wealth is not a significant source of power to workers in the same sense that personal wealth is a source of power to capitalists.

A View from the Bottom

Extensive poverty accompanies the great concentrations of income and wealth. The most common figures on poverty, published by the Social Security Administration (SSA), define it as an income below $3,700 for a nonfarm family of four (with different income cut-offs for different family sizes and residences). In 1969, 24.3 million people, or 12.2% of the population, were living in poverty by these criteria. The SSA allows food expenditures of 80¢ per person per day, and assumes that food makes up one-third of the total budget. We reject poverty lines in the neighborhood of $3,700, and thus most poverty figures published by government agencies, as implausibly low.

A more reasonable definition of poverty is the Bureau of Labor Statistics

[5] Securities and Exchange Commission, *Statistical Bulletin,* May, 1970.

(BLS) subsistence budget for 1967.[6] It totals $5,900 for an urban family of four. The BLS calculates it on a much more detailed, and reasonable, basis than the SSA budget. They assume that, of the $5,900, taxes and social security take $700, leaving $5,200 after tax. Food, assumed to cost less than $1.20 per person per day (this requires very careful shopping and cooking and no meals away from home), takes $1,650 for the year. They assume rent, heat and utilities for an inexpensive 5-room, one-bath apartment, to be under $90 per month, or $1,000 per year. House furnishings and household expenditures add another $300 per year. Clothing and personal care together total $700 for the family, or $175 per person. Transportation, assumed to be by an 8-year-old used car except in cities with good public transportation, costs $450. Medical care and medical insurance cost $475. Less than $700 remains for other expenses.

Most people would agree that a family of four living on the BLS subsistence budget would feel quite poor and be consistently concerned with making ends meet. By 1969, inflation had raised the cost of the BLS budget to $6,500. In that year, approximately 20% of all four-person families had incomes lower than $6,500.

Apologists for capitalism remind us that even though vast numbers of Americans are poor, poverty is declining. While it is gratifying to learn that 1.1 million fewer people were "officially" impoverished in 1969 than in 1968 and that fewer people are dying of starvation, the point is that a wealthy society should do much better.

Inequalities by Class, Race, and Sex

Class and Income

Most people with very high incomes are capitalists who own substantial assets, especially corporate stock, and receive income primarily from those assets.

The only source that describes capitalist income in any useful detail is the Internal Revenue Service.[7] In 1966 fewer than 2% of all taxpayers received 74% of all dividends and 76% of all capital gains. In the following discussion we define the capitalist class as this group of large shareowners.

Table 6 shows the types of income of taxpayers at several income levels. We define "small business income" as interest, rent, and income of farmers, unincorporated businesses, proprietors, and self-employed professionals. "Capitalist income" is dividends and capital gains. Total small business in-

[6] This is the lowest of the three budgets presented in Jean C. Brackett, "New BLS Budgets . . . ," *Monthly Labor Review*, April, 1969. The more commonly quoted "modest, but adequate" budget is the middle of the three budgets, amounting to $9,800 for an urban family of four in 1967. For a discussion of the "modest, but adequate" budget and related problems of defining poverty, see Donald Light, "Income Distribution: The First Stage in the Consideration of Poverty."

[7] See IRS, *Statistics of Income, 1966: Individual Income Tax Returns* (hereafter abbreviated Tax Returns).

TABLE 6
Types of Income, 1966 (in Billions of Dollars)

Size of Taxable Income	Number of Tax Returns	All Types	Wage and Salary	Small Business	Capitalist
Total, all sizes	70,160,000	478.2	381.1	56.8	32.9
Under $20,000	68,230,000	401.1	349.1	35.1	12.3
$20,000–$50,000	1,644,000	48.0	24.7	14.8	7.0
$50,000–$100,000	218,000	15.4	5.3	5.0	4.4
Over $100,000	53,000	13.5	2.1	1.8	9.0

Types of Income, 1966, As Per Cent of Total Income

Size of Taxable Income	All Types	Wage and Salary	Small Business	Capitalist
Total, all sizes	100.0%	79.7%	11.9%	6.9%
Under $20,000	100.0%	87.0%	8.7%	3.1%
$20,000–$50,000	100.0%	51.4%	30.8%	14.5%
$50,000–$100,000	100.0%	34.3%	32.3%	28.4%
Over $100,000	100.0%	15.2%	13.3%	66.8%

SOURCE: Internal Revenue Service, *Statistics of Income, 1966: Individual Income Tax Returns,* Tables 7, 11, 19. The lower table simply converts the data in the upper table to percentages.

come is almost twice as large as total capitalist income, but capitalist income is far more concentrated in the hands of the rich.

Taxpayers who reported under $20,000 in net taxable income, the vast majority, got 87% of their income from wages and salaries and only 3% from capitalist sources. At higher income levels, the share of wages and salaries falls steadily and that of capitalist income rises. The 53,000 taxpayers with net taxable incomes exceeding $100,000 received only 15% of their income from wages and salaries and 67% from dividends and capital gains.

Moreover, these IRS data are biased to minimize the relationship between class and income. About one-third of the capitalist income reported to the IRS was tax-exempt, and therefore excluded from net taxable income. So, many people who reported large capitalist incomes on their income tax returns were classified in Table 6 as having small taxable income. A variety of tax loopholes also permit the wealthy to understate their taxable incomes. Interest on municipal bonds is completely tax-exempt. Exaggerated depreciation and depletion allowances are common. Tax-exempt charitable donations can be padded and overstated.

As a result of these and other loopholes, there were approximately 250 capitalists who reported zero taxable income, but over $100,000 each in capital gains or dividends. These individuals, all of whom are included in the lowest income class in Table 6, received at least $70 million in reported capitalist income, completely tax-free. Doubtless there were others who achieved somewhat less spectacular success in reporting their incomes as tax-exempt; no comprehensive statistics are available on the extent of such behavior.[8]

So those who receive profits (capitalists) earn much higher incomes than those who receive wages and salaries (workers).

It is no accident that incomes from ownership of corporations are so unjustly high. Many of America's most important social and political institutions act systematically to serve capitalist interests. Laws against larceny, for example, are enforced much more vigorously than laws (when they exist) against monopolistic combinations. The corporations are allowed to pollute the air and water, to create demands for such dangerous products as cigarettes, and to offset wage increases or corporate income taxes with price increases. Military spending by the government is an important source of profits, owing to the ambiguous relationship between the Pentagon and its military contractors. American foreign policies, supposedly designed to "contain communism," end up protecting profitable corporate foreign investments. Both mass media and government oppose ideas and behavior that discourage individuals from doing the meaningless work offered by big business. In sum, the economic power of corporate enterprise is reinforced by the other major institutions of our society.

Discrimination Against Blacks

A second pattern of inequality is discrimination against blacks. . . . This overlaps the class inequality discussed above because few blacks . . . are in the capitalist class; but it also accounts for substantial inequality within the working class. The labor market effectively preserves and aggravates inequality between groups of people. The inferior economic position of blacks . . . has survived more than a century after the abolition of slavery.

In 1969 the median income for all black males was $3,900, compared to $6,800 for white males. For workers who held year-round, full-time jobs, the median incomes were as shown in Table 7.

Thus even for workers with stable jobs, black male median income is only

TABLE 7
Median Incomes by Sex and Race, 1969 Workers With Year-Round, Full-Time Jobs

	Male	Female
Black	$5,900	$4,100
White	$9,000	$5,200

SOURCE: *Current Population Reports,* Series P–60, No. 70, p. 5.

[8] See Phillip M. Stern, *The Great Treasury Raid* (New York: Random House, 1964).

67% of white male income and black female income only 80% of white female income.

While lack of schooling is one cause of the black-white income differential (a rather ambiguous cause, as we shall show below), discrimination persists when individuals with the same amount of schooling are compared (see Table 8).

Finishing high school is worth $1,300 per year in higher income to a white male, in the sense that if he completes high school, he can expect his income to be $1,300 higher every year than if he had not finished. By contrast, it is worth only $900 per year to a black male. A college degree is worth $2,500 per year to a black man and $3,800 to a white man. Black college graduates seem to face the most discrimination, but this may result from a higher proportion of whites attending graduate schools.

Discrimination Against Women

The low status of women in the traditional family structure is translated into low pay and menial jobs for those women who work. Most working women are in the labor force not because they are bored with housework but because they must work to support themselves. 51.4% of all women in the 1967 labor force were either unmarried, separated from their husbands, or married to men earning less than $3,000 per year. The breakdown was as shown in Table 9.

Nevertheless, the job market is segmented so that men and women compete only among themselves for different jobs, with women eligible only for the lowest paying jobs. For workers with year-round, full-time jobs, female median income is 58% of male median income. This discrimination persists when we compare median incomes of men and women with the same education (see Table 10).

Restricting our comparison to workers with full-time, year-round jobs clearly understates discrimination against women because the female unemployment rate is much higher than the male rate. In 1969, the adult female unemployment rate was 4.7%, compared to an adult male rate of 2.8%.

TABLE 8
Median Income for All Males (25 Years Old and Over) by Race and Education, 1969

Years of Schooling		Black Male	White Male	Ratio
Elementary—less than 8		3,000	3,600	.82
	8	4,300	5,500	.79
High school	1–3	5,200	7,300	.71
	4	6,100	8,600	.71
College	1–3	7,100	9,600	.74
	4 or more	8,600	12,400	.69

SOURCE: *Current Population Reports,* Series P–60, No. 75, Table 47, p. 105.

TABLE 9
Marital Status of Women in the Labor Force, 1967

Status	Number of Women in the Labor Force	Per Cent of Women in the Labor Force
Total, all women in labor force	27.5 million	100.0%
Single	5.9	21.5%
Married, but husband absent	1.6	5.7%
Widowed	2.5	9.0%
Divorced	1.7	6.0%
Married, but husband earns less than $3,000 per year	2.5	9.2%
Total who must work	14.2	51.4%

SOURCE: *Current Population Reports,* Series P–60, No. 75, Table 47, p. 105.

TABLE 10
Median Income of Civilians (25 Years and Older) With Year-round, Full-time Jobs, 1968

Years of Schooling		Male Income	Female Income	Ratio
Elementary—less than 8		$ 5,300	$3,300	.62
	8	$ 6,600	$3,600	.55
High School	1–3	$ 7,300	$3,900	.53
	4	$ 8,300	$4,800	.58
College	1–3	$ 9,300	$5,500	.59
	4	$11,800	$6,700	.57
	5 or more	$12,800	$8,300	.64
Total		$ 8,100	$4,700	.58

SOURCE: *Current Population Reports,* Series P–60, No. 66, Table 41, p. 98.

Moreover, a higher proportion of women withdraw from the labor force when they cannot find jobs or are forced to accept part-time or seasonal work and, in both cases, are not counted as unemployed.

Sex discrimination does not seem to be declining. The ratio of female to male median wage and salary income for full-time, year-round workers has declined from .63 in 1956 to .58 in 1968. Among the major occupational groups, the relative position of women seems to be improving (slowly) only for professional and technical workers. In the past 10 years, the number of white female unrelated individuals and families headed by a woman below the poverty line has not changed, and the number of such nonwhite females and female-headed families has actually increased. All of the decline in poverty referred to above has affected families headed by men or male unrelated individuals.

Education and Social Mobility

The close relation of education and income distribution is obvious from Tables 8 and 10. For men with full-time, year-round jobs, median incomes in 1968 were $11,800 with a college diploma, $8,300 with a high school diploma, and $6,600 for eight years of schooling. A similar relation is seen for both women and blacks.

The notion of social mobility through education is one of the most widespread beliefs about American society. Is your job terrible and poorly paid? Work hard, save money to put your kids through college, and they will escape into better jobs and comfortable lives. As much as any other idea, this has served to rationalize an alienated, impoverished existence for millions of Americans.

The belief that there is actual mobility through education, however, is a myth. It is true that better-educated people earn higher incomes. But it is also true that children of wealthier families become far better-educated. So the effect of education is to preserve and to legitimize existing inequalities in income distribution.

Table 11 shows that high school seniors are much more likely to enter college if they come from wealthy families. A high school senior from the top income group (family income over $15,000) is over four times as likely to enter college as a senior from the bottom income group (family income under $3,000).

It is not hard to understand why wealthier students stay in school longer. Even in states where public higher education is free, students still have significant living expenses which must be paid by their families. . . .

Family income affects education at all stages. Poor children are more likely to drop out of high school before the twelfth grade or to drop out of college before graduation. Rich children attend the better and more prestigious private universities. They also receive a disproportionate share of the benefits of public higher education.[9]

TABLE 11
College Attendance of High School Graduates by Income, 1966

Family Income in 1965	Percentage of 1966 High School Graduates Who Started College By February, 1967
Under $3,000	19.8
$3,000–$4,000	32.3
$4,000–$6,000	36.9
$6,000–$7,000	41.1
$7,500–$10,000	51.0
$10,000–$15,000	61.3
Over $15,000	86.7
Total, all incomes	46.9%

SOURCE: *Current Population Reports*, Series P–20, No. 185, Table 8.

Public higher education is only one force tending to preserve inequality from one generation to the next. A direct (although rough) measure of intergenerational preservation of status can be seen in Table 12, taken from a Census Bureau study of occupations of men working in 1962.

Seventy-one per cent of the sons of white-collar workers were themselves white-collar workers, while only 37% of the sons of blue-collar workers and 23% of the sons of farm workers (farm owners and employees combined) had white-collar jobs. In other words, the chances of ending up in a white-collar job were almost twice as high for a white-collar worker's son as for a blue-collar worker's son, and three times as high for a white-collar worker's son as for a farmer's son. Of course there has been some movement from

TABLE 12
Occupation of Men Working in 1962 (25–64 Years Old) and of Their Fathers

Father's Occupation When Son Was 16	Son's Occupation in March, 1962			
	Total	White-Collar	Blue-Collar	Farm
White-Collar	100.0%	71.0%	27.6%	1.5%
Blue-Collar	100.0%	36.9%	61.5%	1.6%
Farm	100.0%	23.2%	55.2%	21.6%
Total	100.0%	40.9%	51.4%	7.7%

SOURCE: Calculated from Blau and Duncan, *American Occupational Structure*, Table J2.1, p. 496. The data were obtained from a Census Bureau survey of 20,000 men.

[9] This was shown in a recent study of California higher education, one of the most extensive and progressive systems in the country.

Median income for the entire state was $8,000, but it was $12,000 for families with children in the University of California, the top track of the educational system. The state subsidy, that is, the full cost of education less fees paid by the student, was considerably greater to families with children in the higher tracks, which were also the families with higher incomes. Moreover, public higher education is financed by state and local taxes, which take a higher percentage of income from the poor than from the rich.

Distribution of Benefits From Public Higher Education in California, 1964

	All Families	Families Without Children in Calif. Higher Education	Families With Children in		
			Junior College	State College	Univ. of Calif.
Median family income	$8,000	$7,900	$8,800	$10,000	$12,000
Average subsidy received	—	0	$1,700	$ 3,800	$ 4,900
Subsidy as % of median family income	—	0	12%	31%	41%

SOURCE: W. Lee Hansen and B. Weisbrod, "The Distribution of Costs and Direct Benefits of Public Education: The Case of California," *Journal of Human Resources*, Spring 1969, Tables 5 and 6.

lower status jobs into white-collar jobs; there had to be, since the proportion of the labor force in white-collar jobs has been expanding rapidly.

To some extent Table 12 reflects racial discrimination, since most non-whites are in the blue-collar or farm categories. However, most of the men in each of the three major occupational categories are white; Table 12 suggests the existence of a hierarchy of status, preserved across generations, even within the white male working class.

Summary

We find, then, that American capitalism is characterized by considerable un-justifiable inequality of income and wealth, a state of affairs that is not im-proving over time. Causes of this inequality include social class distinctions between workers and capitalists and economic discrimination against women and minority groups. Legend has it that the United States is the land of equal opportunity; nevertheless, there is very little actual social mobility. Wealth, both personal and corporate, is perhaps the most important source of political power; and, in a vicious cycle, political power is used to preserve existing accumulations of wealth.

Taxation and the Distribution of Income: A Liberal Analysis

JOSEPH PECHMAN

The distribution of income has always been a hotly debated subject. Whatever has happened or is happening to the distribution of income, some people will always assert that the rich are getting a bigger share of the pie than is "fair," while others will seek to show that this is not the case. Few people, however, bother to find out the facts and fewer still understand what they mean.

The same applies to the tax system. Everybody knows that there are loop-

From Joseph Pechman, "The Rich, the Poor, and the Taxes They Pay," *The Public Interest*, No. 17 (Fall 1969), pp. 21–43. Copyright © National Affairs Inc., 1969.

holes in the federal tax laws, but few realize that there are loopholes for persons at all income levels. Even fewer have a clear idea about the effects on the distribution of income of closing the more controversial loopholes. And only the experts know the state-local tax structure is in more urgent need of reform than the federal structure.

This article is intended to put these matters in perspective by summarizing the available information. What has happened to the distribution of income before taxes in recent years, and how has the tax system modified it? What's wrong with the national tax system? What reforms are needed to make it a fairer system? And . . . what would be the shape of a tax distribution that most Americans today might agree to be "fair"?

I. The Distribution of Income

Despite the proliferation of sophisticated economic data in this country, the United States government does *not* publish official estimates of the distribution of income. Such estimates were prepared by the Office of Business Economics for a period of years in the 1950's and early 1960's, but were discontinued because the sources on which they were based were acknowledged to be inadequate. We have data from annual field surveys of some 30,000 households conducted by the Bureau of the Census, as well as from the annual *Statistics of Income* prepared by the Internal Revenue Service from federal individual income tax returns. But both sources have their weaknesses: the Census Bureau surveys systematically understate income, particularly in the top brackets; tax returns, on the other hand, understate the share received by low income recipients who are not required to file. Nevertheless, if used with care, the two sources provide some interesting insights.

Before turning to the most recent period, it should be pointed out that a significant change in the distribution of pre-tax income occurred during the Great Depression and World War II. All experts who have examined the data agree that the distribution became more equal as a result of (a) the tremendous reductions in business and property incomes during the depression and (b) the narrowing of earnings differentials between low-paid workers and higher-paid skilled workers and salaried employees when full employment was reestablished during the war. The most authoritative estimates, prepared by the late Selma Goldsmith and her associates, suggest that the share of personal income received by the top 5 per cent of the nation's consumer units (including families and unrelated individuals) declined from 30 per cent in 1929 to 26.5 per cent in 1935–36; the share of the top 20 per cent declined from 54.4 per cent to 51.7 per cent in the same period. The movement toward greater equality appears to have continued during the war up to about 1944. By that year, the share of the top 5 per cent had dropped another notch to 20.7 per cent, and of the top 20 per cent to 45.8 per cent.

The income concept used by these researchers did not include undistributed corporate profits, which are a source of future dividends or of capital gains for shareholders; if they had been included, the movement of the income distribution toward equality from 1929 to 1944 would have been substantially moderated, but by no means eliminated.[1]

The movement toward equality seems to have ended during World War II, at least on the basis of the available statistics. In 1952, for example, the share of the top 5 per cent was 20.5 per cent and of the top 20 per cent, 44.7 per cent. (The differences from the 1944 figures are well within the margin of error of these data, and can hardly be called significant.)

To trace what happened since 1952, we shift to the census data that provide the longest continuous and comparable income distribution series available to us. The best way to appreciate the trend is to look at the figures for income shares at five-year intervals:

TABLE 1
Before-Tax Income Shares, Census Data (Per Cent)

Year	Top 5 Per Cent of Families	Top 20 Per Cent of Families
1952	18	42
1957	16	40
1962	16	42
1967	15	41

SOURCE: Bureau of the Census. Income includes transfer payments (e.g., social security benefits, unemployment compensation, welfare payments, etc.), but excludes capital gains.

The figures indicate that the share of the top 5 per cent declined slightly between 1952 and 1957, and has remained virtually unchanged since 1957; the share of the top 20 per cent changed very little. Correspondingly, the shares of the groups at the bottom of the income scale (not shown in the table) also changed very little throughout the period.

Tax data are needed to push the analysis further. These data are better than the census data for our purposes, because they show the amount of realized capital gains and also permit us to calculate income shares *after* the federal income tax. But the great disadvantage of the tax data is that the bottom part of the income distribution is underrepresented because of an unknown number of nonfilers. Furthermore, the taxpayer unit is not exactly a family unit, because children and other members of the family file their own income tax returns if they have income, and a few married couples continue to file

[1] The year 1929 must have been the high point of inequality during the 1920's, so that the distribution of income in the more recent period may not have been very different from what it was in the early 1920's if account is taken of undistributed profits. Unfortunately, the available data for those years are simply not good enough to say much more.

separate returns despite the privilege of income splitting, which removed the advantage of separate returns with rare exceptions.

There is really no way to get around these problems, but the tax data are too interesting to be abandoned because of these technicalities. So, we make an assumption that permits us to use at least the upper tail of the income distribution. The assumption is that the top 10 or 15 per cent of the nation's tax units are for the most part similar to the census family units and the cases that differ represent roughly the same percentage of the total number of units each year. Because we have official Department of Commerce estimates of income (as defined in the tax code) for the country as a whole, the assumption enables us to compute income shares before and after tax for the top 1, 2, 5, 10, and 15 per cent of units annually for the entire postwar period.[2]

The tax series confirms much of what we learned from the census series, and adds a few additional bits of information besides. Here are the data for selected years chosen to represent the three sets of federal income tax rates levied, beginning with the Korean War:

TABLE 2
Before-Tax Income Shares, Tax Data (Per Cent)

Year	Top 1 Per Cent of Tax Units	Top 2 Per Cent of Tax Units	Top 5 Per Cent of Tax Units	Top 10 Per Cent of Tax Units	Top 15 Per Cent of Tax Units
1952	9	12	19	27	33
1963	8	12	19	28	35
1967	9	13	20	29	36

SOURCE: *Statistics of Income*. Income excludes transfer payments, but includes realized capital gains in full.

According to tax returns, the share of total income, including all realized capital gains, going to the top 1 per cent of the tax units was about the same for the entire period from 1952 through 1967. But the shares of the top 2, 5, 10, and 15 per cent—which, of course, include the top 1 per cent—all rose somewhat. These trends differ from the census figures which show that the entire income distribution was stable. By contrast, the tax data show that

[2] People with money always feel poorer than they are, and it might be useful to indicate what kinds of income we are talking about for these various categories. For the year 1967, a taxpayer was in the top 1 per cent if his income (including realized capital gains) was over $43,000, the top 2 per cent if his income was over $28,000, the top 5 per cent if his income was over $18,000, the top 10 per cent if his income was over $14,000. The top 15 per cent if his income was over $12,000.

I would assume that most of the readers of this article . . . are included among the rich and super-rich. I also assume they will find this hard to believe.

the 14 per cent of income recipients just below the top 1 per cent—this group reported incomes between $12,000 and $43,000 in 1967—*increased* their share of total income from 24 per cent to 27 per cent.

If the figures are anywhere near being right, they suggest two significant conclusions:

First, in recent years the very rich in our society have not enjoyed larger increases in incomes, as defined in the tax code, than the average income recipient. Although realized capital gains are included in our figures, they do not include nonreported sources, such as tax-exempt interest and excess depletion; correction for these omissions would probably not alter the results very much, because the amounts involved are small relative to the total of reported incomes. Even a correction for the undistributed profits of corporations wouldn't change the result very much because undistributed gross corporation profits have remained between 10 and 13 per cent of total reported income since 1950.

Second, a change in the income distribution may have occurred in what are sometimes called the "middle income" classes. These classes consist of most of the professional people in this country (doctors, lawyers, engineers, accountants, college professors, etc.) as well as the highest paid members of the skilled labor force and white collar workers. The increase in their share of total income from 24 per cent to 27 per cent, if it actually occurred, represents a not insignificant improvement in their relative income status.

Clearly, this improvement in the income shares of the middle classes could come only at the expense of the lower 85 per cent of the income distribution. But this is not the whole story. These figures contain only incomes that are generated in the private economy; they do not include transfer payments (e.g., social security benefits, unemployment compensation, welfare payments, etc.) which are, of course, concentrated in the lower income classes. Correction of the figures for transfer payments might be just enough to offset the increased share of the middle income classes. If this is the case, the constancy of the shares of pre-tax income shown by the census data is fully consistent with the growth in shares of the middle incomes shown by the tax data. And, if this is the explanation of the constancy of the income shares in the census distribution, it means that the lower classes have not been able to hold their own in the private economy; large increases in government transfer payments were needed to prevent a gradual erosion of their income shares.

II. The Effect of Taxes

Since one of the major objectives of taxation is to moderate income inequality, it is appropriate to ask how the tax system actually affects the distribution of income and whether it has become more or less equalizing. We examine first the impact of the federal individual income tax, which is the most progressive element in the nation's tax system and for which data by income classes are readily available, and then we speculate about the effect of the other taxes in the system.[3]

The Federal Income Tax

While everybody grumbles about the federal income tax, few people realize that tax rates have been *going down* for about two decades. Even with the 10 per cent surtax, the rates are lower today than they were from 1951 through 1963. Briefly, the history of the tax is as follows: tax rates reached their peak, and exemptions their low point, during World War II. They were reduced in 1946 and again in 1948, when income splitting and the $600 per capita exemption were also enacted. Rates were pushed up close to World War II levels during the Korean War, but were reduced in 1954 and again in 1964. The surtax that became effective for individuals on April 1, 1968 moved the rates only half way back to the 1954–63 levels.

The structure of the tax has been remarkably stable during this entire period, despite all the talk about closing loopholes. The preferential rate on long-term capital gains was enacted in 1942; income splitting became effective in 1948; interest on state and local government bonds has never been taxed by the federal government; percentage depletion dates back to the 1920's; and the deductions allowed for interest charges, taxes, charitable contributions, medical expenses, and casualty losses date back to 1942 or earlier. The 1954 law introduced a 4 per cent dividend credit, but this was repealed in 1964. (As a compromise, the $50 exclusion for dividends, which was enacted along with the credit, was raised to $100.) A few abuses have been eliminated from time to time, but the revenues involved have not been significant.

The single major victory for tax reform occurred in 1964, when the dividend credit and the deductions for state and local taxes other than income, sales, property, and gasoline taxes were eliminated. All told, these revenue-raising reforms amounted to about $750 million, and they were accompanied by revenue-losing reforms of $400 million (mainly the minimum standard deduction which benefitted only those with very low incomes).

Given this history, it follows that the effective tax rates at specific absolute income levels have been going down since World War II. For example, from 1947 to 1967, the effective rate of tax paid by taxpayers with adjusted gross income of $5,000-$10,000 declined from 13.8 per cent to 9.5 per cent; for those in the $15,000–20,000 class, the decline was from 24.6 per cent to 14.0 per cent; and above $100,000, the decline was from 57.4 per cent to 39.5 per cent. (These figures understate actual declines because adjusted

---

[3] Since the terms are often used loosely, it might be a good idea explicitly to define what *regressive, proportional,* and *progressive* taxation mean. A tax is *regressive* when it takes a larger proportion of a poor person's income than of a rich man's, *proportional* when it takes equal proportions of such incomes, and *progressive* when it takes a larger proportion of a rich man's income than of a poor man's.

gross income excludes half of long-term capital gains that were much larger relative to total income in 1967 than in 1947.)

Although such figures are of considerable interest, they are not directly useful for an analysis of the effect of the tax on the income distribution. For it must be remembered that most people moved up the income scale almost continuously throughout this period; under a progressive tax, they would be taxed more heavily as a result of this upward movement. There is a case for the argument that, as incomes rise, it is only "fair" that progressive tax rates—established on the basis of an earlier income distribution that was considered "fair"—ought to go down somewhat. The key question is: how much? Specifically, has the progressive taxation of increased incomes been offset by the reduction in tax rates, or has there been a "surplus" on the side of either income or taxation?

To answer this question, the effective tax rates were computed for the top 1, 2, 5, 10, and 15 per cent of the income tax units, but in this case the full amount of realized long-term capital gains, and also other exclusions, were included to arrive at a total income concept. The data show that, on this basis, average effective tax rates were substantially lower in 1967 than in 1952 for the top 1 per cent, slightly lower for the next 1 per cent, and roughly constant for the next 13 per cent. Note also that the effective rate of tax paid in 1967 by the top 1 per cent, whose before-tax income was $43,000 and over, was only 26 per cent of their total reported income, including all their realized capital gains.

TABLE 3
Effective Federal Tax Rates on Total Income (Per Cent)

Year	Top 1 Per Cent of Tax Units	Next 1 Per Cent of Tax Units	Next 3 Per Cent of Tax Units	Next 5 Per Cent of Tax Units	Next 5 Per Cent of Tax Units
1952	33	20	16	14	12
1963	27	20	16	14	13
1967	26	18	15	13	12

SOURCE: *Statistics of Income.* Total income is the sum of adjusted gross income and excluded capital gains, dividends, and sick pay.

It is a fairly simple matter to deduct the tax paid by each of these groups from their total income to obtain their disposable income. The results modify the conclusions we drew on the basis of the before-tax incomes in only minor respects. The shares of disposable income of the top 1 per cent remain stable, and the shares of the top 2, 5, 10, and 15 per cent go up from 1952 to 1967. Furthermore, the shares of the "middle income classes"—the 14 per cent between the top 1 and top 15 per cent—rise from 23 to 27 per cent on a disposable income basis, or about as much as on a before-tax basis (Table 4).

TABLE 4
Shares of Total Disposable (i.e., After-Tax) Income (Per Cent)

Year	Top 1 Per Cent of Tax Units	Top 2 Per Cent of Tax Units	Top 5 Per Cent of Tax Units	Top 10 Per Cent of Tax Units	Top 15 Per Cent of Tax Units
1952	7	10	16	24	30
1963	7	10	17	26	33
1967	7	11	17	26	34

SOURCE: *Statistics of Income*. Disposable income is total income less federal income tax paid.

We may conclude that the federal individual income tax has moderated the before-tax income distribution by roughly the same proportions since 1952. Thus, while tax rates at any given absolute income level have declined, the effect of progression has just about offset the decline, leaving the relative tax bite about the same in the top 15 per cent of the income distribution. Furthermore, similar calculations suggest that the post-World War II income tax is just about as equalizing as it was in 1941. The tremendous movement upward in the income distribution pushed much more taxable income into higher rate brackets, but this has been offset by the adoption of income splitting and the increase in itemized deductions.[4]

It should be emphasized that the foregoing data omit large chunks of income that are received primarily by high-paid employees of large business firms. Tax-exempt interest and percentage depletion have already been mentioned. In addition, beginning with the imposition of the very high individual income tax rates and the excess profits tax during World War II, methods of compensation were devised to funnel income to business executives in nontaxable forms. The devices used are well known: deferred compensation and pension plans, stock option arrangements, and direct payment of personal consumption expenditures through expense accounts. There is no question that these devices are used widely throughout the corporate sector. But little is known about the amounts involved, and even less is known about the impact on the distribution of income.

A recent study by Wilbur G. Lewellen for the National Bureau of Economic Research concluded that, even after allowance is made for the new compensation methods, the after-tax compensation (in dollars of constant purchasing power) of top executives in industrial corporations was no higher

[4] But the income tax is surely more equalizing now than it was in 1929, when the top bracket rates were cut to a maximum of 25 per cent. This means that the equalization of the distribution of income between the 1920's and the post-World War II period is even more pronounced on a disposable income basis than it is on a before-tax basis.

in the early 1960's than in 1940. The more important finding from the income distribution standpoint is that stock options, pensions, deferred compensation, and profit-sharing benefits rose rapidly as a percentage of the executives' compensation package from 1940 to 1955, and then stabilized. The study did not attempt to measure the value of expense accounts, and omitted firms in industries other than manufacturing. Nevertheless, the results of the study suggest that extreme statements about the possible effects of these devices on the distribution of income in recent years are not warranted.

The Corporation Income Tax

The corporation income tax was enacted four years before the individual income tax and it has been a mainstay of the federal tax system ever since. It produced more revenue than the individual income tax in 17 out of 28 years prior to 1941; today, it is the second largest source of federal revenue. The general corporation tax was reduced to 38 per cent after World War II. It was raised to 52 per cent during the Korean War and remained there until 1964, when it was reduced to 48 per cent.

Public finance experts have argued the merits and demerits of a corporation tax for a long time, but the issues have not been resolved. Its major purpose in our tax system is to safeguard the individual income tax. If corporate incomes were not subject to tax, individuals could avoid the individual income tax by arranging to have their income accumulate in corporations, and later on selling their stock at the low capital gains rate, or holding on until death at which time the capital gains pass to their heirs completely tax free. Short of taxing shareholders on their share of corporation incomes (a method which is attractive to economists, but is anathema to businessmen and most tax lawyers) and taxing capital gains in full, the most practical way to protect the individual income tax is to impose a separate tax on corporation incomes.

Some people have argued that a large part or all of the corporation income tax is shifted forward to the consumer in the form of higher prices. On this assumption, the corporation income tax is a sales tax—a very peculiar one, to be sure—and is therefore regressive. But the majority view among tax experts is that the corporation income tax comes out of corporate profits, as was intended, so that the tax is borne by shareholders. Despite the large post-World War II increases in the number of shareholders, stock ownership is still concentrated in the highest income classes. This means that the corporation income tax is, to some extent at least, a progressive tax.

The major change in the corporation tax in the last two decades has been the enactment of more generous depreciation deductions in 1954 and 1962 and of the investment credit in 1962. As a result, despite relatively constant rates, the corporation tax has declined as a ratio to gross corporate profits (i.e., profits before deduction of depreciation) from 33 per cent in 1954 to about 27 per cent in 1967. It rose in 1968 to 30 per cent as a result of the imposition of the 10 per cent surtax. The impending expiration of the surtax and repeal of the investment tax credit will just about offset one another, so that the post-surtax ratio will continue at 30 per cent until the continuously growing depreciation allowances will tilt it downward once again. Thus, although the contribution of the corporation tax to the progressivity of the national tax system has declined somewhat (for economic reasons that most economists regard as persuasive), the contribution continues to be on the progressive side.

Estate and Gift Taxes

In theory, estate and gift taxes are excellent taxes because they have little effect on incentives to earn income and, if effective, would reduce the inequality of the distribution of wealth that in turn accounts for much of the inequity in the distribution of income. In practice, the yield of these taxes is disappointing. Tax rates are high, but there are numerous ways to escape them. The result is that the federal government receives little of its revenue from these tax sources—about 1.7 per cent in the current fiscal year. The effective rate of estate taxes on wealth passed each year from one generation to the next must be less than 10 per cent; and the gift tax is even less effective. While these taxes are progressive, they have little effect on the distribution of wealth.

The Social Security Payroll Tax

We now turn to the features of the national tax system that, in combination, more than offset the progressivity of the federal income and estate and gift taxes. The social security payroll tax, which is levied at a flat rate on earnings up to a maximum of $7,800 under present law, was enacted in 1935 as the basic method of financing social security on the principle that the workers were buying their own insurance. This idea is doubtless responsible for the widespread acceptance of social security as a permanent government institution in this country; but the insurance analogy is no longer applicable to the system as it has developed. Present beneficiaries receive far larger benefits than the taxes they paid would entitle them to—a situation that will continue indefinitely as long as Congress raises benefits as prices and wages continue to rise. The trust funds have not grown significantly since the mid-1950's; the payroll taxes paid by the workers have not been stored up or invested, but have been paid out currently as benefits. When benefits promised to people now working come due, the funds for their payment will be provided out of tax revenues as of that future date.

Nevertheless, the insurance analogy has a strong hold on the thinking of the administrators of social security and the Congressional tax-writing committees. Every time a benefit increase is enacted, the payroll tax rates (or the maximum earnings subject to the tax) are raised, in order to balance out the revenues and expenditures for the next 75 years on an actuarial basis. In a relatively short time, the trust funds begin running large surpluses, which then become the justification for another round of benefit increases by Congress. This requires a further increase in rates for actuarial reasons, payroll taxes are again raised, and so on.

As a result of this process, payroll taxes have been raised seven times since the beginning of 1960. The combined employer-employee tax was 6 per cent on earnings up to $4,800 on January 1, 1960; this year the tax is 9.6 per cent on earnings up to $7,800. Most economists believe that the burden of the employer tax, as well as the employee tax, falls eventually on the workers (either by substituting for larger wage increases or inflating prices). Thus, the federal government has been placing more and more weight on this regressive element of the federal tax system.

State and Local Taxes

Although the federal tax system is progressive on balance, the state and local tax system is highly regressive. The states rely heavily on sales taxes, while the local governments rely on property taxes. Personal and corporation income taxes account for only about 11 per cent of state-local revenues from their own sources. This situation is disturbing because the state-local tax system is the growing element of the national system. Whereas the federal government has been able to reduce income tax rates several times beginning in 1954, and has eliminated virtually all of its excise taxes, state governments continue to enact new taxes and to raise the rates of old taxes to keep up with their increasing and urgent revenue needs; meanwhile, local governments keep raising the already excessively burdened property tax.

Federal tax receipts have moved within the narrow range of 19 to 21 per cent of the Gross National Product since 1951. By contrast, state-local receipts rose from 7.1 per cent of the GNP in 1951 to 11.9 per cent in 1968. Assuming that state-local taxes respond more or less proportionately to the rise in the national product (a reasonable assumption), the state and local governments must have increased rates by 68 per cent in these 17 years to push up their tax yields to current levels. The net result is, of course, that a greater degree of regression is being built into the national tax system by the states and local governments as they continue to seek for more revenues.

Parenthetically, it might be observed that the "tax revolt" which has been so much in the news of late must have been a reflection of the increasing burden of state and local taxes. The revolt is allegedly concentrated in the "middle income" classes living in the suburbs. In this, there is a paradox: this group probably pays a smaller proportion of its income in taxes than the poor and near poor (see below), but the taxes they have been paying, or recently began to pay, are highly visible. Their incomes have risen sharply in recent years, so that their federal income taxes are higher in dollar amounts despite the 1964 rate reduction. Six states have enacted new income taxes in the past eight years and ten states have enacted new sales taxes; many others have raised the rates of both taxes substantially. Most of the new suburbanites are now paying property taxes directly as home owners, rather than indirectly as tenants, and property taxes have also been rising everywhere. Tax morale was, therefore, generally at a low ebb when the federal government requested more taxes to finance a budget containing $30 billion to fight an unpopular war. Since the request was in the form of a surcharge on those already paying taxes, and did nothing about those who escaped, the existing inequities in the federal income tax at last became evident to large masses of taxpayers who have no difficulty in communicating their unhappiness to their Congressmen.

Summary of the National Tax System

It is not easy to arrive at an accurate estimate of the impact of the whole tax system at various income levels. Taxes are reported to different federal, state, and local government agencies. No single agency has the responsibility to compel reporting of taxes on a meaningful and consistent basis. A number of isolated attempts have been made by students of public finance to piece together from the inadequate data estimates of the distribution of all taxes by income classes. These studies were for different years, make different assumptions from the incidence of the various taxes, and use different statistical sources and methodologies to correct for the inconsistencies in the data. Nevertheless, they all arrive at similar conclusions regarding the relative tax loads at different income levels.

The most recent estimates were prepared by the Council of Economic Advisers for the year 1965. They show the distribution of taxes by the income classes of families and unattached individuals, income being defined exclusive of transfer payments. The estimates for taxes and transfers separately, and in combination, are summarized in Table 5.

The following are the major conclusions that can be drawn from these and previously published estimates:

1. Since at least the mid-1930's, the federal tax system has been roughly proportional in the lower and middle income classes, and clearly progressive for the highest classes. Federal income tax data suggest that the preferential rate on capital gains, and the exclusion of interest on state and local bonds and other items from the tax base, have produced some regressivity for the very small group at the top of the income pyramid, say, beginning with incomes of $100,000 or more.
2. State and local taxes are regressive throughout the income scale.
3. The combined federal, state, and local tax burden is heaviest in the very bottom and top brackets, and lowest in the middle brackets. This statement is, of course, based on averages for each group and there are wide variations around these averages for specific individuals, depending on the sources of their incomes, the kind of property they own, and where they live.

TABLE 5
Taxes and Transfers as Per Cent of Income, 1965

| Income Classes | Taxes | | | Transfer Payments | Taxes Less Transfers |
	Federal	State and Local	Total		
Under $2,000	19	25	44	126	–83*
$ 2,000– 4,000	16	11	27	11	16
4,000– 6,000	17	10	27	5	21
6,000– 8,000	17	9	26	3	23
8,000–10,000	18	9	27	2	25
10,000–15,000	19	9	27	2	25
15,000 and over	32	7	38	1	37
Total	22	9	31	14	24

SOURCE: *Economic Report of the President,* 1969. Income excludes transfer payments, but includes realized capital gains in full and undistributed corporate profits.
* The minus sign indicates that the families and individuals in this class received more from federal, state, and local governments than they, as a group, paid to these governments in taxes.

4. The poor receive numerous transfer payments (e.g., social security, un-employment compensation, public assistance, etc.) that are financed by this tax system. The net effect of transfers as against taxes is distinctly progressive, because transfer payments make up such a large proportion of total income at the bottom of the income distribution—56 per cent for those with incomes of less than $2,000 in 1965. (To some extent, this progressivity is overstated because the transfers do not always go to the same people who pay taxes, the best example being social security retirement benefits that are received only by retirees—many of whom are not poor—while $1.5 billion of the payroll tax levied to pay for these benefits are paid by the poor.) There is no reason in the abstract, why a nation should not levy taxes on and pay transfers to the same groups; but while the nation wages a war on poverty, it is surely appropriate to consider the possibility of providing additional financial assistance to the poor by *tax reduction* as well as through transfer payments.

III. Reforming the National Tax System

The preceding discussion indicates that the agenda for reforming this country's tax system to correct its regressive features is lengthy and complicated. It involves reconstruction of the tax systems at all levels of government, and the development of new forms of intergovernmental fiscal relations. State and local governments need to rely more heavily on income taxes, relieve the poor of paying sales taxes, and deemphasize the property tax. At the federal level, the most important items on the agenda are to alleviate the payroll tax on the poor, to deliver—at last—on promises made by both political parties to close loopholes in the income taxes, and make the estate and gift taxes more effective.

State and Local Taxes

There are no easy solutions to the state-local problems, given the political constraints under which our federal system operates. At the state level, the trend is for moderate income and sales taxes—34 states already have both, and the number increases every year. Six states have adopted simple per capita credits against income taxes for sales taxes paid (with refunds for those who do not pay income taxes) to alleviate the sales tax burden on the poor. This device eliminates the regressive feature of the sales tax and makes it more acceptable on grounds of equity. Progress on the adoption of state income taxes has been slow, but there has been a new surge of adoptions by the states in the past couple of years as governors and legislators have realized that they cannot get along without the growth-responsive revenues from an income tax.

The states are also beginning to take a more responsible attitude toward their local governments, although the situation is admittedly bad in many parts of the country. More of the states' own revenues should be allocated to local governments through grants-in-aid to prevent the development of city income and sales taxes that tend to drive wealthy taxpayers and businesses to the suburbs. An ideal arrangement, that is already in operation in Maryland for income tax purposes, would be to have statewide income and sales taxes along with modest "piggyback" local taxes—all collected by the state government and subject to state control so that individual communities will not get too far out of line with their neighbors. (As a long-run goal, the federal government should collect state-local, as well as federal, income taxes on the basis of a single return.)

The local governments need to improve local property tax administration to remove the haphazard way in which the tax applies to properties of equal values. The states can help by providing technical assistance and also by forcing the communities to meet minimum standards of administration. Consideration should also be given to the development of new local revenue sources to take some of the pressure off the general property tax. The best alternatives are the "piggyback" income and sales taxes already mentioned, always with the credit or refund for sales taxes paid by the poor.

In addition, it is time to tap the high and rising land values for some of the urgently needed local revenues. The National Commission on Urban Problems, which was chaired by former Senator Paul Douglas, has estimated that land values rose from $269 billion in 1956 to $523 billion in 1966, or about $25 billion a year. This tremendous increase in wealth was not created by the landowners but by society as a whole. This is, of course, the basis of the old "single tax" idea that was oversold by the zealots as a complete and final solution to the nation's tax problems, although correct in principle. The revenue potential of special taxes on land values or on increases in land values is modest, but the approach has merit even if it will not solve the financial problems of our cities and suburbs by itself. It would also discourage the hoarding of land for speculative purposes and thereby encourage more efficient use of land in and around the nation's cities.

But there is no hope for the states and local governments, whatever they do on their own initiative, unless the federal government cuts them in on its superior tax resources. It is true that federal grants to states and local governments have increased rapidly in recent years—from $5 billion in fiscal year 1958 to an extimated $25 billion this year—but the need is even greater than that. To satisfy this need, more money will have to be allocated to the categorical grants already authorized for such programs as education, health, welfare, and housing. Also, a federal-state-local income tax revenue-sharing system should be established to moderate the huge disparities in fiscal capacities of the fifty states and to give governors and local officials unrestricted funds that can be used to help solve their own particular problems. The Nixon administration's proposal, based on a plan devised by a Johnson task force, is a good—though modest—beginning.

Mayors and county managers are suspicious of revenue sharing because they have little faith that the states will distribute the funds fairly. To answer this criticism, various formulas have been devised to require the states to "pass through" at least a minimum percentage of the revenue-sharing grants. Disagreement over the details of the "pass through" should not be allowed to delay the adoption of an idea that will relieve some of the fiscal pressure at the state and local levels and, at the same time, provide revenues from a progressive tax that otherwise would be raised mainly on a regressive basis. Ultimately, the federal government should allocate 2 per cent of the federal individual income tax base to revenue sharing, which would amount to $8 billion at current income levels and as much as $12 billion in 1975.

The Payroll Tax

Much has been said about the need for removing the poor from the income tax rolls, and Congress seems to be prepared to remedy this anachronism. But the more urgent problem is to remove the much heavier payroll tax burden of the poor. The federal income tax bill of the families and individuals who are officially classified as poor is only $200 million a year, as compared with the $1.5 billion they pay in payroll taxes. In addition, the regressive feature of the payroll tax at the higher income levels should be moderated immediately and ultimately eliminated entirely.

Several different approaches might be taken to achieve these objectives.

First, part or all of the payroll tax could be converted into a withholding tax for income tax purposes. No formal change in the payroll tax need be involved; at the end of the year, individuals would receive credit against their income taxes (or a refund if they are not income tax payers) for the amount of payroll taxes paid.

Second, contributions from general revenues might be made, on the basis of a fixed formula, to the social security and other trust funds. Such a possibility was foreseen in the earlier days of social security.

Third, the social security system might be combined with a liberalized and modernized public assistance system or some variant of a negative income tax. The negative income tax payments to the aged in such a system would be financed out of general revenues.

But whatever is ultimately done about the payroll tax as the basic revenue source for social security financing, the poor should be relieved of paying this tax as soon as possible. The principle of a minimum taxable level under the income tax—soon to be raised to the poverty levels—should be carried over into the payroll tax. The Internal Revenue Service is already proficient at handling tens of millions of refunds per year under the income tax; the additional payroll tax refunds would not be an excessive burden.

Taxation and Inequality: A Radical Critique

JOHN G. GURLEY

I. The Rich

In dealing with the individual income tax, one of Pechman's major points is that the nominal or potential tax rates are far above the rates actually paid by the various income groups. If we take total income to be adjusted gross income including all realized capital gains,[1] then potential average tax rates for the single taxpayer run from about 14 to 70 per cent, if all of this income is fully subject to tax. Because, however, much of this income is not subject to tax for one reason or another, or receives favorable tax treatment, the actual average rates start from less than 1 per cent on the lowest income

From John G. Gurley, "Federal Tax Policy," *National Tax Journal,* Vol. 20, No. 3, 1967, pp. 319–27. Reprinted by permission of the author and the publisher.
[1] Plus excludable sick pay and excludable dividends.

group and rise to only 29 per cent on those with incomes of $150,000 to $200,000, and then fall to 27 per cent on the still richer.

At the lower income levels, the actual tax rate is much below the potential mainly because of personal exemptions and personal deductions. These factors continue to exert strength through the middle and upper-middle income ranges, but in addition the income splitting provision and the favorable treatment of realized capital gains become increasingly important. The capital gains provisions clearly dominate the picture at the highest income levels. These provisions permit the rich to pay only half the tax they would otherwise be liable for, and personal deductions lower their taxes still more—to a third of the potential levels.[2] So, in these terms, the individual income tax turns out to be only moderately progressive throughout most of the income classes and actually regressive on incomes above $200,000.

That is where Pechman leaves the story, but there is much more to it than that. Although only a part of the realized capital gains reported in any year is a realization of gains actually made in that year (the rest is a current realization of gains made in previous years), such reported gains on the average greatly understate the year's actual capital gains (realized and unrealized). For example, over the period 1955–65, the average annual capital gains on corporate stock, other business equities, and tangible assets (mainly land) were at least $60 billion.[3] Over the same period, realized capital gains reported by taxpayers were on the average only $10 billion per year.[4] Thus, a year's true capital gains were at least 6 times the reported-realized gains.

When these true capital gains are taken into account, the degree of progression of the individual income tax is reduced still further from where Pechman left it. This may be seen as follows. As incomes rise, net worth rises much faster: net worth is about 2-½ times income on the average in the lower income levels; it is 10–15 times income at the highest income levels. As net worth rises, the "price-sensitive assets"—corporate stock, other business equities, and land (excluding houses)—rise much faster, from about 5 per cent of net worth at the lower end of the income scale to 60 per cent and more at the upper. As price-sensitive assets rise, the rate of capital gain on

[2] This material was reported by Pechman at the 1964 annual meetings of the American Finance Association (and later by Richard Goode, *The Individual Income Tax*). The results are based on a special file of about 100,000 tax returns for 1962. However, one can come close to these results by using the information regularly published by the U.S. Treasury Department in *Individual Income Tax Returns;* the approximation of the excluded portion of capital gains at each income level is the important step.

[3] I have used various sources to obtain this and other estimates in this section. For net worths at various income levels, see "Survey of Financial Characteristics of Consumers," *Federal Reserve Bulletin,* March 1964. See also Robert Lampman, *The Share of Top Wealth-Holders in National Wealth* (NBER, 1962). For indications of capital gains on corporate equities, see *Flow-of-Funds, Assets and Liabilities, 1945–65,* Board of Governors of the Federal Reserve System, October 20, 1966, p. 25, along with the companion publication, *Flow of Funds, Annual 1946–65,* October 20, 1966, p. 28. I have also drawn from Raymond W. Goldsmith and Robert E. Lipsey, *Studies in the National Balance Sheet of the United States,* Vol. I (NBER, 1963), pp. 43–7, 170–75, 181–84, from George Katona and John B. Lansing, "The Wealth of the Wealthy," *Review of Economics and Statistics,* February 1964, and from *Individual Income Tax Returns,* U.S. Treasury Department, IRS, 1964, pp. 8–10, 113–18.

[4] This figure includes the excludable portion of realized capital gains.

them increases. Thus, compared to lower and middle income groups, the rich have huge net worths relative to their incomes, mostly in equities and land, on which they make extremely large capital gains, only a small part of which is realized. So, when true capital gains are substituted for realized capital gains in Pechman's income classes, the incomes at the lower end are raised very little and those at the upper end are raised enormously. Hence, the ratio of taxes paid to true total income rises much more slowly over the entire income range than Pechman shows. The average tax rate at the upper end, instead of being around 30 per cent as Pechman calculates it, is probably around 20 per cent. The fact is that the rich are not being soaked; instead, they are soaking up wealth very rapidly in ever-increasing amounts.

At the present time, there are around 200,000 families with an average income (including all capital gains) of more than $150,000, 80 per cent of which consists of returns on property—capital gains, dividends, interest, rents, and business profits. The average net worth of these super rich is about $1 million, about ⅔ of it in corporate stock, other business equities, and land. These families comprise only ⅓ of 1 per cent of all families, but their net worth is 15 per cent of the total, and they own 30 per cent of all corporate stock held by families, 25 per cent of all other equity in business and professions, and a large share of the land. During most of the postwar period, capital gains on these assets have been huge; some of the gains have been taxed at relatively low rates, but most of them have not been taxed at all and probably never will be.

The individual income tax has hardly made a dent in the buildup of this massive concentration of wealth, despite the façade of progressive rates, principally because the super rich receive over half their incomes in capital gains and have the political power to prevent any serious taxation of these gains. While, as I have said, the individual income taxes paid annually by these privileged families average only 20 per cent of their true incomes, their taxes are of course a much smaller percentage of their net worths—around 2–3 per cent—which is about equal to the inflation-induced capital gains each year on their asset holdings, and which is less than the rates paid on net worth by many, less-affluent families. While in terms of income, the individual income tax becomes regressive only at very high income levels, in terms of wealth or net worth, it becomes regressive at relatively lower levels.

So when Pechman appears so pleased by the "attractive feature" of progression to individual income taxation (p. 50), I can only ascribe it to a temporary lapse into a dreamy, make-believe world. That it may be a temporary lapse is suggested 13 pages later where we find him saying:

> Graduated expenditure taxes are often proposed as a method of avoiding or correcting the defects of the income tax base, particularly in the top brackets where the preferential treatment of capital gains, tax-exempt interest, depletion allowances, and other favorable provisions permit the accumulation of large fortunes with little or no payment of income tax (p. 63).

While in the real world, then, as Pechman recognizes, the individual income tax touches the super rich very lightly, this is doubly true for the estate and gift taxes. In fact, the latter for many years have been something of a joke among public finance experts, a joke which Pechman tells as follows:

> Estate and gift taxes are levied only on a small proportion of privately owned property in the United States. About 3 per cent of the estates of adult decedents and less than one-fourth of the wealth owned by the decedents in any one year are subject to estate or gift taxes. The relatively small size of the tax base is explained in part by the generous exemptions which exclude a large proportion of the wealth transfers, and also by defects in the taxes that permit substantial amounts of property to be transferred free of tax (p. 182).

The reason for this state of affairs is that the super-rich families who have seen to it that their capital gains are largely untouched are exactly the ones who have prevented any substantial taxation of their estates. The super rich have super power, and they have used it. Pechman's explanation is more romantic:

> One can only guess why the estate and gift taxes have not been more successful. A possible explanation is that equalization of the distribution of wealth by taxation is not yet accepted in the United States. In some countries, economic classes tend to be fairly stable with little crossing-over by succeeding generations. In the American economy, membership in economic classes is fluid. The average family in the United States still aspires to improved economic and social status, and the estate and gift taxes are erroneously regarded as especially burdensome to the family which is beginning to prosper through hard work and saving (p. 180).

It is true that the "equalization of the distribution of wealth by taxation is not yet accepted," but it is surely only the wealthy who do not accept it. The millions of poor have not voted against such equalization for any reason, and especially not in the belief that they are part of a fluid upstream. The poor know better than that because they are the children of the poor. And neither is there concerted opposition by middle-class families to a more equal wealth distribution. Instead, there is powerful opposition to any such change in the status quo by the top 1 or 2 per cent of families who own more than 35 per cent of the wealth.

II. The Poor

I have mentioned the poor. About 20 per cent of our families have incomes (including transfer payments) below $3,000, and over 40 per cent of "unrelated individuals" have incomes below $1,500. These 14 million economic units have an aggregate net worth substantially less than that of the few super rich. Indeed, over 40 per cent of the poor have a net worth less than $1,000 per family; only 7 per cent of the poor own any stock at all, and these holdings are very small; they have few liquid assets. A fifth of the poor live in trailers, parts of other families' dwellings, in abandoned shelters, etc.[5]

Nevertheless, the poor pay taxes. They are hardly affected by the estate and gift taxes, but as a group they do pay individual income taxes—on the average, about 3 per cent of their total incomes including transfer payments and capital gains. In addition, these families have been subjected to two sets of highly regressive taxes—the federal excises (including custom duties) and the payroll taxes—which in 1965 brought to the federal government revenues equal to 75 per cent of those collected from the individual income tax. According to estimates presented by Pechman, the poor pay 5–6 per cent of their incomes (including transfers, etc.) in excise taxes and 4–5 per cent in payroll taxes (assuming forward shifting of the employer tax). The super rich also pay these taxes, but such levies are very tiny as a percentage of their incomes. As Pechman points out, these taxes are regressive, and recent increases in payroll taxes "have raised the tax burden on low income wage earners substantially. . . . In 1966, the federal payroll tax will be the highest tax paid by at least 25 per cent of the nation's income recipients, and $350 million will be paid by persons officially classified as living below poverty levels" (pp. 166, 168). He later adds: "Given the present importance of the payroll taxes and the increases in tax rates already scheduled, the effects of these taxes on the distribution of income can no longer be disregarded" (p. 177).

While Pechman does not present estimates of the incidence of state and local taxes, he does claim that as a whole they are regressive (p. 202); and this is no doubt true above a relatively low level of income, considering that consumption and property taxes and charges and fees comprise over 80 per cent of all revenue of state and local governments (excluding that from the federal government). Pechman also presents some evidence that corporations, in the face of a long-term rise in the corporation income tax, have been able to raise rates of return before tax sufficiently to maintain their after-tax returns, probably by more efficient use of capital. Still, it is likely that some or most of this tax has been a burden on owners of capital.

These considerations do not permit any definite statements about the overall relative tax burdens on rich and poor. However, if we confine ourselves to the federal individual income, estate, excise, and payroll taxes, it would seem, from the information presented above, that the poor may spend around 12–14 per cent of their total incomes to pay these taxes, while the comparable tax burden on the super rich is around 25 per cent.[6] If we now try to take

---

[5] In this section, I have drawn from: *Poverty in the United States,* Committee on Education and Labor, Washington, D.C., 1964; Mollie Orshansky, "Counting the Poor: Another Look at the Poverty Profile," *Social Security Bulletin,* January 1965; Michael Harrington, *The Other America;* and Margaret S. Gordon (ed.), *Poverty in America.*

[6] Twenty per cent on income tax, 4 per cent on estate and gift taxes, and 1 per cent on excises and payroll taxes. The estimate on estate and gift taxes is based on information in Pechman, pp. 252, 271, 276.

account of the regressive state and local taxes and the (probably) progressive corporation income tax, it is difficult to see how the richest 200,000 families could have a tax burden as much as twice that of the 14 million poor.[7] This is not much of a difference considering the vast gulf separating the two groups. Furthermore, since the super rich have wealth that, relative to their incomes, is several times higher than that possessed by the poor, it is almost certain that on a wealth basis the poor pay a higher tax rate than the rich.

Although the poor bear on the average a substantial tax burden, the most destitute of them, with little or no regular income, at least do not pay income taxes, and some do receive welfare payments. A recent suggestion for tidying up these programs which are aimed at easing the economic hardship of the lowest income families is the negative income tax. Pechman presents the problem in this way:

> The traditional method of helping poverty-stricken families has been through public welfare and other direct transfer payments (for example, old-age assistance, aid to families with dependent children, medical assistance for the aged, aid to the blind and disabled persons, and general relief). Most of these programs reach specific categories of poor persons; except for general relief, which is inadequate almost everywhere, they provide no assistance to families headed by able-bodied workers who, for reasons of background, training, or temperament, do not participate effectively in the modern industrial economy.
>
> Considerable thought has been given in recent years to the relationship between the welfare system and the income tax system. The two grew up side by side in response to different pressures, but it has become increasingly recognized that one may be regarded as an extension of the other. Direct assistance to low income persons is an extension of progression into the lowest brackets, with negative rather than positive rates . . . (pp. 72–3).

Families whose exemptions and deductions exceed their incomes would, under this scheme, receive a payment from the government based on a new set of tax rates applied to negative incomes. The negative income tax, according to some of its proponents, could replace most of the present welfare programs and thereby allow poor families to spend their money in ways they think best.

This may solve some problems, but they are not likely to be important ones. The main difficulty is that large numbers of the poor are trapped in desolate rural areas and in urban ghettos in a way of life that perpetuates itself and that almost completely isolates them from what is going on in the rest of the country; they have virtually no voice in deciding anything important and little control over their own lives. The negative income tax (not

---

[7] A recent study shows that families with incomes below $3,000 pay the same percentage of their incomes for all state and local taxes plus the federal corporate income tax as do families with incomes of $15,000 and over. See *Tax Burdens and Benefits of Government Expenditures by Income Class, 1961 and 1965*, Tax Foundation, Inc., 1967.

to speak of the various welfare programs) is basically a paternalistic scheme for maintaining the existing class structure; it is a scheme for equating the marginal utilities of the last dollars spent in all directions by people who are without direction and who are living in a physical, intellectual, and spiritual hell.

Compared to the negative income tax and welfare programs, the war on poverty may have more to recommend it, insofar as it stresses dynamic programs of self-help for the poor and encourages them to make their own decisions—and mistakes. If the poor are to become active participants in the economic, social, and political life that is now going on without them, they must be educated, given good health, and encouraged to mobilize themselves and to struggle against society so that they can work their own way out of the underworld in which they have been imprisoned. The risk in this, of course, is that, in gathering strength, the poor will ultimately upset the existing power relationships at both the local and national levels. But if the basic problems of poverty are ever to be solved, the solution will probably have to be along these lines. Taxation, transfer payments, and other budgetary schemes have little to offer.

III. The Corporations

There are today more than 1.2 million U.S. corporations, but the largest 600 of them ($\frac{1}{20}$ of 1 per cent) own half of all corporate net assets and receive half of all corporate net income; each of the largest 600 has on the average net assets of at least $1 billion.[8] These gigantic corporations are controlled largely by the super rich who own most of the stock, and in controlling these 600 corporations they control most of what goes on in the business world.

In recent years, corporations as a whole have prospered greatly. Corporate profits after tax have risen by 80 per cent in the last five years— twice the growth rate of GNP. One result is that manufacturing corporations' rate of return (after tax) on stockholders' equity is now at the highest level since the very early postwar years; in the last five years it has risen from 9 per cent to 14 per cent. And this has occurred in the face of rapidly rising capital consumption allowances and steeply rising interest costs, both of which are part of gross returns to property but neither of which is included in the above rates of return.

Some of this bonanza to corporations since 1961 is attributable to the economy's higher growth rate and to its fuller utilization of resources. A large part, however, as Pechman clearly brings out, is owing to the very favorable tax treatment that corporations have recently received. Since 1954 corporations have increasingly taken advantage of liberalized provisions regarding capital consumption allowances—accelerated depreciation. In addition, in 1962, service lives of "facilities," as guidelines to depreciation, were reduced in manufacturing industries by about 15 per cent, thereby allowing corpora-

[8] See, for recent years, *Corporation Income Tax Returns*, U.S. Treasury Department, IRS.

tions to accelerate capital consumption even more. Further, in 1962, an investment tax credit of as much as 7 per cent of qualified new investment was given to corporations. After 1964 the corporation income tax rate was lowered from 52 per cent to 48 per cent. (And, of course, firms engaged in extracting oil and gas and other minerals from the ground continue to receive a depletion allowance which is much more generous than depreciation allowances.) These measures have enabled corporations to reduce their stated profits by inflating capital consumption allowances, and to pay less taxes on these profits through the tax credit and lower tax rates.

As Pechman shows, the result is that federal corporation income taxes as a percentage of profits before tax plus capital consumption allowances fell from 33 per cent in 1954 to about 26 per cent in 1965 (p. 111). The reduction in taxes paid by corporations, at 1966 levels of profits and investment, as a result of these measures was around $6.5 billion, which becomes $8 billion if the effect of depletion allowances is included.[9] Pechman calculates that the generous depreciation allowances and the investment tax credit have boosted the rate of return on 10-year assets from 10 per cent to 12-½ per cent, which is a remarkable jump of 25 per cent. In brief, corporations have cleaned up in the past several years.

These corporate windfalls, however, probably have stimulated business investment and so contributed to the higher growth rate which the economy has enjoyed since 1961. That is to say, to achieve investment levels compatible with an acceptable output growth rate, it has been thought necessary to "slip" an extra several billion dollars a year to the handful of huge corporations that account for most of the business investment. This raises the general question of whether these and other extravagant payoffs (e.g., capital gains) to the wealthy are too costly a way to achieve our saving-investment goals. This is, of course, an old problem in economics—income distribution vs. growth—but it is especially pertinent to raise it now when many economists, including Pechman, seem so satisfied with the growth performance of the economy and so complacent about the costs of achieving it.

IV. Taxes and Sources of Inequality

At one point, Pechman notes that, while in a democracy such as ours incomes are (naturally?) distributed unequally, income taxes can largely take care of the problem. There are a few points to make about this attitude. First, as I showed above, while income (and wealth) taxation is progressive, when all capital gains are taken into account, the redistribution achieved by such taxation is not impressive. Second, income and wealth taxation is increasingly likely to give rise to allocative inefficiencies as the gap between the pre-tax income distribution and the post-tax one that society wishes to achieve widens. While this gap is not tremendous in our society, it is large enough to insure that our tax-transfer system disturbs work, saving, investment, and

[9] See Pechman, pp. 121–22, 124, for some of the figures. The totals are mine.

other incentives—and, I think, more seriously than Pechman is willing to admit. Third, even if a tax-transfer system could smoothly produce equity out of inequity, many people might prefer another economic system that produced equity to begin with. Finally, while a tax-transfer system may strike, directly or indirectly, at some sources of material inequalities, it is mainly an ameliorative measure, a way of smoothing ruffled feathers without removing the causes of the difficulty.

Why is it that our income distribution, even when lifetime incomes are considered and even when differences in investment in human capital are taken into account, is so bad to begin with? Part of the answer is that, given the demands for various abilities and skills, some of these talents are exceptionally scarce and others most plentiful (at some uniform compensation); so the former receive fabulously high compensations, and the latter virtually nothing. Much of this gross maldistribution of abilities and skills is artificially imposed by privileged groups or by the mores and practices of society. It can be attacked in various ways—by widening educational opportunities, weakening monopolistic positions, reducing discriminatory practices, encouraging initiative by the underprivileged, etc.

The maldistribution of wealth, although partly a result of income inequalities, also contributes importantly to them. High incomes are often based on nothing more than the "talent" that certain people have in inheriting large fortunes. The maldistribution of such "talents" can be corrected by inheritance taxes that mean something, by progressive income taxes that over longer periods weaken abilities to accumulate assets, or by nationalization of land and other means of production.

A final source of income inequalities, though generally not recognized as such, is the pervasiveness of the "capitalist mentality" in our society: the fact that our economy runs mostly on self-interest and material incentives, so that tasks simply don't get done unless there are monetary payoffs for them. Since allocative efficiency demands such payoffs, and since there is such a maldistribution of abilities and skills, gross income inequalities are the result. If people were willing to work for non-material reasons—for the sheer love of it, to serve their country, to serve others, to serve God—material incomes (but not necessarily non-material ones!) could be distributed equitably in the first place, without much if any loss in allocative efficiency, and without the aid of an elaborate tax-transfer system.

While income and wealth taxation may help a bit to dry up these wellsprings of material inequalities, the real attack on them comes from civil rights groups, anti-poverty campaigns, anti-monopoly drives, etc., all working within the context of capitalism; from socialists who call for the nationalization of means of production; and from Maoists, hippies, and others who are rebelling against the capitalist mentality with its heavy emphasis on selfishness and material rewards. It might well be that this last movement poses the ultimate threat to material inequalities—the hippies rather than the Internal Revenue Service.

V. Conclusion

What I have written is a response to parts of Pechman's book; it is not a complete description of it. Although much of the material in the book is, in one way or another, concerned with income distribution, much of it also deals with stabilization and growth problems, with the structure of the various taxes, and with proposals for change. All of these topics are not only treated beautifully but with the voice of authority. Pechman knows what is going on in Washington; in fact, he has been partly responsible for the tax events of the past several years. (But am I right that his tax reform proposals, as presented in the book, are much less sweeping than they used to be? Has Pechman mellowed?) While I have pointed out certain shortcomings of the book, the most important being the romantic and uncritical view of the society we live in, I nevertheless feel that it is a gem as an introduction to the subject—a shining combination of good writing and good thinking.

The Great Tax Swindle

FERDINAND LUNDBERG

If the propertied elite can enforce basic socio-political decisions—such as denying employment in the labyrinthine corporate bureaucracy to large numbers of qualified people on irrational ethnic grounds when the basic laws do not support such discrimination—the experience of history would suggest that they would go farther and also deal themselves enormous tax advantages. For down through history the dominant classes, groups, factions, clans, interests or political elites have always been scrupulously prudent in avoiding taxes at the expense of the lower orders. The aristocracy of France before the French Revolution, for example, gave itself virtually total tax exemption. The burden of supporting a profligate royal court with its thousands of noble pensioners was therefore laid upon commoners, thus supplying not a little fuel for the onrushing tidal wave of blood.

It would be foolish to contend that there is a propertied elite in the United States and then not be able to show that this elite accords itself fantastic

From Ferdinand Lundberg, *The Rich and the Super-Rich* (New York: Lyle Stuart, Inc., 1968), pp. 345–410. Reprinted by permission of the publisher.

tax privileges down to and including total exemption. And, true enough, the large-propertied elements in the United States see to it that they are very lightly taxed—many with $5 million or more of steady income often paying no tax at all for many years while a man with a miserable $2,000 income, perhaps after years of no income, denies his family medical or dental care in order to pay tax!

Taxes "are a changing product of earnest efforts to have others pay them. In a society where the few control the many, the efforts are rather simple. Levies are imposed in response to the preferences of the governing groups. Since their well-being is equated with the welfare of the community, they are inclined to burden themselves as lightly as possible. Those who have little to say are expected to pay. Rationalizations for this state of affairs are rarely necessary. It is assumed that the lower orders will be properly patriotic." And, as anyone may ascertain any day, aggressively expressed patriotism increases markedly in intensity, readily crossing the borderline into spontaneous violence, the further one looks down the socio-economic and cultural scales into the lower middle class and downward.

There is a fundamental view, widely shared and often overtly expressed in schools and in the mass media, that the American socio-political system is, if not completely fair, as fair to everybody as the ingenuity of man can devise. This belief is monumentally false, as analysis of the tax structure alone discloses. . . .

Some Preliminary Remarks

While the American propertied element is not ordinarily completely tax exempt it is subject in general to extremely low taxes. In many salient areas it is *absolutely* tax exempt, like prerevolutionary French aristocrats. This happy condition derives, as Eisenstein often points out, from special obscurely worded congressional dispensations. The situation, far from being mixed or a matter of shading, is absolutely black and white. The United States is widely supposed to have a graduated tax system, based on ability to pay, but there is very little actual graduation in the system and what graduation there is turns out to be against the impecunious.[1]

[1] I prefer the somewhat pretentious-sounding "impecunious" to the simpler "poor man" because it is semantically cleaner, less streaked with the crocodile tears of latter-day politicians and professional social workers. A poor man, after all, is only a man without money and is often very little different in cultural attainment or outlook from many beneficiaries of multiple trust funds. He does not wear a halo; worse, he is never likely to. The recreations of a bayou Negro are little different from those of many denizens of Fifth and Park Avenues; each hunts, fishes, copulates, eats, sleeps, swims and boats and neither is much of a reader, thinker or art patron. The main social difference between them is money and its lack. The defensive idea of some sociologists that there is a "poverty culture," insuring the continued poverty through generations of its participants even though they were given trust funds, must be rejected as untenable. What is called the "poverty culture" is merely the reactive creation of impecunious people rejected for one reason or the other, often arbitrary, from the labor force as unsuitable. But if they were given an ample regular income without the performance of any labor, like members of the trust-fund cult, they would quickly emerge from this "culture," perhaps to comport themselves like "Beverly Hillbillies" or Socialites.

It is not being urged that the results to be shown were obtained through some centralized secret plot of bloated capitalists and paunchy cigar-smoking politicians. For it would indeed take a confidently jocund group of autocrats to deliberately plan the existing tax structure—what conservative tax-expert Representative Wilbur Mills, Democrat of Arkansas, in a bit of judicious understatement has called a "House of Horrors." The late Senator Walter George of Georgia (never regarded as a friend of the common man) called the present scale of exemptions "a very cruel method by which the tax upon the people in the low-income brackets has been constantly increased." Senator Barry Goldwater of Arizona, no liberal, radical, or starry-eyed reformer, said "the whole tax structure is filled with loopholes"; Senator Douglas of Illinois, a liberal and a professional economist, asserted that the loopholes have become "truck holes." Referring to the fantastic depletion allowance, conservative Senator Frank Lausche of Ohio, no extremist or reformer of any kind, said: "It is a fraud, it is a swindle, and it ought to be stopped."

One is, therefore, in fairly sedate baby-kissing company if one says (perhaps overcautiously) that the tax structure is a pullulating excrescence negating common sense, a parody of the gruesomely ludicrous, a surrealist zigzag pagoda of pestilent greed, a perverse thing that makes the prerevolutionary French system seem entirely rational. One takes it that Congressman Mills had something like this in mind with his "House of Horrors."

Representative Mills in further explication of his "House of Horrors" characterization said the tax laws are "a mess and a gyp," with some taxpayers treated as coddled "pets" and others as "patsies."

But the tax laws would have been no surprise or cause for consternation to someone like Karl Marx with his doctrine that government is inherently the executive committee of a ruling class. Indeed, they document that dictum—if not to the hilt—then a good distance up the blade. . . .

To refer to this system, then, as another but bigger Banana Republic is not merely a bit of misplaced literary hyperbole.

The American tax system is the consequence of diligent labors by diversified parties of major property interest working down through the years to gain their ends. Two congressional committees of seemingly over-easy virtue have been their target. A public demoralized by a variety of thoughtfully provided distractions, and liberally supplied with Barnum's suckers and Mencken's boobs, would not know what takes place even if it were fully attentive because it could not understand the purposely opaque syntax of the tax code, the inner arithmetic or the mandarinic rhetoric of the tax ideologists. . . .

The Sales Tax Steal

In order to make this clear initially, we may note that a man who pays sales taxes of $60 a year out of a $3,000 income has paid 2 per cent of his income on this tax. He would incur such an outlay at 5 per cent, enough to buy a good deal of medicine or dental care, on purchases amounting to $1,200. As the same amount of purchases by a man with $100,000 income incurs a tax of only six-hundredths of 1 per cent, the lower income-receiver pays at a rate more than 3,300 per cent higher in relation to income!

In order to incur a recurrent sales tax that would be 2 per cent of his income (at a 5 per cent rate) the $100,000-a-year man would have to buy $40,000 of sales-taxable goods—hard to do unless he buys a Rolls-Royce or a seagoing vessel every year.

But the disparity is often greater even than this, difficult though it may be to believe. The lower income is almost always in already taxed dollars. For on a $3,000 income an individual has already paid $620 in income taxes at the pre-1964 rate, $500 at the post-1964 rate. The $500,000 income, however, is often tax-exempt or, owing to the diversity of its sources, is taxed at a small fraction of the cited 88.9 per cent pre-1964 or 60 per cent post-1964 rates.

As in all these tax matters there are always further ramifications, let us in this instance pursue one, allowing readers to work out the ramifications of others. Whatever is paid in sales taxes in one year is deductible on the federal return the next year and has an in-pocket value to the taxpayer at whatever percentage tax bracket he is in. The individual with $3,000 taxable income is in the 16.6 per cent bracket as of 1966, which means that the following year his sales tax of $60 will be good for $10.00 against his federal taxes. But the $100,000 man who paid $2,000 sales tax on $40,000 (improbable) sales-taxable purchases is in the 55.5 per cent bracket and will on his return receive a federal tax credit worth $1,110. The leveraging influence of the higher brackets greatly reduces the impact of sales taxes on his purse. If he, like the low-income man, bought goods sales-taxed at only $60, he would get a tax credit of $33.30, or more than three times that of the low-income man.

But a married man with four children and a gross income of $5,000, and who paid no federal tax, would get no compensatory reduction in any federal tax at all. Those low-income people, in other words, who have no federal tax to pay, are hit flush on the jaw by the sales tax. A married couple with one child and $2,000 of gross income ($40 per week), not uncommon in the American economy, might pay 5 per cent of sales taxes on $1,000 of goods, clothing and medicine. This would be $50, or more than a week's pay. If one traces indirect taxes they pay through prices and rent, one sees that they pay many weeks' income in taxes.

The sales tax clearly is a heavy levy directly on the least pecunious citizens.

Tax-Exempt Corporations

Corporations as well as individuals *apparently* pay income taxes.

In 1965, for example, the official statistics tell us that every dollar received by the government came from the following sources: individual income taxes,

40 cents; corporation income taxes, 21 cents; employment taxes, 14 cents; excise taxes, 12 cents; miscellaneous taxes, 11 cents; and borrowing, 2 cents. Corporations on the face of it appeared to contribute 21 per cent of federal revenues, and individual income-tax payers 40 per cent. Of these collections, 44 cents went for "national defense."

But corporations do not really pay any taxes at all (or very, very rarely)—surely a novel and (to most people) no doubt a thoroughly wrong-headed, erroneous and even stupid assertion. For are there not daily allusions to corporation taxes and don't official statistics list corporation taxes? Corporations, however, are no more taxed than were the aristocratic prerevolutionary French estates.

The evidence is plain, in open view; there is nothing recondite about the situation. *All* taxes supposedly paid by corporations are passed on in price of goods or services to the ultimate buyer, the well-known man in the street. This is not only true of federal and state taxes (where levied) but it is also true of local real estate and property taxes paid in the name of corporations. The corporations, in nearly all cases, merely act as collection agents for the government.

The scant exceptions to this rule are those corporations (none of the large ones and very few of any) that are losing money or that make a considerably below-average rate of return on invested capital. The money-losers pay no income tax at all, and may be forced to absorb local property taxes. Those making a below-average return may be required to pay some taxes, the payment of which does indeed contribute to the low return. . . .

Landlords and Business Partnerships

It is the same with the revenues of landlords and of business partnerships. Unless they happen to be running at a loss or doing less well than average, all their taxes—local, state and federal—like other costs, are packed into the price of goods or services they sell. The buyer pays the taxes.

Where a landlord owns an apartment building his tenants obviously must pay his taxes as well as all other costs in order to leave him with a profit. Yet it is the landlord who constantly laments about the taxes, which he collects for the government, and the tenants who live lightheartedly unawares. If anyone is to lament about taxes paid, it is obviously they; but they are inattentive to the actual process.

Multiple Taxation

The Eisenhower Administration became very indignant about multiple taxation, holding it to be, if not unconstitutional, at least unfair. It felt stockholders were most unfairly treated in this respect, and puckishly devised a system of dividend credits (4 per cent of dividends discount on the tax itself) that gave very little to many small stockholders but a great deal to a few big ones. A small dividend-received credit remains in the tax laws, but the theory on which it is based—unfair double taxation—is false from beginning to end. For stockholders as such have not, directly or indirectly, paid any tax prior to receiving their dividends. Again, multiple taxation has long prevailed on every hand.

The way these dividend credits worked in 1964 was as follows: Any person receiving dividends could deduct up to $100 of dividends received ($200 for a married couple). Up to $200 of dividends, in short, were tax free for a married couple, and so remained in 1965 and 1966. Beyond this, 2 per cent of all dividends received from domestic taxpaying corporations were deducted *directly from the tax total*. If a man had $1 million of dividend income, he could deduct a flat $20,000 from his final tax. But a married couple receiving $500 of dividends beyond the tax-free base could deduct only $10.

The dividend credit, in other language, was of significant value only to very wealthy people. Before the Eisenhower law was revised, it had twice the value of 1964.

Expressing his indignation, in the 1952 presidential campaign Eisenhower complained that there were more than a hundred different taxes on every single egg sold, and he was probably correct.

But this serves only to point up the fact that it is the rank-and-file consumer who pays most taxes. When, for example, one buys a loaf of bread one pays fractional multiple taxes—the farmer's original land tax; the farmer's income tax (if any); the railroads' real-estate, franchise and income taxes; storage warehouse taxes for the ingredients (income and realty); the bakery's income and realty taxes; the retailers' income and realty taxes; and, possibly, a climactic local sales tax. If all these and many more taxes did not come out of the price of the bread, there would be no gain for anyone along the line of production. So it is the buyer of the bread as of other articles and services who pays the taxes. . . .

Valuable Wives

In the upper income stratosphere, wives (or husbands for wealthy women) are extremely valuable, as Stern shows in detail.

Here is the cash asset value of a spouse at different taxable income levels under pre-1964 law (it is only slightly less now):

Taxable Income	Asset Value of Spouse
$ 10,000.00	$ 11,818.25
25,000.00	131,931.75
75,000.00	1,000,000.00
100,000.00	1,891,875.00
445,777.78	5,996,994.00

But at $1 million of income, the capital value of a spouse, oddly, begins to decline, as follows:

Taxable Income	Asset Value of Spouse
$1,000,000.00	$2,766,153.75
$1,399,555.55 and higher	Zero
Under $ 2,889.00	Zero

The point about capitalizing a wife in these ways is that one can compute at going rates of return what a wife is worth to one in yearly retained income. The wife capitalized at a value of $1 million at 4 per cent is worth $40,000 a year in income to her husband; the $6,996,994-wife is good for $279,877.66. But in the tax bracket below $5,000 a wife is worth in tax benefits only 73 cents per week, no bargain.

Tax Support for Rich Children

A married man with a taxable income of $8,000 under the tax law as of 1965 paid $1,380 (against $1,630 for a single man). If the married man had four children his tax liability was reduced to $924. Under the law four children have gained a married man $456 or $114 per child over the childless married man. But the married man in the $50,000 bracket, who without children paid $17,060 tax, with four children and the same income pays $15,860 tax, a gain for him of $1,200 or $300 per child. His children are worth in tax benefit about three times what the children of the $8,000 man were worth.

Whose Congress writes this sort of a law? Is it a Congress that represents the $8,000-a-year man or the $50,000-a-year man? As I can't ask this question after showing each such disparity, let it be said here that as one crosses the income-mark of about $15,000 the tax laws boldly and brazenly always progressively favor the richer and always absolutely favor unearned income over earned income.

While the tax laws subsidize only very slightly the wives and children of the poorer man at the expense of single people, they do *absolutely* subsidize those of the wealthier. Here is a flat statement of incredible fact: The upkeep of wives and children of the wealthy is subsidized generously by the existing tax laws. It would, in other words, cost a wealthy single man nothing additional if he suddenly married an impecunious widow with four children. He would retain as much in-pocket spending money as he had before marriage and might also gain a fine ready-made family. If a single man earning $8,000 a year and itemizing deductions did this he would gain only $820 compared with a gain of $7,030 for the $50,000-a-year man. Most families live on far less than a $50,000-a-year bachelor would get in annual tax reduction by marrying a hungry widow with four children.

But the lower taxpayers, while computing their paltry marital and children's deductions, perhaps feeling pity for the single persons, get the feeling of "getting away" with something, or at least of getting some concession from the government because they are married and have children. Actually, however, they are only being "conned" by a wily Congress.

In any case, whatever encouragement the tax deduction gives to the birth rate is distinctly against the general interest at a time of obvious over-population and a seemingly intractable unemployment rate of 4 per cent. By all present signs at least 4 per cent of children born, and perhaps more, will not be able to get jobs.

There are many other ways of dividing the formidable army of taxpayers, throwing first this one and then that one a sop, always under a sentimental camouflage. A single person, incidentally, who is contributing less than half to the support of a disabled or aged relative gets no tax rebate. Unless a person is more than half dependent, which would exclude almost everybody, he cannot be deducted.

Other Ways of Income Splitting

The treatment of married people is known as income splitting, producing two incomes that are taxed at lower rates.

One can, once the principle is established, carry out this process of income splitting further, producing three, four or more smaller incomes, less taxed, instead of one that is large and subject to much tax. These ways are all practiced by the wealthy.

While the tax laws basically divide the populace between the single and the married and between the childless and parents, its greatest discrimination is with respect to earned income as against unearned or property-derived income.

This salient feature is carried forward in the extension of income splitting.

One way of income splitting is to allot partnerships in businesses to children, thus giving them a taxable income. If the partnership can be split many ways, among children, grandparents and other dependents, into smaller incomes, substantially smaller taxes will be encountered all around. Retained income for the family group will be much larger.

Another way, as we have seen, is to establish trust funds, and the use of trust funds has grown enormously. While trust funds have many aims, one of the objectives they serve is to split assets and incomes among many people, often among many trust funds for the same person.

But the income of such a recipient is not limited to the trust funds. He may also draw salary, have low-tax capital gains and tax-free income from government bonds or oil-mineral royalties. He may, indeed, draw every kind of income there is, taxable and nontaxable.

Does anyone actually do this? They do much better! As President Roosevelt observed in a message to Congress in 1937 "one thrifty taxpayer formed 64 trusts for the benefit of four members of his immediate family and thereby claimed to have saved them over $485,000 in one year in taxes." But that is ancient history. More recently the Stranahan family, the leading owner of Champion Spark Plug Company, created more than thirty trusts and thus saved $701,227.48 in three years, according to Mr. Stern.

But a certain Dr. Boyce, misled by the logic of the tax laws, in one day established ninety identical trusts to hold a mere $17,000 of stocks and bonds. The $100 dividend exemption left them each tax exempt. Appealed to the tax court, the plan was found "preposterous." "Straining reason and credulity," the learned court said, "it ought to be struck down forthwith." And, as Mr. Stern remarks, "It was."

Another device for income splitting, thus obtaining lower taxes, is to establish many corporations in place of one. In one of many instances a finance business split into 137 corporations to avoid $433,000 of taxes annually, and a retail chain divided itself into 142 corporations to avoid $619,000 annually. The surest way of keeping money today is to steer a proper course through the crazy-quilt tax laws.

Additional Tax Dodges

A man who is sixty-five or over, in the best of health, gets an additional deduction of $600 whether his income is $1,000, $10,000, $100,000 or $1 million, although most people over sixty-five have little income at all beyond meager Social Security. But if he is in chronic poor health, unable to work except spasmodically, and under sixty-five, even if he is sixty-four—no extra deduction. A blind person gets an extra exemption of $600, suggesting to the reader of tax instructions that he lives under a Congress with a heart. But if a person retains his sight and is stone deaf, without hands, has had a stroke or is paralyzed from the waist down he does not get this compassionate exemption.

Whenever such a disparity is pointed out to Congress it usually gladly, in the name of consistency and equity, spreads the inequity to include others. We may, therefore, soon see Congress giving an exemption to all disabled or physically handicapped people, thereby further narrowing the tax base.

The point here is not whether a person is handicapped but whether he has income. What value is an extra exemption to a blind, disabled or aged person who has no income? The only person such an exemption could benefit would be one with an income. And all such special exemptions are taken by persons with incomes—often very substantial incomes. They are props to financial strength, not supports of weakness.

Just how much good the exemptions for over age sixty-five do may be seen by considering the income statistics for 1962, the latest year available. Of 7.4 million male income recipients over sixty-five years old, 18.6 per cent got less than $1,000 gross; 34 per cent, from $1,000 to $2,000; 18.4 per cent, from $2,000 to $3,000; and 9.9, from $3,000 to $4,000—80.9 per cent under $4,000 gross. Of 7,491,000 female recipients 56.2 per cent got less than $1,000; 30 per cent, from $1,000 to $2,000; and 6.7 per cent, from

$2,000 to $3,000—92.9 per cent under $3,000 gross. Much of this income was from tax-free Social Security, which averaged $74.33 per month in October, 1965.

In other words, exemptions for persons over sixty-five can be of significant advantage only to affluent persons, property owners, retired corporation executives on large pensions with big stock bonuses and upper professionals who have managed to save and invest. Like marital income splitting and deductions for children, it is of significant advantage only if one has a large, preferably unearned income.

For a man in the 70-per-cent tax bracket each such exemption is worth in cash 70 per cent. For a person with zero income it is worth zero. In order to benefit slightly from the extra exemptions for being over sixty-five and blind, a single person using the standard deduction must have in excess of $2,000 taxable income. If he receives $4,001, he will pay tax on $1,800 (standard deduction plus three exemptions) or $294. But, having saved $80 by being blind, he will then be in a minority income group of less than 20 per cent of over-aged males! He will, despite the smallness of his income, be in a small, highly privileged income group. If it is a woman with an income of $3,001, she will pay $146— but she will then, despite the smallness of her income, be in a restricted group of less than 8 per cent of over-aged females!

The tax deductions for the aged, blind and retired are of significant benefit only if one belongs to a small group of persons with taxable incomes higher than 81.8 per cent of the males and 92.9 per cent of the females actually do have. The ones most benefited are the affluent aged, blind and retired.

These income statistics for the aged throw a curious light on the propaganda about the United States as a land of opportunity, the richest country in the world and the home of the individual-success system. Under this system, most people, economically, appear to be failures at the end of the road. And were it not for Social Security, the figures in each of the income brackets cited would, on the average, be about $900 less.

Some hidden hand, force or influence appears to cause most people, after a lifetime of effort, to show up very patently as losers. Could prices, taxes and overpersuasive advertising, as well as individual shortcomings, have anything to do with the result? With only 19.1 per cent of over-age males having a gross income above $4,000 and 7.1 per cent of retired females above $3,000, economic success does not appear to have crowned the efforts of most survivors in the most opulent land ever known to history.

In drawing the tax laws Congress is no more being sentimental than when it temporarily exempts the father of twelve from battle duty. Although individual congressmen no doubt have their personal points of view on all of this, collectively Congress in drawing the tax laws is absolutely indifferent to whether one is poor, married, has children or has personal disabilities. But it is not indifferent if one has property or a well-paid position. Then it is most enthusiastically on one's side.

Congress, as we have noted, likes students. It likes them so much that if one is able to gain a scholarship or fellowship he need pay no tax at all on it, an educational exemption, up to $300 a month for thirty-six months and even if the scholarship adds considerably to family income. Scholarships are awarded by many endowed colleges and special bodies, but many corporations now earmark scholarship funds given, for example, to the National Merit Scholarship Fund. Some funds are not earmarked, but the earmarked funds are for the children of employees (usually executives) of the company. The granting of the scholarship has the hidden effect of giving the father an untaxed pay raise and the corporation a pre-tax deduction, paid by consumers and small taxpayers. The father will not now have to pay his own taxed money for tuition. And in known cases students of *lower* standing in test examinations and lower academic standing have drawn earmarked scholarships while students of *higher* standing have drawn none, even as the public supposes the scholarships are awarded on the basis of strictly on-the-record merit.

For nonability factors are taken into consideration in this quarter, too, as in the hiring of people of negative ethnicity. . . .

Lucrative Charities

One may deduct up to 30 per cent of gross adjusted income for contributions to charities, and if contributions exceed 30 per cent in any one year they may be spread over five years. As most taxpayers manifestly cannot make contributions on such a scale, the provision is obviously of service only to the wealthy.

While the contributions may be made to existing bodies, most of the wealthy prudently decide to make them to their own charitable foundations, which are run as helpful adjuncts to their other affairs.

Oddly enough, one's financial power in society increases as one "gives" money to a personally owned foundation, proving that it is more profitable to "give" than to receive. If a certain man has a million-dollar *taxable* income (he has made all deductions), he is liable for $660,980 in taxes under the 1965 law, or nearly 70 per cent flat. But he can still make a charitable contribution for a deduction of $300,000. If he does, his tax will be only $450,980, a tax saving of $210,000. But as he has "given" $300,000 it looks as though he is deprived of $90,000 more than if he had paid straight tax.

But what he has "given" he has given to his own foundation, and he can invest this money in stocks of his own companies and thereby maintain profitable control. Again, the earning power of this $300,000 (at least $15,000 a year) is now tax free itself, greatly increasing its effectiveness. It will recoup his $90,000 out-of-pocket cost in at most six years and thereafter show a tax-free profit. He has more income to dispose of now in "philanthropic" patronage than if he had retained his taxed earnings and invested or spent them, for the proceeds of such retained money would be taxed.

What does his foundation contribute to? It contributes, as actual cases show, to laboratories seeking cures for various diseases. Surely this is entirely worthy, and so it is. But what do the corporations make that he controls? They may make medicines that are sold at a profit for the cure of various diseases, and any discoveries made by the laboratories to which his tax-free foundations "give" money will be utilized by his medicine-making corporations in making further profits. But few such discoveries will be available to impecunious people. It usually takes money to buy medicines.

Big Killings via Interest

Interest received, except from tax-exempt bonds, is taxable. Every man who gets interest from a bank account, a mortgage or on a federal or corporate bond is liable for taxes on it.

Interest paid out, on the other hand, is 100 per cent deductible. The man who buys an automobile or household appliance on the installment plan may deduct the interest paid before computing his income tax, just like the man who deducts for the payment of $100,000 of interest a year on a margined stock-market account. For the latter, the interest is deductible as an expense of doing business, and in the 70-per-cent bracket is worth to him $70,000. His true interest outlay is only 30 per cent of the face amount.

All such big interest payments are of major advantage to the big operators in stocks, real estate and oil lands who borrow a great deal in order to contrive their killings, which are sometimes sure things—as in the case of the metropolitan realty operators who "mortgage out."

Where interest paid as a deduction most obviously divides the population, placing another large number in the role of sucker and an apparent large number among the advantaged, is in the matter of home ownership. While tenants, in the form of rent, pay all costs, including mortgage interest and taxes of the owner, the home owner may deduct on his federal tax return interest he pays on his mortgage and his local real estate taxes. On a $30,000 house in which he has a $10,000 equity the home owner may pay 5 per cent perhaps on a $20,000 mortgage, or $1,000; his taxes may be $500; and he may reasonably figure 3 or 4 per cent for depreciation, repairs and maintenance, or $900–$1,200. His rent, then, exclusive of heating, is minimally $2,400. But if he is married and has a $10,000 taxable income he may first deduct the interest payment of $1,000 and then the real estate tax of $500. At the 22 per cent rate for that bracket the deduction is worth $330, bringing his actual rent down to $2,070 or $172.50 per month. A tenant would have to pay considerably more per month plus some entrepreneurial profit to the owner; he would probably have to pay from $225 to $275 per month, possibly more.

While this seems to give home owners a bit of an edge over tenants (I have omitted items like cost of insurance), Congress is not especially fond of home owners either. It has much bigger game in mind. With home owners sitting contentedly chewing their little tidbit, knowing they are slightly better off taxwise than tenants, the interest deduction meanwhile has opened some large gaps in the tax laws through which profit-hungry elements churn like armored divisions through Stone Age club-wielders.

First, for the wealthy man with many houses and country estates, both the realty tax and interest deductions amount to windfalls. If a million dollars of such residential property is mortgaged up to half at 5 per cent, there is a total interest charge of $25,000. But in the 70-per-cent bracket only $7,500 of this represents an out-of-pocket payment. Whatever the realty tax bill is, only 30 per cent of it represents an out-of-pocket payment. The same situation applies with respect to personally owned cooperative luxury apartments; the general taxpayers defray up to 70 per cent of the interest and realty tax outlay.

The interest and realty tax deductions, then, are extraordinarily valuable—to holders of extensive properties.

But this is only the beginning of the story.

Metropolitan real estate operators, as we have observed, use interest as a lever with which to "mortgage out" and then obtain tax-free income.

Here, in other words, is the real milk of the interest deduction coconut. Whereas the average home owner is getting away with peanuts at the expense of tenants, both tenants and home owners in the end must make up out of other taxes they pay, mainly in the form of prices, what the big operators have been able to avoid paying on their profits.

Congress, although not loving home owners, is surely infatuated with big real estate and stock-margin operators. And why not? It is these chaps who have the money to kick in for campaign funds, always a matter of concern to the officeholder.

One may agree that the ordinary citizen is entitled to complain. He knows he is in some sort of squeeze. But, politically illiterate, he clearly does not realize its nature nor does he see that he won't get out of it by obtaining some petty advantage over the single, the childless, the tenants and other fellow rank-and-file citizens. He cannot understand that it is the very *type* of person he likes as a legislator that is his undoing. For he prefers "con men" to seriously honest men.

Tax-Exempt Bonds

One of the biggest tax-exemption loopholes consists of state and municipal government and school bonds. Here, whether one draws $1,000 or $50 million of income, one pays absolutely no tax ever.

Very few people invest in such bonds and nearly all who do are very rich. Tax-exempt bonds are, clearly, a rich man's investment vehicle and are provided for this very purpose.

In the last available Treasury report issued about such bonds, the top $\frac{1}{10}$ of 1 per cent of the population owned 45 per cent of all outstanding, the top

$\frac{3}{10}$ of 1 per cent owned 66 per cent and the top 1½ per cent owned 87 per cent.[29] In short, no down-to-earth people own such bonds.

How many such bonds are outstanding? As of 1963 there were $85.9 billion outstanding compared with only $17.1 billion in 1945. One can see they are very popular with their buyers. At an average interest rate of 3 per cent, this amounts to $2.577 billion of untaxed annual revenue falling into the hands of wealthy individuals and a few banks and insurance companies.

The ordinary man would not find such investments attractive, as he can get from 4 to 5 per cent on savings. The advantage enters through the leverage exerted by the tax-free feature as one ascends the formal income brackets.

As Mr. Stern has worked it out, for a person with a taxable income of $4,000 a 3 per cent tax-free bond is equal to a stock yielding 3.75 per cent; for a person in the $20,000–$24,000 bracket to 4.8 per cent; for a person in the $32,000–$36,000 bracket to 6 per cent; but to a person in the $88,000–$100,000 bracket it is equal to 10.7 per cent on a stock.

On $140,000–$160,000 income it is equal to 15.8 per cent on a stock, on $300,000–$400,000 income to 30 per cent on a stock and on everything above $400,000 income to 30 per cent on a stock and on everything above $400,000 it is equal to a blessed flat, cold 33 per cent on a stock! Such a percentage return in a tax jungle is obviously worth reaching for.

As these bonds are secured by a lien on all the real estate taxes in their respective jurisdictions, they are absolutely without risk as to capital or payment of interest. In order to make as much taxable money, a high-income person would obviously have to invest in very risky enterprises that paid dividends of at least 33 per cent on invested capital. . . .

Not only is it possible, but it actually happens, that the house servants—chauffeurs, cooks, maids, gardeners—of some ultra-wealthy people pay income taxes and the employers pay none at all, year after year. For this, as one must understand, is a democracy where the lowly pay taxes but many of the rich do not.

In passing, very few Americans can afford to hire servants, and there are in fact few servants in the United States, which some naive souls take as proof of how "democratic" the country is. According to the 1960 census, there were only 159,679 private household workers "living in" in the entire country; they had a median wage of $1,178, were of a median age of 51.6 years and only 26.4 per cent of them were nonwhite. As some large estates harbor huge staffs of servants it is evident that this number distributes among a very small percentage of rich families. Private household workers "living out" numbered at that time 1,600,125, had a median wage of $658, were of a median age of 44.2 years and were 57.3 per cent non-white. This latter group obviously makes up the part-time help of some of the urban middle class.

Even suburban families with two or three children in the $25,000 income-bracket find they cannot pay for a servant after taxes, educational and medical costs, car operation and ordinary running expenses. And even part-time servants in the United States are now a luxury confined to an extremely small group of people. . . .

Depletion and Depreciation Allowances

We have not yet touched upon some of the more spectacular congressionally sanctioned large-scale special tax dispensations.

One of these is the oil depletion allowance. And at the outset it must be made clear that this depletion allowance applies to far more than oil. While it began with oil it now includes all the products of the earth *except*, as Congress finally stipulated, "soil, sod, dirt, turf, water, mosses, minerals from sea water, the air or similar inexhaustible sources." But it does include farm crops, trees, grass, coal, sand and gravel, oyster shells and clam shells, clay and, in fact, every mineral and naturally occurring chemical or fiber on land.

The percentage depletion, according to the Supreme Court, is an "arbitrary" allowance that "bears little relationship to the capital investment" and is available "though no money was actually invested."

But as more than 80 per cent of depletion benefits accrue to the oil and natural gas industries, the discussion can be confined to them.

Dating back to 1919 but with many tax-evading embellishments added since then, the depletion scheme works as follows:

1. The original investment by a company or individual in drilling a well—and under modern discovery methods three out of five wells drilled are producers—is wholly written off as an expense, thereby reducing an individual's or corporation's tax on other operations toward zero. Investment in oil drilling, in other words, offsets other taxable income. If an ordinary man had this privilege, then every dollar he deposited in a savings account would be tax deductible. The law permits, in short, a lucrative long-term investment to be treated as a current business expense.

2. As this was an investment in the well there is to be considered another outlay, or development cost, for *the oil that is in the well*. This cost is purely imaginary, as the only outlay was in drilling the well, but it is nevertheless fully deductible.

3. There remains a continuing, recurrent deduction, year after year, for making no additional investment at all!

The way these steps are achieved is through a deduction of $27\frac{1}{2}$ per cent (the figure was arrived at in 1926 as a compromise between a proposed arbitrary 25 per cent and an equally arbitrary 30 per cent) of the gross income from the well but not exceeding 50 per cent of its net income. If after all expenses, real and imaginary, a well owned by a corporation has a net income of $1 million, the depletion allowance can halve its ordinary liability to a corporation tax and it may maintain prices as though a full tax was paid. Through controlled production of some wells as against others, the tax rate can be reduced still further so that leading oil companies can and have paid as little as 4.1 per cent tax on their net earnings. Some pay no tax at all although earnings are large. Oil prices are "administered" by the companies; they are noncompetitive.

As Eisenstein sets forth this triple deduction, "For every $5 million deducted by the oil and gas industry in 1946 as percentage depletion, another $4 million was deducted as development costs. For every $3 million deducted as percentage depletion in 1947, another $2 million was deducted as development costs." The process continues, year after year, through the life of the well. Income often finally exceeds investment by many thousands of times.

A widowed charwoman with a child, taking the standard deduction which leaves her with $1,500 of taxable income, pays taxes at a much higher rate, 14 to 16 per cent, than do many big oil companies and oil multimillionaires in the great land of the free and the home of the brave.

This depletion deduction "continues as long as production continues, though they may have recovered their investment many times over. The larger the profit, the larger the deduction."

"For an individual in the top bracket, the expenses may be written off at 91 per cent while the income is taxable at 45.5 per cent. For a corporation the expenses may be written off at 52 per cent while the income is taxable at 26 per cent." A company may work this percentage a good deal lower and even to nothing.

We have noted that the Supreme Court has called the depletion allowance "arbitrary"—that is, as having no basis whatever in reason. Eisenstein examines in detail all the excuses given for permitting the depletion and in detail shows them all to be without a shadow of merit. . . . The depletion allowance is a plain gouge of the public for the benefit of a few ultra-greedy overreachers and is plainly the result of a continuing political conspiracy centered in the United States Congress.

What it costs the general public will be left until later.

Even more sweeping results are obtained by means of legally provided accelerated depreciation, long useful in real estate and under the Kennedy tax laws applicable up to 7 per cent annually for all new corporate investments. In brief, whatever a corporation invests in new plant out of its undistributed profits it may take, up to 7 per cent of the investment, and treat it as a deductible item. On an investment of $100 million this would amount to $7 million annually.

The results in real estate alone, as related by Stern, are as follows:

> In 1960, the following events occurred:
> —Eight New York real estate corporations amassed a total of $18,766,200 in cash available for distribution to their shareholders. They paid not one penny of income tax.
> —When this $18,766,200 was distributed, few of their shareholders paid even a penny of income tax on it.
> —Despite this cash accumulation of nearly $19 million, these eight

companies were able to report to Internal Revenue *losses,* for tax purposes, totaling $3,186,269.

—One of these companies alone, the Kratter Realty Corporation, had available cash of $5,160,372, distributed virtually all of this to its shareholders—and yet paid no tax. In fact, it reported a *loss,* for tax purposes, of $1,762,240. Few, if any, of their shareholders paid any income tax on the more than $5 million distributed to them by the Kratter Corporation.

All of this was perfectly legal, with the blessing of Congress.

According to a survey by the Treasury Department, eleven new real estate corporations had net cash available for distribution in the amount of $26,672,804, of which only $936,425 or 3.5 per cent was taxable.

The Great Game of Capital Gains

Capital gains are taxed, as we have noted, at a maximum of 25 per cent, although this rate is lowered corresponding to any lower actual tax bracket; but up to and including people in the highest tax brackets the rate is only 25 per cent. Thus, capital gains are a tax-favored way of obtaining additional income by the small number of people in the upper tax brackets.

Something to observe is that 69 per cent of capital gains go to 8.7 per cent of taxpayers in the income group of $10,000 and up; 35 per cent go to the 0.2 per cent of taxpayers in the income group of $50,000 and up. The cut-rate capital gains tax, like many of these other taxes, is therefore obviously tailored to suit upper income groups only.

The total of capital gains reported to Internal Revenue for 1961, for example, was $8.16 billion. Of this amount $465 million of gains were in the $1 million and upward income group; $1.044 billion in the $200,000 to $1 million income group; $1.63 billion in the $50,000–$200,000 income group; $1.6 billion in the $20,000–$50,000 income group; and $1.3 billion in the $10,000–$20,000 income group. Only $2 billion was in the less than $10,000 income group. It is, plainly, people in the upper income classes who most use this way of garnering extra money.

What is involved in ordinary capital gains is capital assets—mainly stocks and real estate.

The theory behind the low-tax capital gain is that risk money for developing the economy is put to work. If the capital gains tax were applied for a limited period, say, to new enterprises, giving new employment, the theory might be defensible. But, as it is, it applies to any kind of capital asset, to seasoned securities or to very old real estate. Most capital gain ventures start nothing new.

There is some risk in buying any security, even AT&T. The risk here is that it may go down somewhat in price for a certain period; but there is absolutely no risk that the enterprise will go out of business. The theory on which the capital gains tax discount is based is that there is *total* risk; yet most capital gains are taken in connection with basically riskless properties. There would be some risk attached to buying the Empire State Building for $1; one might lose the dollar in the event a revolutionary government confiscated the property. But the amount of risk attached to paying a full going market price for the building is in practice only marginal. One might conceivably lose 10 per cent of one's money if one sold at an inopportune time. But one would not risk being wiped out.

In real estate, capital gains serve as the icing on a cake already rich with fictitious depreciation deductions. Depreciation is supposed to extend over the life of a property. Yet excessively depreciated properties continue to sell at much higher than original prices. When so much capital value is left after excessive depreciation has been taken, there must be something wrong with the depreciation schedule. What is wrong with it is that it is granted as an arbitrary and socially unwarranted tax gift to big operators. It is pure gravy.

Depreciation for tax purposes in real estate is taken at a much more rapid rate than is allowed even by mortgage-lending institutions.

First, a certain arbitrary life is set for a building, say, twenty-five years. But a bank will usually issue a mortgage for a much longer term. On such a new building in the first year a double depreciation—8 per cent—may be taken, but on an old building with a new owner a depreciation rate of one and a half may be taken in the first year. The depreciation taken in the first year and subsequently generally greatly exceeds the net income, leaving this taxless. The depreciation offsets income. For a person in high tax brackets it is, naturally, advantageous to have such tax-free income.

In a case cited of a new $5 million building the tax savings to an 81-percent bracket man amounted to nearly $1 million in five years.

The book value of this building, by reason of accelerated depreciation deductions of nearly $1.7 million, was now $3.3 million. The owner was offered $5 million for the building, the original cost. He decided to accept this offer. The tax deductions he had already taken had saved him 81 cents on the dollar and the tax rate he would get on his "book profit" would cost him only 25 cents on the dollar. The seller's net tax gain was $942,422.78.

The new owner of the building could resume the depreciation cycle again on the basis of the $5 million cost and the old owner could go and start the process again with some other building. Real estate operators repeat this process endlessly. Many buildings in their lifetime have been depreciated many times their value. Best of all, the land remains.

Depreciation charges, deducted from before-tax profits, are an increasingly important way of concealing true earnings, as the *Wall Street Journal* notes (August 29, 1967; 18:3–4). "These funds don't show up as profits in corporate earnings reports, but are regarded by many investors as being nearly as good as profits . . . such funds can be put into new facilities that eventually may bring bigger sales, earnings and dividends for stockholders.

"At no time during the 1948–57 period did depreciation funds amount to more than 80 cents for each dollar of after-tax earnings, Government records show," the *Journal* said. "In some of the earlier years, in fact, depreciation cash came to less than 40 cents per dollar of earnings. But in 1958—the year that the price-earnings ratio climbed so sharply—depreciation for the first time in the post-World War II era approximately equaled the after-tax earnings total. Through the Sixties, depreciation funds remained relatively high, so that for every dollar of corporate earnings there was nearly another dollar of cash for expansion programs or other such programs."

Depreciation, in brief, amounts to a second line of profit, not acknowledged as such and now approximately equaling the acknowledged profit.

While this tax-deductible depreciation feature is not present with the purchase of stocks, the leverage of a loan at interest, as in the case of the real estate mortgage, is often present. For at least half the purchase price of the stock may be financed with a broker's loan at the standard rate of annual interest. The percentage of profit in relation to the input of investment becomes very great.

If 1,000 shares of stock are purchased at $50 a share, with a bank supplying half the money, the investor's share is $25,000. The interest he pays on the $25,000 of bank money is itself deductible. If the stock in six months doubles in value and is sold, the price realized is $100,000. As the bank loan is paid off and the initial investment is recovered there remains a profit of $50,000 or 200 per cent. On this there will be paid a capital gains tax of $12,500, leaving the profit after taxes at 150 per cent (or 300 per cent at a yearly rate).

It isn't usual that a stock doubles in value in six months, but many have done so. A post-tax profit of 150 per cent in as much as five years will amount to 30 per cent tax-free per year, which is not in itself a poor return. Compared with 5 per cent from a bank or a high-grade bond, which is taxable, it is an excellent return, making chumps out of most ordinarily thrifty citizens.

Whether the owner is using only his own money or is borrowing some, he is obtaining a tremendous tax advantage over the ordinary citizen.

The General Results

What is not paid by the higher-ups must be paid by the rank-and-file. The government, despite all the tax loopholes, is never deprived of whatever revenue it says it needs, even for waging fierce undeclared wars of its own bureaucratic making. What revenue the government decides not to take from the influential *finpols* it must take from the poor and needy over which the *pubpols* weep and wail like the Walrus and the Carpenter did over the happy trusting oysters they had eaten.

Stern has reported various shrinkages in the tax base and the attendant cost to the Treasury (which cost must be made up by the patriotic rank and file).

Here these various shrinkages and costs are presented somewhat differently: first, those shrinkages and costs of advantage solely to the wealthy; secondly, those shrinkages and costs participated in and preponderantly of advantage to the wealthy; and, thirdly, those shrinkages and costs generally of advantage only to rank-and-filers.

Lump-Sum Tax Evasions of the Wealthy Only

	Shrinkage of Tax Base (Billion Dollars)	Cost to Treasury (Billion Dollars)
Depletion deductions	$ 3.7	$ 1.5
Intangible oil and gas drilling deductions	–	.5
Excessive expense account deductions	–	.3
Real estate depreciation	–	.2
Dividend credits	–	.5
Capital gains deductions	6.0	2.4
Estate tax evasions	12.5	2.9
Interest on tax-free bonds	2.0	1.0
Undistributed corporate profit*	25.6 (1965)	12.8 (est.)
Totals	$49.8	$22.1

* Stern does not include this significant item.

The wealthier class of taxpayers, in brief, fails to pay $22.1 billion of taxes which it might properly pay. Nor is this all, because it participates in tax loopholes available to others.

According to this approximate computation, which would vary in detail from year to year, there is a total tax diversion from the Treasury of $52.7

Lump-Sum Tax Dodges in Which the Wealthy Probably Have Little Participation

	Shrinkage of Tax Base (Billion Dollars)	Cost to Treasury (Billion Dollars)
Fringe benefits (some participation by well-paid executives)	$ 9.0	$3.0
Interest on life insurance savings	1.5	.4
Sick pay and dividend exclusions (some participation by wealthy)	.9	.3
Standard deduction	12.0	2.6
Unreported dividends and interest (mostly small people)	3.7	.9
Totals	$27.1	$7.2

Lump-Sum Tax Evasions in Which the Wealthy Participate With the Less Wealthy Middle Classes

	Shrinkage of Tax Base (Billion Dollars)	Cost to Treasury (Billion Dollars)
Extra exemptions for the aged and blind (most of these deductions percentagewise and in totality must go to those few with substantial income—the higher the income the greater the deduction)	$ 3.2	$ .9
Nontaxable income from social security, unemployment and veterans' benefits, etc. (except for unemployment benefits, the wealthy participate to some extent)	11.9	3.6
Rent equivalent (deducted mortgage interest, etc.) on owned homes (greatest advantage to wealthy as residents and as real estate operators)	6.5	2.0
Itemized deductions (most profitably used by wealthy)	43.0	11.9
Income-splitting for married people (of most percentage and dollar value for wealthy persons)	–	5.0
Totals	$64.6	$23.4

billion a year. This diversion must be compensated for, with national budgets now rising above $100 billion, and it is compensated for at the expense of the smaller taxpayers, who pay more than $20 billion of corporate and other taxes in price and also pay most of income and excise taxes. The rates on the lower incomes are far higher than they would be if an equitable system of taxation existed.

While the less pecunious classes are able to evade most of $7.2 billion (for which they nevertheless pay elsewhere), the more affluent classes (with the wealthy participating by individual proportions most extensively) evade paying $23.4 billion (for which most of their members pay elsewhere). The wealthiest class as a whole evades directly a total of $22.1 billion, which it unloads on the impecunious and less pecunious classes.

What the extent of its participation is in the evasion of $23.4 by the middle group can only be surmised. If we estimate the participation at only $5 billion then we find the wealthiest have evaded $27.1 billion of taxes in addition to whatever they have merely generally pushed over on the lower orders.

If anyone believes there is suggested here too high a figure of what is really owed in taxes by the wealthy, it should be recalled that the upper 10 per cent of the population owns *all* of the nation's productive private property while 1 per cent of the population owns more than 70 per cent of it. Such being the case one would not reasonably expect that a single employed person who is paid $1,000 in a year—about $20 a week—would be obliged to pay a tax of $12. Nor would one expect that a married man with a salary of $4,000 would be obliged to pay a tax of $350, a month's pay. But so they had to do in 1966 if they took the standard deductions.

To shift the scene a bit, it may be recalled that national elections now require the spending by the political parties of more than $100 million. This is without considering the many costly local elections in off years or parallel with the national elections. The rising figures, often cited, are considered stupendous. These campaign funds are supplied by the wealthy and the propertied who, it should be clear, get a manifold return on what they pay for. As the political parties (in default of effective popular participation) are to all practical purposes theirs, they obtain preferential treatment from government. So it has been all down through history. The United States is not an exceptional case. It is a typical historical case, contrary to what the Fourth of July orators would have one believe, except that the people have been subdued through their own ineptitude. . . .

The Chances of Reform

What are the chances of reforming the tax laws?

Here it must suffice to say that most experts see little prospect of reform. At most there will be further deceptive rearranging and ideological tinkering. And even if taxes were fairly apportioned, past gains would remain in the hands of the advantaged.

A colossal historical inequity like the American tax structure, a mechanism subtly fastened on a people with a view to extracting from them the produce of their labors not necessary for subsistence, is never removed by means of elections or the passage of laws. At least, it never has been thus far in history. The beneficiaries, having gone to a great deal of trouble and expense to devise and maintain this structure, are not going to stand idly by and see it dismantled. They will use every considerable power at their command to defeat all substantial reforms.

In history fantastic, capricious and arbitrary structures such as this have vanished only in some sort of climactic explosion—revolution, conquest or collapse. A far less onerous tax structure in the early American colonies was terminated not by reform but by revolution and war.

Unequal Education and the Reproduction of the Social Division of Labor

SAMUEL BOWLES

The ideological defense of modern capitalist society rests heavily on the assertion that the equalizing effects of education can counter the disequalizing forces inherent in the free market system. That educational systems in capitalist societies have been highly unequal is generally admitted and widely condemned. Yet educational inequalities are taken as passing phenomena, holdovers from an earlier, less enlightened era, which are rapidly being eliminated.

The record of educational history in the U.S., and scrutiny of the present state of our colleges and schools, lend little support to this comforting optimism. Rather, the available data suggest an alternative interpretation. In what follows I will argue (1) that schools have evolved in the U.S. not as part of a pursuit of equality, but rather to meet the needs of capitalist employers for a disciplined and skilled labor force, and to provide a mechanism for social control in the interests of political stability; (2) that as the economic importance of skilled and well educated labor has grown, inequalities in the school system have become increasingly important in reproducing the class structure from one generation to the next; (3) that the U.S. school system is pervaded by class inequalities, which have shown little sign of diminishing over the last half century; and (4) that the evidently unequal control over school boards and other decision-making bodies in education does not provide a sufficient explanation of the persistence and pervasiveness of inequalities in the school system. Although the unequal distribution of political power serves to maintain inequalities in education, their origins are to be found outside the political sphere, in the class structure itself and in the class subcultures typical of capitalist societies. Thus unequal education has its roots in the very class structure which it serves to legitimize and reproduce. Inequalities in education are thus seen as part of the web of capitalist society, and likely to persist as long as capitalism survives.

From the *Review of Radical Political Economics,* Vol. 3, No. 4 (Fall and Winter 1971), pp. 1–26. Reprinted by permission of the publisher.

I. The Evolution of Capitalism and
the Rise of Mass Education

In colonial America, and in most pre-capitalist societies of the past, the basic productive unit was the family. For the vast majority of male adults, work was self-directed, and was performed without direct supervision. Though constrained by poverty, ill health, the low level of technological development and occasional interferences by the political authorities, a man had considerable leeway in choosing his working hours, what to produce, and how to produce it. While great inequalities in wealth, political power, and other aspects of status normally existed, differences in the degree of autonomy in work were relatively minor, particularly when compared with what was to come.

Transmitting the necessary productive skills to the children as they grew up proved to be a simple task, not because the work was devoid of skill, but because the quite substantial skills required were virtually unchanging from generation to generation, and because the transition to the world of work did not require that the child adapt to a wholly new set of social relationships. The child learned the concrete skills and adapted to the social relations of production through learning by doing within the family. Preparation for life in the larger community was facilitated by the child's experience with the extended family, which shaded off without distinct boundaries, through uncles and fourth cousins, into the community. Children learned early how to deal with complex relationships among adults other than their parents, and children other than their brothers and sisters.[1]

It was not required that children learn a complex set of political principles or ideologies, as political participation was limited and political authority unchallenged, at least in normal times. The only major socializing institution outside the family was the church, which sought to inculcate the accepted spiritual values and attitudes. In addition, a small number of children learned craft skills outside the family, as apprentices. The role of schools tended to be narrowly vocational, restricted to preparation of children for a career in the church or the still inconsequential state bureaucracy.[2] The curriculum of the few universities reflected the aristocratic penchant for conspicuous intellectual consumption.[3]

The extension of capitalist production, and particularly the factory system,

[1] This account draws upon two important historical studies: P. Aries, *Centuries of Childhood* (New York, 1970); and B. Bailyn, *Education in the Forming of American Society* (New York, 1960). Also illuminating are anthropological studies of education in contemporary pre-capitalist societies. See, for example, J. Kenyatta, *Facing Mount Kenya* (New York, 1962), pp. 95–124. See also Edmund S. Morgan, *The Puritan Family: Religion and Domestic Relations in Seventeenth Century New England* (New York, 1944).

[2] P. Aries, *Centuries of Childhood*. In a number of places, Scotland and Massachusetts, for example, schools stressed literacy so as to make the *Bible* more widely accessible. (See C. Cipolla, *Literacy and Economic Development* (Baltimore, 1969); and E. Morgan, *The Puritan Family* (ch. 4).) Morgan quotes a Massachusetts law of 1647 which provided for the establishment of reading schools because it was "one chief project of that old deluder, Satan, to keep men from knowledge of the Scriptures."

[3] H. F. Kearney, *Scholars and Gentlemen: Universities and Society in Pre-Industrial Britain* (Ithaca, N.Y., 1971).

undermined the role of the family as the major unit of both socialization and production. Small peasant farmers were driven off the land or competed out of business. Cottage industry was destroyed. Ownership of the means of production became heavily concentrated in the hands of landlords and capitalists. Workers relinquished control over their labor in return for wages or salaries. Increasingly, production was carried on in large organizations in which a small management group directed the work activities of the entire labor force. The social relations of production—the authority structure, the prescribed types of behavior and response characteristic of the work place—became increasingly distinct from those of the family.

The divorce of the worker from control over production—from control over his own labor—is particularly important in understanding the role of schooling in capitalist societies. The resulting social division of labor—between controllers and controlled—is a crucial aspect of the class structure of capitalist societies, and will be seen to be an important barrier to the achievement of social class equality in schooling.

Rapid economic change in the capitalist period led to frequent shifts in the occupational distribution of the labor force, and constant changes in the skill requirements for jobs. The productive skills of the father were no longer adequate for the needs of the son during his lifetime. Skill training within the family became increasingly inappropriate.

And the family itself was changing. Increased geographic mobility of labor and the necessity for children to work outside the family spelled the demise of the extended family and greatly weakened even the nuclear family.[4] Meanwhile, the authority of the church was questioned by the spread of secular rationalist thinking and the rise of powerful competing groups.

While undermining the main institutions of socialization, the development of the capitalist system created at the same time an environment—both social and intellectual—which would ultimately challenge the political order. Workers were thrown together in oppressive factories, and the isolation which had helped to maintain quiescence in earlier, widely dispersed peasant populations was broken down.[5] With an increasing number of families uprooted from the land, the workers' search for a living resulted in large-scale labor migrations. Transient—even foreign—elements came to constitute a major segment of the population, and began to pose seemingly insurmountable problems of assimilation, integration, and control.[6] Inequalities of wealth became more apparent, and were less easily justified and less readily accepted. The simple legitimizing ideologies of the earlier period—the divine right of kings and the divine origin of social rank, for example—fell under the capitalist attack on the royalty and the traditional landed interests. The broadening of the

[4] See B. Bailyn, *Education in the Forming of American Society*, and N. Smelser, *Social Change in the Industrial Revolution* (Chicago, 1959).

[5] F. Engels and K. Marx, *The Communist Manifesto* (1848); K. Marx, *The 18th Brumaire of Louis Bonaparte* (New York, 1852).

[6] See, for example, S. Thernstrom, *Poverty and Progress: Social Mobility in a 19th Century City* (New York, 1969).

electorate of political participation generally—first sought by the capitalist class in the struggle against the entrenched interests of the pre-capitalist period—threatened soon to become an instrument for the growing power of the working class. Having risen to political power, the capitalist class sought a mechanism to insure social control and political stability.[7]

An institutional crisis was at hand. The outcome, in virtually all capitalist countries, was the rise of mass education. In the U.S., the many advantages of schooling as a socialization process were quickly perceived. The early proponents of the rapid expansion of schooling argued that education could perform many of the socialization functions which earlier had been centered in the family and to a lesser extent, in the church.[8]

An ideal preparation for factory work was found in the social relations of the school: specifically, in its emphasis on discipline, punctuality, acceptance of authority outside the family, and individual accountability for one's work. The social relations of the school would replicate the social relations of the workplace, and thus help young people adapt to the social division of labor. Schools would further lead people to accept the authority of the state and its agents—the teachers—at a young age, in part by fostering the illusion of the benevolence of the government in its relations with citizens. Moreover, because schooling would ostensibly be open to all, one's position in the social division of labor could be portrayed as the result not of birth, but of one's own efforts and talents. And if the children's everyday experiences with the structure of schooling were insufficient to inculcate the correct views and attitudes, the curriculum itself would be made to embody the bourgeois ideology. Where pre-capitalist social institutions—particularly the church—remained strong or threatened the capitalist hegemony, schools sometimes served as a modernizing counter-institution.

The movement for public elementary and secondary education in the U.S. originated in the 19th century in states dominated by the burgeoning industrial capitalist class, most notably in Massachusetts. It spread rapidly to all parts of the country except the South. In Massachusetts the extension of elementary education was in large measure a response to industrialization, and to the need for social control of the Irish and other non-Yankee workers recruited to work in the mills. The fact that some working people's movements had demanded free instruction should not obscure the basically coercive nature of the extension of schooling. In many parts of the country, schools were literally imposed upon the workers.

The evolution of the economy in the 19th century gave rise to new socialization needs and continued to spur the growth of education. Agriculture continued to lose ground to manufacturing; simple manufacturing gave way to production involving complex interrelated processes; an increasing fraction of the labor force was employed in producing services rather than goods. Employers in the most rapidly growing sectors of the economy began to re-

[7] B. Simon, *Studies in the History of Education, 1780–1870*, Vol. I. (London, 1960).

[8] Bailyn, *Education in the Forming of American Society.*

quire more than obedience and punctuality in their workers; a change in motivational outlook was required. The new structure of production provided little built-in motivation. There were fewer jobs like farming and piece-rate work in manufacturing in which material reward was tied directly to effort. As work roles became more complicated and interrelated, the evaluation of the individual worker's performance became increasingly difficult. Employers began to look for workers who had internalized the production-related values of the firm's managers.

The continued expansion of education was pressed by many who saw schooling as a means of producing these new forms of motivation and discipline. Others, frightened by the growing labor militancy after the Civil War, found new urgency in the social control arguments popular among the proponents of education in the antebellum period.

A system of class stratification developed within this rapidly expanding educational system. Children of the social elite normally attended private schools. Because working class children tended to leave school early, the class composition of the public high schools was distinctly more elite than the public primary schools. And as a university education ceased to be merely training for teaching or the divinity and became important in gaining access to the pinnacles of the business world, upper class families used their money and influence to get their children into the best universities, often at the expense of the children of less elite families.

Around the turn of the present century, large numbers of working class and particularly immigrant children began attending high schools. At the same time, a system of class stratification developed within secondary education. The older democratic ideology of the common school—that the same curriculum should be offered to all children—gave way to the "progressive" insistence that education should be tailored to the "needs of the child." In the interests of providing an education relevant to the later life of the students, vocational schools and tracks were developed for the children of working families. The academic curriculum was preserved for those who would later have the opportunity to make use of book learning, either in college or in white-collar employment. This and other educational reforms of the progressive education movement reflected an implicit assumption of the immutability of the class structure.

The frankness with which students were channeled into curriculum tracks, on the basis of their social class background, raised serious doubts concerning the "openness" of the social class structure. The relation between social class and a child's chances of promotion or tracking assignments was disguised—though not mitigated much—by another "progressive" reform: "objective" educational testing. Particularly after World War I, the capitulation of the schools to business values and concepts of efficiency led to the increased use of intelligence and scholastic achievement testing as an ostensibly unbiased means of measuring the product of schooling and classifying students. The complementary growth of the guidance counseling profession allowed much of the channeling to proceed from the students'-own-well-counselled-choices, thus adding an apparent element of voluntarism to the system.

The legacy of the progressive education movement, like the earlier reforms of the mid-19th century, was a strengthened system of class stratification within schooling which continues to this day to play an important role in the reproduction and legitimation of the social division of labor.

The class stratification of education during this period had proceeded hand in hand with the stratification of the labor force. As large bureaucratic corporations and public agencies employed an increasing fraction of all workers, a complicated segmentation of the labor force evolved, reflecting the hierarchical structure of the social relations of production. A large middle group of employees evolved comprising the clerical, sales, bookkeeping, and low level supervisory workers.[9] People holding these occupations ordinarily had a modicum of control over their own work; in some cases they directed the work of others, while themselves being under the direction of higher management. The social division of labor had become a finely articulated system of work relations dominated at the top by a small group with control over work processes and a high degree of personal autonomy in their work activities, and proceeding by finely differentiated stages down the chain of bureaucratic command to workers who labored more as extensions of the machinery than as autonomous human beings.

One's status, income, and personal autonomy came to depend in great measure on one's place in the hierarchy of work relations. And in turn, positions in the social division of labor came to be associated with educational credentials reflecting the number of years of schooling and the quality of education received. The increasing importance of schooling as a mechanism for allocating children to positions in the class structure, played a major part in legitimizing the structure itself.[10] But at the same time, it undermined the simple processes which in the past had preserved the position and privilege of the upper class families from generation to generation. In short, it undermined the processes serving to reproduce the social division of labor.

In pre-capitalist societies, direct inheritance of occupational position is common. Even in the early capitalist economy, prior to the segmentation of the labor force on the basis of differential skills and education, the class structure was reproduced generation after generation simply through the inheritance of physical capital by the offspring of the capitalist class. Now that the social division of labor is differentiated by types of competence and educational credentials as well as by the ownership of capital, the problem of inheritance is not nearly as simple. The crucial complication arises because education and skills are embedded in human beings, and—unlike physical capital—these assets cannot be passed on to one's children at death. In an ad-

---

[9] See M. Reich, "The Evolution of the U.S. Labor Force," in R. Edwards, M. Reich, and T. Weisskopf (eds.), *The Capitalist System* (Englewood Cliffs, N.J., 1971, forthcoming).

[10] The role of schooling in legitimizing the class structure is spelled out in S. Bowles, "Contradictions in U.S. Higher Education" (mimeo, 1971).

vanced capitalist society in which education and skills play an important role in the hierarchy of production, then, the absence of confiscatory inheritance laws is not enough to reproduce the social division of labor from generation to generation. Skills and educational credentials must somehow be passed on within the family. It is a fundamental theme of this paper that schools play an important part in reproducing and legitimizing this modern form of class structure.

II. Class Inequalities in U.S. Schools

Unequal schooling reproduces the social division of labor. Children whose parents occupy positions at the top of the occupational hierarchy receive more years of schooling than working class children. Both the amount and the content of their education greatly facilitates their movement into positions similar to their parents'.

Because of the relative ease of measurement, inequalities in years of schooling are particularly evident. If we define social class standing by the income, occupation, and educational level of the parents, a child from the 90th percentile in the class distribution may expect on the average to achieve over four and a half more years of schooling than a child from the 10th percentile.[11] As can be seen in Table 1, social class inequalities in the number of years of schooling received arise in part because a disproportionate number of children from poorer families do not complete high school.[12] Table 2 indicates that these inequalities are exacerbated by social class inequalities in college attendance among those children who did graduate from high school: even among those who had graduated from high school, children of families earning less than $3,000 per year were over six times likely *not* to attend college as were the children of families earning over $15,000.[13]

Because schooling—especially at the college level—is heavily subsidized by the general taxpayer, those children who attend school longer have access—for this reason alone—to a far larger amount of public resources than those who are forced out or drop out early.[14] But social class inequalities in public expenditure on education are far more severe than the degree of inequality in years of schooling would suggest. In the first place, per-student

[11] The data for this calculation refer to white males who were aged 25–34 in 1962. See S. Bowles, "Schooling and Inequality from Generation to Generation," paper presented at the Far Eastern Meetings of the Econometric Society, Tokyo, 1970.

[12] Table 1 understates the degree of social class inequality in school attendance in view of the fact that a substantial portion of the upper income children not enrolled in public schools attend private schools. Private schools provide a parallel educational system for the upper class. I have not given much attention to these institutions as they are not quantitatively very significant in the total picture. Moreover, to deal extensively with them might detract attention from the task of explaining class inequalities in the ostensibly egalitarian portion of our school system.

[13] For recent evidence on these points, see U.S. Bureau of the Census, *Current Population Reports*, Series P-20, Numbers 185 and 183.

[14] W. L. Hansen and B. Weisbrod, "The Distribution of Costs and Direct Benefits of Public Higher Education: the Case of California," *Journal of Human Resources*, Vol. V, No. 3 (Summer 1970), pp. 361–370.

TABLE 1
**Percentage of Male Children Aged 16–17 Enrolled in Public School, and
Percentage at Less Than the Modal Grade Level, by Parent's
Education and Income, 1960**[a]

	% of Male Children Aged 16–17 Enrolled in Public School	% of Those Enrolled Who Are Below the Modal Level
1. Parent's education less than 8 years		
Family Income:		
less than $3,000	66.1	47.4
$3,000–4,999	71.3	35.7
$5,000–6,999	75.5	28.3
$7,000 and over	77.1	21.8
2. Parent's education 8–11 years		
Family income:		
less than $3,000	78.6	25.0
$3,000–4,999	82.9	20.9
$5,000–6,999	84.9	16.9
$7,000 and over	86.1	13.0
3. Parent's education 12 years or more		
Family income:		
less than $3,000	89.5	13.4
$3,000–4,999	90.7	12.4
$5,000–6,999	92.1	9.7
$7,000 and over	94.2	6.9

SOURCE: Bureau of the Census, *Census of Population, 1960,* Vol. PC-(2)5A, Table 5.
[a] According to Bureau of the Census definitions, for 16-year olds 9th grade or less and for 17-year olds 10th grade or less are below the modal level. Father's education is indicated if father is present; otherwise mother's education is indicated.

TABLE 2
College Attendance in 1967 Among High School Graduates, by Family Income[a]

Family Income[b]	Per Cent Who Did Not Attend College
Total	*53.1*
under $3,000	80.2
$3,000 to $3,999	67.7
$4,000 to $5,999	63.7
$6,000 to $7,499	58.9
$7,500 to $9,999	49.0
$10,000 to $14,999	38.7
$15,000 and over	13.3

[a] Refers to individuals who were high school seniors in October 1965 and who subsequently graduated from high school. Source: U.S. Department of Commerce, Bureau of the Census, *Current Population, Report,* Series P-20, No. 185, July 11, 1969, p. 6. College attendance refers to both two- and four-year institutions.
[b] Family income for 12 months preceding October 1965.

public expenditure in four-year colleges greatly exceeds that in elementary schools; those who stay in school longer receive an increasingly large *annual* public subsidy.[15] Second, even at the elementary level, schools attended by children of the poor tend to be less well-endowed with equipment, books, teachers, and other inputs into the educational process. Evidence on the relationship between the level of school inputs and the income of the neighborhoods which the schools serve is presented in Table 3.[16] The data in this table indicate that both school expenditures and more direct measures of school quality vary directly with the income levels of the communities in which the school is located.

Inequalities in schooling are not simply a matter of differences in years of schooling attained or in resources devoted to each student per year of schooling. Differences in the internal structure of schools themselves and in the content of schooling reflect the differences in the social class compositions of the student bodies. The social relations of the educational process ordinarily mirror the social relations of the work roles into which most students are likely to move. Differences in rules, expected modes of behavior, and opportunities for choice are most glaring when we compare levels of schooling. Note the wide range of choice over curriculum, life style, and allocation of time afforded to college students, compared with the obedience and respect for authority expected in high school. Differentiation occurs also within each level of schooling. One needs only to compare the social relations of a junior

TABLE 3
Inequalities in Elementary School Resources: Per Cent Difference in Resource Availability Associated With a One Per Cent Difference in Mean Neighborhood Family Income

Resource	Within Cities (1)	Between Cities (2)
1. Current real education expenditure per student	n.a.	.73[b]
2. Average real elementary school teacher salary	.20[a]	.69[b]
3. Teacher-student ratio	.24[a]	n.a.
4. Real expenditure per pupil on teacher salary	.43[a]	n.a.
5. Verbal ability of teacher	.11[a]	1.20[a]

Sources: [a]John D. Owen, "An Empirical Analysis of Economic and Racial Bias in the Distribution of Educational Resources in Nine Large American Cities" (Center for the Study of Social Organization of Schools, Johns Hopkins University, 1969).

[b] John D. Owen, "Towards a Public Employment Wage Theory: Some Econometric Evidence on Teacher Quality," *Industrial Labor Relations Review* (forthcoming, 1972).

[15] In the school year 1969–70, per pupil expenditures of federal, state, and local funds were $1490 for colleges and universities and $747 for primary and secondary schools. U.S. Office of Education, *Digest of Educational Statistics, 1969* (Washington: U.S. Government Printing Office, 1969).

[16] See also P. C. Sexton, *Education and Income* (New York, 1961).

college with those of an elite four-year college,[17] or those of a working class high school with those of a wealthy suburban high school, for verification of this point.[18]

The differential socialization patterns in schools attended by students of different social classes do not arise by accident. Rather, they stem from the fact that the educational objectives and expectations of both parents and teachers, and the responsiveness of students to various patterns of teaching and control, differ for students of different social classes.[19] Further, class inequalities in school socialization patterns are reinforced by the very inequalities in financial resources decumented above. The paucity of financial support for the education of children from working class families not only leaves more resources to be devoted to the children of those with commanding roles in the economy; it forces upon the teachers and school administrators in the working class schools a type of social relations which fairly closely mirrors that of the factory. Thus financial considerations in poorly supported working class schools militate against small intimate classes, against a multiplicity of elective courses and specialized teachers (except disciplinary personnel), and preclude the amounts of free time for the teachers and free space required for a more open, flexible educational environment. The lack of financial support all but requires that students be treated as raw materials on a production line; it places a high premium on obedience and punctuality; there are few opportunities for independent, creative work or individualized attention by teachers. The well-financed schools attended by the children of the rich can offer much greater opportunities for the development of the capacity for sustained independent work and the other characteristics required for adequate job performance in the upper levels of the occupational hierarchy.

While much of the inequality in U.S. education exists between schools, even within a given school different children receive different educations. Class stratification within schools is achieved through tracking, differential participation in extra-curricular activities, and in the attitudes of teachers and particularly guidance personnel who expect working class children to do poorly, to terminate schooling early, and to end up in jobs similar to their parents.[20]

Not surprisingly, the results of schooling differ greatly for children of different social classes. The differing educational objectives implicit in the social

[17] See J. Binstock, *Survival in the American College Industry* (unpublished manuscript).

[18] E. Z. Friedenberg, *Coming of Age in America* (New York, 1965). It is consistent with this pattern that the play-oriented, child-centered pedagogy of the progressive movement found little acceptance outside of private schools in wealthy communities. See Cohen and Lazerson, "Education and the Industrial Order."

[19] That working class parents seem to favor more authoritarian educational methods is perhaps a reflection of their own work experiences which have demonstrated that submission to authority is an essential ingredient in one's ability to get and hold a steady, well-paying job.

[20] See, for example, A. B. Hollingshead, *Elmtown's Youth* (New York, 1949); W. I. Warner and P. S. Lunt, *The Social Life of a Modern Community* (New Haven, 1949); R. Rosenthal and L. Jacobson, *Pygmalion in the Classroom* (New York, 1968); and W. E. Schafer, C. Olexa, and K. Polk, "Programmed for Social Class: Tracking in High School," *Trans-Action,* Vol. 7, No. 2 (October, 1970).

relations of schools attended by children of different social classes has already been mentioned. Less important but more easily measured are differences in scholastic achievement. If we measure the output of schooling by scores on nationally standardized achievement tests, children whose parents were themselves highly educated outperform the children of parents with less education by a wide margin. A recent study revealed, for example, that among white high school seniors, those whose parents were in the top education decile were on the average well over three grade levels ahead of those whose parents were in the bottom decile.[21] While a good part of this discrepancy is the result of unequal treatment in school and unequal educational resources, it will be suggested below that much of it is related to differences in the early socialization and home environment of the children.

Given the great social class differences in scholastic achievement, class inequalities in college attendance are to be expected. Thus one might be tempted to argue that the data in Table 2 are simply a reflection of unequal scholastic achievement in high school and do not reflect any *additional* social class inequalities peculiar to the process of college admission. This view, so comforting to the admissions personnel in our elite universities, is unsupported by the available data, some of which is presented in Table 4. Access to a college education is highly unequal, even for children of the same measured "academic ability."

The social class inequalities in our school system and the role they play in the reproduction of the social division of labor are too evident to be denied. Defenders of the educational system are forced back on the assertion that things are getting better; the inequalities of the past were far worse. And, indeed, there can be no doubt that some of the inequalities of the past have been mitigated. Yet new inequalities have apparently developed to take their

TABLE 4
Probability of College Entry for a Male Who Has Reached Grade 11[a]

| | | Socioeconomic Quartiles[b] | | | |
		Low 1	2	3	High 4
	Low 1	.06	.12	.13	.26
Ability	2	.13	.15	.29	.36
Quartiles[b]	3	.25	.34	.45	.65
	High 4	.48	.70	.73	.87

[a] Based on a large sample of U.S. high school students as reported in John C. Flannagan and William W. Cooley, *Project TALENT, One-Year Follow-up Studies,* Cooperative Research Project Number 2333, School of Education, University of Pittsburgh, 1966.

[b] The Socioeconomic index is a composite measure including family income, father's occupation and education, mother's education, etc. The ability scale is a composite of tests measuring general academic aptitude.

[21] Calculation based on data in James S. Coleman *et al., Equality of Educational Opportunity,* Vol. II (Washington, 1966), and methods described in S. Bowles, "Schooling and Inequality from Generation to Generation."

place, for the available historical evidence lends little support to the idea that our schools are on the road to equality of educational opportunity. For example, data from a recent U.S. Census survey reported in Table 5 indicate that graduation from college has become increasingly dependent on one's class background. This is true despite the fact that the probability of high school graduation is becoming increasingly equal across social classes. On balance, the available data suggest that the number of years of schooling attained by a child depends upon the social class standing of the father at least as much in the recent period as it did fifty years ago.[22]

The argument that our "egalitarian" education compensates for inequalities generated elsewhere in the capitalist system is so patently fallacious that few will persist in maintaining it. But the discrepancy between the ideology and the reality of the U.S. school system is far greater than would appear from a passing glance at the above data. In the first place, if education is to compensate for the social class immobility due to the inheritance of wealth and privilege, education must be structured so as to yield a negative correlation between social class background of the child and the quantity and quality of her or his schooling. Thus the assertion that education compensates for inequalities in inherited wealth and privilege is falsified not so much by the extent of the social class inequalities in the school system as by their very existence, or, more correctly, by the absence of compensatory inequalities.

Second, if we turn now from the problem of intergeneration immobility to the problem of inequality of income at a given moment, a similar argument applies. In a capitalist economy, the increasing importance of schooling in the economy will exercise a disequalizing tendency on the distribution of income even in the absence of social class inequalities in quality and quantity of schooling. To see why this is so, consider a simple capitalist economy in which only two factors are used in production: uneducated and undifferentiated labor, and capital, the ownership of which is unequally distributed among the population. The only source of income inequality in this society is the unequal distribution of capital. As the labor force becomes differentiated by type of skill or schooling, inequalities in labor earnings contribute to total income inequality, augmenting the inequalities due to the concentration of capital. This will be the case even if education and skills are distributed randomly among the population. The disequalizing tendency will of course be intensified if the owners of capital also acquire a disproportionate amount of those types of education and training which confer access to high-paying jobs. A substantial negative correlation between the ownership of capital and the quality and quantity of schooling received would have been required merely to neutralize the disequalizing effect of the rise of schooling

---

[22] See P. M. Blau and O. D. Duncan, *The American Occupational Structure* (New York, 1967). More recent data do not contradict the evidence of no trend towards equality. A 1967 Census survey, the most recent available, shows that among high school graduates in 1965, the probability of college attendance for those whose parents had attended college has continued to rise relative to the probability of college attendance for those whose parents had attended less than eight years of school. See U.S. Bureau of the Census, *Current Population Reports*, Series P-20, No. 185, July 11, 1969.

TABLE 5
Among Sons Who Had Reached High School, Percentage Who Graduated From College, by Son's Age and Father's Level of Education

					Father's Education			
			Some High School		High School Grad.		Some College or More	
Son's Age in 1962	Likely Dates of College Graduation[a]	<8 Years	% Grad.	Ratio to <8	% Grad.	Ratio to <8	% Grad.	Ratio to <8
25–34	1950–1959	07.6	17.4	2.29	25.6	3.37	51.9	6.83
35–44	1940–1949	08.6	11.9	1.38	25.3	2.94	53.9	6.27
45–54	1930–1939	07.7	09.8	1.27	15.1	1.96	36.9	4.79
55–64	1920–1929	08.9	09.8	1.10	19.2	2.16	29.8	3.35

SOURCE: Based on U.S. Census data as reported in William G. Spady, "Educational Mobility and Access: Growth and Paradoxes," *American Journal of Sociology*, Vol. 73, No. 3 (November 1967).
[a] Assuming college graduation at age 22.

as an economic phenomenon. And while some research has minimized the importance of social class biases in schooling,[23] nobody has yet suggested that class and schooling were inversely related!

III. Class Culture and Class Power

The pervasive and persistent inequalities in U.S. education would seem to refute an interpretation of education which asserts its egalitarian functions. But the facts of inequality do not by themselves suggest an alternate explanation. Indeed, they pose serious problems of interpretation. If the costs of education borne by students and their families were very high, or if nepotism were rampant, or if formal segregation of pupils by social class were practiced, or educational decisions were made by a select few whom we might call the power elite, it would not be difficult to explain the continued inequalities in U.S. education. The problem of interpretation, however, is to reconcile the above empirical findings with the facts of our society as we perceive them: public and virtually tuition-free education at all levels, few legal instruments for the direct implementation of class segregation, a limited role for "contacts" or nepotism in the achievement of high status or income, a commitment (at the rhetorical level at least) to equality of educational opportunity, and a system of control of education which if not particularly democratic, extends far beyond anything resembling a power elite. The attempt to reconcile these apparently discrepant facts leads us back to a consideration of the social division of labor, the associated class cultures, and the exercise of class power.

. . . The social division of labor—based on the hierarchical structure of production—gives rise to distinct class sub-cultures. The values, personality traits, and expectations characteristic of each subculture are transmitted from generation to generation through class differences in family socialization and complementary differences in the type and amount of schooling ordinarily attained by children of various class positions. These class differences in schooling are maintained in large measure through the capacity of the upper class to control the basic principles of school finance, pupil evaluation, and educational objectives.

The social relations of production characteristic of advanced capitalist societies (and many socialist societies) are most clearly illustrated in the bureaucracy and hierarchy of the modern corporation. Occupational roles in the capitalist economy may be grouped according to the degree of independence and control exercised by the person holding the job. There is some evidence that the personality attributes associated with the adequate performance of jobs in occupational categories defined in this broad way differ considerably, some apparently requiring independence and internal discipline, and others emphasizing such traits as obedience, predictability, and willingness to subject oneself to external controls.

[23] See, for example, Robert Hauser, "Educational Stratification in the United States," *Sociological Inquiry*, Vol. 20, Spring, 1970.

These personality attributes are developed primarily at a young age, both in the family and, to a lesser extent, in secondary socializing institutions such as schools. Because people tend to marry within their own class (in part because spouses often meet in our class segregated schools), both parents are likely to have a similar set of these fundamental personality traits. Thus children of parents occupying a given position in the occupational hierarchy grow up in homes where child-rearing methods and perhaps even the physical surroundings tend to develop personality characteristics appropriate to adequate job performance in the occupational roles of the parents. The children of managers and professionals are taught self-reliance within a broad set of constraints; the children of production line workers are taught obedience.

While this relation between parents' class position and child's personality attributes operates primarily in the home, it is reinforced by schools and other social institutions. Thus, to take an example introduced earlier, the authoritarian social relations of working class high schools complement the discipline-oriented early socialization patterns experienced by working class children. The relatively greater freedom of wealthy suburban schools extends and formalizes the early independence training characteristic of upper class families. . . .

The operation of the labor market translates differences in class culture into income inequalities and occupational hierarchies. The personality traits, values, and expectations characteristic of different class cultures play a major role in determining an individual's success in gaining a high income or prestigious occupation. The apparent contribution of schooling to occupational success and higher income seems to be explained primarily by the personality characteristics of those who have higher educational attainments.[24] Although the rewards to intellectual capacities are quite limited in the labor market (except for a small number of high level jobs), mental abilities are important in getting ahead in school. Grades, the probability of continuing to higher levels of schooling, and a host of other school success variables, are positively correlated with "objective" measures of intellectual capacities. Partly for this reason, one's experience in school reinforces the belief that promotion and rewards are distributed fairly. The close relationship between educational attainments and later occupational success thus provides a meritocratic appearance to mask the mechanisms which reproduce the class system from generation to generation.

So far, the perpetuation of inequality through the schooling system has been represented as an almost automatic, self-enforcing mechanism, operating only through the medium of class culture. An important further dimension of the interpretation is added if we note that positions of control in the pro-

[24] This view is elaborated in H. Gintis, "Education, Technology, and Worker Productivity," *American Economic Association Proceedings,* May 1971, pp. 266–279. For other studies stressing the non-cognitive dimensions of the schooling experience, see T. Parsons, "The School Class as a Social System: Some of Its Functions in American Society," *Harvard Educational Review,* Vol. 29, No. 4 (Fall 1959), pp. 297–318; and R. Dreeben, *On What Is Learned in School* (Reading, Mass., 1968).

ductive hierarchy tend to be associated with positions of political influence. Given the disproportionate share of political power held by the upper class and their capacity to determine the accepted patterns of behavior and procedures, to define the national interest, and in general to control the ideological and institutional context in which educational decisions are made, it is not surprising to find that resources are allocated unequally among school tracks, between schools serving different classes, and between levels of schooling. The same configuration of power results in curricula, methods of instruction, and criteria of selection and promotion which confer benefits disproportionately on the children of the upper class.

It is not asserted here that the upper class controls the main decision-making bodies in education, although a good case could probably be made that this is so. The power of the upper class is hypothesized as existing in its capacity to define and maintain a set of rules of operation or decision criteria—"rules of the game"—which, though often seemingly innocuous and sometimes even egalitarian in their ostensible intent, have the effect of maintaining the unequal system.

Notes on the Political Economy of Racism

HAROLD M. BARON

The economic base of racism would have to be subjected to intensive analysis in order to get at the heart of the oppression of black people in modern America. If we employ the language of Nineteenth Century science, we can state that the economic deployment of black people has been conditioned by the operation of two sets of historical laws: the laws of capitalist development, and the laws of national liberation. These laws were operative in the slave era as well as at present. Today the characteristic forms of economic control and exploitation of black people take place within the institutional structure of a mature state capitalist system and within the demographic frame of the metropolitan centers. The economic activities of blacks are essentially those of wage (or salary) workers for the large corporate and

From Harold M. Baron, "The Demand for Black Labor: Historical Notes on the Political Economy of Racism," *Radical America*, Vol. 5, No. 2 (March-April 1971), pp. 1–40. Reprinted by permission of *Radical America*, 1878 Mass Ave., Cambridge, Mass. 02140.

bureaucratic structures that dominate a mature capitalist society. Thus today racial dynamics can be particularized as the working out of the laws of the maintenance of mature state capitalism and the laws of black liberation with the metropolitan enclaves (rather than a consolidated territorial area) as a base. . . .

The changes that took place in the economic deployment of black labor in World War II were clearly an acceleration of developments that had been under way since World War I. In a process of transition, at a certain point the quantity of change becomes so great that the whole set of relationships assume an entirely different character. Such a nodal point took place during World War II, and there resulted a transformation in the characteristic relations of institutional racism from agrarian thralldom to a metropolitan ghetto system.

Within a generation, few of the concrete economic or demographic forms of the old base remained. In 1940, over three-fourths of all blacks lived in the South, close to two-thirds lived in rural areas there, and just under half were still engaged in agriculture. By 1969, almost as many blacks lived outside the South as still resided in that region, and only 4% of the black laborers remained in agriculture, as they had left the farms at a much more rapid rate than whites. Today, only about a fifth of the total black population live in the rural areas and small towns of the South.

The United States, during the Twentieth Century, has become a distinctively urban nation—or, more accurately, a metropolitan nation with its population centered in the large cities and their surrounding configurations. The first three decades of this century witnessed the rapid urbanization of whites; the next three decades saw an even more rapid urbanization of blacks. In 1940 the proportion of the country's black population living in urban areas (49%) was the same as that proportion of whites had been in 1910. Within 20 years, almost three fourths of all blacks were urban dwellers, a higher proportion than the corresponding one for whites. More specifically, the black population has been relocated into the central cities of the metropolitan areas—in 1940, 34% of all blacks resided in central cities; in 1969, 55%. The larger cities were the points of greatest growth. In 1950 black people constituted one out of every eight persons in the central cities of the metropolitan areas of every size classification, and one out of every twenty in the suburbs. By 1969, black people constituted one out of every four in the central city populations of the large metropolitan areas (1,000,000 plus), and about one out of six in the medium-size metropolitan areas (250,000 to 1,000,000), while in the smaller-size metropolitan areas (below 250,000) and the suburbs the proportions remained constant. Today black communities form major cities in themselves, two with populations over 1,000,000, four between 500,000 and 1,000,000 and eight between 200,000 and 500,000. Newark and Washington D.C. already have black majorities, and several other major cities will most likely join their ranks in the next 10 years.

The displacement of blacks from Southern agriculture was only partially due to the pull of labor demand in wartime. Technological innovation, being a necessary condition of production, acted as an independent force to drive the tenants out of the cotton fields. The push off the land occurred in two phases. Initially, right after the war, the introduction of tractors and herbicides displaced the cotton hands from full-time to seasonal work at summer weeding and harvest. The now part-time workers moved from the farms to hamlets and small towns. During the 1950s mechanization of the harvest eliminated most of the black peasantry from agricultural employment and forced them to move to the larger cities for economic survival.

Elimination of the Southern black peasantry was decisive in changing the forms of racism throughout the entire region, for it meant the disappearance of the economic foundation on which the elaborate superstructure of legal Jim Crow and segregation had originally been erected. Not only did this exploited agrarian group almost vanish, but the power of the large landholders who expropriated the surplus it had produced diminished in relation to the growing urban and industrial interests. While the civil-rights movement and the heroic efforts associated with it were necessary to break the official legality of segregation, it should be recognized that in a sense this particular form of racism was already obsolete, as its base in an exploitative system of production had drastically changed. The nature of the concessions made both by the ruling class nationally and by the newer power groups of the South can be understood only in terms of this fuller view of history.

For the United States as a whole, the most important domestic development was the further elaboration and deepening of monopoly state capitalism. As the political economy has matured, technological and management innovation have become capital-saving as well as labor-saving. Capital accumulation declines as a proportion of the gross national product, and a mature capitalist economy enters into a post-accumulation phase of development. Under these conditions the disposal of the economic surplus becomes almost as great a problem as the accumulation of it. Corporations promote consumerism through increased sales effort, planned obsolescence, and advertising. The State meets the problem by increasing its own expenditures, especially in non-consumable military items, by providing monetary support to consumption through subsidies to the well-off, and by spending a certain amount on welfare for the working class and the poor. Markedly lower incomes would add to the surplus disposal problems and would create economic stagnation as well as risking the most disruptive forms of class struggle.

Working-class incomes have two basic minimum levels, or floors. One is that which can be considered the level of the good trade-union contract which has to be met even by non-union firms that bid in this section of the labor market. State intervention is usually indirect in the setting of these incomes, but has grown noticeably in the last few years. The other income floor is set by direct government action via minimum-wage and welfare legislation. In the Northern industrial states where trade unions are stronger, both these income floors tend to be higher than in rural and Southern states.

Although in the mature capitalist society both economic and political imperatives exist for a certain limiting of the exploitation of the working class as a whole, each corporation still has to operate on the basis of maximizing its profits. The fostering of a section of the working class that will have to work at the jobs that are paid at rates between those of the two income floors works to meet the needs of profit maximization. Other jobs that fall into this category are those that might pay at the collective bargaining contract level but are subject to considerable seasonal and cyclical unemployment, and those from which a high rate of production is squeezed under hard or hazardous conditions. In all the developed Western capitalist states, there exists a group of workers to fill the jobs that the more politically established sectors of the working class shun. These marginal workers generally are set apart in some way so that they lack the social or the political means of defending their interests. In Western Europe usually they are non-citizens coming from either Southern Europe or Northern Africa. In England they are colored peoples coming from various parts of the Empire. In the urban centers of the United States race serves to mark black and brown workers for filling in the undesirable slots.

Further, in the distribution of government transfer payments each class and status group strives to maximize its receipts. Therefore the powerless tend to receive a smaller proportion of these funds, and those that are delivered to them come in a manner which stigmatizes and bolsters political controls.

Specifically, in the metropolitan centers in America, there is a racial dual labor market structure. Side by side with the primary metropolitan job market in which firms recruit white workers and white workers seek employment, there exists a smaller secondary market in which firms recruit black workers and black workers seek jobs. In the largest metropolitan areas this secondary black market ranges from one-tenth to one-quarter of the size of the white market. For both the white and black sectors there are distinct demand and supply forces determining earnings and occupational distribution, as well as separate institutions and procedures for recruitment, hiring, training, and promotion of workers.

The distinctiveness of these two labor forces is manifested by many dimensions—by industry, by firm, by departments within firms, by occupation, and by geographical area. Within all industries, including government service, there are occupational ceilings for blacks. In a labor market like that of the Chicago metropolitan area, there are a number of small and medium-size firms in which the majority of the workers are black. However about two-thirds of the small firms and one-fifth of the medium ones hire no blacks at all. In larger firms a dual structure in the internal labor market marks off the position of the black worker along the same lines that exist in the metropolitan labor market.

A review of black employment in Chicago in 1966 finds that blacks tend to work in industries with lower wages, higher turnover, and higher unemployment. Further, they are also over-represented in the industries which exhibit sluggish growth and obviously less chance for advancement. Black men provide a third of the blue-collar workers in such industries as textiles, retail stores, primary metals, and local transportation, while in utilities, advertising, and communication they constitute less than 6%. Black women are even more concentrated in furnishing over half the blue-collar women workers in five industries—personal services, education, retail stores, hotels, and railroads.

In terms of internal labor market segregation, one of the Chicago firms best known as a fair-practice employer has a major installation located in the black community in which blacks constitute 20% of the blue-collar workers and less than 5% of the craftsmen and white-collar workers. A General Motors plant with 7500 workers is reported to have 40% black semi-skilled operatives, but only between 1% and 2% black craftsmen. A foundry firm will have one black clerk out of nearly 100 white-collar workers, while 80% of its blue-collar operators will be black.

The most detailed information we have on racial dualism for an internal labor market is for the Lackawanna plant of Bethlehem Steel Company near Buffalo. The Lackawanna plant is a major employer of black workers in the Buffalo labor market. In 1968 it employed 2600 out of a total black labor force of about 30,000 for the area. Within the plant blacks constituted about 14% of the work force, which runs in the neighborhood of 19,000. The majority of black employees were assigned to only five of the plant's departments, while only 15% of the whites were in the same units. Within the individual units, blacks were given either the hardest or the lowest-paying jobs. In the plant's Coke Oven Department blacks held 252 out of 343 of the labor jobs, while whites held 118 out of 119 craft jobs. Blacks predominated in the battery and coal-handling units, where the top job paid $3.12 an hour. Whites made up the bulk of the work force in the better paying by-products and heating units, where had hourly pay rates ranging up to $3.42 and $3.65.

Basic Steel is a high-labor-turnover industry. From April 1, 1966 to December 31, 1967 the Lackawanna plant hired about 7,000 workers. Black job-seekers obviously identified the firm as being active in this labor market. Although 30% to 50% of the job applicants were black, the initial screening ended up with only 20% blacks among those newly hired. Prospects were screened by a general aptitude test the passing score for which was not validated by any measure of performance. As the labor market tightened, the passing score lowered. About an eighth of those hired were hired without taking the test, and 96% of this category were whites. The Supervisor of Employment also gave clear preference to residents of Angola, a nearly all-white suburb. Once on the payroll, a majority of the newly hired blacks were assigned to one of the five departments in which most of the black workers already were placed. Only 20% of newly hired whites were assigned to these departments, all of which were among the hotter and dirtier locations in the plant.

The dual labor market operates to create an urban-based industrial labor reserve that provides a ready supply of workers in a period of labor shortage and can be politically isolated in times of relatively high unemployment. In a tight labor market the undesirable jobs that whites leave are filled out of this labor reserve so that in time more job categories are added to the black sector of the labor market. If the various forms of disguised unemployment and sub-employment are all taken into account, black unemployment rates can run as high as three or four times those of whites in specific labor markets in recession periods. The welfare and police costs of maintaining this labor reserve are high, but they are borne by the State as a whole and therefore do not enter into the profit calculations of individual firms.

This special exploitation of the black labor force also leads to direct economic gains for the various employers. Methodologically it is very difficult to measure exactly the extra surplus extracted due to wage discrimination, although in Chicago it has been estimated that unskilled black workers earn about 17% less on similar jobs than unskilled white workers of comparable quality. While in a historical sense the entire differential of wage income between blacks and whites can be attributed to discrimination, the employer realizes only that which takes place in the present in terms of either lesser wage payments or greater work output. Estimates of this realized special exploitation range on the order of 10% to 20% of the total black wage and salary income.

The subordinate status of the black labor market does not exist in isolation, but rather is a major part of a whole complex of institutional controls that constitute the web of urban racism. This distinctive modern form of racism conforms to the 300-year-old traditions of the culture of control for the oppression of black people, but now most of the controls are located within the major metropolitan institutional networks—such as the labor market, the housing market, the political system. As the black population grew in the urban centers a distinctive new formation developed in each of these institutional areas. A black ghetto and housing market, a black labor market, a black school system, a black political system, and a black welfare system came into being—not as parts of a self-determining community, but as institutions to be controlled, manipulated, and exploited. When the black population did not serve the needs of dominant institutions by providing a wartime labor reserve, they were isolated so that they could be regulated and incapacitated.

This model of urban racism has had three major components with regard to institutional structures: (1) Within the major institutional networks that operate in the city there have developed definable black sub-sectors which operated on a subordinated basis, subject to the advantage, control, and priorities of the dominant system. (2) A pattern of mutual reinforcement takes place between the barriers that define the various black sub-sectors. (3) The controls over the lives of black men are so pervasive that they form a system analogous to colonial forms of rule.

The history of the demand for black labor in the post-war period showed the continued importance of wartime labor scarcities. The new job categories gained during World War II essentially were transferred into the black sectors of the labor market. Some war industries, like shipbuilding, of course, dropped off considerably. In reconversion and the brief 1948–1949 recession blacks lost out disproportionately on the better jobs. However the Korean War again created an intense labor shortage, making black workers once more in demand, at least until the fighting stopped. The period of slow economic growth from 1955 to the early 1960s saw a deterioration in the relative position of blacks as they experienced very high rates of unemployment and their incomes grew at a slower rate than those of whites. The civil-rights protests had generated little in the way of new demand. Only the coincidence of the rebellions of Watts, Newark, and Detroit with the escalation of the Vietnam War brought about a sharp growth in demand for black labor.

All the available evidence indicates that there has been no structural change of any significance in the deployment of black workers, most especially in private industry. Certain absolute standards of exclusion in professional, management, and sales occupations have now been removed, but the total growth in these areas has been slight except where a black clientele is serviced, as in the education and health fields. The one significant new demand in the North has been that for women clerical workers. This arises from a shortage of this particular kind of labor in the central business districts, which, being surrounded by the black community, are increasingly geographically removed from white supplies of these workers. About 90% of Chicago's black female white-collar workers work either in their own communities or in the central business districts, and are not employed in the rapidly growing outlying offices. In the South the whole pattern of racial regulation in the major cities is shifting over to a Northern model, so that the basic situation of black workers in Atlanta or Memphis is approaching that of the North about a decade ago.

Until the uprisings in the mid-60s, management of racial affairs was carried out either by the unvarnished maintenance of the status quo (except when black workers were needed) or by an elaborate ritual of fair practices and equal employment opportunity. The latter strategy operated as a sort of sophisticated social Darwinism to make the rules of competition for the survival of the fittest more equitable. Actually it blurred institutional realities, channeling energies and perceptions into individualized findings of fact. The black protest movement finally forced a switch to a policy of affirmative action that is supported by legal encouragement. In either case no basic structures have actually been transformed. As a review of studies on the current racial status in several industries finds: "Over the long haul, however, it is apparent that the laws of supply and demand have exercised a greater influence on the quantitative employment patterns of blacks than have the laws of the land."

In the Cold War era the trade-union movement lost its innovative dynamism and became narrowly wage-oriented. Overwhelmingly, the net racial effect of the collective-bargaining agreements was to accept the given conditions in a plant. Only a very few unions, usually from the CIO, conducted any fights for the upgrading of black workers. More usual was the practice of neglecting shop grievances. Within union life itself the black officials who arose as representatives of their race were converted into justifiers of the union administration to the black workers. On the legislative and judicial fronts—that is, away from their day-to-day base of operations—national unions supported the programs of civil-rights organizations and the fair-employment symbolism. In fact by the early 1960s the racial strategies of national trade unions and those of the most-sophisticated corporate leadership had converged.

The actions of the black community itself were destined to become the decisive political initiator, not only in its own liberation struggles but on the domestic scene in general. From World War II through the Korean War the urban black communities were engaged in digesting the improvements brought about by the end of the depression and by the wartime job gains. Both bourgeois and trade-union leadership followed the forms of the New Deal-labor coalition, but the original substance of mass struggle was no longer present.

The destabilization of the whole agrarian society in the South created the conditions for new initiatives. The Montgomery bus boycott was to re-introduce mass political action into the Cold War era. The boldness of the civil-rights movement, plus the success of national liberation movements in the Third World, galvanized the black communities in the major cities. At first the forms of the Southern struggle were to predominate in pro-integration civil-rights actions. Then youth and workers were swept into the movement and re-defined its direction toward black self-determination. The mass spontaneity in the ghetto rebellions revealed the tremendous potential of this orientation.

The ghetto systems and the dual labor markets had organized a mass black proletariat, and had concentrated it in certain key industries and plants. In the decade after World War II the most important strategic concentration of black workers was in the Chicago packing houses, where they became the majority group. United Packinghouse Workers District I was bold in battles over conditions in the plants and supplied the basic leadership for militant protest on the South Side. Even though the UPW was the most advanced of all big national unions on the race question, a coalition of black officials and shop stewards had to wage a struggle against the leadership for substantive black control. This incipient nationalist faction was defeated in the union, and the big meat packers moved out of the city; but before it disappeared the movement indicated the potential of black-oriented working-class leadership. The Packinghouse Workers' concrete struggles contrasted sharply with the strategy of A. Philip Randolph, who set up the form of an all-black Negro American Labor Council and then subordinated its mass support to maneuvers at the top level of the AFL-CIO.

After the ghetto uprisings workers were to re-assert themselves at the point of production. Black caucuses and Concerned Workers' Committees sprang up across the country in plants and installations with large numbers of blacks. By this time the auto industry had created the largest concentration of black workers in the nation on its back-breaking production lines in Detroit. Driven by the peculiarities of the black labor market, the "big three" auto companies had developed the preconditions for the organization of the Dodge Revolutionary Union Movement (DRUM) and the League of Revolutionary Black Workers. The insertion onto this scene of a cadre that was both black-conscious and class-conscious, with a program of revolutionary struggle, forged an instrument for the militant working-class leadership of the Black Liberation Movement. The League also provides an exemplary model for proletarians among other oppressed groups, and might even be able to stimulate sections of the white working class to emerge from their narrow economistic orientation.

The ruling class is caught in its own contradictions. It needs black workers, yet the conditions of satisfying this need compel it to bring together the potential forces for the most effective opposition to its policies, and even for a threat to its very existence. Amelioration of once-absolute exclusionary barriers does not eliminate the black work force that the whole web of urban racism defines. Even if the capitalists were willing to forego their economic and status gains from racial oppression, they could not do so without shaking up all of the intricate concessions and consensual arrangements through which the State now exercises legitimate authority. Since the ghetto institutions are deeply intertwined with the major urban systems, the American Government does not even have the option of decolonializing by ceding nominal sovereignty that the British and French empires have both exercised. The racist structures cannot be abolished without an earthquake in the heartland. Indeed, for that sophisticated gentleman, the American capitalist, the demand for black labor has become a veritable devil in the flesh.

Questions for Discussion

1. What do you think of the statement by Lundberg that all corporation income taxes are ultimately passed on to the consumer?
2. Are there any reasons that justify an unequal distribution of income? If so, does our economic system reflect these reasons accurately?
3. Will a better moral approach to the problems of poverty and discrimination lead to a satisfactory solution to the problem?
4. Is the economic situation faced by blacks substantially different from that faced by other Americans? If so, why?

PART X

Government
and the
Quality of Life—
the Case of
Pollution

The "discovery" in the last few years of the present and increasingly foreboding ecological crisis has necessarily opened new vistas for the intrusion and elaboration of state economic power. While the social costs of industrial and consumer goods pollution had heretofore interested neither economists nor politicians and had received little regard from the public in general, concern about the environment and the effects of our economic system upon it began to grow in the late 1960s. Of necessity, no one could be in favor of pollution or ecological self-destruction and, equally, it became necessarily understood that the only agent capable with dealing with the problem was government itself, in some form or another. The question therefore was not "whether" or not government should take up the problem of polluted streams and air but "how" it should approach this "quality of life question." Even after a fair consensus developed that upheld the obvious but for some reason overlooked fact that pollution was uniquely connected to our business-profit system, it was (and is) by no means clear what the government attack on the problem should be. The argument to tax the polluters (to make them pay the community burden of cleaning up the atmosphere) seems reasonable enough in the abstract but how should such taxes be levied and collected so that they are not ultimately passed on to the consuming public; or, indeed, should they be paid by the public as the final user of the goods?

Such questions strike deeply at long cherished symbols of free enterprise business relations on the one hand and at matters of equity on the other. As is indicated in the first article by the President's Council of Economic

Advisers, there remains among government officials considerable concern as to the lengths to which government ought to go in intervention in market affairs and private property relations. It should be noted that these matters seem to take up much more "official" concern than the basic environmental and ecological problems themselves.

The second article, by Robert Heilbroner, presents a growing liberal-radical view of the issue. It lays a justifiable basis for the increasing concern for environmental issues and it proposes more extensive and "radical" governmental solutions to the problem. The solutions, while abusing some traditional capitalist views toward property rights, still are offered in a conventional context; that is, the author still believes that the elaboration of state controls can and will be made on behalf of society broadly and not just for special interests. Or, at least he believes theoretically that the ecological problem *can* be approached this way with desirable outcomes.

The last two selections are radical critiques. Some readers may be struck by what appears to be a certain fatalistic cynicism in these approaches, for neither holds out much hope for a solution through existing social and political institutions. The Barkley and Weissman article points out there is a certain phoniness to the recent ecological concerns, that the ecology movement is an "official" evasion of the crises caused by modern capitalism by directing efforts towards cleaning up the environment rather than cleaning up the system which fouls the environment. The two approaches, the authors hold, are definitely not the same. The Gellen article goes even further, pointing out that there are profits to be made by the new "pollution-industrial complex," those firms developing antipollution technology which will be purchased by the state to produce a cleaner atmosphere. Thus, the ecology problem becomes just another means for making social transfer payments to firms by the state, and passing ecology costs on to consumers.

Safeguarding the Environment

PRESIDENT'S COUNCIL OF
ECONOMIC ADVISERS

As the economy grows, more waste of various types is produced. This does not cause major problems as long as the population is widely dispersed and the environment is not overloaded. As the population is increasingly concentrated in urban areas, however, the assimilative capacity of the environment in these areas tends to be exceeded. It then becomes more and more important that these limited environmental resources be used to the best advantage.

While it might be tempting to say that no one should be allowed to do any polluting, such a ban would require the cessation of virtually all economic activity. Since society places a value both on material goods and on clean air and water, arrangements must be devised that permit the value we place on each to determine our choices. Additional industrial development, increased use of pesticides on farms, and a growing volume of municipal sewage mean dirtier water downstream and fewer opportunities for recreation. On the other hand, stricter rules for pollution control generally mean either higher taxes or higher prices for goods. What we seek, therefore, is a set of rules for use of the environment which balances the advantages of each activity against its costs in other activities forgone. We want to eliminate pollution only when the physical and aesthetic discomfort it creates and its damage to people and things are more costly than the value of the good things—the abundance of industrial or farm products and efficient transportation—whose production has caused the pollution.

One of the ways that the competing claims on environmental resources could be balanced is through the development of "new towns" and resort communities. In these cases, a developer essentially buys title to a whole community's environment. He then has an economic incentive to avoid excessive damage to that environment. If, for example, he lets a factory buy the right to locate in the community even though it would substantially damage the community's environment, the value of potential residential property will thereby be lowered. Only when the advantages of industrial activity, such as increased income, outweigh the environmental disadvantages would the

From the *President's Council of Economic Advisers Report, 1971.*

developer permit the factory to locate there. The same incentives would operate to limit pollution from such activities as municipal waste disposal.

The concept of unified development does not provide much guidance for solving pollution problems in areas that are already developed. With substantial capital invested in existing industrial facilities, a company that must pay large additional costs for pollution control may find continuing operations economically infeasible. A major change in liability for pollution costs may, in effect, expropriate the capital of some even while it enhances that of others. Nearby homeowners, on the other hand, may feel that pollution has always been harmful, and that its existence in the past does not justify its continuation.

This kind of dispute is central to the pollution problem and has become increasingly widespread as the various users of air and water seek to assert their claims to the limited environmental resources. A solution requires procedures and rules for the use of clean air and water that permit an orderly settlement of the competing claims on these limited resources, and that take account of the fact that these resources are not inexhaustible. The homeowner, the factory owner, and the farmer cannot simultaneously enjoy unlimited use of air and water. Industry and agriculture must recognize the new sense of urgency and concern about environmental problems. At the same time we must not overlook the fact that people also want more and more of the jobs and products of farms and factories.

Social Role of Property Rights

Problems similar to those arising from pollution have frequently been handled by granting private title to limited resources. Agricultural and forest land were once common property with poorly defined usage rights. As demands on these resources grew, their use by one party inflicted damage on others. The adjudication of conflicting claims to these resources by granting private title to them served the important social purpose of providing an incentive for these resources to be used more efficiently.

Air and water resources are harder to divide into meaningful private parcels than land. If each landowner had title to clean air around his property, a factory in New York that would emit air pollutants might have to deal with 8 million "property owners," making it difficult to operate any factories at all.

Because private property arrangements cannot be applied generally to our air and water resources, environmental problems connected with their use have to be solved within a framework of common property. The procedures and rules that we develop for resources regarded as common property must encourage their efficient use, just as would be true if they were private property.

A set of rules for the efficient use of air and water should not only permit no more fouling of air and water than we wish to tolerate, but it should also ensure that the tolerated degree of pollution occurs for the most productive reasons. The rules should also encourage the use of resources to limit the damage done by the pollution that is allowed. Finally, the rules and procedures should not themselves entail a higher cost of administration and enforcement than the cost of having no rules.

Specific Rules

As our society has become increasingly aware of the conflicting claims on air and water, specific rules have been developed for the use of these resources that recognize their limited nature. As early as 1899 a Federal law was passed regulating the disposal of waste in rivers and harbors. However, only with recent legal opinions and legislation has it become clear that the law could be used to reduce pollution, and the President has recently issued an Executive Order to use the law in this way.

Two problems must be faced in setting up rules for use of the environment. First, it must be decided how much pollution, if any, will be tolerated and under what circumstances changes in this amount will be permitted. Toward this end, the Federal Government has established the Environmental Protection Agency. This Agency, together with State and local authorities, develops standards for ambient air and water quality. These standards are statements of environmental quality goals considered desirable for particular areas or for the Nation as a whole. Since past arrangements, which imposed no cost on those who polluted the environment, led to excessive pollution, these air and water quality goals have uniformly sought reduction of pollution. Once such goals are developed, the next problem is to devise a system of rules for attaining them. Particular polluters must be led to change their actions so that, in fact, less pollution is produced. The Federal Government and other authorities have also been active in devising rules to implement attainment of environmental goals.

Foremost among the new rules has been the setting of Government standards applicable to particular pollution sources. Under this system, the Government requires that each source reduce its emissions of pollutants by an amount sufficient to keep the total of all emissions within the environmental quality standard. All sources are ordinarily required to reduce emissions by the same percentage. For example, under recently enacted amendments to the Clean Air Act of 1967, cars of the 1975 model year will have to reduce emissions of carbon monoxide and hydrocarbons by 90 per cent from 1970 levels. While such Government standards have been applied most extensively to automobiles, similar standards are now being developed and implemented for other pollution sources.

This system of Government standards provides one mechanism for attaining environmental goals that recognizes the increasing scarcity of environmental resources. If this system is to generate efficient results, the goal must, of course, be appropriate. That is, the control of emissions that is required at each source must produce a high enough quality of air and water so that further improvement is not worth the costs of further control. If Government standards are to achieve the best use of environmental resources, there must also be substantial uniformity of the cost of control among pollution sources. Where these costs differ, the same environmental quality could be attained more cheaply by having the source with low control costs undertake more control than the source with high costs; but this would not occur if uniform standards were applied to all sources. The standards might, of course, be made nonuniform to account for differences in control cost, but only at considerable administrative cost because the Government agency setting the standards would need detailed knowledge about many different pollution-causing activities. It is also difficult politically to set variable standards. Many, including of course the owner, would think it unfair to penalize a plant with low control costs for its efficiency in pollution control by imposing an especially tough standard on such a plant.

Differences in control cost were perhaps an unimportant problem when attention focused on automobile exhausts. While there are some differences among types of cars in the cost of controlling exhaust emissions, the common technology of the internal combustion engine limited these differences and seemed to justify the application of common standards to all cars. In other cases a pollutant may prove so damaging that a common standard, namely, an outright ban on all discharges, would also be called for even if there are differences in control costs. However, as attention focuses on industrial and agricultural pollutants that are not to be eliminated completely, differences in control cost will prove to be more of a problem. Particular pollutants are emitted from sources with diverse processes, sizes, and ages; and large differences in the cost of control can be expected. For example, sulphur oxides, which are one of the most damaging pollutants of the air, are emitted by electric powerplants, steel mills, nonferrous metal smelters, and home-heating systems. The differences in the size of these sources and the diversity of their processes make it almost certain that a given reduction of sulphur oxides cannot be accomplished at the same cost at each source. It is already known that there are economies of scale in sulphur oxide abatement, so that, for example, a given degree of control could be attained less expensively at one large powerplant than in many home-heating systems.

One way that differences in control costs could be taken into account would be to set "prices" for the use of the air and water. If each potential polluter were faced with a price for each unit of pollutant he discharged, he would have to compare this with the costs of pollution control in his particular circumstance. If control costs were relatively low, he would engage in extensive control to avoid paying the price being charged for polluting. If control costs were high, less control would be undertaken. Since sources with low control costs would carry out more than average control and those with high control costs less than average, a given level of environmental quality could be attained with expenditure of less productive resources than if all sources had to meet a common standard. At the same time, discovery of new techniques to control pollution would be encouraged, because every reduction in pollution would lower the payments for the right to emit pollutants. Of course, a price system, like a system of standards must be employed in a way that is consistent with environmental goals. The right to use air and water must be priced high enough so that the abatement encouraged improves the quality of the environment enough to justify the abatement expenses, while further improvement would not be worth additional expenditures.

There are three methods by which prices may be established for use of air and water: subsidies for control of pollution, charges for emissions of pollution (also called effluent fees), and sales of transferable environmental usage rights.

In the case of pollution abatement subsidies, the "price" paid by the polluter is the subsidy he forgoes. The more he fouls the air and water, the less he receives in subsidies. This approach can attain the efficiency inherent in a price system, but it entails substantial administrative as well as fiscal costs. In order to keep its subsidy payments down, the Government agency will have to incur the expense of ascertaining the level of pollution that would have occurred without any pollution control. As new products and processes are developed, this administrative task would grow more expensive, because in their case no record of past pollution would be available.

Alternatively charges could be levied on pollution. A charge on emissions of harmful substances would limit the amount of emissions indirectly. The higher the charge, the more a polluter would be willing to spend to avoid contaminating the environment (and thereby avoiding the charge). Another alternative would be an environmental usage certificate system. It would limit the amount of pollutants directly, but allow the price for pollution to be set indirectly. Under this system, as under a system of pollution standards, a Government agency would set a specific limit on the total amount of pollutants that could be emitted. It would then issue certificates which would each give the holder the right to emit some part of the total amount. Such certificates could be sold by the Government agency at auction and could be resold by owners. The Government auction and private resale market would thus establish a price on use of the environment. The more pollution a user engaged in, the more certificates he would have to buy. Groups especially concerned about the environment, such as conservation groups, would have a direct method of affecting the environment. They could themselves buy and hold some of the certificates, thus directly reducing the amount of emissions permitted and increasing the cost of pollution.

In general, any choice between emission charges and usage certificates should depend on which is easier to determine: the right price for pollution or the right quantity. If the amount of damage done by a pollutant can be measured easily and it appears that each unit of pollutant does roughly the same damage, an emission charge would be called for. If the damage per unit of pollutant may rise substantially with higher total emissions, a usage certificate system would be in order. Both the charge and the certificate approach would, like a system of standards, reduce the total amount of air and water pollution. However, by introducing a price mechanism, charges or certificates would allow the limited amount of tolerable pollution to be allocated efficiently when differences in the cost of control are present. Such efficiency would reduce the resource cost of pollution control and would therefore enable us to afford cleaner air and water than we could if common standards were imposed in the face of differences in control costs.

Pollution charges and certificates have not yet been widely used in this country, though some municipalities have levied charges on industrial sewage discharge. A system of water pollution charges has been used in the Ruhr basin for some time, and new proposals for pollution charges have been advanced in this country. This Administration has already proposed a tax on lead additives in gasoline which reduce the effectiveness of certain devices used to control auto exhaust emissions. This tax should encourage drivers to switch to unleaded or low-lead gasoline, refiners to produce such gasoline, and carmakers to equip their cars with the low-cost catalytic filters which work only with unleaded gasoline.

There is currently under study a charge on atmospheric emissions of sulphur oxides from combustion of fossil fuels. This charge would be sufficiently high to encourage substantial control of sulphur oxide emissions, and the consequent reduction of damage to health and property should substantially exceed the control costs.

A charge on sulphur oxide emissions provides a good illustration of one of the important benefits of a price system—namely, the information produced by prices about the most efficient way of handling pollution problems. Sulphur oxide emissions are now regulated by Government standards. The State of Washington, for instance, has proposed a standard whereby copper smelters there would be required to control 90 per cent of the sulphur content of copper ore entering smelters. This, according to a study done for the State, could be accomplished at a cost equal to about 2 cents per pound of copper (about 4 per cent of the price). The copper smelters there, however, claim that such a level of control is technologically impossible to attain, and that imposition of the standard would force the smelters to close. Such disputes over Government standards are not surprising where there is uncertainty over control costs. Advocates of the standard will tend to minimize its costs so that the chances of having the standard adopted are increased, while those facing the burden of complying with the standard have an incentive to overstate the costs so that chances are improved of having the standard, and hence their costs, lowered. In the absence of accurate independent information on the costs of control, such disputes are difficult to resolve.

Much of the gap in information could be eliminated quickly if an emission charge were instituted. If, for example, a charge were applied to smelters equivalent to 3 cents per pound of copper when emissions were not controlled, then with 90-per cent control the smelter would save about 2.7 cents in charges per pound of copper produced. If this 90-per cent control could indeed be achieved at a cost of 2 cents per pound, the smelter would not hesitate to incur such costs and thus avoid the larger charge. If, on the other hand, 90-per cent control were "technologically impossible" or cost much more than 2.7 cents per pound, the smelter would engage in less complete control. Perhaps 80-per cent control could be achieved more cheaply than the 2.4 cents in payments which this control would save. However, the company would still have an incentive to find new control methods that might be less costly than its remaining tax burden. Not only would the factual dispute be settled by this charge but incentives would be created for an efficient response to an environmental problem.

While transferable environmental usage certificates have the same kind of efficiency advantages as emission charges, they have not yet been applied to the solution of environmental problems. One area where their use may merit attention is the control of offshore dumping of waste, which constitutes a growing hazard to the environment. It is feared that damage, especially to food sources, may escalate sharply unless steps are taken to limit the waste dumped into the ocean. At the same time, the cost of alternative means of waste disposal differs among the many current users of the ocean. Ocean dumping could be limited and individual differences in the cost of control of dumping taken into account under a certificate system. This would require that anyone who wished to dump wastes in the ocean have a Government license to do so. The license would specify the amount and type of material that could be dumped at a particular ocean site, and the number of such licenses would be limited to permit no more dumping activity than is considered safe. These licenses could be auctioned off by the Government, and sold later by a purchaser who no longer required them.

The Administration has proposed legislation under which licenses will be required for ocean dumping. A possibility worth considering is to make such licenses transferable. If this were done, prospective ocean dumpers would either have to pay the going price for licenses or find a cheaper way of disposing of their waste products. Those who were able to find such alternatives would not buy the licenses; those for whom alternatives were very costly would purchase them. The Government's prime concern should, of course, be limited to the total amount and kind of dumping, not who is doing it.

As choices are made between applying Government standards and instituting prices, the grounds on which the choice is made must be kept clear. Prices for pollution have, for example, been regarded by some as a form of evasion of standards, as a "license to pollute." Actually every system of rules for use of the environment, other than outright and total prohibition of certain uses, involves granting someone the right or "license" for some polluting. The amount of pollution that results does not depend on which system of rules is adopted, but on how each is administered.

It is sometimes said that administration of emission charges is unduly complicated, since they must be varied continually as pollution damages change, and they require close measurement of the pollution against which the charge is to be made. When damage estimates can change frequently, administration of a system of charges can become costly, and a certificate or standard system would save this cost. However, the cost of measuring pollution is not unique to a charge or certificate system. It would be just as great if standards are to be enforced. If measurement of pollution is too expensive to permit an effective system of standards, charges, or licenses, we face a choice between outright prohibition of the pollution, tolerating the present level, or requiring adoption of some conventional control procedure.

Problems in the Application of Rules

As rules for the use of common property are developed, whether these are embodied in Government standards, emission charges, or usage certificates, several problems will have to be resolved. We shall, for example, have to decide at what level of Government the rules will be made. Since these rules require that the gains and losses entailed by different levels of environmental quality be weighed, the Government agency making the rules must be responsive to those who bear the gains and losses. This is especially important because part of the damage from pollution cannot be measured directly but depends on such things as the aesthetic preferences of those affected. As a practical matter, much of the damage from pollution will be "measured" by political pressures from those damaged. Many, though not all, pollution problems are local in character, and therefore determination of the appropriate level of environmental quality in these cases is likely to be more accurate if it is done locally rather than by the Federal Government.

Where the environmental effects of a particular activity are in fact nationwide, as is true when poisons enter the food chain in a river and eventually damage fish caught in a distant waterway, the Federal Government must ensure that certain minimum standards are set. Some degree of uniformity may also be desirable where the cost of altering a given production process or product to meet differing local standards is great. It is not clear, however, that the Federal role should extend beyond the setting of such minimum standards where most benefits and costs of pollution are borne locally. In such cases, a pollution source generates income as well as pollution damage in the community where it is located. The seriousness of the damage will depend in part on such local factors as topography, wind patterns, and population density; and the right amount of control will depend on how much income would be lost to achieve abatement. It would not be sensible to impose the same abatement costs on a factory or farm located in a lightly populated area or where the environment has substantial assimilative capacity as on one in an area without these favorable characteristics.

Where environmental damage crosses local political boundaries but is not national in scope, the appropriate Federal role might be to foster the creation of interstate agencies, such as regional air quality boards and river basin authorities, which would be responsible to residents of areas affected by common environmental problems. The recent amendments to the Clean Air Act of 1967 will permit interstate air quality agencies to set regional air quality standards, which will have to meet minimum Federal standards. It is important, however, that these minimum standards permit these agencies to adopt standards appropriate to local circumstances.

New rules for use of the environment are bound to affect competitive relationships within and among industries, localities, and nations. As industries are forced to bear the costs of using the environment, those who have high costs will lose part of their market to those with lower costs of using the environment. Inevitably, there will be pressures for Government action to prevent this reallocation of production. It should be realized, however, that such reallocation is necessary if environmental resources are to be used efficiently. Government interference with this process should therefore be limited to mitigating the transitional effects.

The same considerations apply internationally as well as domestically. Our high level of material wealth has caused us to place a higher value on clean air and water than they are assigned in countries which have lower incomes or where clean air and water may still be abundant. As this value becomes reflected in the costs imposed on our producers, those for whom the costs of pollution control are high will find it harder to compete with producers in countries where clean air and water are less valuable or where pollution is lower. The resulting reallocation of production among nations should benefit all nations. We will tend to concentrate on the production of goods which make small added demands on our valuable environmental resources, while other countries will produce goods which increase the use of their relatively abundant environmental resources or whose lower incomes make growing industrialization more urgent than extensive control of damage to their environment. International agreements to restrict this reallocation would, however, be desirable when pollutants emitted in one country damage residents of another.

Ecological Armageddon

ROBERT HEILBRONER

Ecology has become the Thing. There are ecological politics, ecological jokes, ecological bookstores, advertisements, seminars, teach-ins, buttons. The automobile, symbol of ecological abuse, has been tried, sentenced to death, and formally executed in at least two universities (replete with burial of one victim). Publishing companies are fattening on books on the sonic boom, poisons in the things we eat, perils loose in the garden, the dangers of breathing. The *Saturday Review* has appended a regular monthly Ecological Supplement. In short, the ecological issue has assumed the dimensions of a vast popular fad, for which one can predict with reasonable assurance the trajectory of all such fads—a period of intense general involvement, followed by growing boredom and gradual extinction, save for a die-hard remnant of the faithful.

This would be a tragedy, for I have slowly become convinced during the last twelve months that the ecological issue is not only of primary and lasting importance, but that it may indeed constitute the most dangerous and difficult challenge that humanity has ever faced. Since these are very large statements, let me attempt to substantiate them by drawing freely on the best single descriptive and analytic treatment of the subject that I have yet seen, *Population, Resources, Environment* by Paul and Anne Ehrlich of Stanford University. Rather than resort to the bothersome procedure of endlessly citing their arguments in quotation marks, I shall take the liberty of reproducing their case in a rather free paraphrase, as if it were my own, until we reach the end of the basic argument, after which I shall make clear some conclusions that I believe lie implicit in their work.

Ultimately, the ecological crisis represents our belated awakening to the fact that we live on what Kenneth Boulding has called, in the perfect phrase, our Spaceship Earth. As in all spaceships, sustained life requires that a meticulous balance be maintained between the capability of the vehicle to support life and the demands made by the inhabitants of the craft. Until quite recently, those demands have been well within the capability of the ship, in its ability both to supply the physical and chemical requirements for continued existence and to absorb the waste products of the voyagers. This is not to say that the earth has been generous—short rations have been the lot of mankind for most of its history—nor is it to deny the recurrent advent of local ecological crises—witness the destruction of whole areas like the erst-while granaries of North Africa. But famines have passed and there have always been new areas to move to. The idea that the earth as a whole was overtaxed is one that is new to our time.

For it is only in our time that we are reaching the limit of earthly carrying capacity, not on a local but on a global basis. Indeed, as will soon become clear, we are well past that capacity, provided that the level of resource intake and waste output represented by the average American or European is taken as a standard to be achieved by all humanity. To put it bluntly, if we take as the price of a first-class ticket the resource requirements of those pas-sengers who travel in the Nothern Hemisphere of the Spaceship, we have now reached a point at which the steerage is condemned to live forever—or at least within the horizon of the technology presently visible—at a second-class level; or a point at which a considerable change in living habits must be imposed on first class if the ship is ever to be converted to a one-class cruise.

This strain on the carrying capacity of the vessel results from the contem-porary confluence of three distinct developments, each of which places tre-mendous or even unmanageable strains on the life-carrying capability of the planet and all of which together simply overload it. The first of these is the enormous strain imposed by the sheer burgeoning of population. The statistics of population growth are by now very well known: the earth's passenger list is growing at a rate that will give us some four billion humans by 1975, and that threatens to give us eight billion by 2010. I say "threatens," since it is likely that the inability of the earth to carry so large a group will result in an actual population somewhat smaller than this, especially in the steerage, where the growth is most rapid and the available resources least plentiful.

We shall return to the population problem later. But meanwhile a second strain is placed on the earth by the simple cumulative effect of *existing* tech-nology (combustion engines, the main industrial processes, present-day agri-cultural techniques, etc.). This strain is localized mainly in the first-class por-tions of the vessel where each new arrival on board is rapidly given a standard complement of capital equipment and where the rate of physical and chemical resource transformation per capita steadily mounts. The strain consists of the limited ability of the soil, the water, and the atmosphere of these favored regions to absorb the outpourings of these fast-growing industrial processes.

The most dramatic instance of this limited absorptive power is the rise in the carbon dioxide content of the air due to the steady growth of (largely industrial) combustion. By the year 2000, it seems beyond dispute that the CO_2 content of the air will have doubled, raising the heat-trapping properties of the atmosphere. This so-called greenhouse effect has been predicted to raise mean global temperatures sufficiently to bring catastrophic potential consequences. One possibility is a sequence of climatic changes resulting from a melting of the Arctic ice floes that would result in the advent of a new Ice Age; another is the slumping of the Antarctic ice cap into the sea with a consequent tidal wave that could wipe out a substantial portion of mankind and raise the sea level by 60 to 100 feet.

These are all "iffy" scenarios whose present significance may be limited to alerting us to the immensity of the ecological problem; happily they are of sufficient uncertainty not to cause us immediate worry (it is lucky they are, because it is extremely unlikely that all the massed technological and human energy on earth could arrest such changes once they began). Much closer to home is the burden placed on the earth's carrying capacity by the sheer requirements of a spreading industrial activity for the fuel and mineral resources needed to maintain the going rate of output per person in the first-class cabins. To raise the existing (not the anticipated) population of the earth to American standards would require the annual extraction of 75 times as much iron, 100 times as much copper, 200 times as much lead, and 250 times as much tin as we now take from the earth. Only the known reserves of iron allow us to entertain such fantastic rates of mineral exploitation (and the capital investment needed to bring about such mining operations is in itself staggering to contemplate). All the other requirements exceed by far all known or reasonably anticipated ore reserves. And, to repeat, we have taken into account only today's level of population: to equip the prospective passengers of the year 2010 with this amount of basic raw material would require a doubling of all the above figures.

I will revert later to the consequences of this prospect. First, however, let us pay attention to the third source of overload, this one traceable to the special environment-destroying potential of newly developed technologies. Of these the most important—and if it should ever come to full-scale war, of course the most lethal—is the threat posed by nuclear radiation. I shall not elaborate on this well-known (although not well-believed) danger, pausing to point out only that a nuclear holocaust would in all likelihood exert its principal effect in the Northern Hemisphere. The survivors in the South would be severely hampered in their efforts at reconstruction not only because most of the easily available resources of the world have already been used up, but because most of the technological know-how would have perished along with the populations up North.

But the threats of new technology are by no means limited to the specter of nuclear devastation. There is, immediate at hand, the known devastation of the new chemical pesticides that have now entered more or less irreversibly into the living tissue of the world's population. Most mothers' milk in the United States today—I now quote the Ehrlichs verbatim—"contains so much DDT that it would be declared illegal in interstate commerce if it were sold as cow's milk"; and the DDT intake of infants around the world is twice the daily allowable maximum set by the World Health Organization. We are already, in other words, being exposed to heavy dosages of chemicals whose effects we know to be dangerous, with what ultimate results we shall have to wait nervously to discover. (There is food for thought in the archaeological evidence that one factor in the decline of Rome was the systematic poisoning of upper-class Romans from the lead with which they lined their wine containers.)

But the threat is not limited to pesticides. Barry Commoner predicts an agricultural crisis in the United States within fifty years from the action of our fertilizers, which will either ultimately destroy soil fertility or lead to pollution of the national water supply. At another corner of the new technology, the SST threatens not only to shake us with its boom, but to affect the amount of cloud cover (and climate) by its contrails. And I have not even mentioned the standard pollution problems of smoke, industrial effluents into lakes and rivers, or solid wastes. Suffice it to report that a 1968 UNESCO Conference concluded that man has only about twenty years to go before the planet starts to become uninhabitable because of air pollution alone. Of course "starts to" is imprecise; I am reminded of a cartoon of an industrialist looking at his billowing smokestacks, in front of which a forlorn figure is holding up a placard that says: "We have only 35 years to go." The caption reads, "Boy, that shook me up for a minute. I thought it said 3 to 5 years."

I have left until last the grimmest and gravest threat of all, speaking now on behalf of the steerage. This is the looming inability of the great green earth to bring forth sufficient food to maintain life, even at the miserable threshold of subsistence at which it is now endured by perhaps a third of the world's population. The problem here is the very strong likelihood that population growth will inexorably outpace whatever improvements in fertility and productivity we will be able to apply to the earth's mantle (including the watery fringes of the ocean where sea "farming" is at least technically imaginable). Here the race is basically between two forces: on the one hand, those that give promise that the rate of population increase can be curbed (if not totally halted); and on the other, those that give promise of increasing the amount of sustenance we can wring from the soil. . . .

I have no doubt that one can fault bits and pieces of the Ehrlichs' analysis, and there is a note of determined pessimism in their work that leads me to suspect (or at least hope) that there is somewhat more time for adaptation than they suggest. Yet I do not see how their basic conclusion can be denied. Beginning within our lifetimes and rising rapidly to crisis proportions in our children's, humankind faces a challenge comparable to none in its history, with the possible exception of the forced migration of the Ice Age. It is with the responses to this crisis that I wish to end this essay, for telling and courageous as the Ehrlichs' analysis is, I do not believe that even they have fully faced up to the implications that their own findings present.

The first of these I have already stated: it is the clear conclusion that the underdeveloped countries can *never* hope to achieve parity with the developed countries. Given our present and prospective technology, there are simply not enough resources to permit a "Western" rate of industrial exploitation to be expanded to a population of four billion—much less eight billion—persons. It may well be that most of the population in the underdeveloped world has no ambition to reach Western standards—indeed, does not even know that such a thing as "development" is on the agenda. But the elites of these nations, for all their rhetorical rejection of Western (and especially American) styles of life, do tend to picture a Western standard as the ultimate end of their activites. As it becomes clear that such an objective is impossible, a profound reorientation of views must take place within the underdeveloped nations.

What such a reorientation will be it is impossible to say. For the near future, the outlook for the most population-oppressed areas will be a continuous battle against food shortages, coupled with the permanent impairment of the intelligence of much of the surviving population due to protein deficiencies in childhood. This pressure of population may lead to aggressive searches for *Lebensraum;* or, as I have frequently written, may culminate in revolutions of desperation.

In the long run, of course, there is the possibility of considerable growth (although nothing resembling the attainment of a Western standard of consumption). But no quick substantial improvement in their condition seems feasible within the next generation at least. The visions of Sir Charles Snow or the Soviet academician Sakharov for a gigantic transfer of wealth from the rich nations to the poor (20 per cent of GNP is proposed) are simply fantasies. Since much of GNP is spatially nontransferable or inappropriate, such a huge levy against GNP would imply shipments of up to 50 per cent of much movable output. How this enormous flood of goods would be transported, allocated, absorbed, or maintained—*not to mention relinquished by the donor countries*—is nowhere analyzed by the proponents of such vast aid.

The implications of the ecological crisis for the advanced nations are not any less severe, although they are of a different kind. For it is clear that free industrial growth is just as disastrous for the Western nations as free population growth for those of the East and South. The worship in the West of a growing Gross National Product must be recognized as not only a deceptive but a very dangerous avatar; Kenneth Boulding has begun a campaign, in which I shall join him, to label this statistical monster Gross National Cost.

The necessity to bring our economic activities into a sustainable relationship with the resource capabilities and waste absorption properties of the world will pose two problems for the West. On the simpler level, a whole series of technological problems must be met. Fume-free transportation must be developed on land and air. The cult of disposability must be replaced by that of reusability. Population stability must be attained through tax and other inducements, both to conserve resources and to preserve reasonable population densities. Many of these problems will tax our ingenuity, technical and socio-political, but the main problem they pose is not whether, but *how soon* they can be solved.

But there is another, deeper question that the developed nations face—at least those that have capitalist economies. This problem can be stated as a crucial test as to who was right—John Stuart Mill or Karl Marx. Mill maintained, in his famous *Principles of Economics,* that the terminus of capitalist evolution would be a stationary state, in which the return to capital had fallen to insignificance, and a redistributive tax system would be able to capture any flows of income to the holders of scarce resources, such as land. In effect, he prophesied the transformation of capitalism, in an environment of abundance, into a balanced economy, in which the capitalist, both as the generator of change and as the main claimant on the surplus generated by change, would in effect undergo a painless euthanasia.

The Marxian view is of course quite the opposite. The very essence of capitalism, according to Marx, is expansion—which is to say, the capitalist, as a historical "type," finds his *raison d'etre* in the insatiable search for additional money-wealth gained through the constant growth of the economic system. The idea of a "stationary" capitalism is, in Marxian eyes, a contradiction in terms, on a logical par with a democratic aristocracy or an industrial feudalism.

Is the Millian or the Marxian view correct? I do not think that we can yet say. Some economic growth is certainly compatible with a stabilized rate of resource use and disposal, for growth could take the form of the expenditure of additional labor on the improvement (aesthetic or technical) of the national environment. Indeed, insofar as education or cultural activity are forms of national output that require little resource use and result in little waste product, national output could be indefinitely expanded through these and similar activities. But there is no doubt that the main avenue of traditional capitalist accumulation would have to be considerably constrained; that net investment in mining and manufacturing would effectively cease; that the rate and kind of technological change would need to be supervised and probably greatly reduced; and that as a consequence, the flow of profits would almost certainly fall.

Is this imaginable within a capitalist setting—that is, in a nation in which the business ideology permeates the views of nearly all groups and classes, and establishes the bounds of what is possible and natural, and what is not? Ordinarily I do not see how such a question could be answered in any way but negatively, for it is tantamount to asking a dominant class to acquiesce in the elimination of the very activities that sustain it. But this is an extraordinary challenge that may evoke an extraordinary response. Like the challenge posed by war, the ecological crisis affects all classes, and therefore may be sufficient to induce sociological changes that would be unthinkable in ordinary circumstances. The capitalist and managerial classes may see—

perhaps even more clearly than the consuming masses—the nature and nearness of the ecological crisis, and may recognize that their only salvation (as human beings, let alone privileged human beings) is an occupational migration into governmental or other posts of power, or they may come to accept a smaller share of the national surplus supply simply because they recognize that there is no alternative. When the enemy is nature, in other words, rather than another social class, it is at least imaginable that adjustments could be made that would be impossible in ordinary circumstances.[1]

There is, however, one last possibility to which I must also call attention. It is the possibility that the ecological crisis will simply result in the decline or even destruction of Western civilization, and of the hegemony of the scientific-technological view that has achieved so much and cost us so dearly. Great challenges do not always bring great responses, especially when those responses must be sustained over long periods of time and require dramatic changes in life styles and attitudes. Even educated men today are able to deny the reality of the crisis they face: there is wild talk of farming the seas, of transporting men to the planets, of unspecified "miracles" of technology that will avert disaster. Glib as they are, however, at least these suggestions have a certain responsibility when compared to another and much more worrisome response: *Je m'en fiche.* Can we really persuade the citizens of the Western world, who are just now entering the heady atmosphere of a high consumption way of life, that conservation, stability, frugality, and a deep concern for the distant future must now take priority over the personal indulgence for which they have been culturally prepared and which they are about to experience for the first time? Not the least danger of the ecological crisis, as I see it, is that tens and hundreds of millions will shrug their shoulders at the prospects ahead ("What has posterity ever done for us?"), and that the increasingly visible approach of ecological Armageddon will bring not repentance but Saturnalia.

Yet I cannot end this essay on such a note. For it seems to me that the ecological enthusiasts may be right when they speak of the deteriorating environment as providing the *possibility* for a new political rallying ground. If a new New Deal, capable of engaging both the efforts and the beliefs of this nation, is the last great hope to which we cling in the face of what seems otherwise to be an inevitable gradual worsening and coarsening of our style of life, it is possible that a determined effort to arrest the ecological decay might prove to be its underlying theme. Such an issue, immediate in the experience of all, carries an appeal that might allow vast improvements to be worked in the American environment, both urban and industrial. I cannot estimate the likelihood of such a political awakening, dependent as these mat-

[1] Let me add a warning that it is not only capitalists who must make an unprecedented ideological adjustment. Socialists must also come to terms with the abandonment of the goal of industrial superabundance on which their vision of a transformed society rests. The stationary equilibrium imposed by the constraints of ecology requires at the very least a reformulation of the kind of economic society toward which socialism sets its course.

ters are on the dice of personality and the outcome of events at home and abroad. But however slim the possibility of bringing such a change, it does at least make the ecological crisis, unquestionably the gravest long-run threat of our times, potentially the source of its greatest short-term promise.

The Eco-Establishment

KATHERINE BARKLEY
AND STEVE WEISSMAN

The environment bandwagon is not as recent a phenomenon as it seems. It began to gather momentum back in the mid-'60's under the leadership of Resources for the Future. "The relationship of people to resources, which usually has been expressed in terms of quantity, needs to be restated for modern times to emphasize what is happening to the quality of resources," warned RFF President Joseph L. Fisher in his group's 1964 report. "The wide variety of threats to the quality of the environment may well embrace the gravest U.S. resources problem for the next generation." The following year, Resources for the Future established a special research and educational program in environmental quality, funded with a $1.1 million grant from its parent organization, the Ford Foundation.

Created by Ford in the early '50's during the scare over soaring materials costs, RFF had just made its name in conservation by organizing the Mid-Century Conference on Resources for the Future, the first major national conservation conference since Teddy Roosevelt and Gifford Pinchot staged the National Governors' Conference in 1908. Held in 1953, the Mid-Century Conference mustered broad support from both the country's resource users and conservers for the national conservation policy already spelled out by President Truman's Materials Policy Commission. It was this Commission, headed by William S. Paley (board chairman of CBS and a founding director of RFF), which had openly affirmed the nation's inalienable right to extract cheap supplies of raw materials from the underdeveloped countries, and which set the background for Eisenhower and Dulles' oft-quoted concern over the fate of the tin and tungsten of Southeast Asia. Insuring adequate supplies of resources for the future became a conservationist byword.

By the mid-'60's, Resources for the Future had begun to broaden its concern to include resource quality, thus setting the tone for a decade of conser-

From *Ramparts,* May 1970, © Ramparts Magazine, Inc., 1970.

vationist rhetoric and behavior. The trustees of the Ford Foundation, an executive committee of such international resource users and polluters as Esso and Ford Motor, established a separate Resources and Environment Division which, since 1966, has nourished such groups as Open Space Action Committee, Save-the-Redwoods League, Massachusetts Audubon Society, Nature Conservancy, and the Environmental Defense Fund. A year later, the Rockefeller Foundation set up an Environmental Studies Division, channelling money to the National Academy of Science and RFF and to Laurance Rockefeller's own pet project, the Conservation Foundation.

The conservationist-planners' new concern over threats to the quality of resources, and to life itself, was actually an outgrowth of their earlier success in assuring cheap and plentiful raw materials. It had become clear that supplies of resources would be less a problem than the immense amount of waste generated as a by-product of those now being refined. The more industry consumed, the more it produced and sold, the larger and more widespread the garbage dumps. Rivers and lakes required costly treatment to make water suitable for use in homes and industry. Smoggy air corroded machines, ruined timberlands, reduced the productivity of crop lands and livestock—to say nothing of its effect on the work capacity of the average man. Pesticides were killing more than pests, and raising the spectre of cumulative disaster. Cities were getting noisier, dirtier, uglier and more tightly packed, forcing the middle class to the suburbs and the big urban landowners to the wall. "Ugliness," Lyndon Johnson exclaimed sententiously, "is costly."

This had long been obvious to the conservationists. Something had to be done, and the elite resource planners took as their model for action the vintage 1910 American conservation movement, especially its emphasis on big business cooperation with big government.

When the 1890 census officially validated the fact that the frontier was closed, a generation of business and government leaders realized with a start that the American Eden had its bounds. Land, timber and water were all limited, as was the potential for conflicts over their apportionment. What resources should timbermen, grazers or farmers exploit? What should be preserved as a memory of the American past? Who would decide these questions? The conservationists—Teddy Roosevelt, Chief Forester Gifford Pinchot and some of the bigger timber, grazing and agricultural interests—pushed heavily for a new policy to replace the crude and wanton pillage which had been part of the frontier spirit. While preservationists like John Muir were fighting bitterly against any and all use of wild areas by private interests, the conservationists wanted only to make sure that the environment would be exploited with taste and efficiency.

Roosevelt and his backers won out, of course. And the strategy they used is instructive: failing initially to muster congressional support for their plan, they mobilized a broadly based conservation movement, supposedly to regulate the private interests which they in fact represented. Backed by the widespread public support it had whipped up, the conservationist juggernaut then began to move the country toward a more regulated—but still private—exploitation of its riches.

Of course, the private interests which had helped draft this policy also moved—to staff the regulatory agencies, provide jobs for retiring regulators, and generally to put the right man in the right niche most of the time. Within short order, the regulatory agencies were captives of the interests they were supposed to regulate, and they were soon being used as a screen which kept the public from seeing the way that small interests were squeezed out of the competition for resources. Their monopoly position thus strengthened by regulatory agencies, these large interests found it easy to pass the actual costs of regulation on to the citizen consumer.

The old American conservation movement had reacted out of fear over resource scarcities; the new movement of the mid-'60's feared, as well, the destruction of resource quality. And the corporation conservationists and their professional planners in organizations like Resources for the Future once again looked to government regulations as an answer to the difficulties they foresaw. Only this time the stakes were much higher than they had been at the early part of the century. Many of the resource planners want an all-encompassing environmental agency or Cabinet level Department of Resources, Environment and Population. Holding enormous power over a wide range of decisions, this coordinating apparatus would be far more convenient for the elite than the present array of agencies, each influenced by its own interest groups.

Who will benefit from this increased environmental consciousness and who will pay is already quite clear to business, if not to most young ecology activists. "The elite of business leadership," reports *Fortune,* "strongly desire the federal government to step in, set the standards, regulate all activities pertaining to the environment, and help finance the job with tax incentives." The congressional background paper for the 1968 hearings on National Policy on Environmental Quality, prepared with the help of Rockefeller's Conservation Foundation, spells out the logic in greater detail: "Lack of national policy for the environment has now become as expensive to the business community as to the Nation at large. In most enterprises, a social cost can be carried without undue burden if all competitors carry it alike. For example, industrial waste disposal costs can, like other costs of production, be reflected in prices to consumers. But this becomes feasible only when public law and administration put all comparable forms of waste-producing enterprises under the same requirements." Only the truly powerful could be so candid about their intention to pick the pocket of the consumer to pay for the additional costs they will be faced with.

The resource planners are also quite frank about the wave of subsidies they expect out of the big clean-up campaign. "There will have to be a will to provide funds," explains Joseph Fisher, "to train the specialists, do the research and experimentation, build the laws and institutions through which more rapid progress [in pollution control] can be made, and of course, build the facilities and equipment." The coming boondoggles—replete with tax incentives, direct government grants, and new products—will make the oil depletion allowance seem tame. And what's more, it will be packaged as a critical social service.

The big business conservationists will doubtless be equally vocal about the need for new bond issues for local water and sewage treatment facilities; lead crusades to overcome reluctance of the average citizen to vote "yes" on bond measures; and then, as bondholders themselves, skim a nice tax-free six or seven per cent off the top.

It isn't just the citizen and taxpayer who will bear the burden, however. Bedraggled Mother Nature, too, will pay. Like the original conservation movement it is emulating, today's big business conservation is not interested in preserving the earth; it is rationally reorganizing for a more efficient rape of resources (e.g., the export of chemical-intensive agribusiness) and the production of an even grosser national product.

The seeming contradictions are mind-boggling: industry is combating waste so it can afford to waste more; it is planning to produce more (smog-controlled) private autos to crowd more highways, which means even more advertising to create more "needs" to be met by planned obsolescence. Socially, the result is disastrous. Ecologically, it could be the end.

Why don't the businessmen simply stop their silly growthmanship? They can't. If one producer slowed down in the mad race, he'd be eaten up by his competitors. If all conspired together to restrain growth permanently, the unemployment and cutbacks would make today's recession look like full employment, and the resulting unrest would make today's dissent look like play time at Summerhill.

They began in the mid-'60's in low key, mobilizing the academicians, sprinkling grants and fellowships at the "better" schools, and coordinating research efforts of Resources for the Future, the Conservation Foundation, RAND, Brookings Institution, the National Academy of Science and the Smithsonian Institution. Major forums were held in 1965 and 1966 on "The Quality of the Environment" and "Future Environments of North America." Research findings were programmed directly into industrial trade associations and business firms.

Then the resource people put their men and programs in the official spotlight: Laurance Rockefeller (founder of and major donor to the Conservation Foundation and also a director of RFF) chaired both the White House Conference on Natural Beauty and the Citizens' Advisory Committee on Recreation and Natural Beauty (which Nixon has rechristened his Citizens' Advisory Committee on Environmental Quality). Conservation Foundation President Russell Train headed up Nixon's Task Force on Resources and

Environment, with help from Fisher and several other directors of RFF and the Conservation Foundation, and then became Undersecretary of Interior.

Then the media were plugged in, an easy task for men who have in their hands the direction of CBS, National Educational Television, *Time-Life-Fortune, Christian Science Monitor, New York Times* and Cowles publications, as well as many of the trade journals and conservation magazines. Independent media, seeing that environment was now news, picked up and broadcast the studies which the conservation elite had produced. Public opinion leaders told their public, in *Business Week's* words, "to prepare for the approval of heavy public and private spending to fight pollution."

Finally, the grass roots were given the word. RFF, Ford and Rockefeller had long worked with and financed the old-time conservation groups, from Massachusetts Audubon to the Sierra Club, and now the big money moved beyond an appreciation of wilderness to a greater activism. When, for example, David Brower broke with the Sierra Club, it was Robert O. Anderson of Atlantic-Richfield and RFF who gave him $200,000 to set up Friends of the Earth (prudently channeling the donation through the organization's tax-exempt affiliate, the John Muir Institute).

When Senator Gaylord Nelson and Congressman Pete McCloskey got around to pushing the National Teach-In, it was the Conservation Foundation, the Audubon Society and the American Conservation Association which doled out the money while Friends of the Earth was putting together *The Environmental Handbook,* meant to be the Bible of the new movement.

The big business conservationists and their professionals didn't buy off the movement; they built it.

Ecology activists out picketing a polluter or cleaning up a creek will have total freedom to make up their own minds about the threats to our environment, and they will have every right to choose their own course of constructive action. Yet they will surely never get a dime from Robert Anderson, or even a farthing from Ford or Rockefeller. And so far, the grass-roots ecology movement has done nothing but echo the eco-elite.

Ecology, unlike most of the fractured scientific field, is holistic. It talks of life and its environment as a totality: how organisms relate to each other and to the system which provides their life-support system. As a discipline applied to human affairs, then, ecology should help us get a whole view of our natural and social environment—from oxygen cycles to business cycles, from the jeopardized natural environment to the powerful institutional environment which creates that jeopardy. If it revealed these interconnections, ecology would become, as it has been called, a "subversive science," subverting the polluters and resource-snatchers who now control the conservation of the nation's wealth. It would point the finger not simply at profit-making polluters or greedy consumers, but at the great garbage-creation system itself—the corporate capitalist economy.

But this is a far cry from the ecology movement as we have inherited it. Ecology, the science of interconnections, becomes a matter of cleaning up beaches and trying to change individuals' habits and attitudes, while ignoring the institutions which created them and practically all environmental damage.

The grass-roots ecology groups do have politics—the politics of consumer boycotts, shareholder democracy and interest group pluralism, all of which show a wonderfully anachronistic faith in the fairness of the market, political and economic. "If Dow pollutes," say the boycotters, "then we just won't buy Saran Wrap." If Super Suds won't make biodegradable soap, we'll buy Ivory. If Ford and Chevy won't make steam cars, we'll buy Japanese imports. From the planned obsolescence in automobiles, to 20 brands of toothpaste, much of what industry produces is insulting to the intelligence while also serving no real need; it is waste, to say nothing of the enormous pollution entailed in overproduction.

Consumer sovereignty has gone the way of the dodo, its passing noted two decades back by that stalwart defender of the new corporate capitalism, John Kenneth Galbraith. Consumers just don't control what gets produced, or how. To educate or build support for some stronger action, boycotts, like the picket line, work well. But to change production habits, an ecology movement will really have to pull the big plug at the other end of the TV transmitter, or better, at the production line itself.

Failing in the economic arena, the ecology groups can of course try their hand directly in the political marketplace. Oil has its lobby, the auto manufacturers theirs. Why not a People's Lobby? Californians have already created one, which is now pushing in Sacramento for a referendum "to make the polluters pay." The Environmental Defense League, geared primarily to the court system, is also defending the environment in Congress. The Sierra Club has already lost its tax-exempt status for being too political, and a number of the older conservation groups are pushing new, streamlined legislation. The strategy seems to be paying off, winning victories here and there. Most of the victories, however, merely strengthen the regulatory agencies, which, after public vigilance peters out, will become tools of the big corporations.

Where boycotts and stockholder strategies simply fail, the interest group politics may lead the ecology movement off the edge of a very well-conserved cliff. Eco-catastrophe threatens to kill us all—and Mother Nature, too. But to engage in the give-and-take of interest group politics, the ecologists must grant serious consideration to and must compromise with the oil interests, auto manufacturers and other powerful business groups. Standard Oil gets Indonesia only if they will market that country's prized sulphur-free oil here; the auto makers can keep producing their one-man-one-car civilization in return for making additional profit (and apparent compromise) on smog control. The world is dying: write your congressman today.

From lobbying, the eco-groups will move into the nearest election, trying to put Paul Ehrlich or David Brower in office. But elections aren't won on single issues. Allies must be wooed, coalitions built. Already parochial and out of sympathy with the blacks and other out-groups, the environmentalists, anxious to infiltrate the electoral system, will become even more respectable and more careful to avoid contamination by "extreme" positions or people. They will become further compartmentalized and will be at dead center, sacrificing even those of their own who refuse to compromise.

Avoiding "politics," the ecologists have taken up the old liberal shuck. Give equal freedom to aristocrats and the people, to bosses and workers, to landlords and tenants, and let both sides win. The scheme, of course, overlooks the one-sided distribution of resources, money and media-power. Some "reformers" will have all they need, but their solution, which will become the solution, is itself a good part of the problem. Profit-seekers and growth-mongers can't co-exist with Mother Nature and her fragile children without doing them irreparable harm.

To save any semblance of democracy, a decent relationship to the environment and perhaps the environment itself—ecology, the "in" movement, must become a movement of the outs. It must be committed to a long-term militant fight on more clearly understood grounds—its own grounds. That too might be impossible. But, as Eugene V. Debs once observed, it's a lot better to fight for what you want and not get it, than to fight for—and get—what you don't want.

The Making of a Pollution-Industrial Complex

MARTIN GELLEN

In January of this year Coca-Cola Company announced its purchase of Aqua-Chem, a leading manufacturer of water treatment equipment and de-salination systems. "The acquisition will permit Coca-Cola to enter the main-stream of envirionmental control systems," declared a spokesman for the company. Perhaps the people at Coke have seen the handwriting on the wall and realize that their livelihood depends on having clean water to make brown. But whatever the precise reasoning, the marriage of Coke and Aqua-Chem is just one among a rash of similar developments on Wall Street where

From *Ramparts,* May 1970, © Ramparts Magazine, Inc., 1970.

pollution control has emerged as one of the hottest growth industries of the '70's. As *Forbes* Magazine put it in a recent cover story, "there's cash in all that trash."

Since the beginning of December 1969, despite a market engaged in a remarkably stubborn downward spiral, stock issues of companies with substantial interests in pollution control have made price advances of often better than 50 per cent. For instance, Research-Cottrell, Inc., the largest of the corporations devoted entirely to environmental systems, has quadrupled its sales in five years. For the pollution control industry as a whole, the average annual growth rate for the next five years is expected to climb to better than 20 per cent, which is almost three times that of most manufacturing groups.

Lester Krellenstein, an engineer and pollution control promoter for the brokerage firm of H. Hentz and Company, believes that President Nixon's appointment of a Council of Environmental Quality triggered the heavy buying. According to Krellenstein, "A great deal of money is going to be made in this business." Present estimates of the potential market start at $25 billion.

But of all the developments in the fledgling industry, by far the most instructive is the corporate integration of polluters and controllers. About two dozen pollution control companies are subsidiaries or divisions of the largest corporations and polluters in the United States. Represented among this latter group are Dow Chemical Co., Monsanto Chemical, W. R. Grace, DuPont, Merck, Nalco, Union Carbide, General Electric, Westinghouse, Combustion Engineering, Honeywell, Beckman Instruments, Alcoa, Universal Oil Products, North American Rockwell, and many others. Although these super-corporations currently make less in sales from pollution control than do smaller firms like Research-Cottrell and Wheelabrator, their superior access to capital, resources, markets, management skills and political power will invariably be translated into a superior competitive position as the ecology movement flowers and the control industry grows.

The pollution control industry is really an extension of both the technological capabilities and the marketing patterns of the capital goods sector of the economy. Most of the companies involved in pollution control are not only polluters themselves but are the same firms which supply the chemicals, machines, plant fuels and parts for even bigger polluters, such as General Motors, U.S. Steel, Boeing, Standard Oil, Philco-Ford, American Can Co. and Consolidated Edison. For many of these firms, pollution control is merely one aspect of a program of "environmental diversification," which is generally accompanied by heavy investment and aggressive acquisition programs.

Koppers, for instance, is an engineering and construction firm that designs municipal sewage plants as well as air and water purification systems. Among its many specialties in pollution abatement is the production of gas removal devices for electric utilities, steel plants, coke plants and foundries. At the same time, however, Koppers is one of the world's leading builders of steel-making equipment and is responsible for designing over 25 per cent of all basic steelmaking facilities in the U.S., as well as half of the present domestic coke plants in operation. Thus it gets the business coming and going. Since 80 per cent of the coke plants in the nation will require modernization in the '70's, and the steel industry expects to increase its overall capacity by 50 per cent, Koppers can expect good profits designing the pollution control systems needed to curb the pollution caused by all the new coke ovens, steel furnaces and foundries which it will construct.

It is the chemical industry, however, that best illustrates the consequences of the incest between the pollution control business and the industrial polluters. First, the chemical industry is in the enviable position of reaping sizable profits by attempting to clean up rivers and lakes (at public expense) which they have profitably polluted in the first place. To facilitate this, practically every major chemical company in the U.S. has established a pollution abatement division or is in the process of doing so. Dow Chemical, for example, produces a wide variety of products and services for water pollution abatement, including measuring instruments, specialty treatment chemicals, and a special biological filter medium called SURF-PAC. The company designs, engineers, builds and services waste water treatment plants and is currently supervising municipal sewage plants in Cleveland and working on waste disposal problems for lumber companies in Pensacola, Florida, and West Nyack, New York. All of these projects are funded by the Federal Water Pollution Control Administration (FWPCA).

Thus, the chemical industry—which ranks second in production of polluted waste water and generates close to 50 per cent of the biological oxygen demand in industrial water before treatment—has, at the same time, established a dominant position in the water pollution control business.

A second consequence of placing the "control" of pollution in the hands of big business is that the official abatement levels will inevitably be set low enough to protect industry's power to pollute and therefore its ability to keep costs down and revenues high. According to a recent study by the FWPCA, if the chemical industry were to reduce its pollution of water to zero, the costs involved would amount to almost $2.7 billion per year. This would cut profits almost by half.

Fortunately for the chemical industry, the present abatement target is only 75 per cent reduction in water pollution through "secondary treatment" methods which will clean up the solids but leave the phosphates, nitrogen compounds and a host of other poisonous substances which secondary treatment can't possibly catch.

Of course, it is precisely the profit incentive as the criterion of what shall and shall not be produced that makes it impossible to stop the proliferation and profusion of poisons in even the most obvious places. Thus, the chemical industry has polluted the housewife's food package not only through the unintended absorption of pesticide residues, but also through innumerable colorings, additives (like the cyclamates) and preservatives designed to increase food purchases and consumption, in order to buoy up sagging sales curves.

The package itself, which is a sales boosting device par excellence, can be both the most polluting and dangerous feature of all. As a piece de resistance the chemical industry produces the non-biodegradable plastic container, which comes in all sizes, shapes and colors, and, if made from polyvinyl plastic, like Dow's Saran-Wrap, can be deadly in the most literal sense of the word. When Saran-Wrap is accumulated as trash and burned, it produces phosgene gas—a poison gas used in World War I and currently stockpiled by the Department of Defense. Exposure for only a short duration to 50 parts of phosgene per million parts of air will cause death. The chemical industry currently makes approximately five billion pounds of polyvinyl plastic per year and output is expected to rise by seven per cent this year alone.

Another consequence of business control of cleaning up the environment is cost to the public. Most municipal water treatment plants in large urban areas are currently constructed to handle an excess capacity frequently 100 per cent greater than the volume of waste actually produced by their resident populations. Much of this surplus capacity is used by big business (especially the chemical industry) to dispose of its wastes. Although industries are charged for this use, it is the consumers and taxpayers, through federal grants and state bonds, who bear the cost of construction and maintenance of the treatment facilities. Thus the public pays the polluters to construct the treatment facilities necessitated by the polluters in the first place.

Thus pollution control, developed as a complementary industry, is a way to insure that the favorable balance between cost, sales and profits can be maintained and business can continue as usual—indeed, better than usual, for pollution control means new investment outlets, new income and new profits; the more waste, the better. Pollution control as conceived by the pollution control industry is merely an extension of the same pattern of profit-seeking exploitation and market economics which is at the root of the environmental crisis itself.

The most salient fact about the crisis that now threatens to overwhelm us is that it is first and foremost a product of the so-called free-enterprise system. "American business," as *Fortune* admits, "since it organizes and channels a high proportion of the total action of this society, has been and still is deeply implicated in depredations against the environment." It is not technology per se, but the way technology is employed (its organization and channeling) that creates the problems. Take, for example, the automobile. What logic determined man's use, as his central mode of transportation, of a device which threw concrete highways across the plains, cut up the forests, poisoned the atmosphere, congested the cities and created the sprawling conurbations that have smothered the land? Was it safe? Computed as fatalities per mile, the death rate for cars is 25 times that for trains and 10 times that for planes. Was it efficient? A traffic study made in 1907 shows that horse-drawn vehicles in New York moved at an average speed of 11.5 miles per hour. Today, automobiles crawl at the average daytime rate of six miles per hour.

At the beginning of the '60's it was estimated that in a single day, motor vehicles burned about seven million gallons of gasoline and in the process produced enough carbon monoxide to pollute the air to a depth of 400 feet over an area of 681 square miles. One-third of the entire land area of Los Angeles (two-thirds of the downtown section) had been absorbed by cars and trucks and the facilities to service them. The area was so congested that plans were laid to spend another $7.5 billion over the next decade on highway construction. The highway program would cost $10,000 per family, while during the same period only $3090 per family would be spent in Los Angeles County for schools, hospitals, parks, water supply, recreation and all other facilities. And Los Angeles is no worse in this respect than other city or urban areas. New York is now spending $100 million per mile to construct a crosstown highway. But in the peak hours, 87.6 per cent of the people entering the central business district come by public transport (71 per cent by subway).

Is there any rationality in all this? There is. But it is a private rationality. The essence of the private property system is that social technology and production are privately or corporately organized and channeled through the market. Thus, in launching his new product, Henry Ford had only private costs to reckon (i.e., the costs to him in labor, materials, etc.). The individual consumer who bought the car had only to reckon his personal preferences versus the purchase price. The question of who would pay the costs of roads, of restructuring cities and organizing the flow of traffic, was taken care of by Ford, the rubber industry, the glass industry, the concrete industry and related interests getting together and twisting the arm of the government. They saw to it that the public would pay for solving the problems created by the new machine.

The costs of pollution are borne by our lungs and in individual cleaning bills; the costs of lack of safety are paid in individual hospital bills and individual deaths. Suppose Ford had been forced from the outset to reckon the social costs (at least the ones that could be quantified) and to put that in the price of his autos. At that price, people would have bought trains as their mass transportation, or more reasonably, they would have been forced to structure their cities and communities in a way which would have enabled them to walk to virtually all of the places necessary.

The problems created by the market system are thus like original sin: their implications keep spreading and diversifying. Now, when the demand for cars shows signs of being saturated, the market strategists get to work and—by changing models, manipulating consumers and planning the obsolescence of their product—generate the need for more and more cars, ad infinitum. The waste in resources is staggering (it has been estimated that style changes in autos alone cost $4 billion annually) and the increase in pollution incalculable.

The pollution control industry itself reflects this irrationality in production for profit. It, too, is a growth industry. It, too, depends for its existence on society's capacity to make waste. The production of steel, copper, aluminum, asbestos and beryllium components for air pollution systems and sewage plants will probably create more air pollution and kill more rivers. The waste involved in the production of all the specialty chemicals and biological agents needed for water treatment alone is staggering. Moreover, the waste in resources required to operate $100 billion worth of control systems will certainly not reduce the despoliation of the environment.

Instead of reorganizing the productive system for social ends, thereby eliminating the problem of waste production and distribution at its source, pollution control under business auspices amounts to no more than rationalizing and improving waste production by making it less ugly, less harmful, less objectionable, and more pleasant for everybody. The object of this kind of pollution control is to make pollution "functional" in society, to institutionalize it, to change it into a necessary and regular part of the everyday world. There is no more effective way to do that than to make it possible for a whole industry to make money out of it. To the military-industrial complex, we can now add an eco-pollution-industrial complex, with a vested interest in continuing economic growth and environmental malaise.

The philosophical justifications for this "solution" are already well developed. As President Nixon's science adviser, Dr. Lee A. DuBridge, puts it, "Let's face it—waste products are a fact of life we have to recognize. . . . Clearly, the U.S. will be producing more waste in the future—not less." The purpose of pollution control, DuBridge explains, is simply to "determine reasonable levels of pollution consistent with good health." Such a logic simultaneously justifies the political economy of waste, effectively de-politicizes the issues of the environment, and defines the problem of pollution in terms of technological solutions and bureaucratic directives. As such it is the normal logic of a society whose business, as Coolidge once said, is business.

Following every failure of the business system in a major social area, the government has stepped in to create a new social-industrial complex, passing the costs of rehabilitation and correction on to the taxpaying public, and reserving the benefits for the corporations. Like the defense suppliers and the educational-manpower conglomerates, the pollution control industry now enjoys the good fortune of being legislated into success. Lavish profits will come from ready-made markets bolstered by special laws controlling pollution levels of factories, special tax write-offs for the industrial buyers of abatement equipment, and plenty of R&D money for the pollution controllers themselves. As government outlays on abatement grow, so will the profits accruing to the pollution control industry. With Uncle Sam posing as Mr. Clean, the crisis of the environment can't help being profitable.

At the National Executives Conference on Water Pollution Abatement, convened last fall by the Department of Interior in order to "bring the environmental programs of business and government into close alignment," John Gillis, president of Monsanto Chemical Co., led the business executives in calling for immediate federal financial aid in the form of quick tax write-offs and investment credits. The Tax Reform Bill passed by Congress early this winter answered the call. While abolishing the seven per cent investment credit, Congress instituted a special five-year amortization allowance for pollution control equipment, which will actually allow a lot of corporations somewhat larger tax deductions than did the investment credit. In addition, some 22 states also offer such subsidies for installation of pollution control equipment. California, for example, provides for a special five-year write-off, while Connecticut gives anti-polluters a five per cent tax credit.

With the prospects of rising R&D expenditures by the federal government, everyone is getting into the act. Anaconda and Alcoa have recently established environmental divisions. Esso Research has started a five-year planning study to determine the National Air Pollution Control Administration (NAPCA) needs in the area of nitrogen oxide emission control. The presence of aerospace corporations and other major defense contractors like Dow, G.E. and Westinghouse on the federal pollution control payroll is of course more than mere coincidence. Currently, the aerospace industry receives about 25 per cent of all the research contracts awarded by NAPCA. Aerojet-General, Avco Industries, Bendix Corporation and Litton Industries are some of the more prominent newcomers to the field. For Litton, Bendix and Aerojet-General, pollution control is a spin-off from their government-sponsored programs for development of biological weapons. Aerojet-General has also received over a million dollars in contracts from the Federal Water Pollution Control Administration for control of toxic agents in water supplies.

After riot control, pollution control is another area in which North American Rockwell, builder of Apollo and one of the country's biggest defense contractors, expects to make "important social contributions as well as profits," according to Robert T. Chambers, chairman of Envirotech, which is NAR's new pollution abatement subsidiary. Envirotech will market some of the measuring devices which NAR has developed through work for FWPCA, NAPCA, the Defense Department's chemical and biological warfare programs, and the space program. Just to keep it all in the family, President Nixon is reportedly planning to place the coordination of pollution control R&D programs under the aegis of the National Aeronautics and Space Administration instead of setting up a special agency for this purpose.

Nixon is also arranging to whip up a little business for investment bankers. As a part of Nixon's $10 billion program for municipal sewage plant construction, state and local governments will finance their $6 billion share of the deal through tax-exempt bonds. The President will also establish an Environmental Funding Authority to buy up any of the bonds which the locals can't sell. The EFA will probably handle a good number of them, since the municipal and state government bond markets are currently glutted. Its own funds would come from the sale of bonds at the even higher non-municipal rates. The Treasury Department . . . would make up the difference between the interest the EFA would receive on local bonds and what it would have to pay out on its own. In other words, the taxpayers would once again pay the bill.

Thus, pollution control programs illustrate the ways in which government promotes the welfare of business at the expense of the taxpaying public. The non-taxpaying poor will also suffer. It's all a matter of priorities. More federal spending for pollution control will mean less for the war on poverty. "Ultimately," pontificates the *Wall Street Journal,* "preservation of the environment may have to take absolute priority over social stability and welfare."

The crisis of the environment must be viewed in terms of a paradox central to modern society. The mobilization of the productive energies of society and the physical forces of nature for the purpose of accumulating profits or enhancing private power and privilege now conflicts directly with the universal dependence of men upon nature for the means of their common survival. A society whose principal ends and incentives are monetary and expansionist inevitably produces material and cultural impoverishment—in part precisely because of the abundance of profitable goods. To make an industry out of cleaning up the mess that industry itself makes is a logical extension of corporate capitalism. What is needed, however, is not an extension of what is already bad, but its transformation into something better.

Questions for Discussion

1. What do you think would be the economic and social effects of the pollution policy laid out in the Council of Economic Advisers' Report if it were widely established? Who does it appear will pay for the cleaning of the environment?
2. Marx's and J. S. Mill's views toward the economic basis of society radically differ. In what sense would their solution to the ecology problem also differ?
3. How do you react to Heilbroner's call for a "New Deal" for the environment?
4. Why do Barkley and Weissman believe that the ecology movement "misses the real problem" and is doomed to failure?
5. What is the pollution-industrial complex?
6. Who should pay for the costs of pollution? How?

Government and the World Economy

While domestic politics in the United States have shifted with the downswinging of the economy to a recent focus on domestic issues, foreign policy was no doubt the crucial issue of the late 1960s. The war in Vietnam was, of course, the reason that international concerns achieved such status in both newspaper editorials and idle conversation.

There is little doubt that, while such issues as Vietnam, Cuba, the Common Market, the Middle East, and foreign aid will only in extraordinary circumstances outrank in public discussion the problems of unemployment, inflation, racial discrimination, and poverty, the events of the past decade have led to a new recognition among Americans of the importance of international relations.

The selections in this section were chosen because they highlight two of the more crucial questions involved in the public consideration of the American government's role in the world.

The first of these is the question of just what our foreign policy is and ought to be. Is the United States (or was it ever) an essentially benign force in the world or is it an imperialistic nation, seeking only to extend its power and influence?

The second question relates to the domestic distribution of the costs and benefits of our foreign policy. Wars, ambassadors and their staffs and materials, the United States Information Agency, and American contributions to such international agencies as the United Nations, the World Bank, and the International Monetary Fund are of course paid through tax monies so that the debate over the distribution of the costs of various policies is considered in Part IX of this book. The question more specifically relevant to these readings is whether foreign policy tends to shore up a domestic "establishment," that is, the corporate elite.

Senator Fulbright, in the first article, argues that we have overextended ourselves in our role as international policemen and have presented the worst of ourselves to the world view. Thus, it seems, we are an essentially benevolent nation temporarily gone astray.

The senator's opposition to the war in Vietnam is, of course, well known. The reader should, however, note the clear differences between his position and that of the following article by Harry Magdoff. Fulbright approaches the war through an answer to the first question above, while Magdoff, typical of radical writers, insists that neither the Vietnam War nor any other aspect of foreign policy can be appropriately discussed without considering the second question. Magdoff argues that the key to understanding United States policy is a recognition of the need of "monopoly capital" to both provide itself with necessary raw materials cheaply and to find new markets for its output.

Charles P. Kindleberger, the eminent professor at Massachusetts Institute of Technology and author of the most widely read textbook in international economics, denies the imperialist thesis, or the "simplistic economic materialistic view," as he refers to it. Economics and foreign policy can, says Kindleberger, be separated and, in fact, decisions made about conditions abroad often result in the economic aspects being ignored.

The last article, by Magdoff and fellow editor of the *Monthly Review,* Paul Sweezy, is included because it discusses the multinational corporation, seen by many writers as a significant institutional development affecting the traditional national industry-national government relationship in the international economy. Some writers have argued that the internationalization of the corporation may lessen the degree of cooperation between American firms and the American government.

The Arrogance
of Power

J. WILLIAM FULBRIGHT

America is the most fortunate of nations—fortunate in her rich territory, fortunate in having had a century of relative peace in which to develop that territory, fortunate in her diverse and talented population, fortunate in the institutions devised by the founding fathers and in the wisdom of those who have adapted those institutions to a changing world.

For the most part America has made good use of her blessings, especially in her internal life but also in her foreign relations. Having done so much and succeeded so well, America is now at that historical point at which a great nation is in danger of losing its perspective on what exactly is within the realm of its power and what is beyond it. Other great nations, reaching this critical juncture, have aspired to too much, and by overextension of effort have declined and then fallen.

The causes of the malady are not entirely clear but its recurrence is one of the uniformities of history: power tends to confuse itself with virtue and a great nation is peculiarly susceptible to the idea that its power is a sign of God's favor, conferring upon it a special responsibility for other nations— to make them richer and happier and wiser, to remake them, that is, in its own shining image. Power confuses itself with virtue and tends also to take itself for omnipotence. Once imbued with the idea of a mission, a great nation easily assumes that it has the means as well as the duty to do God's work. The Lord, after all, surely would not choose you as His agent and then deny you the sword with which to work His will. German soldiers in the First World War wore belt buckles imprinted with the words *"Gott mit uns."* It was approximately under this kind of infatuation—an exaggerated sense of power and an imaginary sense of mission—that the Athenians attacked Syracuse and Napoleon and then Hitler invaded Russia. In plain words, they overextended their commitments and they came to grief.

I do not think for a moment that America, with her deeply rooted democratic traditions, is likely to embark upon a campaign to dominate the world in the manner of a Hitler or Napoleon. What I do fear is that she may be drifting into commitments which, though generous and benevolent in intent,

455

are so far-reaching as to exceed even America's great capacities. At the same time, it is my hope—and I emphasize it because it underlies all of the criticisms and proposals to be made in these pages—that America will escape those fatal temptations of power which have ruined other great nations and will instead confine herself to doing only that good in the world which she *can* do, both by direct effort and by the force of her own example.

The stakes are high indeed: they include not only America's continued greatness but nothing less than the survival of the human race in an era when, for the first time in human history, a living generation has the power of veto over the survival of the next. . . .

The enormity of the danger of extinction of our species is dulled by the frequency with which it is stated, as if a familiar threat of catastrophe were no threat at all. We seem to feel somehow that because the hydrogen bomb has not killed us yet, it is never going to kill us. This is a dangerous assumption because it encourages the retention of traditional attitudes about world politics. . . .

The attitude above all others which I feel sure is no longer valid is the arrogance of power, the tendency of great nations to equate power with virtue and major responsibilities with a universal mission. The dilemmas involved are pre-eminently American dilemmas, not because America has weaknesses that others do not have but because America is powerful as no nation has ever been before, and the discrepancy between her power and the power of others appears to be increasing. One may hope that America, with her vast resources and democratic traditions, with her diverse and creative population, will find the wisdom to match her power; but one can hardly be confident because the wisdom required is greater wisdom than any great nation has ever shown before.

Innocents Abroad

There are signs of the arrogance of power in the way Americans act when they go to foreign countries. Foreigners frequently comment on the contrast between the behavior of Americans at home and abroad: in our own country, they say, we are hospitable and considerate, but as soon as we get outside our own borders something seems to get into us and wherever we are we become noisy and demanding and we strut around as if we owned the place. The British used to say during the war that the trouble with the Yanks was that they were "overpaid, oversexed, and over here." During a recent vacation in Mexico, I noticed in a small-town airport two groups of students on holiday, one group Japanese, the other American. The Japanese were neatly dressed and were talking and laughing in a manner that neither annoyed anybody nor particularly called attention to themselves. The Americans, on the other hand, were disporting themselves in a conspicuous and offensive manner, stamping around the waiting room in sloppy clothes, drinking beer, and shouting to each other as if no one else were there.

This kind of scene, unfortunately, has become familiar in many parts of the world. I do not wish to exaggerate its significance, but I have the feeling that just as there was once something special about being a Roman or a Spaniard or an Englishman, there is now something about the consciousness of being an American abroad, something about the consciousness of belonging to the biggest, richest country in the world, that encourages people who are perfectly well behaved at home to become boorish when they are in somebody else's country and to treat the local citizens as if they were not really there.

One reason Americans abroad may act as though they "own the place" is that in many places they very nearly do: American companies may dominate large segments of a country's economy; American products are advertised on billboards and displayed in shop windows; American hotels and snack bars are available to protect American tourists from foreign influence; American soldiers may be stationed in the country, and even if they are not, the population are probably well aware that their very survival depends on the wisdom with which America uses her immense military power.

I think that when any American goes abroad, he carries an unconscious knowledge of all this power with him and it affects his behavior, just as it once affected the behavior of Greeks and Romans, of Spaniards, Germans, and Englishmen, in the brief high noons of their respective ascendancies. It was the arrogance of their power that led nineteenth-century Englishmen to suppose that if they shouted at a foreigner loud enough in English he was bound to understand, or that now leads Americans to behave like Mark Twain's "innocents abroad," who reported on their travels in Europe that

> The people of those foreign countries are very, very ignorant. They looked curiously at the costumes we had brought from the wilds of America. They observed that we talked loudly at table sometimes. . . . In Paris they just simply opened their eyes and stared when we spoke to them in French! We never did succeed in making these idiots understand their own language.[1]

The Fatal Impact

Reflecting on his voyages to Polynesia in the late eighteenth century, Captain Cook later wrote that "It would have been better for these people never to have known us." In a book on European explorations of the South Pacific, Alan Moorehead relates how the Tahitians and the Australian aborigines were corrupted by the white man's diseases, alcohol, firearms, laws, and concepts of morality, by what Moorehead calls "the long down-slide into Western civilization." The first missionaries to Tahiti, says Moorehead, were "determined to recreate the island in the image of lower-middle-class Protestant England. . . . They kept hammering away at the Tahitian way of life until

[1] Mark Twain, *The Innocents Abroad* (New York: The Thistle Press, 1962), p. 494.

it crumbled before them, and within two decades they had achieved precisely what they set out to do."[2] It is said that the first missionaries to Hawaii went for the purpose of explaining to the Polynesians that it was sinful to work on Sunday, only to discover that in those bountiful islands nobody worked on any day.

Even when acting with the best of intentions, Americans, like other Western peoples who have carried their civilizations abroad, have had something of the same "fatal impact" on smaller nations that European explorers had on the Tahitians and the native Australians. We have not harmed people because we wished to; on the contrary, more often than not we have wanted to help people and, in some very important respects, we have helped them. Americans have brought medicine and education, manufactures and modern techniques to many places in the world; but they have also brought themselves and the condescending attitudes of a people whose very success breeds disdain for other cultures. Bringing power without understanding, Americans as well as Europeans have had a devastating effect in less advanced areas of the world; without knowing they were doing it, they have shattered traditional societies, disrupted fragile economies and undermined peoples' self-confidence by the invidious example of their own power and efficiency. They have done this in many instances simply by being big and strong, by giving good advice, by intruding on people who have not wanted them but could not resist them.

The missionary instinct seems to run deep in human nature, and the bigger and stronger and richer we are, the more we feel suited to the missionary task, the more indeed we consider it our duty. Dr. Chisholm relates the story of an eminent cleric who had been proselyting the Eskimos and said: "You know, for years we couldn't do anything with those Eskimos at all; they didn't have any sin. We had to teach them sin for years before we could do anything with them."[3] I am reminded of the three Boy Scouts who reported to their scoutmaster that as their good deed for the day they had helped an old lady to cross the street.

"That's fine," said the scoutmaster, "but why did it take three of you?"

"Well," they explained, "she didn't want to go."

The good deed above all others that Americans feel qualified to perform is the teaching of democracy. Let us consider the results of some American good deeds in various parts of the world.

Over the years since President Monroe proclaimed his doctrine, Latin Americans have had the advantages of United States tutelage in fiscal responsibility, in collective security, and in the techniques of democracy. If they have fallen short in any of these fields, the thought presents itself that the fault may lie as much with the teacher as with the pupils.

When President Theodore Roosevelt announced his "corollary" to the Monroe Doctrine in 1905, he solemnly declared that he regarded the future

[2] Alan Moorehead, *The Fatal Impact* (New York: Harper & Row, 1966), pp. 61, 80–81.

[3] Brock Chisholm, *Prescription for Survival* (New York: Columbia University Press, 1957), pp. 55–56.

interventions thus sanctified as a "burden" and a "responsibility" and an obligation to "international equity." Not once, so far as I know, has the United States regarded itself as intervening in a Latin American country for selfish or unworthy motives—a view not necessarily shared, however, by the beneficiaries. Whatever reassurance the purity of our motives may give must be shaken a little by the thought that probably no country in human history has ever intervened in another except for motives it regarded as excellent.

For all our noble intentions, the countries which have had most of the tutelage in democracy by United States Marines have not been particularly democratic. These include Haiti, which is under a brutal and superstitious dictatorship; the Dominican Republic, which languished under the brutal Trujillo dictatorship for thirty years and whose second elected government since the overthrow of Trujillo is threatened, like the first, by the power of a military oligarchy; and of course Cuba, which, as no one needs to be reminded, has replaced its traditional right-wing dictatorships with a communist dictatorship.

Maybe, in the light of this extraordinary record of accomplishment, it is time for us to reconsider our teaching methods. Maybe we are not really cut out for the job of spreading the gospel of democracy. Maybe it would profit us to concentrate on our own democracy instead of trying to inflict our particular version of it on all those ungrateful Latin Americans who stubbornly oppose their North American benefactors instead of the "real" enemies whom we have so graciously chosen for them. And maybe—just maybe—if we left our neighbors to make their own judgments and their own mistakes, and confined our assistance to matters of economics and technology instead of philosophy, maybe then they would begin to find the democracy and the dignity that have largely eluded them, and we in turn might begin to find the love and gratitude that we seem to crave.

Korea is another example. We went to war in 1950 to defend South Korea against the Russian-inspired aggression of North Korea. I think that American intervention was justified and necessary: we were defending a country that clearly wanted to be defended, whose army was willing to fight and fought well, and whose government, though dictatorial, was patriotic and commanded the support of the people. Throughout the war, however, the United States emphasized as one of its war aims the survival of the Republic of Korea as a "free society," something which it was not then and is not now. We lost 33,629 American lives in that war and have since spent $5.61 billion on direct military and economic aid and a great deal more on indirect aid to South Korea. The country, nonetheless, remained until recently in a condition of virtual economic stagnation and political instability. Only now is economic progress being made, but the truly surprising fact is that having fought a war for three years to defend the freedom of South Korea, most Americans quickly lost interest in the state of the ward for whom they had sacrificed so much. It is doubtful that more than a handful of Americans now know or care whether South Korea is a "free society."

We are now engaged in a war to "defend freedom" in South Vietnam. Unlike the Republic of Korea, South Vietnam has an army which fights without notable success and a weak, dictatorial government which does not command the loyalty of the South Vietnamese people. The official war aims of the United States government, as I understand them, are to defeat what is regarded as North Vietnamese aggression, to demonstrate the futility of what the communists call "wars of national liberation," and to create conditions under which the South Vietnamese people will be able freely to determine their own future.

I have not the slightest doubt of the sincerity of the President and the Vice-President and the Secretaries of State and Defense in propounding these aims. What I do doubt, and doubt very much, is the ability of the United States to achieve these aims by the means being used. I do not question the power of our weapons and the efficiency of our logistics; I cannot say these things delight me as they seem to delight some of our officials, but they are certainly impressive. What I do question is the ability of the United States or any other Western nation to go into a small, alien, undeveloped Asian nation and create stability where there is chaos, the will to fight where there is defeatism, democracy where there is no tradition of it, and honest government where corruption is almost a way of life.

In the spring of 1966 demonstrators in Saigon burned American jeeps, tried to assault American soldiers, and marched through the streets shouting "Down with American imperialists," while a Buddhist leader made a speech equating the United States with the communists as a threat to South Vietnamese independence. Most Americans are understandably shocked and angered to encounter expressions of hostility from people who would long since have been under the rule of the Viet Cong but for the sacrifice of American lives and money. Why, we may ask, are they so shockingly ungrateful? Surely they must know that their very right to parade and protest and demonstrate depends on the Americans who are defending them.

The answer, I think, is that "fatal impact" of the rich and strong on the poor and weak. Dependent on it though the Vietnamese are, American strength is a reproach to their weakness, American wealth a mockery of their poverty, American success a reminder of their failures. What they resent is the disruptive effect of our strong culture upon their fragile one, an effect which we can no more avoid having than a man can help being bigger than a child. What they fear, I think rightly, is that traditional Vietnamese society cannot survive the American economic and cultural impact.

The evidence of that "fatal impact" is seen in the daily life of Saigon. A *New York Times* correspondent reported—and his information matches that of other observers on the scene—that many Vietnamese find it necessary to put their wives or daughters to work as bar girls or to peddle them to American soldiers as mistresses; that it is not unusual to hear a report that a Vietnamese soldier has committed suicide out of shame because his wife has been working as a bar girl; that Vietnamese have trouble getting taxicabs because drivers will not stop for them, preferring to pick up American soldiers who will pay outrageous fares without complaint; that as a result of the American influx bar girls, prostitutes, pimps, bar owners, and taxi drivers have risen to the higher levels of the economic pyramid; that middle-class Vietnamese families have difficulty renting homes because Americans have driven the rents beyond their reach, and some Vietnamese families have actually been evicted from houses and apartments by landlords who prefer to rent to the affluent Americans; that Vietnamese civil servants, junior army officers, and enlisted men are unable to support their families because of the inflation generated by American spending and the purchasing power of the G.I.s. One Vietnamese explained to the *New York Times* reporter that "Any time legions of prosperous white men descend on a rudimentary Asian society, you are bound to have trouble." Another said: "We Vietnamese are somewhat xenophobe. We don't like foreigners, any kind of foreigners, so that you shouldn't be surprised that we don't like you."[4]

Sincere though it is, the American effort to build the foundations of freedom in South Vietnam is thus having an effect quite different from the one intended. "All this struggling and striving to make the world better is a great mistake," said George Bernard Shaw, "not because it isn't a good thing to improve the world if you know how to do it, but because striving and struggling is the worst way you could set about doing anything."[5]

One wonders how much the American commitment to Vietnamese freedom is also a commitment to American pride—the two seem to have become part of the same package. When we talk about the freedom of South Vietnam, we may be thinking about how disagreeable it would be to accept a solution short of victory; we may be thinking about how our pride would be injured if we settled for less than we set out to achieve; we may be thinking about our reputation as a great power, fearing that a compromise settlement would shame us before the world, marking us as a second-rate people with flagging courage and determination.

Such fears are as nonsensical as their opposite, the presumption of a universal mission. They are simply unworthy of the richest, most powerful, most productive, and best educated people in the world. One can understand an uncompromising attitude on the part of such countries as China or France: both have been struck low in this century and a certain amount of arrogance may be helpful to them in recovering their pride. It is much less comprehensible on the part of the United States—a nation whose modern history has been an almost uninterrupted chronicle of success, a nation which by now should be so sure of its own power as to be capable of magnanimity, a nation which by now should be able to act on the proposition that, as George Ken-

---

[4] Neil Sheehan, "Anti-Americanism Grows in Vietnam," *The New York Times*, April 24, 1966, p. 3.

[5] George Bernard Shaw, *Cashel Byron's Profession* (1886), Ch. 5.

nan said, "there is more respect to be won in the opinion of the world by a resolute and courageous liquidation of unsound positions than in the most stubborn pursuit of extravagant or unpromising objectives."[6]

The cause of our difficulties in Southeast Asia is not a deficiency of power but an excess of the wrong kind of power, which results in a feeling of impotence when it fails to achieve its desired ends. We are still acting like Boy Scouts dragging reluctant old ladies across streets they do not want to cross. We are trying to remake Vietnamese society, a task which certainly cannot be accomplished by force and which probably cannot be accomplished by any means available to outsiders. The objective may be desirable, but it is not feasible. As Shaw said: "Religion is a great force—the only real motive force in the world; but what you fellows don't understand is that you must get at a man through his own religion and not through yours."[7]

With the best intentions in the world the United States has involved itself deeply in the affairs of developing nations in Asia and Latin America, practicing what has been called a kind of "welfare imperialism." Our honest purpose is the advancement of development and democracy, to which end it has been thought necessary to destroy ancient and unproductive modes of life. In this latter function we have been successful, perhaps more successful than we know. Bringing skills and knowledge, money and resources in amounts hitherto unknown in traditional societies, the Americans have overcome indigenous groups and interests and become the dominant force in a number of countries. Far from being bumbling, wasteful, and incompetent, as critics have charged, American government officials, technicians, and economists have been strikingly successful in breaking down the barriers to change in ancient but fragile cultures.

Here, however, our success ends. Traditional rulers, institutions, and ways of life have crumbled under the fatal impact of American wealth and power but they have not been replaced by new institutions and new ways of life, nor has their breakdown ushered in an era of democracy and development. It has rather ushered in an era of disorder and demoralization because in the course of destroying old ways of doing things, we have also destroyed the self-confidence and self-reliance without which no society can build indigenous institutions. Inspiring as we have such great awe of our efficiency and wealth, we have reduced some of the intended beneficiaries of our generosity to a condition of dependency and self-denigration. We have done this for the most part inadvertently: with every good intention we have intruded on fragile societies, and our intrusion, though successful in uprooting traditional ways of life, has been strikingly unsuccessful in implanting the democracy and advancing the development which are the honest aims of our "welfare imperialism. . . . "

[6] George F. Kennan, "Supplemental Foreign Assistance Fiscal Year 1966—Vietnam," *Hearings Before the Committee on Foreign Relations,* United States Senate, 89th Congress, 2nd Session on S. 2793, Part I (Washington: U.S. Government Printing Office, 1966), p. 335.
[7] George Bernard Shaw, *Getting Married* (1911).

If America has a service to perform in the world—and I believe she has—it is in large part the service of her own example. In our excessive involvement in the affairs of other countries we are not only living off our assets and denying our own people the proper enjoyment of their resources, we are also denying the world the example of a free society enjoying its freedom to the fullest. This is regrettable indeed for a nation that aspires to teach democracy to other nations, because, as Edmund Burke said, "Example is the school of mankind, and they will learn at no other."[8]

[8] Edmund Burke, "On a Regicide Peace" (1796).

The New Imperialism

HARRY MAGDOFF

The urge to dominate is integral to business. Risks abound in the business world. Internal and external competition, rapid technological changes, depressions, to name but a few, threaten not only the rate of profit but the capital investment itself. Business therefore is always on the lookout for ways of controlling its environment—to eliminate as much risk as possible. In industry after industry, the battle for survival has also been a battle for conquest, from which the giant corporations best fitted for their environment have emerged. Their ways and habits are the result of a process of adaptation to the battle for survival and growth; these ways and habits have been built into their organizational structures and their modes of operation as ways of guaranteeing and sustaining victory.

1. The most obvious first requirement to assure safety and control in a world of tough antagonists is to gain control over as much of the sources of raw materials as possible—*wherever these raw materials may be, including potential new sources.*[1]

Controlling raw materials sources is both a protective device against pressure of competitors as well as a weapon of offense to keep non-integrated competitors in line. Ownership of and control over raw material supplies is,

From Harry Magdoff, *The Age of Imperialism,* Chapter 2, pp. 34–66. Copyright © 1969 by Harry Magdoff; reprinted by permission of Monthly Review Press.
[1] Note that giant U.S. corporation learned early in the game the desirability of controlling their raw material supplies. Vertical integration, including control over the mining of their own raw materials, was characteristic of the giants in oil, fertilizer, steel, copper, paper, explosives, and other industries.

as a rule, an essential prerequisite for the ability of a leading firm or group of leading firms to limit new competition and to control production and prices of the finished products. Moreover, the very size of the large vertically integrated firms gives them the resources to explore and develop potential new supplies throughout the world.[2] The history of the oil industry is of course a classic illustration, but this principle applies also to the aluminum, steel, copper, and other industries.

2. The pattern of most successful manufacturing businesses includes conquest of foreign markets. This is so even where there is as large an internal market as in the United States. In the mass market auto industry, for example, foreign markets exercised an important influence from the earliest days. The sixth Ford car built was shipped to a Canadian distributor. The Ford Motor Company in its first year of operation started making arrangements for building up its foreign markets.[3]

Despite the very high rate of domestic population increase and the opportunities available in the underdeveloped regions of this country, the drive to develop exports of manufactures took root during the very first flush of industrial maturity—less than a decade after the end of the Civil War. In 1871 little over 7 per cent of United States exports consisted of finished manufactures; by 1890 this per cent rose to almost 12 per cent; by 1900 to almost 19 per cent.[4] The succession of depressions from 1873 to the turn of the century produced two responses: internally, a wave of consolidations and the move towards Big Business; externally, the drive to capture export markets, including those of industrialized Europe.[5]

The dynamics of this search for export markets varies from industry to industry, and has different degrees of importance at various stages in the evolution of an industry and in different phases of the business cycle. What must be understood in any case is the special significance for industry to maintain these export markets. Lenin's generalization on this point is most appropriate: "The growth of internal exchange, and particularly of international exchange,

---

[2] When Lenin gives his explanation of the transformation from competition to monopoly, he notes: "Concentration has reached the point at which it is possible to make an approximate estimate of all sources of raw materials (for example, the iron ore deposits) of a country and even, as we shall see, of several countries, or of the whole world. Not only are such estimates made, but these sources are captured by gigantic monopolist combines." *Imperialism, The Highest Stage of Capitalism,* New York, 1939, p. 25. Later in the essay: "Finance capital is not only interested in the already known sources of raw materials; it is also interested in the potential sources of raw materials, because present-day technical development is extremely rapid, and because land which is useless today may be made fertile tomorrow if new methods are applied . . . and large amounts of capital are invested." *Ibid.,* p. 83.

[3] Mira Wilkins and Frank Ernest Hill, *American Business Abroad, Ford on Six Continents,* Detroit, 1964, p. 1.

[4] Matthew Simon and David E. Novack, "Some Dimensions of the American Commercial Invasion of Europe, 1871–1914: An Introductory Essay," in *Journal of Economic History,* December, 1964, Table 2.

[5] Note also: "The composition of manufactured exports has been changing ceaselessly since 1879 in a fairly consistent direction—away from products of animal or vegetable origin and toward those of mineral origin. Among those of mineral origin, the trend has been away from commodities closely tied to the production of raw materials, such as petroleum products, to metal products, including machinery and vehicles; and within the metal products group the shift has been to the more complex machinery and vehicles." Robert E. Lipsey, *Price and Quantity Trends in the Foreign Trade of the United States,* Princeton, 1963, pp. 59–60.

is the characteristic distinguishing feature of capitalism. The uneven and spasmodic character of the development of individual enterprises, of individual branches of industry and individual countries, is inevitable under the capitalist system."[6]

Foreign markets are pursued (with the aid and support of the state) to provide the growth rate needed to sustain a large investment of capital and to exploit new market opportunities. In this process, the dependence on export markets becomes a permanent feature, for these markets coalesce with the structure of industrial capacity. In one period exports may be the only way out of disaster; in another they may be the best way to maintain the flow of profits. But as the filling of foreign orders becomes built into the capacity and overhead of the business firm, the pressure to maintain these foreign markets over the long run becomes ever more insistent—especially as competitors arrive on the scene.[7]

3. Foreign investment is an especially effective method for the development and protection of foreign markets. The clearest historic demonstration of this was the export of capital for railways, which stimulated at the same time the demand for rails, locomotives, railway cars, and other products of the iron, steel, and machine industries.[8]

But this method of penetrating foreign markets becomes ever more prevalent in the age of the giant corporation, characterized as it is by intensification of national rivalries. The role of foreign investment to capture and exploit sources of raw materials is evident. More than this, though, is the urgency of foreign investment to withstand the competition, or to pre-empt markets, in the countries where competitive corporate giants also exist.

The foreign corporate giants can swing their own weight in controlling their own domestic markets, or in their preferential markets—such as in colonies, dependencies, or "spheres of influence." They can also use their political strength to set up protective tariffs and other trade barriers against outsiders. For these reasons, the ability to compete in other countries and to exercise the kind of market control needed by the giant corporations calls for a program of foreign investment. The competition between corporate giants resolves itself either in cartel arrangements or in permanent invasion of each others' markets via the route of foreign investment. Moreover, this procedure becomes more feasible in the age of Big Business, thanks to the large masses of capital available to large corporations from their own profits or from what they can mobilize in cooperation with financial institutions.

[6] *Op. cit.*, p. 62.

[7] It is customary to think of competition and monopoly as direct opposites. This is quite proper according to dictionary definitions. However, in Marxist literature, the terms competition and monopoly are used to designate different phases of capitalist society. In neither of these phases is there either pure competition or pure monopoly. Indeed, it is the very essence of the theory of imperialism to recognize that competition exists within the monopoly phase. Competition is between giants of the same industry (within and outside the nation) and between industries (steel vs. aluminum vs. plastics, for example).

[8] Thus, all the iron material for India's railroads was imported from England. Even in the United States, which had a growing iron industry, iron rails were imported from England. South Wales iron masters took part of their payment for this iron in the form of bonds of the railroad companies.

The foregoing reasons for the spurt of foreign investment in the age of imperialism are far from exhaustive. There is naturally the attractiveness of increasing profit rates through taking advantage of lower labor costs abroad. Observe, for example, how The Chase Manhattan Bank slips in information on wage rates in South Korea in its report spelling out the attractiveness of investing in that country.

> In fact, the main impetus for Korea's economic growth comes from the determination and drive of its businessmen and officials. Americans comment on the dexterity and aptitude of Korean workers, who are available at cash rates averaging 65¢ a day in textiles and 88¢ a day in electronics. These human characteristics produce industrial results.[9]

Attractive as lower costs are, their appeal is not necessarily the main attraction of foreign investment. It is merely one of the influences. Much more important is the spur of developing raw material resources, creating demand for exports, and taking advantage of "monopoly" situations. The latter arises due to cost advantages of Big Business, exclusive patents, superior technology, or preferred market demand stimulated by establishment of desired brands via sales promotion. Finally, foreign investment arises from the pressure to establish trade in markets protected by tariff walls or trade preferences. (United States investment in Canada, for example, is a convenient arrangement for participating in British Empire trade.)

The commonly held notion that the theory of imperialism should be concerned largely with investment in underdeveloped countries just isn't correct. The fact is that profitable investment opportunities in such countries are limited by the very conditions imposed by the operations of imperialism. Restricted market demand and industrial backwardness are products of the lopsided economic and social structures associated with the transformation of these countries into suppliers or raw materials and food for the metropolitan centers.

Our purpose here is not to analyze exhaustively all the factors involved in foreign investment. Rather, it is to suggest that there are clear reasons for the spurt of foreign investment in the age of imperialism—as a consequence of the opportunities and pressures accompanying the rise of Big Business. This is not prompted by the malice of the businessman, but by the normal and proper functioning of business in the conditions confronted. The patterns of these investments should be examined in their historical context, in light of the actual situations business firms deal with, rather than in the more usual terms of an abstraction concerning the pressure of surplus capital.[10]

---

[9] *Korea, Determined Strides Forward,* The Chase Manhattan Bank, May, 1967, p. 3.

[10] For a critique of the "surplus capital" abstraction and suggestions for more significant analysis of current developments, see Paul A. Baran and Paul M. Sweezy, "Notes on the Theory of Imperialism" in *Problems of Economic Dynamics and Planning, Essays in Honour of Michal Kalecki,* Oxford, 1966. Reprinted in *Monthly Review,* March, 1966.

4. The drive for foreign investment opportunities and control over foreign markets brings the level of political activity on economic matters to a new and intense level. The last quarter of the 19th century sees the spread of protective tariffs.[11] Other political means—threats, wars, colonial occupation—are valuable assistants in clearing the way to exercise sufficient political influence in a foreign country to obtain privileged trade positions, to get ownership of mineral rights, to remove obstacles to foreign trade and investment, to open the doors to foreign banks and other financial institutions which facilitate economic entry and occupation.

The degree and type of political operation naturally vary. In weak outlying territories, colonial occupation is convenient. In somewhat different circumstances, bribery of officials or loans (via banks or state institutions) are appropriate.[12] Among the more advanced countries, alliances and interest groups are formed.

The result of these developments is a new network of international economic and political relations. The network itself changes in shape and emphasis over time as a result of wars, depressions, and differential rates of industrialization.[13] The forms also vary: colonies, semi-colonies, "a variety of forms of dependent countries—countries, which, officially, are politically independent, but which are in fact, enmeshed in the net of financial and diplomatic dependence,"[14] and junior and senior partners among the imperialist powers. The significant theme is the different degrees of dependence in an international economy, an international economy in continuous ferment as a result of the battles among giant corporations over the world scene and

[11] It is one of the significant ironies of these times that the wave of protectionism followed on the heels of the widespread adoption of the international gold standard. "The agrarian crisis and the Great Depression of 1873–86 had shaken confidence in economic self-healing. From now onward the typical institutions of market economy could usually be introduced only if accompanied by protectionist measures, all the more so because since the late 1870's and early 1880's nations were forming themselves into organized units which were apt to suffer grievously from the dislocations involved in any sudden adjustment to the needs of foreign trade or foreign exchanges. The supreme vehicle of the expansion of market economy, the gold standard, was thus usually accompanied by the simultaneous introduction of the typical protectionist policies of the age such as social legislation and customs tariffs." Karl Polanyi, *The Great Transformation*, Boston, 1957, p. 214.

[12] For documentation and analysis see George W. F. Hallgarten, *Imperialismus Vor 1914*, Munich, 1963; and Herbert Feis, *Europe The World's Banker, 1870–1914*, New York, 1965.

[13] On the question of uneven rate of development: "Thus, Great Britain stood in much the same relation to most of the regions of Europe around 1850 that Europe and the United States bore to the Orient and South America a half century later." L. H. Jenks, *The Migration of British Capital to 1875*, New York, 1927, pp. 187–188.

[14] Lenin, *op. cit.*, p. 85. It is noteworthy that Lenin specifically rejects the definition advocated by Karl Kautsky which confines imperialism to the acquisition of raw materials supplying colonies; that is, the attempt by industrialized capitalist countries to control and annex agrarian regions. He debates this point in terms of the conditions existing prior to and during World War I: "The characteristic feature of imperialism is precisely that it strives to annex *not only* agricultural regions, but even highly industrialized regions (German appetite for Belgium; French appetite for Lorraine), because (1) the fact that the world is already divided up obliges those contemplating a *new* division to reach out for *any kind* of territory, and (2) because an essential feature of imperialism is the rivalry between a number of great powers in the striving for hegemony, i.e., for the conquest of territory, not so much directly for themselves as to weaken the adversary and undermine *his* hegemony. (Belgium is chiefly necessary to Germany as a base for operations against England; England needs Baghdad as a base for operations against Germany, etc.)" *Ibid.*, pp. 91–92.

the operations of these corporations along with their state governments to maintain domination and control over weaker nations.

The oversimplification which identifies imperialism with colonialism pure and simple neither resembles Lenin's theory nor the facts of the case. Similarly fallacious is the version of Lenin's theory that imperialism is in essence the need of advanced countries to get rid of a surplus which chokes them, and that this surplus is divested through productive investments in colonies.

The stage of imperialism, as we have tried to show, is much more complex than can be explained by any simple formula. The drive for colonies is not only economic but involves as well political and military considerations in a world of competing imperialist powers. Likewise, the pressures behind foreign investment are more numerous and more involved than merely exporting capital to backward countries. There is no simple explanation for all the variations of real economic and political changes, nor is it fruitful to seek one. The special value of Lenin's theory is the highlighting of all the principal levers that have moved international economic relations. These levers are the ones associated with the new stage of monopoly and the essential ways monopoly operates to achieve, wherever and whenever feasible, domination and control over sources of supply and over markets. The fact that these are still the principal levers explains why the theory is still relevant. But the particular forms in which these factors operate and become adapted to new conditions requires continuous re-examination. . . .

Demand for External Sources of Raw Materials

One of the features of imperialism that persists unabated to this day is the reliance of the giant corporation for its monopolistic position, including the size of its profits, on foreign sources of raw materials. What is new in today's imperialism is that the United States has become a "have-not" nation for a wide range of both common and rare minerals.

A strange sort of reasoning crops up these days in academic discussions of this subject because advanced industrialized countries are importing a smaller value of raw materials in proportion to output of final products than in the past. This trend reflects increasing efficiency in the industrial uses of raw materials resulting from: (1) improvements in technology and design; (2) increased complexity of consumer products (that is, more manufacturing work is applied to a given amount of raw materials); (3) development of synthetic materials (rubber, plastics, fibers); and (4) improved organization of scrap collection and utilization.

This increasing efficiency in raw materials use is undoubtedly important. It has a serious bearing on the prosperity and viability of the underdeveloped primary commodity producing countries. It is an important contributor to the differential rates of growth between the industrialized and non-industrialized countries. It is involved in the increasing financial dependency of many underdeveloped economies, which will be discussed below. But a strange leap in reasoning is needed to conclude that the strategic role of raw materials has changed for the advanced countries. No matter how efficient industry becomes in the use of aluminum or in the extraction of alumina from bauxite, you can't make aluminum without bauxite and you can't make an airplane without aluminum. And when in the United States, 80 to 90 per cent of the bauxite supply comes from foreign sources, the assurance of such supply is of crucial importance to the aluminum industry, the airplane industry, and the country's military power.

Another factor often cited as tending to minimize the raw materials problem is the technical achievements in the processing of low-grade ores, and the use of substitute materials (e.g., plastics for metals). Significant technical strides have indeed been made but, as the data we are about to present will show, these achievements have not reversed the trend. With all the amazing accomplishments of scientists and the wonders of electronics and atomic energy, they still have not discovered how to make ordinary metals behave, except within narrow limits, according to the will of the user.

What may seem dramatic in the laboratory or in a pilot plant is often a far cry from what is needed in practice to transform an entire industry. Managers of business may plan for the future, but they live in the present. Any president of a big corporation who did not aggressively pursue acquisition of foreign leases for raw materials because in the historical long run a domestic substitute will probably be found, would most properly be fired from his job.

Thinking in terms of national planning (for the good of the people) or in abstract economic analysis (in terms of cost curves) does not help to understand the impact of foreign raw materials supplies on the policies of business and government. The question boils down to the nature of control and behavior in business, and the government's realistic response to the operational needs of business. Thus, great developments in the exploitation and use of shale oil, which may some day eliminate domestic dependency on foreign sources, do not and will not diminish the rivalry among oil firms to acquire every bit of oil under land or sea they can lay their hands on. The decisive issues are not consumer and social needs but the controls business firms desire in order to manage world production and prices for the sake of greater profits.

While monopolistic behavior patterns produce the eager drive for foreign supply sources, the shift of the United States from a "have" to a "have-not" nation has likewise resulted in an intensification of the urgency to obtain and control foreign resources. . . .

Up until the 1920's, the United States was a net exporter of minerals; the change in trend is postponed by the depression when consumption of raw material declined. The situation, however, reverses significantly during the war years. But the new situation faced by the United States, simultaneous with its new role as organizer and leader of the imperialist network, shows up dramatically in the 1950's, when in place of its former position as a net exporter, close to 13 per cent of domestic consumption is supplied by imports. . . .

Back in the years just before the war, net imports of iron ore amounted to about 3 per cent of the close to 52 million tons of iron ore extracted from domestic sources. In 1966, net imports were equal to 43 per cent of the 90 million tons mined in the country. (The latter includes the mining of such taconite as we have learned and choose to use productively.) The exhaustion of high-quality domestic ore supplies occasioned a dramatic rise in foreign investment to develop more efficient and richer sources of iron ore in Canada, Venezuela, Brazil, and Africa. The purpose, as it developed, was not only to exploit more profitable sources of supply but to map out greater control over this essential raw material as a preventive measure: each large domestic producer naturally anticipates similar moves by other domestic and foreign producers.

It is true that in recent years technical innovations have increased the utility of domestic ores. Nevertheless, the tendency to increasing reliance on foreign sources of supply persists, partly to get one's money's worth out of an investment already made, partly as a protective device to keep the lesser quality ore sources in reserve, and partly for immediate financial advantage where foreign ores are more economical. As specialists in the field see it, in the absence of a further breakthrough in technology that would make the very low grade iron ore, derived from taconite and similar rock, decidedly cheaper than foreign ore, the prognosis is for increased reliance of our steel industry on foreign sources of ore. Thus, it is anticipated that about half of the iron ore to be consumed in 1980 will be met by foreign sources, and that by 2000 the import ratio will reach 75 per cent.[15]

The dramatic reversal in the self-sufficiency of the United States with respect to raw materials was succinctly summarized in a report by the staff of the President's Commission on Foreign Economic Policy:

> This transition of the United States from a position of relative self-sufficiency to one of increasing dependence upon foreign sources of supply constitutes one of the striking economic changes of our time. The outbreak of World War II marked the major turning point of this change.
>
> Both from the viewpoint of our long-term economic growth and the viewpoint of our national defense, the shift of the United States from the position of a net exporter of metals and minerals to that of a net importer is of overshadowing significance in shaping our foreign economic policies.
>
> We have always been almost entirely dependent on imports for tin, nickel, and the platinum group of metals. In addition, our requirements for asbestos, chromite, graphite, manganese, mercury, mica, and tungsten have been generally covered by imports. Prior to World War II this was about the extent of our list of strategic materials, that is mineral substances of which our requirements are wholly or substantially supplied

[15] Hans H. Landsberg, *Natural Resources for U.S. Growth*, Baltimore, 1964, p. 206.

by foreign sources. At present by contrast, *the United States is fully self-sufficient only in coal, sulfur, potash, molybdenum and magnesium.* (Emphasis added.)[16]

Strategic Materials

The Defense Department operates with a list of strategic and critical materials as a guide to the stockpiling program. These are the materials which are assumed to be critical to the war potential of this country and where supply difficulties can be anticipated. However, war products are not the only ones for which these materials are strategic. Many civilian products in today's technical environment rely on the same materials. (Mica, for example, appears on this list. Mica is used in the electrical industry in condensers, telephones, dynamos, and in electric toasters.) . . .

For more than half of these items, 80 to 100 per cent of the supply in this country depends on imports. For 52 out of the 62 materials, at least 40 per cent has to be supplied from abroad. And, according to a report of the International Development Advisory Board (a special commission set up by the President in the 1950's), *three quarters of the imported materials included in the stockpile program come from the underdeveloped areas.* The political and military response to this fact is clearly formulated by the President's Board: ". . . it is to these countries that we must look for the bulk of any possible increase in these supplies. The loss of any of these materials, through aggression, would be the equivalent of a grave military set-back."[17]

The facts presented here are of course no mystery to business or to the government planners and coordinators of policy. President Truman established in 1951 the Materials Policy Commission, cited above, to study the materials problem of the United States and its relation to other non-Communist countries. The resulting five-volume report was issued with much publicity in the midst of the Korean War. The theme of raw materials sources as an ingredient of foreign policy crops up not only with respect to direct United States requirements but also as it concerns United States responsibility as the leader of the "free world" to see to it that Western Europe's and Japan's supplies of raw materials are assured. Consider, for example, this frank statement by former President Eisenhower:

> One of Japan's greatest opportunities for increased trade lies in a free and developing Southeast Asia. . . . The great need in one country is for raw materials, in the other country for manufactured goods. The two regions complement each other markedly. By strengthening of Vietnam and helping insure the safety of the South Pacific and Southeast Asia,

[16] The Commission on Foreign Economic Policy, *Staff Papers Presented to the Commission,* Washington, D.C., February, 1954, p. 224.

[17] International Development Advisory Board, *Partners in Progress,* Washington, D.C., March, 1951, p. 46.

we gradually develop the great trade potential between this region . . . and highly industrialized Japan to the benefit of both. In this way freedom in the Western Pacific will be greatly strengthened.[18]

And finally, two more citations—one from the Republican side and one from the Democratic side of policy making. The Rockefeller Brothers Fund report on foreign economic policy offers these propositions:

> Europe's economic security today depends on two indispensable factors: (1) her own intellectual and technical vitality and economic enterprise; and (2) an international structure which will enable Europe to have access to foreign markets on fair terms and adequate supplies of materials, if Europe can offer reasonable value in return for them.
>
> Nevertheless, the economic situation of the industrialized nations remains precarious. If Asia, Middle Eastern and African nationalism, exploited by the Soviet bloc, becomes a destructive force, European supplies of oil and other essential raw materials may be jeopardized.[19]

W. W. Rostow, President Johnson's closest adviser on national security affairs, seems to be well aware of the underpinning of the imperialist network as it applies to raw materials and to the special role of the United States in today's imperialism. Testifying before the Joint Congressional Committee, Rostow explained the relations between industrialized and underdeveloped nations as follows:

> The location, natural resources, and populations of the underdeveloped areas are such that, should they become effectively attached to the Communist bloc, the United States would become the second power in the world. . . . Indirectly, the evolution of the underdeveloped areas is likely to determine the fate of Western Europe and Japan and, therefore the effectiveness of those industrialized regions in the free world alliance we are committed to lead. If the underdeveloped areas fall under Communist domination, or if they move to fixed hostility to the West, the economic and military strength of Western Europe and Japan will be diminished, the British Commonwealth as it is now organized will disintegrate, and the Atlantic world will become, at best, an awkward alliance, incapable of exercising effective influence outside a limited orbit, with the balance of the world's power lost to it. In short, our military security and our way of life as well as the fate of Western Europe and Japan are at stake in the evolution of the underdeveloped areas. We evidently have a major national interest, then, in developing a free world coalition which embraces in reasonable harmony and unity the industrialized states of

[18] Address at the Gettysburg College Convocation, April 4, 1959, in Public Papers of the Presidents of the United States, *Dwight D. Eisenhower 1959*, Washington, D.C., 1960, p. 314.
[19] Rockefeller Brothers Fund, *Foreign Economic Policy for the Twentieth Century*, Garden City, New York, 1958, p. 11 for the first item, p. 16 for the second.

Western Europe and Japan on the one hand, the underdeveloped areas of Asia, the Middle East, and Africa, on the other.[20]

United States as the Leading Capital Exporter

Along with the political and military changes after the Second World War, when the United States assumed the role of undisputed leader of world capitalism, came the clear-cut pre-eminence of the United States as a capital exporter. While the urgent need to develop foreign raw material sources contributed to the momentum of capital exports after the war, the acceleration of investment in foreign manufacturing ventures added a new dimension to the internationalization of capital. . . .

Despite the fact that the United States was a debtor nation until after the First World War, it had already started to get its feet wet in this field, beginning with the onset of its participation in the imperialist way of life.

The interwar years, and the consequent change in position to that of a creditor nation, gave the United Sates its opportunity and it raced ahead to the point where it was getting close to the position of the oldest and best entrenched capital exporter. By 1960, United States foreign investments accounted for almost 60 per cent of the world total. (These data apply to both portfolio and direct investment. Direct investment—the ownership of branches and subsidiaries—was the most important factor in this expansion of United States investment. Hence, if the data were shown for direct investment alone, the United States share would be even larger. While all the information is not available for the post-1960 period, it seems clear that the United States share has kept on increasing in these years as well.)

Because of this huge expansion of investment in manufacturing industries abroad, the United States is able to compete in foreign markets directly rather than by exports alone. . . .

But the United States is not the only contender for these markets. . . . English firms invest in France and West Germany. Belgium invests in France, West Germany, and England. However, the position of the United States as a foreign investor in Europe is overwhelming. As might be expected, the concentration of investment by a small number of giant firms has resulted in the United States firms' having quite impressive shares of the market in particular industries in Europe. . . . United States firms control over half of the automobile industry in Britain, close to 40 per cent of petroleum in Germany, and over 40 per cent of the telegraphic, telephone, electronic, and statistical equipment business in France (the control of computing machines in France is 75 per cent).

The tie-in between monopolistic trends and the flow of investment to Europe is indicated by the following: in the three biggest European markets

---

[20] Subcommittee on Foreign Economic Policy of the Joint Economic Committee, Congress of the United States, 84th Congress, 2nd Session, *Hearings,* December 10, 12, and 13, 1956, pp. 127–131.

(West Germany, Britain, and France) 40 per cent of United Sates direct investment is accounted for by three firms—Esso, General Motors, and Ford. In all Western Europe, 20 United States firms account for two thirds of United States investment.[21]

In short, the internationalization of capital among the giant firms is of a much higher order today than was the case fifty years ago when Lenin wrote his work on imperialism.

[21] Christopher Layton, *Trans-Atlantic Investment,* Boulogne-sur-Seine, France, 1966, p. 18.

Imperialism

CHARLES P. KINDLEBERGER

The Economic Drive

The domination of peoples beyond a country's national borders is a fact of history called imperialism or colonialism. After the breakup of formal empires and the granting or taking of independence by colonies, there often remain economic relationships which are alleged to involve latent or actual economic or political domination. This is called neo-imperialism or neo-colonialism. One question with respect to imperialism is whether it was caused by economic rather than purely political drives such as aggrandizement. The issue over neo-imperialism is whether it exists.

That there is an economic element in imperialism is an undeniable fact. Marx and especially Lenin thought, however, that economic materialism explained it all. Imperialism was the last stage of capitalism. Marx, and the British economist Hobson, found the cause in underconsumption. Capitalist enterprise, while highly productive, paid out too little of the value of its output to be able to sell its products at home and had to seek overseas markets. Lenin's emphasis went more to the problem of disposing surplus value abroad through investment of finance capital. In either case, political domination (if need be with military force) was necessary to protect markets for goods and savings.

Neo-imperialism operates through national corporations, sometimes called

Excerpted from Chapter 5, "Imperialism" by Charles P. Kindleberger in *Power and Money: The Politics of International Economics and the Economics of International Politics* by Charles P. Kindleberger; © 1970 by Basic Books, Inc., Publishers, New York. Also by permission of Macmillan London and Basingstoke.

multi-national or international, though they all have strong national roots. In some formulations the need is less for markets than for raw materials. Exploitation of foreign workers enables the imperialist nation, through its large national corporations, to fill its requirements for primary products (when its own resources are nearing exhaustion) at low cost and with high profit.

Variation on these themes is endless. If the nation as a whole does not gain from imperialism or neo-imperialism, dominant groups within it do. Aggressive foreign policy is undertaken by government in the interest of the ruling capitalist class, of which it is the handmaiden. Or imperialist expansion may be political, and international corporations are the tool of government, rather than the reverse.

The Leninist theory that imperialism is a stage of capitalist evolution encounters difficulty both from precapitalist empires—Holy Roman, Roman, Greek, Egyptian, Persian, and so on back into the mists of antiquity—and from socialist expansion or imperialism as exemplified by the Soviet Union and China. Perhaps the most aggressive countries in recent years have been Fascist Italy, National Socialist Germany, and pre-war Japan (which was capitalist but with a primitive rather than highly developed form, and a large role for the state). While there is some evidence that Japanese expansion was a reaction to her loss of the market for silk in the depression and British colonial resistance to her efforts to penetrate those markets, these attempts at domination seem to have been a function of nationalism rather than economic organization.

Political scientists sometimes distinguish among military, economic and cultural forms of imperialism, and among economic gain, "animal drives," defensive strategy, and a mission of bringing civilization to the rest of the world as causes. Most non-Marxist observers believe that, while imperialist expansion has an economic element, politics has primacy over economics. In their view, politics is politics and business is business. The economic materialists, on the other hand, insist that politics is business, and vice versa. There is something to it, perhaps, but not a great deal. . . .

Foreign Investment

Marxian theory put emphasis on the outlet for goods; Leninist theory emphasized the problems faced by finance capital in preventing a decline of the rate of interest to the vanishing point. Finance capitalists in their struggle for profitable outlets would bring their countries into conflicts which escalated into war.

Professors Jacob Viner and Eugene Staley have investigated this charge in some detail for the period prior to World War I and find it unconvincing. Apart from the Boer War, there is virtually no support. In fact the evidence makes the conclusion inescapable that governments used finance, rather than the other way round. Bismarck cut off loans to Czarist Russia as a means of applying diplomatic pressure; the Quai d'Orsay in its turn urged the French market to support Russia and the Little Entente with the savings of French peasants. Robbins quotes Wölf-Metternich in a private communication to Von Bülow: "High finance shakes its knees whenever any kind of political complication comes up." Hobson expressed the view that the Rothschilds could have vetoed World War I if it had not been to their advantage, but there is no demonstration of the mechanism and the idea is not persuasive on the face of it.

The conventional criticism of foreign investment in European intellectual circles runs counter to the Leninist view and to the effect that foreign investment hurt the leading countries of Europe by depriving entrepreneurs of the capital needed to take advantage of investment opportunities at home. The question is raised "Did Foreign Investment Pay?" On the whole, the conclusion is that it did. The Marxist-Leninist view is correct to the extent that in Britain and France rates of profit and investment were low, and higher returns could be earned abroad. This was partly, however, the result of a decline in entrepreneurial thrust; there was no lack of investment push in Germany and the United States. And while much of foreign investment was wasted in loans to Czarist Russia, the state of Mississippi, and overtouted business ventures all over the world, the average rate of return was higher than at home. Some investments in tin, rubber, gold, copper, oil, etc., paid off handsomely. Cairncross calculated that the British investor earned £4 billion in forty years from 1870 to 1913, or roughly £100 million a year on the average, as against a national income which started at £900 million in 1870 when the income on foreign investment was low and rose to £2.3 billion in 1913. The detailed figures are complicated by the need to weigh interest and dividends and capital appreciation as well, the latter possibly distorted by the choice of beginning and end years. Excluding capital appreciation, the rate of return in interest and dividends was 5.6 per cent in government bonds, 4.9 per cent in railroads, and 5.4 per cent in miscellaneous, which compares favorably, but not dramatically so, with domestic yields of 3.26 per cent on British government consols (perpetual bond), 4.3 per cent on railroads, 4.7 per cent on railroad preferred stocks, and nearly 6 per cent on common railroad shares.[1]

Foreign investment often had limited benefits for the native population. In some cases it had almost no effect, positive or negative, as where it took place in an enclave. In Peru, the guano industry used European capital, British ships, Chinese labor, and foreign markets, hardly involving the local economy at all. In mines and plantations large amounts of local labor were used. Where foreign investors built railroads, they tended to serve the needs of foreign traders, rather than those of the domestic population. In India, the railroads were laid to connect the interior to the ports of Bombay and Calcutta, to make transport cheap for commodity exports, rather than to con-

---

[1] Cairncross, *Home and Foreign Investment, 1870–1913* (Cambridge: Cambridge University Press, 1953), pp. 230 ff.

nect the major centers of the domestic economy. The same was true, of course, for railroads in countries producing bananas and meat.

The worst about this period of investment is that those undertaking it felt superior to the local populations and had no compunction in ignoring their interests. History is replete with what are now shameful episodes of cheating, lying, failure to disclose, bribery, taking advantage of ignorance and gullibility, and of weaknesses of local enterprise and local government (where it existed). Local customs were flouted. Most of these actions, which so poison political and economic relations between the developed and the less developed countries today, were taken by reason of inattention to any but the imperialist or colonial interest. It was not deliberately criminal or immoral, so much as myopic or egocentric. In a world where communication was limited among different peoples, and the sense of likeness had not developed, local peoples were treated as objects rather than people, as strangers whose interests counted for nothing. There was expected to be no feedback. That expectation was wrong. There were many episodes in which all parties to the investment benefited and a number in which none did.

Neo-Imperialism

Since World War II, the empires and colonial systems have been dismantled. In part this was done voluntarily, by the imperial powers; largely these powers were unable to prevent assertion of independence. In Southeast Asia the defeat of white military might by the Japanese early in the Asian war lost prestige for the imperialist. Freedom was promised to some for support during the war and to make good on promises of political parties of liberal opinion. Whatever economic forces may have contributed to imperialism, they could not prevent its dissolution.

But there is the view that the more it changes, the more it's the same thing. Modern trade and investment are regarded in some quarters as the old imperialism and colonialism under new forms. Baran and Sweezy have asserted that the world has moved from national imperialism to enterprise imperialism. The more usual term is neo-imperialism or neo-colonialism, which imply that economic relations in trade and investment cloak political relationships of control and dependence.

A French journalist, M. Claude Julien, the expert of *Le Monde* on the United States and Latin America, is a major exponent of this view. M. Julien has absorbed and sympathizes with a number of Latin American economic doctrines regarding the terms of trade between manufactures and primary products, and the need of less developed countries to borrow interest on past indebtedness to maintain their balances of payments. Many of these have been developed by M. Raul Prebisch, the highly original Argentine economist who has been Secretary General, first of the Economic Commission for Latin America and then of the United Nations Conference on Trade and Development and the Agency which it established. From this vantage point the views have spread from Latin America to Africa and Asia.

Julien claims that the United States antipathy to colonialism, expressed in its support for Indonesia against the Dutch in 1946, and restraint of France and Britain in the Suez crisis of 1956, is essentially phony. Having invented neo-colonialism in its relations with Cuba and the Philippines, at the end of the last century it had no need of colonialism. Trade and investment relationships substitute for the political ties that used to bind. The United States desperately needs this neo-colonialism or neo-imperialism to supply itself with primary products which are approaching exhaustion within its borders. Investments abroad obtain these materials at low prices, with high profits for the producers, but impoverishment for those who own the land or supply the labor. The United States interest in Cuba did not go beyond sugar and the richest nickel mines in the world (*sic*). Unlike some economic determinists, like Hobson who thought the Rothschilds could have stopped World War I, Julien does not think that the United States intervention in Vietnam was narrowly motivated by tin. He asserts, however, that the domino effect which makes no sense politically or militarily is valid in economic terms, and that South Vietnam is supported at great cost in United States blood and treasure to ensure access to Southeast Asian supplies of tin, rubber, copper, bauxite, oil, coal, manganese, nickel, gold and silver.

The thesis has attractive simplicity, but it is difficult to sustain in logical analysis or empirical demonstration. Low-cost raw materials can provide large profits for their owners, or cheap inputs for consumers goods to sustain a high level of living, but not both. United States dependence on imported raw materials was examined at length by the Paley Commission at the time of the Korean War when there was fear that the country might be cut off from Southeast Asia and suffer severely from material shortages. The conclusion was reached, however, that raw-material supplies were not a serious problem for the United States. The man-in-the-street notion that an economy, like Mother Hubbard, can run out of supplies, misunderstands the workings of the price system. So long as markets are open, one can never run out of anything: what happens is that the price goes up. A high price stimulates output and limits consumption. When raw materials become relatively scarcer, the prices of raw materials rise to economize their use and to stimulate production of the goods themselves and of synthetic substitutes.

The less developed countries, and particularly Latin America under the intellectual leadership of Prebisch, have continually complained about a downward trend in the relative prices (the so-called terms of trade) of raw materials as against manufactured goods. Prebisch believes that this trend is the result of persistent differences in monopoly power, greater in manufactures than in primary products. The evidence for this view is weak. Monopoly exists in both classes of commodities—where it does not already exist in primary products, it is likely to be provided by government intervention—and there is little evidence that it is greater in one than the other, despite

more administered pricing in manufactures than primary products. If anything, raw-material and foodstuff prices are held well above market-clearing
levels by export taxes, production controls, stockpiling, and the like. The Organization of Petroleum Exporting Countries (OPEC) maintains crude petroleum prices well above long-run marginal cost to which it would fall under
competitive conditions, and as it is likely to do as new entrants outside the
"cartel" come into production. Coffee, cocoa and similar tropical foodstuffs,
plus tin, are also above long-run competitive levels. Sugar is produced more
efficiently in Cuba than elsewhere in the world, but there is no shortage (i.e.,
the price is low) even without the normal Cuban contribution to world
output.

One can interpret United States preoccupation with the Panama Canal and
the Guantanamo naval base in Cuba as straightforward imperialism in the
national security interest, with some economic overtones implicit in the added
cost of transporting goods overland if the Panama Canal were closed. But
the more satisfactory explanation, on the philosophical principle that simpler
explanations are superior to complex, is the need to gain mobility for the
navy between oceans. The economic dimension is a side issue. No economic
materialist has found an economic rationale for the base at Okinawa. Raw-
material interests may lead away from neo-colonialism and to independence
for former colonies, as the Philippine example demonstrates: the pressure
for independence came from beet-sugar interests in the mountain states, anxious to ease the relatively efficient Philippine industry out from behind the
United States tariff. Moreover, raw-material interests can line up on two sides
of an issue, as illustrated by domestic and international companies on the
question of quotas on oil for "national defense" or producer and processor
companies' tariff on copper. Again, the overseas interests of the oil companies
in getting along with the Arabs were allowed to go untended because of political and non-economic involvement in Israel.

Countries engaged in raw-material production have a problem. Entry is
relatively easy. World population growth which favors rising terms of trade,
seems to have less effect than improved technology which lowers production
costs, produces synthetic substitutes, and increases efficiency in utilization.
As world income per capita rises, the demand for foodstuffs increases less
than that for other goods and services, according to Engel's law. Colin Clark
once thought that the developed countries would be squeezed by adverse
terms of trade as the less developed countries shifted resources out of primary
production into manufactures too rapidly. This has happened briefly in india,
for example, where until recently the improvement in production in agriculture was neglected. On balance the trend seems still to favor manufactures.
Occasional rising demand and production shortage will lead to rising prices
in such commodities as copper and nickel. By and large, however, easy entry
into primary production, abetted by foreign investment, and difficulty in expanding manufactured output in the less developed countries means that the
terms of trade tend to favor the developed countries. Entry is relatively easy,

exit difficult. When primary-product prices rise, expanded new output brings them down. When prices fall, the resources involved are slow to switch to other occupations. If countries cannot readily switch their resources between industries, their terms of trade tend to inch downward. . . .

The less developed countries have benefited greatly from foreign investment in recent years, and this is quite apart from all training, employment, and social overhead investment effects, through taxing profits, exports or both. Oil is certainly not typical, but it alone counts for an impressive rise in income; the Middle East governments' income rose from $1,022 millions in 1957 to nearly $3 billion in 1966.[2] In 1969, the Iranian government negotiated with the oil companies with a resolute demand to raise its take from oil to $1 billion a year.

Nor is neo-imperialism proof against confiscation of foreign properties in the host countries; witness Mexico, Iran, Ceylon, Cuba, Indonesia, Peru, and so on. No marines have been forthcoming and there has been great reluctance on the part of the executive branch of government to apply the Hickenlooper amendment on foreign aid, or cancellation of the sugar quota as the Congress requires in protection of United States investments.

The less developed countries not unnaturally complain about foreign investments, but want more. In fact, the United States finds itself urging them not to go so far in giving tax advantages, subsidies and encouragements to new investors from abroad that they erode the tax basis on which economic development in part rests. It is easier to promise to pay rewards for future investments, to be sure, than it is to sustain those to investments that already exist.

Pax Americana

We may dismiss, then, the case that the United States goes abroad to rid itself of embarrassing surpluses, to sustain the rate of profit at home, or to obtain vital raw materials—each of which has an element of truth in it, to be sure, but no monopoly. The possibility of imperialism remains. Like Britain in the nineteenth century, the United States maintains an active diplomatic and often military interest in matters around the world even though it lacks possessions, colonies or dominions. There are troops in Europe and Asia, South Korea, Japan, Okinawa, the Philippines as well as South Vietnam. The Sixth Fleet patrols the Mediterranean and the Seventh the China Seas. The Strategic Air Command flies over halfway around the world, and occasionally drops an unarmed nuclear bomb by accident. Intervention takes place with Marines in Lebanon and troop carriers in the Congo, not to mention the Dominican Republic. The United States concerns itself with local disputes between India and Pakistan, Israel and its Arab neighbors, Peru and Paraguay, civil war in the Congo and Nigeria.

[2] Edith T. Penrose, *The Large International Firm in Developing Countries: The International Petroleum Industry* (London: Allen and Unwin, Ltd., 1968), pp. 200, 249.

The economist is not professionally concerned with whether this is *The Arrogance of Power* as Senator Fulbright has characterized it, or an evident necessity to fill the balance of power left by reduced British, French, and Dutch power around the world after two wars, and to prevent the intrusion of Soviet and Chinese power into the vacuum. Ronald Steel in *Pax Americana* pays almost no attention to economic issues. He touches on foreign aid, on trade barriers in Latin America, and on "economic colonialism" limited to United States investments in European manufacturing. Mainly he criticizes the foreign policy of the United States as neurotically ideological. The United States, he asserts, overreacts and over-intervenes, well beyond the serving of her own interests, wherever it can safely and effectively oppose the expansion of Communism.

But of course there are economic aspects. At a minimum there is the cost and pressure on the balance of payments. The United States has gone to considerable length to patch up the balance of payments. Britain decided on withdrawal from its bases in Singapore and Aden on the ground that it can't afford it. $30 billion a year for Vietnam is substantial. The maintenance of fleets, and stationing of troops, bases, and keeping SAC going all cost money. U.S. foreign aid of $2½ to $3 billion may or may not be connected with the imperial role, although Canada, Sweden and a number of smaller powers contribute to aid for economic development on moral grounds and without large designs.

On the benefit side, the question is how much is insurance against future wars and their cost, how much protection against loss of economic assets, and how much an investment in expansion for economic benefit. There is no way to decide. My instinct, or political prejudice, suggests that Nature abhors a vacuum, including one of power, and that the United States is assisting the work of Nature in its worldwide intervention. It can make mistakes, as in Vietnam, but in its own interest and that of the world it must exercise its power to stabilize and to prevent the outbreak of large wars. This is the use of power to preserve the status quo, if one likes, though aid to Europe and to developing countries is designed to be more positive in building other sources of independent foreign-policy initiative and stability. In this view, the short-run economic interests of the United States—more markets, higher profits, cheaper materials, more outlets for investment—count for something, but for far less than the objective of political stability.

Whereas Julien considers that *L'Empire americain* was designed to obtain economic benefits without colonies, another Frenchman, Amaury de Riencourt, believes in *The American Empire,* the title of his book, but with a different role for business concerns. De Riencourt notes that the United States was not consciously imperialist, or it would not have dismantled its armed forces after V-E Day and not tried so hard to reconstruct European economies. He believes the United States to be an unconscious imperial power, and where conscious reluctant ("although many took to it as cats to milk"). The point for us is that the United States foreign policy is not run by a military-industrial complex, a power elite, or an Establishment to serve its economic interests. Rather the contrary, the United States government uses American firms with foreign investments as one among many instruments to carry out its foreign policy.

A number of European countries and especially Canada complain that the United States uses the foreign subsidiaries of United States corporations to extend its power into other jurisdictions. . . .

In instructing American firms to forbid their subsidiaries to sell to China and Cuba, to borrow abroad and remit home profit for balance-of-payments reasons, to adhere to United States anti-trust policies even in other jurisdictions, and so on, the United States seeks to apply its laws inside other countries. At the same time, it has an obligation to protect the interests of its nationals abroad. According to this view, the United States uses foreign policy to protect foreign investments and foreign investments to protect foreign policy.

As an example of the possibility that there need be no unique causation running between foreign investments and foreign policy, de Riencourt offers a scenario of what might happen in this country's foreign policy toward the Republic of South Africa. Simpleminded Marxism, which has strongly influenced general views on the subject, assumes that United States policy toward South Africa functions on behalf of United States investors in that country— such firms as Engelhard Industries (owned by Charles Engelhard, a friend of former president Lyndon B. Johnson) and the Chase Manhattan Bank which, through a partly-owned London subsidiary, the Standard Bank, has an interest in banking in the country, and has taken part in a consortium which extended a line of credit to the South African Treasury. This view, held by groups ranging from the Presbyterian Church board to the Students for Democratic Society, is espoused with special tenacity by organized black groups in the United States who maintain in addition that recognition of and dealings with the Republic of South Africa imply support for the Nationalist Party policy of apartheid, or enforced segregation of whites, colored and Bantu.

All this ignores one issue on which the United States is firmly opposed to the Republic of South Africa: the question of raising the price of gold from $35 an ounce to something perhaps on the order of $70. The Republic of South Africa wants such an increase to gain more income; the United States opposes it for monetary reasons. (If foreign policy were made exclusively on racial lines, there might be something to be said for raising the gold price to improve the unhappy plight of the Bantu—though the idea is too sophisticated to be acceptable. Inflation breaks down racial barriers by giving incentive to businesses to hire black workers contrary to the laws forbidding it. A higher price for gold would mean more inflation in the Republic and more pressure on the discriminatory regulations. But killing the cat by stuffing it with cream is too sophisticated and hence unacceptable.) The matter will come up again under the discussion of the political implications of international monetary arrangements, but it is evident that the United States has resisted an opportunity to benefit investors in South African mines.

De Riencourt has an alternative scenario to suggest as a possibility. Suppose that the Republican Party were to swing away from the Southern strategy and contest the black vote with the Democrats. Whichever party was in office might find it politically rewarding and necessary in mollifying the mass of black voters to adopt a militant stance in opposition to the Republic of South Africa. An occasion for it might be taken in the continuous resolutions passed by the United Nations terminating the Republic's trusteeship of South-West Africa and the General Assembly vote of 1967 recommending blockade to enforce its decision. It is not inconceivable that the United States would send troops to South-West Africa under the aegis of the United Nations. Nothing guarantees that business interests come first.

Politics and Economics

On the whole the Marxist-Leninist interpretation of imperialism and its extension to the neo-imperialism of foreign investment after the dissolution of empires is not very convincing. To be sure, particular interests supported imperialism for reasons of private gain. But it is impossible to prove, as opposed to assert, that interests had control of the decision-making machinery of government. They influence decision, along with other forces; there is grave doubt that they consistently control.

By the same token, it is difficult to find political controls in economic relationships between independent states. The government of the investor seeks to protect his interests. It has other concerns as well, in the preservation of peace, or the status quo, or good relations, and these are not in all times and places subsidiary to its support of the economic welfare of its citizens. This eclectic and agnostic view will not budge the True Believer who has found the answer in the simplest economic materialist view. That cannot be helped.

Notes on the Multinational Corporation

EDITORS OF *MONTHLY REVIEW*

First of all, then, we need to understand the precise nature and limits of the multinationality of the multinational corporation. It *is* multinational in the sense that it operates in a number of nations with the purpose of maximizing the profits not of the individual units on a nation-by-nation basis but of the group as a whole. As we shall see, from this characteristic flow some of the most important consequences of the multinational corporation; indeed we can say that it is this alone which constitutes a valid reason for using the term multinational. For in all other decisive respects we are dealing with national corporations. In particular, ownership and control are located in one nation, not dispersed throughout the corporate system. There are two exceptions to this generalization: Royal Dutch Shell and Unilever, in both of which British capital and Dutch capital genuinely share ownership and control through complex parallel headquarters structures. But these exceptions are among the oldest of multinational corporations, and the pattern has not been copied by any of the two to three hundred which have emerged in the half century since the First World War. In particular and contrary to widespread expectation, the European Common Market has not given rise to new multinationals in which ownership and control are shared in two or more countries. There have been mergers and takeovers across national boundaries, and of course many of the European giants have working arrangements with their counterparts in other countries; but we know of no new instance in which a real division of ownership and control has taken place.

Here we meet head-on one of the most persistent themes of the apologetic literature. It is true, these writers say, that up to now the multinationals have been owned and controlled in one of the advanced capitalist countries, but the *trend* is toward a genuine internationalization of both stockholding and management. In support of this contention two sets of facts are cited: the large-scale investment, amounting to many billions of dollars, by foreigners

From *Monthly Review*, Vol. XXI, No. 5 (October 1969), pp. 1–13, and Vol. XXI, No. 6 (November 1969), pp. 1–13. Copyright © 1969 by Monthly Review, Inc.; reprinted by permission of Monthly Review Press.

(mainly Europeans) in U.S. stocks; and the hiring by the multinationals of more and more local people at the middle- and even upper-management levels in their foreign subsidiaries. Assuming the continuation of these activities, the apologists argue that in a relatively short time the national grip on the multinational corporations will be broken and they will become, so to speak, citizens of the world rather than of any particular country.

There is no need to quarrel about the facts here, though they are considerably less massive than is sometimes asserted or implied. What is really at issue is their interpretation. As to stockholdings, the following excerpt from a story in the *New York Times* of February 22, 1968, is instructive:

> Experts of the United Nations Economic Commission for Europe say there is a link between the flow of European capital into American equities and the direct investments of the big United States companies in Europe.
> "Europeans," the experts say . . . , "buy the stocks of the big United States companies, which are precisely the ones that invest in Europe."
> This means, in effect, that European capital joins with United States management to invest in Europe, it is asserted.

Since European stockholders, like their counterparts in the United States, normally have no influence on the composition or policies of managements, what this means is that many European capitalists, instead of investing directly in European industry, put their capital at the disposal of Americans who invest in Europe. "Internationalization" of ownership thus turns out to be one of many ways in which U.S. capital gains control over foreign capital.

As far as the hiring of local personnel to staff foreign subsidiaries is concerned, this has absolutely nothing to do with sharing control, which remains undivided in the parent company. Of course if boards of directors and top managements of parent companies began to blossom with foreigners, that would be something else which would call for serious analysis. But this has not happened. A few foreigners probably sit on the boards of some of the multinationals, but we have not run across a single case of foreigners occupying top management positions. . . .

None of this should be taken to imply that the existence of this second and inferior "class" of executives in the multinational company is of no importance. On the contrary these people make up a significant section of the native bourgeoisie in every country where multinationals operate. Their interests (jobs, salaries, bonuses, promotions) lie with the parent company; only to the extent that they serve it well and faithfully can they expect to advance and prosper. But, as we shall see, the interests of the parent company often contradict those of the countries in which they operate. It follows that while multinational corporations do not, as so often claimed, internationalize their managements, they do *de*nationalize a section of the native bourgeoisies in the countries they penetrate. This of course weakens these native bourgeoisies and makes it that much harder for them to resist demands and pressures emanating from more powerful countries. . . .[1]

The very idea of a unit of capital divorced from any nationality—which, according to some apologetic theories, is what the multinational corporation is in the process of becoming—is a contradiction in terms. Capital is a fundamental part of a particular set of relations of production which, far from being natural and eternal, is historical and alterable. These relations of production, implying as they do the exploitation of some classes and groups by other classes and groups, were established through violent struggles and can be maintained in existence only through a sufficiently powerful apparatus of coercion, i.e., a state. Capital without a state is therefore unthinkable. But in the world as it is constituted today only nations have states: there is no such thing as a supranational state. It follows that to exist capital must have nationality. If, for example, the state of the nation to which it belonged were to collapse, capital would lose its indispensable protector. It would then either be incorporated into the capital of another nation or it would cease to be capital by coming under the jurisdiction of a revolutionary regime dedicated to the abolition of the entire set of relations of production of which capital is one part. Finally, capital of one nationality can operate in other nations only because all the capitalist classes maintain basically similar sets of relations of production and because they find it, on the whole, in their mutual interest to permit this kind of international movement of capital.

As Marx showed—and it was certainly one of his most important contributions—it is of the very essence of capital to expand. There are two basic reasons for this. First, the power and standing of the capitalist (owner or functionary of capital) is proportional to the magnitude of his capital. The way to rise in capitalist society is therefore to accumulate capital. And second, any capitalist who stands still is in danger of being wiped out. As Marx put it in a brilliant passage:

> The development of capitalist production makes it constantly necessary to keep increasing the amount of capital laid out in a given industrial undertaking, and competition makes the immanent laws of capitalist production to be felt by each individual capitalist as external coercive laws. It compels him to keep constantly extending his capital, in order to preserve it, but extend it he cannot except by means of progressive accumulation. (*Capital*, Kerr ed. Vol. 1, p. 649.)

These considerations are as valid for the corporate capitalist as for the individual capitalist of an earlier period. And they are deeply embedded in the ideology of the business world where the worship of growth has attained the standing of a secular religion. "The only real security for this company

---

[1] The section of the native bourgeoisie which identifies its interests with foreign companies rather than with its own class and nation is not limited to those in the direct employ of the foreign companies. It also includes a variety of others such as suppliers, subcontractors, lawyers, etc., who depend on the foreign subsidiaries for the major part of their incomes.

or any other company," says the annual report of a major corporation which we have quoted in these pages before, "is through healthy, continuous, and vigorous growth. A company is just like a human being. When it stops growing, when it can't replenish itself through growth, then it starts to deteriorate. . . . There is no security where there is no opportunity for growth and development and continual improvement."[2]

In the abstract terms of Marxist economic theory, growth means that a part of the surplus value accruing to a unit of capital in one period is added to capital in the next period. The larger capital now brings in a greater amount of surplus value which permits a still larger increment of growth, and so on. Marxist theory has traditionally focused on the overall consequences for the whole economy of such behavior by the individual units of capital. What has been unduly neglected are the implications of this spiral process (capital/surplus value/added capital) for what bourgeois economics calls the theory of the firm. The following highly schematic sketch may serve to indicate lines along which fruitful work can advance.

We start—as both Marx and the classical economists did—with the firm in a competitive industry. Its output is small relative to the total, and its product is more or less indistinguishable from that of all the other firms catering to the same market. Under these circumstances each firm will produce up to the point where the cost of turning out an additional unit is equal to the market price (beyond that point cost would exceed price and hence entail a reduction of profit). This is the famous equilibrium position which in textbook economics is too often treated as the end of the subject rather than the beginning.

The profitable course for the capitalist who finds himself in this position is clearly marked: he must bring down his costs and thus increase his profit margin (it is assumed that he can sell whatever he produces at the going price, so he has no sales problem). And cost reduction normally means expanding the scale of production and introducing new and improved techniques. Those who successfully follow this course prosper and grow, while those who lag behind fall by the wayside.

This process, however, cannot continue in this way indefinitely. There comes a time when the expansion in the size of the average firm, brought about by the growth of the successful ones and the elimination of the failures, alters the situation in a fundamental way. The individual firm is no longer one small producer among many, all taking the going price as a datum to which they adjust in the most profitable manner. Instead, each firm now produces a significant proportion of the industry's total supply, and each must take into account the effect of its own output on the market price. This opens up new problems and possibilities which have been more or less adequately studied under such headings as imperfect or monopolistic competition, oligopoly, and monopoly. Here we need only point out that in addition to

[2] From the 1965 annual report of Rockwell-Standard Corporation, since merged with North American Aviation to form North American Rockwell Corporation.

continuing to seek lower production costs, the rational course for every firm to follow is to get itself as nearly as possible into the position of a monopolist, either individually (through differentiating its product from those of rivals) or collectively (through acting openly or tacitly in collusion with rivals). It follows that for the purposes of theoretical analysis the appropriate assumption is that the typical firm acts like a monopolist, maximizing profits at a level of output which falls well short of the volume at which the cost of producing an additional unit equals market price. When this situation prevails in most of the important industries, capitalism has entered its monopoly stage.

From our present point of view what needs to be stressed is that in the monopoly stage, the problem of growth presents itself to the firm in a radically different light. It is no longer simply a question of progressively reducing costs and expanding output of a homogeneous product. Cost reduction of course remains as important as ever, but now the maximization of profit requires a go-slow policy with respect to the expansion of output. It follows that the monopolistic firm can no longer count on being able to grow while remaining within the confines of the industry of its origin and early development. Not that expansion within the industry is entirely precluded, but it is strictly limited by cost and demand factors which are totally unrelated to the firm's ability and hence desire to grow, that is to say, by its profitability. The monopolistic firm is therefore driven by an inner compulsion to go outside of and beyond its historical field of operations. And the strength of this compulsion is the greater the more monopolistic the firm and the greater the amount of surplus value it disposes over and wishes to capitalize.

Here, it seems to us, we have the fundamental explanation of one of the decisive phenomena of recent capitalist history: the tendency of the corporation as it gets bigger to diversify both industrially and geographically—or, in current terminology, the tendency to become on the one hand a conglomerate and on the other hand a multinational corporation. The great majority of the 200 largest nonfinancial corporations in the United States today—corporations which together account for close to half the country's industrial activity—have arrived at the stage of both conglomerateness and multinationality. . . .

This is not to argue that the drive for investment abroad by monopolistic firms is stimulated solely by pressures emanating from the search for investment outlets for surplus funds. For example, capital will move to areas where it is feasible to exploit low wages and other cost advantages. And the monopoly stage adds yet another dimension. Under monopoly conditions in a given industry, it is usual to find not one but several dominant companies. It follows that when one of the leading firms invests in a foreign country, competing giants in the same industry are prompted to follow suit to make sure that they get their "proper" share of the local market. Furthermore, tariff barriers, patent rights, and other local conditions create circumstances in which the corporate giants find that they can best control the market in a foreign country through investment rather than mere exports. One of the outstanding features of the giant corporation, indeed, is that it has the means to try to control the market over a large part of the world; and, for its own security and profit, it continuously strives to do so.

It is important to understand that under monopolistic conditions the axiom according to which capital always moves from low-profit to high-profit industries and regions no longer holds. Monopoly by definition impedes the free flow of capital into protected high-profit situations; and, as we have already seen, the monopolist sitting inside these bastions is careful not to invest more than the traffic will bear, while seeking outlets elsewhere for his surplus capital. It is therefore not only possible but probably quite common for capital to move in directions opposite to those indicated by traditional economic theory. This fact alone is enough to knock into a cocked hat that supposedly sacrosanct tenet of bourgeois thought according to which any movement of capital in search of maximum profits automatically guarantees a more efficient allocation of resources. (There are other reasons why this idea, considered as a general proposition, is fallacious, but they do not concern us here.) Unless otherwise stated, what follows relates entirely to giant corporations which have reached the monopolistic stage and are in the process of spreading into both new industries and new geographical areas. This is the actual situation of most of the giants that dominate the U.S. economy, and it is increasingly true of the large corporations of Western Europe and Japan.

The spreading process can take two forms. The initiating corporation can establish a new enterprise in the industry or country it is entering, or it can buy up an existing enterprise. We know of no empirical studies dealing with this matter, but it is our impression that the preferred way is generally to buy up an existing enterprise. And there is a good reason for this. Establishing a foothold from scratch in a new field or new place can be costly and time-consuming, while buying one that already exists is quick and easy. In this connection it matters little whether the enterprise in question is doing well or badly; in fact, there is much to be said for a weak company since it can be acquired more cheaply. In any case, the parent corporation usually plans to reorganize the new subsidiary to conform to its own style and to make the most of the advantages which its superior size and strength confer upon it.

What are these advantages? It is usual to think of the large corporation thriving and growing because of its ability to take advantage of the economies of large-scale *production,* and of course there is considerable merit to this line of reasoning. But when it comes to expanding into new fields, the economies of scale may have little or nothing to do with success or failure. For one thing the technology of the new field may be entirely different from that of the base industry and may not lend itself to the development of mass-production methods. And for another, when a corporation sets up shop to produce its accustomed product abroad, it will deliberately tailor its techniques according to the size of the market rather than export its domestically developed mass-production methods. The decisive advantages of the giant corporation lie elsewhere than in production proper. Chief among them are (not necessarily in order of importance, which will vary from case to case) the following: (1) Plenty of capital to invest and almost unlimited access to credit on favorable terms in both domestic and foreign money markets. (2) A pool of experienced managerial talent which can be deployed anywhere in the corporate empire according to need. (3) A large and effective sales apparatus which is similarly available to all units of the corporate empire. And (4) research and development facilities which can be put to work to solve all sorts of technological and marketing problems. The small independent corporation is likely to be deficient in all these respects and hence quite incapable of competing on even terms with a rival which is a subsidiary of one of the giant conglomerate multinationals. It follows that whenever one of the latter enters a new field it tends to forge ahead rapidly until it occupies a leading position along with a few other giants. At this time competitive behavior gives way to monopolistic behavior. The newly matured subsidiary begins to generate more profits than it can safely invest, with the surplus flowing back into the central pool of capital maintained by the parent company. At this time the subsidiary which began by being an outlet for surplus capital becomes a source of additional surplus capital and hence a spur for the corporation as a whole to find still new areas into which to expand—in short, to become still more conglomerate and multinational. Logically, this process should come to an end either with all major industries in all capitalist countries dominated by a few hundred giant corporations, or with the overthrow of capitalism on an international scale. At the moment we seem to be moving more rapidly toward the first denouement than the second. Judd Polk of the United States Council of the International Chamber of Commerce is responsible for the following estimates which, at least as far as orders of magnitude are concerned, seem quite reasonable:

> Over the past two decades international investment and its output have been growing about twice as fast as world GNP [Gross National Product]. The effect has been to produce an internationalized sector of production that is now of a very substantial order of magnitude and is continuing to grow in relation to total world output. Already it appears that almost a quarter of all production in the market world is accounted for by the output of international companies. If we look to the end of this century, envisioning the growth of world GNP to continue at its typical pace of the 1960s, and similarly the output of international investment at its typically faster rate of the 1960s we get a picture roughly estimable as follows [table omitted]. The final figure (53 per cent) shows a world economy better than half internationalized.[3]

By "internationalized" Polk of course means gobbled up by a relative handful of U.S., Western European, and Japanese multinational corporations.

As things are going now, this is the realistic prospect. . . .

[3] Judd Polk, "The Internationalization of Production," mimeographed, issued by the U.S. Council, International Chamber of Commerce, May 7, 1969.

The multinational corporation, in brief, is the key institution of finance capital in the second half of the 20th century; and Lenin's characterization in *Imperialism* (1917) requires little modification to fit it: "The concentration of production; the monopolies arising therefrom, the merging or coalescence of the banks with industry—such is the history of the rise of finance capital and such is the content of this term."

There are of course profound conflicts of interest between multinational corporations and the foreign countries in which they operate. Most of the apologetic literature attempts to play them down as either of little importance or amenable to remedial action, but none can deny their existence. Here is a fairly comprehensive list of such conflicts, cast in the form of "six major fears" felt by the foreign countries:[4]

1. Fear that the international corporation will take too much and leave too little. The fear is often expressed that the big foreign corporation will take away the national resources (oil, iron ore, foodstuffs, etc.), all the profits, the most able local people (hence the brain drain), and leave only the crumbs in the form of low wages, low compared to the wages the same corporations pay at home.[5]

2. Fear that the international corporation will crush local competition and quickly achieve a monopolistic dominance of the local market if not the local economy. "Who can compete with the enormous technical resources of a giant corporation whose annual sales are more than the French national budget?"

3. Fear of becoming dependent on foreign sources for modern technology needed for national defense, and for being competitive in world markets.

4. Fear that the international corporation's local subsidiary will be used as an instrument of foreign policy by the government of the parent company. For example, in the case of a U.S. subsidiary, fear that the U.S. government will prohibit sales to certain markets (Red China, Cuba, North Korea, North Vietnam, etc.); or that the U.S. government will prohibit the parent from sending certain technology to the subsidiary which technology would be useful locally for national defense or for other purposes; or fear that the U.S. government will prevent the U.S. parent from sending new capital to the local subsidiary, and will require the local subsidiary to remit virtually all of its earnings home thus damaging the balance of payments of the local government.

5. Fear that the good jobs will be given to nationals of the parent company and not to local nationals.

6. Fear that decisions will be taken by the parent company in callous disregard for their impact on the local town, province, or even on the

[4] "The International Corporation and the Nation State," prepared by Business International, New York, May 1968 (mimeographed).

[5] A classic example of the reality underlying this fear—the rape of Cyprus by Cyprus Mines Corporation, a Los Angeles-based multinational—was analyzed in these pages a few years ago. See "Foreign Investment," Review of the Month, MR, January 1965.

national economy. For example—a decision to close down a factory and put thousands of workers out of jobs.

Needless to say, none of these fears is the product of fevered imaginations; all are grounded in much bitter experience. At bottom the conflicts of interest which they reflect are related to the most fundamental characteristic of the multinational corporation, that policies for all the units in the corporate empire are formulated by a central management with a view to benefiting the whole (i.e., the parent corporation) rather than the separate parts. From the point of view of the central owners and managers, this is obviously the correct course to pursue, indeed the only possible course since there could be no other conceivable reason for putting the multinational entity together in the first place. But for the parts—and for the communities and countries in which they operate—it means that they quite literally have no interests which have to be taken into account in the formulation of their own policies. This is not the place for a catalogue of the concrete ways in which the interests of the subsidiaries, considered as separate capitalist enterprises, may be (and at one time or other actually have been) overridden by the interests of the parent. But a couple of examples, taken again from a source friendly to the multinational corporations, will indicate the kind of thing that is involved.

> Every sovereign [nation] is aware that a multinational corporate group which is able to provide export markets for the product of the host country is also capable of withholding such markets and cutting off the jobs that depend on such exports. If Nigeria should eventually become a lower cost producer of widgets than Italy, the corporate group may shift the locus of its operations out of Italy into Nigeria.
>
> Along similar lines, a multinational group that can provide foreign capital to the host government's economy is also thought capable of draining capital away for use elsewhere; hence the perennial accusations of "decapitalization" with which foreign investors are confronted in Latin America.[6]

This last paragraph points to the ultimate conflict of interest between the multinational corporation and the host country. As Paul Baran so eloquently demonstrated, the key to a country's economic development lies in the size and utilization of its surplus. We see now that to the extent that its economy is penetrated by multinational corporations, control over *both* size and utilization passes into the hands of others who are owners or functionaries of capital of a different nationality. Under these circumstances it can be said that multinational corporations are the enemy, perhaps not of *any* development in the host countries but at least of any development which conforms to the interests of any class or group within the country other than those who have been denationalized and coopted into the service of foreign capital.

[6] Raymond Vernon, "Multinational Enterprise and National Sovereignty," *Harvard Business Review,* March–April 1967, p. 163.

The conflicts of interest between multinational corporations and the foreign countries in which they operate generate many-sided political struggles, particularly in the underdeveloped countries where the relative weight of the multinationals is greatest. Here the local bourgeoisies tend to be split and largely incapable of independent action or initiative. An important section works, directly or indirectly, for foreign capital; and much of the remainder is paralyzed by fear of social revolution. Hence the political stance of the local bourgeoisie is generally pro-imperialist and reactionary. Its rule is therefore naturally favored by the countries in which the multinationals have their headquarters. For practical purposes this means that the chief backer of local bourgeoisies in the underdeveloped countries is the United States, since the great majority of multinationals are U.S. companies. . . .

To complete the picture on the U.S. side, we need only remind ourselves that the government of the United States is controlled by the very same corporations which have spread their tentacles out to every corner of the globe. This is of course not recognized by U.S. political "science," but it is well known, if not often proclaimed, by those who are directly concerned with the business of government. . . .

As actual or potential opposition to the local bourgeoisies and their U.S. backers there are various classes and strata in the underdeveloped countries: peasants and workers, petty bourgeoisie, students and intellectuals, some members of the military. Short of making a revolution, which is their ultimate threat and must sooner or later become their goal, the peasants and workers are largely excluded from the political arena, though some elements from these classes may lend support to nationalistic regimes based primarily on the petty bourgeoisie and led by intellectuals and military people. The objective of such regimes, or of those trying to form such regimes, is not to dispossess or oust the multinational corporations, which would involve a life-and-death struggle against imperialism, but to reduce their scope, to limit their freedom of action, and, by applying various economic and political pressures, to force them to operate more in the national interest than they would if left to their own devices. A good example of such a regime is the military dictatorship which seized power in Peru earlier this year. Among its first acts was the taking over of the properties of the International Petroleum Corporation, a subsidiary of Standard of New Jersey, which had been embroiled in a quarrel over taxes with Peruvian governments for more than half a century and in the process had become the chief target of Peruvian nationalism. The regime also embarked on a land reform which impinges on the interests of another multinational, W. R. Grace & Co. But at the same time it has made clear that it intends no large-scale attacks on foreign capital, though the threat (from foreign capital's point of view) always exists that the situation will get out of hand and the regime, or a more radical one that might follow it, will plunge ahead with an all-out nationalization program.

Against this background it can be seen that for the multinational corporation a world of nations is a world full of pitfalls and dangers. Their most fundamental requirement is freedom to do business wherever and whenever they choose, unrestrained by any external authority. . . .

But nations cannot grant these sweeping freedoms without denying their essence as nations, i.e., as collectivities with pretensions to sovereignty, which means simply the right to run their own affairs without interference from those outside the nation. Multinational corporations and nations are therefore fundamentally and irrevocably opposed to each other. The logic of each, carried to its final conclusion, is to destroy the other. Or, to put the point differently, the historic course of the global capitalist system is leading to one of two outcomes: world empire or world revolution.

Questions for Discussion

1. Can the United States plead "temporary insanity" in the case of Indochina, or is the American involvement the result of natural and permanent forces
2. such as those suggested by Magdoff?
   Is a world of free trade the best for all concerned?
3. Even if Magdoff and Sweezy are correct that the development of truly multinational corporations has been exaggerated, what kind of implications would such a development have for world affairs? For United States foreign policy?

PART XII

A Concluding Essay

Before questions can be answered they must be posed, and before debates can lead to fruitful interchange the participants must agree on what the issues are.

Ideological disputes, and that is what this book primarily contains, are often confusing to the observer precisely because the fundamental questions have not been agreed upon. This problem is especially important in a book of readings such as this one, where individual contributions have not been prepared in direct response to one another, but have appeared in various sources at different times, and with different immediate purposes in mind.

It is the purpose of the editors in this final essay to attempt to make clear to the reader the underlying differences in approach and purpose of the various contributors to this volume as well as to discuss, in a critical way, the general point of view of the discipline of economics on the basic questions raised. This will be done by first indicating what seem to be the principal differences among what we have called the conservative, liberal, and radical positions, and then by discussing how the subject matter of economics, as it is commonly taught, relates to these differences.

Conservatives, Liberals, and Radicals

In characterizing the ideological stances of the individual writers in this book this tripartite classification has been used because it seemed to the editors to be the most descriptive. As with any such generalized categorization, however, this division is likely to obscure both important differences among individuals placed in the same category and similarities among those pigeonholed differently. This cannot be helped since we want to speak of ideological currents rather than engage in biography, to discuss forests rather than trees. We must, however, make more clear the important distinguishing characteristics that define our categories.

Radical, conservative, and liberal are often used synonomously with the terms left, middle, and right, referring to positions along a political "spectrum." One of the principal determinants of one's position on the spectrum is his attitude toward government, as one moves from left to right less government involvement is preferred. The conservative and the radical are therefore seen as opposites, with the liberal occupying the role of compromiser, adopting points from each.

This simplistic overview is, at times, more confusing than helpful, especially when considering the issues at hand. As an example of where the spectrum approach breaks down, consider the writings of Murray Rothbard in Part III and James O'Connor in Part VI, both of whom conclude that government in the United States exploits the many to the benefit of the privileged few. This may sound more left than right—more radical than conservative—but even Milton Friedman's critique of too much government is often that a particular form of government intervention unjustifiably redistributes income from the poor to the rich.

The key to understanding this paradox is in correctly identifying two separate questions to which these ideologies address themselves. The first may be stated most directly as "What does government do?" and is to be contrasted with the second, "What *should* government *ideally* do?" In examining the generalized responses of our ideological postures to these questions in order, some important distinctions will be made clear.

What Does Government Do?—The Character of Government in the United States

There is one point on which everyone should agree, government, in particular the federal government, is an extremely powerful institution today. This agreement is possible because a *quantitative* approach to the question "How powerful is government?" is both possible and meaningful if the question is restated as "How *big* is government?" The introductory essay interpreted the question in this way and marshalled evidence to indicate the trends in the size of government.

On the more important *qualitative* question, however, of whether government is *too* powerful or not powerful enough, such agreement is not so easy to obtain. Yet it is surely this last interpretation of the question that is most important.

Both the conservative and the radical find the current role of government distasteful and view with alarm any trend toward increasing federal government influence; they can agree that government is too powerful. The liberal, on the other hand, while admitting to some misguided *policies,* is optimistic about government power and proposes its enlargement.

When a new problem rises to the public attention one sees at first the liberal and the radical in an alliance to increase awareness and concern. Once a "solution" has been found, however, the radical will be heard echoing the conservative laments of more government bureaucracy, because some new federal government program is nearly always the liberal-directed solution.

This apparent convergence of radical and conservative views is only superficial, because it is in the reasons for their dissatisfaction that they disagree. It is their answers to the second question which distinguish them.

What Should Government Do?—On the Ideal Form of Government

Lord Acton's familiar dictum that "power corrupts, and absolute power corrupts absolutely" is the warning cry of the conservative. To him the radical's complaint that government is used by the upper classes to their own ends is not consistent with the demand for socialistic institutions or the elimination of private property since this, in the conservative view, would represent an even greater concentration of power. And, as Milton Friedman puts it, "The power to do good is also the power to do harm. . . . The great tragedy of the drive to centralization, as of the drive to extend the scope of government in general, is that it is mostly led by men of good will who will be the first to rue its consequences." The radical considers the conservative incredibly naive, especially in his belief in *laissez-faire*. The radical interpretation of American economic growth is that it has been precisely the intervention of government which has kept the system afloat, and the radical's rejection of the system itself is the basis for his criticism of this intervention. To the conservative, the government's role has rarely been crucial and even when well-intentioned has in fact distorted or slowed the growth that would have occurred autonomously.

A complaint that conservatives and liberals have in common is that the radical rarely spells out explicitly his own vision of the most appropriate institutional arrangement. The radical, in defining his objectives, more often focuses on what would not be: private property, a large defense and police establishment, racial or sexual discrimination, poverty, and so on. This evasion in fact points to what are the crucial issues for the radical. He is interested in the *system* and interprets individual *policies* as mere elaborations of the system itself. To both the liberal and the conservative the best system has been found and the thing to do is to find that variant of the existing system, that set of policies, which will ensure its continued viability. This explains the liberal's typical exasperation with the radical, for when the radical points to a problem the liberal immediately asks what policy can be adopted and what government organization created to deal with the problem. The radical's response is that within the existing system none is possible, at least none that would bring about a permanent and just solution, because the system does not really have enough options. The source of nearly all problems is the exploitation of man by man inherent in the competitive, private-property economy. The *a priori* importance of the discipline of economics to these questions should be clear; the conservative and the liberal are aligned against the radical on the question of whether the system can work, while the liberal and the conservative disagree on what policy mix within the system is best.

It behooves us at this point, therefore, to turn to a discussion of the actual practice and teaching of the discipline in order to evaluate its contribution to the debate.

Economics and Economists on the Role of Government

We have been, perhaps, unfair to the radical in saying that he offers no alternatives. He can point to other examples of institutional arrangements, most obviously the Soviet Union and the countries of Eastern Europe, China, and Yugoslavia, and often does. This is not, however, a book on comparative economic systems, so that this method of approaching the question, although an entirely valid one, will not be followed, though we must admit that that is another arena in the discipline in which this debate is carried out. We have intended to show, however, that the way in which economics is studied, the questions to which it is directed, mitigate against a careful analysis of the radical point of view.

It is rare indeed to find an introductory textbook in economics that does not begin essentially as follows:

Economics is the study of the manner in which scarce resources are allocated to alternative ends. It attempts to answer the questions: (1) What shall be produced, of the myriad of possible combinations, with these scarce resources? (2) Since a given quantity of a given good can be produced with different combinations of the resources, which combination shall be chosen? (3) How shall the bundle of goods thus produced be distributed among the members of the society? and, perhaps, (4) What quantity of the available nonperishable resources shall be used in the current time period and what quantity saved for the future?

The distinction is then typically made between two (and only two) ways in which these questions can be answered by a society, by leaving the answers to the "market" or to a government. In our society, the explanation typically proceeds, these answers are by and large left to the market, with the exception of a few mysterious cases where "externalities" mean that the market does not lead to optimal results. The role of the government is to ensure that the rules of the system are followed, that is, to promote the attainment of the necessary conditions for perfect competition and to produce those goods and services (or to regulate and otherwise control their production), where externalities are involved. The major part of the introductory course will, however, be devoted to an explanation of how the market carries out this decision making. To put the icing on the cake, a few examples of markets where extensive government intervention has occurred, most usually in agriculture, will be considered in order to show how the unfettering of the market would achieve better results.

This all sounds very conservative, and indeed it is. The liberals have their heyday in the macro section, where a rather automatic government could contract and expand in order to achieve economic stability if only the conservatives could be convinced of the correctness of the theory. This government, ethically neutral and mindless of pleas for special privilege, looks only at aggregate indicators, charts and graphs, in order to decide how much to spend. The answer is usually that it should spend more.

Introductory courses, in response to student demands for "relevancy," more and more profess an orientation to "problems." This usually means that the student is forced to buy yet another book, which will contain articles explaining how much poverty there is, the differences in black-white, male-female, and North-South average incomes. The book will document the existence of underdeveloped countries, the problems of pollution and over-population, and will require the student on the final examination to remember which writer said what. If the problems ever leave the realm of "outside reading" and become part of the lecture topic, or are "integrated" in the textbook, the purpose or at least the *result* of doing so will be to indicate that the whole problem and its possible solutions could be understood with the aid of one or a few simple supply-demand diagrams.

In economics the answer to nearly every question, including how large the government should be, depends on the size or sign of a parameter, the slope or shape of a curve. It is this characteristic of economics that leads to claims like that of George Stigler, "that economics as a positive science is ethically—and therefore politically—neutral. The corpus of economic analysis can be turned to a thousand contradictory ends." For couldn't statistical evidence tell us the size of the parameter or the slope of the curve and therefore decide the question once and for all?

That the debate over the appropriate role of government has continued should be evidence enough that this is not the case. And the reason for this is not that the statistical and mathematical tools are missing; the explanation lies at the beginning—in the interpretation of the basic questions and the elaboration of the subquestions to be considered.

The *weltanschauung* or paradigm, the questions that are posed and the way in which they are posed, of economics does not permit the asking of the radical's questions. This is both because some questions are outlawed and reveal the ignorance of the asker when raised and because some questions simply never come up. As an example of the first sort, consider "What is a fair or just price of a loaf of bread?" This is a real question and surely an important one in everyday life. It was, however, forever banned from economics classrooms, at least since 1890, when Alfred Marshall published his *Principles of Economics,* the cornerstone of modern microeconomic theory. The student who would ask such a question on the last day of class in economics would be surely ridiculed.

A more enlightening example, however, is the question of just income distribution, similarly banished in perpetuity. The reason the economist refuses to answer the first question is because it is irrelevant, and the second he finds outside his expertise. Who am I, protests the fair and modest professor, to say who should have the higher and who the lower income?

The trouble with this attitude is that it closes the debate, at least so far as the radical is concerned. For the radical's whole point of view, the direction of his attention, is based upon his observation that the existing distribution of income *is* unjust. All his theoretical and empirical laborings proceed from that judgment, and when he asks "Why?" he is led to look at government in an entirely different way than is the economist.

It is of course true, as economists protest, that one distribution of income cannot be objectively proved superior to another, but this begs the question. Joan Robinson has said, "I can't define an elephant, but I know one when I see one." Similarly, the radical *knows* that there are better distributions of income than the one with which we are living, and he *knows* that resources are better spent in relieving urban and rural poverty, in cleaning up the environment, and in the alleviation of racism and sexism than on bombs and bullets and an entire industry like advertising, devoted to explaining to people what it is they want to buy. It cannot be *proved* that such alterations of the allocation of resources would increase the public welfare. But then what *can* be proved?

As economics textbooks do, it can be shown that under perfect competition, in the absence of externalities, an unambiguously "better" allocation of resources is achieved than under most monopolistic arrangements. No one, of course, claims that the necessary conditions for perfect competition exist. What is proposed is "workable" competition, something approximating perfect competition as closely as possible. Yet the proposition that a little bit more competition always means a better allocation of resources is logically invalid; it cannot be proved. This completely plausible proposition is, however, the basic faith of the economist. As substantiation of his faith he points to the laudable performance of the American economy, to the high relative standard of living of even the lower classes when compared to much of the rest of the world.

This amounts to an admission that the real proof of the pudding is in the eating, that the real test of economic theory is in the way the economy actually works. This suggests that the correct way to analyze government in the American economy is to ask what it has done and what it is doing and to whom the benefits and costs are accruing. It suggests that we ask whether a great deal of government expenditure in fact represents the socialization of the costs of production, whether the government agencies designed to control and regulate private enterprise in fact lend support and protection to their "clients," that is, those they are supposed to regulate.

This is not, however, the way the relation of business and government is examined in economics. Assuming that this is the purpose of government agencies, economics texts ask, rather, what is the optimal, most efficient, set of policies to carry out such regulation?

This, to the radical, is lunacy. The state is the prisoner of the corporate elite and acts in the interests of that elite. Some of those interests are not in conflict with efficiency as the economist defines the word, but very many are. And, more importantly, most of those interests are in conflict with the "good society" as envisioned by the radical.

The scope of the conflict between radicals and economists can also be appreciated by considering another important topic on the radical agenda, that of imperialism. Traditional economics does not even take up the question and therefore presumptuously denies its existence or importance.

Perhaps it could be demonstrated that a world of sovereign governments who have in mind the maximum welfare of their total populations is the way the world works (though we certainly doubt it), so that, except for a few highly technical exceptions, free trade is the best of all possible worlds. But if that premise is never questioned, if the radical's alternative model of an increasingly small number of giant oligopolies who through the American and other capitalist governments assert their authority in the underdeveloped world is never even considered, then the question cannot be resolved.

Radicals may be misled on this and many other questions. They may have the wrong answers, but we must conclude that at least they focus on the right questions.

It is the conclusion of the editors that the way economics is traditionally taught, and in particular the way in which the question of the relationship of government to business is approached, biases subsequent discussion away from the radical point of view. By focusing on the "economic" (read, "efficiency") effects of various alternative policies the discipline makes the following implicit assumptions:

First, on having reached a conclusion about the "optimal" policy mix, this is what will be adopted, or, at least, such efficiency questions will be the primary criterion.

Second, since this is the framework within which the alternative policies are compared for their efficiency effects, the economy is characterized by a high degree of competition, or government will move to ensure its attainment.

Third, consumers' patterns of tastes and preference, which were arrived at autonomously, along with the real opportunity costs of production are the principal determinants of what gets produced.

With some inevitable individual differences, liberals and conservatives would agree in spirit with these assumptions, while most radicals would disagree almost totally. An adequate analysis of the radical point of view is therefore made impossible. This is true despite the profession's claim to "ethical and, therefore, political neutrality."

Bibliographical Essay

General

The increasing integration of government and the private economy has drawn greater attention lately but there is by no means a plethora of writings on this topic. It is recommended, however, that the reader examine the March 1972 issue of the *Journal of Economic Issues,* which is devoted largely to this topic. Especially noteworthy in this issue are articles by Daniel Fusfeld, Seymour Melman, Jack Barbash, and Howard Sherman. Probably the best known books examining this problem are John Kenneth Galbraith's *American Capitalism: The Concept of Countervailing Power* (Boston: 1958); and *New Industrial State* (Boston: 1971). Many of Galbraith's ideas are drawn from the earlier works of Thorstein Veblen, particularly Veblen's *Theory of Business Enterprise* (New York: 1904). Other general works on this topic include Robert T. Averitt, *The Dual Economy* (New York: 1968); Morton Baratz, *The American Business System in Transition* (New York: 1970); David T. Bazelon, *The Paper Economy* (New York: 1965); and Michael D. Reagan, *The Managed Economy* (New York: 1963).

Marxist and radical critiques of the growth of state economic power are becoming more numerous and decidedly more relevant. Probably the two best general presentations are Paul Baran's *Political Economy of Growth* (New York: 1968), and Paul Baran and Paul Sweezy, *Monopoly Capital* (New York: 1966). James O'Connor's *Fiscal Crisis of the State* (New York: 1973) presents a good survey of the growth of state economic power from a Marxist perspective. A number of left political journals have devoted whole issues or at least considerable space in recent months to the emergence of the corporate state. Among the most literate and nonsectarian of these are *Monthly Review, Socialist Revolution, Radical America,* and the review and conference papers of the *Union for Radical Political Economics* (URPE).

The Ideological and Historical Background of the Corporate State

For a conventional historical perspective of the problem of growing business-government integration, we recommend the work of Thomas Cochran, especially his recent work, *Business in American Society* (New York: 1971). A radical interpretative approach is offered in Gabriel Kolko's *Triumph of Conservatism*

(New York: 1965). Other books on the ideology and history of the corporate state's development are: James Weinstein, *The Corporate Ideal in the Liberal State 1900–1918* (Boston: 1968); William A. Williams, *The Contours of American History* (Cleveland: 1961); Adolf A. Berle, Jr., *Power Without Property* (New York: 1959); Richard Hofstadter, *Social Darwinism in American Thought* (Boston: 1955); David Finn, *The Corporate Oligarch* (New York: 1969); James W. Prothro, *Dollar Decade: Business Ideas in the 1920's* (Baton Rouge, La.: 1954); and John R. Bunting, *The Hidden Face of Free Enterprise* (New York: 1964).

Government and the Maintenance of the Level of Economic Activity

For further insights into the traditionalists' view the following works are suggested: Gardner Ackley, *Macroeconomic Theory* (New York: 1961); B. H. Wilkins and Charles B. Friday, eds., *The Economists of the New Frontier: An Anthology* (New York: 1963); Alvin H. Hansen, *Fiscal Policy and Business Cycles* (New York: 1941); Nicholas Kaldor, *Essay on Economic Stability and Growth* (Homewood, Illinois: 1960); John Maynard Keynes, *The General Theory of Employment, Interest, and Money* (New York: 1964); Alvin H. Hansen, *A Guide to Keynes* (New York: 1963); and Robert Lekachman, *The Age of Keynes* (New York: 1966).

For a radical analysis of Keynesian economics and government's role in economic activity see Paul A. Baran's, *The Longer View* (New York: 1969); Paul Mattick, *Keynes and Marx* (Boston: 1969); and Paul Sweezy, *Theory of Capitalist Development* (New York: 1942).

Government and Business—Regulation and Control

Though direct controls of the economy during peacetime have been used only recently, there are some analyses of government's regulation and control of business: Richard J. Barber, *The American Corporation: Its Power, Its Money, Its Politics* (New York: 1970); H. H. Liebhafsky, *American Government and Business* (New York: 1971); Morton Mintz and Jerry S. Cohen, *America Inc.: Who Owns and Operates the United States* (New York: 1971); Charles N. Davisson and Ross Wilhelm, *Economic Effects of the Wage-Price Guideposts* (Ann Arbor, Mich.: 1967); Robin Marris, *The Economic Theory of "Managerial Capitalism"* (New York: 1968); and George Meany, Roger M. Blough, and Neil H. Jacoby, *Government Wage-Price Guideposts in the American Economy* (New York: 1967).

Some dated materials of useful quality and still pertinent are Robert A. Brady, *Business as a System of Power* (New York: 1943); and Adolf A. Berle, Jr., and Gardiner C. Means, *The Modern Corporation and Private Property* (New York: 1932).

Government and the Military-Industrial Complex

The student who wishes to delve deeper into the current raging issue of the government and the military-industrial complex should refer to three works by

Seymour Melman, *The Defense Economy* (New York: 1970); *Our Depleted Society* (New York: 1965); and *Pentagon Capitalism* (New York: 1970). Other works in this area are Jacob K. Javits, Charles J. Hitch, and Arthur F. Burns, *The Defense Sector and the American Economy* (New York: 1968); Sidney Lens, *The Military Industrial Complex* (Philadelphia: 1970); Kenneth E. Boulding, ed., *Peace and the War Industry* (Chicago: 1970); Michael Kideon, rev. ed., *Western Capitalism Since the War* (Baltimore: 1970); and Richard J. Barnet, *The Roots of War* (New York: 1972). Some older works which the student might find still applicable are Jules Backman et al., *War and Defense Economics* (New York: 1952); and A. C. Pigou, *The Political Economy of War* (New York: 1941).

The Government and Economic Equality

The student who wishes to explore this topic from the viewpoint of government's taxing role might find it useful to read Joseph A. Pechman, *Federal Tax Policy* (Washington: 1962); Harvey W. Peck, *Taxation and Welfare* (New York: 1925); Harold M. Groves, *Financing Government* (New York: 1964); Jerome A. Hillestein, *Taxes, Loopholes and Morals* (New York: 1963); Alan A. Tait, *The Taxation of Personal Wealth* (Urbana, Ill.: 1967); and J. K. Butlers et al., *Taxation and Business Concentration* (Princeton: 1962).

One interested in studies of the economic elite may find it enlightening to study F. W. Taussig and C. S. Joslyn, *American Business Leaders* (New York: 1932); E. D. Baltzell, *An American Business Aristocracy* (New York: 1962); F. Hunter, *The Big Rich and the Little Rich* (New York: 1965); Lloyd W. Warner and James C. Abegglen, *Big Business Leaders in America* (New York: 1955); T. B. Bottomore, *Elites and Society* (Baltimore: 1966); Joseph Schumpeter, *Imperialism and Social Classes* (New York: 1951); William Miller, ed., *Men in Business,* new ed. (New York: 1962); C. W. Mills, *The Power Elite* (New York: 1956); and Ferdinand Lundberg's *America's Sixty Families* (New York: 1937); and *The Rich and the Super-Rich* (New York: 1968).

Some earlier materials that should not be overlooked are Gustavus Myers, *A History of the Great American Fortunes* (New York: 1936); and Matthew Josephson, *The Robber Barons* (New York: 1934).

Government and the World Economy

The concept and implications of the multinational firm are arousing much interest today. Some works in this area are Charles P. Kindleberger, *American Business Abroad* (New Haven: 1969); Mira Wilkins, *The Emergence of Multinational Enterprise: American Business Abroad from the Colonial Era to 1914* (Cambridge, Mass.: 1970); Jack N. Behrman, *National Interests and Multinational Enterprise* (Englewood Cliffs, New Jersey: 1970); Edith T. Penrose, *The Large International Firm in Developing Countries* (Cambridge, Mass.: 1968); John H. Dunning, ed., *The Multinational Enterprise* (London: 1971); and Louis Turner, *Invisible Empires* (New York: 1970).

If one wishes to view this topic from the aspect of American expansion, the following books will aid the student: Harry Magdoff, *The Age of Imperialism* (New York: 1969); Claude Julien, *America's Empire* (New York: 1971); J.

J. Servan-Schreiber, *The American Challenge* (New York: 1969); David Horowitz, ed., *Corporations and the Cold War* (New York: 1969); Paul A. Baran, *The Political Economy of Growth* (New York: 1968); Richard W. Van Alstyne, *The Rising American Empire* (New York: 1960); and George Thayer, *The War Business* (New York: 1969).

One should not overlook the interpretative historical works of William A. Williams, *The Contours of American History* (Cleveland: 1961); *The Tragedy of American Diplomacy* (Cleveland: 1959); and *The Roots of the Modern American Empire* (New York: 1969).

1 2 3 4 5 6 7 8 9 10